0267-0001-REXJ-EMB6-LXTG-VKDV

LearnTCI Access Code

0267-0001-REXJ-EMB6-LXTG-VKDV

Student Edition

Econ Alive!®
The Power to Choose

TCi™

Director of Product Development Liz Russell
Managing Editor Laura Alavosus
Project Editor Mali Apple
Developmental Editor Kate Connell
Copyeditors Rachel Farber, Tara Joffe
Editorial Associates Anna Embree, Sarah Sudano
Production Manager Lynn Sanchez
Art Director John F. Kelly
Senior Graphic Designers Paul Rebello, Christy Uyeno
Graphic Designers Sarah Wildfang, Don Taka
Photo Editor Margee Robinson
Art Editor Eric Houts
Audio Director Katy Haun

TCi™ Teachers' Curriculum Institute
P.O. Box 50996
Palo Alto, CA 94303

ISBN 978-1-934534-26-7
1 2 3 4 5 6 7 8 9 10 -QW- 12 11 10 09

Program Director
Bert Bower

Program Author

Phillip J. VanFossen is the James F. Ackerman Professor of Social Studies Education and director of the James F. Ackerman Center for Democratic Citizenship in Purdue University's College of Education. He also serves as the associate director of the Purdue University Center for Economic Education (and holds a courtesy appointment in the Krannert School of Management at Purdue), where he teaches introductory economics courses for the Economics Department. A former middle and high school social studies teacher, Dr. VanFossen has authored, co-authored, and edited two books, four nationally distributed curricula, and more than 50 research articles, textbook chapters, and monographs in economic education.

Dr. VanFossen has spent much of his professional career on projects designed to increase the economic literacy of American citizens, conducting hundreds of teacher workshops on economic education across the United States. With a focus on developing an economic way of thinking about the world, Dr. VanFossen leads students to increase their economic literacy and see that they all have the "power to choose."

Writing Manager
Diane Hart

Contributing Writers
David Fasulo
Brent Goff

Creative Development Manager
Kelly Shafsky

Curriculum Developers
Nicole Boylan
Julie Cremin
Amy George
Nathan Welbourne

Teacher and Content Consultants
Amber Baumann
Elsik High School
Houston, Texas

Bruce L. Damasio
Maryland Council for Economic Education
Towson, Maryland

Karl Grubaugh
Granite Bay High School
Granite Bay, California

Colleen Guccione
National-Louis University
Chicago, Illinois

Cathy Hix
Swanson Middle School
Arlington, Virginia

Cassie Lanzas
Grant High School
Portland, Oregon

Derek Miyahara
Los Altos High School
Los Altos, California

Jose Luis Navarro IV
Sylmar High School
Sylmar, California

Carmen Newstreet
Coral Springs High School
Coral Springs, Florida

Gary N. Petmecky
Parkview High School
Lilburn, Georgia

Fred H. Walk
Illinois State University
Normal, Illinois

Scholars
Bill Bosshardt, PhD
Florida Atlantic University

Barry Brown, PhD
Murray State University

Steven Cobb, PhD
University of North Texas

Toni Criss, PhD
University of Southern Florida,
St. Petersburg

Gregory DeCoster, PhD
Bowdoin College

Tawni Hunt Ferrarini, PhD
Northern Michigan University

Indranil Ghosh, PhD
Winston-Salem State University

Vereda King, PhD
North Carolina A&T State University

Winnie Lee, PhD
New Mexico State University

Jane Lopus, PhD
California State University East Bay

Zagros Madjd-Sadjadi, PhD
Winston-Salem State University

Sandra Odorzynski, PhD
St. Norbert College

Gregory Price, PhD
Morehouse College

Meghan Starbuck, PhD
New Mexico State University

Robert Whaples, PhD
Wake Forest University

Edward Zajicek, PhD
Winston-Salem State University

Cartographer
Mapping Specialists
Madison, Wisconsin

Internet Consultant
Clinton Couse
Cedar Valley Community School
Edmonds School District
Edmonds, Washington

Researcher
Carla Valetich
Pittsboro, North Carolina

Contents

Key Concepts

Figures

The Economic Fundamentals

Chapter 1

How can you think like an economist?

An Economic Way of Thinking

■ 1.1 Introduction

Why are some people and nations wealthy and others poor? This simple-sounding question has no easy answer. In fact, over the past two centuries, some of the world's best thinkers have wrestled with it. Their answers have generated many of the ideas and principles at the heart of the social science we call **economics**.

Among the first to consider this question in depth was a political economist and philosopher named Adam Smith. Born in Scotland, Smith taught at the University of Glasgow and later became Scotland's commissioner of customs. He is best known for his book *An Inquiry into the Nature and Causes of the Wealth of Nations,* better known today as *The Wealth of Nations.*

Smith's book was published in 1776, the same year the Declaration of Independence was written. The connection between *The Wealth of Nations* and the Declaration does not stop there. In his book, Smith argued that competition is the key to a healthy **economy**. Nations prosper when buyers and sellers are free to do business in the marketplace without government interference. In the newly independent and liberty-loving United States, Smith's ideas about competition and free markets took root and grew vigorously.

In *The Wealth of Nations,* Smith made many observations about people that still ring true today.

Everyday economic activity takes many forms.

Speaking of Economics

economics
The study of how people choose to use their limited resources to satisfy their unlimited wants.

economy
A system used to manage limited resources for the production, distribution, and consumption of goods and services.

positive economics
The branch of economics that uses objective analysis to find out how the world works. The goal is to describe how things are.

normative economics
The branch of economics that applies value judgments to data in order to recommend actions or policies. The goal is to advise how things ought to be done.

scarcity
The condition that results because people have limited resources but unlimited wants.

tradeoff
The exchange of one benefit or advantage for another that is thought to be better.

cost-benefit analysis
A way to compare the costs of an action with the benefits of that action. If benefits exceed costs, then the action is worth taking.

incentive
Any factor that encourages or motivates a person to do something. Prices, taxes, and laws create incentives that influence how people behave.

For example, Smith observed,

Every man is rich or poor according to the degree in which he can afford to enjoy the necessaries, conveniencies, and amusements of human life.

In his 18th-century prose, Smith made the point that people want not only the basic necessities of life—food, clothing, and shelter—but also things that make life easier, or more convenient, and that entertain them. The more of such things they have, the richer they are, at least in economic terms.

Smith was not the first to explore everyday economic events. But he developed a way of thinking about those events that had a lasting impact and earned him the title "the father of modern economics." Economists still read *The Wealth of Nations* to refresh their thinking about fundamental economic principles.

This chapter explores some of these principles and how they can help you develop an economic way of thinking. Along the way, the words of Smith and other economists are included to offer you guidance. The more you learn about how to think like an economist, the better you will become at making sound decisions in almost every area of your life.

■ 1.2 What Is Economics All About?

When most people think about economics, they see numbers, graphs, and equations. Indeed, in this book, you will encounter a fair number of graphs and the occasional equation. But that is not what economics is all about. In their popular book *Freakonomics*, economist Steven Levitt and journalist Stephen Dubner argue that economics "is about stripping a layer or two from the surface of modern life and seeing what is happening underneath." This is what Adam Smith did in 1776 and what economists continue to do today.

Everyday Mysteries and Economic Enigmas

When they strip away a layer from the surface of modern life, economists often uncover curious mysteries and enigmas. These **economic enigmas** are puzzles or riddles that might be explained through an economic analysis. For economist Steven Landsburg, finding and solving such mysteries is what economics is all about:

First, it is about observing the world with genuine curiosity and admitting that it is full of mysteries. Second, it is about trying to solve those mysteries in ways that are consistent with the general proposition that human behavior is usually designed to serve a purpose.
 —Steven E. Landsburg, *The Armchair Economist: Economics and Everyday Life*, 1993

Some of the mysteries that Landsburg refers to are large and abstract. For example, why does an economy grow for a long time and then start to shrink? Others deal with smaller, everyday enigmas that an ordinary person might wonder about. For example, one question Landsburg pursues is, why does popcorn sold at the movies cost more than at a grocery store? Another is, why are so many products sold for $2.99 and so few for $3.00?

Not all economists think of their job as investigating economic enigmas. But most would agree that economics has a lot to do with asking questions that reveal what the *Freakonomics* authors call "the hidden side of everything."

The Granger Collection, New York

Adam Smith is revered today as the father of modern economics. His ideas have been so important that Michael Hart ranked him as number 30 in his book *The 100: A Ranking of the Most Influential Persons in History*. Thomas Jefferson, the primary author of the Declaration of Independence, also made Hart's list—at number 64.

Economic Enigma 1: Why does popcorn cost so much at movie theaters? One answer is that theater owners make money by selling either tickets or food. By overcharging for popcorn, they keep ticket prices low to attract people who would otherwise not be able to afford a night out at the movies.

Economic Enigma 2: Why do prices often end in 99 cents? One theory links 99-cent pricing to the invention of cash registers. Pricing goods at 99 cents instead of $1.00 made it hard for clerks to pocket a customer's dollar bill rather than ringing up the price on the register and giving the customer change.

How People Use Limited Resources to Satisfy Unlimited Wants

Economics has traditionally been defined as the study of how people—individually and in groups—choose to use their limited resources to satisfy their unlimited wants. This concept of economics goes back at least to the ancient Greek author Xenophon, whose book *Oeconomicus* described how a household should manage its resources.

A **resource** is anything used to produce an economic good or a service. Resources are limited, or scarce, because they exist in finite amounts. Only so many workers, minerals, machines, and other resources can be used at any given time to produce goods and services. Resources also have alternative uses. Trees, for example, can be used to build houses, to make paper, or to burn for fuel.

Despite the scarcity of resources, people's wants are unlimited. At any one moment, we may have enough of certain things to satisfy us. But we would still like more of other things. Even the wealthiest people want more—perhaps a fancier vehicle or a bigger home.

Economists divide their study of how people use their scarce resources into two main branches. **Microeconomics** looks at economic decision making by individuals, households, and businesses. **Macroeconomics** focuses on the workings of an economy as a whole.

Economists look at how individuals and whole societies try to satisfy their unlimited wants given their limited resources. This issue is so central to human existence that Alfred Marshall, an influential 19th-century economist, described economics as "a study of mankind in the ordinary business of life."

The Science of Decision Making

Look again at the traditional definition of economics. Notice that it also involves studying how people choose to use their resources. When people cannot have everything they want, they must make choices. Some economists argue that economics is mainly about how we make these choices. They would define economics as the science of decision making.

As a consumer, you are continually making decisions. Should you buy a sandwich or a salad for lunch? If a salad, should it be lettuce or spinach? Should you top it with tomatoes, onions, or peppers? What about the dressing? These decisions may seem relatively trivial. But what about larger decisions, such as should you look for a weekend job? Or should you accept a credit card offer you got in the mail? Economists have developed ways of thinking about such choices that can lead to better decision making.

What Is and What Should Be: Positive Versus Normative Economics

Economists spend a great deal of time describing how things are and why. But sometimes, they are also asked to offer advice on what should be done to make things better. Consider the following two

Figure 1.2

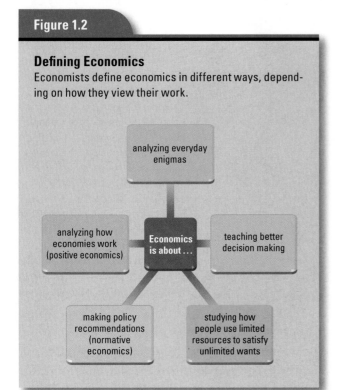

Defining Economics
Economists define economics in different ways, depending on how they view their work.

analyzing everyday enigmas

analyzing how economies work (positive economics)

Economics is about . . .

teaching better decision making

making policy recommendations (normative economics)

studying how people use limited resources to satisfy unlimited wants

questions, which a school board facing a budget crisis might ask of an economic analyst:

Question 1: What impact will increased enrollment, salary increases, and rising maintenance costs have on next year's budget?

Question 2: What actions should we take now to reduce expenses in order to balance next year's budget?

To answer the first question, the economic analyst would gather facts about the number of new classes needed to cope with rising enrollment, the salaries of school employees, maintenance costs, and other expenses. This type of analysis, which describes how things are, is known as **positive economics**.

To answer the second question, the economic analyst would not only gather facts but also analyze the various choices the school board has for cutting costs. Having laid out the choices and their possible impacts, the analyst would then make a recommendation to the board on where to cut costs. This type of analysis, which focuses on how things ought to be done, is known as **normative economics**.

Most economists are engaged in positive economics. But many others have taken on the role of policy advisers to government officials. In this role, they go beyond the objective facts to recommend actions based

on what they believe to be the best way to achieve the officials' desired objectives.

1.3 What Seven Principles Guide an Economic Way of Thinking?

People often think of economics as a limited field of study concerned with money, taxes, banking, and trade. These subjects *are* central to economics. But in studying them, economists have developed principles that apply to much more than money or business. Taken together, these principles represent an economic way of thinking about the wider world. This way of thinking can help you see ordinary events in a new way—sort of like putting on a special pair of glasses. Try looking for these principles as you take an imaginary summer road trip. Try to see events along the way as an economist might see them.

Principle 1: Scarcity Forces Tradeoffs

This first principle recognizes that although our desires for things are unlimited, the resources needed to fulfill our desires are scarce. Because of this **scarcity** of resources, there will never be enough of everything to satisfy everyone completely. We will always be forced to make choices as to what we want most. Whenever you choose one thing over another, you are making a **tradeoff**. You are giving up one thing to get another that you want even more. The **scarcity-forces-tradeoffs principle** reminds us that limited resources force people to make choices and face tradeoffs when they choose.

Economists have another name for the scarcity-forces-tradeoffs principle: the **no-free-lunch principle**. This name stems from the observation that every choice—even that of accepting a free lunch—involves tradeoffs. Even if the lunch was free to you, someone had to pay for the meal. And in making that choice, that someone had to go without something else. Looked at in this way, there is no such thing as a "free" lunch.

You may not realize it, but you make choices all the time based on the scarcity-forces-tradeoffs principle. What, for example, should you do next summer? Should you get a job at the mall? The pay might be good, but the work might be boring. Should you find an internship in a career area that interests you? The pay might be low, but the experience could be valuable. Should you volunteer to help build housing for the homeless? Although there is no pay, you would like working with your hands and helping others. Time is scarce. You can take only one of these jobs. Will it be good pay, valuable work experience, or a sense of satisfaction helping others? The tradeoff for choosing one alternative is giving up the other two.

Now consider another option for the summer after you graduate—a road trip with your best friend to follow your favorite band on tour. How might the scarcity-forces-tradeoffs principle come into play if you were to buy a used car for the trip? Say you find two cars that fit your budget. One is a luxury sedan that averages 15 miles per gallon of gas. The other is an economy model that gets nearly twice the mileage of the large sedan. You cannot buy both. In making a choice, you will have to trade off roominess for good gas mileage or the other way around.

Principle 2: Costs Versus Benefits

The scarcity-forces-tradeoffs principle forces us to make choices. But how do we decide which alternative to choose? Economists assume that individuals make choices based on the expected costs and benefits. The **costs** of something are what you spend in money, time, effort, or other sacrifices to get it.

The **benefits** are what you gain from something in terms of money, time, experience, or other improvements in your situation. The **costs-versus-benefits principle** tells us that people choose something when the benefits of doing so are greater than the costs.

To calculate costs and benefits, economists use a tool known as a **cost-benefit analysis**. This analysis might begin with a formal listing of the costs and benefits involved in a choice, as shown in Figure 1.3. Or it might be a quick, informal assessment of the costs and benefits. Either way, the analysis should lead to a calculation of which side "outweighs" the other. For example, what are the costs of sleeping an hour longer on a school day? Would you not take a hot shower? Would you lose out on study time? What benefits might you gain? Would you get needed rest or have more energy? A rational choice is one in which the benefits are greater than the costs.

Think about how the costs-versus-benefits principle might come into play during your proposed road trip. Each evening, you and your friend face the choice between pitching a tent at an inexpensive campground or paying more for a motel room with a soft bed and a shower. Your decision would depend on your own analysis of the costs and benefits of each arrangement. The choice here is personal. Do the benefits of renting a motel room outweigh the higher cost?

Figure 1.3

Analyzing Costs and Benefits

Every choice entails costs (something lost) and benefits (something gained). A cost-benefit analysis involves identifying those costs and benefits and weighing them against each other. The best choice is that in which the benefits outweigh the costs.

Sleeping One Hour Later

Costs	Benefits
No time for a good breakfast	Pleasure of sleeping longer
No long morning shower	Lower water bill
No study time for tests before school	May do better on tests if well rested
Less time to dress	Less time to worry what to wear
More likely to be late for class	Less likely to fall asleep in class

Principle 3: Thinking at the Margin

Most everyday choices involve thinking in terms of a little more of this or a little less of that, rather than all or nothing. For example, you may find yourself having to decide whether to study one more hour, buy one more shirt, or eat one more slice of watermelon. In economic terms, when we decide to add (or subtract) one more unit to (or from) what we already have, we are thinking "at the margin." The **margin,** in this case, is the border or outer edge of something. The **thinking-at-the-margin principle** tells us that most of the decisions we make each day involve choices about a little more or a little less of something rather than making a wholesale change.

Making decisions at the margin involves comparing marginal costs and benefits. The **marginal cost** is what you give up to add one unit to an activity. The **marginal benefit** is what you gain by adding one more unit. Suppose you have just spent two hours studying for an economics test. Should you study another hour or go to bed? The answer depends on whether you think the marginal benefit of the extra hour of sleep—maybe doing a bit better on the test—will exceed the marginal cost of that hour—perhaps being less well rested for the test.

Now think about your road trip. You and your friend have organized your trip around all six cities where your favorite band is performing. But then the band announces that it is extending its tour to one more city. The added concert is not in your plans, but you would really hate to miss it. Here is a decision you must make at the margin. Is the marginal benefit of attending the seventh concert worth the added costs in time and money?

Principle 4: Incentives Matter

As we have seen, costs and benefits influence our behavior. That is, they act as an **incentive,** something that motivates a person to take a particular course of action. The **incentives-matter principle** simply says that people respond to incentives in generally predictable ways.

When economists want to understand why people do what they do, they start looking for incentives. This principle led Landsburg to write, "Most of economics can be summarized in four words: 'People respond to incentives.'" Levitt and Dubner would agree:

> *Incentives are the cornerstone of modern life. And understanding them—or, often, ferreting them out—is the key to solving just about any riddle, from violent crime to sports cheating to online dating.*
> —Steven D. Levitt and Stephen J. Dubner,
> *Freakonomics,* 2006

Why, for example, would hundreds of people stand in line on a city sidewalk in the heat of summer for several hours just to get a concert ticket? Certainly they would not behave this way without some sort of powerful incentive.

Incentives come in many forms, both positive and negative. Teachers use points and grades as positive

Incentives matter in everything we do. Why else would people stand in line for hours under a hot sun to buy tickets to a rock concert?

incentives to encourage students to complete their assignments. Honor societies and awards are also positive incentives used by schools to motivate students to achieve their highest levels.

Governments use negative incentives, such as fines and jail time, to discourage people from breaking laws. You are reminded of this one morning when your road trip hits a speed trap. While driving along, you suddenly see a police motorcycle with flashing lights behind you. The officer tells you that you were driving 65 miles per hour in a 50-mile-per-hour zone. Worse yet, you were in a construction zone, where fines are doubled. Your decision to ignore the speed limit signs will cost you a hefty $150 fine. You decide that is more than enough incentive for you to watch your speed from now on.

Principle 5: Trade Makes People Better Off

Why doesn't your family make all its own clothes, build all its own furniture, grow all its own food, and produce its own medicines? Adam Smith answered that question two centuries ago:

> *It is the maxim of every prudent master of a family never to attempt to make at home what it will cost him more to make than to buy. The taylor [tailor] does not attempt to make his own shoes, but buys them of the shoemaker. The shoemaker does not attempt to make his own clothes, but employs a taylor.*
> —Adam Smith, *The Wealth of Nations*, 1776

As Smith understood, none of us is equally skilled at doing everything. Nor should we try to be. It makes more sense to concentrate on what we do best and then trade with others for what they do best. The **trade-makes-people-better-off principle** tells us that by focusing on what we do well and then trading with others, we will end up with more and better choices than by trying to do everything for ourselves.

Your road trip gives you a firsthand appreciation of this principle when you run into car trouble. One morning, you turn the key and nothing happens. Neither you nor your friend is a mechanic, so you push the car to the nearest gas station and look for help. The mechanic on duty quickly diagnoses the problem as a dead battery. You offer to trade your two tickets for that night's concert for a new battery. The mechanic agrees, and your car is soon running again. You are disappointed about missing the concert, but everyone involved agrees that trading the battery for the tickets makes you all better off than you were that morning.

Principle 6: Markets Coordinate Trade

When you think of markets, you probably conjure up the image of a supermarket or farmers market. Economists take a more expansive view of markets. To them, a **market** is any arrangement that brings buyers and sellers together to do business with each other. A market can exist in a single place, like a weekend flea market. Or it can exist in cyberspace, such as an online auction site.

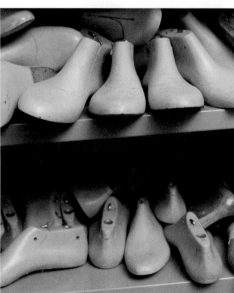

Looking at these tools used by tailors and shoemakers reminds us that trade makes people better off. Without trade, we would be spending much of our time sewing our own clothes and making our own footwear.

When markets operate freely, or with limited government interference, buyers and sellers can trade with each other until both are satisfied with their sales and purchases. The result is an efficient market that serves everyone's interests without guidance from a person or an institution. The **markets-coordinate-trade principle** states that markets usually do better than anyone or anything else at coordinating exchanges between buyers and sellers.

Just how markets do all this coordination was not clear to people in Adam Smith's day. He used the metaphor of an **invisible hand** guiding human affairs to explain this mystery. On your road trip, you feel the invisible hand at work when you visit a supermarket. As you push your cart through the aisles, you see fresh mangos from Mexico, bananas from Belize, shrimp from Thailand, cheese from France, and salmon from Alaska. You wonder how a grocery store manages to stock its shelves with so many fresh foods from around the world at prices you are willing to pay. The answer is simple: markets coordinate trade with remarkable efficiency.

Markets are remarkably efficient at coordinating the activities of buyers and sellers over vast distances. These Korean pears traveled halfway around the world to reach customers in the United States.

Principle 7: Future Consequences Count

In general, people are shortsighted. They tend to make decisions by looking only at the immediate costs and benefits. But decisions made today often have longer-term effects that should also be considered. The **future-consequences-count principle** tells us that decisions made today have consequences not only for today but also in the future.

To economist Henry Hazlitt, this principle separates the good economist from the bad. He wrote,

> *The bad economist sees only what immediately strikes the eye; the good economist also looks beyond. The bad economist sees only the direct consequences of a proposed course; the good economist looks also at the longer and indirect consequences . . . The art of economics consists in looking not merely at the immediate but at the longer effects of any act or policy.*
> —Henry Hazlitt, *Economics in One Lesson,* 1979

Part of thinking like an economist involves trying to imagine all the possible consequences of a decision. But nothing about doing this is easy. Consider a law passed in 1968 in Vermont that banned roadside billboards and other large signs in order to protect the state's scenic beauty. Since then, businesses have instead built sculptures, including a giant squirrel in red suspenders and a 19-foot-high genie, to attract the attention of passersby.

The result of the Vermont law was an example of what economists call the **law of unintended consequences**. This law says that actions of people and governments always have effects that are not expected, or that are "unintended." Economists spend much of their time trying to predict these unintended consequences.

Your decision to take a road trip had a variety of consequences—some intended, others not. In the short term, you found out what it was like to be on your own, away from your family. You learned a lot about being independent, handling difficult situations, and making your own way in the world. When you open your insurance bill months later, however, you realize that your trip has had a long-term, unintended consequence. The cost of your insurance has gone up because one day last summer you chose to ignore a speed limit sign.

Seven Principles of Economic Thinking

Each stop on this road trip illustrates one of the seven principles of economic thinking. The trip begins with a tradeoff between comfort and economy in a car and ends with the long-term consequence of a speeding ticket—higher insurance rates.

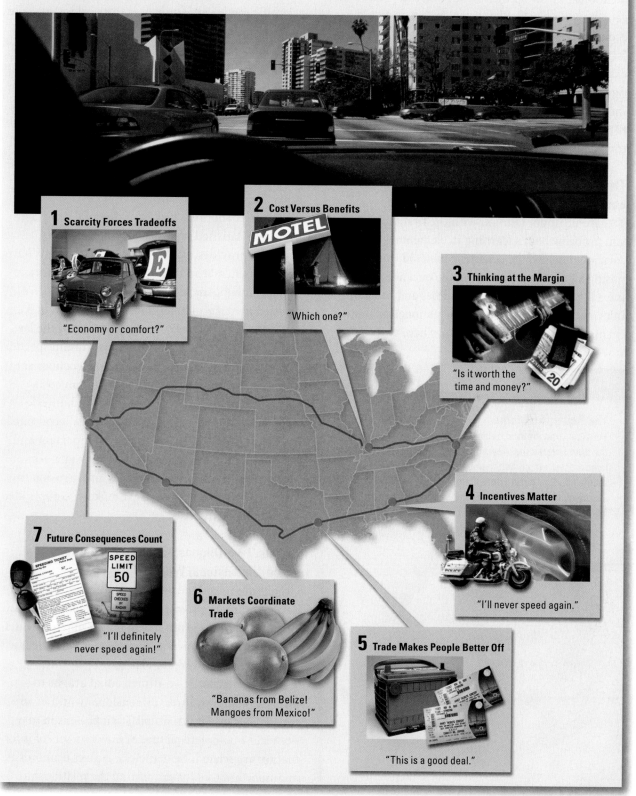

1 Scarcity Forces Tradeoffs

"Economy or comfort?"

2 Cost Versus Benefits

MOTEL

"Which one?"

3 Thinking at the Margin

"Is it worth the time and money?"

4 Incentives Matter

"I'll never speed again."

5 Trade Makes People Better Off

"This is a good deal."

6 Markets Coordinate Trade

"Bananas from Belize! Mangoes from Mexico!"

7 Future Consequences Count

SPEED LIMIT 50

SPEED CHECKED BY RADAR

"I'll definitely never speed again!"

■ 1.4 What Tools Do Economists Use?

The law of unintended consequences illustrates just how complicated—and frustrating—the work of an economist can be. You might wonder why economists do not just throw up their hands and say, "I quit!" But economists actually like their job and enjoy solving economic enigmas.

To do their job properly, economists need ways to examine economic events, to simplify them, and to figure out how a given economic decision can affect the world. To do this, they need a set of tools. Three of the most effective tools that economists use are the scientific method, graphs, and economic models.

The Scientific Method: Question, Hypothesize, and Observe

You are no doubt familiar with the first tool, which you probably began learning in elementary school. As shown below, the **scientific method** involves posing a question, researching the question, developing a hypothesis, conducting studies and collecting information, analyzing the information, and then evaluating the hypothesis. You may have applied the scientific method by growing bean plants, examining bacteria under a microscope, or measuring waves in a wave tank. Through such laboratory experiments, you collected **data,** or factual information, that gave you vital insights into the physical world and its processes.

Economists, like other scientists, rely on the scientific method to study how the world works. But they have a big handicap. Usually, they cannot conduct laboratory experiments to make observations or test their theories. For example, an economist might have a theory that raising highway speed limits would improve the economy, in part by enabling the speedier transport of goods from farms and factories to stores. But how might she test that theory? It is highly unlikely that government officials would permit an economist to turn the highway system into a huge laboratory.

When economists lack experimental data, they have to be satisfied with whatever data society naturally provides. For this reason, economists have become skilled at analyzing existing and historical data. As it happens, a law that was passed in 1974 resulted in a national maximum speed limit of 55 miles per hour. In 1995, Congress repealed the law, allowing each state to set its own maximum speed. Many states raised their limits, giving economists the chance to analyze how transportation costs varied before and after the speed limit changed.

Through such "natural experiments," economists have learned what kinds of data are important and have developed ways to examine those data. As economist Steven Levitt noted, "Knowing what to measure and how to measure it makes a complicated world much less so."

Graphs: Two-Dimensional Representations of a Three-Dimensional World

Graphs are useful tools for analyzing and displaying data. A **graph** is a visual representation of the relationship between two given sets of data. One or both sets of data are also known as variables. A **variable** is a quantity that can vary, or change.

Economists use two-dimensional graphs to simplify the complex, three-dimensional world in which we live. Because it is a simplification, a graph may not yield a complete picture of how two sets of information are related. Nonetheless, it gives economists an important tool for examining the relationship.

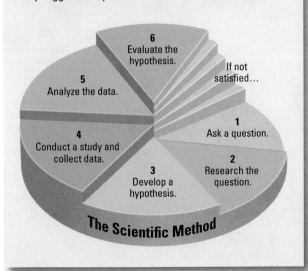

Key Concept

The Scientific Method
The scientific method begins with curiosity about why the world works the way it does. Questions lead to hypotheses, which can then be tested by conducting studies and gathering data about economic activities. As the diagram suggests, the conclusion from one study may trigger new questions and new rounds of research.

6 Evaluate the hypothesis.

If not satisfied…

5 Analyze the data.

1 Ask a question.

4 Conduct a study and collect data.

2 Research the question.

3 Develop a hypothesis.

The Scientific Method

Consider how economists might analyze the relationship between the amount of education a person has and that person's annual income. They would start by gathering information. The table in Figure 1.4 shows data for the year 2005. The two variables in this table are level of education and income. Each dollar figure in the table represents the average annual income of every person at that education level who had an income in 2005.

The same data can be plotted on a coordinate system, like the graphs shown with the table. A coordinate system consists of two perpendicular

Figure 1.4

Using a Graph to Show Economic Data

One of an economist's most important tools is the graph. Graphs are used to show how two variables—in this case, education and income—relate to one another. Notice how the data in the table are plotted on a graph to represent this relationship in a visual way.

Average Annual Income by Education Level, 2005

Level of Education	Income
Some high school	$17,300
High school graduate	26,900
Some college	30,600
Associate's (two-year) degree	36,600
Bachelor's (four-year) degree	52,700
Master's degree	66,800
Doctoral degree	91,400

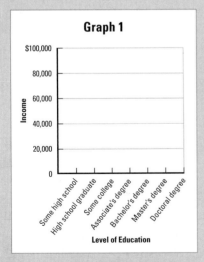

Graph 1

The x-axis shows the education levels from the data table. The y-axis shows the range of average annual incomes, from $0 to $100,000.

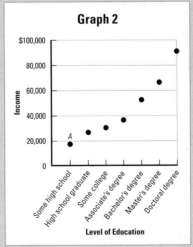

Graph 2

Each point on the graph corresponds to both education and income level. Point A, for example, shows that adults with some high school education earned, on average, less than $20,000 in 2005.

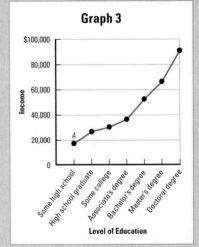

Graph 3

Connecting the points on the graph creates a curve. From this curve, you can easily draw your own conclusions about the importance of education on your future earning power.

lines that can be used to locate a point in space. Each of the two perpendicular lines is called an **axis**. The horizontal line is the *x*-axis, and the vertical line is the *y*-axis.

Once the data in the table are plotted as a set of points in the coordinate system, the points can be joined to form a curve. A **curve** is any line representing data points plotted on a graph. As you can see in Graph 3 in Figure 1.4, a curve doesn't have to be curved. In fact, straight lines on a graph are also called curves. The shape of this curve tells us that, on average, the more education people have, the higher their incomes will be.

As useful as graphs are at representing relationships, they have their limitations. The graphs in Figure 1.4 do not, for example, shed light on factors other than education that might have affected income in 2005. Suppose an unusually harsh winter had slowed construction projects and delayed spring planting across the country that year. The impact of such a slowdown would have fallen most heavily

Economists create models to try to understand how the world works. The theory behind the rational-behavior model is that people make decisions based on their self-interest. But can this model explain why these volunteers decided to help beautify Gulfport, Mississippi? Not really. Despite its limitations, the model helps economists predict and explain human behavior.

on construction workers and farmworkers, many of whom lack college degrees. As a result, their 2005 incomes would have been lower than usual for reasons quite unrelated to education.

Economic Models: Simplified Representations of Reality

Economists use models to help them understand how the world works. An **economic model** is a simplified representation of reality that often allows economists to focus on the effects of one change at a time. Models also help economists structure their thinking. A model can take the form of an equation, a computer program, or a diagram. It can also consist mainly of a written description.

One widely accepted descriptive model is called *homo economicus*. This is Latin for "economic man," although it applies to all human beings. It is also called the **rational-behavior model**. This model is a tool for understanding the mystery of human behavior. It theorizes that people behave in ways that are rational, or based on reason. That is, people make decisions that they think will fulfill their wants and needs to the greatest extent possible. They behave in ways that serve their own interests, without taking into account the well-being of others.

The rational-behavior model, with its focus on self-interest, arose after the time of Adam Smith. But the pursuit of self-interest plays a key role in Smith's descriptions of the free market. As if guided by an "invisible hand," self-interested market activity ends up benefiting all of society. This is the point Smith made in describing the typical businessperson:

> *It is his own advantage, indeed, and not that of the society, which he has in view . . . He intends only his own gain, and he is in this, as in many other cases, led by an invisible hand to promote an end which was no part of his intention.*
> —Adam Smith, *The Wealth of Nations*, 1776

Models are an approximation of how people, in general, act. As such, models cannot accurately predict all behavior all of the time. Economists who construct models must make assumptions. Consider the model just described, which assumes that people always act for their own benefit. Economists know that the rational-behavior model does not deal with social values, such as charity, that might curb self-interest. Nor does it deal with decisions based on limited or false information.

Faced with these missing factors, the economist shrugs and says, *"Ceteris paribus,"* which is Latin for "other things being equal" or "other relevant factors remaining unchanged." This is the economist's way of saying, "Let's focus on understanding what happens if we change one aspect of the mystery and keep all other aspects the same." The economist thinks, "Maybe if I can understand this one aspect, I can begin to understand the larger mystery." The point of economic models is to aid in examining economic effects, one change at a time, and in making predictions about the consequences of that change.

Good economic models are useful for both explaining and predicting how the economy operates. The rational-behavior model works pretty well at predicting how people generally react to incentives or how they use cost-benefit analyses to make decisions. By and large, we do these things without even consciously thinking about them. When this happens, we are behaving as this economic model would predict.

According to this model, humans make decisions based on their own best interests. So, is thinking like an economist in your best interest? Certainly it is, if it helps you make better decisions. You have had a brief introduction to the principles and tools that help economists look at the world in a special way. In the rest of this book, you will use those principles and tools to develop your own understanding of how the world works. In the process, you will become a better consumer and citizen. That seems like a pretty good tradeoff for the time you will spend in this course.

Summary

Economics is both a social science and a way of thinking about how the world works. It can help us unravel everyday mysteries and make better decisions about matters large and small.

What is economics all about? Economics is the study of how individuals and societies use their limited resources to satisfy their unlimited wants. Positive economics looks at the way things are and why. Normative economics looks at the way things ought to be. In examining how people make decisions about production and consumption, economists attempt to get beneath the surface of everyday life.

What principles guide an economic way of thinking? Economists have identified several principles that can help us understand how people make choices and how their decisions affect others. They include the following:

- scarcity forces tradeoffs
- benefits should outweigh costs
- decisions are often made at the margin
- incentives matter
- trade makes people better off
- markets coordinate trade better than anything or anyone else
- decisions made today have consequences in the future

What tools do economists use? Economists use the scientific method to analyze economic events and predict outcomes. They use graphs to analyze the relationship between two sets of data. They also use economic models to better understand how the world works. An economic model can take various forms, such as a diagram, an equation, or a description.

Is college the right choice for you?

Have you already decided that you are definitely going to college? Or are you just as certain that you want to leap directly into the world of work? Perhaps you have some doubts about which path is right for you. Whatever your situation, know that you have the power to choose.

As you have read in this chapter, people make decisions based on expected costs and benefits. On the opposite page is a table to help you analyze the costs and benefits of going to college versus entering the workforce. But first, read the article by Ryan Allis, a young man who grew up believing that he would go to college. While in high school, Allis applied to several colleges and got an acceptance—and a big scholarship offer—from the University of North Carolina (UNC). He then began to have doubts about his decision.

Should I Go to College?

by Ryan Allis

You might ask why I was even considering the possibility of not going to college. I was a good student and had a chance to go to a great university on a near-full ride. Here is where my story really begins.

You see, since August of 2001 I had been working with a guy who had developed a product that was effective in treating arthritis in humans and pets. He had heard that I owned a website development business by reading an article on me in the local newspaper and asked me to come in and meet with him. I set up a website about his product and got a shopping cart and merchant account for the site so we could take orders online . . .

After I got the initial site up I began to market it . . . We also started a monthly newsletter and sweepstakes and began to write a lot of informational content for the website. We set up two informational websites, one on arthritis and the other on arthritis in pets, and drove each to the top of the search engines for our targeted keywords.

Things progressed slowly the first few months but soon picked up. In January we did $31,130 and in April alone we did $87,578. These sales were on one product with just the owner, myself, and one person to ship out the product. Our net profit was 51% and we were growing at 20% per month. In short, we were doing very well.

So it was now April and I saw that the company was taking off . . . I was seventeen and had the chance to make a couple hundred thousand dollars in salary and commission if I would just defer college for a year. Now you can see why I was seriously considering not going to college right away after knowing my whole life that I would . . .

My Decision

However, I wanted something more than this and knew there was much more to life than money . . . In the end, I chose to accept the offer and on August 14, 2002, my eighteenth birthday, I drove up to Chapel Hill, North Carolina, with my dad and moved into the Ehringhaus dorm.

So why did I choose to go to UNC? If I had the chance to earn more at age 18 than the average person with an MBA [Master's in Business Administration], why did I forgo this opportunity to go off to college? . . .

New Knowledge, New People and New Surroundings

I know now that I made the right decision. Although I still become frustrated at not having enough time to work on my businesses or read what I want to read, I know I have done what has been best for me. College really makes one go through many formative and developmental changes. I have learned how to take care of myself. I have learned that I must put the twisty-tie back on the bread or else it will mold. I have learned that I should not put whites in with my colors in a hot wash. I have learned who I am.

Just as important, I have developed a network of contacts and built strong relationships that will be a great asset to me in the future. I have found other students like me and have made some friends that may turn out to be my business partners in years to come . . .

Why I Am in College

In sum, I feel that these first three months of college have been a great experience for me. I have learned how to take care of myself and how to live away from my parents. I have met some great people and built some key relationships. I learned how to use the resources of UNC and will be studying what I want to study next semester yet still working towards my degree . . .

College Is Not for Everyone

In case there is anyone reading this that is considering starting their own company and not going to college, let me say this. Be very careful. For most people I would say that both a college degree and the college experience would be extremely beneficial . . . I may have been part of a select group that already had such specialized skills and such knowledge about the way the world worked that I might have been fine without going to college. If you feel you are in this group by all means go for it.

Ryan P. Allis is the author of Zero to One Million: How I Built a Company to $1 Million in Sales . . . and How You Can, Too.

Analyzing the Costs and Benefits of Going to College

You probably know many of the benefits of leaving home to become a full-time college student. But have you analyzed the costs as well?

- Copy this cost-benefit table, and fill in the costs and benefits that are listed. Also add any others you think of.
- Assign each cost and benefit a score of 1 (not very important) to 5 (extremely important).
- Add your scores in both columns. What conclusions can you draw by comparing the results?

Costs and Benefits of Going to College

Costs	Score	Benefits	Score
Cost of tuition, books, room and board, and travel to school		Greater lifetime earnings with a college degree	
Earnings lost by not joining the workforce full-time after high school		Better job opportunities once college is completed	
Lost opportunity for on-the-job training and the development of workplace skills		More opportunity to develop thinking, writing, and professional skills	
Less time to pursue nonacademic interests and hobbies		More time to pursue academic interests	
Less opportunity to spend time with old friends from high school		More opportunity to make new friends from different places	
Less time for spending with family at home		More opportunity to make family proud	

Chapter 2

Why can't you always get what you want?

Economic Decision Making

■ 2.1 Introduction

In 2004, a music magazine compiled a list titled the "500 Greatest Songs of All Time." The song chosen as the 100th greatest begins with a choir singing something economists have been saying for years:

> *And you can't always get what you want,*
> *Honey, you can't always get what you want*
> *You can't always get what you want*
> *But if you try sometime, yeah,*
> *You just might find you get what you need!*
> —Mick Jagger and Keith Richards, "You Can't
>   Always Get What You Want," 1969

As simple as it sounds, this chorus explains why everyone has to make choices—even Mick Jagger, Keith Richards, and the other members of the self-styled "Greatest Rock and Roll Band in the World."

What you may not know about Michael Philip Jagger is that he was once a student of economics. Born into a middle-class family in Dartford, England, Jagger was raised to be a teacher like his father, earning high enough marks in school to win a scholarship to the prestigious London School of Economics.

Jagger was studying accounting and finance in 1961 when a chance meeting with a boyhood friend named Keith Richards changed his life. "So I get on the train to London one morning, and there's Jagger and under his arm he has four or five albums," Richards later recalled. "He's got Chuck Berry and Little

The Rolling Stones, like the musicians who inspired them, had to make important decisions about their careers.

goods
Physical articles that have been produced for sale or use. Three examples are food, clothing, and cars.

services
Work done by someone else for which a consumer, business, or government is willing to pay. Three examples are teaching, gardening, and childcare.

factors of production
The resources used to produce goods and services. Economists define these resources as land, labor, and capital.

entrepreneurship
The willingness and ability to take the risks involved in starting and managing a business.

capital
The tools, machines, and buildings used to produce goods and services.

productivity
A measure of the efficiency with which goods and services are produced. Productivity is often stated as the quantity produced per person per hour.

opportunity cost
The value of the next best alternative that is given up when making a choice. This is the measure of what you must give up to get what you most want.

production possibilities frontier (PPF)
A simple model of an economy that shows all the combinations of two goods that can be produced with the resources and technology currently available.

Mick Jagger's decision to choose music worked out far better than he or his parents could ever have imagined. Since 1963, the Rolling Stones have sold more than 200 million albums. In late 2007, it was announced that the band had earned a record-breaking $437 million on its just-completed "A Bigger Bang" tour. This was enough to earn the Rolling Stones a spot in the next edition of *Guinness World Records*.

Walter, Muddy Waters." Fans of American rhythm and blues music were few and far between in England at that time. Finding another one was like coming across a long-lost brother.

Jagger invited Richards to join a few of his friends who played music together for fun. Once Richards did so, life began to change. "You could feel something holding the band together," a friend observed. "Keith sounded great." This worried Jagger's mother, who had noticed that after teaming up with Richards her son had begun to think of music as more than just a hobby.

A year after this meeting, a new R&B band billing itself as the Rolling Stones began to appear at London clubs. Then, in 1963, the Stones released their first record. Jagger now faced a difficult choice: finish his degree or drop out of college to pursue a career in music. He later said of his decision,

> It was very, very difficult because my parents obviously didn't want me to do it. My father was furious with me, absolutely furious. I'm sure he wouldn't have been so mad if I'd have volunteered to join the army. Anything but this. He couldn't believe it. I agree with him: It wasn't a viable career opportunity.

Despite his parent's misgivings, Jagger chose music —and the rest, as they say, is history.

This chapter is about the choices and decisions we all face in our lives. It explores why, as the song says, we can't always get what we want. And it looks at how we can use the economic way of thinking to decide what we want most and what we are willing to give up to get it.

■ 2.2 Why Is What We Want Scarce?

Every time we go shopping, most of us come up against the hard truth of the Rolling Stones song "You Can't Always Get What You Want." Difficult as it may be to believe, even a person as successful as Mick Jagger can't have everything. Even he has to make choices sometimes. But why is this so? Why do any of us have to choose at all?

Our Wants Always Exceed Our Resources
The simple answer to that question is that our wants—our desire for things that meet our needs or make us happy—are unlimited, while our means of fulfilling those desires are not. Some of our wants are necessary for survival. Each of us, for example, needs food, water, and shelter to survive from day to day. But beyond those basics, what we desire to have or experience is limited only by our imaginations.

Although our wants may be unlimited, our ability to satisfy them is not. We have only limited amounts of resources to use in fulfilling even our fondest desires. Time, for example, is a limited resource. Whether rich or poor, a person has only 24 hours each day to use in work or play. Money is also limited. Even the very rich can't afford an endless supply of everything. They, like the rest of us, experience scarcity, a situation in which the supply of something is not sufficient to satisfy their wants.

With Resources Limited, Scarcity Is Everywhere

It is hard for most people to see scarcity the way economists do. You shop in stores that are overflowing with **goods,** or physical objects produced for sale. You look around your classroom and see that nearly everyone has paper and pencils. Many of your classmates probably have cell phones. How can these goods be scarce if everyone seems to have them?

Similarly, most of us have access to a multitude of **services,** or activities done for us by others. Teachers, doctors, hair stylists, bus drivers, plumbers, nurses, and police officers all provide services we take for granted. Some are even offered to us without charge. So how can economists see these services as scarce?

And yet, goods and services *are* scarce. They are scarce because the resources needed to produce them—

land, labor, materials, and machines—are scarce. Should you doubt that this is true, try asking someone who owns one of these resources to turn it over to you for free. The answer will almost surely be no.

Scarcity would exist even if everyone in the world were suddenly as rich as Mick Jagger. Suppose every new multimillionaire wanted to build an elegant mansion to live in. Could they all do so? Probably not. While one essential resource for such a project (money) is now less scarce, other essential resources (land, lumber, concrete, glass, skilled workers, and time, to name just a few) are still just as scarce.

Shortages Are Temporary, While Scarcity Is Forever

While scarcity may seem like an abstract idea, most of us have experienced a shortage. A **shortage** is a lack of something that is desired, a condition that occurs when there is less of a good or service available than people want at the current price. When a record store runs out of Rolling Stones CDs while the band is performing live in that city, the result is a shortage.

Shortages occur for many reasons. A fashion fad can cause a shortage by suddenly increasing the number of people who want to buy the trendy item. The shortage lasts until either enough items are produced for everyone who wants them or the fad ends.

The women in India who walk miles each day to draw water from this well understand very well that water is a scarce resource. For them, scarcity is a visible and inescapable fact of life.

Wars and natural disasters can cause shortages by disrupting the production or movement of goods. Katrina, the Category 5 hurricane that ravaged the Gulf Coast in 2005, shut down major oil refineries, leading to gasoline shortages across the nation. In addition, customers at a national restaurant chain could not get their favorite Cajun side dishes of gumbo and red beans and rice because supplies from New Orleans had been cut off.

As annoying as shortages may be, they are usually a temporary condition. A shortage ends once production is resumed or new sources of supply are found. In contrast, scarcity is forever. No matter how well people use their limited resources, there will never be enough of everything to satisfy all of their wants.

■ 2.3 How Do We Satisfy Economic Wants?

Take a quick break from reading this book, and let your eyes wander around wherever you happen to be just now. What do you see? Walls, windows, furniture, books, paper, pens, pencils . . . the list could likely go on and on. None of these goods magically appeared at this moment for your comfort and convenience. All of them were produced to satisfy somebody's wants. The question is, how is this done?

Inputs, Outputs, and the Production Equation

Economists answer this question by looking at the inputs and outputs of the production process. **Inputs** are the scarce resources that go into the process. Economists call these productive resources the **factors of production** and divide them into three basic categories: land, labor, and capital. **Outputs** are the goods and services produced using these resources.

Economists use the production equation to represent the process of combining resources (inputs) to produce goods and services (outputs). In its simplest form, the **production equation** looks like this:

$$\text{land} + \text{labor} + \text{capital} = \text{goods and services}$$

Some economists consider **entrepreneurship**—the willingness to take the risks involved in starting a business—to be a fourth factor of production.

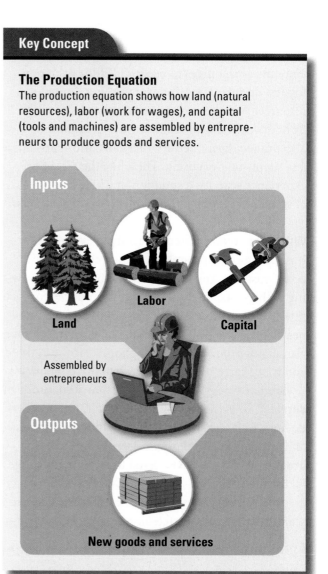

The Production Equation
The production equation shows how land (natural resources), labor (work for wages), and capital (tools and machines) are assembled by entrepreneurs to produce goods and services.

Inputs

Labor

Land

Capital

Assembled by entrepreneurs

Outputs

New goods and services

Entrepreneurs assemble the other inputs to create new goods and services.

Land Resources: The "Gifts of Nature"

As seen by economists, **land** is far more than real estate. It means all of the "gifts of nature" that are used to produce goods and services. These gifts include such familiar natural resources as air, soil, minerals, water, forests, plants, animals, birds, and fish. Others are less obvious, such as solar energy, wind, geothermal energy, and the electromagnetic spectrum used to transmit communication signals.

Natural resources vary in their abundance and availability. A few, such as sunlight and wind, are **perpetual resources** that are both widely available and in no danger of being used up. Others, including

The company that owns this oil field is harvesting both nonrenewable and renewable energy resources. The oil being pumped out of the ground cannot be replaced. In contrast, the wind driving the turbines that generate electricity will never be used up.

forests, fresh water, and fish, are **renewable resources** that, with careful planning, can be replaced as they are used. A few resources, mostly metals, can be recycled for use again and again. Still others, especially fossil fuels like oil, coal, and natural gas, are **nonrenewable resources**. Once they are used, they are gone forever.

The value of natural resources depends on someone knowing how to plug them into the production process. Vast pools of oil have lain under the surface of Earth for millions of years. But until someone developed the tools and technology needed to extract that oil from deep under the ground and turn it into a useful fuel, it had little value.

Figure 2.3A

Identifying Nature's Gifts in a Pencil
The common pencil is produced by assembling natural resources from many parts of the world. The resources that come from plants are renewable. The mineral resources—zinc, copper, pumice, clay, and graphite—are not.

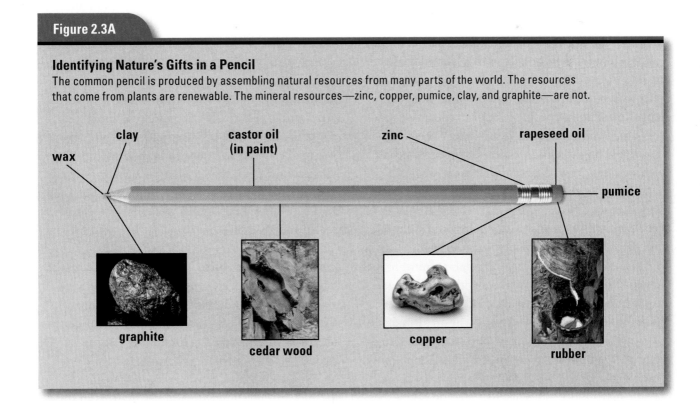

Figure 2.3B

Assessing America's Human Capital

Since 1940, this country's human capital—as measured by formal schooling—has increased steadily. Americans with college degrees can expect to earn at least one million dollars more over their lifetimes than high school graduates.

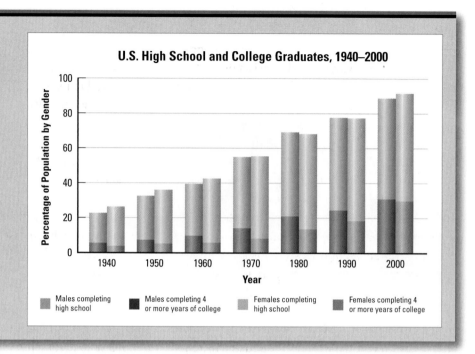

U.S. High School and College Graduates, 1940–2000

Sources: Susan B. Carter et al., eds., *Historical Statistics of the United States, Millennial Ed.,* Vol. 2. New York: Cambridge University Press, 2006. Eva E. Jacobs, ed., *Handbook of U.S. Labor Statistics,* 9th ed., Lanham, MD: Bernan Press, 2006.

Legend:
- Males completing high school
- Males completing 4 or more years of college
- Females completing high school
- Females completing 4 or more years of college

Labor Resources: Putting Human Capital to Work

The time and effort people devote to producing goods and services in exchange for wages is called **labor.** This includes both physical labor, such as planting crops and building houses, and mental activity, such as writing legal briefs and programming video games.

The quantity of labor available in a country depends on the size of its population and people's willingness to work. The quality of that labor depends on how skilled these workers are, or what economists refer to as human capital. **Human capital** is the knowledge and skill that people gain from education, on-the-job training, and other experiences. "It is what you would be left with if someone stripped away all of your assets," says economist Charles Wheelan, "and left you on a street corner with only the clothes on your back." What human capital would Mick Jagger be left with in that situation? He could still write and perform songs that people want to hear.

The importance of human capital is almost impossible to overstate. Workers with high human capital are more productive and earn more money than those with few skills. This is why an airline pilot makes more money than a taxi driver, although they offer similar services. Airline pilots are not only more highly trained, but they also move far more people many more miles in a day than do cabbies.

There is a strong **correlation,** or relationship, between a country's level of human capital and its standard of living. In contrast, the correlation between a country's natural resources and living standards is weak. This explains why a country like Japan, which is poor in resources but rich in human capital, is among the world's wealthiest nations, while Nigeria, which is rich in oil but poor in human capital, is among the poorest.

Economist Gary Becker, who won a Nobel Prize for his work in human capital, estimates that about 75 percent of the wealth of a modern economy consists of the education, training, and skills of its people. "We really should call our economy a 'human capitalist economy,' for that is what it mainly is," he says. "Indeed, in a modern economy, human capital is by far the most important form of capital in creating wealth and growth."

Capital Resources: Tools, Machines, and Buildings

When most Americans use the word *capital,* they are thinking about money that they could invest in stocks, bonds, real estate, or businesses to produce future wealth. Economists sometimes refer to money used in this way as **financial capital.**

To an economist, however, money by itself does not produce anything. What matters in the production process are the tools, machines, and factory buildings that money can buy. To avoid confusion, these concrete productive resources are sometimes called **physical capital** or **capital goods**.

Looked at this way, capital consists of the tools, machines, and buildings used in the production of other goods and services. That last part—used in the production of other goods and services—matters. If you buy a car to drive to school and social events, it is a consumer good. If you buy a car to deliver pizzas for a restaurant, it is a capital good.

Capital takes a surprising number of forms. It includes tools as simple as a screwdriver and machines as complicated as a supercomputer. Factories, office towers, warehouses, bakeries, airports, and power plants are forms of capital. So are roads, electrical grids, sewer systems, and the Internet.

Since the beginning of the Industrial Revolution, capital has replaced labor in one area after another. This process began in the textile industry in England, where water-powered spinning machines and mechanical looms replaced spinners and weavers in the production of cloth. More recently, automated teller machines have taken over many services once handled by bank tellers. Robots have replaced assembly-line workers in automobile assembly plants. Each advance in physical capital, however, has created new needs for labor. Someone has to design, produce, and maintain the new machines.

Putting It All Together: Entrepreneurship

Entrepreneurship is a specialized and highly valued form of human capital. It involves the combining of land, labor, and capital in new ways to produce goods and services. Entrepreneurs perform several roles in the production process, including the four listed below.

Innovator. Entrepreneurs think of ways to turn new inventions, technologies, or techniques into goods or services that people will want.

Strategist. Entrepreneurs supply the vision and make the key decisions that set the course for new business enterprises.

Risk taker. Entrepreneurs take on the risks of starting new businesses. They invest their time, energy, and abilities—not to mention their own and often other people's money—not knowing whether they will succeed or fail.

Sparkplug. Entrepreneurs supply the energy, drive, and enthusiasm needed to turn ideas into realities. As entrepreneur Nolan Bushnell, founder of Atari and Chuck E. Cheese's Pizza Time Theaters, has observed,

> *The critical ingredient is getting off your butt and doing something. It's as simple as that. A lot of people have ideas, but there are few who decide to do something about them now. Not tomorrow. Not next week. But today. The true entrepreneur is a doer, not a dreamer.*

Entrepreneurs come in all sizes and ages. YouTube was founded in 2005 by three entrepreneurs in their 20s: Chad Hurley, Steve Chen, and Jawed Karim. First headquartered in a garage office, YouTube quickly became one the fastest-growing sites on the Web, with over 100 million video clips being viewed daily by mid-2006.

© Martin Klimek

Working Smarter Boosts Productivity

Because all three factors of production are scarce, we will never be able to produce all of the goods and services people might want. But by using these inputs more efficiently, we can increase the productivity of our economy. **Productivity** is a measure of the output of an economy per unit of input. It is determined by dividing total output by one of the three inputs involved in its production: land, labor, or capital.

$$\text{productivity} = \frac{\text{output}}{\text{input}}$$

Productivity is stated as a ratio of output per unit of input. For example, in measuring the productivity of a lumber mill, you would begin with its output in a given period of time—in this case, the number of board feet of lumber produced in a week. You would then divide the output by one input, such as the hours of labor needed to produce that output. The mill's productivity would be the ratio of board feet produced per hour.

Because productivity is a ratio of output to input, it can be raised in two ways. The first is by getting more output from the same inputs. In the case of the lumber mill, this might be accomplished by organizing the production process in a more efficient manner. By doing so, the same number of hours of labor (one of the mill's inputs) could produce more board feet of lumber (the mill's output) each week.

The second way to raise productivity is by getting the same output from fewer inputs. Looking again at the lumber mill, this could be done by finding a way to get more board feet of lumber out of each tree that the mill workers harvest. This improvement would enable the mill to produce the same amount of lumber (its output) using fewer trees (an input) and fewer workers to cut down the trees (another input).

■ 2.4 What Do We Give Up When We Make a Choice?

Some decisions in life are easy. You probably don't fret much over which option to choose from a school lunch menu. Other decisions are agonizing. Think back to the choice facing Mick Jagger when he realized he did not have enough time to both continue his studies and be the lead singer in a band. It was "very, very difficult," he said later, because his parents wanted him to stay in college. But there was another reason this decision was so tough. In making his choice, Jagger had to give up something he valued (education) to get something he valued even more (a chance to become a rock star).

Maximizing Utility: What We Want When We Choose

The way economists see the world, people seek to make themselves as well off as possible by maximizing the utility of their decisions. They usually define **utility** as the satisfaction or pleasure one gains from consuming a product or service or from taking an action. But utility is more than that. We also gain utility by making choices that, while not all that pleasurable, are likely to improve our lives. Getting a vaccination or studying for a test may not be your idea of fun, but both should make you better off in the long run.

Maximizing utility is seldom easy. Whether choosing which television program to watch or which college to attend, we seldom have enough information to be absolutely sure we have made the best choice. This was true for Mick Jagger as well. When choosing between school and music, he had no way of knowing how successful the Rolling Stones would become. Nonetheless, he made the best judgment he could about the utility of one alternative over the other. In retrospect, he seems to have gotten it right.

Key Concept

Productivity
Productivity measures the efficiency of production as a ratio of output to input. In a lumber mill, the output is lumber. One input is labor. Productivity in this case is the amount of lumber produced per hour of labor.

Productivity of a Lumber Mill

Outputs
Total board feet of lumber

Inputs
Total hours of labor

Productivity
Board feet of lumber produced per hour

Tradeoffs: What We Give Up When We Choose

As the scarcity-forces-tradeoffs principle reminds us, every decision we make—even one as simple as deciding to read this book—involves giving up one thing for another. To gain time to read, you are giving up all of the other things you could be doing right now. Each of those alternatives not chosen is a tradeoff.

Like individuals, businesses face tradeoffs as they try to maximize the utility of their land, labor, and capital. Suppose an automaker decided that it could best use all of its factories and workers to build pickup trucks instead of cars. The tradeoff of its decision would be the loss of its passenger car business.

Societies face tradeoffs as well. The classic example used by economists is the guns-versus-butter tradeoff, in which a society must choose between using its resources to produce guns (military goods) or butter (civilian goods). If the society chooses guns, it maximizes its security, but at the cost of lowering living standards. If it chooses butter, the society maximizes living standards, but at the cost of reducing security.

Opportunity Cost: The Best Thing We Give Up to Get What We Want

You may have noticed that each decision made by a society in the guns-versus-butter example involved a cost. The same is true for the decisions you make. When you choose one course of action, you lose the utility, or benefits, of the alternatives you did not choose. Were you to rank those alternatives, one would likely stand out as more attractive than the rest. While you might think of this option as your second best choice, an economist would see it as your opportunity cost.

The **opportunity cost** of any action is the value of the next best alternative that you could have chosen instead. Whether you have 2 alternatives or 200, your opportunity cost is simply the value of the next best one. Think back to Mick Jagger's decision. His opportunity cost of pursuing a singing career was the future utility of the college degree he never earned. Similarly, the opportunity cost of the automobile company that decided to produce only trucks was the money it would have made by continuing to produce cars.

Understanding the opportunity costs of the choices you face every day can help you make better decisions. Put yourself in this situation. There is a new video game you want to buy. You can download the game from an online store for $49.95. You can order the game CD from a computer catalog for $42.95 plus $3.00 shipping, but it will take at least a week to get to your home. Or you can buy it today for only $35.95 at a big box store in a nearby town, but it will take an hour of your time and about $4.00 of gas to drive there and back.

One way to sort through these alternatives is to lay them out on a decision matrix like the one in Figure 2.4. The matrix lists all the alternatives

---

Figure 2.4

Identifying Tradeoffs and Opportunity Costs

This decision matrix shows the tradeoffs associated with each of three purchase alternatives.

- Buying at a big box store is cheapest. Choose this if you are happy to trade off your time for money.
- Buying online is fastest. If you choose this, your opportunity cost will be the money you could have saved had you chosen the next best option.

Video-Game-Purchase Decision Matrix

	Price	Delivery Cost	Transaction Time	Delivery Time
Online store	$49.95	$0	5 minutes	7 minutes for download
Catalog	$42.95	$3.00 (shipping)	10 minutes	1 week for shipping
Big box store	$35.95	$4.00 (gas money)	1 hour or more	none

involved in the decision as well as the criteria, or factors, that might be used in evaluating those alternatives. In this instance, the factors are price, delivery cost, transaction time (how long it will take you to complete the purchase), and delivery time. The decision matrix doesn't tell you which alternative to choose, but it does clarify what you will gain and lose by choosing one over another.

After analyzing the alternatives, you decide you really want to buy the game today. If you choose to download it from the online store, your opportunity cost is the $10 you would have saved by driving to the big box store. If you choose to buy it from the store, your opportunity cost is the hour you would have saved by downloading the game.

Knowing the opportunity cost of each alternative still does not tell you what to do. That depends on the value of $10 or an hour's time to you. Should you have a better use for that hour, such as working at a job that pays $15 an hour, you probably would be better off downloading the game. If not, you might decide that trading an hour of your time for a savings of $10 is the better choice.

Making "How Much" Decisions at the Margin

Note that in the video-game-purchase scenario, you were not facing an all-or-nothing, "buy the game or do without" decision. Instead, you were employing the thinking-at-the-margin principle by looking at the marginal utility of one purchase alternative over another. **Marginal utility** is the extra satisfaction or pleasure you will get from an increase of one additional unit of a good or service. One alternative in the scenario left you with more time compared to the others. Another left you with more money.

An understanding of marginal utility begins with the recognition that the amount of satisfaction we get from something usually depends on how much of that something we already have. Suppose you are so thirsty after a workout that you buy yourself a large bottle of apple juice. The first glass provides you with a high level of utility by quenching your thirst. The second glass is still satisfying, but its marginal utility is less because you are no longer so thirsty. The third or fourth glass has less utility as your thirst disappears and your stomach fills up. The fifth glass, should you go on drinking, might have a **negative utility** by making you feel sick.

As this example shows, the marginal utility of something diminishes as we get more of it. This explains why a homeless person is more likely to pick up a dollar bill off the sidewalk than a millionaire is. The dollar has a relatively high marginal utility to a person with little money. Conversely, the marginal utility of an extra buck to a person who already has a million dollars is relatively low. An economist would

---

Key Concept

Tradeoffs and Opportunity Costs
Having trouble deciding on what to do next with your life? Know that you are not alone. In making this decision, you need to consider all of your options and the tradeoffs they present. Your opportunity cost will be the value to you of your next best choice once you make your decision.

The Decision Maker	**The Choice**	**The Tradeoffs**		
What to do after finishing high school?	Go to college.	Join a band?	Work at a bank?	Travel the world?

Opportunity cost: The value to you of your next best alternative, whether measured in money, utility, or happiness.

The Law of Diminishing Marginal Utility
The law of diminishing marginal utility tells us that the more we consume of something, the less satisfaction we will get from each additional unit of it.

Slice 1: Very high utility   Slice 2: High utility   Slice 6: Low utility   Slice 10: Negative utility

see this difference in behavior as an example of the **law of diminishing marginal utility**. According to this law, as the quantity of a good consumed increases, the marginal utility of each additional unit decreases.

Most of the choices we face every day are "how much" decisions *at the margin*. Think back to the video game example. How much more would you be willing to pay to get the game right now? How much longer would you be willing to wait to get the game for less? Whenever you find yourself asking "how much" questions like these while considering a choice, you are thinking at the margin.

■ 2.5 How Can We Measure What We Gain and Lose When Making Choices?

In 1719, approaching the somewhat advanced age of 60, Daniel Defoe published what would become one of the great classics of English literature: *The Life and Strange Surprising Adventures of Robinson Crusoe*. The novel tells the story of a sailor who spent 28 years marooned on a remote tropical island.

The tale may have been inspired by the true story of Alexander Selkirk, a Scottish sailor who was left on a small island off the coast of Chile by his shipmates in 1704. For the next four years and four months, Selkirk survived using whatever resources the island

had to offer. He became, in essence, a one-person economy. This makes him the ideal subject for exploring an economic model used to measure what we gain and lose when we decide how to use the resources available to us.

This illustration by American artist N. C. Wyeth first appeared in a 1920 edition of *Robinson Crusoe*. Castaway Alexander Selkirk, who may have inspired the novel, had no more capital goods than shown here with which to create his one-person island economy.

Measuring Tradeoffs Using the Production Possibilities Frontier

The **production possibilities frontier (PPF)** is an economic model, in the form of a line graph, that shows how an economy might use its resources to produce two goods. The graph shows all possible combinations of those goods that can be produced using the available resources and technology fully. It also helps us see the tradeoffs involved in devoting more resources to the production of one good or the other.

Figure 2.5A shows a PPF for Alexander Selkirk's one-person economy. It focuses on the production of two foods that were critical to his survival: clams and wild turnips. In this hypothetical example, Selkirk can use the four hours he spends each day gathering food to harvest either turnips or clams. Using his crude digging stick, he can dig up an average of 10 turnips an hour in the forest or 10 clams an hour on the beach.

The sloping line on the graph shows the various combinations of turnips and clams that Selkirk can produce in a day. That line, known as the **production possibilities curve,** is straight in this simple case. In the more complex example you will look at next, the line bows outward in a curve. This line is also called the production possibilities *frontier* because it represents the best that this economy can do with its current factors of production. Without better tools (capital) or more time devoted to food gathering (labor), Selkirk will never produce more than any combination of turnips and clams shown along the line graph.

Measuring Opportunity Costs Using the PPF

A PPF can also be used to measure the opportunity costs of different production choices. Consider a hypothetical country that can use its resources to produce just two goods: cell phones or bananas. Its land can be used for cell phone factories, banana plantations, or some combination of both. Its workers can be trained to assemble phones, raise bananas, or both. Its capital goods consist of assembly-line equipment, farm machinery, or some of each.

The graphs in Figure 2.5B show the different production possibilities for this two-goods economy, depending on how the country's resources are allocated. Notice the bowed-out shape of the curve in this PPF. This shape indicates that the tradeoffs in this economy are not the same at every point on the curve. As a result, the opportunity cost—what the country gives up—when choosing to produce more of either good changes as one moves along the curve.

Why would this be so? One reason might be that not all of the country's land is equally well suited for bananas or factories. Banana trees planted on poor land may not produce well. Factories located far from cities may have difficulty finding workers.

Another reason might be that the country's workers are not equally well trained for banana and cell phone production. Suppose the country decides to increase its output of bananas. To do so, it would have to move workers from its factories to its plantations. The factory workers would arrive at the plantations with very different skills (such as knowing how to assemble electronic components) than the experienced plantation workers. They would likely be less productive than workers who have been raising bananas for some time.

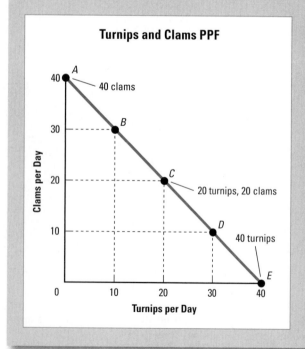

Figure 2.5A

Analyzing PPFs and Tradeoffs
Selkirk's production possibilities frontier shows all the combinations of turnips and clams that his one-person economy can produce.
- At Points *A* and *E,* Selkirk devotes his time to producing just one food, either 40 clams or 40 turnips.
- At Point *C,* he divides his time evenly between turnips and clams. His tradeoff compared to Point *A* is a loss of 20 clams in exchange for a gain of 20 turnips.

Turnips and Clams PPF

Measuring Economic Efficiency Using the PPF

The production possibilities frontier can also help us see how efficient our choices are. **Economic efficiency** is the result of using resources in a way that produces the maximum amount of goods and services. Every point on the PPF represents an efficient use of

Figure 2.5B

Analyzing PPFs and Opportunity Costs
The shape of this PPF indicates that the opportunity cost of producing more of one product is greater at some points along the curve than at others.
- Moving from Point *B* to Point *C* increases banana production by 200 pounds at the modest opportunity cost of 60 cell phones.
- Moving from Point *E* to Point *F* increases banana production by only 20 pounds at the much larger opportunity cost of 300 cell phones.

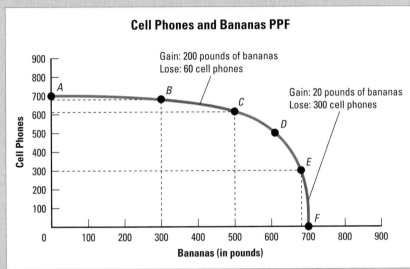

Analyzing PPFs and Efficiency
A PPF shows what an economy can produce using its resources as efficiently as possible.
- At Point *G*, the economy is not producing as many cell phones or bananas as it could.
- Point *H* represents a level of production that is not possible for this economy.

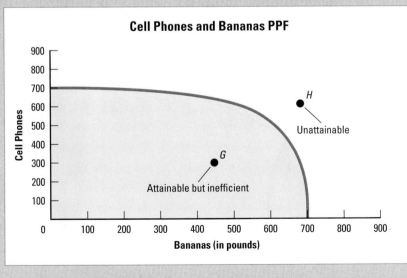

resources to produce that combination of outputs.

But what if an economy does not use its resources efficiently—or wishes to produce more than is currently possible given its resources? Both of those situations are illustrated in the second graph of Figure 2.5B.

Figure 2.5C

Analyzing PPFs and Changes in Productivity
Changes in productivity can shift part of a PPF to the right or left. In this graph, the productivity of banana plantations has been improved by the introduction of trees that bear more fruit. There is no change in the productivity of cell phone factories.
- Note that the PPF remains fixed at Point A while increasing between Points F and F_1.
- The productivity gains of banana growers can be measured anywhere along the curve by calculating the difference between the original PPF and the new PPF.

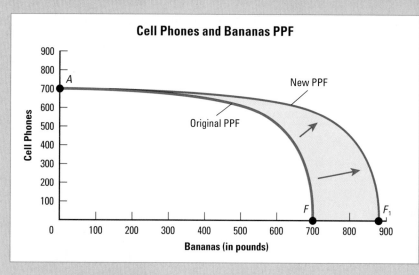

Analyzing PPFs and Changes in the Economy
Changes in a country's economy can shift an entire PPF to the right or left.
- A shift to the right is good news. It means that output is expanding and the economy is growing.
- A shift to the left is bad news. It means that output is shrinking and the economy is heading into harder times.

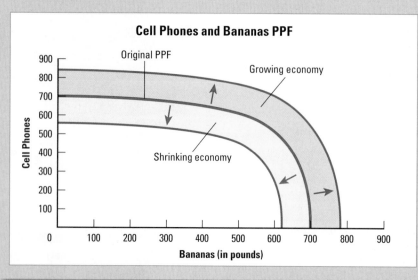

Every point in the shaded area inside the PPF represents a less efficient, but still attainable, production possibility. This reduced efficiency might be the result of a natural disaster or of a slowdown in the economy and a rise in unemployment. Whatever the reason, within this shaded area, the economy is not functioning at full efficiency.

Every point outside the PPF represents an unattainable production possibility. The economy's resources are already being used to the max to reach the points on the curve. Beyond those points, the economy cannot produce more without added resources or improvements in efficiency.

Reflecting Economic Change Using the PPF

A PPF is a snapshot of an economy's production possibilities at a specific moment in time. In the real world, these possibilities are constantly changing as economic conditions change. Improvements in productivity might mean more of one good can be produced using the same resources. Or the economy as a whole might expand or shrink. Both of these situations are illustrated in Figure 2.5C.

When an economy grows, economists say that the PPF has "shifted to the right." Productivity increases, jobs are more plentiful, and living standards improve. Likewise, when an economy shrinks, the PPF "shifts to the left." Productivity falls, unemployment rises, and living standards decline. A number of factors can cause such shifts, many of which you will study in the chapters ahead.

What is important to remember at this point is that while you can't always have everything you want, the decisions you make in life may influence what you get. The most important of those decisions, from an economic point of view, is how to maximize your human capital—and with that, your future earning power. You may never make enough money to get everything you want. But with enough human capital, you should be able, as the song says, to "get what you need."

Summary

Life is full of choices and decisions. The study of economics helps us see why we have to choose among alternatives. It also gives us tools for thinking about what we stand to gain and lose when making life's decisions.

Why is what we want scarce? Scarcity exists because our wants, which are infinite, exceed our resources, which are finite. Unlike shortages, which are temporary in nature, scarcity is an inescapable fact of life. It means we can never have everything we might want.

How do we satisfy economic wants? Goods and services are produced by bringing together the three factors of production: land, labor, and capital. Entrepreneurship is an essential part of the production process. Entrepreneurs combine land, labor, and capital in new ways to create products that satisfy economic wants.

What do we give up when we make a choice? Every choice involves tradeoffs among alternatives. When making a decision, people generally try to maximize the utility, or satisfaction, they hope to gain by choosing one alternative over another. The opportunity cost of any decision is the value of the next-best alternative.

How can we measure what we gain and lose when making choices? Economists use an economic model known as the production possibilities frontier to measure what we gain and lose when deciding how to use the factors of production in different ways. The model shows the tradeoffs and opportunity costs involved in producing more of one good at the expense of another. It also reminds us that even when an economy is working at peak efficiency, it won't be able to produce everything that we might want.

Are you maximizing the utility of your free time?

For many teenagers, the time they don't spend in school is a scarce resource. By 2004, the percentage of teenagers using that precious time to work for wages or to look for work had dropped to the lowest on record. This article explores some of the reasons why, including both the tradeoffs and opportunity costs of working or using nonschool time in other ways.

As you read the article, think about how you choose to use your free time. Are your choices maximizing your utility for today? Or building your human capital for tomorrow?

Full Activity, Study Schedules Have Many Teens Just Saying No to Jobs

by Barbara Hagenbaugh,
USA TODAY, April 7, 2005

Many teens today are working harder than ever—just not for a paycheck. Teens are studying more, are taking heavier course loads and are involved in more extracurricular activities than ever before. But the percentage of teenagers working or looking for work has steadily fallen in the past two decades . . .

What is in question is whether teens are missing out on important lessons learned from early work experience. Jeylan Mortimer, a sociology professor . . . at the University of Minnesota, . . . has found that working moderate amounts during high school was beneficial not just while the students were in school but beyond.

Teens who worked learned key basics, what she calls "generic learning," such as showing up on time and dealing with supervisors. They also developed stronger self-esteem and other traits that carried beyond their teen years . . . "They learned how to deal with people, they developed interpersonal skills, they learned how to overcome shyness."

But while some economists, sociologists and psychologists say it is important to learn those lessons at an early age, others argue that the type of work teens do generally doesn't help that much later in life . . . If students are focusing their attention on school and other worthwhile activities, their lack of work experience might not be harmful in the long run.

"This could be a good thing," says Erica Groshen, an economist at the Federal Reserve Bank of New York . . . "for employers and for society as a whole if it means we are getting more and better education for our workers."

Not Enough Time

Brian Cavanagh-Strong, 18, of Ann Arbor, Mich., has worked a total of three weeks in his life, but he's hardly sitting around watching reruns of *Friends.*

The high school senior gets all A's and takes a heavy course load, including advanced journalism, advanced Latin poetry, a one-on-one advanced calculus course, and writing. After school, he participates in theater, currently rehearsing two hours a day . . . practices jazz piano at least $1\frac{1}{2}$ hours a day in addition to playing in a band, then studies for a few hours. All of those activities leave little time for work, he says . . .

Cavanagh-Strong's parents give him a monthly allowance for expenses. In return, he works around the house . . .

The decline in teens working is not a result of rich kids getting handouts from mom and dad . . . From 1990 to 2002 [the drop] was much more pronounced among kids from families whose income ranks in the bottom quarter than those from the highest. Middle-income kids had the greatest likelihood of working . . .

Pressure to achieve—at school, in sports and in other activities—is one of the key theories for why fewer teens have jobs:

School . . . There is evidence that kids are working harder in school. In 2004, the number of Advanced Placement tests taken by high school students was up 65% from five years earlier . . . The more hours students spent on homework, the less likely they were to have jobs . . .

College pressure . . . Many students think colleges see holding offices in extracurricular groups, such as Spanish Club and band, as more valuable than working six hours a week as a cashier . . .

But Andrew Flagel, dean of admissions at George Mason University outside Washington, D.C., says working can be an important asset on applications.

"It doesn't sound to anyone like working at the local diner is sexy enough," he says. "But I've read wonderful essays from students who talk about the difference they made in doing their jobs."

College is costly . . . With costs mounting, the expectation that students can save for college working part time while in high school and make a dent in their expenses has eroded significantly. To some students, it makes more sense to spend the time studying for the SATs rather than working . . .

While some research has shown that working while in school helps students manage their time better, leading them to earn better grades and make more money when they graduate, other studies have shown teen work has no effect and might hurt students when they try to go to school at the same time.

"I personally don't think it does them much good . . . ," says Jeffrey Arnett, a psychology professor at the University of Maryland . . . "The work itself is usually mindless drudgery." . . .

But Atlanta honors student Stephanie Binkow, 16, thinks her time working Saturdays at Dolce, a gourmet food, candy and chocolate shop, is well worth it. That's not because the money helps pay for trips to Starbucks with friends or to fill the gas tank or to save for college. "I get to see what life will be like when I'm 25 or 30," the high school sophomore says.

Barbara Hagenbaugh reports on economic issues for USA TODAY.

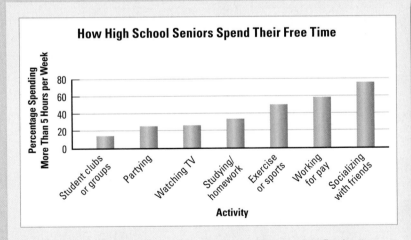

How High School Seniors Spend Their Free Time

Three-fourths of high school seniors say they spend more than five hours a week socializing with friends. Working for pay and participating in sports come in second and third.

Who or what decides what you get?

Economic Systems

3.1 Introduction

It is a Saturday afternoon, and across the United States, supermarkets are hopping. Parking lots are full. Inside, brightly lit shelves are neatly stocked with every imaginable foodstuff and household item. Shoppers maneuver their carts through the aisles, deciding which products to buy from a seemingly endless array of choices.

It was on a day like this in 1989 that Boris Yeltsin, a popular political leader from the Soviet Union and formerly chief of the Moscow Communist Party, visited a supermarket in Houston, Texas. It was one of many stops on a two-week tour of the United States.

To Yeltsin, the sight of ordinary people doing their weekly grocery shopping was anything but ordinary. In fact, to someone who had lived his whole life under communism, it was a revelation. A local newspaper reported that Yeltsin wandered the aisles, shaking his head in amazement. He sampled cheese and produce. He stared at the meat displays. He stopped customers to ask about the items in their carts and how much they cost. He asked the manager whether special training was necessary to run a supermarket.

Yeltsin's reaction was understandable. By the late 1980s, the state-run Soviet economy was in shambles. Consumer goods were scarce. People had to wait in long lines to buy food and other necessities. Store shelves were frequently empty of all but one or two poorly made goods. Even the privileged Communist Party elite did not enjoy such abundance as could be found in the average American supermarket.

The U.S. economy offers grocery store customers an abundance of choices.

In the late 1980s, Boris Yeltsin challenged the leaders of the Soviet Union over the slow pace of economic reforms. A visit to the United States in 1989 convinced him that communism was doomed to failure. After the collapse of the Soviet Union in 1991, Yeltsin became the first-ever freely elected president of Russia.

The stark contrast between American and Russian living standards was, Yeltsin later wrote, "shattering."

> When I saw those shelves crammed with hundreds, thousands of cans, cartons, and goods of every possible sort, for the first time I felt quite frankly sick with despair for the Soviet people. That such a potentially super-rich country as ours has been brought to a state of such poverty! It is terrible to think of it.
> —Boris Yeltsin, *Against the Grain,* 1990

The visit confirmed for Yeltsin the painful truth about the Soviet economic system: it was a complete failure. In Houston and other American cities, he saw a very different economic system at work.

In this chapter, you will explore different economic systems. You will see why one has succeeded where the other has failed. And you will find out who, in our society, determines what you get.

■ 3.2 Who Gets What? How Do Societies Decide?

If resources were unlimited, we could all have whatever we want. But as the scarcity-forces-tradeoff principle reminds us, resources are limited. Just as scarcity forces individuals to make choices about what to have and what to give up, it also forces societies to make choices. The larger and more advanced a society is, the more numerous and complex these choices may be. In the end, however, these choices boil down to three basic questions.

The Three Fundamental Economic Questions: What to Produce, How, and for Whom?

In deciding how to allocate limited resources, every society—from a tribe of people living in the Kalahari Desert to a modern industrial nation like the United States—must answer three fundamental economic questions. Each society answers these questions differently, depending on its priorities. The questions, however, are the same for everybody.

What goods and services are to be produced? Because of scarcity, no society can produce everything its people might want. This raises the question: What goods and services are most wanted and needed? For example, should the United States conserve wilderness areas for recreational purposes or open them up to logging or oil exploration? Should the U.S. steel industry produce more car parts or more beams for skyscrapers? What do consumers want or need more: sneakers or diapers? Teachers or dentists? Books or video games? With millions of possible products and many different interests competing for the same limited resources, the choices seem endless.

Even the simplest societies face difficult choices. Vanuatu is a nation of several small islands in the South Pacific. Vanuatu's economy has long depended on agriculture, but tourism is growing in importance. The question looming over Vanuatu's people is about what will benefit them more—putting more resources into growing food, or expanding tourist services? As a society, Vanuatuans must decide.

How are goods and services to be produced? The answer to this question is not as simple as it may seem. You know that goods and services are produced by combining the factors of production: land, labor, and capital. But how is this done, exactly, and in what combination?

Consider wheat production. How should land, labor, and capital be used to raise this essential grain? Should wheat be grown mainly on giant factory farms?

The Three Basic Economic Questions

Every society—no matter how rich or poor—must answer three basic economic questions about the goods and services its people want.

What will be produced? Even with our limited resources, billions of things might be produced. Who or what decides which wants to fulfill and which to leave unsatisfied?

How will it be produced? There are many ways to produce a desired item. Who decides how the factors of production will be organized to make what people want?

For whom will it be produced? Once an item is produced, the question remains: who should get it? The first person in line? The highest bidder? The person who needs it most?

That is the way an American agribusiness raises wheat. But in a different society—say, in France—wheat is more likely to be grown on smaller family farms. Think about another example: hats. Should hats be crafted individually, by hand, or in factories by machines? Each society has to decide for itself the answer to such questions.

At this point, you are probably wondering why a society as a whole has to make decisions about hats. Don't hat manufacturers decide how to produce headwear? In the United States, they do. But that is because our society gives them that choice. Not all societies work this way.

For whom are goods and services to be produced? In other words, who gets what? This last question is a difficult one, because it inevitably raises the slippery question of fairness: who *deserves* what? Again, every society finds its own answer.

Goods and services are distributed in a variety of ways. The ability to pay is the approach most of us know best. It essentially says that anyone who can afford to buy a hat can have one.

Another approach is equal distribution. This approach was adopted by the Soviet Union before its collapse. Unfortunately, goods were in such short supply that lines formed for everything. Instead of distributing goods equally, the system favored those

who got in line early and had time to wait. As a result, some people got more than their share, while others got nothing.

This brings us to yet another form of distribution: first come, first served. As in the Soviet Union, this approach often prevails when quantities are limited. Goods such as concert and theater tickets are usually sold this way.

In addition, there is distribution according to need. A soup kitchen does this when it provides meals to the homeless. So does a public school that provides classroom aides for special education students.

A Society's Answers Depend on Its Economic Goals

The way a society answers the three economic questions will necessarily depend on its economic aspirations and social values. Most societies try to address some or all of the following six economic goals.

Economic freedom. In our society, we place a high value on **economic freedom**—the ability to make our own economic decisions without interference from the government. When you choose to buy something, whether it is a music download or a used car, you are exercising this freedom. When you choose to sell your car or go into business selling cars or anything else, you are exercising this freedom. A society that values economic freedom gives individuals and businesses the right to make decisions about how to use their resources, without government intervention.

Economic efficiency. An efficient economy makes the most of society's resources. It delivers the goods, literally, by allocating resources in such a way that the greatest number of consumers get what they want with the least amount of waste. Because unemployed workers are a wasted resource, an efficient economy strives for **full employment,** which exists when all who want to work can find jobs.

Economic equity. The term equity concerns fairness and justice. **Economic equity** involves the fair and just distribution of a society's wealth. A society that values economic equity seeks to give everyone his or her fair share of the economic pie. But what constitutes a fair share? Is it fair that corporate executives make millions while retail workers earn minimum wage? Is it fair that women, as a group, earn less than men? People often disagree on questions of equity, which makes it a difficult goal to achieve.

Economic growth. An economy is said to grow when it produces more and better goods and services. **Economic growth** is desirable because over time it leads to an improved standard of living. A century ago, middle-class Americans lived without cars, electricity, kitchen appliances, and indoor plumbing (not to mention antibiotics, frozen foods, and the Internet). A key element of economic growth is scientific and technological innovation. New ideas and inventions bring new and improved products into the market, creating economic growth and raising living standards.

Economic security. Every society has people who cannot provide for themselves. They may be too young, too old, too sick, or too poor to meet all of their basic needs. A society that puts a high value on **economic security** seeks to provide its less fortunate members with the support they need in terms of food, shelter, and health care to live decently. This is another economic goal about which people often disagree. As Figure 3.2 shows, in the United States, access to affordable health insurance, which most people need to pay for health care, differs greatly from state to state. Even when Americans agree that access to health care should be provided to everyone, they do not agree on how this goal should be accomplished.

Economic stability. No one likes economic uncertainty. Societies therefore strive for its opposite: economic stability. **Economic stability** means that the goods and services we count on—electricity on demand, food and clothing in the stores—are there when we want them. Our jobs are there when we go to work each day. Prices are predictable, allowing us to plan ahead for purchases.

Most societies consider these goals when making economic choices. But societies differ in the degree of importance they attach to each goal. Sometimes progress toward one goal can be achieved only at the expense of another. For example, when the government taxes our wages in order to pay unemployment

In a society that values economic freedom, people are free to own, buy, and sell property. Sellers are also free to decide what price they are willing to set.

Figure 3.2

Mapping and Graphing Economic Insecurity

Almost everyone agrees that access to affordable health care is essential to economic security. Yet nearly 45 million Americans under the age of 65 lacked health insurance in 2005. How best to close the health care gap became a major issue in the 2008 presidential campaign.

- Find your state on the map. How did it stack up in terms of insurance coverage in 2005?
- Study the graph. What does it tell you about your chances of joining the ranks of the uninsured after you leave school?

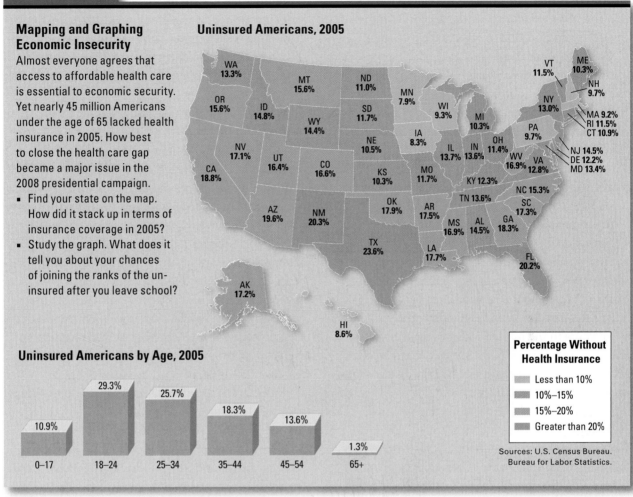

Uninsured Americans, 2005

Uninsured Americans by Age, 2005

0–17: 10.9%
18–24: 29.3%
25–34: 25.7%
35–44: 18.3%
45–54: 13.6%
65+: 1.3%

Percentage Without Health Insurance

- Less than 10%
- 10%–15%
- 15%–20%
- Greater than 20%

Sources: U.S. Census Bureau. Bureau for Labor Statistics.

---

benefits, it is contributing to society's economic security. But it is also encroaching on our economic freedom to control our own resources. Societies, like individuals, must weigh the tradeoffs and opportunity costs of pursuing any particular set of economic goals.

■ 3.3 Who Decides What in Different Economic Systems?

In the process of answering the three economic questions, every society develops an economic system. An **economic system** is the way a society coordinates the production and consumption of goods and services. Economic systems are as old as humankind, so you might expect there to be many different models. But if we strip away all the cultural differences that exist between all the societies that ever were, we find that history has produced only three basic types of eco-

nomic systems. There are those built on tradition, those based on the command of rulers, and those organized by free markets. Each system answers the three economic questions differently. And each emphasizes different economic goals.

Traditional Economies: Decision Making by Custom

The first and oldest economic system is the traditional economy. Traditional economies have existed since the first clans of hunter-gatherers emerged in Africa. In a **traditional economy,** custom and tradition dictate what to produce, how to produce it, and for whom.

Most traditional economies that survive today belong to indigenous people who live much as their ancestors did hundreds or thousands of years ago. The Maasai of East Africa, for example, are a semi-nomadic herding people. Livestock, primarily cattle, is the mainstay of their economy. Maasai wealth is measured in cattle and children. The traditional

Maasai diet consists primarily of meat, blood, and milk from cattle. The Maasai's answer to the question of *what to produce* is cattle, because it is their centuries-old tradition to raise cattle.

As for the question of *how to produce,* people in traditional economies engage in farming, herding, fishing, hunting, and the gathering of wild plants. Exactly who does what is determined by social customs. Labor is often divided along gender lines. Among the Maasai, for example, men build enclosures to protect the cattle from lions. Boys graze the cattle. Women and girls milk the cattle. Among the Khoi-San people of the Kalahari Desert in Southern Africa, men hunt and women gather.

For whom to produce is another question decided by tradition. Social hierarchies play an important role. A good illustration of this is the way meat is distributed among the Khoi-San people of the Kalahari. After a hunt, the kill is divided up, with a large share going to the hunter. He gives some to relatives, and they give part of theirs to other relatives, all according to the accepted social order. In the end, everyone gets enough to eat.

The highest goals of people in a traditional economy are economic stability and security. Most want nothing more than to live as they always have, following traditional ways of life, in harmony with nature. For most traditional societies, though, this goal is increasingly difficult to attain. Traditional economies have become shrinking outposts of the past surrounded by the modern world. As modern economies exert an ever-growing influence, traditional societies are struggling to find a path to economic survival.

Command Economies: Decision Making by Powerful Rulers

The next economic system to develop is what economists call a command economy. In a **command economy,** decisions about what, how, and for whom to produce are made by a powerful ruler or some other authority.

The earliest command economies originated in Mesopotamia, Egypt, China, and India about 5,000 years ago. As these civilizations became highly advanced, centralized governments arose that were headed by powerful rulers. These rulers imposed their economic choices on society. This happened even as tradition still guided economic activity at the lower levels of society.

Rulers at the top of these early civilizations—kings, pharaohs, emperors—commanded the populace to devote economic resources to building projects or military adventures. Many thousands of people might be conscripted to build a pyramid, defensive wall, irrigation canal, temple, or road. In a preindustrial age,

This herder is one of the Maasai people of East Africa. Livestock has been the mainstay of the Maasai economy for centuries. Cattle are used for food, building materials, and trade. Like people in other traditional economies, the Maasai decide what, how, and for whom to produce based on long-standing customs and traditions.

The Great Pyramid of Giza was built as a tomb for the Egyptian pharaoh Khufu around 2560 B.C.E. Historians estimate it took 20 years and tens of thousands of workers to construct the pyramid. In ancient command economies, economic decisions were made by powerful rulers who used their power to force people to labor on monumental works, many of which still stand.

such projects took vast quantities of human labor. Often, many people would be drafted into a ruler's army and sent into battle in distant lands.

The primary goal of these ancient command economies was to accumulate wealth and goods for the ruling class while preserving economic stability. The many monuments these societies left behind are a testament to both the productive power of these economies and the excesses of their rulers.

Market Economies: Decision Making by Individuals

The newest economic system to emerge in human history is the market economy. A **market economy** depends not on tradition or command to coordinate its activities but on the decisions of individual producers and consumers. Note that when economists speak of "the market," they are referring to the economic system within which buyers and sellers exchange goods and services. This is distinct from an everyday market, which is a place where people buy and sell goods.

In a **free market economy,** the workings of the market are not planned or directed. No one—no single person, business, or government agency—tells producers or consumers what to do. Economic deci-sions are made voluntarily, one at a time, by millions of individuals guided by self-interest.

The highest goals of a market economy are economic freedom and efficiency. Individuals and businesses are left at liberty to decide what, how, and for whom to produce. The producers of goods and services make these decisions based largely on consumers' spending decisions. Because you are free to buy what you want, producers must compete for your dollars. This competition means that you, the consumer, have many choices. It also forces pro-ducers to use resources efficiently. If they do not, a competitor will find a way to offer the same good or service at a price that consumers will be more will-ing to pay.

In a free market, individuals are encouraged to pursue the jobs that allow them to make the most of their human capital. If one employer fails to pay them what they think they are worth, they can quit and seek employment elsewhere. Or they can start their own businesses, perhaps even offering new products or services to consumers.

You might expect that the result of all this indi-vidual decision making and competition would be chaos. But as the markets-coordinate-trade prin-ciple reminds us, just the opposite is true. Markets are highly efficient at producing a great variety of goods and services that people find attractive and at prices they are willing to pay. It was this coordinat-ing power of markets that Adam Smith famously described as "the invisible hand." He wrote,

> *Every individual . . . neither intends to promote the public interest, nor knows how much he is promoting it . . . He intends only his own gain, and he is in this, as in many other cases, led by an invisible hand to promote an end which was no part of his intention . . . By pursuing his own interest he frequently promotes that of the society more effectually than when he really intends to promote it.*
>
> —Adam Smith, *The Wealth of Nations,* 1776

The Flow of Money and Goods in a Market Economy

The reason markets work so well is that one person's output always becomes another person's input. Goods are produced and consumed. Money comes in and

Figure 3.3

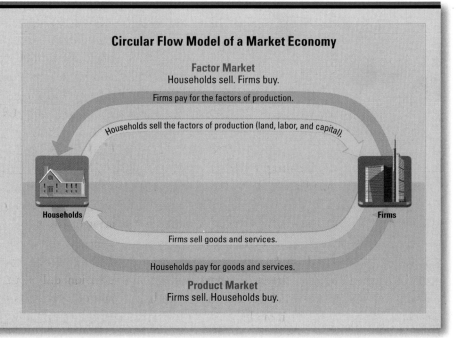

Modeling a Market Economy

This economic model shows how money, goods, and resources circulate in a market economy. The model assumes that households own the factors of production.

- The clockwise flow represents the movement of products and resources. Goods and services flow from firms to households. Land, labor, and capital flow from households to firms.

- The counterclockwise flow represents the movement of money. Money flows from households to firms in payment for goods and services. It flows from firms to households as payment for land, labor, and capital.

Circular Flow Model of a Market Economy

Factor Market
Households sell. Firms buy.

Firms pay for the factors of production.

Households sell the factors of production (land, labor, and capital).

Households

Firms

Firms sell goods and services.

Households pay for goods and services.

Product Market
Firms sell. Households buy.

goes out. This flow keeps the economy running. Economists use the **circular flow model,** like that in Figure 3.3, to illustrate these interactions.

In the simplified market economy shown in the model, there are two kinds of participants: households and firms. A **household** is made up of a person or of a group of people living together. The model assumes that households own the factors of production. A **firm** is an organization that uses these factors to make and sell goods or services.

The model also shows two kinds of markets. One is the **product market,** in which goods and services are sold by firms and purchased by households. Your local mall or supermarket is part of the product market. The other is the **factor market,** in which households sell their land, labor, and capital to firms. A household, for example, might rent land to a firm. Or members of a household might sell their labor to a firm for wages. They might loan money to a firm in exchange for interest payments. Or they might buy a firm's stock in the hopes of receiving dividend payments. The funds paid to households—whether in the form of rent, wages, interest, or dividends—are known as **factor payments**.

Follow the arrows of the diagram to see the circularity. Households buy products from firms with money that they receive in the factor market. Firms

acquire land, labor, and capital from households using money that they receive in the product market. For example, you (as part of a household) might buy a pair of jeans from a firm with money that you earned by working at a local ice cream parlor (another firm). The ice cream parlor, in turn, pays you for your labor with money that it receives from selling ice cream cones to other households.

All these transactions are conducted by people and businesses who want something for themselves. People work so they can buy things. Firms employ people so they can make things to sell. In a market economy, everybody chooses what is best for him- or herself. As Adam Smith wisely observed, "It is not from the benevolence of the butcher, the brewer, or the baker, that we expect our dinner, but from their regard to their own interest."

Capitalism Gives Rise to Socialism and Communism

Market economies emerged in Europe in the 1700s and began to grow rapidly in the 1800s. This economic growth was a direct result of the **Industrial Revolution**. During the Industrial Revolution, new inventions and manufacturing processes spurred the growth of industry. Individual investors, called **capitalists,** grew wealthy by accumulating capital, including machinery, factories, railroads, and the like. The term **capitalism** came to be synonymous with the free market economic system.

The headlong growth of capitalism had profound effects on society. As more and better goods became widely available, people's standard of living improved. But capitalism did not improve the quality of life for everybody. The workers who filled the factories and mills labored under harsh conditions. Hours were long, and wages were low. Critics of capitalism blamed the capitalists for exploiting workers and keeping them in poverty.

In 1848, economist Karl Marx and philosopher Friedrich Engels published *The Communist Manifesto,* in which they advocated the overthrow of capitalism. They proposed an alternative vision of society known as socialism. **Socialism** is a political and economic philosophy that calls for property to be owned by society as a whole, rather than by individuals, for the equal benefit of all.

To bring about this socialist vision of society, Marx and Engels called on workers everywhere to revolt against their governments. Once the workers had gained power, private property and the free market would be replaced with national ownership of industry and more equal distribution of income.

The final phase of socialism, in the view of Marx and Engels, is **communism,** a political and economic system in which all property and wealth are owned by all members of society. In a communist society, class differences—and the conflicts they create—disappear. Once that happens, government is no longer needed to keep order. Instead of self-interest, people in a communist society are guided by Marx's famous slogan: "From each according to his ability, to each according to his needs."

Modern Command Economies: Decision Making by the State

The ideas of Marx and Engels spurred the development of political movements dedicated to the creation of a workers' paradise. But when the first successful communist revolution took place in Russia in 1917, it did not lead to the utopian society Marx had envisioned. Instead, the revolutionaries formed an authoritarian government that pursued its socialist goals with brutal force. The renamed Union of Soviet Socialist Republics, or Soviet Union for short, became the first modern command economy.

In the Soviet Union, private ownership of property was forbidden. The state owned the factors of production. **Economic planning** was done by government committees of economists, production experts, and political officials. These central planning committees attempted to perform the functions of a market.

The Granger Collection, New York

This Soviet-era billboard celebrates the heroes of the world's first socialist command economy. Karl Marx and Frederick Engels, authors of *The Communist Manifesto,* appear to the left. Vladimir Lenin, the revolutionary first leader of the Soviet Union, is to their right. Joseph Stalin, who ruled the Soviet Union with an iron fist until his death in 1953, is shown at the far right.

They decided what goods and services should be produced. They decided which farms and factories should get which resources to produce what was planned. Committees also controlled prices and wages and decided how goods and services should be distributed.

In theory, this kind of planning was supposed to ensure economic equity and security—two important goals of a modern command economy. But the reality was very different. The planning committees could not keep track of the millions of products and prices in the Soviet system. Two Soviet economists described what happened when Goskomsten, the committee in charge of prices, raised the price that the government would pay hunters for moleskins.

> State purchases increased, and now all the distribution centers are filled with these pelts. Industry is unable to use them all, and they often rot in warehouses before they can be processed. The Ministry of Light Industry has already requested Goskomsten twice to lower purchasing prices, but the "question has not been decided" yet. And this is not surprising. Its members are too busy to decide. They have no time: besides setting prices on these pelts, they have to keep track of another 24 million prices.
> —Nikolai Shmelev and Vladmir Popov,
> The Turning Point: Revitalizing
> the Soviet Economy, 1990

In this planned economy, shortages were common. Long lines would form to buy whatever goods suddenly became available. But once a customer got to the front of that line, choice was limited or nonexistent.

Planners made matters worse by ignoring the incentives-matter principle. The wages paid to workers were determined by government committees, not by a worker's ability or output. A poor worker could not be fired for slacking off. Nor could a good worker be rewarded for working hard. Under this system, workers had little or no incentive to produce high-quality goods. They also lacked any incentive to innovate in order to increase productivity. As a result, production was slow, and the goods produced were often shoddy, far inferior to those produced in a market economy.

The Soviet Union and other command economies did succeed in increasing economic equity and economic security for their people. But what good is a guaranteed income if there is nothing to buy? What markets do effortlessly, command economies struggle to do, usually with dismal results. Central planning was so inefficient and wasteful that the Soviet Union economy eventually collapsed. Since then, virtually all modern command economies have either failed or struggled to introduce market-based reforms.

Three Economic Systems and Their Goals

Over time, human societies have developed three types of economic systems. In each system, decisions about what, how, and for whom to produce goods and services are made differently. Each system also emphasizes different economic goals, as shown here.

Traditional Economy
Economic decisions are based on tradition and custom.

Command Economy
Economic decisions are made by a single authority, such as a government agency.

Market Economy
Economic decisions are made by individual producers and consumers interacting freely in the marketplace.

■ 3.4 How Do Mixed Economies Divide the Decision Making?

No country in the world today relies on a purely traditional, market, or command economic system. These systems represent theoretical extremes. Nearly all countries have mixed economies that fall somewhere in between these extremes. In a **mixed economy,** both the government and individuals play important roles with regard to production and consumption. But who decides what varies from one country to another.

Government's Role in a Mixed Economy: Protection, Regulation, and Public Benefits

Every nation with a mixed economy forges its own balance between market freedom and government involvement. At the minimum, governments are needed to establish the institutions that enable markets to operate. Such institutions include a legal system to enforce laws and a stable system of currency. Most of us never think about these things, but markets cannot function without them.

In many countries, people expect government to go further. They want it to step in when the market operates in ways that society finds unacceptable.

For example, many nations outlaw child labor. Some governments limit the amount of pollution that industries can discharge. In the United States, the government regulates the manufacture of cosmetics, foods, and drugs because consumers want to know that products on the market are safe. Not all governments regulate to the same degree. Each society decides how far it wants its government to go in curtailing the freedom of the market.

Finally, government provides certain goods and services that markets do not always provide or do not provide enough of. Examples include **public works,** or government-financed projects such as dams, highways, and sewer systems. The market does not provide these goods because, as Adam Smith explained, the cost of providing them "could never repay the expence to any individual or small number of individuals."

What a government provides varies from country to country. In Canada and much of Europe, health care is provided free to every citizen. Some governments provide free college education or free day care. Governments that provide a high level of goods and services also tax heavily to pay for those goods and services. Again, these are economic choices that every nation makes differently.

A public lending library is an example of a valuable service to society that a free market is not likely to provide. Each society has to decide what goods and services it wants its government to provide.

Figure 3.4A

Modeling a Mixed Economy

This economic model shows how government affects the flow of money, goods, and resources in a mixed economy.

- Households supply taxes and labor to the government.
- Firms supply taxes and products to the government.
- The government supplies services to households and firms. It also pays households and firms for their labor and products, as well as sending transfer payments to households.

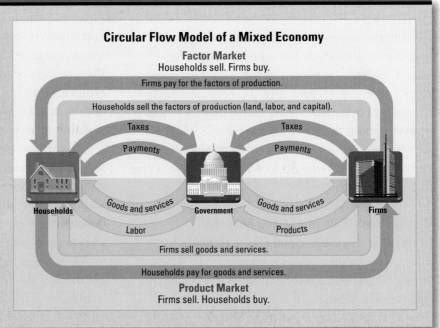

Circular Flow Model of a Mixed Economy

Factor Market
Households sell. Firms buy.

Firms pay for the factors of production.

Households sell the factors of production (land, labor, and capital).

Taxes · Payments · Taxes · Payments

Households · Goods and services · Government · Goods and services · Firms

Labor · Products

Firms sell goods and services.

Households pay for goods and services.

Product Market
Firms sell. Households buy.

The Flow of Goods and Money in a Mixed Economy

How does government participation in the economy change the flow of money and goods? The answer to this can be seen by adding government to the circular flow model. The revised circular flow model in Figure 3.4A shows a mixed economy with three participants: households, firms, and government.

A government enters the flow of money and products through an economy in a number of ways. It purchases land, labor, and capital from households in the factor market. In the United States, the federal government employs almost 2 million people, making it the nation's largest employer. A government also purchases goods and services from firms in the product market. As the nation's largest employer, the federal government is also its largest customer, spending hundreds of billions of dollars a year on goods and services.

Governments also combine land, labor, and capital to produce and distribute goods and services. As an example, suppose a town decides it needs a library. The town government buys land and hires architects and builders in the factor market. Later, the town buys books, shelves, computers, and furniture in the product market. Finally, it hires librarians in the factor market. The end result is a public service that the entire community can enjoy.

Now follow the flow of money in a mixed economy. You will see that a government collects taxes from both households and firms. It uses some of this money to pay for the goods and services it buys from firms. It may also transfer some money back to households as payment for government benefits. Social Security checks, welfare payments, and unemployment benefits are examples of government **transfer payments**.

The Mixed Economy Continuum: From Free to Repressed

Although most of today's economies can be described as mixed, the "mix" of market freedom and government control varies greatly from one nation to the next. In 2008, the Heritage Foundation and the *Wall Street Journal* published their annual Index of Economic Freedom. This index is a kind of scorecard that ranks the economic freedom of the world's nations. It is a useful tool for understanding the variety of mixed economies.

Near the top of the rankings is Australia, which was rated the fourth-most-free economy. Free markets dominate Australia's mixed economy. All banks are privately owned. The economy is open to foreign investment and trade. Private property is very secure. Starting a business is easy, taking an average of only two days.

At the very bottom of the list is North Korea, which came in last of the 157 ranked nations. A communist country since 1948, North Korea still has a tightly controlled command economy. The government directs all industries and businesses. Nearly all foreign trade is forbidden. Private property is severely restricted.

What about countries that fall somewhere in between, such as Japan, South Africa, and France? All three have mixed economies dominated by the market system. All have relatively high levels of economic freedom and secure property rights. But they also have high tax rates, which are used to pay for an array of public services and benefits, such as government-provided health care. In these nations,

people have decided that achieving economic equity and security for more members of society is worth giving up some measure of their individual wealth.

Further down in the rankings is China, which is rated "mostly unfree." China, which has had a communist government since 1949, is in transition from a command economy to a market-oriented system. But its mixed economy is still dominated by an authoritarian government. All Chinese banks are owned by the state. Private property is not secure. Internet use is tightly controlled by the government.

Still, China allows more economic freedom than many countries. Iran, for example, is rated "repressed." Its economy is dominated by the state. The oil and gas industries are owned by the government, as are

Figure 3.4B

Mapping Economic Freedom

Whereas most countries today have mixed economies, the level of economic freedom their citizens enjoy varies widely. The Index of Economic Freedom ranks countries based on 10 indicators, including the ease of starting a new business, protection of property rights, and freedom from corruption. The 2008 rankings—from a high of 90 percent to a low of 3 percent—are displayed on the map.

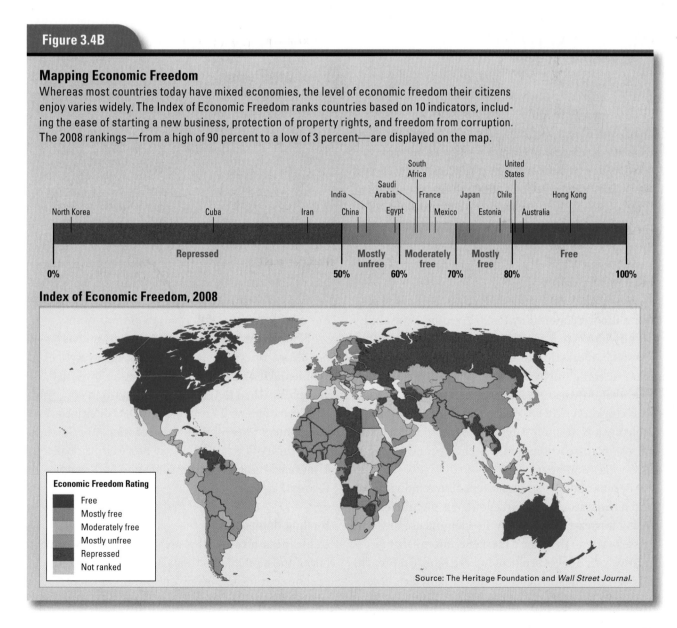

Index of Economic Freedom, 2008

Source: The Heritage Foundation and *Wall Street Journal*.

almost all banks. As in repressed North Korea, foreign investment in Iran is severely restricted. Iran's legal system does not uphold property rights or contracts.

Only six countries in the *2008 Index of Economic Freedom,* plus Hong Kong, were rated "free." In addition to Australia, these countries are Singapore, Ireland, the United States, New Zealand, and Canada. What do these countries have in common? All have mixed economies dominated by free markets. Most have democratic forms of government. They are also all among the wealthiest nations in the world. As Adam Smith might have predicted, the societies with the most economic freedom are also among the most prosperous.

■ 3.5 What Are the Key Characteristics of the U.S. Economic System?

The high ranking of the United States on the Index of Economic Freedom is not surprising. Americans dearly value their economic freedom, so much so that we even describe our economy as a free enterprise system. In a **free enterprise system,** individuals own the factors of production and make decisions about how to use those factors within the framework of the law. Seven key characteristics of a free enterprise system are explored below.

Economic Freedom
As the term free enterprise suggests, the essence of our nation's economic system is freedom—the ability of individuals to act in their own best interest in free markets. In practical terms, this means we can buy what we want and from whom we want. If we do not like what one firm is selling, we can take our business elsewhere. We are free to start businesses or to seek any job we choose. Firms are free to make what they want, hire whomever they choose, and set their own wages and prices.

Because our economic system allows individuals and businesses so much freedom, it is often referred to as a **laissez-faire** economy. Economists use the term laissez-faire to describe a market economy that is relatively free of government intervention. (In French, laissez-faire means "let them do.") But in fact, laws exist that limit what producers and consumers can

do in this country. Stores are not free to sell alcohol to teenagers. Businesses are not free to hire child laborers. Economic freedom does not give anyone the right to break the law. But it does allow us to act in our economic best interest within the law.

Competition
Because virtually anyone can enter the market at any time, many rival sellers usually vie for customers' business. The resulting competition is a hallmark of the free enterprise system.

Competition provides an incentive for businesses to create new and better products and ways of serving customers. For consumers, this means more goods and services to choose from. Competition also encourages producers to use their resources efficiently in order to lower costs. When lower costs translate into lower prices, consumers win again.

Equal Opportunity
In 1776, the Declaration of Independence declared,

We hold these truths to be self-evident, that all men are created equal, that they are endowed by their Creator with certain unalienable Rights, that among these are Life, Liberty and the pursuit of Happiness.

Most Americans today understand these words to mean that we are born equal in terms of our rights, freedoms, and the opportunity to make the best of our talents and abilities. Our belief in the United States as a "land of opportunity" is deeply rooted in our country's history as a nation of immigrants.

Nonetheless, our free enterprise system has not always offered equal opportunity to everyone. Women, African Americans, and other minority groups have had to fight discrimination in education and employment. Through the efforts of citizens and government intervention, these barriers to economic opportunity have fallen. Today every citizen has the same legal right to gain an education and compete in the marketplace.

Binding Contracts
In business, a **contract** is an agreement between a buyer and a seller. Contracts are used in all kinds of economic transactions. Even the slip of paper you sign when you use a credit card is a contract. In our

free enterprise system, people are free to decide what contracts they want to enter into—but once agreed on, a contract is binding. That means both sides have to fulfill their ends of the deal.

Because free enterprise depends on buyers and sellers honoring their agreements, it is important to have a legal system that upholds contracts. U.S. courts recognize the binding nature of contracts.

The American Free Enterprise System

The American tradition of free enterprise is as old as America itself. Its characteristics are so ingrained in our way of life that we seldom think about them. Yet they define our way of life.

Limited Government
Government laws and agencies regulate, but do not operate, U.S. businesses.

Economic Freedom
We are free to work where we want, buy what we want, and sell what we want.

Competition
Firms are free to compete with one another for our business. When they do, consumers benefit.

Binding Contracts
We have the right to enter into contracts to buy and sell goods and services. Such contracts are legally binding.

Downloading MP3s

Equal Opportunity
We all have the same legal rights to seek an education and compete in the marketplace.

Profit Motive
The desire for profit drives the free enterprise system. It provides our incentive to work and create new businesses.

Property Rights
We have the right to buy, sell, and control the use of our property, including intellectual property.

"'How I Spent My Summer Vacation,' by Lilia Anya, all rights reserved, which includes the right to reproduce this essay or portions thereof in any form whatsoever, including, but not limited to, novel, screenplay, musical, television miniseries, home video, and interactive CD-ROM."

This young author is not taking any chances with her intellectual property. By copyrighting her school essay, she is protecting her property rights in the print, broadcast, and electronic media.

They also recognize that people and businesses can run into financial problems and become unable to pay their debts. Bankruptcy is the legal process by which such situations can be resolved.

Property Rights

A necessary element of a free enterprise system is the right to own property. **Property rights** are the rights of those who own land, buildings, or other goods to use or dispose of them as they choose.

In other countries, past and present, rulers have had the power to seize another person's property for their own use. The U.S. Constitution protects against this abuse of power. It guarantees access to the courts in case of disputes about property. It further guarantees that an owner will be paid for property that is taken by the government for public use. These constitutional guarantees are crucial to the free market. Why would people buy homes or start businesses, unless they were certain they would get to keep their property?

The Constitution also provides for the protection of intellectual property by empowering Congress to enact patent and copyright laws. **Intellectual property** refers to creations of the mind that have com-

mercial value. A **patent** gives an inventor the sole right to make, use, or sell his or her invention for 20 years. A **copyright** similarly gives the creator of a literary or artistic work the sole right to reproduce, distribute, perform, or display the copyrighted work. Current copyrights last for 70 years beyond the life of the author.

Why do we need intellectual property laws? Think about what would happen without them. As soon as a new invention (or book or song) became public, others would copy it and put it on the market. The inventor (or writer or composer) would get no reward for his or her efforts. Without a reward, inventors and creative individuals would have no incentive to invent new things or create new works. Patents and copyrights encourage creativity and innovation by guaranteeing that inventors and artists can profit from their creations.

Profit Motive

If any one force could be said to drive a free enterprise system, it is the profit motive. **Profit** is the money earned by a business after subtracting its costs of operation. The desire to make a profit is known as the **profit motive**. The profit motive is closely tied to the incentives-matter principle. Profits are our incentive to work or start businesses in the hope of making money for ourselves.

Some people confuse the profit motive with greed or with stealing wealth from others. Most economists, however, see the profit motive as a positive force in society. It is, they remind us, the reason most businesses exist. As Adam Smith observed, people produce goods and services not out of the kindness of their hearts, but in order to improve their economic situation—to make a profit.

Limited Government

The final key characteristic of a free enterprise system is a relatively limited role for government in the economy. In the United States, the government does not try to control firms. Nor does it often compete with firms. Government intervention in the economy is generally limited to seven areas.

Protecting property rights and contracts. The government enforces laws that protect property owners and patent and copyright holders.

Promoting the general welfare. The government

funds projects and programs that benefit society as a whole.

Preserving competition. The government enacts laws that protect and preserve a competitive marketplace.

Protecting consumers, workers, and the environment. The government requires businesses to ensure that their products do not harm consumers. It also imposes regulations on firms to promote workplace safety and reduce pollution.

Stabilizing the economy. The government works to keep the economy growing steadily rather than alternating between periods of boom and bust.

Looking at these seven characteristics of a free enterprise system brings us back to the question we started with: *Who or what decides what you get?* In our economic system, the answer is both a *who* and a *what.* The *what* is the market, made up of millions of individuals who buy and sell goods every day on a strictly voluntary basis. The *who* is you, your family, and your friends, all exercising your freedom of choice as consumers. In the chapters ahead, you will learn more about how the choices you and others make in the market help determine what you might get tomorrow.

Summary

Because resources are always scarce compared to people's wants, all societies must make choices about what to have and what to give up. How those choices get made depends on a society's economic system.

How do societies decide who gets what? Every society is faced with three economic questions: *What goods and services should be produced? How should they be produced? Who should get what is produced?* How a society answers those questions depends on its economic goals. These goals include economic freedom, efficiency, equity, growth, security, and stability.

Who decides what in different economic systems? Over time, societies have developed three economic systems to answer these questions. In a traditional economy, decisions are dictated by custom and the ways of ancestors. In a command economy, a powerful ruler or government makes decisions. In a market economy, decisions are made by the interactions of individual producers and consumers. Each system emphasizes different economic goals.

How do mixed economies divide the decision making? Most countries today have a mixed economy, in which both the government and individuals have a voice in economic decisions. Who decides what varies greatly. Some countries, including the United States, minimize government regulation of the market. Others, such as China, still exercise considerable government control over economic activities.

What are the key characteristics of the American economic system? Americans describe their economy as a free enterprise system. This system has seven key characteristics.

- Economic freedom to buy and sell what we want and work where we want
- Competition among firms, which try to attract customers with new and better products
- Equal opportunity to make the best use of our talents, abilities, and education
- Property rights that allow us to buy, own, and sell goods and intellectual property
- Binding contracts, which give us confidence that others will abide by their agreements
- The profit motive, which provides an incentive to work and start new businesses
- Limited government that regulates without controlling individuals, firms, or the market

What does it take to go from unfree to free?

After the Soviet Union collapsed in 1991, the new nations that emerged from the wreckage were able to make their own political and economic choices for the first time in decades. All chose to move from a command economy toward a market economic system. In most cases, the transition has been bumpy. But one success story stands out from the rest: Estonia.

In this article, Estonia's former prime minister Mart Laar describes Estonia's amazing economic transformation. As you read the article, look for clues as to "how Estonia did it." Then ask yourself what it took for Estonians to go from unfree to free in a decade.

How Estonia Did It

by Mart Laar

There are countries where impossible dreams have been achieved. In the *2002 Index of Economic Freedom,* for the first time, a former communist country had a free economy. Even more remarkable, it was not only a "free economy," but one of the freest in the world.

This country is called Estonia, and I had the honor to serve two terms as its Prime Minister. Estonia's ranking in sixth place in the *2003 Index of Economic Freedom* makes it one of Europe's most free-market–oriented economies. Ten years ago, however, we were probably among the most "unfree" of the world's economies.

Estonian history has not been easy. In 1940, independent Estonia was occupied by the Soviet Union . . .

But after 50 years of Soviet occupation, Estonia was in ruins. Our economy was a shambles, the spirit of our people spoiled by the socialist heritage. Shops were empty of goods, and money no longer had any value . . . People stood for hours and hours in lines to buy food.

Within 10 years, Estonia has changed beyond recognition . . . Estonia is now a modern and vibrant young country . . .

Three Key Lessons

A large number of experts and politicians have asked how we did it . . .

Some key lessons emerged. One is to take care of politics first and then to proceed with economic reform. Don't underestimate the importance of a new, modern constitution and democratic legislature with free elections.

In some transition countries, the importance of the rule of law has not been understood, and this has been a huge mistake . . . There can be no market economy and democracy without laws, clear property rights, and a functioning justice system.

The second lesson is summed up by a well-known advertising slogan: "Just do it." In other words, be decisive about adopting reforms and stick with them despite the short-term pain they bring. To put it briefly: no pain, no gain. Of course, that is easy to say and hard to do.

The most basic and vital change of all, however, must take place in the minds of people. In the era of socialism, people were not used to thinking for themselves, taking the initiative, or assuming risks.

Tallinn, the capital of Estonia

Many people had to be shaken free of the illusion—common in post-communist countries—that, somehow, somebody else was going to come along and solve their problems for them. It was necessary to energize people, to get them moving, to force them to make decisions and take responsibility for these decisions.

To achieve this change, we had to wake up the people. First, competition had to be supported. In 1992, Estonia abolished all import tariffs and became one big free trade zone. Foreign competition pressed local enterprises to change and restructure their production. At the same time, Estonia stopped all subsidies, support, and cheap loans to enterprises, leaving them with two options—to die or to begin working efficiently. Surprisingly, a lot of them chose the second option.

At the same time, we had to make clear that if somebody works more and earns more, he will not be punished for this. Radical tax reform was introduced . . .

At the same time, countries in transition not only must deal with their current problems, but must have the courage to look into the future as well. If you are severely underdeveloped, you can make a tremendous leap to the future by moving immediately to the most modern technologies.

Trade, Not Aid

To do this, one should not rely too much on foreign aid . . . Shipments of outdated computers to any transition country can secure them a permanent seat in the Third World. "Trade, not aid," was proclaimed by Estonia in 1993 and characterizes its forward thinking.

As a result, Estonia has made a real jump to modern technology, and this gave us our advantage. The government uses no paper; all members of the government use computers during meetings and sessions. One-third of Estonians use mobile telephones, many of them made in Estonia, while 44 percent of our exports are electronics . . .

Of course, to implement such changes is not easy. I can say to you: You will not be very popular with such politics. A government that implements such policy can become unpopular and be ousted from power. But this is not important. More important is that your country is changed beyond recognition. Looking back, you can say: This was a dirty job, but someone had to do it. The train that you pushed to start it moving will not be stopped, and this is actually the only thing that matters.

Mart Laar served as prime minister of Estonia from 1992 through 1994 and from 1999 to 2002.

Chapter 4

How does trade make people better off?

Gains from Trade

4.1 Introduction

Being a jack-of-all-trades sounds like a good thing, doesn't it? It seems as if having a wide range of knowledge and skills, as well as the ability to perform many kinds of tasks, would lead to a more productive life. Yet it is not necessarily so. It might be true if you lived alone on a desert island. But for the rest of us, being able to do everything for ourselves might not be an advantage.

To illustrate this fact, economists Robert Frank and Ben Bernanke give us the example of Birkhaman, a man from a poor village in rural Bhutan, a south Asian country that lies north of India and east of Nepal. Birkhaman worked as a cook for a Peace Corps worker stationed in Nepal. Not only was Birkhaman an excellent cook, he could also do many other things. He could butcher a goat, make furniture, thatch a roof, and build a house. He could also sew clothing, fix appliances, craft objects from tin, and even prepare home remedies. In short, Birkhaman was a jack-of-all-trades who had a much wider range of skills and abilities than most Americans.

Frank and Bernanke pointed out that although Birkhaman was very talented, he was by no means unique in Nepal. Many Nepalese can perform a variety of tasks that we, as Americans, would hire others to do. What accounts for this difference?

It might seem that the Nepalese do more things for themselves because Nepal is a poor country where many people cannot afford to pay others for their services. But the economists offered another explanation. They argued that poverty is the result—and not the cause—of the jack-of-all-trades phenomenon

In rural Nepal, people produce most of what they need themselves.

specialization
The development of skills or knowledge in one aspect of a job or field of interest. People who specialize become expert in a particular activity.

division of labor
The allocation of separate tasks to different people. Division of labor in the production of a good or service is based on the principle of specialization.

voluntary exchange
The act of willingly trading one item or service for another. Both parties in a voluntary exchange expect to gain from it.

barter
The direct exchange of goods or services without the use of money. Barter is typical in traditional economies.

money
A generally accepted medium of exchange that can be traded for goods and services or used to pay debts. Money is critical in a market economy.

economic interdependence
The characteristic of a society in which people rely on others for most of the goods and services they want. This interdependence results from specialization and trade.

absolute advantage
The condition that exists when someone can produce a good or service using fewer resources than someone else.

comparative advantage
The condition that exists when someone can produce a good or service at a lower opportunity cost than someone else.

In mountainous areas of Nepal, many members of the Sherpa ethnic group work as porters and guides for mountaineering expeditions. Specializing in this way allows Sherpas to earn a better living than most Nepalese.

in Nepal. "The Nepalese do not perform their own services because they are poor," Frank and Bernanke wrote. "Rather, they are poor largely *because* they perform their own services."

Instead of doing almost everything themselves, Frank and Bernanke argued, poor Nepalese would be better off specializing in the production of particular goods and services. They could then trade among themselves to obtain any goods and services they do not produce. The result, as the trade-makes-people-better-off principle tells us, would be more wealth and a better standard of living.

It may be nice to know how to do many things, but that does not mean it is in your economic interest to do them. In this chapter, we will examine how specialization and trade can make people better off than they would otherwise be.

■ 4.2 How Does Specialization Lead to Economic Interdependence?

If you had lived in the United States 200 years ago, there is a good chance you and your family, like Birkhaman, would have been much more self-sufficient. You might have grown your own food, built your own house, made your own tools, and performed many other tasks for yourself rather than relying on others.

Although self-sufficiency may be an appealing idea, it is not necessarily economically productive.

In fact, societies that emphasize self-sufficiency are less productive and have a lower standard of living than those that rely on specialization and trade. Why should this be the case?

Specialization Improves Productivity

In *The Wealth of Nations*, Adam Smith wrote about the advantages of **specialization,** an approach to production in which individual workers become highly skilled at a specific task. Smith illustrated this principle by describing a pin factory.

> *One man draws out the wire, another straight[en]s it, a third cuts it, a fourth points it, a fifth grinds it at the top for receiving the head; to make the head requires two or three distinct operations . . . I have seen a small manufactory of this kind where ten men only were employed . . . [who] could, when they exerted themselves, make among them . . . up-wards of forty-eight thousand pins in a day . . . But if they had all wrought [worked] separately and independently, and without any of them having been educated to this peculiar business, they certainly could not each of them have made twenty, perhaps not one pin in a day.*
> —Adam Smith, *The Wealth of Nations,* 1776

Smith's description illustrates the **division of labor** that arises from specialization. It also underscores the great efficiency and productivity that result when workers divide the individual tasks that make up a job and become expert at those specific tasks. Smith's pin workers were far more productive when each worker specialized in one step of the manufacturing process.

What was true for Smith's pin factory in the late 1700s is also true for an entire economy today. An economy can produce more with the same inputs of land, labor, and capital when each person or business specializes in a skill or task. As productivity increases, more products and services become available to more people, and living standards rise for society as a whole.

If specialization is so great, shouldn't all societies specialize? The answer, said Smith, has to do with population density and isolation from large markets. He observed, for example, that specialization in the late 1700s was more developed in large British cities than in less-populated rural areas, such as the Scottish Highlands.

In the lone houses and very small villages which are scattered about in so desert a country as the Highlands of Scotland, every farmer must be butcher, baker and brewer for his own family . . . A country carpenter . . . is not only a carpenter, but a joiner, a cabinet maker, and even a carver in wood, as well as a wheelwright, a ploughwright, a cart and waggon maker.

In big cities, however, where the market for each of these jobs was large, different specialists would have performed these tasks. These workers could specialize because they knew that there were enough customers to sustain them. But markets in rural Scotland were too small, and the region too isolated, to support a range of specialists. Therefore, people had to perform a variety of tasks to earn a living and to satisfy their wants.

A similar scenario exists in Nepal, one of the most remote and isolated countries in the world. Nepal actually has a higher population density than many countries, including the United States. But the country's rugged, mountainous terrain and relatively undeveloped transportation system limit contact among different regions and with neighboring nations. These factors make trade difficult and help keep Nepal's markets small, thus discouraging specialization.

The United States presents a very different picture. Even the most remote parts of this country are linked to other regions and the rest of the world through an advanced system of transportation and communications. This system promotes trade and the growth of markets and encourages the development of a highly specialized economy.

This specialization is evident in the variety of jobs performed by American workers. The U.S. Department of Labor's *Occupational Outlook Handbook* lists thousands of types of jobs. These jobs range from familiar occupations like carpenter, engineer, and teacher to more specialized jobs like budget analyst, recreational therapist, and violin repairer. The people

At the start of the Industrial Revolution, factories using specialized machines began to replace hand spinners and weavers in the production of cloth. These old mechanical looms can still be seen in operation at the Boott Cotton Mills Museum in Lowell, Massachusetts.

who work in these jobs are specialists, each pursuing a particular career.

Specialization Encourages Trade

When people specialize, they no longer produce everything for themselves. As a result, they must trade with others to obtain those things they do not produce. They trade not only to satisfy their own wants but also so they can focus on what they do best. As economist and author Charles Wheelan pointed out, "We trade with others because it frees up time and resources to do things that we are better at."

Wheelan noted that we could, in theory, do many more things for ourselves. We could raise our own livestock, for example, and not have to pay others for meat, milk, and cheese. But that would require an enormous amount of time and energy, and the opportunity cost—as measured by all the other things we could be doing—would be very high. After all, what do most of us know about meat and dairy production? In the end, we are better off when we specialize in activities suited to our skills and trade for everything else.

Trade is a **voluntary exchange** in which both parties give up something in order to get something else they want. People trade because it is in their mutual interests. As economists James Gwartney,

Richard Stroup, and Dwight Lee pointed out in their book *Common Sense Economics,* "The foundation of trade is mutual gain. People agree to an exchange because they expect it to improve their well-being."

In traditional economies, trade often takes the form of **barter,** the direct exchange of one good or service for another. For example, a farmer and a shepherd might agree to barter by exchanging a basket of potatoes for a bag of wool. Barter works well when there is a **coincidence of wants**—that is, when "you have something I want and I have something you want."

In market economies, barter is replaced by the use of money. **Money** is a medium of exchange that can be traded for goods or services or used to pay debts. Money is useful only when its value is generally accepted throughout society. It facilitates trade because it is easy to carry and convenient to use for commercial transactions.

Trade Creates Economic Interdependence

Whether carried out through barter or with money, trade leads to **economic interdependence**. When we specialize and trade, we depend on other people or countries to produce many of the goods and services we want. A modern economy consists of a complex web of economic links that connect producers and consumers throughout society and across borders.

"Everybody is specializing these days."

Figure 4.2

Origins of the American Breakfast
A typical American breakfast consists of food products from many different places. In that sense, it reflects the specialization, trade, and interdependence that characterize the U.S. economy.

Florida oranges

Colombian coffee

Kansas wheat

Idaho potatoes

Nebraska pork

Iowa eggs

This economic interdependence is apparent in a typical American breakfast. We might begin with a glass of juice made from Florida oranges. We might follow that with toast made from Kansas wheat, eggs from Iowa, or hash browns made from Idaho potatoes. We might also have coffee made from Colombian coffee beans. In other words, our breakfast depends on food produced by people in many different places.

Like Adam Smith, our country's founders believed that trade and economic interdependence are essential to the nation's economic growth. In the years just after independence, they had experienced the problems created when states erected trade barriers against each other. These **trade barriers,** which included tariffs and other measures to limit interstate trade, were designed to protect local industry and promote self-sufficiency. But they prompted conflicts between states and made it difficult for the country to develop a unified national economy.

The framers of the Constitution encouraged the growth of a national market by giving Congress alone the power to regulate interstate commerce. Article I, Section 8, also known as the **Commerce Clause,** states, "Congress shall have Power . . . To regulate Commerce with foreign Nations, and among the several States." This clause empowers the national government to promote trade and economic interdependence among the states. To that end, the federal government maintains an interstate highway system and regulates navigation on interstate rivers and lakes. These government actions contribute to a large and prosperous national economy.

■ 4.3 How Do People and Nations Gain from Specialization and Trade?

Remember Alexander Selkirk? He was the castaway you read about in Chapter 2 who was stranded on a desert island in the early 1700s. Because Selkirk was alone and had no contact with the outside world, he had no chance to improve his standard of living through trade.

Suppose, however, that a second castaway, Pirate Jack, washed up on the island one day. Now Selkirk would not only have someone to talk to; he would also have a potential trading partner. But would trade make life better for either Selkirk or Pirate Jack? To find out, consider the following scenario.

The Castaways' Dilemma: Self-Sufficiency or Interdependence

Shortly after Pirate Jack's arrival, Selkirk tells him about the island's two main economic activities: gathering wild turnips and digging clams. Right away, the castaways face a critical question: would they be better off working separately and fending for themselves or joining forces and working together?

Figure 4.3A

Calculating the Castaways' Productivity
Alexander Selkirk was less productive than Pirate Jack at food production. Pirate Jack had an absolute advantage in both turnip gathering and clam digging.

Selkirk's and Pirate Jack's Productivity

	Turnips	Clams
Selkirk	10 per hour 40 per day	10 per hour 40 per day
Pirate Jack	30 per hour 120 per day	15 per hour 60 per day

As it turns out, Pirate Jack is a more efficient worker than Selkirk. He is younger, stronger, and better at almost everything, including gathering turnips and digging clams. As a result, he enjoys an **absolute advantage** in food production.

Figure 4.3A shows how many turnips and clams each castaway is able to collect in a given amount of time. Selkirk can gather 10 turnips or dig 10 clams in one hour, for a total of 40 turnips or 40 clams in a four-hour workday. Pirate Jack can gather 30 turnips or dig 15 clams in an hour. In four hours, he can collect 120 turnips or 60 clams.

At first, the two men decide to work together and equally share the food they produce. Pirate Jack soon begins to wonder, however, whether he might be better off moving to the other side of the island and working for himself. Based on his absolute advantage as a food producer, he concludes that it is in his interest to go it alone. At the time, three centuries ago, most people would have agreed with Pirate Jack's decision.

What Pirate Jack Missed: The Benefits of Comparative Advantage

A century later, however, new economic insights might have led Pirate Jack to a different conclusion. Those insights came from the pioneering work of the English economist David Ricardo, who, in 1817, developed the theory of comparative advantage.

Comparative advantage is defined as the ability to perform a task at a lower opportunity cost than someone else is able to perform that task. Opportunity cost, you will remember, is the value of what you give up to do something. As a producer, you have an absolute advantage if the time and labor required for you to produce something is less than it is for another producer. But you have a comparative advantage if your opportunity cost is less than another producer's opportunity cost. Ricardo's breakthrough was to see that, regardless of absolute advantage, people could benefit from specializing in those activities in which they had a comparative advantage.

Ricardo developed this principle in response to new English import tariffs known as Corn Laws. These tariffs placed a tax on imported grain in order to raise its price and protect English grain growers, who could not compete with cheaper foreign grain. This tariff helped farmers and wealthy landowners. But it hurt factory workers, who could not grow their own food and had to pay more for their bread.

Ricardo argued that allowing cheap grain to enter

Figure 4.3B

Graphing the Castaways' Production Possibilities

These PPFs show the amounts of turnips and clams that Selkirk and Pirate Jack can produce in a four-hour day.

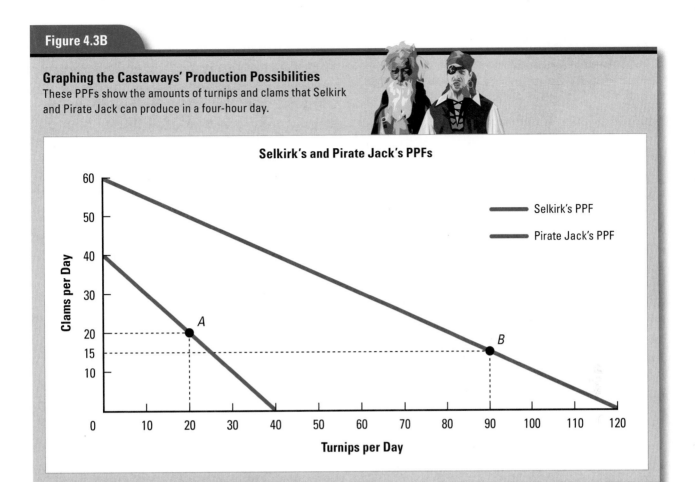

Selkirk's and Pirate Jack's PPFs

— Selkirk's PPF
— Pirate Jack's PPF

England would force the English to cut back on grain production and to instead concentrate their resources on manufacturing, which was increasingly where their advantage lay. In other words, English producers should specialize in goods in which they had a comparative advantage and then trade with foreign producers. The results, Ricardo said, would benefit society as a whole.

Calculating the Opportunity Costs of Going It Alone

The production possibilities frontiers (PPFs) in Figure 4.3B show how Ricardo's theory can be applied to Selkirk and Pirate Jack. Remember that a PPF shows how much of two products or services a person or an economy can produce in a given amount of time.

Selkirk's PPF shows that he can produce 40 turnips or 40 clams in four hours. If he divides his time between the two activities, he can produce a combination of turnips and clams in varying amounts. For example, Point A on the graph indicates that Selkirk can collect 20 turnips and 20 clams in a typical workday.

According to Pirate Jack's PPF, in addition to his daily rate of 120 turnips or 60 clams, he can produce mixed quantities, such as 90 turnips and 15 clams. This mixed quantity is represented by Point B.

The PPFs clearly show Pirate Jack's absolute advantage in food production. But do they indicate any comparative advantage for either Selkirk or Pirate Jack? To answer this question, we must first calculate the opportunity cost associated with each activity.

Selkirk's data show that for every 10 turnips he gathers, he gives up the opportunity to dig 10 clams. So his opportunity cost for each turnip is 1 clam, and his opportunity cost for each clam is 1 turnip.

Pirate Jack has different opportunity costs. For every 30 turnips he gathers, he gives up the opportunity to dig 15 clams. That means that Pirate Jack's opportunity cost for each turnip is $\frac{1}{2}$ clam, while his opportunity cost for each clam is 2 turnips. The opportunity costs for both men are shown in Figure 4.3C.

Figure 4.3C

Calculating the Castaways' Opportunity Costs
Selkirk and Pirate Jack have different opportunity costs for gathering food. A comparison of their opportunity costs shows where each man's comparative advantage lies.

Selkirk's and Pirate Jack's Opportunity Costs

	Cost of One Turnip	Cost of One Clam
 Selkirk	1 clam	1 turnip
 Pirate Jack	$\frac{1}{2}$ clam	2 turnips

As the table above shows, Pirate Jack's opportunity cost for gathering turnips is lower than Selkirk's: $\frac{1}{2}$ clam for Pirate Jack versus 1 clam for Selkirk. This gives Pirate Jack a comparative advantage over Selkirk in gathering turnips. On the other hand, Selkirk's opportunity cost for digging clams is lower: 1 turnip for Selkirk versus 2 turnips for Pirate Jack. This means that Selkirk has a comparative advantage over Pirate Jack in digging clams, even though he does not have an absolute advantage.

Specialization Based on Comparative Advantage Benefits Both Trading Partners

According to Ricardo's theory, Selkirk and Pirate Jack should each specialize in the activity in which he has a comparative advantage. That would mean that Selkirk should dig clams and Pirate Jack should gather turnips. They could then trade with each other to obtain the product they do not produce. But would this arrangement work to their benefit?

The table in Figure 4.3D shows how each castaway might gain from trading based on comparative advantage. The first two columns of data provide production and consumption values for both men if they do not specialize and trade. These columns contain the values represented by Points A and B from Figure 4.3B.

The next two columns show production and consumption values if the castaways agree to specialize and then trade 17 clams for 25 turnips. The

Figure 4.3D

Calculating the Castaways' Gains from Trade
By specializing and trading, the castaways are able to produce and consume more food. Neither man, however, has to work any harder than he would if he fended for himself.

Selkirk's and Pirate Jack's Gains from Trade

		Without Specialization and Trade		With Specialization and Trade		Gains
		Production	Consumption	Production	Consumption	
 Selkirk	Turnips	20	20	0	25	+5
	Clams	20	20	40	23	+3
 Pirate Jack	Turnips	90	90	120	95	+5
	Clams	15	15	0	17	+2

Figure 4.3E

Graphing Gains from Trade
Based on Comparative Advantage

The theory of comparative advantage says that both producers and consumers stand to benefit from specialization and trade. These PPFs show the gains from trade possible for Alexander Selkirk and Pirate Jack.

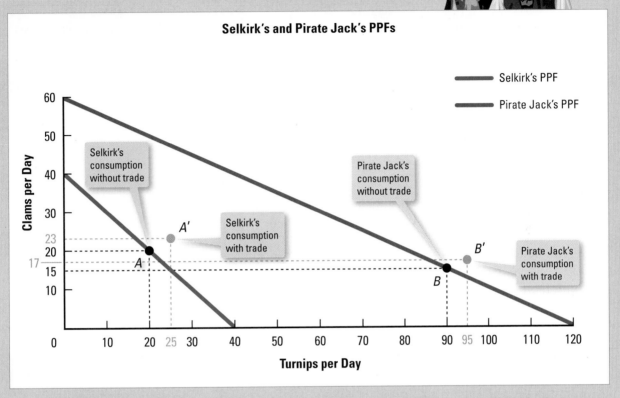

Selkirk's and Pirate Jack's PPFs

production values show how much each man can produce by specializing. The consumption values indicate how much of both products the men could have if they then traded with each other.

The last column shows what each man has gained from this trade. Selkirk now has the 25 turnips he got from Pirate Jack, along with the 23 clams he did not trade. His decision to trade has resulted in a gain of 5 turnips and 3 clams.

As for Pirate Jack, after trading 25 turnips to Selkirk, he still has 95 left, 5 more than he would have had if had chosen to go it alone. He also has the 17 clams he got from Selkirk, 2 more than he would have had without trade. So both castaways have gained from specialization and trade.

The PPFs in Figure 4.3E show the original production possibilities for the castaways, along with

the increased amounts they receive through trade. Those new amounts, represented by Points *A'* and *B'*, sit outside the PPF curve, thus indicating the gains the castaways have made as a result of trade.

Comparative Advantage Applies to Nations as Well as Individuals

What is true for individuals is also true for nations, including the United States. When the principle of comparative advantage is allowed to guide who produces what—for example, Florida farmers growing oranges and Idaho farmers growing potatoes—society usually benefits.

Some of the factors that give rise to comparative advantage, such as climate and natural resources, may be fairly obvious. The main reason Florida has an advantage over Idaho in orange production is that

Climate conditions in Florida are well suited to growing oranges. This gives Florida a comparative advantage over most other states in orange production.

oranges grow better in warm climates. Likewise, Nevada has a comparative advantage in gold production because of its gold deposits. Saudi Arabia excels in oil production because of its abundant oil reserves, while Canada can exploit its vast forests to produce timber. When it comes to farming, mining, forestry, and fishing, geography determines where comparative advantage lies.

Other factors—including education, wage levels, and technology differences—also play a role in determining comparative advantage. The United States, with its many colleges and universities, has a highly skilled, high-wage workforce. This gives the United States a comparative advantage in the development of advanced technologies, such as computer systems. Less-developed nations, on the other hand, tend to have relatively unskilled, low-wage workforces. Such countries often have a comparative advantage in the production of assembly-line goods, like clothing, that do not require highly skilled labor.

The beauty of comparative advantage, as economists see it, is that it stands to benefit all trading partners. Countries that seem to have it all— abundant natural resources, high human capital— can actually gain more by specializing in what they do best and trading with other countries. But even countries with no absolute advantages can come out ahead by finding what *they* can produce at a lower opportunity cost than other countries—their comparative advantage—and trading.

■ 4.4 How Does Trade Make Us Wealthier?

The principle that trade makes people better off is fundamental to the economic way of thinking. Another way to state this principle is to say that trade raises our standard of living and makes us wealthier. To appreciate this, try imagining life without the volume of trade we enjoy today.

What would it be like? You might wake up in the morning to a cold house that your family built for itself. Because there would be no gas or electricity, which is only available through trade, you would build a fire from wood you helped to gather and chop. For breakfast you would eat food that your family produced itself, perhaps in a backyard garden. Of course, you would have no appliances to cook with— no toaster or microwave—because these things also depend on trade. You would put on clothes made at home, perhaps using wool from sheep you raised. Then, unless your family owns a horse—cars and bikes are out of the question—you would probably walk to school.

This imaginary scenario gives an idea of how much harder and poorer life would be without trade.

The fact is that trade does make us wealthier. Trade does this in three main ways.

- It puts goods in the hands of those who value them.
- It increases the quantity and variety of goods.
- It lowers the cost of goods.

Trade Moves Goods to People Who Value Them

Trade can increase the value of goods, even when nothing new is produced. Think about a second-hand item you might buy at a flea market or garage sale or through an online classified ad. The fact that this item is for sale and that you are willing to buy it means that it has more value to you than to the person who is selling it. Otherwise, there would be no exchange. Trades of this kind move goods from people who value them less to people who value them more. Even though the product has merely changed hands, its value has increased.

Here is a simple example of how a voluntary exchange can increase the value of goods. Imagine that you own a baseball cap that is practically new but does not fit you. A friend of yours owns a soccer ball she no longer wants. She wants your hat and you want her soccer ball. So you trade. Why? Because you expect to be happier or better off afterward.

When we trade for things we value, our wealth increases. Most people define **wealth** as money and the things money can buy. But economists define wealth more broadly. Economist Michael Bade defined wealth as the total value of all the things a person owns. Notice that he did not say the total *monetary* value. This implies that wealth, which is often measured in dollars and cents, can also be measured in other ways. As economist Paul Heyne pointed out, "Wealth, in the economic way of thinking, is whatever people value," which is another way of saying that trading for a used soccer ball can make you wealthier if a soccer ball is what you really want.

Trade Increases the Quantity and Variety of Goods Available

At the start of this chapter, you read about Birkhaman, the jack-of-all-trades who was skilled at many jobs. In Nepal, where he lived, modern consumer goods are relatively scarce, especially in rural areas. In contrast, the United States and other highly developed nations are awash in consumer goods of all kinds. In part, this is the result of specialization, which allows us to produce more goods for our own use and for trade with other countries. This trade, in turn, gives

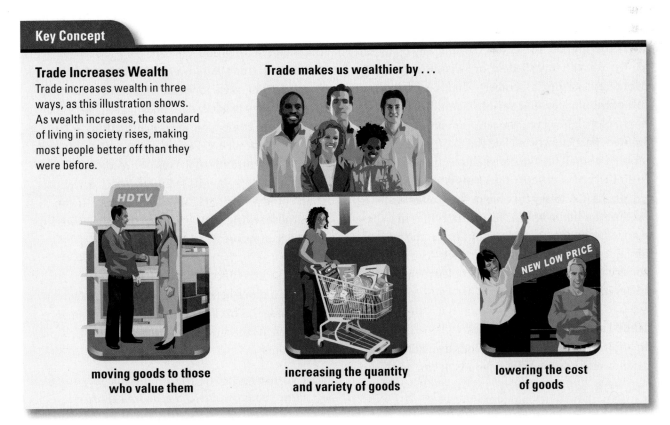

Key Concept

Trade Increases Wealth
Trade increases wealth in three ways, as this illustration shows. As wealth increases, the standard of living in society rises, making most people better off than they were before.

Trade makes us wealthier by . . .

moving goods to those who value them

increasing the quantity and variety of goods

lowering the cost of goods

Figure 4.4

Assessing the Impact of Trade on Cell Phone Use

The impact of trade on the goods and services available to consumers can be seen in the evolution of the cell phone. Introduced in 1983, the first cellular phone weighed two pounds, sold for $3,995, and did nothing but make phone calls. Today's cell phones weigh under five ounces, sell for less than $200, take photos, send text messages, and provide access to e-mail, the Internet, television, and radio. As cell phone producers introduced smaller, cheaper phones, the number of U.S. cell phone subscribers soared.

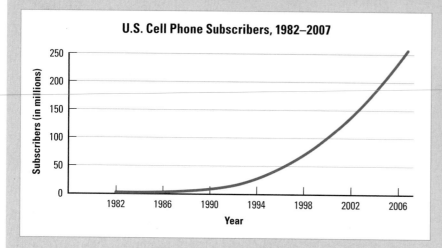

U.S. Cell Phone Subscribers, 1982–2007

Source: CTIA, The Wireless Association.

us access to a range of goods from around the world. As a result, the quantity and variety of goods available to us is enormous.

Just think about the choices you have as a consumer. If you want to buy cheese, for example, you can go to a supermarket and choose from many different kinds. You can buy cheddar or Swiss, Brie or Colby, Monterey Jack or Camembert. And those are only a few of the choices. The variety is mind-boggling.

In Nepal, however, the selection is much more limited, particularly outside the main cities. At a store in a small village, for example, there might be just one type of cheese or perhaps none at all.

This is not to say that life in the United States is better than life in Nepal. The point is that in a specialized economy with abundant trade, the variety and quantity of goods are far greater. As a result, the society is wealthier, and most people are materially better off.

Trade Lowers the Cost of Goods

In addition to making more goods available, trade also lowers the cost of those goods. It can do this in two ways.

First, trade lowers the cost of goods by opening markets to less costly goods from other places. Countries that have a comparative advantage in the production of certain goods may be able to provide those goods to American consumers at a lower cost than American producers can.

Second, trade can lower the cost of goods by expanding markets for products. Larger markets, in turn, allow producers to take advantage of the savings that come with **mass production,** or large-scale manufacturing. For example, a company that produces thousands of loaves of bread each day might be able to buy its flour at a much lower cost than could a small neighborhood bakery. It can then pass those savings along to consumers by lowering the price of its bread.

Trade Creates More Winners than Losers

Overall, nations benefit by expanding trade across their borders. This is true for both rich and poor countries. As the authors of *Common Sense Economics* point out,

Expansion of world trade has made more and more goods available at economical prices.

The poor, in particular, have benefited, and worldwide the income of levels of several hundred million poor people have been lifted above minimum subsistence (incomes of less than a dollar per day) during the last decade. U.S. residents, too, benefit from expanded trade. International trade is a good example of how we improve our own well-being by helping others improve theirs.

—James Gwartney, Richard Stroup, and Dwight Lee, *Common Sense Economics*, 2005

Not everyone gains from expanding global trade, however. Cheap imports from countries with a comparative advantage may take business away from American producers and even force them out of business. When U.S. factories close, American workers lose their jobs. This is one reason why workers and communities affected by plant closings often oppose free trade.

In general, however, most economists agree that expanding trade is good for Americans and the U.S. economy as a whole. Although some people are harmed by foreign competition, most Americans benefit. Furthermore, notes economist Tim Harford,

It is simply not possible for trade to destroy all of our jobs and for us to import everything from abroad and export nothing. If we did, we would have nothing to buy the imports with. For there to be trade at all, somebody in America must be making something to sell to the outside world.

—Tim Harford,
The Undercover Economist, 2006

Economists point out that as the economy changes, old jobs may be lost, but new ones are created. If producers follow the principle of comparative advantage and specialize in businesses in which their opportunity cost is lowest, the increased trade that results should produce far more winners than losers.

If trade makes people better off, what does this mean for you? It suggests that you, too, can use comparative advantage to improve your life prospects. To find your comparative advantage, you must first decide what you like to do and can do well. If you focus on your strengths and specialize in what you do well, you will be making use of your comparative advantage and thinking like an economist.

Summary

We live in a world in which people and nations are economically interdependent. Such interdependence comes about as a result of specialization and trade. The benefits of trade can be seen in increased wealth and a higher standard of living for society as a whole.

How does specialization lead to economic interdependence? When people specialize, the resulting division of labor increases productivity. However, those who specialize must trade to obtain what they do not make themselves. This trade gives rise to economic interdependence, as people come to depend on one another for goods and services.

How do people and nations gain from specialization and trade? The principle of comparative advantage is what enables producers to gain from specialization and trade. By producing goods or services that have the lowest opportunity cost and then trading, people and nations end up being more efficient and productive.

How does trade make us wealthier? Trade makes societies wealthier by moving goods to people who value them the most. Trade also increases the quantity and variety of goods and lowers the cost of goods.

What is your comparative advantage?

Comparative advantage is an important principle in the world of economics. But how important is it to you personally? And how would you go about finding your comparative advantage?

In this article, economists James Gwartney, Richard Stroup, and Dwight Lee make the case that comparative advantage is just as important to you as it is to businesses or nations. Following the article is a skills inventory that will help you begin to figure out your own comparative advantage.

Discover Your Comparative Advantage

by James Gwartney, Richard Stroup, and Dwight Lee

The principle of comparative advantage is most often used to explain why free trade makes it possible for people in different countries to produce larger outputs and achieve higher living standards . . . Two countries can each gain by trading with one another, even if one country is the best at producing everything and another is the worst at producing everything.

The principle of comparative advantage is just as important to the wealth of individuals. Finding the occupational or business activity in which you have a comparative advantage and specializing in it will help you earn more money than otherwise, regardless of how good you are in absolute terms.

Like nations, individuals will be able to achieve higher income levels when they specialize, that is, concentrate their efforts on those things they do best.

To pick one extreme, suppose that you are better than everyone else in every productive activity. Would that mean that you should try to spend some time on each activity? Or to go to another extreme, someone could be worse than everyone else in every productive activity.

Would that individual be unable to gain from specialization because he or she would be unable to compete successfully in anything? The answer to both questions is no.

No matter how talented you are, you will be *relatively* more productive in some areas than others. Similarly, no matter how poor your ability to produce things, you will still have a comparative advantage . . .

In other words, your comparative advantage is determined by your comparative abilities, not your absolute abilities.

Tiger Woods: To Golf or to Caddy?

For example, Tiger Woods has the skills not only to be the world's best golfer but also the best caddy. Who could do a better job than Tiger at giving you advice on your swing, on which club to use, and how to line up your putts?

But Tiger Woods has a comparative advantage in playing golf, not caddying. He would be giving up far more value by caddying than he gives up by golfing; that is, his opportunity cost for caddying is far greater than his opportunity cost for playing golf.

Similarly, the caddies on the

pro tour may not have the caddying potential of Tiger Woods; but since their skills as caddies are far better than their skills as golfers, they sacrifice less value when caddying, and so that is where their comparative advantage lies. For them the opportunity cost of caddying is lower than that for playing golf.

Obviously, individuals will always be better off if they are really good at something that is highly valued by others. This explains why people like Tiger Woods make a lot of money. But even a person who is not very good at anything will be better off by specializing where his or her disadvantage is smallest compared to others and by

trading with others who have different specialties.

Comparative Advantage Works for Everyone

Some people may feel that they are at a disadvantage when they trade with those who make a lot more money than they do. But . . . trade benefits both parties. And generally, the more accomplished and wealthy the people you trade with, the better off you are because your service is often worth more to them than to those who are less accomplished and wealthy . . .

The worst thing you can do is convince yourself, or be convinced by others, that you are somehow a victim and

therefore unable to become wealthy through your own effort and initiative. Some people start out with fewer advantages than others, but . . . even those who are less advantaged, for whatever reason, can do extremely well financially if they make the effort and apply themselves intelligently.

You need to take charge of your career development and figure out how you can best develop your talents and use market cooperation to achieve your goals. No one else cares more about your personal success than you do. Neither does anyone else know more about your interests, skills, and goals.

Discovery of career opportunities where you have a comparative advantage involves more than figuring out those things that you do best. It also involves discovering the productive activities that suit your interests and give you the greatest fulfillment. If you enjoy what you do and believe it is important, you will be happy to do more of it and work to do it better. Real wealth is measured in terms of personal fulfillment.

James Gwartney, Richard Stroup, and Dwight Lee are professors of economics and authors of the book Common Sense Economics *(St. Martin's Press, 2005).*

Tiger Woods is one of the world's best golfers. Although he might also be an excellent caddy, it makes little sense for him to take time away from his golfing, because that is where his comparative advantage lies.

Complete a Skills Inventory

One way to help you figure out your comparative advantage is to complete a skills inventory. A skills inventory is a series of statements about your skills and attributes that will help you identify your strengths.

List the five headings (Communication Skills and so on) and the numbers 1 through 20 on a sheet of paper. Then assess your strengths by writing a score from 1 (strongly disagree) to 5 (strongly agree) beside each statement number.

When you have finished the inventory, analyze the results. Where do your strengths lie? Which skills and attributes do you think might give you a comparative advantage when you are seeking a job or deciding on a career?

Skills Inventory

Communication Skills

	strongly disagree		agree		strongly agree
1. I have strong oral communication skills.	1	2	3	4	5
2. I have strong written communication skills.	1	2	3	4	5

Learning and Thinking Skills

	strongly disagree		agree		strongly agree
3. I generally learn new things quickly.	1	2	3	4	5
4. I am good at math.	1	2	3	4	5
5. I am skilled at using a computer.	1	2	3	4	5
6. I have strong research skills.	1	2	3	4	5
7. I have good problem solving and applied reasoning abilities.	1	2	3	4	5
8. I have strong critical thinking skills.	1	2	3	4	5

Social Skills

	strongly disagree		agree		strongly agree
9. I work well with others.	1	2	3	4	5
10. I have strong leadership skills.	1	2	3	4	5
11. I get along well with customers.	1	2	3	4	5

Workplace Skills

	strongly disagree		agree		strongly agree
12. I have strong time management skills.	1	2	3	4	5
13. I am a good planner.	1	2	3	4	5
14. I am detail oriented.	1	2	3	4	5
15. I am good at managing big projects.	1	2	3	4	5
16. I have strong manual or mechanical skills.	1	2	3	4	5

Personal Attributes

	strongly disagree		agree		strongly agree
17. I am flexible and adaptable.	1	2	3	4	5
18. I am highly creative.	1	2	3	4	5
19. I am strongly motivated and enthusiastic.	1	2	3	4	5
20. I am very self-confident.	1	2	3	4	5

How Markets Work

Chapter 5

*What are demand and supply, and
what factors influence them?*

Demand and Supply

5.1 Introduction

In late 2005, a new album release made a big splash in the music world—and sent a small ripple through the economy. The release was *Some Hearts,* country singer Carrie Underwood's first CD. *Some Hearts* was reported to be the fastest-selling debut country album in history. It started out at number 2 on *Billboard*'s chart of the top-selling 200 albums. Within three weeks of its appearance in stores, fans had bought nearly 315,000 copies. For the next three years, *Some Hearts* would be the best-selling country music album by a female singer. By 2008, Underwood had sold more than 6 million *Some Hearts* CDs in the United States alone.

For Underwood, the rise to stardom came suddenly. In high school she had dreamed of becoming a singer but set that dream aside to go to college. She continued to sing for family and friends, and performed during summers in a country music show. But demand for her talents was limited to a small, local market.

In her senior year, Underwood read a news story about upcoming auditions for *American Idol,* a television show in which singers compete to become the next big music star. She was chosen to be contestant in the summer of 2004 and, in 2005, won the competition.

In a matter of months, Underwood went from being an unknown to being a star. After completing her college degree and releasing her first album, she began a concert tour. In 2006, she performed in more than 150 shows, including holiday shows for U.S. troops in Kuwait and Iraq. The following year, she released her second best-selling album, *Carnival Ride.*

As avid consumers of music, teenagers contribute to the demand for new musical groups and CDs.

Millions of Americans watched as country singer Carrie Underwood learned she had won the *American Idol* competition in 2005. After that win, demand for her vocal talents soared. Fans flocked to her concerts and bought millions of her CDs.

How much would you have been willing to pay to see Carrie Underwood perform when she was still an unknown? Not a lot, certainly. Perhaps $5 if a friend had given her show a rave review.

Now assume that after her appearances on *American Idol,* you became a fan. How much would you have been willing to pay then? In 2008, tickets to Carrie Underwood concerts cost around $45 and up. Thousands of people paid this much and more to see her perform. The demand for Underwood's singing had clearly increased since her *American Idol* victory.

Carrie Underwood's rise to stardom is more than just a country music success story. From an economist's point of view, it is also an illustration of demand and of how demand can change. In this chapter, you will read more about demand and its partner, supply. You will explore how price and other factors influence what consumers demand and what producers are willing to supply.

■ 5.2 How Do Demand and Price Interact?

Most people's understanding of demand comes from their own experience as consumers. Consumers, after all, are the ones who decide what to buy and how much to spend. Demand, in this everyday sense, is whatever consumers decide they want. But how do consumers—how do *we*—make those decisions?

Consider this scenario. You are shopping for CDs.

You see *Some Hearts* for sale for $15. Do you buy it? Would you be more likely to buy it if it were priced at $11? What about if it were priced at $18? If you respond the way economists expect you to, the lower the price, the more likely you would be to buy the CD. This is a key idea in understanding the relationship between demand and price.

Demand: What We Are Willing and Able to Buy at Various Prices

Anyone who has ever gone shopping knows that making a purchase depends on two things. You have to be willing to buy the item in question, and you have to be able to pay for it.

Those two characteristics of consumers— willingness and ability—both matter to economists. You may want the Underwood CD, for example, but if you don't have $15, you can't buy it. You see a Rolling Stones CD priced at $9, but you don't like the Rolling Stones enough to spend the money. For you to contribute to the demand for either CD, you have to be both willing and able to buy.

What does it mean to contribute to the demand for something? Let's say that you do, after all, buy a copy of *Some Hearts* for $15. That one copy, at that one price, is what an economist would call your quantity demanded. **Quantity demanded** is the amount of a good or service that consumers are willing and able to buy at a specific price. If a different store were to charge $11 for *Some Hearts,* and consumers bought

30 copies, then that amount at that price—30 copies at $11—would be the quantity demanded.

When the quantities demanded at all the various prices at which a good is sold are added together, the result is demand. **Demand** is the amount of a good or service that consumers are willing and able to buy at all prices in a given period.

Demand is expressed in terms of a time frame, such as "per day" or "per week." To say that consumers bought 315,000 copies of *Some Hearts* does not, to an economist, convey demand. But 315,000 copies purchased in three weeks is demand. Enormous demand, in fact. And every consumer who bought *Some Hearts* during that period, at any price, contributed to it.

Using a Demand Schedule to Determine One Consumer's Willingness and Ability to Buy

Price is obviously important to consumers. How important? A simplified model of a market can show us how prices influence consumers' buying decisions.

Suppose that Tyler is the sole consumer in a market with one product, tacos. Assume that the tacos sold in this market are all exactly alike. This is the *ceteris paribus,* or other-things-being-equal, assumption. Also assume that price is Tyler's only consideration. All other influences on Tyler's buying—and there could be many—are held constant.

Tyler eats tacos several times a week at a taqueria owned by Jasmine. One day Jasmine conducts a customer survey to find out how Tyler might react to a price change. The survey asks how many tacos per week Tyler would be willing and able to buy at various prices.

The results of Jasmine's survey are shown in the table in Figure 5.2A. Economists call this kind of table a **demand schedule**. An individual demand schedule lists the quantities of a good that one person will buy at various prices. Tyler's demand schedule shows that at a price of $1.00, his quantity demanded is nine tacos. That is, he can be expected to buy nine tacos per week when the price is $1.00. Notice that as the price increases, the quantity of tacos that Tyler is willing and able to buy decreases.

The data from Tyler's demand schedule are plotted on the graph in Figure 5.2A. Each pair of variables in the demand schedule—quantity and price—is a pair of coordinates marking a point on the graph. The line that is formed by connecting the points is called a demand curve. A **demand curve** shows the relationship between price and the quantity that buyers are willing and able to buy. Put another way, it shows how price influences the quantity demanded. As the price changes, the quantity demanded moves up or down along the demand curve.

Notice that this demand curve happens to be a straight line. Demand curves can be straight or curved. As you might expect, this demand curve shows that Tyler is able and willing to buy a lot more tacos at $0.50 apiece than at $3.00 apiece.

Figure 5.2A

Graphing Individual Demand

A demand schedule and graph show how much of something consumers in a market are able and willing to buy at various prices. In this case, the market has just one consumer, Tyler.

- When plotted on a graph, the data from Tyler's demand schedule form a demand curve.
- Each point on the curve shows the relationship between price (on the vertical axis) and quantity demanded (on the horizontal axis).

Tyler's Demand Schedule

Price (per taco)	Quantity (tacos per week)
$0.50	11
1.00	9
1.50	7
2.00	5
2.50	3
3.00	1

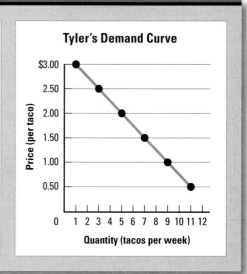

Tyler's Demand Curve

Figure 5.2B

Graphing Market Demand

Market demand is the sum of the individual quantities demanded in a market. In this case, the market is made up of the four consumers listed on the demand schedule.

- When plotted on a graph, the data from the schedule form a demand curve for Jasmine's tacos.
- Point *A* on the curve represents 30 tacos (7 + 7 + 6 + 10) demanded at $1.50 per taco. At this price, Jasmine can expect to sell 30 tacos a week.

Market Demand Schedule

Price (per taco)	Tyler		Amber		Kayla		Luis		MARKET
			Quantity (tacos per week)						
$0.50	11	+	10	+	11	+	13	=	45
1.00	9		9		8		11		37
1.50	7		7		6		10		30
2.00	5		6		5		7		23
2.50	3		4		4		6		17
3.00	1		3		4		5		13

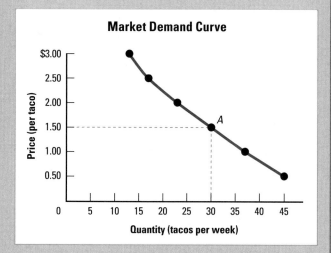

Market Demand Curve

Market Demand: The Sum of All Consumers' Willingness and Ability to Buy

In the real world, of course, Jasmine would need more than one customer to stay in business. Suppose she opens the doors of her taco stand to the general public, a move that gains her three more customers: Amber, Kayla, and Luis. She now needs to consider the market demand for her tacos. **Market demand** is the sum of all the individual quantities demanded in a market. When economists refer to demand, they are usually talking about market demand.

Knowing market demand helps businesses make plans because it tells them how many goods all consumers will buy at various prices. To determine that broader demand, a business might track sales of a product at various prices. Or a business owner might conduct a survey.

Jasmine again uses a survey to determine the demand for her tacos. A schedule of the data is shown in Figure 5.2B. It shows the sum of the quantities demanded at each price by each of the four consumers. This sum is the market demand for Jasmine's tacos.

The accompanying graph shows the same market demand data. Each point on the curve represents the quantity of tacos demanded at a particular price. As you might expect, there is a clear relationship between price and demand for Jasmine's tacos.

The Law of Demand: As Price Increases, Quantity Demanded Decreases

One thing is clear from both of the demand graphs you just looked at. As the price of tacos increases, the quantity demanded decreases. As the price decreases, the quantity demanded increases. Price and quantity demanded move in opposite directions. This inverse relationship between price and quantity demanded is so strong that economists refer to it as the **law of demand**. Economist David Henderson calls the law of demand the "most famous law in economics, and the one that economists are most sure of."

Why do price and quantity demanded move in opposite directions? The answer can be found in three factors that affect consumers' spending behavior.

The law of diminishing marginal utility. Sometimes a consumer has to decide whether or not to buy something, like a music CD at a particular price. Other times, however, as the thinking-at-the-margin principle tells us, consumers are faced with the choice not of whether to buy, but of how much to buy. This raises the question of marginal utility.

How much utility, or satisfaction, is there in consuming "just one more"? The law of diminishing marginal utility tells us that with most goods and services, the more we have already consumed, the less satisfaction we are likely to get from consuming yet another additional unit. This explains why each helping of food you eat at an all-you-can-eat buffet is less enjoyable than the one before. Does this mean that people will not buy ever-larger quantities of a good or service? No. But it does imply that they will do so only if the price is low enough.

The income effect. Because of scarcity, people's incomes are limited. They have only so much money to spend. If the price of a good or service increases, they will not be able to continue to buy the same quantity as they did at the original price.

The substitution effect. Sometimes two different goods can satisfy the same want. Such products are called **substitute goods**. Rubber flip-flops, for example, can satisfy the same want as leather sandals for many people. What happens if the price of sandals increases relative to the price of flip-flops? At some point, people will substitute the cheaper good for the relatively more expensive one.

All three factors cause consumers to react in predictable ways to a change in the price of a good or service. As consumers buy more in response to a decrease in price—or less in response to an increase in price—the quantity demanded is said to "move along the demand curve." Economists call this movement along the curve a **change in quantity demanded**. Only a change in price causes a change in quantity demanded.

■ 5.3 What Can Cause Demand to Change?

As the law of demand recognizes, price is key when people are deciding what and how much to buy. But other factors can influence demand as well. Suppose, for example, that a street fair were held on the block where Jasmine's taqueria is located. She might be mobbed with customers. The demand for her tacos would certainly increase. Or suppose a blizzard brought the city to a halt. Jasmine would have very few customers for a day or two, and the demand for tacos at all prices would decrease. How would these changes in demand be reflected on a graph?

If the price of leather sandals were to rise, consumers might decide they don't need them after all if a cheaper substitute is available. This would cause the quantity of leather sandals demanded to decrease.

Graphing Changes in Demand: Shifting Demand Curves

Movement along a demand curve shows how the quantity demanded changes as the price of a good or service changes. But sometimes a factor other than price—such as a spike or a drop in the number of customers—causes an entire demand curve to shift to a new position on the graph. Economists call this shift a **change in demand**. A change in demand occurs when quantities demanded increase or decrease at all prices.

The market demand schedule in Figure 5.3 shows the changed demand for tacos. The original market demand schedule for Jasmine's tacos appears in the middle column. The column to the left shows the decrease in market demand for the week of the blizzard. The column to the right shows the increase for the week of the street fair.

Each demand curve on the accompanying graph corresponds to one of the three demand schedules. The demand curve in the middle shows the original market demand for tacos. The curve to the right shows an increase in quantity demanded at every price. And the curve to the left shows a decrease in quantity demanded at every price.

Both the decrease and the increase in market demand have caused the entire demand curve to move. When this happens—when a factor other than price alters demand—economists say the demand curve has shifted. An increase in demand shifts the demand curve to the right. A decrease in demand shifts the demand curve to the left.

Demand Shifters: Factors that Cause a Change in Demand

Economists have identified several **demand shifters** that can cause a change in demand for a good or service. We will consider each demand shifter as if it were independent of all the rest—*ceteris paribus*. But in fact, as any economist will tell you, everything is interconnected.

Changes in income. Generally, an increase in income increases people's demand for goods and services, and vice versa. This makes sense. If you like movies, for

---

Figure 5.3

Graphing Changes in Market Demand

An increase or decrease in market demand can cause the entire demand curve to shift to the right or the left. The original market demand for Jasmine's tacos is shown by the dark purple demand curve labeled D_1. The light purple curves labeled D_2 and D_3 represent changes in demand.

- Follow the dashed lines from Points A and B to the x-axis. Note that the quantity demanded at Point B and every other point on D_2 has decreased by 10 tacos.
- Do the same for Points A and C. What change in demand do you see between D_1 and D_3?

Market Demand Schedule

Quantity (tacos per week)

Price (per taco)	Decreased Market Demand	Original Market Demand	Increased Market Demand
$0.50	35	45	55
1.00	27	37	47
1.50	20	30	40
2.00	13	23	33
2.50	7	17	27
3.00	3	13	23

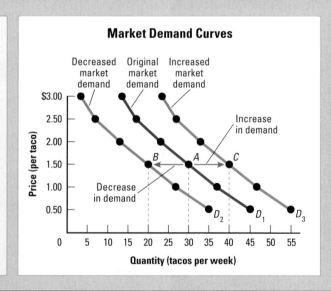

Market Demand Curves

Demand Shifters

All but one of the factors listed here are demand shifters. These shifters can cause an increase or a decrease in demand at every point along a demand curve.

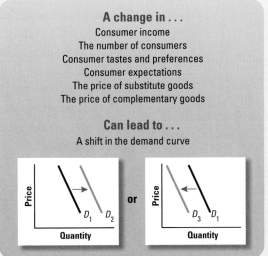

A change in . . .
Consumer income
The number of consumers
Consumer tastes and preferences
Consumer expectations
The price of substitute goods
The price of complementary goods

Can lead to . . .
A shift in the demand curve

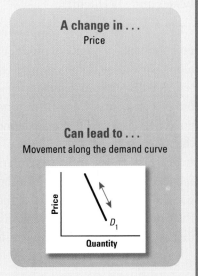

A change in . . .
Price

Can lead to . . .
Movement along the demand curve

example, you probably go to more movies when you are working and earning money than when you are not.

When the economy is growing and jobs are being created, more people earn more income. The demand for many goods and services increases at all prices. That is, their demand curves shift to the right. The opposite also holds true. In an economic downturn, incomes—and demand—can decrease. The demand curves for many goods and services shift to the left.

Changes in the number of consumers. A change in the number of consumers can cause market demand to shift. You saw this effect in the taco stand scenario, when the street fair brought in more customers and the blizzard prevented customers from coming. In some markets, this effect is seasonal. In a summer resort town, for example, market demand for hotels and restaurants increases when summer brings an influx of consumers. When summer ends and the tourists leave town, demand decreases sharply.

Changes in consumer tastes and preferences. Consumers do not necessarily buy the same products year after year. Thirty years ago, only a small number of Americans ate sushi, and they did so mainly at Japanese restaurants. Today sushi is so popular that it is sold in many supermarkets. This change in consumer tastes has caused an increase in demand for sushi. The demand curve for sushi has steadily shifted to the right.

Advertising can play a powerful role in shaping consumer preferences. Suppose, for example, that a producer of sunglasses were to launch an advertising campaign with celebrity endorsements. At all price levels, quantity demanded would likely increase. The demand curve would shift to the right.

Changes in consumer expectations. Prices don't actually have to rise or fall to cause consumers to change their behavior. Consumers may decide to buy or not to buy based on the *expectation* of a price change. Let's say you go into a store with the intention of buying a particular video game. You find the game, which is priced at $39.99. A salesperson informs you that this game will go on sale next week for $29.99. You put the video game back. The expectation that the price will soon go down has, for the moment, lessened your demand.

Changes in the price of substitute goods. A change in the price of one product in a pair of substitute goods can cause the demand curve for the other good to shift. Take burritos and tacos, for example. If the price of burritos were to increase, the law of demand tells us that people would buy fewer burritos. (This would cause movement along the demand curve for burritos.) At the same time, assuming that the price of tacos did not change, consumers would tend to buy more tacos. Market demand for tacos would increase, and the demand curve for tacos would shift to the right. Other pairs of substitute goods include fish and chicken, sweatshirts and jackets, and movie tickets and DVD rentals.

Changes in the price of complementary goods. A **complementary good** is a product that is consumed along with some other product. Tennis rackets and tennis balls are complementary goods. So are hamburgers and buns. Demand for one complementary good increases and decreases along with demand for the other. So, for example, if the price of printers were to decrease, the quantity of printers demanded would increase. As a result, demand for the ink cartridges that go with the printers would also increase. Assuming the price of the cartridges remains unchanged, the demand curve for cartridges would shift to the right.

5.4 How Do Supply and Price Interact?

Opposite every consumer in a market exchange is a producer. Producers supply the goods and services that consumers demand. They decide what to sup-

ply and how much to produce. How do they make those decisions?

Price plays a critical role for producers, just as it does for consumers. Jasmine, for example, might be willing to sell a certain quantity of tacos for $2.00 apiece. But would she be willing to sell the same quantity at $1.00 apiece? Economists can safely predict that her answer would be no. The lower the price, the fewer tacos Jasmine would be willing to sell. This is a key idea in understanding the interaction between supply and price.

Supply: What Producers Are Willing and Able to Sell at Various Prices

When we look at the supply side of the market, we find that the same concepts and terms that apply to consumers also apply to producers. The same *ceteris paribus* assumptions apply as well. All tacos are the same—and price, for now, is Jasmine's only consideration. All other variables that might influence supply, including the cost of ingredients, are held constant.

Suppose, then, that a customer wants to buy as many tacos as Jasmine is willing to supply in a week

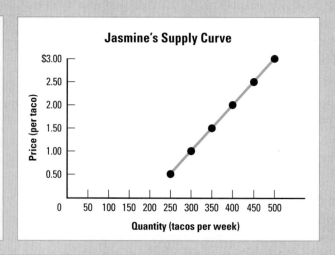

Figure 5.4A

Graphing Individual Supply

A supply schedule and graph show how much producers of a good or service are able and willing to supply at various prices. In this case, the market has just one producer, Jasmine. When plotted on a graph, the data from Jasmine's supply schedule form a supply curve.

- Each point on the supply curve shows the relationship between price (on the vertical axis) and quantity supplied (on the horizontal axis).
- At any point below the supply curve, Jasmine's profit is so low that she has little motivation to increase her production.

Jasmine's Supply Schedule

Price (per taco)	Quantity (tacos per week)
$0.50	250
1.00	300
1.50	350
2.00	400
2.50	450
3.00	500

for a big party. Jasmine is only willing to supply 300 tacos at $1.00 apiece. Her profit at that price is so low that she is not interested in producing more. At a price of $3.00, however, she is willing to supply 500 tacos to the party giver. Each of these amounts is a quantity supplied. **Quantity supplied** is the amount of a good or service that producers are willing and able to offer for sale at a specific price.

When we add up the quantities that Jasmine and all other taco producers are willing and able to sell at all prices, the result is supply. **Supply** is the amount of a good or service that producers are willing and able to offer for sale at all prices in a given period. Like demand, supply is always expressed in terms of a specific time period, such as weeks or months.

Using a Supply Schedule to Determine One Producer's Willingness and Ability to Sell

A look at Jasmine's supply schedule can help us understand how price and supply interact. A **supply schedule** is a table that shows the quantities supplied at different prices in a market. The individual supply schedule in Figure 5.4A shows the quantities that Jasmine will supply at different prices. At a price of $2.00, for example, Jasmine's quantity supplied is 400 tacos. In other words, she is willing and able to offer 400 tacos for sale per week at that price. Notice that as

the price increases, the quantity of tacos that Jasmine is willing and able to offer for sale also increases.

The data from Jasmine's supply schedule are plotted on the accompanying graph. Each pair of variables from the schedule—quantity and price—is a pair of coordinates marking a point on the graph. The line formed by connecting the points is a supply curve. A **supply curve** shows the relationship between the price and the quantity that producers are willing and able to supply. This supply curve shows that Jasmine will offer many more tacos for sale at a price of $3.00 each than she will at a price of $0.50 each.

Market Supply: The Sum of All Producers' Willingness and Ability to Supply

Jasmine's taqueria has thus far been operating in an imaginary one-producer market. A more realistic scenario would be a market with multiple producers, each one contributing to the market supply of tacos. **Market supply** is the sum of all the individual quantities supplied. When economists refer to supply, they are usually talking about market supply.

Economists studying markets have several methods of determining market supply. One is to keep track of production figures—how many goods each firm in a market is producing. Another is to survey firms to find out their quantities supplied at different prices.

Figure 5.4B

Graphing Market Supply

Market supply is the sum of the individual quantities supplied in a market. In this case, the market is made up of the three producers listed on the supply schedule. When plotted on a graph, the data from the schedule form a market supply curve for tacos.

- Point A on the curve represents 750 tacos (350 + 125 + 275) supplied at a price of $1.50. That is how many tacos the market is willing and able to supply per week at that price.
- As the price increases, the three producers' profits rise. This increase in profit makes the producers willing to supply more tacos at higher prices.

Market Supply Schedule

Price (per taco)	Quantity (tacos per week)			
	Jasmine's Taqueria	Aleta's Taqueria	Joshua's Taqueria	MARKET
$0.50	250 +	0 +	100 =	350
1.00	300	50	150	500
1.50	350	125	275	750
2.00	400	175	375	950
2.50	450	275	475	1,200
3.00	500	400	600	1,500

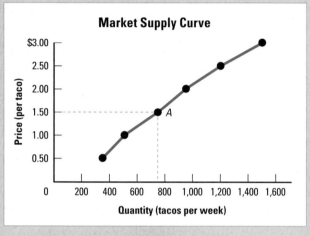

Market Supply Curve

Suppose that Jasmine now has two competitors in the taco market: Aleta and Joshua. A survey of these three producers might result in the supply schedule shown in Figure 5.4B. The schedule shows each producer's individual supply per week and the resulting total market supply.

The accompanying graph shows the same data as a market supply curve. Each point on the curve represents a quantity of tacos supplied at a given price. As you might expect, the graph shows a clear relationship between price and supply of tacos.

The Law of Supply: As Price Increases, Quantity Supplied Increases

Jasmine's supply curve and the market supply curve share an important similarity. In both, the quantity of tacos supplied increases as the price of tacos increases.

As the price decreases, the quantity supplied decreases. Price and quantity move in the same direction. Economists refer to this direct relationship between price and quantity as the **law of supply**. The law of supply holds true as long as all other influences on supply remain constant.

Why do price and quantity supplied move in the same direction? Economists cite two main reasons: production decisions by existing producers, and market entries and exits.

Production decisions by existing producers. In a market-based economy, every producer's primary goal is to maximize profits. Firms earn profits based partly on **revenue,** the amount of money received in the course of doing business. Bringing in more revenue is likely to increase profits. So when prices increase, the desire to make a profit leads producers to increase their production of goods. They expect their profits to increase as a result. Likewise, when prices fall, producers are likely to cut production.

Market entries and exits. When the price of a good or service increases, new firms may enter a market because they see the potential for profit. For example, a building firm might enter the housing construction market to take advantage of rising home prices. Suppose the firm were to build 20 new homes and offer them for sale at $500,000 each. This would increase the quantity of houses supplied at that price. The reverse can also happen when prices drop. Producers may exit the market, decreasing the quantities supplied at certain prices.

The law of supply tells us that producers react in predictable ways to a change in the price of a good or service. As producers supply more at higher prices, and less at lower prices, the quantity supplied is said to "move along the supply curve." Economists call this movement along the curve a **change in quantity supplied**. The only factor that causes a change in quantity supplied is price.

■ 5.5 What Can Cause Supply to Change?

As the law of supply recognizes, price is important to producers when they are deciding how much of a good or service to offer for sale. But factors other than price can also influence supply. Think about what would happen if Jasmine were to close her taqueria. The market supply of tacos would decrease at all prices. Likewise, if a new taqueria were to open, the market supply of tacos would increase at all prices. What would these changes in supply look like on a graph?

Graphing Changes in Supply: Shifting Supply Curves
When the price of a product changes, the quantity supplied moves along the supply curve. But often a variable other than price—such as a change in the number of producers—can cause market supply at all prices to increase or decrease. Economists call this a **change in supply**. A change in supply causes the entire supply curve to shift to a new position. The graph in Figure 5.5 illustrates this effect.

Figure 5.5

Graphing Changes in Market Supply
An increase or decrease in market supply can cause the entire supply curve to shift to the right or the left. The original market supply for tacos is shown by the dark blue supply curve labeled S_1. The light blue curves labeled S_2 and S_3 represent changes in demand.

- Follow the dashed lines from Points *A* and *B* to the *x*-axis. Note that the quantity supplied at Point *B* and every other point on S_2 has decreased by 200 tacos.

- Do the same for Points *A* and *C*. What change in supply do you see between S_1 and S_3?

Market Supply Schedules

Quantity (tacos per week)

Price (per taco)	Decreased Market Supply	Original Market Supply	Increased Market Supply
$0.50	150	350	550
1.00	300	500	700
1.50	550	750	950
2.00	750	950	1,150
2.50	1,000	1,200	1,400
3.00	1,300	1,500	1,700

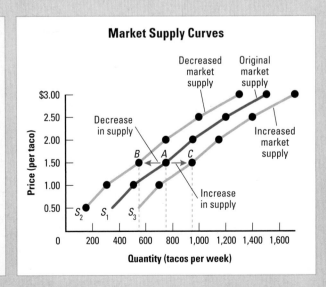

Market Supply Curves

The schedule in Figure 5.5 contains market supply data for our imaginary taco market. The original market supply of tacos is shown in the middle column. The decrease and increase in market supply are shown in the columns to the left and right.

The three supply curves on the graph correspond to the three market supply schedules. The original market supply data were used to plot the supply curve in the middle. The supply curve on the left shows the decrease in quantity supplied at every price. And the supply curve on the right shows the increase in quantity supplied at every price.

These changes in supply caused the entire supply curve to move. When this happens—when a factor *other* than price causes the quantities supplied at every price to change—economists say that the supply curve has shifted. When supply increases, the supply curve shifts to the right. When supply decreases, the supply curve shifts to the left.

Supply Shifters: Factors that Cause a Change in Supply

Economists point to several factors that can cause a change in supply of a good or service. Six of these **supply shifters** are listed below.

Changes in the cost of inputs. Any change in the cost of a factor of production—land, labor, or capital—will result in a change in the market supply of a product. Profit is the key to this process. Lower production costs increase profits. Higher profits are an incentive to produce more. Thus a decrease in production costs causes an increase in supply. The supply curve shifts to the right.

In the same way, an increase in production costs causes a decrease in supply. For example, an increase in the price of coltan, a metallic ore used in the manufacture of electronic devices, would cause cell phone production costs to increase. Profits would go down. The quantity of cell phones that producers would be willing and able to supply at all prices would likely decrease. The supply curve would shift to the left.

Changes in the number of producers. Another factor that affects supply is the number of producers in a market. Producers enter a market when they think there is a profit to be made. This happened with the lightweight, handheld computers known as PDAs. The PalmPilot, introduced in 1996, was not the first PDA, but it was the first one to enjoy robust sales. Its success attracted many other producers into the PDA market. The market supply of PDAs increased dramatically.

Changes in conditions due to natural disasters or international events. Natural disasters such as hurricanes, floods, and wildfires can decrease supply. Consider what would happen to the supply of orange juice

---

Key Concept

Supply Shifters
All but one of the factors listed here are supply shifters. These shifters can cause an increase or a decrease in supply at every point along a supply curve.

A change in . . .
The cost of inputs
The number of producers
Conditions due to disasters or crises
Technology
Producer expectations
Government policy

Can lead to . . .
A shift in the supply curve

or

A change in . . .
Price

Can lead to . . .
Movement along the supply curve

Factors as diverse as natural disasters and new technology can cause a shift in supply. A frost, for example, can decrease the supply of Florida orange juice by destroying much of the state's citrus crop. In contrast, a technological advance, such as the use of industrial robots to assemble automobiles, can increase supply by improving productivity.

if a sudden cold snap were to wipe out half the Florida orange crop. Supply would decrease—producers of orange juice would supply fewer cartons of juice at every price.

International crises such as wars and revolutions can have a similar effect. For example, what if a rebel group were to block the main port of a major copper-producing country? Firms producing copper wire and copper pipes would supply smaller quantities at every price.

Changes in technology. Technological advances can reduce the amount of labor needed to produce a good, thereby lowering costs and increasing productivity. A prime example of this kind of technology is the robot. Automobile manufacturers today use thousands of robots for spot welding, painting, assembly, and other tasks. This technology allows automakers to produce more vehicles with the same amount of human labor. This, in turn, lowers the cost of production, which leads to an increase in supply.

Changes in producer expectations. Producers often make supply decisions based on the expectation that prices will rise or fall. For example, what if wheat farmers were offered a low price for their crop? Farmers might take part of their crop off the market and put it into storage. Expecting higher prices in the

future, wheat farmers would supply less to the market today. The supply curve for wheat would shift to the left. Expectations that future prices will fall leads to the opposite effect—producers supply more to the market in the short term, hoping to make a profit before prices decrease.

Changes in government policy. Governments can directly affect supply in two ways. One is by offering producers a **subsidy**—a cash payment aimed at helping a producer to continue to operate. The U.S. government, for example, pays large subsidies to farmers. Farm subsidies do not necessarily increase supply, however. Sometimes farmers are paid *not* to farm their land to keep supply low and prices high.

Governments also use excise taxes to reduce the supply of certain goods. An **excise tax** is a tax on the manufacture or sale of a good. It adds to the production cost of every unit produced, thereby causing supply to decrease.

■ 5.6 What Is Demand Elasticity? What Factors Influence It?

You no doubt already have a good idea of what elasticity means in the everyday world—rubber bands and bungee cords come immediately to mind. In the world of economics, elasticity retains this idea of "stretchiness." Economists define **elasticity** as the degree to which a quantity demanded or a quantity supplied changes in response to a change in price. The degree of elasticity tells economists how responsive consumers and producers will be to a change in the price of a good or service.

Elasticity of Demand: A Measure of Consumer Sensitivity to Price Changes

The economist Alfred Marshall first developed the idea that demand is elastic more than a century ago. He introduced the term elasticity to describe the way quantity demanded responds to changes in price. Economists since Marshall have referred to **elasticity of demand** as a measure of consumers' sensitivity to a change in price.

How sensitive are you to price changes? The answer most likely depends on what you want to buy. If the price of toothpaste were to increase by 50 percent, for example, you would probably buy it anyway. The demand for necessities like toothpaste tends to be **inelastic,** meaning that it responds slightly or not at all to a change in price.

How sensitive would you be to changes in prices for these goods? Probably not very. Demand for goods that seem essential to daily life (such as salt), or for which there are few good substitutes (such as toothpicks), tends to be relatively inelastic.

In contrast, if your favorite energy bars were marked up by 50 percent, you might decide to buy something else instead. Your demand in this case would be **elastic,** or responsive to a change in price.

Calculating and Graphing Elasticity of Demand

To an economist, the terms *elastic* and *inelastic* have precise mathematical definitions. To calculate the degree of elasticity of demand, economists use the following formula:

$$\text{demand elasticity} = \frac{\text{percentage change in quantity demanded}}{\text{percentage change in price}}$$

If the result of this calculation is greater than 1, demand is said to be elastic. If the result is less than 1, demand is inelastic. In Figure 5.6, you can see how these calculations work out for the toothpaste and energy bar examples you read about above.

Figure 5.6 also illustrates how elasticity can be graphed using a demand curve. The first graph shows a demand curve for toothpaste. A 50 percent increase in the price of toothpaste produces only a 10 percent decrease in the quantity demanded. The result is a demand curve with a steep slope. The quantity of toothpaste demanded moves only slightly along this steep curve when the price increases or decreases.

The second graph shows a demand curve for energy bars. Here, a 50 percent increase in price produces a 80 percent decrease in the quantity demanded. The result is demand curve with a flatter slope. The quantity of bars demanded moves much farther along this curve in response to price changes than is the case with toothpaste.

Economists use several terms to describe degrees of elasticity. In addition to elastic and inelastic, they speak of perfectly elastic, perfectly inelastic, and unitary elastic. **Unitary elastic demand** occurs when the percentage change in price exactly equals the percentage change in quantity demanded. The result of the elasticity calculation in such instances is exactly 1.

The only way to know for certain whether a demand curve is elastic or inelastic is to plug the percentages into the formula and do the math. But as a general rule of thumb, the flatter the curve, the more likely it is that demand is elastic. The steeper the curve, the more likely it is that demand is inelastic.

Figure 5.6

Exploring Elasticity of Demand

Elasticity of demand measures how sensitive consumers are to a change in price. The degree of elasticity can be graphed by looking at how quantity demanded changes as price changes. It can also be calculated using this formula:

$$\text{demand elasticity} = \frac{\text{percentage change in quantity demanded}}{\text{percentage change in price}}$$

A result of greater than 1 is elastic. A result of less than 1 is inelastic.

Example 1: Inelastic Demand

Suppose the price of toothpaste were to rise from $2.00 to $3.00. This is a 50 percent increase in price. Also suppose consumers reacted to this price rise by buying 9 percent fewer tubes of toothpaste. The elasticity calculation would look like this:

$$\text{demand elasticity} = \frac{9\%}{50\%} = 0.18$$

The result is less than 1. This means demand for toothpaste in this market is relatively inelastic. The relatively steep slope of the demand curve for toothpaste confirms this finding.

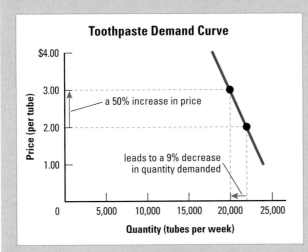

Toothpaste Demand Curve

a 50% increase in price

leads to a 9% decrease in quantity demanded

Price (per tube) — Quantity (tubes per week)

Notice that we follow the practice of dropping the negative sign that would be used to indicate a decrease. So the price change of negative 9 percent (−9%) becomes simply 9 percent. Elasticity is therefore always expressed as a positive number.

Example 2: Elastic Demand

Now suppose the price of energy bars rose 50 percent, from $2.00 to $3.00. And suppose consumers reacted to this price increase by buying 80 percent fewer bars. The elasticity calculation would look like this:

$$\text{demand elasticity} = \frac{80\%}{50\%} = 1.4$$

The result is greater than 1. This means demand for energy bars in this market is relatively elastic. The flatter slope of the demand curve for energy bars confirms this finding.

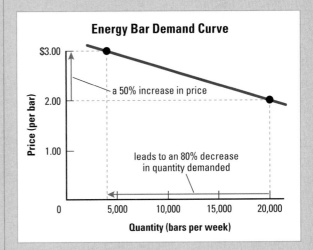

Energy Bar Demand Curve

a 50% increase in price

leads to an 80% decrease in quantity demanded

Price (per bar) — Quantity (bars per week)

Measuring Elasticity of Demand with the Total Revenue Test

Knowing how elastic demand is for various goods can help producers price their products at a level that maximizes their revenue. To gauge the impact of prices on their revenue, producers use a business tool known as the **total revenue test**.

To measure the elasticity of demand for toothpaste, for example, a producer using the total revenue test would create a revenue table like those shown below. Like a market demand schedule, a **revenue table** lists the possible prices for a given product and the market demand at each price. But it has an additional column for total revenue at each price level. **Total revenue** is calculated by multiplying the quantity of a good sold by the price of the good. For example, a toothpaste producer who sells 22,000 tubes of toothpaste per week at $2.00 per tube earns a total revenue of $44,000 per week.

The revenue table for toothpaste shows that as the price of toothpaste increases, total revenue also increases. This response to price changes tells us that demand for toothpaste in this market is inelastic. Even a large change in price leads to a relatively small change in the quantity demanded. In this case, toothpaste producers can maximize their total revenue by selling fewer units at higher prices.

The revenue table for energy bars tells a different story. It shows that as the price of the bars increases, total revenue decreases. The demand for energy bars in this market is very elastic—a small change in price leads to a large change in the quantity demanded. This producer will earn a higher total revenue by selling more energy bars at lower prices.

Any producer thinking about changing the price of a product needs to know whether demand for that product is inelastic or elastic. When demand is inelastic, price and total revenue move in the same direction. When demand is elastic, price and total revenue move in opposite directions.

Factors that Influence Elasticity of Demand

Why is consumer demand more elastic for some goods than for others? The following factors help economists predict the elasticity of demand for a good or service.

Availability of substitutes. Demand for products that have close substitutes tends to be elastic. If the price of a sports drink goes up, for example, many

---

Key Concept

Elasticity of Demand and the Total Revenue Test

The total revenue test is a way to calculate elasticity of demand. The total revenue of a good or service is calculated by multiplying the quantity sold by the price.

- The table on the left shows a product with relatively inelastic demand: toothpaste. Raising the price of this product in this market will likely have a small effect on sales and increase total revenue.
- The table on the right shows a product with relatively elastic demand: energy bars. Lowering the price of this product in this market will likely increase sales and total revenue.

Revenue Table for Toothpaste

Price (per tube)	×	Quantity (tubes sold per week)	=	Total Revenue (per week)
$1.50		23,000		$34,500
2.00		22,000		44,000
2.50		21,000		52,500
3.00		20,000		60,000
3.50		19,000		66,500

Revenue Table for Energy Bars

Price (per bar)	×	Quantity (bars sold per week)	=	Total Revenue (per week)
$2.00		20,000		$40,000
2.25		16,000		36,000
2.50		12,000		30,000
2.75		8,000		22,000
3.00		4,000		12,000

Sports drinks, fruit juices, and bottled water are all satisfactory substitutes for each other. If the price of one thirst quencher goes up, consumers can easily switch to another. Because of the availability of so many substitutes, the demand for any one of these drinks is relatively elastic.

consumers will switch to bottled juice or water. Milk, however, has no close substitutes. When its price increases, most consumers of milk continue to buy it. Demand for milk is inelastic.

Price relative to income. Consumers are more responsive to changes in price when buying "big ticket" items, which eat up more income, than when making minor purchases. If you were considering buying a laptop computer, for example, a price decrease of 20 percent might very well motivate you to buy. Your demand in this case would be elastic. Your demand for an inexpensive item like soap, however, would be inelastic. You might not even notice if its price were to increase or decrease 20 percent.

Necessities versus luxuries. When a product is perceived as a necessity, demand for it tends to be highly inelastic. Demand for luxuries, in contrast, is elastic. People will always buy food, a necessity, even if prices increase. Luxuries like fancy watches, on the other hand, are goods we can live without. If their price goes up, we can easily stop buying them.

Time needed to adjust to a price change. Elasticity of demand can change over time. When gas prices increased sharply in 2008, many people found it difficult to reduce their gas consumption in response. They still needed gas to drive to work, shop, and get around. Nor could they instantly exchange their big gas guzzlers for more fuel-efficient vehicles. Over time, however, people adjusted to the price rise. They formed

carpools, began using public transportation, and bought smaller cars that used less fuel. As they did so, the demand for gas gradually became more elastic.

■ 5.7 What Is Supply Elasticity? What Factors Influence It?

Economists apply the principle of elasticity to supply in the same way they apply it to demand. **Elasticity of supply** is a measure of the sensitivity of producers to a change in price. It tells economists how much a producer will change the quantity supplied in response to a change in price.

Elasticity of Supply: A Measure of Producers' Sensitivity to Price Changes

The law of supply tells us that quantity supplied moves in the same direction as price. As prices rise, producers are motivated to increase production levels in the hope of making higher profits. Thus a producer whose supply is elastic will likely respond to an increase in price with an increase in quantity supplied.

Yogurt makers, for example, are flexible producers. They can churn out more yogurt fairly easily in response to even a small increase in price. They can also slow production just as quickly if the price of yogurt decreases. The supply of yogurt, in this case, is relatively elastic.

Not so for antiques. The supply of genuine antiques is limited, and their numbers do not increase much over time. An antiques dealer cannot simply create more antiques to take advantage of increasing prices. Antiques dealers, therefore, are not very responsive to changes in price because their supply of antiques is inelastic.

The supply of bananas may be equally inelastic, but for different reasons. Growers can increase the quantity supplied by expanding their banana plantations. But there will be a lag time between planting new banana trees and harvesting more fruit. Until the new plantations begin to produce, the supply of bananas will remain relatively inelastic.

Calculating and Graphing Elasticity of Supply

Economists calculate elasticity of supply the same way they do demand, using the following formula:

$$\text{supply elasticity} = \frac{\text{percentage change in quantity supplied}}{\text{percentage change in price}}$$

If the result is greater than 1, supply is said to be elastic. If the result is less than 1, it is inelastic. If the result is exactly 1—the percentage change in price equals the percentage change in quantity supplied—the result is **unitary elastic supply**. In Figure 5.7, you can see how these calculations work out for yogurt and bananas.

Figure 5.7 also illustrates how elasticity of supply can be graphed using a supply curve. The first graph shows a supply curve for bananas. You can see that even a 50 percent rise in the price of bananas yields a relatively small change in the quantity supplied. The result is a supply curve with a steep slope. The quantity of bananas supplied moves only slightly along this steep curve when the price increases or decreases.

The second graph shows a supply curve for yogurt. Here a 50 percent change in price causes a relatively large change in the quantity supplied. The result is a supply curve with a flatter slope. The quantity of yogurt supplied moves much farther along this curve in response to price changes than is the case with bananas.

As with demand curves, economists classify supply curves according to their degree of elasticity. The only way to know for certain whether a supply curve is elastic or inelastic is to run the numbers. But as a general rule, we can say that the flatter the supply curve, the more likely it is that supply is elastic. The steeper the curve, the more likely it is that supply is inelastic.

Factors that Influence Elasticity of Supply

Why is the supply of some goods elastic and other goods inelastic? Several things can influence the elasticity of supply at different points in the **supply chain**. The supply chain is the network of people, organizations, and activities involved in supplying goods and services to consumers. The supply chain begins with the delivery of needed inputs to the producer, continues through the production process, and ends with the distribution of the finished product to consumers. Along the way, supply can be affected by any or all of the following factors.

Availability of inputs. Are the inputs needed at the beginning of the supply chain readily available? If the answer is yes, then supply of the product based on those inputs will probably be elastic. Suppliers can offer more or less of the good or service in response to a price change without too much trouble.

If key raw materials or other essential inputs are less available, supply is likely to be inelastic. The supply of medical care is a good example. The most important input for good medical care is a trained physician. Medical schools turn out only so many new doctors each year. Producing more in response to a sudden rise in fees for medical services would be difficult.

Mobility of inputs. The ease with which inputs and products move through the supply chain also affects elasticity. A new highway, for example, might cut the time needed to ship oats, soybeans, and other inputs from farmers to the manufacturing plants where energy bars are produced. As a result, energy bar producers would be able to respond more quickly to changes in the price of energy bars.

Storage capacity. How easy it is to store products as they move through the supply chain has an impact on elasticity as well. Toothpaste, for example, can easily be stored in distribution-center warehouses. Producers can readily hold back or supply more tubes in response to price changes. Bananas, in contrast, are perishable. This makes it harder for producers to adjust their supply as prices change.

Figure 5.7

Exploring Elasticity of Supply

Elasticity of demand measures how sensitive producers are to a change in price. The degree of elasticity can be graphed by looking at how quantity supplied changes as the price changes. It can also be calculated using this formula:

$$\text{supply elasticity} = \frac{\text{percentage change in quantity supplied}}{\text{percentage change in price}}$$

A result of 1 or greater is elastic. A result of less than 1 is inelastic.

Example 1: Inelastic Supply

Suppose banana growers react to a 50 percent rise in the price of bananas by supplying only 25 percent more fruit to consumers. The elasticity calculation would look like this:

$$\text{supply elasticity} = \frac{25\%}{50\%} = 0.5$$

The result is less than 1. This means supply is relatively inelastic. The steep slope of the supply curve for bananas confirms this finding.

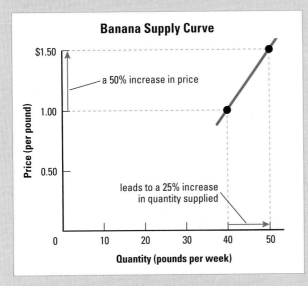

Example 2: Elastic Supply

Suppose yogurt producers react to a 50 percent rise in the price of yogurt by increasing their supply by 150 percent. The elasticity calculation would look like this:

$$\text{supply elasticity} = \frac{150\%}{50\%} = 3$$

The result is greater than 1. This means supply is elastic. The flatter slope of the yogurt supply curve bears out this result.

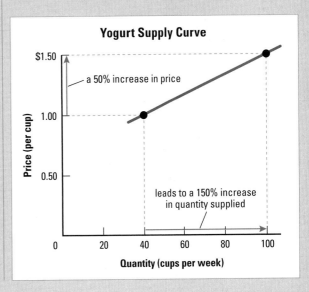

Supply Chains

A supply chain is made up of the people, organizations, and activities that create and distribute goods and services. A supply chain begins with consumer demand for a product. It ends with the delivery of that product to consumers. The diagram shows a simplified supply chain for energy bars.

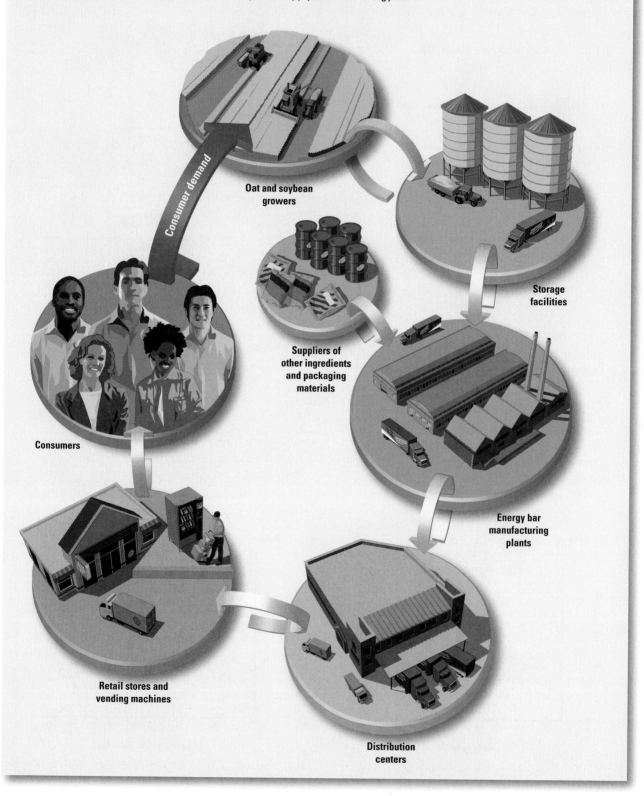

Oat and soybean growers

Consumer demand

Storage facilities

Suppliers of other ingredients and packaging materials

Consumers

Energy bar manufacturing plants

Retail stores and vending machines

Distribution centers

Time needed to adjust to a price change. The supply of many products is inelastic when the price actually changes, but it may become more elastic with the passage of time. The supply of bananas, for example, may be inelastic in the short run. But given enough time, banana producers will either increase or decrease their production to adjust to changes in the price of bananas.

At this point in your life, you probably do not have to worry about such factors as the mobility of inputs or storage capacity. The key thing to remember now is that the two most important forces in a market economy are demand and supply. Consumers, always looking for a bargain, are generally willing to demand more when the price goes down. Producers, always looking to increase profits, are generally willing to supply more when the price goes up. In the next chapter, you will see how demand interacts with supply to determine what you pay for the goods and services you most want.

Summary

Demand and supply are the two forces that make market-based economies work. Demand reflects what consumers are willing and able to purchase at various prices. Supply reflects what producers are willing and able to produce at various prices. Price is related to the quantity of goods that consumers want and producers will provide, though other variables can have a significant influence as well. Economists use elasticity as a tool for measuring how responsive consumers and producers are to price changes.

How do demand and price interact? The law of demand states that as the price of a good or service increases, the quantity demanded decreases. As the price decreases, the quantity demanded increases. The inverse relationship of quantity demanded and price can be shown in a demand schedule and graphed as a demand curve.

What can cause demand to change? Demand in a market changes when quantities demanded at all prices increase or decrease. On a graph, a change in demand causes the demand curve to shift. Significant demand shifters include income, the number of consumers, and the price of substitutes.

How do supply and price interact? The law of supply states that as the price of a good or service increases, the quantity supplied increases. As the price decreases, the quantity supplied decreases. The direct relationship of quantity supplied and price can be shown in a supply schedule and graphed as a supply curve.

What can cause supply to change? Supply in a market changes when quantities supplied at all prices increase or decrease. On a graph, a change in supply causes the supply curve to shift. Significant supply shifters include cost of inputs, number of producers, and new technology.

What is demand elasticity? What factors influence it? Demand elasticity is a measure of how responsive consumers are to changes in price. Demand elasticity is influenced by such factors as the availability of substitutes, the product's price relative to income, whether the product is a necessity or a luxury, and the time needed to adjust to a price change.

What is supply elasticity? What factors influence it? Supply elasticity is a measure of how responsive producers are to changes in price. Supply elasticity is influenced by such factors as the availability and mobility of inputs, a producer's storage capacity, and the time needed to adjust to a price change.

Can the demand you help to create change the world?

Every time you buy something, you add to the demand for whatever it is you are buying. Your choices matter, because what you demand affects what producers choose to supply. Have you ever thought about using your power to shape demand to change how the goods you buy are produced? If so, you may be ready to join the ranks of consumers who shop to change the world.

A Beginner's Guide to Shopping with a Conscience

What do organic food, recycled paper, Fair Trade coffee, and eco-friendly laundry soap have in common? They are all products that appeal to ethical consumers—people who shop with a conscience. Ethical consumers make an effort to purchase goods and services that are produced without doing harm to people, animals, or the environment.

Estimates of the number of ethical consumers in the United States range from 40 million to about 70 million. Consumer activist Ellis Jones compares their shopping dollars to votes in the marketplace.

> *As citizens, on average, we might vote once every four years, if at all. As consumers, we vote every single day with the purest form of power . . . money. The average American family spends around $18,000 every year on goods and services. Think of it as casting 18,000 votes every year for the kind of world you want to live in.*

—Ellis Jones, *The Better World Shopping Guide,* 2007

Take the Shopping-with-a-Conscience Quiz
Do you see shopping as a chance to do the right thing? Take this short quiz to find out.

1. Would you be willing to read product labels to find out what company produced the products, where, and how?

2. Would you make an effort to buy products from a company that supports good causes?

3. Would you switch brands to avoid buying products from a company that behaves unethically or illegally?

4. Would you be willing to pay more for products that you know were produced under good working conditions?

5. Can you name a company that stands out in your mind as a good corporate citizen?

If you answered yes to most or all of these questions, then you are among the growing number of consumers worldwide who shop to change the world for the better.

Look for These Labels

Being an ethical consumer is easier if you know what to look for on the labels and packages of the products you buy.

Recyclable

After they have been used, recyclable products can be reprocessed into new products. Products with a recycling label do not necessarily contain recycled materials themselves. They benefit the environment only if they are recycled after use. The most common recyclable items are cans, bottles, plastic containers, and paper goods.

Green, Eco-friendly

Both of these terms indicate that a product was produced in an environmentally friendly way, such as by using recycled materials. You are likely to find green or eco-friendly labels on cleaning, personal care, and paper products.

Fair Trade, Fair Trade Certified

Look for Fair Trade labels on such agricultural products as coffee, tea, fresh fruit, sugar, and rice. They tell you that the farmers who raised these crops were treated fairly and received fair prices for what they produced.

Recycled Content

The recycle symbol inside a circle indicates that a product has been completely or partially manufactured from recycled materials. Recycled-content products range from paper napkins to park benches.

Cruelty-free

Products carrying this label were developed and produced without animal testing. The leaping bunny was chosen for the cruelty-free logo because rabbits have long been used to test the safety of cosmetics.

Organic

This term applies to crops and animals that were raised without the use of pesticides, chemical fertilizers, antibiotics, or growth hormones. Products carrying the organic label are certified to be at least 95 percent organic by the U.S. Department of Agriculture.

Energy Efficient

Energy-efficient products are designed to do their job with little or no wasted energy. The Energy Star symbol is used by the U.S. Environmental Protection Agency and the U.S. Department of Energy to identify energy-efficient products. It appears on household appliances as well as on energy-efficient homes.

Chapter 6

How do you know when the price is "right"?

Markets, Equilibrium, and Prices

6.1 Introduction

If you were to drive into Albion, Nebraska, from the south or west, the first thing you would see would be the swelling clouds of steam from the new ethanol plant on the edge of town. Ethanol, which in the United States is made primarily from corn, is a bio-fuel—a fuel made from recently living organisms or their by-products. Ethanol is in growing demand as a gasoline additive to help meet energy needs.

Ethanol, and the corn it is made from, is one of the main reasons that Albion, a farm town of 2,000 people in central Nebraska, is growing. On a hillside overlooking Albion, huge new homes are going up. In town, residents are renovating and expanding their houses. The town is getting a full-time dentist and now has a fine jewelry store and a gourmet coffee shop.

"There's a buzz in Albion," says Brad Beckwith, a corn and soybean farmer. He and farmers like him are reaping profits for the first time in decades. With the demand for corn increasing, grain prices are sky-rocketing to historic levels. Beckwith and his wife are taking advantage of the boom while it lasts. They recently bought a new home, installed a hot tub, and purchased a big-screen television.

How does the rising demand for corn affect consumers? Think about all the foods you eat that are made from corn, such as corn flakes, corn muffins, and tortillas. Soda, candy, and hundreds of other processed foods contain high fructose corn syrup. And then there is popcorn. The corn used for popcorn is

The growing demand for corn to make ethanol, a gasoline additive, is affecting food prices.

Speaking of Economics

market equilibrium
The point at which the quantity of a product demanded by consumers in a market equals the quantity supplied by producers.

equilibrium price
The price at which the quantity of a product demanded by consumers equals the quantity supplied by producers.

equilibrium quantity
The quantity of a good or service demanded by consumers and supplied by producers when the market is in equilibrium.

price controls
Government-imposed limits on the prices that producers may charge in the market.

price floor
A minimum price set by the government to prevent prices from going too low. Minimum wage laws set a price floor for wages paid to workers.

price ceiling
A maximum price set by the government to prevent prices from going too high. Rent control laws set a price ceiling on the amount of rent a landlord can charge a tenant.

rationing
The controlled distribution of a limited supply of a good or service.

black market
An illegal market in which goods are traded at prices or in quantities higher than those set by law.

Is ethanol really the solution to our pollution problems, as some people hope? Research suggests that it may not be because the ethanol-making process itself creates so much pollution. Other potential biofuel alternatives include prairie grass and cattle manure.

different from that used in ethanol, and popcorn producers have to pay farmers more to plant it instead of corn for ethanol. Higher prices for corn mean increased prices for these foods at the grocery store.

Ranchers also pay more for corn, which they use to feed cattle, pigs, and chicken. The higher cost of feeding livestock is then passed on to consumers in the form of higher prices for beef, pork, and chicken.

There is no guarantee that corn prices will stay high, of course. Agricultural markets can be unstable, with swings in supply and demand that lead to rising and falling prices. Or as Beckwith puts it, "It's gone up so fast, what's to say it won't go down fast, too?" If ethanol does not prove to be as efficient a fuel as people hope, the demand for corn may slow.

There will always be factors affecting the prices of the products you buy. In this chapter, you will learn what these factors are. You will see how supply and demand interact to set prices and how changes in supply and demand can cause prices to change. This chapter will help you understand what "the price is right" really means.

■ 6.2 What Happens When Demand Meets Supply?

If you have ever been to a farmers market or a flea market, you have probably seen people haggling over a price. You also surely noticed that it took an agreement between a buyer and a seller before a deal was made. If the buyer did not like the price, he or she might have walked away. If the seller had not wanted to accept the buyer's offer, no sale was made. You may think of such encounters as simple purchases. But to an economist, they represent the coming together of demand and supply.

Market Equilibrium: The Point Where Buyers and Sellers Agree

In a market where consumers and producers are completely free to buy and sell goods and services, demand and supply work together to determine prices. This is true whether the market is a local farmers market or a global market. The very interaction of demand and supply drives prices to a point called **market equilibrium**. At this point of equilibrium, the quantity of a good or service that consumers are willing and able to buy equals the quantity that producers are willing and able to sell. The quantity demanded, in other words, equals the quantity supplied.

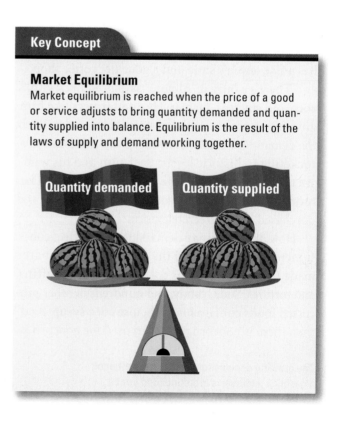

Key Concept

Market Equilibrium
Market equilibrium is reached when the price of a good or service adjusts to bring quantity demanded and quantity supplied into balance. Equilibrium is the result of the laws of supply and demand working together.

Quantity demanded

Quantity supplied

Market equilibrium can be compared to the point reached by a balance scale when each side holds an object of equal mass. The beam of the scale is level. It does not tip up or down. The opposing forces balance each other to create stability. Likewise, when a market is in equilibrium, demand and supply are balanced. Both consumers and producers are satisfied. Neither side has any reason to tip the scale.

Consider watermelons being sold at a weekly farmers market. Suppose that when the season opens, local farmers charge $6.50 per seedless watermelon, hoping to sell 350 melons at this price. You and other customers try to bargain the price down, but the farmers won't budge. Most customers walk away, and the farmers sell only 50 melons.

The next week, the farmers bring 300 new melons and reduce the price to $6.00 a melon. The price is still too high for you and many others. The farmers sell 100 melons and have 200 left over.

Two weeks later, the farmers bring 200 fresh melons to the market and reduce the price to $5.00. All 200 melons get sold, and everyone who wanted to buy a melon got one. The farmers decide to keep the price at $5.00 and bring 200 melons to market each week. At this price, the quantity of melons

demanded by buyers equals the quantity supplied by farmers. The melon market at this farmers market has reached equilibrium.

What if the farmers were to reduce the price even more? Let's assume they want to quickly sell 100 melons. They reduce the price to $4.00 a melon. At this price, customers are eager to buy. They demand 300 melons, 200 more than the farmers have to sell. You don't get a watermelon because they are sold out.

The demand and supply schedule in Figure 6.2 shows the quantity of melons demanded and supplied at each price in the market. When these data are plotted on a graph, the resulting demand and supply curves intersect. This point of intersection is the point at which the market is in equilibrium. At the equilibrium point, the quantity of melons demanded equals the quantity supplied.

The price marked by the equilibrium point on a supply and demand graph is known as the **equilibrium price**. At this price, supply and demand are in balance. This price is also known as the **market-clearing price** because at this price, the market will be "cleared" of all surpluses and shortages. At the farmers market, for example, no customer who wants a melon will go home empty-handed when melons are sold at the

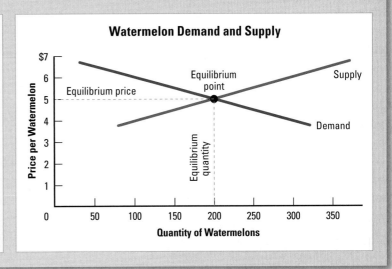

Figure 6.2

Reaching Market Equilibrium
A market reaches equilibrium when the quantity demanded by consumers equals the quantity supplied by producers. On the graph, equilibrium is found at the point where the demand and supply curves intersect.
- What is the equilibrium price at this point?
- What is the equilibrium quantity?

Watermelon Demand and Supply Schedule

Price	Quantity Demanded	Quantity Supplied
$4.00	300	100
4.50	250	150
5.00	200	200
5.50	150	250
6.00	100	300
6.50	50	350

A car purchase often involves intense bargaining over price between buyers and sellers. This car buyer and seller have reached agreement on a price that satisfies them both.

equilibrium price of $5.00. Nor will any farmers go home with leftover melons.

The quantity marked by the equilibrium point on the same graph is called the **equilibrium quantity**. At this quantity, the amount of a good or service supplied by producers balances the quantity demanded by consumers. Both the graph and the schedule show that in this example, the equilibrium quantity is 200 melons.

Prices Move to Bring Markets into Balance

When supply matches demand, consumers and producers both come away satisfied. True, consumers would always be happier to pay less and producers would always be happier to charge more. But in a competitive market, prices are negotiated, not dictated by one side or the other.

A farmers market is a good place to witness the communication that passes between consumers and producers. If a farmer sets prices for a product, such as a watermelon, too high for most shoppers, some consumers will try to drive the price down with hard bargaining. Others will look the goods over in silence and then walk away. On the other hand, if a farmer sets prices too low, early-bird bargain hunters will flock to the stall, sweeping up every melon in sight. The farmer who knows how to read these

signals will respond by adjusting the price of melons up or down to match the current demand.

Such interaction between consumers and producers will eventually establish the equilibrium price for watermelons in that market. This equilibrium price—the price at which shoppers agree to buy all the melons the farmer agrees to sell—is the "right" price for both parties.

What goes on at a farmers market is a simplified version of the communication that takes place between all producers and consumers. In a larger market, this kind of negotiation happens more slowly and perhaps less personally than at a local farmers market. But the process is the same. Consumers and producers send each other numerous "trial and error" messages.

Consider, for example, a new product on the toy market—an electronic dog that can be trained to roll over. If the producer of this toy dog were to price it at $100, and few consumers were to purchase it, consumers would be sending a message to the producer to reduce the price or be left with dogs on the shelf. On the other hand, if consumers were to form lines out the door to purchase the toy at that price, they would be sending a message to producers that the price may be too low.

The interaction between consumers and producers automatically pushes the market price of a good or service toward the equilibrium price. **Market price** is the price a willing consumer pays to a willing producer for the sale of a good or service.

The process by which markets move to equilibrium is so predictable that economists sometimes refer to markets as being governed by the law of supply and demand. This is a shorthand way of saying that in a competitive free market, the law of supply and the law of demand will together push the price of a good or service to a level where the quantity demanded and the quantity supplied are equal.

Economist Alfred Marshall, who helped develop modern theories of supply and demand, famously compared supply and demand to the blades of a pair of scissors. It would be impossible to determine, he wrote, whether it is the top blade or the bottom blade that cuts through a piece of paper. The two blades operate in unison. In the same way, the laws of supply and demand operate together to arrive at equilibrium.

■ 6.3 What Happens When the Price Isn't "Right"?

Economists think of the equilibrium price as the "right" price because it is the price that producers and consumers can agree on. Sometimes, however, producers set a market price that is above or below the equilibrium price. Economists refer to this state of affairs as **disequilibrium**. When disequilibrium occurs in a market, the quantity demanded is no longer equal to the quantity supplied. The result is either a shortage or a surplus.

When the Price Is Too Low, Shortages Result

Have you ever stood in a long line waiting for the latest video game release? Or have you gone to a theater to see a blockbuster movie only to find the tickets sold out?

Economists call situations like these—in which the quantity demanded at a specific price exceeds the quantity supplied—**excess demand**. Consumers experience excess demand as a shortage. A shortage occurs when there are too many consumers chasing too few goods. To economists, excess demand is a sign that the price of a good or service is set too low.

For example, suppose the owners of a juice bar concoct a new smoothie called Blueberry Blast. They price it at $1.50. Soon the line of customers waiting to buy the $1.50 smoothie is out the door, every day. The owners realize they have a problem—excess demand. The quantity demanded greatly exceeds the quantity they are willing and able to supply at this price. They may not be able to afford additional

When a price is set too high or two low, the result is disequilibrium. The quantity demanded and supplied are no longer in balance. For a juice bar owner, the challenge is to find the price at which the number of drinks supplied equals the number of drinks demanded by customers.

staff to accommodate all the customers, or to pay for all the smoothie supplies. The low price results in reduced profits for the owners.

The first graph in Figure 6.3 illustrates this problem. At $1.50 per smoothie, customers will buy 5,000 drinks per month. The juice bar owners supply only 1,000 smoothies at this price. The result is a shortage for the many customers who want smoothies and are not able to buy them.

The juice bar owners could solve their excess demand problem by increasing the price of their smoothies until they have fewer long lines throughout the day. Doing this would bring them closer to the equilibrium price, at which the quantity demanded equals the quantity supplied.

When the Price Is Too High, Surpluses Result

Have you ever looked through a clearance rack for bargains on clothes? Or have you looked for laptops or cell phones on a Web site that sells overstocked electronic goods? These marked-down products have something in common. They were all initially offered for sale at prices above what consumers were willing to pay. The result was **excess supply,** a situation in which the quantity supplied at a specific price exceeds the quantity demanded. Producers experience excess supply as a surplus. A surplus occurs when there are too few consumers willing to pay what producers are asking for their goods.

Suppose that the juice bar owners, in trying to solve their excess demand problem, raise the price

---

Figure 6.3

Graphing Excess Demand and Supply

These graphs show what happens when the price of smoothies is set either above or below the equilibrium price. The result is either excess demand or excess supply.

- What happens to supply when the price is set $1.00 above equilibrium?
- What happens to demand when the price is set $1.00 below equilibrium?

Smoothie Demand and Supply Schedule

Price	Quantity Demanded	Quantity Supplied	Outcome
$1.50	5,000	1,000	shortage from excess demand
2.00	4,000	2,000	
2.50	3,000	3,000	equilibrium
3.00	2,000	4,000	surplus from excess supply
3.50	1,000	5,000	

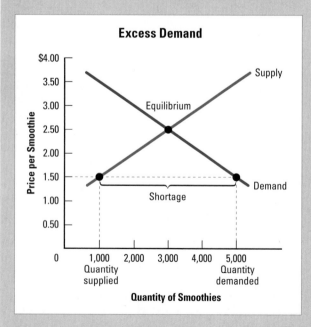

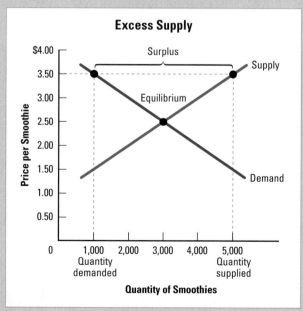

of a Blueberry Blast to $3.50 per drink. Business slows, and they soon discover that they are not selling enough drinks. The quantity demanded by customers is much less than the quantity the juice bar owners want to supply at this price. The excess supply results in a surplus of blueberry smoothie ingredients. Boxes of fresh blueberries go bad in the refrigerator and blenders stand idle on the counter.

The second graph in Figure 6.3 shows that at $3.50 per smoothie, the juice bar owners are willing and able to produce 5,000 drinks. But customers buy only 1,000 smoothies, resulting in a surplus. If the owners choose to reduce the price, more customers would be willing and able to buy. The price would then move toward the equilibrium price, at which quantity demanded equals quantity supplied.

What price should the juice bar owners set for their Blueberry Blast? Figure 6.3 shows that the "right" price is $2.50. At that price, the quantity of smoothies demanded—3,000—equals the quantity supplied.

The Time It Takes to Reach Equilibrium Varies

In a free market, surpluses and shortages are usually temporary. When a market is in disequilibrium, the actions of many producers and consumers serve to move the market price toward equilibrium. How long it takes to restore the equilibrium price varies from market to market.

Owners of a local juice bar might be able to change their blueberry smoothie prices every month until the price is "right." In contrast, a national fast-food chain might take much longer to find the "right" price for every item on its menu. Menus, signs, and advertising would need to be changed for all the many restaurants. Whether prices change quickly or slowly, however, once they move toward equilibrium, shortages and surpluses start to disappear.

■ 6.4 How Do Shifts in Demand or Supply Affect Markets?

In our hypothetical markets for watermelons and smoothies, equilibrium was restored by adjusting prices, thereby changing the quantity demanded and the quantity supplied in those markets. On a graph, a change in quantity demanded is shown as a move-ment from one point to another along the demand curve. Similarly, a change in quantity supplied is shown as a movement from one point to another along the supply curve. When quantity demanded and quantity supplied move to the same point—the intersection of the curves—equilibrium is reached.

Suppose, though, that instead of changes in quantity demanded and quantity supplied, a market experiences a change in demand or supply. Such a change would shift the entire demand or supply curve to a new position on the graph. This shift, in turn, would have an effect on market equilibrium.

Three Questions to Ask About Demand and Supply Shifts

Anything that brings about a shift in the demand curve is a demand shifter. Loss of income, a spike in the population, a popular new fad—any of these events could shift demand by altering consumer spending patterns. Likewise, anything that shifts the supply curve is a supply shifter. Important supply

During the Beanie Baby craze of the 1990s, demand for these small stuffed animals soared. To maintain excitement about the toy, the maker of Beanie Babies kept prices low and limited supplies. The result was a frenzy of excess demand among collectors.

shifters include changes in the number of producers and changes in the cost of inputs.

When an event causes the demand or supply curve to shift, the point of equilibrium changes. To analyze such a change, economists ask three questions:

- Does the event affect demand, supply, or both?
- Does the event shift the demand or supply curve to the right or to the left?
- What are the new equilibrium price and quantity, and how have they changed as a result of the event?

Analyzing the Effect of a Change in Demand on Equilibrium Price

One of the most powerful factors that can influence market demand is changing consumer tastes. Consider, for example, what might happen if new medical research were to identify blueberries as a powerful "brain food." How would this event affect the blueberry smoothie market? Think back to the three questions.

Does the event affect demand, supply, or both? The new research affects the demand for blueberry smoothies. After reading the published report, consumers buy more foods made with blueberries because they think eating blueberries will make them smarter. The research has little or no immediate impact on the supply of such products.

Does the event shift the demand or supply curve to the right or to the left? The event shifts the demand curve to the right. In Figure 6.4A, the demand for blueberry smoothies before the research was reported is represented by the initial demand curve, labeled D_1. The demand after the report's release is shown by the new curve, labeled D_2. The D_2 curve is to the right of the D_1 curve. This shift to the right indicates an increase in demand.

What are the new equilibrium price and quantity, and how have they changed as a result of the event? Due to increased demand, the new equilibrium price—found at the intersection of the new demand curve and the supply curve—is $3.00. The new equilibrium quantity is 4,000 smoothies. This is an increase over the initial equilibrium price of $2.50 and equilibrium quantity of 3,000 smoothies.

Notice that if the juice bar owners had kept the price of smoothies at $2.50 after demand had increased, a shortage would have occurred. At $2.50, consumers would have demanded 5,000 smoothies, but the producers would have been willing and able to supply only 3,000. By raising the price to $3.00, the producers found the "right" price—the equilibrium price, at which the quantity demanded equals the quantity supplied.

Figure 6.4A

Graphing the Effects of a Shift in Demand

The graph shows how a shift in the demand for blueberry smoothies can affect market equilibrium. Here, the shift is caused by new research calling blueberries "brain food."

- Find the initial equilibrium price and quantity.
- Note what happens to both the equilibrium price and the equilibrium quantity when the demand curve shifts to the right.
- What are the new equilibrium price and quantity?

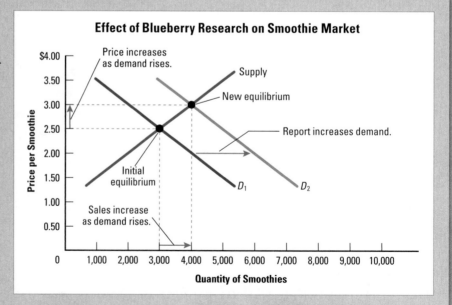

Effect of Blueberry Research on Smoothie Market

Analyzing the Effect of a Change in Supply on Equilibrium Prices

Among the many variables that can shift market supply are extreme weather conditions, such as hurricanes, floods, and freezing temperatures. Consider how a prolonged summer drought in major blueberry-producing states might affect the market for blueberry smoothies. Suppose the blueberry harvest is half of the average amount. What impact would this have on the market?

Does the event affect demand, supply, or both?
The drought and subsequent bad harvest affect supply by driving up the cost of blueberries, one of the raw materials used in the production of blueberry smoothies. As a result of higher input costs, the juice bar owners supply fewer smoothies at every price. The drought has no impact on demand because the higher cost of blueberries does not change the number of smoothies people want to buy.

Does the event shift the demand or supply curve to the right or to the left? Because the number of smoothies produced has decreased at every price, the supply curve moves to the left. This is shown on the graph in Figure 6.4B. The new supply curve, labeled S_2, is to the left of the initial supply curve, labeled S_1.

What are the new equilibrium price and quantity, and how have they changed as a result of the event?
The new equilibrium price for blueberry smoothies is $3.00. At this price, the new equilibrium quantity is 2,000 smoothies. Before the drought, the equilibrium price was $2.50 and the equilibrium quantity was 3,000 smoothies. The drought has caused the equilibrium price to increase and the equilibrium quantity to decrease.

If producers had not raised the price of smoothies, a shortage would have occurred. At $2.50, there would have been demand for 3,000 smoothies, but a supply of only 1,000. In other words, the price was no longer "right" at $2.50. At $3.00, the quantity of smoothies demanded and supplied became equal.

Analyzing the Effect of Changes in Both Demand and Supply

Finally, consider a scenario in which a combination of events causes changes in the demand and supply of blueberry smoothies at the same time. The first event is the publication of a bestselling book that calls the blueberry "a miracle fruit" that promotes good health. The second event is the announcement by a supermarket chain that it is opening juice bars in most of its local stores. To determine the impact of these two events on the smoothie market, think again of the three questions.

Do the events affect demand, supply, or both? The events are likely to affect both demand and supply. The book, like the research report in the earlier scenario, motivates consumers to buy more blueberry smoothies, thus increasing the quantity demanded at all prices. The juice bars opening in supermarkets cause an increase in the number of producers, thus increasing the quantity of smoothies supplied at all prices.

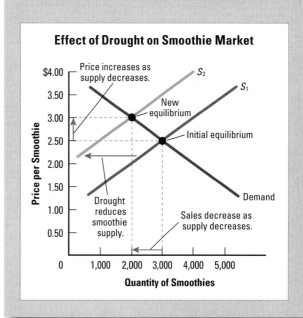

Figure 6.4B

Graphing the Effects of a Shift in Supply
The graph shows how a shift in the supply of blueberry smoothies can affect market equilibrium. In this case, the shift is caused by a drought that damages the blueberry crop.
- Find the initial equilibrium price and quantity.
- Note what happens to both the equilibrium price and the equilibrium quantity when the supply curve shifts to the left.
- What are the new equilibrium price and quantity?

Effect of Drought on Smoothie Market

Figure 6.4C

Graphing the Effects of Shifts in Demand and Supply

The graph shows how a combined demand and supply shift can affect market equilibrium. In this case, the publication of a book on the health benefits of blueberries causes the shift in demand. The shift in supply is caused by the opening of new juice bars in supermarkets.

- What is the initial equilibrium price and quantity?
- Note what happens to the market equilibrium when both the demand and supply curves shift to the right.
- What is the new equilibrium price and quantity?

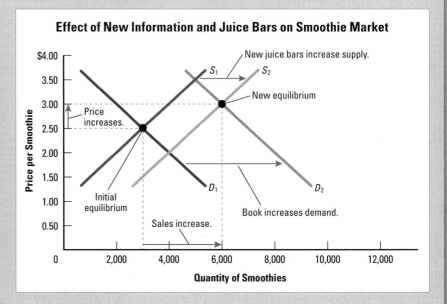

Effect of New Information and Juice Bars on Smoothie Market

Do the events shift the demand or supply curve to the right or to the left? Because these events cause an increase in both quantity demanded and quantity supplied at all prices, both the demand curve and the supply curve shift to the right. This is shown on the graph in Figure 6.4C. The new demand and supply curves, labeled D_3 and S_3, are to the right of the initial demand and supply curves, labeled S_1 and D_2. This indicates an increase in both demand and supply.

What are the new equilibrium price and quantity, and how have they changed as a result of the event? While both demand and supply have increased, demand for smoothies has increased even more than supply has. The graph in Figure 6.4C shows an increase of the equilibrium price from $2.50 to $3.00 and an increase of the equilibrium quantity from 3,000 to 6,000 smoothies. If the juice bar owners had not raised the price by 50¢, a shortage of 2,000 smoothies would have occurred.

In the real world, demand and supply are continually shifting in response to events. The impact of such shifts is not always immediately clear. It usually takes time for economists to discern the precise effects of demand and supply shifters on markets. When a product's demand and supply both increase, economists are safe in predicting that the

equilibrium quantity of that product will increase. But they can't tell with any certainty how the equilibrium price will change. In our simplified model of a market, the equilibrium price increased. In a real market, the equilibrium price could increase, decrease, or stay the same.

■ 6.5 What Roles Do Prices Play in a Modern Mixed Economy?

Think about the last time you went shopping. What were you shopping for? Clothes? New athletic shoes? A birthday gift for a friend? Whatever it was, you probably found a lot to choose from. Athletic shoes, for example, come in dozens of styles and brand names. In the end, how did you decide what to buy? If you are like most consumers, price was an important component of your decision, perhaps even the deciding factor.

As consumers, most of us think of prices simply as indicators of what we have to pay to get what we want. Economists see prices differently. Looking at prices from the point of view of an economist, we find they perform a number of important roles in a modern mixed economy.

Prices Convey Information to Consumers and Producers

A primary role of price is to convey information. Both consumers and producers use this information to help make decisions. It may be an overstatement to call prices a "language," but prices do send a signal. The high price of Manhattan real estate, for example, signals that this particular good is in short supply. The low price of rubber flip-flops sends the opposite signal. As economist Thomas Sowell puts it, "Prices are like messengers conveying news."

To consumers, price signals the opportunity cost of a purchase. The opportunity cost of buying any product, remember, is the next best use for the money you spend. You may not think twice about buying something inexpensive, like a pack of shoelaces, because you give up little opportunity with the dollar you spend. On the other hand, before buying a pricey item like a flat-screen television, you would probably shop around, research brands, and seek out the lowest price. When the opportunity cost of buying is high, people tend to think carefully before parting with their money.

Prices convey information to producers as well. Prices tell producers what consumers want. Automobile manufacturers, for example, pay attention to which models and features sell at high prices and which need to be marked down in order to attract buyers. Prices are a way for automakers to gauge

consumer preferences. Without monitoring prices, carmakers wouldn't know which models to produce more of and which to cut back on.

Producers also use prices to appeal to the consumers they hope will buy their products. A firm that produces backpacks, for example, might offer a stylish model at a low price, targeted to preteens who want packs for school. The same firm might produce heavy-duty backpacks for serious adult hikers and offer them at higher prices. In each case, price sends a message about products and their intended markets.

Consumers, for their part, are used to interpreting these messages. They know that producers are trying to appeal to a wide range of tastes and budgets. Consumers use price to sort through the resulting variety of goods in the marketplace. Faced with a vast selection of running shoes ranging in price from around $19 to over $200, for example, most consumers will narrow their searches to a limited price range. The choice of how much to spend may, in part, be based on what a person can afford. But it also reflects the consumer's expectation of what will be available at that price.

Prices Create Incentives to Work and Produce

As the incentives-matter principle reminds us, people respond to incentives. In a market-based economy, prices function as an incentive because they represent potential for profit. Rising prices in

The two cameras shown here are priced very differently. The low price of the disposable camera on the right signals consumers that it is to be used for casual snapshots. The high price of the camera on the left signals that it is equipped for professional-level photography.

a market motivate existing firms to produce more, and they encourage new firms to enter the market. Falling prices, in turn, serve as incentives for firms to cut back on production or even to leave a market to look for better opportunities elsewhere.

When home prices increase, for example, the change signals construction firms, architects, builders, and tradespeople that there are profits to be made in the housing market. Existing firms build more houses, and new firms get into the act. When prices in the same housing market decrease, the reverse happens. Construction firms build fewer houses. Architects, builders, and tradespeople look for other markets for their talents, such as house renovations and commercial construction.

Just as changing prices motivate producers, prices in the form of wages and salaries motivate workers. The opportunity to earn a higher "price" can inspire people to enter the workforce or seek higher-paying jobs. On the other hand, low wages can act as disincentives for people to seek work.

Prices Allow Markets to Respond to Changing Conditions

Prices allow markets to adjust quickly when major events such as wars and natural disasters interfere with the production or movement of goods, wreaking havoc on supply. Figure 6.5 shows what happened to gas prices in late summer 2005, when the U.S. Gulf Coast was slammed by two powerful hurricanes. The first, Hurricane Katrina, shut down most crude oil production in the Gulf of Mexico and damaged oil refineries from Texas to Florida. Immediately afterward, a government official described the uncertainty facing the oil industry.

They don't know how many platforms are down, how many refineries are down, and how long it'll take to get the power back on. It depends on how much damage, particularly hidden damage . . . some of the undersea pipeline damage can be hard to detect.
—Michael Burdette, *USA TODAY,*
Aug. 29, 2005

Four weeks later, just as the industry was starting to recover, Hurricane Rita struck, causing additional disruptions to the oil supply. The two hurricanes brought a halt to almost 30 percent of the U.S. oil-refinery capacity.

For the next few weeks, gas prices fluctuated, sometimes wildly, as oil companies struggled to bring the quantity of gas demanded in line with

Figure 6.5

The Impact of Hurricanes Katrina and Rita on Gas Prices
In August 2005, Hurricane Katrina slammed into the Gulf Coast, destroying offshore oil rigs and damaging oil refineries. The next month, Hurricane Rita struck. Combined, the hurricanes disrupted almost 30 percent of the U.S. oil refinery capacity. The line graph shows how gas prices fluctuated as the market adjusted to these changing conditions.

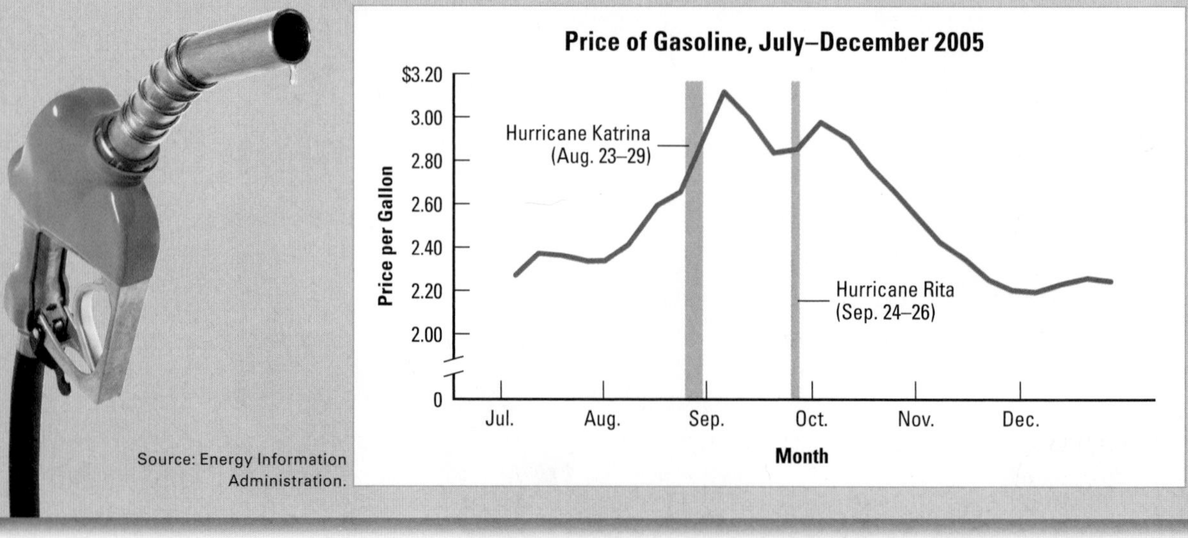

Price of Gasoline, July–December 2005

Hurricane Katrina (Aug. 23–29)

Hurricane Rita (Sep. 24–26)

Source: Energy Information Administration.

Prices

Prices act as messengers in our economy. They convey information that consumers, producers, and workers need to make the most efficient use of their scarce resources.

For consumers, prices
- convey information about products.
- signal the opportunity cost of a purchase.
- allocate products in short supply to those who value them most.

For producers, prices
- signal what consumers want most in a product.
- are used to target different markets.
- indicate when to increase or decrease production.

For workers, prices
- create incentives to enter the labor force.
- signal the level of demand for their skills and work experience.
- inspire search for higher-paying jobs.

what refiners were able to supply. One newspaper reported, "Confused drivers in Georgia saw prices that had climbed as high as $5 a gallon suddenly drop back to $3 in the span of 24 hours." Fluctuating prices frustrated consumers, but they allowed the market to adjust to the disruption in supply caused by the hurricanes.

By early November 2005, the industry had largely recovered, with only 5 percent of oil-refining capacity still disabled. The retail price of gasoline that month averaged $2.30 per gallon. A month later, the average price had dropped to $2.23 per gallon, lower than it had been before Hurricane Katrina. This new, low equilibrium price reflected the fact that in addition to the increase in supply as U.S. facilities went back on line, refiners throughout the world had rushed fuel to the United States in the months after the hurricanes. As the supply of gasoline increased, prices at the pump went down.

By throwing the gasoline market into disequilibrium, Hurricanes Katrina and Rita illustrated the key role that prices play in correcting both shortages and surpluses. Prices give markets the flexibility they need to reach equilibrium even under changing conditions.

Prices Allocate Scarce Resources Efficiently

Perhaps the most important role of price in a market-based economy is to guide resources to their most efficient uses. Consider, for example, the market for dairy products, such as yogurt, ice cream, and cheese. The firms whose dairy products are in greatest demand will buy the most milk in order to make products to meet that demand. Guided by prices that communicate what consumers want, dairy producers automatically allocate milk—a scarce resource used to make many different products—to its most valued use.

Or consider the earlier example of car manufacturers who use prices to decide which models to produce and in what quantities. These production decisions are, at bottom, decisions about how best to use limited resources. As Thomas Sowell explains,

Without really knowing why consumers like one set of features rather than another, producers automatically produce more of what earns a profit and less of what is losing money. That amounts to producing what the consumers want and stopping the production of what they don't want. Although the producers are only looking out for themselves and their companies' bottom line, nevertheless from the standpoint of the economy as a whole the society is using its scarce resources more efficiently because decisions are guided by prices.
—Thomas Sowell, *Basic Economics*, 2007

6.6 How Does Government Intervention Affect Markets?

On the whole, when prices are allowed to freely rise and fall to their equilibrium levels, they do an effective job of allocating scarce resources to their best uses. On occasion, however, governments intervene in the market in an attempt to influence prices. They do this by placing limits on how high or low certain prices may be. These limits are called **price controls**.

Why Governments Intervene in Markets

The temptation to impose price controls is, as the economist Henry Hazlitt reminds us, nothing new.

> *The record of price controls goes as far back as human history. They were imposed by the Pharaohs of ancient Egypt. They were decreed by Hammurabi, king of Babylon, in the eighteenth century B.C. They were tried in ancient Athens.*
>
> —Henry Hazlitt, *The Wisdom of Henry Hazlitt*, 1993

In modern economies, governments usually impose price controls when they are persuaded that supply and demand will result in prices that are unfairly high for consumers or unfairly low for producers. For example, in the 1970s the U.S. government imposed price controls on gasoline in response to reduced shipments of foreign oil due to crises in the Middle East. This action was taken to protect consumers from price swings. The government has also imposed price controls during wars in attempts to ensure that goods are distributed fairly during periods of shortage.

Governments can control prices in two ways: by setting price floors or price ceilings. Both methods affect supply and demand.

Price Floors Lead to Excess Supply

When a government wants to keep prices from going too low, it sets a price floor. A **price floor** is a minimum price consumers are required to pay for a good or service. A price at or above a price floor is legal, while a price below the price floor is illegal.

Price floors are meant to push prices up, ensuring that producers receive a benefit for providing a good or service. Pressure to impose price floors usually arises when producers feel the market isn't providing them with adequate income. Suppose, for example, that the equilibrium price of wheat were to fall so low that wheat farmers were struggling to survive. The government could intervene to establish a price floor for wheat.

The minimum wage is another type of price floor. The **minimum wage** is a government-imposed legal floor on the hourly wage rate, which is the price the market pays for labor. The rationale for the minimum wage is that in some low-skill job markets, where workers outnumber jobs, supply and demand would drive the equilibrium wage so low that many workers would be earning too little to live decently.

While price floors may benefit some people, the larger effect of a price floor is excess supply. To see why, consider the impact of an increase in the minimum wage on both workers and employers. As the minimum wage rises, more people apply for minimum wage jobs. The result is an increase in the supply of low-skill job seekers. At the same time, employers reduce the number of minimum wage workers they hire in an effort to keep their wage costs from rising. The result is a decrease in demand for low-skill workers.

Figure 6.6A illustrates the effect of this combined increase in supply and decrease in demand. At the equilibrium wage rate of $5.00 per hour, the quantity of workers demanded—3 million—equals the quantity supplied. At the minimum wage of $6.00 per hour, however, 4 million workers are supplied— that is, willing and able to work—but only 2 million workers are demanded—that is, hired. This leaves a surplus of 2 million unemployed people.

A price floor above the equilibrium price of wheat would have the same effect. Farmers would produce more wheat to sell, but buyers would buy less, resulting in a surplus of wheat.

Price Ceilings Lead to Excess Demand

When a government wants to keep prices from going too high, it sets a price ceiling. A **price ceiling** is a maximum price consumers may be required to pay for a good or service. A price at or below a price ceiling is legal. A price above the ceiling is not legal.

Governments impose price ceilings to enable consumers to buy essential goods or services they wouldn't be able to afford at the equilibrium price. Price ceilings are usually established in response to

Figure 6.6A

Analyzing the Impact of a Price Floor
A price floor is a minimum price set by the government on a good or service. Minimum wage is an example of a price floor. The graph shows how setting minimum wage above the equilibrium wage affects the job market.

- How does the price floor in the graph affect the quantity of workers supplied? The quantity demanded?
- Is the result a shortage or a surplus of workers?

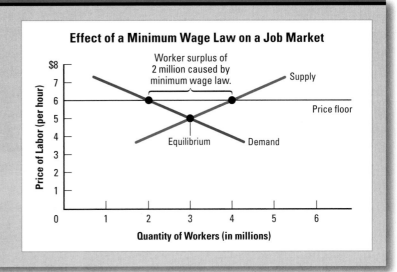

Effect of a Minimum Wage Law on a Job Market

a crisis, such as war, natural disaster, or widespread crop failure. Such supply-shifting events can lead to price increases that may cause a financial burden for a great many people while enriching a select few.

The best-known form of price ceilings in the United States today is rent control. **Rent control** regulations make it illegal to charge more than a specified monthly amount for rental housing. In New York City, rent control was introduced during World War II to protect poor families. Over time, the regulations were eased somewhat. But a half-century later, some 2.5 million New Yorkers were still living in more than a million rent-regulated apartments.

Figure 6.6B illustrates the effect of rent control on the rental housing market in a typical city. As you might have guessed, imposing a rent ceiling that is below the equilibrium rent leads to excess demand. The artificially low rents attract young people eager to leave home and live independently or retirees hoping to reduce their expenses—in short, anyone who likes a bargain—into the rental market.

At the same time, the supply of apartments in the market decreases as landlords who are unwilling to rent at such low prices seek other ways to use their properties. Some, for example, might decide to convert their apartments to condominiums to sell.

Figure 6.6B

Analyzing the Impact of a Price Ceiling
A price ceiling is a maximum price set by the government on a good or service. Rent control laws are an example of price ceilings. The graph shows how establishing a rent ceiling below the equilibrium rent affects the apartment market.

- How does the price ceiling in the graph affect the quantity of apartments demanded? The quantity supplied?
- Is the result a shortage or a surplus of apartments?

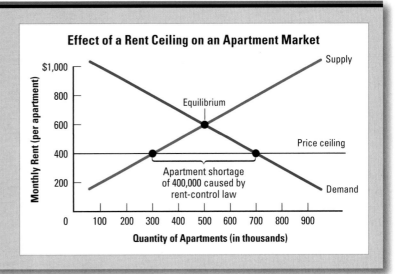

Effect of a Rent Ceiling on an Apartment Market

Moreover, fewer potential landlords enter the rental market because of the difficulty of making a profit under rent control laws. The result is excess demand and a shortage of apartments.

Dealing with Excess Supply and Demand: Rationing and Black Markets

Price controls lead to surpluses and shortages because they prevent markets from reaching a market-clearing price. The excess supply and demand that arise must be addressed outside the market. This happens in various ways.

In the case of an agricultural surplus that results from price floors, the government may limit supply by restricting how much farmers are allowed to grow. Or the government may buy the crop surplus at the price floor to store for later use or to give to a developing country as foreign aid. Such aid often has the effect of undercutting farmers in countries that cannot compete with cheap American surplus grain.

When shortages occur, the government may impose rationing. **Rationing** is the controlled distribution of a limited supply of a good or service. For example, during the 1973 oil crisis, price ceilings on gasoline led to a severe gas shortage. The government instituted a rationing system based on license plate numbers to cope with the shortage. During World War II, the government rationed tires, gasoline, sugar, and other goods that were in short supply because they were being used for the war effort.

Rationing can be a costly means of allocating scarce goods. A giant bureaucracy, the Office of Price Administration (OPA), had to be set up during World War II to enforce the rationing regulations. Thousands of rationing boards were created, operated by 60,000 employees and 200,000 volunteers.

Shortages can also give rise to black markets. A **black market** is an illegal market in which goods are traded at prices or in quantities higher than those set by law. There was a thriving black market during World War II for meat, sugar, and gasoline, among other products. Some people bought and sold meat through bootleg suppliers. People also made counterfeit ration coupons. In one month alone in 1944, the OPA counted 3 million counterfeit coupons.

Why Ending Price Controls Is Difficult

At this point you might be wondering why, if price controls are so harmful to markets, the government doesn't just get rid of them. The answer to this question has more to do with politics than economics.

The political pressure on elected officials to intervene in the market when prices rise and fall rapidly can be intense. And although price controls are inefficient, many people believe that they further the goal of economic equity in such situations.

Moreover, some people—farmers, people who live in rent-controlled apartments, workers who earn minimum wage—clearly benefit from price controls. Labor unions also support minimum wage laws because such laws are believed to push all wages upward. The combined voices—and votes—of those who support price controls are enough to make most politicians reluctant to repeal them.

Rationing became a way of life for Americans during World War II. Ration books filled with stamps like those shown here were issued to each household. Rationed items could not be purchased without those stamps. Most people accepted rationing as a necessary part of the war effort. Nonetheless, a black market soon sprang up to provide goods in high demand to customers who had more cash than coupons.

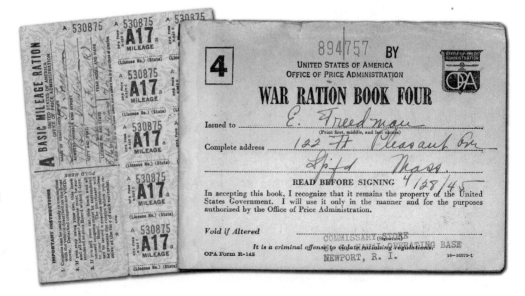

Most economists, as you would expect, take a dim view of price controls. When a government tries to set prices, economists warn, it is likely to set them too high or too low. The inevitable result will be shortages or surpluses. Markets, on the other hand, when left alone, will naturally gravitate to the "right" price.

This takes us back to the question we started with, *How do you know when the price is "right"?* The simple answer is that the price is right when the market reaches equilibrium. The process of reaching equilibrium, however, is anything but simple. It involves the individual decisions of countless producers and millions of consumers just like you. In the next chapter, you will learn more about how markets work and what happens when they work less perfectly than the model of supply and demand suggests they should.

The minimum wage is a price floor set by the government on the hourly wage rate for labor. The minimum wage is intended to benefit low-wage workers, but critics claim it may not always do so.

Summary

In a free market, demand and supply automatically move prices to equilibrium, the point at which quantity demanded equals quantity supplied.

What happens when demand meets supply? Demand and supply interact to drive prices for goods and services to the equilibrium level. On a graph, this equilibrium point is found at the intersection of the demand and supply curves. The equilibrium price, also known as the market-clearing price, may be thought of as the "right" price.

What happens when the price isn't "right"? Disequilibrium occurs when prices are set above or below the equilibrium price. When prices are too low, excess demand leads to shortages. When prices are too high, excess supply leads to surpluses.

How do shifts in supply or demand affect markets? Many kinds of events can cause demand and supply curves to shift to the right or left. Markets adjust to such changed conditions by seeking a new equilibrium point.

What role do prices play in a modern mixed economy? Prices convey information to consumers and producers as to what to buy and produce. Prices motivate workers and firms to enter markets, and they help markets respond to changing conditions. They guide resources to their most efficient uses.

How does government intervention affect markets? Governments sometimes implement price controls when prices are considered unfairly high for consumers or unfairly low for producers. Price floors, such as minimum wage laws, prevent prices from going too low, but lead to excess supply. Price ceilings, such as rent control laws, prevent prices from going too high, but lead to shortages.

Is a minimum wage hike good or bad for you?

The minimum wage has been controversial since the first national minimum wage law went into effect in 1938. The following passages look at this controversy from two points of view. As you read them, think about your own life. Would a hike in the minimum wage be good for you by boosting wages? Or would it hurt you by making it harder for you to find a job?

A Just Minimum Wage: Good for Workers, Business and Our Future

by Holly Sklar and Paul H. Sherry

The federal minimum wage faced fierce opposition in the 1930s, and opponents predictably try to block raises in the minimum today. Opponents stereotype minimum wage workers as teenagers who don't need or deserve higher wages. Opponents claim business can't afford a higher minimum wage. They claim a higher minimum wage will destroy small business, increase unemployment, harm less educated workers, fuel inflation and aggravate poverty. Real world experience shows the claims are wrong.

Most Minimum Wage Workers Are Adults

As if to justify miserly pay, minimum wage critics often stereotype minimum wage workers as teenagers living with their families and working for fun money. In fact, the typical minimum wage earner is an

A Glimmer of Hope: The Unusual Backlash Against Minimum Wage

by Thomas Sowell

A survey has shown that 85 percent of the economists in Canada and 90 percent of the economists in the United States say that minimum wage laws reduce employment. But you don't need a Ph.D. in economics to know that jacking up prices leads fewer people to buy. Those people include employers, who hire less labor when labor is made artificially more expensive . . .

There is no free lunch. Higher labor costs mean fewer jobs.

Since all workers do not have the same skill or experience, minimum wage laws have more impact on some than on others. Young, inexperienced and unskilled workers are especially likely to find it harder to get a job when wage rates have been set higher than the value of their productivity . . .

In the United States, the group hardest hit by minimum wage laws are black male teenagers. Those who refuse to admit that the minimum wage is the reason for high unemployment rates among young blacks blame adult woman, not a teenager.

- Three out of four minimum wage workers are age 20 and older.
- While women make up just under half the total workforce, two out of three minimum wage workers are women.
- Most minimum wage workers have high school degrees or more, including 7 percent with a bachelor's degree or higher . . .

As for Teenagers
Teenagers shouldn't be paid less for doing the same job as an adult whether they are in the Army or working at a gas station. Many teenage minimum wage workers are already out of school and working for a living . . .

The United States does not provide universal public college education. While most high school graduates go on to college, a significant number can't afford to, however good their academic record. A U.S. Department of Education study, which followed a group of students since the 8th grade, provides fresh evidence of the link between socioeconomic status and higher education: The worst scoring students from high socioeconomic status families complete college as frequently as the best students from low socioeconomic status families.

Many teenagers are working minimum wage jobs in order to pay for college . . . The lower the minimum wage, the more hours students have to work at jobs while attending high school and college.

Holly Sklar is senior policy adviser for the Let Justice Roll Living Wage Campaign. Paul H. Sherry is the founding coordinator of the Let Justice Roll Living Wage Campaign.

racism, lack of education and whatever else occurs to them.

The hard facts say otherwise. Back in the 1940s, there was no less racism than today and black teenagers had no more education than today, but their unemployment rate was a fraction of what it is now—and was no different from that of white teenagers.

What was different back then? Although there was a minimum wage law on the books, the inflation of that era had raised wage rates well above the specified minimum, which had remained unchanged for years.

For all practical purposes, there was no minimum wage law. Only after the minimum wage began to be raised, beginning in 1950, and escalating repeatedly in the years thereafter, did black teenage unemployment skyrocket.

Most studies show unemployment resulting from minimum wages. But a few studies that reach different conclusions are hailed as having "refuted" the "myth" that minimum wages cause unemployment.

Some of these latter studies involve surveying employers before and after a minimum wage increase. But you can only survey employers who are still in business. By surveying people who played Russian roulette and are still around, you could "refute" the "myth" that Russian roulette is dangerous.

Minimum wage laws play Russian roulette with people who need jobs and the work experience that will enable them to rise to higher pay levels. There is now a glimmer of hope that more people are beginning to understand this, despite political demagoguery.

Thomas Sowell is an economist, political writer, and commentator. He is a senior fellow at Stanford University's Hoover Institution.

Chapter 7

What happens when markets do not work perfectly?

Market Structures and Market Failures

7.1 Introduction

If you have a cell phone, at some point in the past you may have thought about changing your service provider. Perhaps you wanted to get a new phone that your company did not offer, or maybe you wanted to switch to a cheaper plan. Or perhaps you were annoyed because your provider had raised your rates or altered other terms of your contract. But changing companies might have meant breaking your contract and paying a stiff penalty. So most likely, you swallowed your frustration and did nothing.

Sound familiar? If so, you were not alone. As Bob Sullivan, an investigative reporter specializing in technology and business, has observed, millions of Americans have found themselves stuck in "cell phone jail" with no easy way out. In this situation, says Sullivan in *Gotcha Capitalism* (2007),

> *You don't act like a rational consumer in a normal, functioning market economy. You don't go buy the new phone, or get the cheap new plan. You don't reward the more efficient company with your business. You can't. You're in jail.*
>
> *Imagine if you couldn't switch coffee shops or grocery stores without paying hundreds of dollars in penalties. Preposterous? No—not in the world of cell phones.*

The cell phone service market is structured differently from other markets.

Speaking of Economics

market structure
The organization of a market, based mainly on the degree of competition. There are four basic market structures.

perfect competition
A market structure in which many producers supply an identical product. This is the most efficient structure, with prices set by supply and demand.

monopoly
A market structure in which a single producer supplies a unique product that has no close substitutes. In an unregulated monopoly, the producer sets prices.

oligopoly
A market structure in which a few firms dominate the market and produce similar or identical goods. This structure is more competitive than a monopoly.

monopolistic competition
A market structure in which many producers supply similar but varied products. This structure is the closest to perfect competition.

market failure
A situation in which the market fails to allocate resources efficiently.

externality
A cost or benefit that arises from production or consumption of a good or service that falls on someone other than the producer or consumer.

public goods
Goods and services that are used collectively and that no one can be excluded from using. Public goods are not provided by markets. Examples include national defense and clean air.

Cell phone providers and clothing manufacturers operate in distinctly different markets. Wireless service providers offer consumers few choices and require binding contracts. In contrast, clothing companies give shoppers many choices, with no strings attached.

What is going on here? How could cell phone companies operate differently from, say, coffee shops or grocery stores or car dealerships? The cell phone companies defended their behavior by arguing that they provided phones to their customers at low, subsidized rates. Thus, the companies had to cover the costs of these phones if people were to break their contracts. Although there is some truth to this argument, it is not the real reason people found themselves trapped in cell phone jail. The real reason was that in 2007 a few major companies dominated the cell phone industry, and these companies all acted pretty much the same.

What about the freewheeling competition that is the hallmark of a market economy? What about the laws of supply and demand? Well, the truth is that even in a free market economy, not all industries and markets are equally competitive. And when they are not equal, it is usually the consumer who suffers.

In this chapter, you will read about various types of markets and how and why they differ. You will also learn about the effects of imperfect and inefficient markets on our economy and society.

■ 7.2 What Is Perfect Competition, and Why Do Economists Like It So Much?

Fortunately, most businesses are more consumer friendly than cell phone companies were when Sullivan wrote his 2007 book. Take T-shirt producers, for example. If you go shopping for a T-shirt, you will find hundreds of colors, styles, and designs to choose from, in a wide range of prices. The T-shirt industry is very competitive, with many different producers. It is apparent that cell phone service providers and T-shirt producers operate in different markets, with different levels of competition. What accounts for these differences?

The Characteristics That Define Market Structure

An economist would answer those questions by pointing out that the T-shirt and cell phone industries have different market structures. **Market structure** refers to the organization of a market, based mainly on the degree of competition among producers.

Economists define market structure according to four main characteristics.

Number of producers. The number of producers in a market helps determine the level of competition. Markets with many producers are more competitive.

Similarity of products. The degree to which products in a market are similar also affects competition. The more similar the products are, the greater the competition among their producers.

Ease of entry. Markets differ in their ease of entry, which is a measure of how easy it is to start a new business and begin competing with established businesses. Markets that are easy to enter, with few restrictions, have more producers and are thus more competitive.

Control over prices. Markets also differ in the degree to which producers can control prices. The ability to influence prices—usually by increasing or decreasing the supply of goods—is known as **market power**. The more competitive the market, the less market power any one producer will have.

Based on these characteristics, economists have identified four basic market structures: perfect competition, monopoly, oligopoly, and monopolistic competition. These structures are shown on the spectrum below, from most competitive to least competitive. As you read, keep in mind that these four models are not always easy to identify in the actual economy. In some cases, a market will have mixed features, making it hard to tell how competitive it is.

Perfect Competition:
Many Producers, Identical Products

The most competitive market structure is **perfect competition**. In a perfectly competitive market, a large number of firms produce essentially the same product. All goods are sold at their equilibrium price, or the price set by the market when quantity supplied and quantity demanded are in balance. Economists consider perfect competition to be the most efficient market structure in terms of allocating resources to those who value them most.

Although many markets are highly competitive, perfect competition is relatively rare. It exists mainly among producers of agricultural products, such as wheat, corn, tomatoes, and milk. Other examples of perfectly competitive markets include commercial fishing and the wood pulp and paper industry.

Perfect competition has four main characteristics.

Many producers and consumers. Perfectly competitive markets have many producers and consumers. Having a large number of participants in a market helps promote competition.

Identical products. Products in perfectly competitive markets are virtually identical. As a result, consumers do not distinguish among the products of different producers. A product that is exactly the same no matter who produces it is called a **commodity**. Examples include grains, cotton, sugar, and crude oil.

Easy entry into the market. In a perfectly competitive market, producers face few restrictions in entering the market. Ease of entry ensures that existing producers will face competition from new firms and that a single producer will not dominate the market.

No control over prices. Under conditions of perfect competition, producers have no market power. They cannot influence prices because there are too many other producers offering the same product. Instead, the market forces of supply and demand determine the price of goods. Producers are said to be **price takers** because they must accept, or take, the market price for their product.

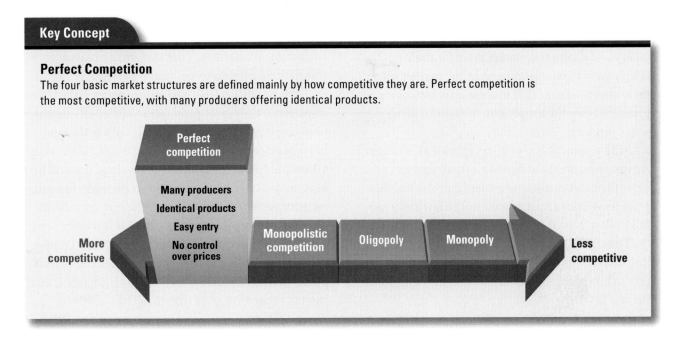

Key Concept

Perfect Competition
The four basic market structures are defined mainly by how competitive they are. Perfect competition is the most competitive, with many producers offering identical products.

In addition to these characteristics, one other feature distinguishes highly competitive markets: easy access to information about products and prices. A person shopping for a car, for example, can easily find out the range of models, features, and prices available. Such information is readily accessible at car dealerships, in published reports, and on the Internet. Information gathering involves trade-offs, however. Consumers must balance the time and expense of gathering such information with the money saved by finding a good deal.

Economists refer to the costs of shopping around for the best product at the best price as **transaction costs**. The Internet has helped reduce transaction costs by making product and price information more readily available. Instead of driving to various stores or making multiple phone calls, consumers can often make price comparisons over the Internet with less time and effort.

A Competition Case Study: The Milk Business

To get a better idea of how perfect competition works, consider the market for milk. To begin with, the milk market has many producers—about 65,000 dairy farms in the United States. They all offer the same basic commodity. Milk from one farm is pretty much the same as milk from any other farm.

Furthermore, no farm produces enough milk to dominate the market and achieve market power. There are simply too many farms, and the overall quantity of milk produced is too great for any one producer to influence prices by increasing or decreasing supply. So dairy farmers must be price takers and accept the market price for their milk. If they were to charge more than the market price, their buyers—firms that process milk into dairy products—would simply buy milk from some other producer.

Milk production also offers relative ease of entry. Anyone who wants to become a dairy farmer can enter the market, assuming that he or she has the resources. Even a farmer with only a few cows can sell milk to a local milk processor.

Thus, milk production satisfies the four criteria for perfect competition: many producers, identical product, no control over prices, and easy entry into the market.

Barriers to Entry Can Limit Competition

Our look at dairy farming hints at some of the obstacles that can restrict access to a market and limit competition. Such obstacles are known as **barriers to entry**.

One possible barrier is **start-up costs,** or the initial expense of launching a business. It is much less expensive, for example, to open a bicycle repair shop than it is to open a bicycle factory. An entrepreneur with little financial capital might find it difficult to get into bicycle manufacturing because of the high cost of building a factory.

The mining industry offers an example of another barrier to entry: control of resources. If existing mining companies already control the best deposits of iron, copper, or other minerals, it will be hard for new firms to enter the market.

Technology can pose yet another barrier. Some industries are more technology driven than others. The need for specialized technology or training may make it difficult to enter these markets. The computer industry is one example. Not only does the manufacture of computers require advanced technology, it also requires specialized knowledge that can be obtained only through years of education. These factors may act as a barrier, keeping new firms out of the computer market.

The Benefits of Perfect Competition

As the name suggests, perfect competition is rare in its purest form. Because it is the most efficient market structure, economists consider perfect competition to be the benchmark, or standard, for evaluating all markets. That said, many markets are competitive enough to be "nearly perfect."

Such nearly perfect markets are beneficial in two ways. First, they force producers to be as efficient as possible. When producers can sell only at the equilibrium price, the only way to maximize profits is by allocating resources to their most valued use and by keeping production costs as low as possible. Second, because perfect competition is efficient, consumers do not pay more for a product than it is worth. The equilibrium price of a product in a perfectly competitive market accurately reflects the value the market places on the productive resources—land, labor, and capital—that have gone into it.

Economists Robert Heilbroner and Lester Thurow summed up the benefits of perfect competition:

In a purely competitive market, the consumer is king. Indeed the rationale of such a market is often described as consumer sovereignty.

The term means two things. First, in a pure competitive market the consumer determines the allocation of resources by virtue of his or her demand—the public calls the tune to which the businessman dances. Second, the consumer enjoys goods that are produced as abundantly and sold as cheaply as possible. In such a market, each firm is producing the goods the consumer wants, in the largest quantity and at the lowest cost possible.

—Robert Heilbroner and Lester Thurow, *Economics Explained: Everything You Need to Know About How the Economy Works and Where It's Going,* 1998

■ 7.3 What Is a Monopoly, and Why Are Some Monopolies Legal?

Most markets are not perfectly competitive. Because these markets do not allocate goods and services in the most efficient way, they are examples of what economists call imperfect competition. Economists define **imperfect competition** as any market structure in which producers have some control over the price of their products. In other words, those producers have market power. The most extreme version of imperfect competition—and the opposite of perfect competition—is monopoly.

Monopoly: One Producer, A Unique Product

A **monopoly** is a market or an industry consisting of a single producer of a product that has no close substitutes. The term *monopoly* comes from a combination of the Greek words *mono,* meaning "alone," and *polein,* meaning "to sell." Literally, then, a monopoly is the only seller of something.

Monopolies share four main characteristics.

One producer. There is no competition in a monopoly. A single producer or firm controls the industry or market. An economist might say that the monopolistic firm is the industry.

Unique product. A monopoly provides the only product of its kind. There are no good substitutes, and no other producers provide similar goods or services.

High barriers to entry. The main factor that allows monopolies to exist is high barriers to entry that limit or prevent other producers from entering the market.

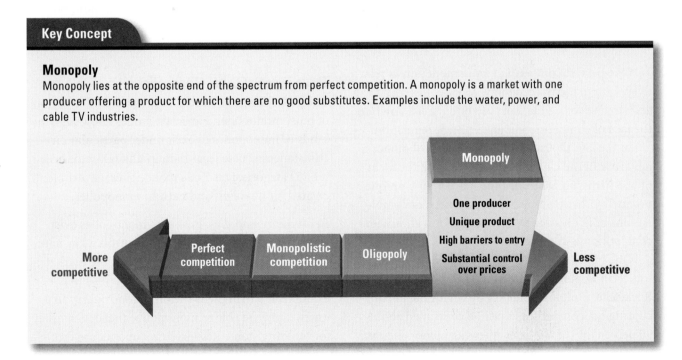

Key Concept

Monopoly
Monopoly lies at the opposite end of the spectrum from perfect competition. A monopoly is a market with one producer offering a product for which there are no good substitutes. Examples include the water, power, and cable TV industries.

More competitive → Perfect competition → Monopolistic competition → Oligopoly → **Monopoly** (One producer, Unique product, High barriers to entry, Substantial control over prices) → Less competitive

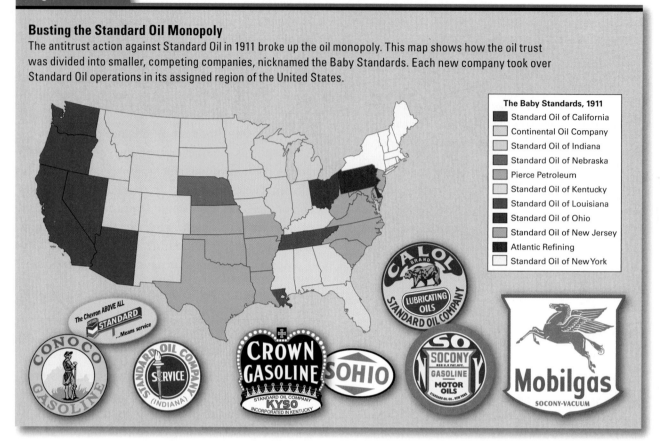

Figure 7.3

Busting the Standard Oil Monopoly

The antitrust action against Standard Oil in 1911 broke up the oil monopoly. This map shows how the oil trust was divided into smaller, competing companies, nicknamed the Baby Standards. Each new company took over Standard Oil operations in its assigned region of the United States.

The Baby Standards, 1911
- Standard Oil of California
- Continental Oil Company
- Standard Oil of Indiana
- Standard Oil of Nebraska
- Pierce Petroleum
- Standard Oil of Kentucky
- Standard Oil of Louisiana
- Standard Oil of Ohio
- Standard Oil of New Jersey
- Atlantic Refining
- Standard Oil of New York

Substantial control over prices. Monopolistic firms usually have great market power because they control the supply of a good or service. They can set a price for a product without fear of being undercut by competitors. Unlike competitive firms, monopolistic businesses are **price setters** rather than price takers.

Like perfect competition, pure monopoly is relatively rare in today's economy. Monopolies may form and survive for a time, but they often break down in the face of competition or government regulation.

In the late 1800s, however, a number of monopolies arose in the United States. Some took the form of one firm that controlled the market for a unique product. Others took the form of **trusts,** or combinations of firms, that worked together to eliminate competition and control prices.

One of the most famous, and feared, monopolies was John D. Rockefeller's Standard Oil Company. Rockefeller built his monopoly by buying out or bankrupting his competitors until he controlled about 90 percent of U.S. oil sales. Viewing monopolies as

harmful to the public interest, Congress enacted **antitrust laws** to limit their formation. In 1911, the federal government took Standard Oil to court for antitrust violations and broke up its oil monopoly. Figure 7.3 shows the results of that famous trust-busting case.

Three Types of Legal Monopolies

The government still seeks to prevent the formation of most monopolies. However, it does allow certain kinds of monopolies to exist under particular circumstances. These legal monopolies fall into three broad categories: resource monopolies, government-created monopolies, and natural monopolies.

Resource monopolies. Resource monopolies exist when a single producer owns or controls a key natural resource. Other firms cannot enter the market because they do not have access to the resource. For example, if a firm owns the only stone quarry in a town, it may be able to monopolize the local market for building stone. Resource monopolies are rare, however, because the economy is large and supplies of resources are not usually controlled by one owner.

Government-created monopolies. Government-created monopolies are formed when the government grants a single firm or individual the exclusive right to provide a good or service. The government does this when it considers such monopolies to be in the public interest. Government-created monopolies may be formed in three ways.

Patents and copyrights. These legal grants are designed to protect and promote intellectual capital. They give inventors or creators the right to control the production, sale, and distribution of their work, thus creating a temporary monopoly over that work. For example, a patent issued to a pharmaceutical company gives that company the sole right to produce and sell a particular drug for a period of 20 years. Such patents encourage investment in research and development. In the same way, a copyright grants exclusive rights to an artist, writer, or composer to control a creative work, such as a painting, a novel, or a song, for a period of time.

Public franchises. A **public franchise** is a contract issued by a government entity that gives a firm the sole right to provide a good or service in a certain area. For example, the National Park Service issues public franchises to companies to provide food, lodging, and other services in national parks. School districts may issue public franchises to snack food companies to place their vending machines in public schools. In each case, a single firm has a monopoly in that particular market.

Licenses. A **license** is a legal permit to operate a business or enter a market. In some cases, licenses can create monopolies. For example, a state might grant a license to one company to conduct all vehicle emissions tests in a particular town. Or a city might license a parking lot company to provide all the public parking in the city. Licenses ensure that certain goods and services are provided in an efficient and regulated way.

Natural monopolies. The third type of monopoly is a **natural monopoly**. This kind of monopoly arises when a single firm can supply a good or service more efficiently and at a lower cost than two or more competing firms can. For example, most utility industries are natural monopolies. They provide gas, water, and electricity, as well as cable TV services, to businesses and households. Because natural monopolies are efficient, governments tend to view them as beneficial.

A natural monopoly occurs when a producer can take advantage of economies of scale to dominate the market. The term **economies of scale** refers to the greater efficiency and cost savings that result from increased production. A firm that achieves economies of scale lowers its average cost per unit of production by increasing its output and spreading fixed costs over a larger quantity of goods.

Grand Canyon Lodges in the Grand Canyon National Park is a public franchise. Its contract with the government gives it a monopoly on lodging, dining, transportation, and other amenities in the park.

You can see how economies of scale work by looking at the cost of supplying water to a new subdivision of 50 homes. Suppose it costs a water company $100,000 to build a network of pipes that will bring water to the subdivision. In addition, installing a water meter at each home costs $1,000. The total cost of supplying water to the first home is $100,000, plus $1,000 for a meter, or $101,000 total.

Now look at the cost per home as the number of homes increases. A water meter for the second home costs $1,000, bringing the total cost for two homes to $102,000, or $51,000 per home. A water meter for the third home costs another $1,000, bringing the total cost for three homes to $103,000, or $34,333 per home. By the time the water company gets to the 50th home, its total cost is $150,000—$100,000 for pipes and $50,000 for 50 meters. The cost per home has decreased to $3,000.

Consider, now, what would happen if two companies were to compete to bring water to the subdivision. Each company would have to build its own network of pipes. The fixed costs of bringing water to the subdivision would essentially double, but the number of homes served would stay the same. As a result, the economies of scale would be substantially reduced. For that reason, it makes sense for the government to allow water companies, like other utilities, to do business as natural monopolies.

A Monopoly Case Study: Microsoft Corporation

Our government permits certain monopolies that are judged to be in the public interest to exist. In most other circumstances, monopoly is illegal. As in the Standard Oil Company case, the government may take action to break up a monopoly.

Consider the case of Microsoft, the giant computer software firm. In the 1980s, Microsoft received a copyright for its computer operating system known as Windows. Microsoft then made deals with computer makers to sell machines with Windows already installed on them. In this way, Microsoft gained control of about 90 percent of the market for operating systems. Microsoft's monopoly power allowed it to charge more for Windows than it might have in a more competitive market.

Microsoft also used its market power to drive potential competitors out of the market. In 1994, a

Bill Gates, the chairman and cofounder of Microsoft, testifies at his company's antitrust trial in August 1998. The trial judge found Microsoft guilty of engaging in monopolistic practices.

software company called Netscape began selling a new computer application known as a Web browser to computer users. A Web browser enables computer users to find and view Internet sites from around the world. Microsoft effectively drove Netscape out of business by bundling its own version of a browser, Internet Explorer, into its Windows operating system. As part of Windows, Internet Explorer came already installed on most new computers, severely reducing the market for browsers from Netscape or any other software company.

In late 1997, the U.S. Department of Justice accused Microsoft of trying to stifle competition by expanding its monopoly power into the Internet market. In 1998, Justice Department lawyers charged Microsoft with antitrust violations and took the company to court. In its defense, Microsoft argued that it had merely added new features to its operating system. It claimed that the integration of its Web browser was a natural and logical step in efforts to improve its products and satisfy its customers.

In November 1999, the trial judge found that Microsoft had violated antitrust laws. He ordered the company to be broken into two separate businesses: one that sold the Windows operating system and another that sold applications software. Microsoft appealed the decision to a higher court, which overturned the breakup order but upheld the antitrust verdict.

In 2002, Microsoft settled its case with the government by agreeing to change the way it dealt with other software firms. The company's troubles did not end there, however. It was later hit by several private antitrust suits and was fined in Europe for anticompetitive actions.

Consequences of Monopoly for Consumers

The government's case against Microsoft focused mainly on the company's aggressive efforts to drive other firms out of the market. But the case also underscored the negative effects of monopoly for consumers. Because a monopolistic firm has considerable market power, it can set prices without fear of lower-priced competition from other firms. As a result, consumers may be forced to pay more for a good or service provided by a monopoly than they would in a competitive market.

Furthermore, because such firms face little or no competition, they have less incentive to innovate or to satisfy consumers. Viewing their customers as a "captive market," monopolies may offer consumers products of lesser quality or fewer product choices than they would if the market were more competitive.

■ 7.4 What Is an Oligopoly, and How Does It Limit Competition?

The third market structure—oligopoly—is similar to monopoly. It is another form of imperfect competition in which firms exercise considerable market power. However, unlike monopolies, oligopolies are quite common in the real economy. We do business with oligopolies whenever we take a domestic airline flight, buy a new car, or consume a can of soda.

Oligopoly: Few Producers, Similar Products

An **oligopoly** is a market or an industry dominated by just a few firms that produce similar or identical products. Oligopoly is one of the less-competitive market structures. On our spectrum of structures, it lies closer to monopoly than to perfect competition.

Like monopolies, oligopolies often arise because of economies of scale, which give bigger producers an advantage over smaller ones. In an oligopoly, however, there is at least some competition. In addition, firms in an oligopoly do not have to be large. As an example, if two hardware stores control all the hardware business in a town, then together they make up an oligopoly.

The modern American economy has many oligopolies. As mentioned above, the airline, automobile, and soft drink industries are oligopolies. So are the

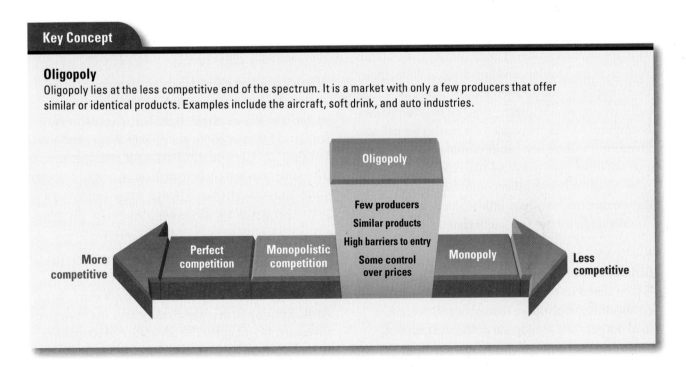

Key Concept

Oligopoly
Oligopoly lies at the less competitive end of the spectrum. It is a market with only a few producers that offer similar or identical products. Examples include the aircraft, soft drink, and auto industries.

Oligopoly

Few producers
Similar products
High barriers to entry
Some control over prices

More competitive

Perfect competition

Monopolistic competition

Monopoly

Less competitive

Figure 7.4

Identifying an Oligopoly

One way to tell whether a market is controlled by an oligopoly is to determine what percentage of market share the four largest firms control. This percentage is called the four-firm concentration ratio. A concentration ratio of greater than 60 percent usually indicates an oligopoly.

- Note the highest concentration ratio. Four firms control 93 percent of the market for washers and dryers.
- Compare the concentration ratios for pet food and soap detergent. How do those markets differ in terms of the numbers of companies competing for market share?

Concentration Ratios of Selected Industries, 2002

Industry	Percentage of Market Controlled by the Four Largest Firms	Firms in the Market
Washers and dryers	93	13
Light bulbs	89	57
Aircraft	81	184
Computers	76	465
Bicycles and motorcycles	72	348
Cacao bean products	69	138
Dog and cat food	64	176
Bottled water	63	201
Soap detergent	61	699

Source: U.S. Census Bureau.

industries that produce light bulbs, tennis balls, and large passenger jets.

If you go to a sporting goods store to buy tennis balls, for example, you will likely find just four brands: Wilson, Penn, Dunlop, and Spalding. In 2008, these four companies controlled the U.S. market for tennis balls. In aircraft manufacturing, just two companies, Boeing and Airbus, dominated the market for jetliners. Likewise, just three companies dominated the carbonated soft drink market: Coca-Cola, Pepsi, and Cadbury-Schweppes. Although other companies may be part of these industries, they have little impact on the market.

Oligopolies share four main characteristics.

Few producers. In an oligopoly, a small number of firms control the market. In general, an industry is considered an oligopoly if the four top producers together supply more than about 60 percent of total output. The proportion of the total market controlled by a set number of companies is called

the **concentration ratio**. For example, the four-firm concentration ratio in the light bulb industry is 89 percent. Figure 7.4 shows concentration ratios for various oligopolies.

Similar products. Producers in oligopolies offer essentially the same product, with only minor variations. For example, light bulbs are all very similar. They may come in different shapes and sizes, but they are all close substitutes for one another. The same goes for kitchen appliances, soap, computer chips, and cola drinks. Though some consumers prefer Coca-Cola to Pepsi and vice versa, the two drinks are actually very nearly the same.

High barriers to entry. It is hard for new firms to break into an oligopoly and compete with existing businesses. One reason may be high start-up costs. Existing firms may already have made sizable investments and enjoy the advantage of economies of scale. For example, it would cost many millions of dollars to open a new computer chip factory and compete with the two industry leaders, Intel and Advanced Micro Devices. In addition, customers might be reluctant to give up their loyalty to the old brands and try something new.

Some control over prices. Because there are few firms in an oligopoly, they may be able to exert some control over prices. Firms in an oligopoly are often influenced by the price decisions of other firms in the market. This interdependence between firms in setting prices is a key feature of oligopoly.

Cooperative Pricing: When an Oligopoly Acts Like a Monopoly

When firms in an oligopoly compete for customers, the result can be a fairly competitive market. Often, however, oligopolies behave more like monopolies. Rather than lower their prices to try to win a larger share of the market, firms in an oligopoly may drive prices upward to levels above the market equilibrium price. They may do this in three ways: price leadership, collusion, and cartel formation.

Price leadership. In an oligopoly dominated by a single company, that firm may try to control prices through **price leadership**. The dominant firm sets a price, and the other, smaller firms follow suit. If the industry leader sets the price high, the other firms benefit. Sometimes, however, the dominant firm may cut prices to take business away from its

competitors or even force them out of business. If the other firms also lower their prices, the market is said to be experiencing a **price war**. Price wars are hard on producers but beneficial for consumers.

Collusion. Firms in an oligopoly may also try to control the market through collusion. **Collusion** occurs when producers get together and make agreements on production levels and pricing.

Collusion is illegal because it unfairly limits competition. Nevertheless, firms sometimes try to get around the law. In 2002, for example, several large music companies were accused of collusion aimed at keeping the price of recorded compact discs artificially high. Although the companies denied any wrongdoing, they agreed to end the questionable practices that led to the collusion charges.

Cartel formation. A **cartel** is an organization of producers established to set production and price levels for a product. Cartels are illegal in the United States, but they do sometimes operate on a global scale, most often in the commodities markets. For example, nations that produce coffee, sugar, and tin have all tried to form cartels in the past.

The Organization of the Petroleum Exporting Countries is the best-known modern cartel. OPEC consists of about a dozen countries that agree to set quotas on oil production and exports. By setting limits on the supply of oil, OPEC exerts a major influence on world oil prices.

The Organization of the Petroleum Exporting Countries is an international cartel that seeks to control oil supplies and prices. OPEC oil ministers meet regularly to assess global demand for oil and assign production quotas. The quotas set an upper limit on each country's oil production. This 2008 meeting of OPEC oil ministers took place in Vienna, Austria.

The market power of a cartel like OPEC underscores the potentially harmful effects of oligopolies on consumers. When firms in an oligopoly work together to control the market, they act much like a monopoly. As such, they can use their market power to limit competition and raise prices.

■ 7.5 What Is Monopolistic Competition, and How Does It Affect Markets?

The fourth market structure, monopolistic competition, is the one we encounter most often in our daily lives. When we eat in a restaurant, buy gas at a gas station, or shop at a clothing store, we are doing business in monopolistically competitive markets.

Monopolistic Competition: Many Producers, Similar but Varied Products

In **monopolistic competition,** a large number of producers provide goods that are similar but varied. Like oligopoly, this market structure falls between the extremes of perfect competition and monopoly. However, it lies on the more competitive end of the spectrum.

The shoe business is a good example of monopolistic competition. If you go to a discount shoe store, you will find hundreds of pairs of shoes on display, made by many different companies. Each company has

marked its shoes with its own **brand,** or trade name. Each has worked to make its line of shoes distinctive in style, color, material, or quality of construction. Because of these differences, shoes are not commodities. Therefore, the shoe industry does not fit the model of perfect competition. At the same time, the sheer number of shoe producers indicates that the shoe industry is neither a monopoly nor an oligopoly.

You might well wonder why a market like this would be called monopolistic. The main reason is that the goods offered by the competing brands are distinct enough to appear unique. As a result, customers may develop **brand loyalty,** favoring one company over all others. Such customer loyalty gives the favored company some degree of market power. In effect, the company "monopolizes" its brand and can charge more for it.

Monopolistic competition is especially common in service industries, such as banks, auto repair shops, and supermarkets. But as our shoe example indicates, it also exists in many manufacturing industries.

Monopolistic competitions share four basic characteristics.

Many producers. Monopolistically competitive markets have many producers or sellers. In a big city, many restaurants compete with one another for business. The same is true for gas stations and hotels.

Differentiated products. Firms in this type of market engage in **product differentiation,** which means they

Key Concept

Monopolistic Competition
Monopolistic competition lies at the more competitive end of the spectrum. It is a market with many producers offering similar but slightly different products. Examples include the shoe, book, and restaurant industries.

More competitive ← Perfect competition | **Monopolistic competition** — Many producers, Differentiated products, Few barriers to entry, Some control over prices | Oligopoly | Monopoly → Less competitive

In monopolistically competitive markets, firms use nonprice competition to attract customers. This supermarket sets itself apart from the competition by selling natural and organic foods and projecting an eco-friendly image.

seek to distinguish their goods and services from those of other firms, even when those products are fairly close substitutes for one another. For example, a pizza stand and a taco stand both offer fast foods. A customer may have a taste for one type of food over the other, but either will provide a suitable lunch.

Few barriers to entry. Start-up costs are relatively low in monopolistically competitive markets. This allows many firms to enter the market and earn a profit. For example, it does not cost much to get into the custom T-shirt business. That means that an entrepreneur with a good set of T-shirt designs may be able to open a shop or create a Web site and sell enough shirts to make a profit.

Some control over prices. Because producers control their brands, they also have some control over prices. However, because products from different producers are close substitutes, this market power is limited. If prices rise too much, customers may shift to another brand. In addition, there are too many producers for price leadership or collusion to be feasible.

Increasing Market Share Through Nonprice Competition

To compete with rival firms, producers in monopolistically competitive markets have to take price into consideration. But they also engage in **nonprice competition,** using product differentiation and advertising to attract customers. By convincing consumers that

their brand is better than others, these producers hope to increase their firm's **market share,** or proportion of total sales in a market.

Nonprice competition typically focuses on four factors.

Physical characteristics. There are many kinds of products that consumers will pay more for because of their unique physical characteristics. For example, a pair of running shoes may stand out from its competitors because of the shoe's unique design, color, or materials. A consumer who likes that particular shoe may not consider buying any other pair, regardless of price.

Service. Some producers offer better service than others and can therefore charge higher prices. For example, a fast food chain and a sit-down restaurant both offer food, but the more expensive restaurant also offers table service. Upscale grocery stores may offer their customers free food samples or special services, such as food delivery and catering. Some department stores provide personal shopping assistants to help customers make selections. Such enhanced services may appeal to consumers who are willing to pay for them.

Location. Gas stations, dry cleaners, motels, and other businesses may compete with one another based on location. Although they offer the same basic product or service, a firm may win customers because it is located near a highway, a shopping mall, or some other convenient spot.

Status and image. Sometimes companies compete on the basis of their perceived status or trendiness. One brand may be regarded as more exclusive, more "natural," or more fashionable than another. For example, a handbag from an expensive boutique may have greater status in a customer's eyes than a similar bag from a discount store. Another customer may willingly pay more for designer jeans, even though a similar product without the designer label might be had for much less money.

These perceived status differences are usually established through advertising. Although advertisers often provide information about their products in ads, their main goal is to increase their sales and market share.

◼ 7.6 Market Failures: What Are Externalities and Public Goods?

As our survey of market structures shows, most market structures fall into the broad category of imperfect competition. Because these structures do not allocate goods and services in the most efficient way, economists call them **market failures**. But imperfect competition is not the only form of economic inefficiency. Externalities and public goods are also evidence of market failure.

Externalities: Costs and Benefits That Spill Over

An **externality** is a side effect of production or consumption that has consequences for people other than the producer or consumer. You might think of externalities as spillover effects, either costs or benefits, resulting from the actions of companies or individuals.

Externalities occur in many ways and take many forms. When a factory dumps chemical waste into a river and the polluted water affects the health of people who live downstream, that is an externality. If a neighbor plants a new flower garden and the results please you, that is also an externality. If that same neighbor holds a party with loud music that keeps you up at night, that is an externality, too. In fact, it is an externality if you hear the music at all, whether you like it or not.

Now consider a more complicated example of spillover effects. Suppose that a corn syrup factory, run by a firm that we will call Acme Corn Syrup

Positive and Negative Externalities

Externalities, or spillover effects of production or consumption, come in many forms—some positive, others negative.

- Immunizations provide a positive externality. They protect the community—not just the recipients—from illness.
- Factory pollution is a negative externality. It imposes a cost on people other than the producer and consumer.

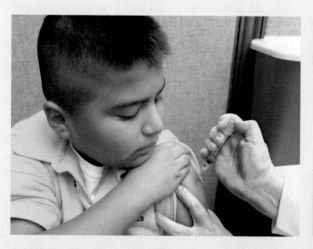

Company, produces an unpleasant odor. Every day that odor drifts into a nearby neighborhood. The odor is an externality by itself, but it has other side effects as well. Because of the smell, some people in the area decide to sell their homes. The odor is so bad, however, that no one wants to buy the houses. As a result, housing prices fall.

An economist would consider the decline in property values around the factory to be a cost of corn syrup production, but it is not a cost paid by Acme Corn Syrup Company. Rather, this cost is external to the company and is borne by homeowners in the community. That external cost is an externality.

There are two types of externalities: negative and positive. A **negative externality** is a cost that falls on someone other than the producer or consumer. This cost may be monetary, but it may also simply be an undesired effect. Most of the examples discussed above are negative externalities.

A **positive externality,** on the other hand, is a benefit that falls on someone other than the producer or consumer. If you enjoy hearing the music from a neighborhood party, that spillover sound is a positive externality. Other examples include the broader benefits of getting an education or developing a less-polluting car. Students who get a college education benefit directly by getting higher-paying jobs. But if their success also results in greater economic prosperity for their communities, that is a positive externality. In the same way, if a car company designs a new car that emits fewer pollutants, the company may benefit from increased sales. But society benefits, too, as a result of reduced air pollution.

Another type of positive externality is known as a technology spillover. The benefit from a **technology spillover** results when technical knowledge spreads from one company or individual to another, thereby promoting further innovations. For example, other car companies might expand on the less-polluting car design to make additional improvements in pollution control. Those improvements are a technology spillover.

How Externalities Reflect Inefficiency

Although positive and negative externalities have very different results, they are both examples of inefficiency and market failure. That is because they fail to factor all costs of production and all benefits to

A college education is a good example of a positive externality. Each individual's consumption of a good—in this case, higher education—will create a benefit for society in the form of a more productive workforce.

consumers into the model of supply and demand.

To understand what this means, consider the case of negative externalities generated by our imaginary corn syrup company. When Acme produces corn syrup, it incurs a private cost. This private cost, however, does not take into account the external cost paid by others as a result of Acme's pollution.

If Acme were to factor in this external cost, its total cost of production would increase. To make up for this extra cost, Acme would have to increase the price of corn syrup. In response to a price increase, the quantity of corn syrup demanded would most likely decrease. Acme would then have to lower its output to match the shrinking demand.

The fact that these changes in price and quantity demanded do not occur under ideal market conditions is a sign that the market is not working efficiently. The result is that goods that generate negative externalities tend to be overproduced, because their full cost is not reflected in the market price.

The reverse is true of goods and services that generate positive externalities. They tend to be underproduced relative to their benefits. Consider a beekeeper who sells honey for a living. The money

Private and Public Goods

Private goods, which are provided by the market system, differ in two key ways from public goods, which are generally provided by governments.

Private Goods

Available only to purchasers
(excludable)

Consumption by one person prevents another from consuming
(rival in consumption)

Public Goods

Available to everyone
(nonexcludable)

Consumption by one person does not prevent another from consuming
(nonrival in consumption)

she makes from her business is her private benefit. The beekeeper's neighbors, however, receive an external benefit when her bees pollinate their flowers and fruit trees at no cost. They may wish that she would double her number of hives. But unless the beekeeper can reap a private benefit from doing so, she is unlikely to expand her business no matter how much it might benefit her neighbors.

The Problem of Public Goods

Another example of market failure involves **public goods**—goods and services that are not provided by the market system because of the difficulty of getting people who use them to pay for their use.

Examples of public goods include fire and police services, national defense, and public parks. Public goods are the opposite of **private goods,** or goods and services that are sold in markets.

Economists make two key distinctions between public and private goods. First, private goods are **excludable**. This means that anyone who does not pay for the good can be excluded from using it. A grocery store, for example, will sell apples only to customers willing to pay for them. Public goods, on the other hand, are **nonexcludable**. Think of streetlights. How could you prevent some people from using the light from streetlights? You could not. This makes them nonexcludable.

A Fourth of July fireworks show put on by a city is an example of a public good. The city could make the show a private good by setting up a fence and selling tickets, but it could not prevent "free riders" from watching the show from outside the gates.

Second, private goods are said to be **rival in consumption,** which means that a good cannot be consumed by more than one person at the same time. Thus, for example, if you buy an apple and eat it, that apple is no longer available for anyone else to eat. In contrast, public goods are **nonrival in consumption**. One person's use of a streetlight's glow does not diminish another's ability to use its light as well.

Based on these two characteristics, you can see why parks and sidewalks are considered public goods. No one can be excluded from using them, and anyone can enjoy their benefits without depriving anyone else.

Private firms do not provide us with these public goods for a simple reason: they have no way to make the people who benefit from nonrival and nonexcludable goods pay for them. Economists call this situation the **free-rider problem**. If streetlights were a private good, for example, the company that provided them would want to charge the people who use them. But street lighting is not excludable. Anyone who passes under a streetlight can take a "free ride" by using the light and not paying for it. Because of these free riders, no private business will provide street lighting. The result, from the point of view of economists, is a market failure.

Externalities and public goods remind us that markets do not always work perfectly. As a matter of fact, they do not work perfectly much of the time. However, this does not mean that the market system is fatally flawed. Despite its weaknesses, the market system is still the most effective, efficient, and flexible way for all of us to get the things we want and need.

Summary

There are four basic market structures, each with different characteristics. Because only one of these structures is perfectly competitive, economists classify the other three as examples of imperfect competition and, therefore, as market failures.

What is perfect competition, and why do economists like it so much? Perfect competition is the most efficient and competitive market structure. It consists of many producers who provide identical goods, usually referred to as commodities. Prices are established by the interaction of supply and demand.

What is a monopoly, and why are some monopolies legal? A monopoly is the opposite of perfect competition. In a monopoly, a single producer provides a unique product and therefore has significant control over prices. The government permits certain kinds of monopolies to exist because they are believed to serve the public interest.

What is an oligopoly, and how does it limit competition? An oligopoly is a market dominated by a small number of producers who provide similar, but not identical, goods. Firms in an oligopoly often set prices based on other firms' pricing decisions. Because oligopolies can dominate markets, their effect may be much like that of a monopoly.

What is monopolistic competition, and how does it affect markets? Monopolistic competition is a market in which many producers provide a variety of similar goods. Such markets are characterized by the use of nonprice competition to differentiate products and build brand loyalty. To the extent that firms "monopolize" their own brands, they may have some control over prices, but such markets remain relatively competitive.

Market failures: What are externalities and public goods? Externalities are side effects of production and consumption. They may be positive or negative. Public goods are goods that are available for all people to consume, whether or not those people pay for the goods. Externalities and public goods are both symptoms of market failure.

What is the best way to address global warming?

Global warming may be the ultimate negative externality. Most scientists agree that fossil fuel emissions are heating up the planet to a dangerous degree. Experts are divided, however, on what to do about it. As you read this article, ask yourself which of the solutions posed might be most effective. Can government incentives really get the market to clean up its act?

Global Warming: A Real Solution

by Robert F. Kennedy Jr.,
***Rolling Stone*, June 18, 2007**

In early May [2007], 100 of the nation's top business leaders gathered for a summit at a private resort nestled on 250 acres in California's Napa Valley. The attendees, gathered at the invitation of Silicon Valley venture capitalists, included CEOs and other top executives from such Fortune 500 corporations as Wal-Mart, Proctor & Gamble and BP. They had been invited to discuss ways to end America's fossil-fuel addiction and save the world from global warming. But in reality they had come to make money for their companies—and that may turn out to be the thing that saves us.

For three days, the executives listened as their colleagues and business rivals described how they are using new technologies to wean themselves from oil and boost their profits in the process. DuPont has cut its climate-warming pollution by seventy-two percent since 1990, slashing $3 billion from its energy bills while increasing its global production by nearly a third.

Wal-Mart has installed new, energy-efficient light bulbs in refrigeration units that save the company $12 million a year, and skylights that cut utility bills by up to $70,000 per store. The company, which operates the nation's second-largest corporate truck fleet, also saved $22 million last year just by installing auxiliary power units that allow drivers to operate electric systems without idling their vehicles. In a move with even more far-reaching potential, Wal-Mart has ordered its truck suppliers to double the gas mileage of the company's entire fleet by 2015. When those trucks become available to other businesses, America will cut its demand for oil by six percent.

The executives gathered at the retreat weren't waiting around for federal subsidies or new regulations to tilt the market in their direction. Business logic, not government intervention, was driving them to cut energy costs and invest in new fuel sources . . .

As the discussions at the summit demonstrated . . . America doesn't need to wait for futuristic, pie-in-the-sky technologies to cut its reckless consumption of oil and coal. Our last, best hope to stop climate change is the free market itself. There is gold in going green, and the same drive to make a buck that created global

Wind farms generate electricity using a renewable resource. Many states offer economic incentives to encourage the market for renewable energy.

warming in the first place can now be harnessed to slow the carbon-based pollution that is overheating the planet . . .

So why, if we can profitably slash planet-warming pollution, does the world face a climate crisis? The answer is simple: market failure.

The global climate crisis is the result not of an orderly free market, but of a distorted market run amok. A truly free market is the planet's best friend. Free markets promote efficiency. "Efficiency," after all, means the elimination of waste—and pollution is waste . . .

Here are six modest, tried-and-true mechanisms we can implement to quickly foster free-market solutions to global warming:

Feebates California is considering imposing a $2,500 fee on

Hummers and other low-efficiency automobiles—and then rebating that money to drivers who choose to purchase more efficient cars like hybrids. This cross between a fee and a rebate motivates manufacturers to develop less-polluting vehicles and is a perfect example of how to give consumers an incentive to conform their self-interest to the public interest, turning every driver into a guerrilla warrior in the battle against global warming.

Cap and Trade One of the most effective tools for harnessing markets to save civilization is a mandatory cap on planet-warming pollution—one that begins by cutting emissions now and then reduces them eighty percent by 2050. Establishing mandatory limits in all industrial sectors would create a huge market for products and tech-

nologies that use less energy and emit far less carbon. In addition, companies that figure out how to cut their emissions to below their limit will earn credits that can be sold to those companies that can't meet their quota, creating a powerful incentive to actually beat the pollution limits . . .

Clean Incentives Revenues from the sale of carbon credits under the cap-and-trade system should be used to create market-based financial incentives to speed the development and adoption of promising new technologies . . . All across Europe, citizens are scrambling to cover their roofs and homes with solar collectors and transform their residences into mini power plants . . . Connecticut already offers a rebate of up to $46,500 for homeowners who go solar, and Congress could boost the rapid expansion of existing technologies by providing similar incentives for solar water heaters, residential wind turbines, geothermal systems, modern electronic lighting and improved insulation . . .

Decoupling Utilities currently make money only by producing and selling us more electricity—giving power companies little incentive to promote energy efficiency. California, however, has decoupled profits from energy sales, creating a new kind of market that rewards efficiency. Utilities make money not by selling power but by helping consumers use it more productively in their homes. The result: Californians use almost half as many kilowatts as other Americans. "We've been able to keep energy demand flat for thirty years with a rapidly growing population, while the average per-capita energy consumption for the rest of the nation has soared by fifty percent," says Tom King, CEO of Pacific Gas and Electric. "And we haven't even made a dent in the potential that's out there—we can go beyond anything anybody's ever projected."

Net Metering California also took an early lead in this area, allowing homeowners who install solar panels or wind turbines to sell their excess electricity back to the utility. The electric meter actually spins backward when the home is generating more electricity than it consumes, and customers are billed only for the net amount of energy they consume from the utility's grid. "Our objective is to give every homeowner the incentive to turn their house into a clean-energy power station,"

says King. "We can not only replace gasoline and dramatically reduce carbon emissions, but we'll also have a grid that is more decentralized and hence more resilient."

Performance Standards The quickest way to improve the energy efficiency of appliances, cars, trucks and buildings is to establish minimum standards based on the current state of technology. Rather than prescribing specific solutions, performance standards harness the market by establishing targets and rewarding companies that create the best emissions-cutting technology. The government has successfully done this for energy-intensive appliances like refrigerators, which now consume seventy-five percent less energy than they did twenty-five years ago . . .

The challenge facing us today is . . . to create a rational marketplace—one that serves the broader interests of our nation by unleashing the innovative power of American entrepreneurs to transform our energy economy. Done right, this transformation will not only curb global warming, it will create an engine of sustainable economic growth for generations.

Robert F. Kennedy Jr. is an environmental lawyer and a professor at Pace University School of Law.

WITH THE PRICE OF GAS, I DECIDED TO GET A "HYBRID"! SO I BOUGHT MY HYBRID BIKE THAT RUNS ON HALF PEANUT BUTTER AND HALF JELLY!

GAS REG. 4¹ʰ

© John Darkow/caglecartoons.com

Economic Institutions and Organizations

Chapter 8

How should you spend, save, and invest your money?

Money, Banking, Saving, and Investing

8.1 Introduction

If you had a paperclip to trade, what do you think you could get for it? If your answer is not much, think again. Kyle MacDonald, an unemployed 25-year-old from Montreal, Canada, traded one red paperclip for a house. Well, actually he started with the paperclip, and 14 trades later he ended up with a house.

How did he do it? MacDonald posted each of his trade offers online using a popular trading site and his own Web site. His purpose was clear from the start. "I'm going to make a continuous chain of 'up trades' until I get a house," he wrote on July 12, 2005.

MacDonald promised to go anywhere to make a trade. While visiting Vancouver, British Columbia, he traded the red paperclip for a pen shaped like a fish. Then he went to Seattle, Washington, for a sculpted doorknob. He traveled to Massachusetts for a camping stove, California for a generator, and New York for supplies to throw a party.

The next trade, for a snowmobile, really got things rolling. The trader was a well-known radio and television personality in Quebec. Soon the national media in Canada and the United States were running stories about the "paperclip guy."

The trades then came fairly quickly—a trip to a town in British Columbia, a van, a recording contract, and a year's free rent of a house in Phoenix,

People spend, save, and invest their money in various ways.

Arizona. MacDonald was nearing his goal. In the next few months, he "up traded" an afternoon with rock star Alice Cooper for a fancy motorized snow globe, the globe for a movie role, and the movie role for—yes—a house. Through barter, with no exchange of money, MacDonald had turned a red paperclip into a house. In one year's time.

Kyle MacDonald's triumph proved that barter is alive and well in our market economy. But did it also show that money is obsolete? Not at all. If anything, MacDonald showed how much we need money—even to accomplish a wildly successful series of barters. Throughout his adventure in bartering, MacDonald relied on money to meet his everyday wants and needs. He used money to pay for his food, clothing, shelter, phone calls, and airplane trips across the continent. Money made his bartering adventure possible.

MacDonald spent money chasing his dream. That was his choice. You, too, have probably made choices about what to do with your hard-earned cash. Those choices will only become more complicated as you take on more responsibility for supporting yourself. This chapter may help make that transition easier by giving you some insight into how you might choose to spend, save, and invest your money.

Starting with a red paperclip, Kyle MacDonald traded his way up to this house. "It's 'official,'" he wrote on his Web site. "I traded one movie role for one house with the town of Kipling Saskatchewan on July 12, 2006."

■ 8.2 What Makes Money . . . Money?

Kyle MacDonald managed to get the house he wanted using barter. To do this, he relied on a coincidence of wants. People wanted what he had, and he wanted what they had. MacDonald also relied on the publicity his adventure generated. Media stories of the "paperclip guy" brought him lots of eager traders.

Of course, MacDonald could have used money to buy a house. With money, you don't need coincidence or publicity to get the things you want. Producers gladly accept money in return for goods and services. When economists define money, they focus on that acceptability. Money, they say, is anything that is generally accepted as a means of payment. Economists further describe money according to its main functions and characteristics.

Money Has Three Basic Functions

Money is obviously useful to us in our economic lives. In fact, it's hard to imagine living without it. Money functions in three key ways: as a medium of exchange, as a standard of value, and as a store of value.

Medium of exchange. Money is a medium, or means, of exchange. It enables us to carry out trade and commerce easily, much more easily than through barter. For example, rather than trying to find someone willing to take, say, a dozen pairs of flip-flops in trade for a new backpack, you can just hand a store clerk a quantity of dollars—the established medium of exchange in the United States. U.S. dollars are this country's **legal tender**—they must be accepted as money for purchases and as payment for a debt.

Standard of value. Money also serves as a standard of value. It allows us to measure and compare the value of all kinds of goods and services using one scale. If we had no standard of value, it would be much harder to compare prices. For example, imagine seeing advertisements from two stores. One advertises a backpack for sale for nine pairs of flip-flops. The other has the same backpack advertised for five T-shirts. Without a common standard of value, how would you know which backpack costs more?

Store of value. Something is a store of value if it holds its value over time. A banana would be a poor store of value because it spoils quickly. A rotten banana has

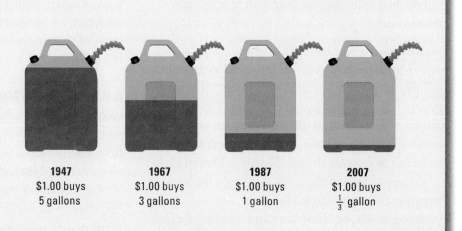

Purchasing Power

Purchasing power is the value of a unit of money, such as a dollar, measured in terms of what it can buy. Ideally, a dollar in your pocket today will have the same purchasing power a year or more from now. In reality, slowly rising prices tend to erode purchasing power over time. You can see this erosion of purchasing power by examining how much gasoline a dollar would buy over time.

1947
$1.00 buys
5 gallons

1967
$1.00 buys
3 gallons

1987
$1.00 buys
1 gallon

2007
$1.00 buys
$\frac{1}{3}$ gallon

lost much or all of its original value. Money, however, holds its value over time.

Put another way, money maintains its purchasing power over time. **Purchasing power** refers to the quantity of goods and services that can be bought with a particular sum of money. The $5 you have in your pocket today will buy $5 worth of goods or services now and for some time into the future. This stability allows you to hold on to your money, knowing you can spend it just as well tomorrow as today.

Although money stores value very well, it is not a perfect store of value, because prices tend to rise over time. For example, your $5 will always get you $5 worth of pencils. But the number of pencils you can get for that price may decrease over time.

Money Has Six Main Characteristics

For money to perform its three primary functions well, whatever people use as money should exhibit the six characteristics listed below. As you read about these characteristics, think about how well they apply to a substance that was once widely used as money: salt.

Acceptability. The most important characteristic of money is acceptability. In order for you to buy something, the seller must be willing to accept what you offer as payment. In the same way, when you sell your services—your labor—you must be willing to accept what your employer offers as payment, or wages, in exchange.

In ancient times, traders throughout the Mediterranean region accepted salt as a medium of exchange. Roman soldiers received, as part of their wages, an allotment of salt known as a *salarium*. From that Latin term comes the English word *salary*.

Scarcity. Whatever is used as money needs to be scarce enough to be valued by buyers and sellers. Throughout history, many cultures have used gold or silver as a medium of exchange. The relative scarcity of these metals adds to their value. If gold and silver were as common as sand, these metals would cease to be used as money.

In ancient times, salt was scarce in many parts of the world. Yet the demand for salt was great. People seasoned and preserved foods with salt and used it in religious ceremonies. Scarcity, coupled with high demand, made salt a valued commodity.

Portability. To be convenient as a medium of exchange, money must be portable. People must be able to carry it with them easily.

Salt is portable—to some extent. But imagine lugging several large bags of salt with you to the mall. And think about the mess you might make paying for a pair of jeans with three cups of salt. By today's standards, salt fails the portability test.

Durability. If money is to serve as a store of value, it must be durable. Moreover, any medium of exchange must be able to withstand the physical wear and tear of being continually transferred from person to person.

Salt can last a long time, but only if kept dry. Think how you would feel if a rainstorm dissolved and washed away your fortune. Salt fails the durability test.

Divisibility. To be useful as a medium of exchange, money must be easy to divide into smaller amounts. To understand why, imagine an economy that uses glass bowls as its medium of exchange. Buyers in that economy would be unable to buy anything worth less than one bowl, because the seller would be unable to provide change. Shards of broken glass would be too hazardous to use as change for something worth just half of a bowl.

A bag of salt, on the other hand, can be split into ever-smaller amounts. This ease of divisibility once made salt a useful medium of exchange.

Uniformity. A dollar is a dollar is a dollar. We take for granted that each dollar bill is the same as the next. Why is such uniformity important? Consider an economy in which pumpkins are the chosen medium of exchange. Pumpkins come in all sizes and weights. Could a large pumpkin be exchanged for more goods than a small pumpkin? How would producers and consumers agree on the value of any one pumpkin?

Like dollar bills, all salt is pretty much the same. Thus salt passes the uniformity test, as it does the tests of acceptability, scarcity, divisibility, and—for ancient traders—portability. Historically, salt had most of the characteristics of a useful medium of exchange.

A Brief History of Money

Gold, silver, and salt have all served as money at some time in history. So have shells, cattle, beads, furs, and tobacco. Economists categorize all of these items of exchange as **commodity money**. A commodity—a good that has value in trade—becomes commodity money when it is used as a medium of exchange. The value of commodity money is about the same as the value of the commodity it consists of.

Commodity money was used for thousands of years, all over the world. Of all the many commodities used as money, precious metals such as gold and silver were historically preferred over other forms of commodity money. These metals had all the useful characteristics of money. They were scarce, portable, durable, divisible, and, best of all, acceptable. In the form of bars and coins, these metals could even be made uniform.

Key Concept

The Six Characteristics of Money

Economists have identified six characteristics that allow money to serve as a medium of exchange, a standard of value, and a store of value. The most important of the six is acceptability. If people won't accept something as money, then it's not money. Some forms of money exhibit the six characteristics better than others.

	Acceptability	Scarcity	Portability	Durability	Divisibility	Uniformity
Rice in Japan	✓	☐	☐	☐	✓	✓
Wampum belt in North America	☐	✓	✓	✓	☐	☐
Spanish pieces of eight	✓	✓	☐	✓	✓	✓
Modern-day euro	✓	✓	✓	✓	☐	✓

Figure 8.2

Safeguarding U.S. Currency

In the 1990s, the Treasury Department began redesigning U.S. currency to make it harder for counterfeiters to create fake bills. The redesigned $20 bill went into circulation in 2003. Which aspect of the redesign do you think would be the most difficult for a counterfeiter to copy?

Color
Color adds complexity to the bill's design.

Watermark
The watermark, or design pressed into the paper, becomes visible when the bill is held up to the light.

Security thread
A small strip embedded in the bill glows green when held under ultraviolet light.

Microprinting
Tiny words printed on the bill are hard to replicate.

Color-shifting ink
The number 20 in the lower right corner shifts from copper to green when the bill is tilted up and down.

As trade flourished in Europe during the Renaissance, wealthy merchants and nobles needed safe places to store their gold and silver bars and coins. In the larger cities, private banks arose to meet this need. A **bank** is a business that receives deposits and makes loans. A **loan** is a transaction in which a lender gives money to a borrower, who agrees to repay the money at some point in the future.

These early banks accepted depositors' precious metals and in return gave the depositors elaborate paper receipts known as **banknotes**. The banks promised to exchange these banknotes for gold or silver "on demand"—that is, whenever the holder asked for such an exchange.

Economists call banknotes given in exchange for gold and silver **commodity-backed money**. The notes had minimal value in and of themselves. One could not eat them, wear them, or otherwise consume them. As commodity-backed money, they had value only as a medium of exchange.

These banknotes were the forerunners of modern printed money issued by governments. But there is a big difference between the two. Paper money today is no longer backed by gold, silver, or any other commodity. It has value only because it is generally accepted as a means of payment.

That acceptance comes in part because governments declare that the paper notes they issue *are* money. You can read this declaration, for example, on any bill issued by the U.S. government:

This note is legal tender for all debts, public and private.

In the past, such government decrees were known as fiats. Thus paper money issued without the backing of gold or silver came to be known as **fiat money**.

U.S. dollars may not be backed by gold or silver, but they are backed by the full faith and credit of the U.S. government. As long as consumers believe they can purchase goods and services with dollars, people will continue to use dollars as a medium of exchange.

What Counts as Money Today

When people nowadays think of money, they most often think of cash, in the form of paper bills or metal coins. Together, bills and coins circulating throughout the economy are known as **currency**.

Currency, however, is only part of a nation's **money supply,** or the total amount of money in the economy. What else counts as money? The answer depends on the kinds of **assets** economists choose to count as money in addition to currency.

The most common measure of money used by economists today is known as M1. Besides coins and bills, **M1** includes **liquid assets** that can be used as cash or can easily be converted into cash.

Currency makes up about half of the M1 money supply. Most of the rest consists of what economists call **checkable deposits,** or deposits in bank checking accounts. Depositors can write checks on these accounts to pay bills or make purchases. A **check** is a signed form instructing a bank to pay a specified sum of money to the person named on it. Checks themselves are not considered money, but the deposits they access are.

Traveler's checks are also included in the M1 money supply. Travelers buy these checks, usually from a bank, and then use the checks like cash to pay for goods and services. The M1 money supply, then, is made up of currency, checkable deposits, and traveler's checks.

Which of these is money? Using the M1 definition, only currency, deposits in checking accounts, and traveler's checks are liquid enough to qualify as money. Credit cards, checks, and debit cards can be used to access cash, but are not themselves money.

What about money deposited in savings accounts? Savings account deposits are considered **near-money**. Although savings account funds can usually be transferred to a checking account fairly easily, they are not used directly to buy things. For example, you cannot go into a store with your savings account statement and buy a pair of shoes. Because people's savings are not as liquid as cash, economists put them into a second category known as the M2 money supply. **M2** consists of M1 plus money saved in various kinds of accounts or funds.

You *can* buy a pair of shoes with a **credit card**. But even though people sometimes call their credit cards "plastic money," economists do not regard credit cards as a form of money.

To see why, consider what the term *credit* means. **Credit** is an arrangement that allows a person to buy something now with borrowed money and pay for it later or over time. Each purchase with a credit card creates a loan that the user must pay back to the bank, store, or other business that issued the card. The credit card is a convenient means for taking out such a loan—so convenient that since 2003, credit card purchases have outnumbered those made with checks or cash. But the card itself is not money.

You can also buy shoes with a **debit card**. A debit card allows you to access the money in your bank account. Used at a store, a debit card electronically transfers funds from your account to the store's account. Although it is a handy tool for accessing money, a debit card, like a check, is not itself considered part of the money supply.

■ 8.3 How Does the Banking System Work?

What do you notice when you enter a bank? Perhaps you pass an automated teller machine in the lobby. ATMs can dispense cash, accept deposits, and make transfers from one account to another. You may see desks and offices on the main floor. There are probably bank tellers behind a counter ready to assist you. Beyond the counter, there may be a large vault for storing money and other valuables.

The process seems fairly straightforward. Money comes in. Money goes out. The bank keeps track of every penny. But what goes on behind the scenes? How does your bank fit into the whole banking system?

The Elements of the Banking System

Banks are **financial institutions**—firms that deal mainly with money, as opposed to goods and services. Like all financial institutions, a bank must have a charter, or agreement, from the state or federal government that spells out how it will operate and how it will be regulated.

There are several kinds of banks, including commercial banks, savings and loans, mutual savings banks, and credit unions. Historically commercial banks served business and industry. The others focused on consumers, encouraging them to embrace the idea of **saving**—putting money aside for later use. Today the differences between the various types of banks have almost vanished. All banks work with businesses and consumers, and all offer the same basic kinds of services.

Banks Offer a Range of Services

Banks serve consumers in a variety of ways. They cash checks, issue credit cards, change foreign currency into dollars and vice versa, and provide safe-deposit boxes for storing valuables. Banks also offer the convenience of electronic banking through ATMs, debit cards, direct deposit of paychecks, and automatic payment of bills. Customers can use the Internet to monitor their accounts, pay bills, and transfer money from one account to another.

A bank's main function, however, is to serve as a **financial intermediary**—an institution that brings together sellers and buyers in financial markets. The sellers and buyers that banks bring together are savers and borrowers. Banks help transfer assets from one to the other. Specifically, banks receive deposits from savers and make loans to borrowers. These are the two main services that banks deliver.

Banks Receive Customers' Deposits

A time-tested way to save money is to deposit it in a bank. Banks offer three kinds of deposits: checkable deposits, savings deposits, and time deposits. Each bank has its own rules about when savers can withdraw deposited money. As a result, accounts vary in their **liquidity,** or the ease with which they can be converted into cash. They also vary in their return, or the amount of earnings they generate.

Checkable deposits. A checkable deposit is an amount

Financial Intermediaries

A financial intermediary is a "middleman" that brings together savers who have surplus money to loan and borrowers who have a need for that money. Banks, credit unions, and savings and loan associations all act as financial intermediaries.

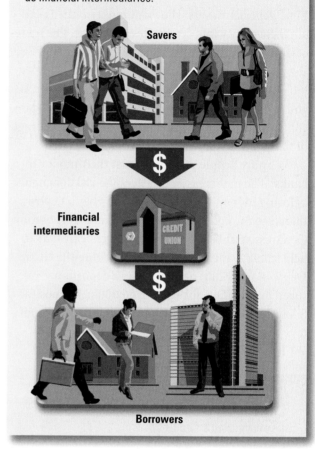

Savers

Financial intermediaries

Borrowers

of money placed in a checking account. Checkable deposits are highly liquid. That is, they can easily and quickly be converted into cash. You can withdraw money deposited in a checking account on demand, any time you wish. This withdrawal once called for writing a check, but today most checking accounts can be accessed electronically using the Internet, a debit card, or an ATM.

Money in a checking account, however, earns little or no interest. **Interest** is money paid periodically in return for the use of borrowed funds. Checkable deposits, then, provide safety and liquidity, but not much in the way of earnings.

Savings deposits. Money deposited in a savings account earns more interest than checkable deposits, although the return is still low. Funds can be held for any length of time, and the entire deposited amount can be withdrawn on demand.

Savings deposits are only slightly less liquid than checkable deposits. Savers usually make withdrawals from savings accounts by using ATMs or by presenting withdrawal slips to bank tellers.

Time deposits. Savers who want higher returns can put their money into certificates of deposit. The trade-off for these higher returns is lower liquidity. CDs, also known as time deposits, tie up cash for a set period of time—typically several months or longer. If you take your money out of a CD before the end date, you will pay a penalty that amounts to a percentage of the interest you would have earned.

Why are people willing to trust their money to banks? The main reason is safety. The **risk,** or chance of losing money, is very low with any bank deposit, thanks to the Federal Deposit Insurance Corporation. Congress established this federal agency in 1933 to help stabilize the banking system during the Great Depression. Today, nearly all bank deposits are insured by the FDIC for up to $100,000 per depositor. Should a bank fail, the FDIC guarantees that depositors will get their money back up to that amount.

Banks Make Loans to Borrowers

Banks use the money deposited by savers to make loans to other customers. Bank loans come in three forms: commercial loans, consumer loans, and mortgage loans.

Commercial loans. Businesses often take out **commercial loans** to buy machinery, equipment, and materials or to pay labor costs. Before making such a loan, banks consider the firm's financial condition and borrowing history as well as the general state of the economy.

Consumer loans. Individual borrowers take out **consumer loans** to make major purchases such as a new car or boat. These loans are often called **installment loans,** because most are paid back in equal monthly installments, or payments. Before making a consumer loan, the bank looks at the individual's **credit history**. This is a history of the person's past borrowing along with his or her record of repaying loans on time and in full.

Individuals can take out loans to buy smaller items by making their purchases with a credit card. Using a credit card is easy—so easy that many people charge more than they can afford. Those who cannot

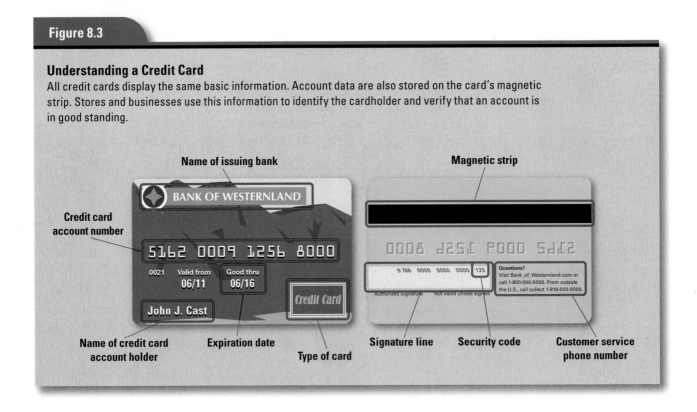

Figure 8.3

Understanding a Credit Card
All credit cards display the same basic information. Account data are also stored on the card's magnetic strip. Stores and businesses use this information to identify the cardholder and verify that an account is in good standing.

Name of issuing bank

Magnetic strip

Credit card account number

BANK OF WESTERNLAND

5162 0009 1256 8000

0021   Valid from 06/11   Good thru 06/16

John J. Cast

Credit Card

0008 d25C F000 5dC2

9 766 0000 0000 0000   123

Questions?
Visit Bank_of_Westernland.com or call 1-800-000-0000. From outside the U.S., call collect 1-818-000-0000.

Authorized Signature   Not valid unless signed

Name of credit card account holder

Expiration date

Type of card

Signature line

Security code

Customer service phone number

pay off their credit card bills each month are charged interest on their unpaid balances by the bank that issued the card. Interest rates for credit card debt are generally much higher than for other kinds of loans. For many cardholders, the result of overcharging is an ever-increasing pile of debt.

Mortgage loans. Banks also offer longer-term loans to consumers and businesses in the form of mortgages. A **mortgage** is a loan used to buy a house, an office building, land, or other real estate. The term of a mortgage typically ranges from 15 to 30 years.

As with any loan, a mortgage is part **principal**— the amount of money actually borrowed—and part interest on the principal. You might be surprised at the total cost of paying off a home mortgage. A house purchased for $220,000 with a traditional 30-year mortgage at a fixed interest rate of 5 percent per year, and paid in monthly installments, could end up costing the buyer more than $400,000 by the time the loan is paid off.

How Banks Make a Profit

In their role as financial intermediaries, banks channel funds from savers to borrowers by taking money deposited into various accounts and using it to make loans. In the process, banks profit by charging more interest on loans than they pay on deposits. For borrowers, interest represents the cost of using someone else's money. For savers, interest represents payment for letting someone else use their money.

How, you might wonder, can a bank lend out depositors' money and still promise to return that money to its depositors on demand? The answer is that banks don't lend out all the money they take in. They are required by law to keep a certain fraction of it in reserve to cover depositors' withdrawals from their accounts. For example, suppose you deposit $1,000 into a checking account. Your bank may be required to keep one-tenth, or $100, in reserve. That would leave $900 for the bank to lend out and charge interest on.

This system—whereby banks keep a fraction of deposits in reserve and make loans with the rest—is known as **fractional reserve banking**. The system keeps enough money available for withdrawals while allowing banks to profit from the rest. The fraction that banks are required to keep on hand is set by the

This family bought a new home with the help of a long-term bank loan called a mortgage. Homebuyers who take out mortgages must pay back the principal, or amount borrowed, as well as interest on the principal. Over the course of several years, interest can add considerably to the overall cost of a home purchase.

Federal Reserve System, which was established in 1913 to oversee the banking system.

The Federal Reserve: Our Nation's Central Bank

The Federal Reserve System, commonly known as the Fed, is the central bank of the United States. A central bank does not serve individual consumers and businesses, and making a profit is not one of its goals. The Fed's customers are the nation's thousands of banks, and its goals involve keeping the entire banking system stable and healthy. The Fed provides several important financial services.

Holding reserves. The Fed requires each bank to keep a fraction of its deposits in reserve. Some of that reserve takes the form of currency in the bank's vault, and some goes into an account set up for the bank at the Fed. In this way, the Fed serves as a bank for banks.

Providing cash and loans. When a bank needs cash to meet withdrawal demands, the Fed supplies it from the bank's account. The Fed also lends money to banks when they run short of funds.

Clearing checks. If you write a check to a store and the store deposits the check into its account with a different bank, the Fed takes care of transferring funds from your bank to the store's bank. This process is known as **check clearing**. The Fed clears billions of checks each year.

Linking banks electronically. The Federal Reserve and nearly all of the nation's banks are linked electronically. Using this electronic network, banks can quickly transfer funds from one financial institution to another.

The Fed Manages the Banking System

The Federal Reserve does more than provide services. It also manages the banking system to ensure that banks operate according to sound financial principles.

Another important job of the Fed is to control the nation's money supply. It does this in part by setting reserve requirements, the minimum fraction of deposits that banks must keep in their own vaults or at the Federal Reserve. The Fed also issues Federal Reserve notes, the paper currency we know as dollars. Through all of its activities the Fed aims to provide liquidity—to make sure consumers and businesses have ready access to money.

The Fed's structure aids in the task of managing the banking system. A seven-member Board of Governors oversees the Federal Reserve System from its headquarters in Washington, D.C. From there, it formulates Fed policies related to the money supply and sets reserve requirements.

Twelve regional Federal Reserve Banks carry out many of the system's day-to-day activities. Each Reserve Bank provides financial services to its region's banks and supervises their operations. Reserve Banks also feed economic information about their regions to the Board of Governors.

About 30 percent of the banks in the United States are members of the Federal Reserve System. Members include all national banks—commercial banks chartered by the federal government—and many state-chartered banks. All commercial banks, whether Fed members or not, enjoy the same privileges when it comes to borrowing from the Fed and must follow the Fed's regulations. And when the Fed takes steps to adjust the money supply, all banks feel the effects.

■ 8.4 How Is Saving Important to the Economy—And to You?

Thirty years ago, Americans saved more of their incomes than they do today. Economists know this by measuring Americans' **personal saving rate**—the proportion of a household's income that its members save each year.

Figure 8.4A shows that in the early 1980s, the personal savings rate often topped 10 percent. By

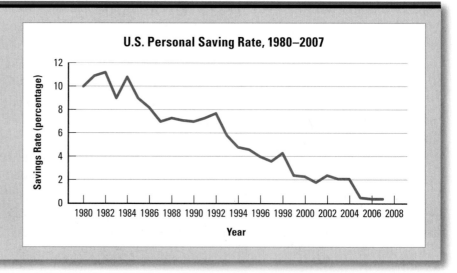

Figure 8.4A

Tracking the U.S. Saving Rate
Americans aren't saving the way they used to. As this graph shows, the percentage of income that we put into savings has dropped to almost nothing in recent years. And yet saving for the future is vitally important—both to individuals and the economy.

U.S. Personal Saving Rate, 1980–2007

This family is celebrating a major event: the graduation of one of its members from college. A college education is an important but costly goal for many young people. Colleges often help students reach that goal by offering loans and scholarships. But they usually expect parents—and their children—to cover some costs as well. Saving for college is one way to avoid having to pay off large student loans after graduation.

2005, it had fallen to less than 1 percent. That means the average American household is setting aside almost none of its income for the proverbial rainy day. Should we be concerned about our general lack of thrift? Does the future-consequences-count principle matter when it comes to saving?

Saving Helps the Economy Grow

The money you and others set aside in savings accounts, retirement plans, and other forms of saving is not just important to you personally. It also contributes to the nation's overall economic growth.

How does this work? Personal savings provide funds that banks can lend to businesses for expansion—what economists call investment in capital goods. When businesses invest in capital goods, the economy grows. For example, suppose a company borrows money to build a new factory. The new factory increases the company's output. More goods are produced and sold, creating growth in the economy.

Building a factory also generates growth indirectly. It provides revenue to a host of other producers, from construction companies to equipment suppliers. Those producers can then launch their own expansions. A new factory also creates jobs. The workers' wages flow to local businesses. Wages also flow into the bank accounts of the workers themselves. Banks use these deposits to start another round of lending and even more economic growth.

Saving Can Help You Reach Important Goals

To most Americans, the idea of saving money is less exciting than the idea of spending it. As our personal saving rate suggests, we are a nation of consumers. Saving part of one's income, however, does not mean never consuming it. In fact, some economists define saving as "consuming less now in order to consume more in the future."

We all have goals for the future. Perhaps your goal is to become a lawyer, an engineer, or a teacher. To do that you will need a college degree. Maybe your goal is to buy your own car or house. Maybe you dream of traveling the world or starting a business. Whatever your goal, it is likely to require money. Setting aside a portion of your income now to cover later expenses is saving for the future.

Saving Can Help You Weather Hard Times

Do you know anyone who lived through the Great Depression? That person could tell you about hard times—businesses ruined, homes and life savings lost, few jobs, and little hope. The Depression affected nearly everyone in the United States to some degree.

Even when the economy is strong overall, financial misfortune can strike at any time—when a company lays off workers, when a business fails, or when a family gets hit with huge medical bills. Such events often come unexpectedly. Unless you are ready, you could find yourself facing real financial hardship.

To be prepared for a financial emergency, experts advise building up a "rainy-day fund"—an easily accessible stockpile of savings. Most advisers say your fund should contain at least six months' worth of salary. Others suggest that $2,000 to $3,000 is enough as long as you also have insurance to cover catastrophes. All experts agree, however, that a rainy-day fund should be used only for real emergencies. As financial adviser David Bach observes,

> *The reason most people don't have any emergency money in the bank is that they have what they think is an emergency every month . . . A real emergency is something that threatens your survival, not just your desire to be comfortable.*
>
> —David Bach, *The Automatic Millionaire*, 2004

Saving Can Help You Fund Your Retirement

Have you ever considered what you will live on when you retire? At this point in your life, that question must seem like a remote concern. "First," you might answer, "let me finish my education and choose a career."

Retirement is indeed a long way off. But in just a few years you will likely be working full time—earning, spending, and, if you are wise, saving. If you are really looking ahead, you will be saving for your eventual retirement.

Americans today are living longer than ever before. Many people starting careers today will live for 20 or more years after they stop earning a paycheck. To maintain even a modest lifestyle during those years will take a lot of money. The earlier you begin accumulating that money, the more you will have when the time comes to retire.

Most retired people support themselves using three sources of money, making retirement something like a three-legged stool. The three "legs" are Social Security, company retirement plans, and personal savings.

Social Security. Social Security is a government program that provides cash payments to retired workers. It is funded by taxes paid by workers and their employers. Social Security is a pay-as-you-go plan. This means that the Social Security taxes you pay each year are not saved for your future retirement. Instead, this money is paid out in benefits to current retirees.

Company retirement plans. At one time, most large companies offered pension plans to their employees. A pension plan is a retirement plan to which the employer makes contributions for the future benefit of its employees.

Today the most common company retirement plan is the 401(k) plan. This plan gets its name from section 401(k) of the Internal Revenue Code—the main body of our nation's tax laws. In a 401(k) plan,

Key Concept

Funding Retirement
This cartoon illustrates the three main sources of retirement income for most Americans. Having all three in place when you stop working is your best guarantee of a well-funded retirement.

Personal savings
Assets accumulated over a lifetime, including private retirement plans such as IRAs

Social Security
A government program that provides monthly benefits to retirees

Company retirement plans
Retirement plans offered by businesses that are funded by the employer, the employees, or both

©TCI/Scott Willis

employees have money automatically taken out of their paychecks and put into retirement investment accounts. Employers may also contribute to the plan by matching all or part of an employee's contribution.

One benefit of a 401(k) plan is that participants may subtract their contributions from their taxable income when they file their tax returns. The effect is to lower the amount of income tax they are required to pay. Financial experts encourage all employees to put money into a 401(k) if their employer offers such a plan.

Personal savings. The third source of retirement funds is personal savings. Such savings may include a variety of financial assets, including private retirement plans—plans that are *not* employer-sponsored.

An Individual Retirement Account is a private retirement plan sponsored by the federal government. Anyone who earns income can put money into an IRA. To encourage Americans to do so, the government has built tax advantages into IRA plans. Depending on the type of plan they choose, participants may either deduct the amount of their IRA contributions from their taxable incomes or take money out of their accounts tax free when they retire. For this reason IRAs are often referred to as tax-sheltered savings accounts.

IRAs, pensions, and other retirement plans come in many forms, each with its own set of rules. These rules govern such things as the amount you can contribute each year, how the account is taxed, and when you can begin to withdraw money from the account. Retirement savers should choose the plan that best suits their circumstances and meets their long-term goals.

Creating a Budget with Saving in Mind

A **budget** is a plan for spending and saving, based on one's income and estimated expenses. It covers a specific time period, typically a month or year. For those who really want to take control of their day-to-day finances, making a budget is essential.

The first step in creating a budget is to estimate your monthly income and expenses. This means keeping track of all income as well as all expenditures for a month. Figure 8.4B shows a typical budget for a young adult. It includes a mortgage or rent payment, a car loan payment or transportation expenses, as well as food, clothing, and other items.

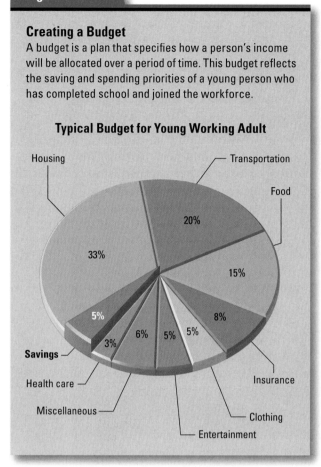

Figure 8.4B

Creating a Budget
A budget is a plan that specifies how a person's income will be allocated over a period of time. This budget reflects the saving and spending priorities of a young person who has completed school and joined the workforce.

Typical Budget for Young Working Adult

- Housing 33%
- Transportation 20%
- Food 15%
- Insurance 8%
- Clothing 5%
- Entertainment 5%
- Miscellaneous 6%
- Health care 3%
- Savings 5%

When most people construct a budget, they make the mistake of calculating only the cost of goods and services consumed. They subtract those expenses from their income, and what is left—if anything—goes toward savings.

To become a successful saver, however, saving needs to be an entry in your budget right from the beginning—perhaps even your first budget item. Setting aside money each month as savings might be difficult, but the effort will be well worth it. Nothing could be more important to your financial future.

◼ 8.5 How Do Americans Invest Their Savings?

Learning how to save money for future use is an important first step in reaching your long-term goals. But saving alone is not enough. You will also need to learn how to invest the money you save. **Investing** involves using the money you have saved to earn even more money.

Investing Offers Rewards—And Poses Risks

People invest money in everything from rare coins to real estate because they expect a favorable financial return in the future. If you decide to invest in a college education, for example, you probably expect that your investment will improve your job prospects and future income. Likewise, when people invest in an old coin or a home, they assume that someday it will be worth more than they paid for it.

The same holds true when people invest their savings in financial securities. **Securities** are investments that give their holders the right to receive some form of return, or profit. The two most common kinds of securities are stocks and bonds. People who invest in securities count on getting back the amount they invested plus interest or some other form of return on their investment. That return is their reward for making the investment.

Not all investments, however, turn out as people hope and expect. Nearly every kind of investment involves some sort of risk. The price of rare coins or houses, for example, can go down as well as up.

In general, there is a strong relationship between risk and reward. The higher the potential reward an investment offers, the higher the risk of losses rather than gains. In choosing what to invest in, therefore, it is important to weigh the various risks against the potential rewards.

Investment Basics: The Power of Compounding

You need not take great risks to ensure a safe return on your investments—if you are patient. You can invest your money conservatively and let the passage of time increase its value. The trick is to take advantage of the power of compounding.

Compounding refers to the ability of an investment to generate earnings that can be reinvested to earn still more earnings. Banks make this happen when they offer to pay depositors compound interest, rather than simple interest, on their savings. **Compound interest** is interest paid not only on the original amount deposited in the savings account, but also on all interest earned by those savings.

Compounding works like this. Suppose that on your 20th birthday you were to deposit $1,000 in a savings account that pays 6 percent compound interest once a year. In one year's time, you would earn $60 in interest ($1,000 multiplied by 0.06). Rather than take your $60 out of the account to spend, you leave it there to compound. The account now contains $1,060.

The next year, your savings account would earn 6 percent on $1,060—your original deposit plus the interest already accumulated. In that second year, you would earn $63.60 in interest, bringing the total in your account to $1,123.60.

In reality, many banks compound interest on a daily rather than annual basis. That means you earn interest today on the interest the bank paid you yesterday. In the example above, the result of daily compounding would be to raise the rate of return on your savings to more than 6 percent. **Rate of return** is a measure of the change in the value of an investment over time. It is usually expressed as a percentage of value gained or lost in a year.

Doubling Your Money: The Rule of 72

Suppose, now, you left your savings in the bank to compound year after year. In time, you would double your investment. But how long would this take? To find out, you could use the **rule of 72**. This rule says to divide the number 72 by the annual rate of return on the investment. The answer is the number of years it will take to double the original investment.

Using the rule of 72, you calculate that at a 6 percent annual rate of return, it would take 12 years for the $1,000 in your savings account to double to $2,000. In another 12 years, the account would double again to $4,000. By the time you reached the age of 68, your investment of $1,000 would have doubled two more times to $16,000. You would not have done a thing, yet you would have accumulated 16 times your original investment.

Now consider what you would have at age 68 had you earned only simple interest on your account. Your $1,000 deposit would have earned $60 a year for 48 years, or a total of $2,880 in interest payments. Added to your original $1,000, your account would total $3,880. That is less than a quarter of the $16,000 you would have earned by compounding.

Compounding works not only for savings accounts, but for other kinds of investments as well. By reinvesting your earnings year after year, your investments can grow surprisingly fast.

Compounding and the Rule of 72

Compounding involves the reinvestment of returns from an asset to earn still higher returns. The rule of 72 tells how long it will take to double an investment through compounding. As the illustration shows, the higher the expected rate of return, the faster your investment will double.

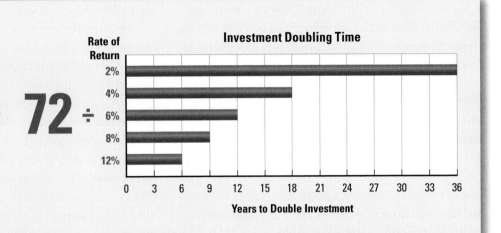

72 ÷

Investment Doubling Time

Rate of Return	
2%	
4%	
6%	
8%	
12%	

Years to Double Investment

FDIC-Insured Savings and Government Bonds: The Safest Investments

Fifty years ago, average Americans had relatively few ways to invest their savings. The $1,000 that you just turned into $16,000 would probably have been invested in a bank savings account. A savings account is still not a bad choice today, especially for people with a very low tolerance for risk. Bank deposits insured by the FDIC are among the safest investments you can make. Even if the bank loses all your savings, the FDIC—backed by the resources of the federal government—will reimburse you up to $100,000.

Those who are reluctant to risk their savings might also choose to invest in government bonds. A **bond** is a loan in which the borrower promises to pay the lender a fixed rate of interest over the term of the loan and then repay the principal at the end of the term, or date of maturity.

When you buy a bond, you are lending money to the issuer of the bond. You might think of a bond as an IOU that pays interest. The business of issuing and buying bonds takes place in the bond market.

When the federal government needs to borrow money, it issues bonds. Known as U.S. Treasury bonds, they are the safest bonds a person can invest in, because the government can print money or raise taxes if needed to pay back the loan at maturity. Treasury bond terms range from 10 to 30 years.

The federal government also borrows money by issuing Treasury bills and Treasury notes, which have shorter terms than Treasury bonds. Treasury bonds, bills, and notes all offer fairly low **yields,** or interest rates, but they are considered risk free.

Government bonds are a safe investment. A bond is like an IOU with interest. It declares that the government will repay the amount of the bond at a certain rate of interest on a specific date. Bonds have sometimes been used to raise money during wartime, as this poster from World War I shows.

State and local governments also issue bonds to raise funds for public projects such as the building of schools, bridges, and highways. Known as **municipal bonds,** these securities are viewed as a bit riskier than Treasury bonds. They attract investors, however, because the interest earned on municipal bonds is exempt from federal income taxes. Nor is the interest taxed by the state in which the bond was issued.

Corporate Bonds: Moderate Risk for More Return

Like governments, corporations borrow money by selling bonds. Because corporations can, and do, go out of business, **corporate bonds** are riskier to invest in than government bonds. Should the corporation issuing the bond fail, the bondholders could lose some or all of their investments. Because of this higher risk, investors expect a higher rate of return on corporate bonds than on government bonds.

The risk of buying a corporate bond varies according to the financial health of the corporation that issues it. To help investors assess that risk, rating companies examine bond issuers to evaluate their ability to repay their loans.

High-quality corporate bonds are classified as investment grade. The ratings on these bonds range from AAA to BBB. Investment-grade bonds do not offer investors high returns, but the risk of the borrower failing to repay the loan is relatively low. For this reason, many people feel fairly safe investing in these top-rated bonds.

Lower-quality bonds are classified high-yield or **junk bonds**. The ratings on these bonds range from BB to C. As the name *high-yield* suggests, these bonds offer higher potential returns in exchange for a moderately higher risk that the company might fail.

Stocks: Historically the Highest Returns

Bonds are debt-related securities. **Stocks,** in contrast, are securities that represent ownership in a business. When a company issues shares of stock,

Trading in the stock market takes place at a number of stock exchanges in major cities throughout the world. The oldest organized U.S. stock exchange is the New York Stock Exchange, shown here.

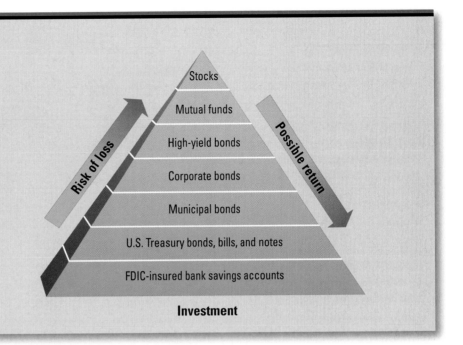

Figure 8.5A

Comparing Investment Risks and Returns

There is a positive relationship between risk and return in financial investments. The higher the risk that an investment might lose money, the greater the possible return demanded by investors. Without the incentive of a higher return, investors would have no reason to take their money out of safe bank accounts to invest in riskier bonds or stocks.

Risk of loss

Possible return

Stocks
Mutual funds
High-yield bonds
Corporate bonds
Municipal bonds
U.S. Treasury bonds, bills, and notes
FDIC-insured bank savings accounts

Investment

---

it is not borrowing money. Rather, it is selling ownership rights. The investors who buy the company's stock become its **shareholders**. These shareholders own the company.

As part owners of a company, shareholders have the right to receive a portion of the firm's profits. That portion of profits is known as a **dividend**. Investors usually receive dividends in the form of a dollar amount for each share owned. To take advantage of the power of compounding, investors often choose to reinvest dividends, using them to buy additional shares of the company stock. The more shares an investor holds, the more dividends he or she receives.

While many profitable companies pay dividends on their stock, many others do not. Instead they invest their profits back into the company to help it grow. Investors who buy non-dividend-paying stocks assume that the price of the stock will rise as the company grows in size, making their shares worth more over time.

Historically, stocks have offered investors a higher rate of return than bonds. Figure 8.5A shows the real rate of return generated by stocks over several decades. The **real rate of return** is the annual percentage return adjusted for the effects of inflation. You will read more about inflation and its effects on prices in Chapter 13.

During some periods, stock prices have marched fairly steadily upward. These happy times for stock investors are known as **bull markets**. At other times, stock prices have dropped just as steadily downward. These painful periods for investors are known as **bear markets**.

Since 1899, bull markets have outnumbered and outlasted bear markets. But past performance is no guarantee of future returns from stocks. Stock prices are variable. Even stable, well-managed companies can have bad years and see their stock prices plunge. Investors who want the higher returns that can be had by investing in stocks must also be willing to accept the higher risks.

Investing in the Stock Market

The most common way to buy and sell stocks is through a securities brokerage. A **brokerage** is a company that buys and sells stocks and bonds for investors. Brokerages employ **stockbrokers** to help investors make and carry out investment decisions.

The actual buying and selling of stocks and bonds takes place in a **stock market**. The most famous stock market in the United States is the New York Stock Exchange. It is located on Wall Street in New York City. The NYSE handles the exchange of more than 2 billion shares of stock, on average, every trading day.

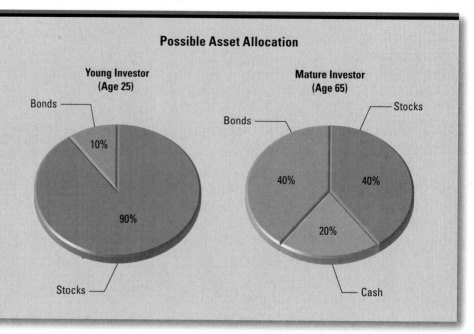

Figure 8.5B

Deciding How to Allocate Your Assets

These graphs show how two investors might allocate their assets. The investors have the same goal—a comfortable retirement—but are at very different stages of life. The older investor is ready to retire now and can't afford much risk. The younger investor has 40 years to accumulate assets for retirement and can therefore afford a higher level of risk. An investor's actual asset allocation would depend not just on age, but also on the person's financial goals and risk tolerance.

Possible Asset Allocation

Young Investor (Age 25): Bonds 10%, Stocks 90%

Mature Investor (Age 65): Bonds 40%, Stocks 40%, Cash 20%

To many Americans, the New York Stock Exchange *is* the stock market. But another exchange, the NASDAQ, also handles billions of shares per day. Many high-tech stocks are traded on the NASDAQ.

The Securities and Exchange Commission, a federal agency established during the Great Depression, regulates the stock market. An important part of the SEC's mission is to make sure all investors have access to the same financial information about firms issuing stock. Firms provide such information in a legal document known as a **prospectus**. A prospectus allows investors to make informed decisions about whether to buy or sell a firm's stock.

Investing in Mutual Funds

Many Americans lack the time or interest to research which stocks or bonds to buy on their own. Instead, they invest in stock or bond mutual funds. A **mutual fund** is a collection of securities chosen and managed by a group of professional fund managers. Shares in a mutual fund can be bought and sold much like shares of stock.

Mutual funds are popular with investors as a way of achieving **diversification**. Diversification simply means investing in a wide variety of financial assets. Investing in many stocks or bonds reduces the risk that a poor performance by any one asset will wipe out your savings.

Every mutual fund is designed to achieve certain financial goals. Those goals vary from fund to fund, as do the risks and potential rewards. Stock funds typically emphasize growth and income from rising stock prices and dividends. Bond funds offer income at a lower risk than stock funds. Money market mutual funds behave much like bank savings accounts. They pay higher interest rates than most banks but are not insured by the FDIC. With some 10,000 mutual funds available, there is something for nearly every investor.

How can an investor tell how well a mutual fund is doing? One way is to compare the fund's performance against a broad market index. A **market index** measures changes in the value of a group of stocks, bonds, or other investments from a specific starting point.

The most often quoted stock index, the Dow Jones Industrial Average, was begun in 1896. The DJIA tracks the stock prices of 30 large U.S. corporations. The Standard & Poor's 500 stock index dates back to 1957. The S&P 500 tracks the stock prices of 500 large firms traded on the stock exchange. Other indexes track different groups of securities such as foreign stocks and bonds.

Indexes tell investors how well the market for a class of stocks or bonds is doing as a whole. If a mutual fund consistently fails to match the overall returns of its market, investors may want to question how well that fund is being managed.

Spreading the Risk Through Asset Allocation

You may have heard the proverb "Don't put all your eggs in one basket." That old saying applies to today's investors. Financial planners warn their clients not to invest all their savings in just stocks, just bonds, or any other single type of investment. The risk of that one investment losing money is simply too great. Instead, they advise following an approach to diversification known as asset allocation.

Asset allocation involves dividing the assets in a person's portfolio among different types of investment. The goal is to reduce the risk of investing while still earning good returns. Stocks, bonds, and cash are the three main asset categories. Cash here refers to assets that have fairly high liquidity, including savings deposits, CDs, and money market mutual funds.

Asset-allocation decisions are personal. They depend on an investor's age, risk tolerance, and financial goals. A young person saving for retirement, for example, can afford to risk more than a retired person. If one asset loses money, a young person has far more time to recover than a retiree who depends on personal savings for income. Figure 8.5B shows possible asset allocations for two people with the same goal—a comfortable retirement—but at very different stages in their lives.

Ultimately it is up to you to decide how to spend, save, and invest your money. In making these decisions, the key to success is information. The better informed you are in money matters, the more likely you will be to make decisions that will enable you to live well today while still saving and investing for the future.

Summary

Money serves many functions in a modern economy. People spend money to meet their daily needs. They also save and invest money to meet their future goals.

What makes money . . . money? Money serves as a medium of exchange, a standard of value, and a store of value. To fulfill these functions well, what we use as money should have six characteristics: acceptability, scarcity, portability, durability, divisibility, and uniformity. Over time, money has evolved from commodity money to commodity-backed money to fiat money. Our money supply today, known as M1, is made up of currency, checkable deposits, and traveler's checks.

How does the banking system work? As financial intermediaries, banks receive deposits and turn them into loans. Banks make a profit by charging borrowers more interest than they pay to depositors. The Federal Reserve determines the fraction of deposits that banks must keep in reserve. The Fed also provides services to banks, oversees and regulates banks, and controls the money supply.

Why is saving important to the economy—and to you? Savings provide money for loans that help businesses and the economy grow. Personal saving can also help you reach important financial goals, weather hard times, and fund your retirement. Creating a budget that includes regular saving can help you gain control of your finances.

How do Americans invest their savings? Americans invest in a variety of financial assets, including savings accounts, government bonds, corporate bonds, stocks, and mutual funds. Each has its own level of risk and expected reward. Diversifying to balance risk and reward in a portfolio can be accomplished through asset allocation.

How will the choices you make today affect your credit score tomorrow?

Have you ever owned a credit card, opened a charge account at a store, or taken out a loan? If you haven't yet, you most likely will someday. And when you do, you will be assigned a credit score. A credit score is a number that lenders look at to judge your creditworthiness—or how likely you are to repay your debts.

As you read about credit scores and one young person's credit adventures, think about the choices you are making today. How might they affect your credit score in the future?

Frequently Asked Questions About Credit Scores

Your credit score is important. But many people don't find out how important it is until they try to take out a loan and learn that they have a poor credit history.

What is a credit score?
A credit score is a number assigned to a consumer to show how safe it is to lend that person money. Credit-scoring organizations employ different systems to indicate levels of creditworthiness. The most widely used system assigns credit scores ranging from 300 to 850. The higher the number, the better the score.

Who uses my credit score?
Any business that is concerned about your ability to pay your bills might check your credit score. This includes lenders, landlords, telephone companies, and utility companies.

How can I establish good credit?
The best way to prove you are a good credit risk is to take on debt and then pay it off. Start off slowly, with an easy-to-manage loan. You might open a charge account at a local store or acquire a gasoline charge card. Then apply for a major credit card with a low credit limit.

How can I keep my credit score high?
These guidelines will help you develop a good credit history.

- **Make at least the minimum payment each month.** Credit card companies do not require that you pay your bill in full each month. But they do expect you to make a minimum payment to keep the account open. But beware—if you don't pay in full, you'll have to pay interest on the remaining balance. You are better off paying the full amount if you can.
- **Pay on time.** Punctuality counts in the credit-scoring business. Each bill has a due date. Try to pay each bill by that date. Especially avoid being more than 30 days late.
- **Keep your unpaid balance low.** The total amount you owe on a credit card should not exceed 25 to 30 percent of your credit limit.
- **Limit the number of credit cards you have.** Having many credit card accounts open at the same time will reduce your credit score. It suggests that you might have trouble paying your bills sometime down the road.

Dylan's Adventures with Credit

Dylan is a fictional character. However, the story of his first year working after finishing school offers real-world lessons about using credit. The credit history below shows how Dylan's choices that year affect his credit score.

Dylan's Credit History

Monthly Activity	Effect on Dylan's Credit Score
June: Builds a credit history Dylan has built up a credit history in the past year by using a gasoline credit card. He pays his bill in full and on time.	👍
July: Applies for a major credit card Dylan applies for and is issued a major credit card with a $1,000 credit limit. When his first statement arrives, he promptly pays off the entire balance.	👍
August: Maxes out credit card Dylan throws a party at a restaurant to celebrate his girlfriend's birthday. To pay for it, he "maxes out" his credit card—charging expenses right up to his $1,000 credit limit.	👎
September: Makes the minimum payment Dylan makes the minimum payment on his credit card on time.	👍
October: Lowers credit card balance Dylan works overtime to pay off the unpaid balance on his credit card. He gets the balance down to $200 by the end of the month.	👍
November: Bounces a check Dylan writes a check to pay for car repairs only to discover that he doesn't have enough money in his checking account to cover the amount. His check bounces.	👎
December: Overspends for the holidays Dylan uses his credit card to buy lots of holiday gifts for family and friends. His unpaid balance rises to over $800.	👎
January: Shops for more credit cards Dylan concludes that he needs more credit, so he applies for two more credit cards. He receives both and begins using them.	👎
February: Pays at least the minimum on his cards Dylan makes the minimum payment on all of his credit card bills. But with the interest charged on his unpaid balances, his debt level is rising.	👍
March: Missed credit card payment One of Dylan's credit card bills gets lost in a pile of junk mail. By the time he makes his payment, it is six weeks late.	👎
April: Uses income tax refund to pay down debt Dylan receives an income tax refund and uses the money to pay off the unpaid balance on one of his credit cards.	👍
May: Continues to pay down debt Dylan cuts expenses this month and manages to reduce the unpaid balance on his other two major credit cards.	👍

How do entrepreneurs use their resources to start businesses?

Entrepreneurs and Business Organizations

9.1 Introduction

In the early 1970s, WLAC-TV in Nashville was looking for a new coanchor for a television news program. They hired a local talent, an articulate young college student and former Miss Black Tennessee. No Nashville television station had ever featured an African American woman as news anchor before. Certainly no 19-year-old had ever coanchored the news. But the station decided to take a chance. In 1973, a young Oprah Winfrey made her television debut on Channel 5 news in Nashville.

Winfrey was not a great success at reading the news, but she stuck with it, determined to have a career in television. Four years later, she moved to WJZ in Baltimore to coanchor the news there. Again she struggled. She tended to get emotional and to stray from the script. Once she even cried on the air.

Winfrey was eventually taken off the news desk and given a morning chat show, *People Are Talking*, to cohost. After the first show, she told herself, "I've found what I was meant to do." Winfrey's relaxed, friendly on-air manner was a hit with viewers, and *People Are Talking* became the most popular talk show in the Baltimore market.

The rest, as they say, is history. In 1984, Oprah moved to Chicago and within two years was hosting the most-watched daytime talk show in the country. She also landed a role in the movie *The Color Purple*, for which she was nominated for an Oscar. By the late 1980s, Winfrey was one of the highest-paid performers in the entertainment industry.

Oprah Winfrey is a successful entrepreneur in the entertainment industry.

sole proprietorship
A business owned and managed by one person.

liability
The legal responsibility to repay debts and to pay for damages resulting from a lawsuit.

partnership
A business owned by two or more co-owners who share profits from the business and are legally responsible for the business's debts.

corporation
A business owned by shareholders who have limited liability for the firm's debts. Because it is considered a legal entity, a corporation can conduct business affairs in its name.

multinational corporation
A corporation that does business in more than one country.

business franchise
An arrangement in which a parent company, or franchiser, distributes its products or services through independently owned outlets. The outlet owners, or franchisees, pay for the exclusive right to use the parent company's trade name and sell its products or provide its services.

cooperative
A business organization that is jointly owned and operated by a group of individuals for their mutual benefit.

nonprofit organization
An organization that functions much like a business but does not operate to make a profit.

If Oprah Winfrey had stopped there, she still would have been an outstanding success story. But she did not stop there. In 1988, Winfrey made the leap from entertainer to entrepreneur. She founded her own company, Harpo Productions, becoming the first African American woman to own a television studio and only the third woman to own a major film production studio. Her corporation has since grown to include magazine publishing and online media.

In some ways, Oprah Winfrey is not a typical entrepreneur. By the time she started her own business, she had already risen to the top of her industry. Her wealth and influence made it likely, at least initially, that her media company would succeed. By contrast, many entrepreneurs start from scratch, often borrowing money to start a business.

Winfrey does possess the enormous drive that entrepreneurship requires. It is what enabled her to overcome poverty and a troubled childhood to become a success in business. As Winfrey put it,

> Don't complain about what you don't have. Use what you've got . . . Every single one of us has the power for greatness, because greatness is determined by service—to yourself and others.
>
> —Oprah Winfrey, *Reader's Digest*, February 1989

Winfrey is one of millions of entrepreneurs driven by their dreams and talents to start their own businesses. In this chapter, you will read more about the vital role of entrepreneurs in business. You will explore the advantages and disadvantages of different types of business organizations. And you will look at the rights and responsibilities of owning a business, no matter what its size and structure.

■ 9.2 What Does It Take to Start a New Business?

Unlike Oprah Winfrey, Linda Alvarado faced considerable obstacles when she tried to start her own business. At 24, Alvarado had nearly everything she needed to start her own construction company. She had skills, education, experience—but no money. Because she was a woman, no bank would lend her the money to start a business in an industry dominated by men.

Alvarado's parents mortgaged their home so they could lend her $2,500. In 1976, Alvarado founded Alvarado Construction. Her firm went on to become one of the most successful construction firms in the country. How did she do it? "Perseverance and persistence have kept me going," Alvarado says. Those qualities, among others, are what it takes to start a business.

The Essential Role of Entrepreneurs in Business Creation

What exactly is an entrepreneur? An entrepreneur is someone who takes on the responsibility and the risk of starting a business with the expectation of making a profit. Entrepreneurs come from every field of endeavor. The most successful are innovators and creative thinkers. Entrepreneurs play a critical role in the economy. By creating businesses, they meet consumer demand for goods and services, create jobs, and spur economic growth.

Thomas Edison, for example, was not only a prolific inventor but also a brilliant entrepreneur. His genius lay in his ability to turn laboratory discoveries into practical inventions that people could use.

Consider the use of electricity to light homes and businesses. Edison did not invent the first incandescent lightbulb, but he did invent the first long-lasting lightbulb that could be used indoors. He also designed the first central power station and, with it, a distribution system for bringing electricity into homes and offices. Edison thus created an entire industry out of a single invention. His entrepreneurial vision also shaped the early sound recording and motion picture industries.

Mary Kay Ash, founder of Mary Kay Cosmetics, was a different kind of innovator. Ash's brainstorm was to tap into the entrepreneurial energy of women. In 1963, frustrated at the unequal treatment she received as a woman working in sales, Ash started her own company with a $5,000 investment. She bought the rights to special skin-care lotions and creams and hired women to teach customers about the products, rather than pressuring customers to buy. Ash believed in "praising people to success" and rewarded her top saleswomen with pink Cadillacs. Her approach to business was unusual—and successful. At the time of Ash's death in 2001, Mary Kay Cosmetics had made more than $1 billion in sales.

Bill Gates, cofounder of Microsoft, was one of the first to see the enormous potential of the personal computer. In 1975, when Gates was 19 years old, he and friend Paul Allen formed Microsoft and began developing software. Gates was certain that someday computers would be used in every home and office —and he wanted to be the one to put them there. For Gates's visionary leadership in the information technology revolution, *Time* magazine named him one of the 100 most influential people of the 20th century.

The Characteristics of Successful Entrepreneurs

What do Linda Alvarado, Bill Gates, and Mary Kay Ash have in common? They share certain traits that helped them to succeed. Although there is no single personality profile of the successful entrepreneur, most of them possess the characteristics that follow.

Ambition. Successful entrepreneurs are highly motivated people with the ability to see the big

Gallery of Entrepreneurs
Entrepreneurs are innovators who create new businesses and even new industries. As this gallery suggests, they are often motivated by more than a simple desire to make money.

Andrew Carnegie (1835–1919) was an industrialist, philanthropist, and founder of Carnegie Steel. One of the wealthiest men in the world, Carnegie was as dedicated to giving money away as he was to making it. "The man who dies thus rich dies disgraced," he said. His legacy includes the establishment of public libraries, schools, and universities, as well as funding for the arts.

The Granger Collection, New York

Madam C. J. Walker (1867–1919), the daughter of former slaves, became a businesswoman, philanthropist, and the first woman millionaire. Persistence and hard work were keys to her success. "I had to make my own living and my own opportunity!" she said. "Don't sit down and wait for the opportunities to come. Get up and make them!"

Vera Wang (1949–) is an award-winning fashion designer. Since 1990, when her wedding gown salon opened in New York, she has expanded her business to include fragrances, jewelry, shoes, and housewares. "Don't be afraid to take time to learn," Wang says. "It's good to work for other people. I worked for others for 20 years. They paid me to learn."

Steve Jobs (1955–) cofounded Apple Computer in 1976 and later went on to cofound Pixar Animation Studios. Known as a stubborn individualist, Jobs left Apple in 1985 after clashing with the company's management. But he returned to the company in 1997. "I'm convinced that the only thing that kept me going was that I loved what I did," he says. "You've got to find what you love."

Chapter 9 Entrepreneurs and Business Organizations **165**

picture and to stay focused on the end result. They set goals for themselves and never stop striving to achieve those goals.

Self-confidence. Successful entrepreneurs believe in themselves. They feel certain that they can accomplish what they set out to do.

A willingness to take risks. Entrepreneurs are not afraid to risk their time, money, and energy on a new business idea. "The important thing is not being afraid to take a chance," says Debbi Fields, the founder of Mrs. Fields Cookies. "Remember, the greatest failure is to not try. Once you find something you love to do, be the best at doing it."

Energy and self-discipline. Entrepreneurs thrive on hard work. "The first requisite for success," said Edison, "is to develop the ability to focus and apply your mental and physical energies to the problem at hand—without growing weary."

Perseverance. Entrepreneurs do not give up. "When you reach an obstacle," advised Mary Kay Ash, "turn it into an opportunity. You have the choice. You can overcome and be a winner, or you can allow it to overcome you and be a loser."

Problem solving ability. The ability to come up with solutions to problems marks all successful entrepreneurs. As Linda Alvarado put it, "I believe I will outwork most people in finding a solution."

Organizational skill. Most entrepreneurs own and operate their own businesses. Thus the ability to manage time, resources, and people effectively and efficiently is critical to their success. "Good management," said John D. Rockefeller, founder of Standard Oil Company, "consists in showing average people how to do the work of superior people."

Ability to motivate others. Entrepreneurs are good at inspiring others to join their team. "As we look ahead into the next century," says Bill Gates, "leaders will be those who empower others."

The Risks and Rewards of Starting a Business

Not everyone who sets out to be a business entrepreneur ends up a success. As Figure 9.2 shows, only 44 percent of new businesses survive after four years of being in business. That means 56 percent of new start-ups—more than half—fail. "Once you've hit five years, your odds of survival go way up," observes economist David Birch. "Only two to three percent of businesses older than five shut down each year."

The risk of failure is not the only challenge facing those who hope to become entrepreneurs. Raising money to finance a new business can be difficult, and new business owners are often beset by financial insecurity. Finding the right employees can also be a challenge. In addition, people who run their own businesses typically work long hours, often with little or no pay.

Madam C. J. Walker, an African American

Figure 9.2

Analyzing the Survival of Business Start-Ups
Starting a new business is risky. As the graph shows, business start-ups have a high mortality rate. Of 212,182 new businesses started in the second quarter of 1998, fewer than half were still operating four years later. By 2005, the survival rate had dropped to 31.2 percent.

Source: Amy E. Knaup and Merissa C. Piazza, "Business Employment Dynamics Data: Survival and Longevity, II," *Monthly Labor Review,* vol. 130, no. 9 (Sep. 2007).

Survival Rates of Businesses Begun in 1998

Businesses Surviving (percentage) / Length of Survival

1 Year (1999), 2 Years (2000), 3 Years (2001), 4 Years (2002), 5 Years (2003), 6 Years (2004), 7 Years (2005)

founder of a hair-care product company and the first woman to become a millionaire, put it this way: "There is no royal, flower-strewn path to success . . . If I have accomplished anything in life, it is because I have been willing to work hard."

With all the drawbacks to starting a business, why would anyone want to be an entrepreneur? The answer lies in the incentives-matter principle. Running a successful business of one's own can bring great rewards. The most obvious reward is the nearly unlimited potential to make money. Look no further than Oprah Winfrey and Bill Gates for proof of that. Yet money is not what motivates most entrepreneurs. They simply love what they do. Says Winfrey, "I would do what I'm doing even if I weren't getting paid."

Part of the personal satisfaction of entrepreneurship comes from the freedom it affords. As a business owner, you are your own boss. You set your own hours, and you do what makes you happy. Entrepreneur Stephen Fairchild, for example, was always an avid spelunker, or cave explorer. In 1972, he sold everything he owned and quit his job to take over a company operating tours of Boyden Cavern, a cave in Giant Sequoia National Monument. He is now head of a company that owns other show caves and operates tours of a gold mine. "Being a 'cave entrepreneur' is the perfect marriage of hobby and career," Fairchild says. "I take extreme pride in what I do, but

more important, I thoroughly enjoy what I do!"

Many entrepreneurs also take satisfaction in knowing that they are contributing to the economy. New businesses can breathe economic life into depressed areas, creating new jobs and helping to support existing businesses. Successful business owners often become community leaders who invest in community projects and give to local charities.

For Jerry Greenfield, cofounder of Ben & Jerry's, a successful ice cream company, the chance to make positive change through business leadership was exciting. "We measured our success not just by how much money we made, but by how much we contributed to the community," says Greenfield. "It was a two-part bottom line."

■ 9.3 What Kinds of Businesses Are Best Organized as Sole Proprietorships?

Businesses come in all shapes and sizes, ranging from small home-based businesses to huge companies with offices around the world. Economists categorize businesses based on how they are organized. Most U.S. business organizations fall into one of three general categories: sole proprietorships, partnerships, or corporations. The most common is the **sole proprietorship,** a business owned and managed by one person.

Sole proprietorships are businesses owned and operated by one person. Many small, service-oriented businesses, like this automobile repair shop, are organized in this way.

Sole Proprietorships: One Owner, One Operator

In a sole proprietorship, the owner of the business—the proprietor—earns all the profits and is responsible for all the debts. This form of business can be simple to establish and easy to manage, with relatively low start-up costs.

This is the kind of business Timothy Redel chose when he started his photography business. Redel had traveled all over the world working as an assistant for other photographers before he went into business as a sole proprietor. To do so, he borrowed $10,000 from a bank. With these funds, he bought cameras and lighting equipment and set up shop, using his small apartment as a studio. He went on to become a highly successful photographer whose work has appeared in many national magazines.

The ease of starting a sole proprietorship is probably why about 7 out of 10 businesses are organized this way. It is a form of business that appeals to people who have a marketable skill or trade and want to work for themselves rather than a boss. A sole proprietor might be a plumber, a pet sitter, a caterer, a farmer, a consultant, or an artist like Redel.

Advantages of Sole Proprietorships

For anyone thinking of starting a business, the sole proprietorship offers a number of advantages.

Ease of start-up. There is little paperwork involved in starting a sole proprietorship. Though requirements vary by city and state, the basics include

- obtaining a **business license** or **business permit,** a legal document that allows a business to operate in that state, city, or town.
- obtaining any necessary **zoning permits**. Local governments often designate certain areas, or zones, for specific business purposes.
- registering the **business name**. If a business carries the owner's legal name—as in Timothy Redel Photography—this step is not necessary. If not, the proprietor must submit a "doing business as" form to the local government office.

Few restrictions. Sole proprietorships are the least regulated form of business. However, some regulations do apply to specific industries. For example, any business that serves food is subject to health department regulations.

Full decision-making power. A sole proprietor makes all business decisions without having to consult with partners or shareholders. The freedom to make decisions quickly in response to market changes can be a great advantage for a business owner.

Full profits and individual taxation. A sole proprietor keeps all the profits generated by the business after paying taxes. Sole proprietors pay personal income tax on their earnings. The business itself pays no taxes.

Ease of closing. Sole proprietors can dissolve their businesses easily if they choose to do so. However, they must pay off business debts and taxes.

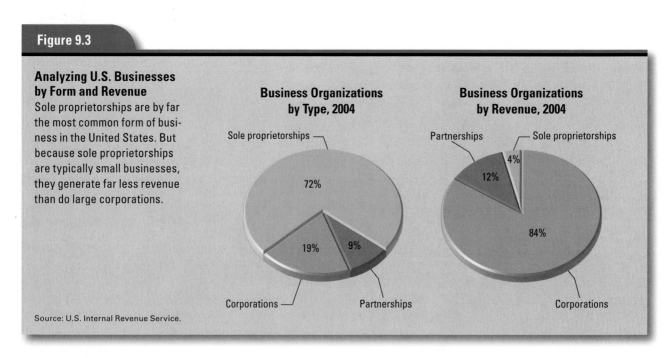

Figure 9.3

Analyzing U.S. Businesses by Form and Revenue
Sole proprietorships are by far the most common form of business in the United States. But because sole proprietorships are typically small businesses, they generate far less revenue than do large corporations.

Business Organizations by Type, 2004
Sole proprietorships — 72%
Corporations — 19%
Partnerships — 9%

Business Organizations by Revenue, 2004
Partnerships — 12%
Sole proprietorships — 4%
Corporations — 84%

Source: U.S. Internal Revenue Service.

Sole Proprietorship

A sole proprietorship is a business owned and operated by one person. The owner keeps the profits, if any, and is liable for debts.

- Advantages include ease of opening, few regulations, and decision-making control by the owner.
- Disadvantages include modest growth potential and a limited business life.

Disadvantages of Sole Proprietorships

Sole proprietorships also have disadvantages. Below are the three main drawbacks of this form of business.

Unlimited liability. The legal obligation to pay debts is known as **liability**. Sole proprietors have **unlimited liability,** or full responsibility for paying any debts their businesses take on. If a business does not have enough assets to repay its debts, the owner must use his or her personal assets—such as a home, car, or bank account—to do so. Unlimited liability is the tradeoff a sole proprietor makes for having complete control and reaping all the profits.

Many sole proprietors reduce their liability by organizing their business as a **limited liability company**. As in a sole proprietorship, the proprietor of an LLC pays personal income tax on the business's profits. But the proprietor's liability is limited to whatever he or she has invested in the company. This feature of LLCs has made them increasingly popular with business owners in recent years.

Limited growth potential. Because the success of a sole proprietorship rests on just one person—often a novice entrepreneur with limited assets—investors may be reluctant to lend money to a sole proprietor. Sole proprietorships can thus have difficulty obtaining the capital needed to expand. Business growth often depends on profits that can be reinvested in the enterprise.

Limited life. A sole proprietorship almost always ceases to operate if the owner dies, goes bankrupt, or is unable to run the business for any reason. New management does not usually take over this type of business. This lack of permanence may discourage some people from seeking work in a sole proprietorship. It may also make lenders reluctant to make loans to businesses with a single owner.

■ 9.4 What Kinds of Businesses Are Organized as Partnerships?

In 1988, brothers Wing Lam Lee , Ed Lee, and Mingo Lee decided to go into the restaurant business together. The brothers were surfers who had grown up in Brazil, had surfed in Mexico, and had worked in their family's Chinese restaurant. All of these influences came together in their first restaurant: Wahoo's Fish Taco in Costa Mesa, California. Wahoo's featured a Mexican-Brazilian-Asian menu with grilled fish tacos as the specialty. The restaurant was so successful that by 2008, the partners had opened more than 50 Wahoo's.

Partnerships like that of the Lee brothers are well known in the business world. Ben Cohen and Jerry Greenfield, friends since middle school, founded Ben & Jerry's. Google, the Internet search company, was founded by partners Larry Page and Sergey Brin. Partnerships are the second most common form of business organization in the United States.

Partnerships: Multiple Owners, Shared Profits

A **partnership** is a business owned by two or more co-owners. Partners share profits from the business. They also share liability for any debts the business incurs. Family-owned businesses, small stores, farms, and medical practices are common examples of business partnerships. Law firms, accounting firms, and money-management firms also frequently form partnership agreements.

Partnerships may be formed by an oral agreement. However, the more common practice is to draw up a legally binding written agreement. There are different kinds of partnerships, each of which confers different

Ben Cohen and Jerry Greenfield learned how to make ice cream from a $5 correspondence course in 1977. Twenty years later, sales of Ben & Jerry's ice cream topped $174 million.

responsibilities on the partners. The following are the three most common kinds of business partnerships:

General partnership. A **general partnership** is a form of business in which all co-owners have unlimited liability for any business debts. The owners, or **general partners,** are also active in the operations of the business.

Limited partnership. A **limited partnership** has at least one general partner and one or more limited partners. The **limited partners** contribute financial capital but leave day-to-day business operations to the general partners. For this reason, limited partners are also known as **silent partners**.

The main advantage of being a limited partner is **limited liability** for debts owed by the partnership. Limited partners can lose only the amount of money they invested in the business should it be sued or go bankrupt.

Limited liability partnership. In a **limited liability partnership,** co-owners are allowed to operate like general partners while enjoying the protection of limited liability. An LLP is well suited to businesses in which all partners want to take an active role in managing the business. Professionals, such as

attorneys, doctors, dentists, and accountants, often form LLPs.

Advantages of Partnerships

Like sole proprietorships, partnerships offer entrepreneurs a number of advantages.

Ease of start-up. Partnerships are relatively easy to establish. The same business permits that are required for a sole proprietorship are also required for a partnership. In addition, business and legal experts recommend that a legal agreement, known as **articles of partnership,** be drawn up. Articles of partnership usually specify
- each partner's contribution in assets and labor.
- each partner's share of the profits and losses.
- each partner's authority and duties.
- how partners will settle disagreements.
- what happens in the event that a partner dies or leaves.
- how assets will be divided if the business fails.

If articles of partnership are not drawn up, most states have guidelines regarding partner rights and responsibilities that automatically go into effect.

Few restrictions. Partnerships are subject to few government regulations. However, like sole

"It seems pretty easy to make partner here."

"Making partner" is the goal of most professionals who join a limited liability partnership. But becoming a partner is seldom as easy as this cartoon implies.

proprietorships, they must meet industry-specific regulations, such as health codes.

Shared decision-making power. "Two heads are better than one" is the philosophy guiding most partnerships. Partners can pool their experience and skills in making the decisions that guide the business.

Specialization. Partners often bring different areas of expertise to a business. For instance, one partner may be good at managing people, whereas another may be a marketing whiz. Partnerships allow partners to do what each does best for the company's overall benefit.

Individual taxation. Partners share in the profits according to whatever arrangement they have made. Each partner pays income taxes on his or her share. The business itself does not have to pay taxes.

Increased growth potential. People who go into business together each bring financial assets to the enterprise—their own assets as well as those of family and friends. Banks therefore see less risk in lending money to a partnership than to a sole proprietorship, which draws on the assets of just one person. For the same reason, suppliers are more willing to extend credit to a partnership.

With greater access to capital, partnerships often find it easier to expand their operations than do sole proprietorships. They are also better able to attract and hire talented employees, some of whom may aspire to become partners themselves some day.

Disadvantages of Partnerships
Partnerships also have drawbacks.

Unlimited liability for general partners. Unless a partnership is a LLP, at least one partner—the general partner—has unlimited liability for debts. Should the business run into financial problems, general partners stand to lose not only what they have invested but also their personal assets outside the business.

Conflict between partners. Like any relationship, a business partnership has the potential for conflict. Partners who see eye to eye when they first go into business may come to disagree about management style, work habits, ethics, or the firm's general goals and direction. Partnership agreements do not address such issues. Good communication and an honest effort to resolve conflicts are essential if a partnership is to survive.

Continuity issues. Partnerships are a temporary form of business. If one partner dies or decides to leave a partnership, the remaining partners will need to buy out the former partner's share. The value of this share may be difficult or impossible to determine. Moreover, the remaining partners may not have the liquid assets needed to buy it. Survival may depend on finding a new partner with the financial resources to purchase the outgoing partner's share of the business.

■ 9.5 Why Are Large Businesses Organized as Corporations?

Sometimes sole proprietors or partners realize that they need more financial capital to grow their businesses than they can provide on their own. One way to raise these funds is to seek venture capital. **Venture capital** is money from an individual investor or organization that invests in promising new businesses in exchange for a share of ownership. Another common way to raise money is to sell shares in the company to the public on the stock market. In either case, this is the time for the company to be reorganized as a corporation.

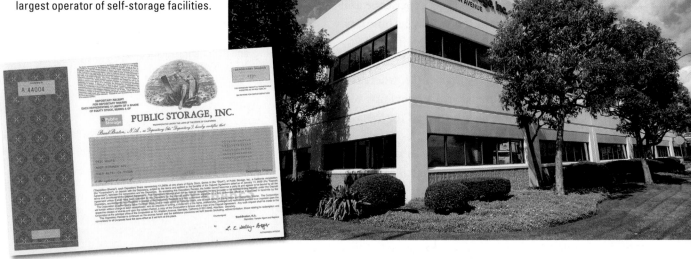

A stock certificate is a legal document that shows the number of shares of stock a shareholder owns in a corporation. This certificate indicates ownership of shares in Public Storage, the world's largest operator of self-storage facilities.

Corporations: Ownership by Shareholders

The word *corporation* has its roots in the Latin word *corpus,* which means "body." The root of the word reflects the modern legal definition of **corporation**: a company treated under the law as a single body with its own powers, separate from its owners. A corporation can enter into a contract. It can buy and sell property, just as an individual can.

Corporations are owned by shareholders who purchase shares of company stock. When a business becomes a corporation, it may offer for sale anywhere from several thousand to several million shares of stock. Such a stock offering might bring the company millions or even billions of dollars in new financial capital. It is easy to see why companies looking to expand might choose incorporation.

Ben & Jerry's offers a good example. Begun in 1978 as a partnership, the ice cream company became a corporation in 1984. That year, it offered stock to Vermont residents only, raising $750,000 for a new manufacturing facility. The following year, Ben & Jerry's stock was offered for sale to the general public. Using the revenue from stock sales, the company expanded its operations, distributing its ice cream outside of New England for the first time.

There are two kinds of business corporations. A **privately held corporation** is owned by an individual or a small group of individuals. It allows only a select group of people, often members of a family,

to purchase stock. The stock is usually not for sale to the general public. A privately held corporation is also known as a **closely held corporation**.

If a privately held corporation grows significantly, it may take steps to become, or may be sold to, a publicly held corporation. A **publicly held corporation** offers stock for sale to the general public and has many shareholders. This is the type of corporation Ben & Jerry's became when it sold stock to the public. Stock in publicly held corporations is typically bought and sold through a stock exchange.

How Corporations Are Organized

Corporations all tend to be organized in much the same way. As shown in Figure 9.5A, the typical corporation is a hierarchy with different levels of employees. Every employee in a corporation reports to a higher-level employee. That person reports to an even higher-level employee, and so on. At the top of the corporate hierarchy sits the board of directors, which reports to the shareholders.

A **board of directors** is a governing body that is elected by the shareholders. The board oversees management of the corporation. It also establishes corporate policy and makes sure the company's resources are being managed effectively.

In many corporations, the board of directors is made up of "inside" as well as "outside" directors. An **inside director** is someone from within the firm, such as the company's founder or a senior-level manager. An **outside director** is someone from outside the firm who can provide an independent perspective.

One of the board's most important responsibilities is to select the corporation's **chief executive officer**. The CEO is the highest-ranking person in charge of managing a corporation.

The CEO usually appoints other **corporate officers**—senior executives who oversee specific areas of the business. For example, the chief financial officer (CFO) is in charge of a company's finances. The chief operating officer (COO) manages the day-to-day operations of a company. Other departments that are typically headed by corporate officers include marketing, legal, and information technology.

These corporate officers, along with other senior executives, make up the senior management of a corporation. Reporting to them is a broad swath of managers known as **middle management**. This next level includes vice presidents, department heads, and managers of various ranks. Middle management is responsible for supervising the day-to-day activities of the firm's workers.

Advantages of a Corporation

Businesses organized as corporations offer a number of advantages over sole proprietorships and partnerships.

Limited liability. A corporation's owners—the shareholders—are liable only for the amount of money they have invested. For example, suppose an investor buys 100 shares of stock at $30 a share. If the corporation goes bankrupt, the investor will lose that $3,000 investment. His or her personal assets are never at risk. The corporation is liable for its debts, however, because the law considers it a legal entity, like a person.

Growth potential. Because corporations can use the sale of stock to raise financial capital, they have far greater potential for growth than do other forms of business. For example, Google offered stock to the public in 2004 in what is called an **initial public**

Figure 9.5A

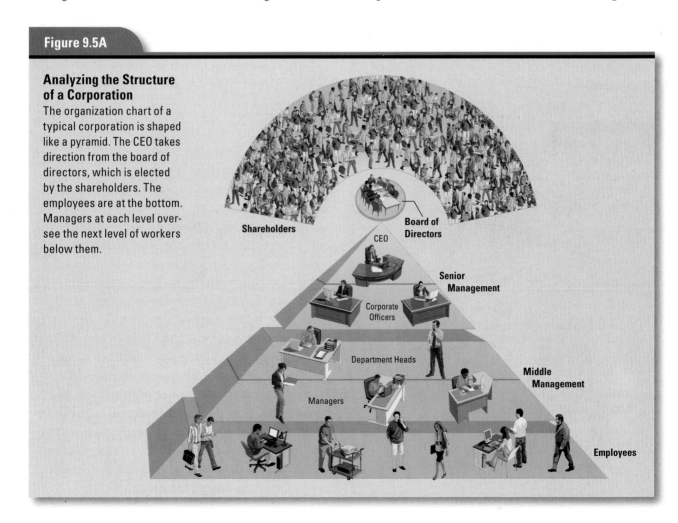

Analyzing the Structure of a Corporation
The organization chart of a typical corporation is shaped like a pyramid. The CEO takes direction from the board of directors, which is elected by the shareholders. The employees are at the bottom. Managers at each level oversee the next level of workers below them.

Shareholders

Board of Directors

CEO

Senior Management

Corporate Officers

Department Heads

Middle Management

Managers

Employees

offering. On the first day of Google's IPO, 22 million shares were sold. This sale raised about $1.2 billion for the company.

Professional management. Whereas sole proprietors and partners must manage their businesses themselves, corporations are run by professional managers. These managers often specialize in a particular area, such as finance or public relations. With this expertise, corporations can increase efficiency to a level that often is not possible in smaller organizations.

Long life. Unlike sole proprietorships and partnerships, corporations continue to exist when founders die or owners sell their shares. As legal entities, corporations have permanence. For example, the company that became IBM Corporation was founded in 1888 and incorporated in 1911. Today it is the largest information technology employer in the world. This ability of corporations to continue indefinitely supports growth and long-range planning efforts.

Disadvantages of a Corporation

Although incorporation provides businesses with important advantages, it also has disadvantages.

Complexity of start-up. Businesses that want to incorporate are legally required to follow certain procedures.

- They must develop a prospectus. This document outlines for potential investors the main features of the enterprise and contains information about the stock being offered.
- They must apply for a business license. All states require new corporations to file a set of documents called **articles of incorporation,** also known as a corporate charter. A **corporate charter** details the company's objectives, structure, and planned operations. It also specifies the number of shares of stock that may be issued. When state officials approve the charter, the company becomes a legal corporation.
- They must create **corporate bylaws,** or rules that govern the management of the corporation. Bylaws deal with such topics as how to conduct shareholder meetings, how to elect directors, what officers the organization will have, and what the duties of those officers will be.
- They must hold a meeting of shareholders to elect a board of directors.
- They must issue stock certificates to shareholders. A **stock certificate** is a legal document that certifies ownership of a specific number of shares in the corporation.

Loss of control. Once a business has been incorporated, the role of the original owner or founder may change. Decisions once made by the founder become the responsibility of the board of directors and the professional management team. For the founder, the change usually means giving up some control of the company.

More government regulation. Corporations are subject to more government regulation than are other types of businesses. For example, corporations are required to hold annual shareholder meetings. They must maintain detailed records of business transactions. Publicly held corporations must also file regular reports with the Securities and Exchange Commission, the federal agency that regulates the stock market.

Double taxation. Corporations face heavier taxes than do sole proprietorships or partnerships. As legal entities, corporations are required to pay taxes on their profits. In addition, shareholders must pay income tax on any dividends they receive. Taxation at the corporate level and again at the shareholder level is known as **double taxation**.

Key Concept

Corporation

A corporation is a legal entity owned by shareholders who buy stock in the company. Shareholders share profits, if any, but have only limited liability for debts.

- Advantages include professional management and permanence.
- Disadvantages include the complexity of start-up and the double taxation of profits.

Figure 9.5B

Mapping a Multinational Corporation

In the past, most multinational corporations were based in Western Europe and North America. In recent decades, however, many Asian companies have gone global. The map shows the worldwide reach of LG Electronics, a multinational corporation based in South Korea.

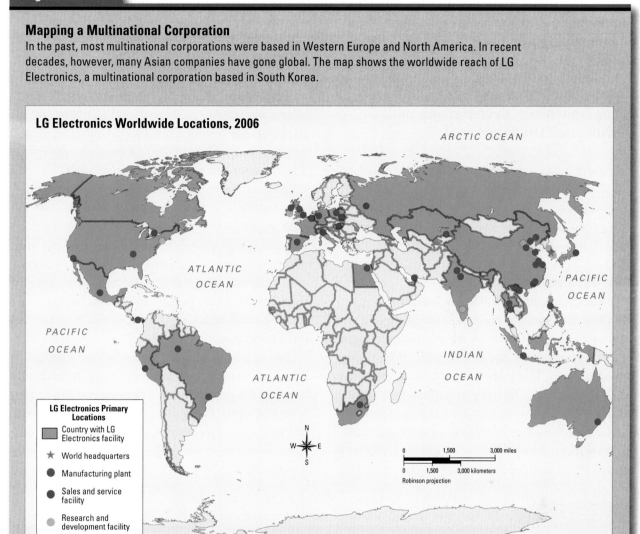

LG Electronics Worldwide Locations, 2006

LG Electronics Primary Locations
- Country with LG Electronics facility
- ★ World headquarters
- Manufacturing plant
- Sales and service facility
- Research and development facility

Multinational Corporations: Doing Business on a Global Scale

Business enterprises that operate in more than one country—known as **multinational corporations**—are not new. They have existed since the 1600s, when English and Dutch trading companies first established outposts in the East Indies.

However, in the past few decades, the number of global businesses has skyrocketed. In 1990, there were about 3,000 multinational corporations. In 2003, there were more than 63,000, with 821,000 branches and 90 million employees around the globe. Contrary to what many people think, not all of them are corporate giants like Coca-Cola and Exxon. Most are smaller firms having fewer than 250 employees.

As Figure 9.5B shows, such corporations typically have headquarters in their "home" country. They then operate production facilities or deliver services in at least one other country. Each branch of a multinational must obey the laws of the country in which it is located, including tax laws.

Multinational corporations have advantages that other firms do not have. Their global reach gives them access to more markets, with greater potential for increased sales and growth. Access to multiple markets also makes it less likely that a multinational will go bankrupt than will a smaller firm operating in a single market. Moreover, multinational corporations often have access to cheaper labor and raw materials than they would find in their home countries.

Locations in multiple countries may also reduce their transportation costs. For all these reasons, the number of global corporations is likely to continue to increase.

9.6 What Purposes Are Served by Franchises, Cooperatives, and Nonprofit Organizations?

Not every business enterprise falls neatly into one of the three business models described in this chapter. There are also other types of business organizations that people adopt to achieve specific goals. One model is the business franchise.

Business Franchises: One Parent Company with Many Outlets

In a **business franchise,** a parent company grants to an independent business owner the exclusive right to use its trade name and sell its products in a designated location. This is the kind of arrangement that such companies as Holiday Inn, McDonald's, and Dunkin' Donuts use to distribute their products.

Under a franchise agreement, a parent company, or **franchiser,** grants a license to operate an outlet in return for an initial payment and ongoing fees. The business owner who buys the license and distributes the franchiser's products is the **franchisee**. The franchise model is well suited to businesses whose products or services can easily be replicated, or "cloned." Motel rooms, hamburgers, and donuts are just such products.

Franchise agreements are popular because they offer advantages to both the parent company and the local franchise owner. Franchising enables a parent company to expand rapidly and more cheaply than if it had to own and operate new outlets itself.

At the same time, franchising gives people who want to own a business the opportunity to do so with some support. Franchisers help new owners get started with management training, budgets, and advertising campaigns. Moreover, many franchises have a record of profitability and a built-in customer base. For the would-be business owner, buying a franchise may be less of a financial risk than starting one's own business.

There are also disadvantages to franchising. Franchisers charge high fees for the right to use their name. The bigger the name, the more expensive the franchise rights. Franchisees must also pay **royalties,** or a percentage of earnings, to the parent company. These costs are on top of the usual costs of operating a business.

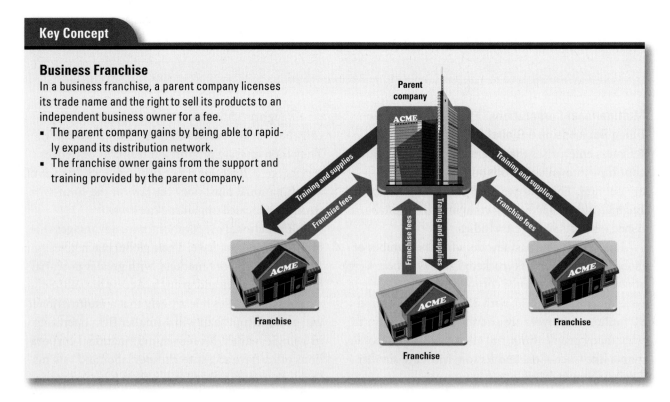

Key Concept

Business Franchise
In a business franchise, a parent company licenses its trade name and the right to sell its products to an independent business owner for a fee.
- The parent company gains by being able to rapidly expand its distribution network.
- The franchise owner gains from the support and training provided by the parent company.

Some 650 cranberry growers in North America market their crop through the Ocean Spray agricultural cooperative. When founded in 1930, the co-op's main product was cranberry sauce. Today it markets a wide range of juices along with dried cranberries.

In addition, being a franchise owner means giving up some independence. Franchise agreements usually require franchisees to follow strict rules and procedures. For some aspiring entrepreneurs, this lack of independence may be a big drawback.

Cooperatives: Share Ownership for Shared Benefits

Another popular form of business organization is the cooperative, or co-op for short. A **cooperative** is a business that is owned and operated by a group of individuals for their shared benefit. Some 120 million Americans were members of some type of co-op in 2005.

Cooperatives are businesses, but with some important differences. Co-ops are not in business to make a profit. Rather their goal is to meet their members' needs for affordable goods and services. Co-ops are run democratically, with members electing other members to a board of directors.

Many people who join co-ops are consumers looking to increase their buying power. Consumer co-ops sell goods to their members at reduced prices. They can do this because they purchase bulk quantities at a lower cost. The requirements of membership in a consumer co-op vary. Some co-ops require members to work a certain number of hours, whereas others require a yearly membership fee. Food co-ops, housing cooperatives, and discount price clubs are types of consumer cooperatives.

Other kinds of consumer co-ops provide services instead of goods. Such services include health care, childcare, and insurance services. Credit unions, or financial cooperatives, make low-cost loans to their members. Electric cooperatives, found mainly in rural areas, provide low-cost electricity to their members. In 2008, electric co-ops delivered electricity to 40 million Americans.

Producers also form cooperatives. The most common producer cooperative is the agricultural co-op, also known as a farm organization. Some agricultural co-ops function like consumer co-ops, providing farmer members with low-cost seeds and equipment. Other agricultural co-ops help to market and sell members' products. Some well-known food brands, such as Sun-Maid, Land O' Lakes, and Ocean Spray, are agricultural co-ops. Ocean Spray, the producer of juice drinks, is owned by about 750 cranberry and grapefruit growers in the United States and Canada.

Nonprofit Organizations

Yet another common business model is the nonprofit organization. A **nonprofit organization** functions like a business, except that it does not operate to make a profit. Instead, nonprofits are established to support particular public or private goals. Human rights, the arts, the environment, religion, and medical research are just a few of the areas in which nonprofits are active. Nonprofits range from global organizations like the Red Cross to local soup kitchens and animal shelters, as you can see in Figure 9.6.

Although some nonprofit groups are organized informally, many seek nonprofit status from the federal government. Nonprofit organizations may be tax exempt, which means they are not required to pay income tax. However, tax-exempt nonprofits are limited to how much income they can earn and how they may use their earnings. Most groups are funded, at least in part, by donations.

A nonprofit may be organized in a variety of ways: as a corporation, a cooperative, a trust, or a foundation. Conservation nonprofits are often organized as land trusts. For example, the Nature Conservancy is a land trust that works to protect wilderness areas and waterways around the world as nature preserves.

A **foundation** is an organization that is created and supported by donated funds or property. Foundations are often created by people who have made fortunes in business. Bill and Melinda Gates, for example, created a foundation dedicated to "bringing innovations in health and learning to the global community." Since its founding in 1994, the Bill and Melinda Gates Foundation has given billions of dollars to groups working to improve health care and education in developing countries and in the United States.

Other kinds of nonprofit organizations support the interests of businesses and professional people. A **business association** represents the interests of businesspeople in a geographical area. Such organizations often go by the title of Chamber of Commerce.

A **trade association** represents the interests of people working in a particular industry. Trade associations include groups like the Alliance of Automobile Manufacturers and the Motion Picture Association of America. Such groups use advertising, education, and political lobbying to promote their interests.

People who work in a profession, such as medicine or teaching, often join a **professional organization**. These nonprofits establish standards of training and ethics for professionals in their fields. They also work to improve conditions for people in their profession. The American Nurses Association, for example, represents nearly 3 million registered nurses. It promotes the rights of nurses in the workplace and lobbies Congress on health care issues that affect nurses.

Labor unions are organizations of workers in a specific industry. A labor union seeks to improve working conditions, wages, hours, and benefits for its members. Labor unions are active in a wide range of industries. Actors, miners, police officers, and aerospace workers, for example, are all represented by unions.

■ 9.7 What Rights and Responsibilities Do Businesses Have in a Free Enterprise System?

In 2007, Facebook, the social-networking Web site, launched an advertising system called Beacon. Under this system, every time a Facebook user purchased a product from a partner company, such as eBay or Amazon, the user's Facebook friends were automatically notified. Many Facebook members saw this as a violation of privacy. For example, one member bought a diamond ring for his wife, and the surprise was spoiled when his wife and all his friends were informed. Thousands of members signed online petitions protesting the new system.

Figure 9.6

Analyzing Nonprofits
Nonprofit organizations are active in many fields. However, the majority of people employed by nonprofits work for organizations that provide health care services.

Nonprofit Paid Employment by Field, 2004

- Hospitals 33.2%
- Nursing homes and clinics 21.4%
- Social services 12.6%
- Education and research 16.5%
- Business, trade, and professional organizations 6.9%
- Arts, entertainment, and recreation 2.5%
- Other 7%

Source: Lester M. Salamon and S. Wojciech Sokolowski, "Employment in America's Charities: A Profile" (Baltimore: Johns Hopkins Center for Civil Society Studies, Dec. 2006).
Note: Percentages do not add to 100 due to rounding.

At first Facebook, which stood to gain huge revenues from advertisers through Beacon, refused to change the system. But when the controversy prompted three big advertisers to threaten to pull out, CEO Mark Zuckerberg did an about-face. He apologized to users and modified the system so that a user could turn off Beacon. Threatened with the loss of revenue, he gave in to his customers' demands.

The Rights of Businesses

Zuckerberg's missteps with Beacon raised an interesting question: What rights do businesses have when it comes to using information about their customers? In a free enterprise system, businesses clearly have many of the same rights that individuals have. These include the right to own property and to enter into and enforce contracts. Following are other specific rights of business.

The right to advertise. The First Amendment's guarantee of freedom of speech did not originally protect the right of businesses to advertise. In recent decades, however, courts have ruled that advertising is "commercial speech." As such, it is protected under the Constitution. With certain exceptions, such as ads for alcohol and tobacco, the government places few restrictions on how companies can market their products.

The right to hire and fire employees. Most states have "employment at will" regulations that protect a business's right to hire or fire employees as its needs change. They also protect an employee's right to quit a job for any reason. The main exception to this rule is when a contract exists between a business and an employee. Unless the contract states otherwise, the employee cannot be fired until the contract ends.

The right to screen employees. Businesses have a legal obligation to provide a safe workplace for their employees and clients. To do so, they have the right to perform background checks on job candidates as well as drug testing on job applicants and employees.

The right to be fairly compensated for property. The Fifth Amendment prohibits the government from taking private property for public use without paying a fair price for it. This right to fair compensation applies to businesses as well as individuals. It ensures that business owners and shareholders will not lose their investment should the government need to take over their property.

Figure 9.7

Identifying Intellectual Property Symbols

Businesses use a variety of symbols to identify and protect their intellectual property. The most important are illustrated here.

TM	Used to identify an unregistered trademark that identifies the source of a good.
SM	Used to identify an unregistered service mark that identifies the source of a service.
®	Indicates that a trademark or service mark has been registered with and is protected by the federal government.
©	Used to indicate that a written or visual work is protected under copyright laws.
℗	Used to indicate that a sound recording is protected under copyright law.

Patent Pending Indicates that a patent has been applied for but has not yet been issued.

US Patent 1234567 Indicates that a patent has been issued in the United States.

The right to protect intellectual property. Businesses are free to use patent, copyright, and trademark laws to protect their exclusive rights to intellectual property. A **trademark** is a distinctive name or symbol that identifies a firm and its products or services and that has been legally registered as the property of that firm. Other forms of protected intellectual property include trade secrets, company logos, designs, and inventions—in short, any intellectual product that has commercial value.

The Responsibilities of Businesses

The list of rights does not answer the question raised by Facebook users about Beacon and its use of information related to their shopping habits. Nonetheless, the users who signed protest petitions clearly felt that Zuckerberg had a responsibility to act on their privacy concerns.

Businesses, like individuals, have many responsibilities. Some are based on our expectations about how a business should behave. Others are enshrined in law.

Obtaining licenses and permits. Businesses must obtain all licenses and permits required by law. For example, a business that uses or stores hazardous materials is required to get a fire department permit. People practicing certain trades or professions, such as plumbers, electricians, and doctors, must be licensed. Such regulations are intended to ensure public safety.

Paying taxes. Business owners are responsible for paying all taxes that apply to their businesses. These may include income, sales, and property taxes. Businesses that do not pay their taxes are subject to penalties and fines.

Dealing honestly. Businesses have a responsibility to deal honestly with their customers and suppliers. Businesses that intentionally misrepresent facts, conceal information, publish false or misleading ads, or otherwise try to cheat people are committing fraud. Business fraud is against federal and state law and is subject to prosecution.

Honoring contracts. Businesses, like individuals, may choose whether to enter into a contract. However, once entered into, a contract is legally binding. Businesses thus have an obligation to honor their contracts with customers, suppliers, and others. When a contract is broken, the injured party may take legal action.

Creating an equal opportunity workplace. Federal law requires businesses to treat all employees equally. Discrimination on the basis of race, gender, age, ethnicity, religion, or disabilities is illegal. Companies have a responsibility to make sure their employment practices—such as hiring, firing, pay, and promotions —are nondiscriminatory.

Protecting whistle-blowers. An employee who reports an employer's misconduct to legal authorities is known as a whistle-blower. In the past, whistle-blowers were often fired for speaking out. However, federal and state laws now protect them from such retaliation.

Ensuring product safety. Businesses are responsible for making sure the products they sell are safe. Federal and state laws govern product safety. When a product is found to be unsafe or defective, the manufacturer may be held liable for any harm it may have caused.

It Is Legal—But Is It Ethical?

In our free enterprise system, businesses are legally permitted to do a great many things. Cosmetics companies may test products on animals. Farmers may use pesticides on crops. Retail stores may pay wages that are too low for employees to live on. But does that mean businesses *should* do these things? On the other hand, there are a great many things that are not required by law—such as giving to charity. But does that mean businesses *should not* do them?

As these questions imply—and as Zuckerberg learned in the Facebook controversy—there is often a difference between what is legal and what is ethically or morally right. This distinction lies at the heart of the growing corporate responsibility movement.

Corporate responsibility is the idea that businesses should take responsibility for the impact of their actions on society. It requires looking beyond a firm's responsibility to its shareholders and considering the needs of its stakeholders. A **stakeholder** is anyone who has an interest in, or is affected by, a company's actions. Stakeholders include employees, customers, suppliers, competitors, and the community in which the business operates.

A growing number of businesses are striving to be good "corporate citizens" by considering the interests of stakeholders. Stonyfield Farm is one example. This organic yogurt manufacturer gives 10 percent of its profits to groups that work to protect the environment.

Many companies address issues of corporate responsibility by creating codes of business ethics. **Business ethics** are principles of right and wrong that guide the actions of a company and its employees.

Visualscope Studios, a company that provides Web site design and search engine services to businesses, created the code of ethics below.

We treat our clients and web site visitors with honesty and respect at all times.

We honor and respectfully exercise any authority and/or privileges provided to us by our clients.

We will be upfront with our rates and fees from the project initiation, so you will be clear on what our roles and expectations are.

We will maintain a high level of competence, as well as staying current with new trends in the web design and development industry.

We will always work to the best of our abilities to ensure the timely delivery and success of every web project.

We will protect sensitive information given by clients and customers as private and confidential.

Are ethical business practices important to Americans? The answer seems to be yes. In a 2008 study, people were asked how much they were willing to pay for a pound of coffee based on what they knew about the company's ethical standards. The study showed that they would pay, on average, $9.71 for coffee produced by a company that treated its workers fairly and followed eco-friendly production practices. In contrast, they would pay only $5.89 for a pound of coffee from a company that ignored business ethics. In addition, companies known as socially responsible may have an edge when it comes to attracting a talented and local workforce.

Studies have shown that ethical business practices are important to clients and consumers. Firms with a reputation for high ethical standards also attract talented employees, giving those firms a competitive edge in the market.

At this point in your life, business ethics are probably not something you need to think much about. But as you move into the world of work, that may change. In the next chapter, you will explore the business world from the working person's perspective. You will learn about human capital, the labor market, and how you might fit into the labor market one day.

Summary

Entrepreneurs are the hardworking visionaries who create new business enterprises. Such enterprises may be sole proprietorships, partnerships, corporations, business franchises, cooperatives, or nonprofit organizations.

What does it take to start a new business? The qualities needed to succeed in business include creativity, determination, and energy. Starting a business is financially risky, but success offers rewards, including unlimited earning potential and a sense of accomplishment.

What kinds of businesses are best organized as sole proprietorships? Sole proprietors tend to be people with a marketable skill who want to work for themselves. They reap the profits and are liable for debts. Small businesses and farms make up the majority of sole proprietorships.

What kinds of businesses are organized as partnerships? In a business partnership, two or more owners share profits and liability. Such businesses may be organized as general, limited, or limited liability partnerships. Family-owned businesses, law firms, and medical practices are common examples of partnerships.

Why are large businesses organized as corporations? The corporation is well suited for a large business because it can sell stock to raise financial capital, thus allowing for growth. It is a legal entity independent of its owners—the shareholders—and can thus exist indefinitely.

What purposes are served by franchises, cooperatives, and nonprofit organizations? Business franchises allow a franchiser to create a distribution network at low cost, while providing business opportunities to franchisees. Cooperatives provide benefits to their members. Nonprofits pursue particular public or private goals but do not operate to make a profit.

What rights and responsibilities do businesses have in a free enterprise system? Businesses have the legal right to advertise, to hire and fire, to screen employees, and to protect intellectual property, among other rights. Legal responsibilities include obtaining licenses and permits, paying taxes, honoring contracts, and using nondiscriminatory employment practices. Many companies have established ethical codes of conduct to guide their actions.

Should businesses be run for shareholders or for other stakeholders?

The idea that corporations have a responsibility beyond making money for shareholders has passionate advocates, as well as fierce critics. As you read the following excerpts, think about how you would run a business if you could. Which viewpoint lines up with your values and why?

The Social Responsibility of Business Is to Increase Its Profits

By Milton Friedman, in *The New York Times Magazine*, Sep. 13, 1970

What does it mean to say that "business" has responsibilities? Only people can have responsibilities. A corporation is an artificial person and in this sense may have artificial responsibilities, but "business" as a whole cannot be said to have responsibilities, even in this vague sense. The first step toward clarity in examining the doctrine of the social responsibility of business is to ask precisely what it implies for whom.

Presumably, the individuals who are to be responsible are businessmen, which means individual proprietors or corporate executives. Most of the discussion of social responsibility is directed at corporations, so in what follows I shall mostly . . . speak of corporate executives.

In a free-enterprise, private-property system, a corporate executive is an employee of the owners of the business. He

Rethinking the Social Responsibility of Business: Putting Customers Ahead of Investors

By John Mackey, in *Reason*, Oct. 2005

In 1970 Milton Friedman wrote that "there is one and only one social responsibility of business—to use its resources and engage in activities designed to increase its profits so long as it stays within the rules of the game, which is to say, engages in open and free competition without deception or fraud." That's the orthodox view among free market economists: that the only social responsibility a law-abiding business has is to maximize profits for the shareholders.

I strongly disagree . . . I believe that the enlightened corporation should try to create value for all of its constituencies. From an investor's perspective, the purpose of the business is to maximize profits. But that's not the purpose for other stakeholders—for customers, employees, suppliers, and the community . . .

We have not achieved our tremendous increase in shareholder value by making shareholder value the primary purpose of our business . . . The most successful businesses has direct responsibility to his employers. That responsibility is to conduct the business in accordance with their desires, which generally will be to make as much money as possible while conforming to the basic rules of the society, both those embodied in law and those embodied in ethical custom . . .

Of course, the corporate executive is also a person in his own right. As a person, he may have many other responsibilities that he recognizes or assumes voluntarily—to his family, his conscience, his feelings of charity, his church, his clubs, his city, his country. He may feel impelled by these responsibilities to devote part of his income to causes he regards as worthy, to refuse to work for particular corporations, even to leave his job, for example, to join his country's armed forces. If we wish, we may refer to some of these responsibilities as "social responsibilities." But in these respects he is acting as a principal, not an agent; he is spending his own money or time or energy, not the money of his employers or the time or energy he has contracted to devote to their purposes. If these are "social responsibilities," they are the social responsibilities of individuals, not of business . . .

The difficulty of exercising "social responsibility" illustrates, of course, the great virtue of private competitive enterprise— it forces people to be responsible for their own actions and makes it difficult for them to "exploit" other people for either selfish or unselfish purposes. They can do good—but only at their own expense.

Milton Friedman (1912–2006), an American economist, received the 1976 Nobel Prize in economics.

---

put the customer first, ahead of the investors . . .

At Whole Foods, we measure our success by how much value we can create for all six of our most important stakeholders: customers, team members (employees), investors, vendors, communities, and the environment . . .

Many thinking people will readily accept my arguments that caring about customers and employees is good business. But they might draw the line at believing a company has any responsibility to its community and environment. To donate time and capital to philanthropy, they will argue, is to steal from investors . . .

A company's assets do belong to the investors, and its management does have a duty to manage those assets responsibly. In my view, the argument is not wrong so much as it is too narrow . . . There can be little doubt that a certain amount of corporate philanthropy is simply good business and works for the long-term benefit of the investors . . . It's a question of finding the appropriate balance and trying to create value for all of our stakeholders . . .

The business model that Whole Foods has embraced could represent a new form of capitalism, one that more consciously works for the common good instead of depending solely on the "invisible hand" to generate positive results for society. The "brand" of capitalism is in terrible shape throughout the world, and corporations are widely seen as selfish, greedy, and uncaring. This is both unfortunate and unnecessary, and could be changed if businesses and economists widely adopted the business model that I have outlined here.

John Mackey is chair, CEO, and cofounder of Whole Foods Market, which has stores in the United States, Canada, and the United Kingdom.

Chapter 10

Why is it important to develop your human capital?

HELP WANTED

Human Capital and the Labor Market

10.1 Introduction

In 2003, Catherine Omega, a striking brunette wearing a form-fitting bodysuit, joined a group of pioneers who were settling a new online virtual world known as Second Life. Like the real world, Second Life has land, seas, mountains, deserts, towns, and cities. People who join Second Life inhabit this virtual world through digital representatives, or avatars. Residents, as members are called, design their avatars to look however they might wish to appear in their online lives.

Catherine Omega was the avatar of a high school dropout in Vancouver, British Columbia, named Catherine Winters. Unfortunately for Winters, just as her Second Life was taking shape, her real life was coming apart. She became homeless and for a time lived on Vancouver's streets. Then she took shelter in an abandoned apartment building that lacked electricity.

Despite the bleakness of her situation, Winters was eager to find a way to return to Second Life. First she needed to find a source of electricity, which wasn't difficult, she later recalled, "because I had my multimeter and I know enough not to touch live wires."

Next Winters needed a computer and a way to connect to the Internet. "It turns out that a computer capable of running Second Life is difficult to come by when you're homeless," she notes. But she was able to assemble a computer from junk parts discarded by computer stores at a nearby recycling facility.

Human capital plays a critical role in the labor market.

Speaking of Economics

labor force
The portion of the population that has paid work or is seeking work. Active members of the military are not considered part of the labor force.

offshoring
Relocating work and jobs to another country.

equilibrium wage
The rate of pay that results in neither a surplus nor a shortage of labor. If the wage for a job is set above equilibrium level, too many workers will apply. If it is set below, too few will apply.

fringe benefits
Nonwage compensations offered to workers in addition to pay. Examples include health insurance plans and paid vacations.

wage gap
A difference in the wages earned by various groups in society.

affirmative action
Policies designed to promote the hiring of individuals from groups that have historically faced job discrimination. Such groups include minorities, women, and people with disabilities.

collective bargaining
Negotiations between an employer and a group of employees, usually represented by a labor union, to determine the conditions of employment.

right-to-work law
A law that prohibits employers from making union membership a requirement for getting or keeping a job. Twenty-two states have right-to-work laws.

Catherine Winters developed her human capital as a programmer in the online virtual world known as Second Life. She later used those skills to launch a career in Web development.

Once she had her computer up and running, it wasn't hard to pick up a wireless Internet connection from a nearby building.

Back on Second Life, Catherine Omega became known for her programming ability. Soon other Residents were hiring Winters in real life to do programming for them. In 2006, Winters found a full-time job as the Second Life coordinator for a Vancouver Web developer. By then she had moved into her own apartment. "It's pretty tiny," she said of her new home, "but it's clean and all mine."

While she was homeless, Winters had developed her human capital to the point where she could start a new career. Although her story is unusual, it has relevance for anyone thinking about entering the labor force. In this chapter, you will read about trends that are shaping the labor market today. You will also learn how you can develop your own human capital as you prepare to enter the workforce.

■ 10.2 What Trends Are Shaping Today's Labor Market?

Before Second Life was launched in 2003, few people would have believed that someone could make money working in a virtual world. Catherine Winters and many other Second Life Residents have done just that. The technology that makes Second Life possible has opened career opportunities that existed only in science fiction not long ago.

New technology has often been a driving force behind changes in the job market, creating new jobs even as it makes others obsolete. But changing technology is just one of many trends that have helped to shape the U.S. labor market in recent decades.

A Larger, More Diverse Labor Force

One long-term trend has been the steady growth of the nation's labor force, which has increased along with the nation's population. The **labor force** consists of those people age 16 and over who have jobs or who are actively looking for work. The labor force does not include unpaid workers, such as homemakers and volunteers. Nor does it include active members of the military or prison inmates. Between 1986 and 2006, the U.S. labor force grew by 34 million people.

A key reason for this growth has been the increased participation of women in the workforce. In 1960, when many women worked as homemakers, women made up 33 percent of the workforce. As women increasingly sought jobs outside the home, that figure rose. By 2006, women made up 46 percent of the labor force. Figure 10.2A shows the percentage of working-age women in the labor force over the span of a half-century.

Members of minority groups have also joined the workforce in growing numbers since 1960. Latinos, for example, are expected to comprise 16 percent of the labor force by 2016. This is more than double the percentage of three decades earlier.

Older Americans will also remain an important part of the working population over the next decade. Many members of the baby boom generation will retire during this period. But some baby boomers are expected to extend their working lives beyond the traditional retirement age of 65.

In contrast, the labor force participation of younger Americans is expected to decrease by 2016. The main reason for this projected decline is increased college enrollments. Rather than going directly into the workforce, many high school students are now choosing to continue their educations.

A Shift from Manufacturing to Service Jobs

The number of workers involved in the production of factory goods has declined. At the same time,

Figure 10.2A

Tracking Workforce Participation by Gender

This graph shows the labor force participation rates for men and women since 1956 and projected to 2016. The labor force includes the portion of the population that is working or looking for work.

- Note that in 1956, the gap between men and women was close to 50 percent.
- By 2016, that gap is projected to narrow to around 13 percent.

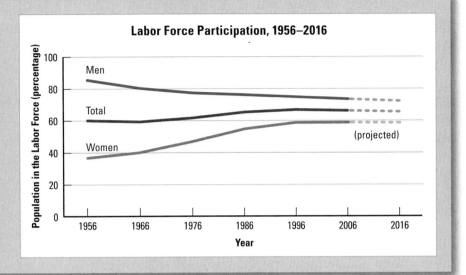

Labor Force Participation, 1956–2016

Source: Bureau of Labor Statistics.

the number of workers who provide services has increased. Jobs in the service sector include food preparation, banking, and health care.

This shift toward services continues a long evolution that began with the Industrial Revolution. By the late 1800s, manufacturing was replacing farming as the nation's most important economic activity. Manufacturing dominated the economy through most of the 1900s.

Beginning in the latter half of the 20th century, however, businesses that provide services have become the major source of jobs and economic growth. Economists expect this trend to continue. Figure 10.2B shows how the shift to service jobs is likely to affect future employment opportunities.

The fact that fewer Americans work in manufacturing these days does not mean that factory output is declining in this country. Just the opposite is true.

Figure 10.2B

Analyzing Future Job Growth

This graph shows how job opportunities are expected to grow (or shrink) in various occupations. Service occupations include jobs that directly assist the public such as police officers, health care aides, and cooks.

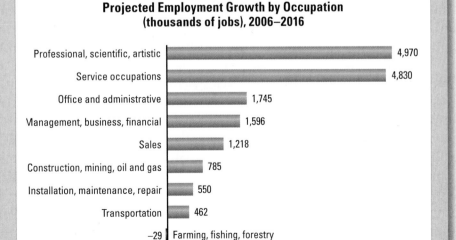

Projected Employment Growth by Occupation (thousands of jobs), 2006–2016

Source: Bureau of Labor Statistics.

Between 1970 and 2008, manufacturing output increased roughly threefold, making the United States the largest producer of manufactured goods in the world as of 2008. American-made products range from industrial machinery to motorcycles to T-shirts.

Because of gains in productivity, fewer workers are needed to turn out all these goods. Workers today are better educated and trained than they were a generation ago. Businesses have invested in labor-saving technologies, such as computers and robots. By some estimates, factory workers today are four times more productive than in the 1950s.

Factory workers have traditionally earned higher wages than most service workers. But this doesn't mean that all service jobs pay low wages. The service sector includes professional fields such as law, medicine, and information technology. In these fields, the most qualified workers command high salaries.

The Bureau of Labor Statistics, which tracks employment trends, predicts that jobs in the service sector will continue to expand. Figure 10.2C shows the 20 fastest-growing occupations based on BLS projections, most of which are service jobs.

The Growing Importance of Knowledge Workers

Another key trend in the labor market is the growing need for **knowledge workers**. Management consultant Peter Drucker coined this term in 1959 to describe people who work with information or who develop or apply information in the workplace. Financial advisers, for example, develop information when they analyze stock market returns. They apply that knowledge when they provide investment advice to clients.

Knowledge workers are a subset of workers in the service sector. They include people like Catherine Winters who work in the information technology field, such as computer programmers and systems analysts. Writers, researchers, teachers, lawyers, and scientists are also knowledge workers. The demand for knowledge workers is expected to grow as the handling of information becomes an increasingly important part of the economy.

Increased Outsourcing, Temping, and Telecommuting

Another set of trends in the labor market has to do with changes in the way people work. Many people spend less time working at the office and more time working at home than they did a decade ago. They also change jobs more frequently than was the case for previous generations.

One key development in recent years is the growth of **outsourcing**. This term refers to the business practice of sending work once done by company employees to outside contractors. Firms decide to outsource work when they believe an outside supplier can do the work more efficiently and at a lower cost than can be done within the company. For example, a medical practice might decide to outsource its billing operations to a firm that specializes in medical billing. Similarly, a school district might decide to outsource its legal work to an outside law firm. Outsourcing generates work for independent contractors. It may also result in the loss of jobs for in-house employees.

The use of **temporary workers** is also common. Temp workers are employed for limited periods of time for a variety of reasons. They may be hired for a project, to fill in for a sick or an absent employee, or to augment a firm's workforce during a busy time.

People choose temp work for many reasons. Many enjoy learning new skills as they move from one job to the next. Others value the flexibility they have in deciding who to work for and when. They also like being able to take time off for any reason at any time without asking anyone's permission. Temps are generally paid as well as or better than permanent employees doing the same job. And some view temping as a good way to try out a job before joining a firm as a regular employee.

Telecommuting is another growing practice in the labor market. Telecommuters do much or even all of their work at home, using phones and computers to remain connected to their workplaces. Telecommuting is especially common among knowledge workers. Writers, for example, can deliver drafts of their work by e-mail without ever stepping into their employer's office.

The Globalization of Work: Offshoring, Inshoring, and Foreign Competition

Globalization is yet another trend that is transforming the labor market. **Globalization** is the process by which people around the world, along with their economic activities, are becoming increasingly interconnected. As globalization increases, the factors of production—land, labor, and capital—move across borders with greater ease than ever before.

One key aspect of globalization is the growing practice of **offshoring,** or relocating work and jobs to other countries. Offshoring occurs in two ways. An American firm can move part of its operations to a facility it sets up in another country. Or it can contract with a company in another country to handle some aspect of its operations.

Firms move work offshore to reduce costs. The sportswear company Nike, for example, contracts with factories in more than 50 countries, including

Figure 10.2C

Identifying Fast-Growing Occupations

This graph shows the 20 fastest-growing occupations by 2016 as identified by the Bureau of Labor Statistics. Note that most of these fast-growing jobs are in the service sector.

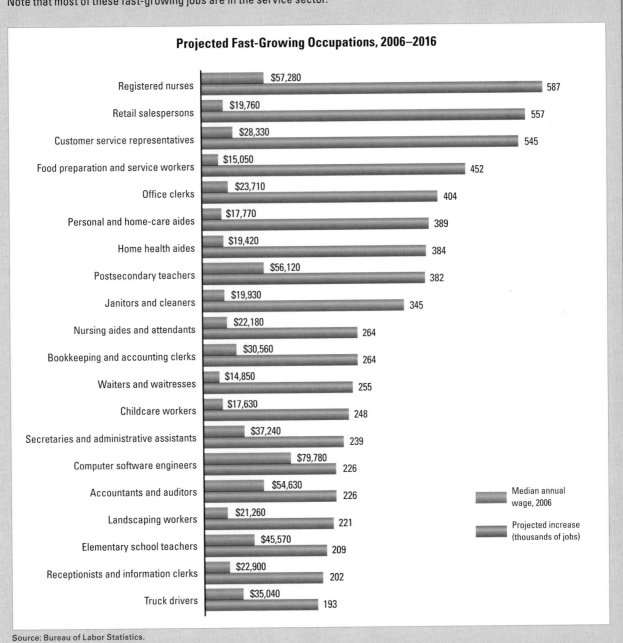

Projected Fast-Growing Occupations, 2006–2016

Occupation	Median annual wage, 2006	Projected increase (thousands of jobs)
Registered nurses	$57,280	587
Retail salespersons	$19,760	557
Customer service representatives	$28,330	545
Food preparation and service workers	$15,050	452
Office clerks	$23,710	404
Personal and home-care aides	$17,770	389
Home health aides	$19,420	384
Postsecondary teachers	$56,120	382
Janitors and cleaners	$19,930	345
Nursing aides and attendants	$22,180	264
Bookkeeping and accounting clerks	$30,560	264
Waiters and waitresses	$14,850	255
Childcare workers	$17,630	248
Secretaries and administrative assistants	$37,240	239
Computer software engineers	$79,780	226
Accountants and auditors	$54,630	226
Landscaping workers	$21,260	221
Elementary school teachers	$45,570	209
Receptionists and information clerks	$22,900	202
Truck drivers	$35,040	193

Source: Bureau of Labor Statistics.

Offshoring and Inshoring

In a global economy, jobs move more easily than ever before across national boundaries. Offshoring occurs when jobs are moved out of the country. Inshoring occurs when jobs are brought into the country. Either way, jobs are moving to places where workers have a comparative advantage.

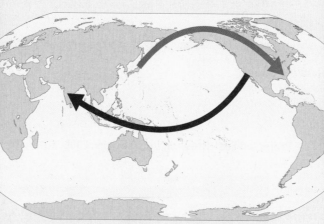

Offshoring of jobs occurred when U.S. companies moved some of their customer service call centers to India.

Inshoring of jobs occurred when Japanese automaker Toyota moved the assembly of some cars to Kentucky.

Vietnam and China. These are countries where Nike can achieve higher output for every dollar it spends on labor than it can in the United States. As Charles Wheelan explains,

> There are industries in which American workers are not productive enough to justify their relatively high wages, such as manufacturing textiles and shoes. These are industries that require relatively unskilled labor, which is more expensive in this country than in the developing world. Can a Vietnamese peasant sew basketball shoes together? Yes—and for a lot less than the American minimum wage.
>
> —Charles Wheelan, *Naked Economics: Undressing the Dismal Science,* 2003

Offshoring is also occurring in the service sector. Many computer programming and call-center operations, for example, have been offshored to India. With a large number of well-educated, English-speaking workers available at relatively low wages, India has a comparative advantage in these services.

Moving work offshore has both costs and benefits. It lowers the cost of production of many goods. This, is turn, translates into lower prices for American con-

sumers. The tradeoff for that benefit, however, is a loss of jobs in some sectors of the economy.

Globalization also brings jobs into the U.S. labor market. Many foreign firms have opened operations in this country. They do so to take advantage of the high levels of human capital available here. This process, known as **inshoring,** creates jobs for American workers. Foreign automakers, for example, employ more than 50,000 workers in their U.S. manufacturing plants.

As globalization increases, American businesses will face growing competition from foreign producers. This competition may cause job losses in some U.S. industries. But it will also create new jobs in others. Looking at the big picture, economists argue that foreign competition is good for businesses and economies. It forces producers to become more competitive by developing their own comparative advantages.

■ 10.3 What Determines How Much Workers Earn?

When Catherine Winters received a job offer in 2006, the company that wanted to hire her suggested a salary that she was free to accept or reject. How did the company decide how much to offer? How did she decide whether the offer was fair? Both questions could be answered by looking at the wage rates for other, similar positions in the job market. In general, wage rates are determined by the same principle that determines the price of goods and services: supply and demand.

Wages Reflect the Value of What Workers Produce

A number of factors influence wage rates. One has to do with the skills and training required for a job. Economists categorize jobs according to four general skill levels.

Unskilled. These jobs require no specialized skills or training. Most workers at this level earn a low hourly wage. Examples of unskilled jobs include janitors, busboys, and seasonal farmworkers.

Semiskilled. Workers at this level have some specialized skills and training, including the ability to use simple tools or equipment. Employees are supervised, and wages are paid on an hourly basis. Jobs include cashiers, construction workers, taxi drivers, and fast food cooks.

Skilled. This level requires specialized skills and training. Workers need little or no supervision, but most are still paid on an hourly basis. Examples include police officers, carpenters, bank tellers, and factory workers who operate complicated machinery.

Professional. This level includes "white collar" jobs that require advanced training and specialized skills. Professional workers receive a salary. Jobs include doctors, lawyers, teachers, airline pilots, and computer specialists.

In general, wages are based on skill level. As skills and training increase, so do wages. More importantly, however, workers command wages that reflect the market value of what they produce. Surgeons are paid more than nurses, for example, because the market places a higher value on surgery than it does on general nursing care.

For the same reason, more productive workers tend to receive higher wages than less productive workers. As economist Robert Frank notes, "Workers tend to be paid in rough proportion to the value they add to their employer's bottom line."

Competition among employers to hire workers also helps to raise wages. Figure 10.3A illustrates this point by looking at the effect of competition on wages for apple pickers. In this scenario, Farmer A begins the harvest season by paying his apple pickers $7.00 an hour. Farmer B, faced with a shortage of workers, decides to offer $8.00 an hour. Lured by the higher wages, a number of workers leave Farmer A and go to work for Farmer B. As a result of this competition for workers, Farmer A must also raise wages in order to attract and retain new workers.

Figure 10.3A

Analyzing the Effect of Competition on Wages
Competition for apple pickers helps determine market wages. The same is true in other competitive labor markets.

| Farmer A pays apple pickers a wage far below the value of their harvest. | Farmer B attracts apple pickers from Farmer A by offering a higher wage. | Farmer A and others raise their wages to compete for pickers. | Apple pickers receive a wage that better reflects the value they produce. |

How Demand and Supply Work in the Labor Market

Farmer A and Farmer B are imaginary, but they illustrate a real dynamic that shapes the labor market: the interaction of supply and demand. Employers create the demand for labor, and workers seeking jobs create the supply. Wages move toward equilibrium in the labor market just as prices move toward equilibrium in the market for goods and services.

The demand for labor comes from businesses and government agencies that compete with each other to hire workers. Demand changes over time with the state of the economy. When the economy is doing well, the quantity of labor demanded goes up. And just as an increased demand for goods tends to raise prices, an increased demand for labor tends to boost wages. In the case of Farmers A and B, competition for apple pickers forced wages up.

Conversely, wages tend to fall when the supply of labor increases or the demand for labor decreases. When the number of people seeking jobs exceeds the quantity demanded, employers can offer lower wages and still find people who are willing to work.

Immigration can play a role in increasing the labor supply and lowering wage rates. In recent decades, competition for jobs from new immigrants has helped to depress wages at the lower end of the labor market. That is one reason why many less-skilled workers oppose increased immigration.

The labor supply is also affected by the tradeoff between work and leisure. When wages are low, people may be less inclined to work and more inclined to pursue other activities. When wages are high, however, workers tend to sacrifice leisure activities in favor of work.

In making such decisions, people are following the costs-versus-benefits principle. For example, suppose you plan to spend time with your friends one afternoon when a neighbor offers you a job cleaning her garage. If she were to offer $5 for an afternoon of work, you would probably say no. But if she were to offer $100, you would probably take the job. In this case, the benefit of earning $100 would outweigh the cost of not seeing your friends.

Over time, wages tend to move toward equilibrium, the point at which the quantity of labor demanded equals the quantity of labor supplied. An **equilibrium wage** is a wage rate that results in neither a surplus nor a shortage of qualified workers. If the wage for a

---

Figure 10.3B

Comparing Equilibrium Wages

When wages reach equilibrium, the number of people willing to work at that wage equals the number of people that employers are willing to hire at that wage. That equilibrium point is generally higher in occupations that require extensive education and training.

- Note that the supply of lawyers is low relative to demand, which drives wages up.
- The supply of security guards, in contrast, is high relative to demand, which pushes wages down.

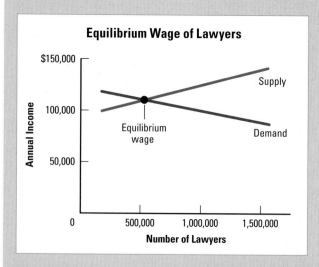

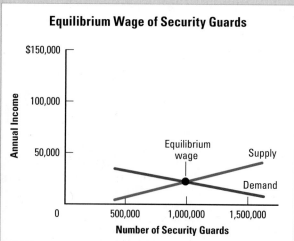

job is too high, a surplus of workers will apply for the job and employers will lower the wage. If the wage is too low, too few people will apply, and the wage will have to rise to attract more workers. Only when the wage reaches equilibrium will demand and supply be in balance.

The graphs in Figure 10.3B show equilibrium wages for two occupations: lawyer and security guard. The wages for these jobs differ for two main reasons. First, the skill level and training required of lawyers is much greater than that required of security guards. Lawyers invest a great deal of time and money in their education. Therefore the supply of lawyers is smaller than the supply of security guards. The second reason is that lawyers perform a higher-value service than security guards do. People are willing to pay more for a lawyer than a security guard. Since the lawyer's labor is more highly valued, the labor warrants a higher wage.

Other Factors that Affect Wages

A number of other factors can also affect wages, including minimum wage laws, working conditions, and cost of living.

Minimum wage laws. Minimum wage laws passed by the federal and state governments can raise wages for low-skill jobs above the equilibrium level. State minimum wage rates vary and may differ from the federal rate. Most workers qualify for the minimum wage, but exceptions exist. Workers who do not qualify include people who are self-employed, such as babysitters and newspaper carriers, and the employees of very small businesses. Around half of all Americans who earn the minimum wage are young workers between the ages of 16 and 24.

Working conditions. Jobs with working conditions that are uncomfortable, stressful, or dangerous may also pay higher wages than less-demanding jobs at similar skill levels. For example, Alaskan crab-fishing crews earn more than fishing crews elsewhere, in part because working conditions are so dangerous in the seas off Alaska. Similarly, air traffic controllers work under highly stressful conditions and receive relatively high wages to compensate for that stress.

Location and cost of living. In some parts of the United States, employers may be willing to pay extra to attract qualified workers. A rural hospital, for example, may pay doctors more than a city hospital because the remote location limits the supply of doctors.

The cost of living in a region also affects wages. Living costs in California, for example, are higher than in Alabama. Wages reflect this difference. For example, software engineers in California made an

Crab fishing is one of the most lucrative but dangerous jobs in the world. Violent winter storms and subzero temperatures make working conditions perilous. To compensate for these dangers, Alaskan crab-fishing crews earn higher wages than those who fish in less hazardous waters.

© Mike Baldwin / Cornered

PAYROLL

EX

BALDWIN

*"That $20 deduction is for new benefits—
like the $10 raise you just got."*

Many jobs come with benefits in addition to a salary or wages. Such benefits usually include health insurance and paid vacation time. The rising cost of benefits is squeezing employers, who may compensate by holding down wages—or even, as this cartoon implies, rolling them back.

average of around $75,000 in 2008, compared to just over $56,000 for software engineers in Alabama.

Rising cost of fringe benefits. The cost of fringe benefits also affects wages. **Fringe benefits** are nonwage compensations offered to workers in addition to their pay. Typical benefits include health insurance, paid vacation time, and retirement plans.

The cost of such benefits has risen in recent years. Health insurance in particular has become increasingly expensive. In 1960, employers nationwide spent $23 billion on health insurance for their workers. In 2006, employers spent $537 billion on health insurance. These rising costs have helped to depress wages in some industries, as employers compensate for high health care costs by holding down wages.

Foreign competition. Competition for jobs in the global market also helps to depress wages. As more companies offshore key tasks to low-wage countries, wage rates in the United States face downward pressure. For example, many American furniture manufacturers now offshore production to low-wage

countries such as China. Faced with factory closings, furniture workers in the United States may agree to accept lower wages in order to keep their jobs.

The Wage Gap and Affirmative Action

Historically, wages have also been influenced by discrimination against certain groups in society. **Wage discrimination** occurs when some workers are paid less to do the same job as other workers because of their ethnicity, gender, or other personal characteristics.

The Civil Rights Act of 1964 outlawed discrimination based on gender, race, religion, and country of origin. Nevertheless, a **wage gap**—a difference in the wages earned by different groups in society—still exists. In 2007, for example, the median weekly income for white men working full-time was $788. For white women, the figure was $626.

A gender-based wage gap exists in every group surveyed: Asian American, white, African American, and Hispanic. Wage gaps also exist among the four groups, with Asian Americans earning the highest median salaries and Hispanics the lowest. The bar graph on the opposite page illustrates the wage gap by gender and ethnicity.

If discrimination is illegal, why does the wage gap persist? Economists attribute it in part to different levels of human capital among different groups. For example, African Americans, on average, have less education than whites and Asians. This education gap is itself a legacy of discrimination that denied blacks equal access to education for many years. Women, on average, have less job experience than men. This "experience gap" exists in part because women have only entered the labor force in large numbers in recent decades. Women are also more likely to interrupt their careers to raise children.

Even though differences in human capital contribute to the wage gap, studies show that discrimination still exists in the labor market. Many economists contend that the remedy for this problem is market competition. They argue that firms that discriminate will not be able to compete in the long run because they do not take advantage of the whole pool of qualified workers. Firms that do not discriminate will be more profitable than those that do.

Nevertheless, there are limits to the power of market forces to end discrimination. The United

The Wage Gap

The term *wage gap* is used to describe the unequal earnings of various groups in society.

- The line graph shows that the wage gap between men and women has narrowed since the 1970s. According to some economists, when the wages of men and women of similar age and background are compared, the wage gap shrinks to just a few percentage points.
- The bar graph shows the 2007 median weekly wages of men and women by ethnic group.

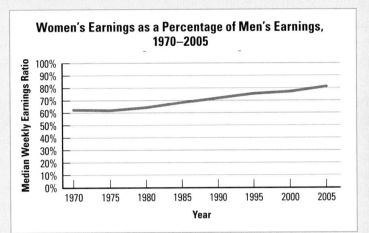

Women's Earnings as a Percentage of Men's Earnings, 1970–2005

Source: Institute for Women's Policy Research.

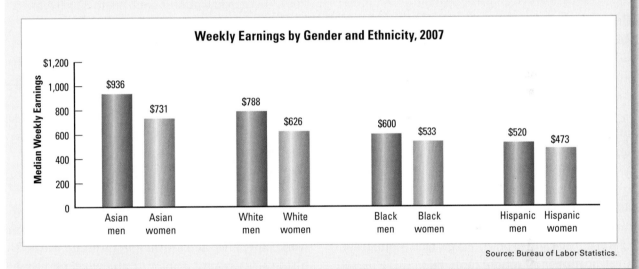

Weekly Earnings by Gender and Ethnicity, 2007

Source: Bureau of Labor Statistics.

States has antidiscrimination laws to help fill the gap. **Affirmative action** initiatives are also intended to prevent discrimination. These initiatives call on employers to take positive steps to increase the presence of historically underrepresented groups in employment, education, and business.

Affirmative action policies have aroused controversy. This is especially true for policies that give preferential treatment to women and minorities. This type of affirmative action has come under attack from critics who say it discriminates against white males. In a series of landmark cases, the U.S. Supreme Court has narrowly upheld affirmative action in such areas as college admissions. But the debate continues as to whether affirmative action is the appropriate means to achieve equal opportunity for all.

■ 10.4 How Can You Increase Your Human Capital?

Though she probably did not realize it at the time, Catherine Winters took a major step toward a career when she got involved with Second Life. The skills she developed through Second Life expanded her human capital and eventually led to a steady job. Developing one's human capital is the key to success in the job market. But how does a person go about doing that?

The Starting Point: Aptitudes, Interests, and Aspirations

Developing your human capital is a lifelong pursuit. It continues as long as you are expanding your skills, experience, and knowledge.

The first step in building your human capital is to identify your aptitudes, interests, and aspirations. In other words, start by thinking about what you are good at, what you like to do, and what you hope to accomplish in your working life.

This assessment can only be done through honest self-evaluation. It is important to be realistic about your skills and abilities, but it is also important to pursue your dreams. It is not always easy to assess yourself. Fortunately, there are some tools that can help. Career counselors can offer useful advice and help steer you in the right direction. Many self-help books focus on helping readers to find and develop a career path. Aptitude tests and skills inventories can also help you analyze your abilities and interests.

Becoming Qualified:
Education, Certification, and Licensing

Education is one of the main routes to developing human capital. A good general education gives you many tools for success in the working world. A more advanced education will help you progress even further. There are many ways to advance your education beyond high school. Besides the traditional four-year college or university, there are community colleges, technical institutes, job-training programs, and online courses.

Higher education may also qualify you for certification or licensing to practice a particular profession. **Certification** is an official recognition that a person is qualified in his or her field. In some professions, certification is required by law. Teachers, for example, must be state certified to teach in public schools. Doctors must pass state licensing exams to practice medicine. In other fields, certification is voluntary. However, certification is usually recommended as a way for aspiring professionals to show their competence and commitment to their field.

Education will also help you earn more money. The difference in wages paid to high school and college graduates has grown over the years. In general, wages are rising faster for more educated, more skilled workers than for less educated, less skilled workers. In 1980, men with college degrees earned an average of 44 percent more than men without degrees. By 2003, this gap had almost doubled, to 82 percent.

The value of a college degree is increasing for several reasons. As U.S. businesses seek a comparative advantage in the global economy, the demand for well-educated knowledge workers is growing. Many employers believe that a college education makes workers more productive. Others see a college degree as a sign of motivation and general ability. Either way, a college degree serves as a screening device that employers can use to identify high-value employees.

Gaining Work Experience and On-the-Job Training

Another way to build your human capital is through work experience and on-the-job training. When hiring new workers, employers often look for people

All states require certification or a license to practice certain professions. After graduating from nursing school, this registered nurse had to pass a national licensing exam to get a job. Licensing exams help ensure that people in certain professions are competent in their fields.

Building Human Capital

Building your human capital is a lifelong project. This illustration shows how a young person might develop the human capital needed to land a job as an emergency medical technician (EMT).

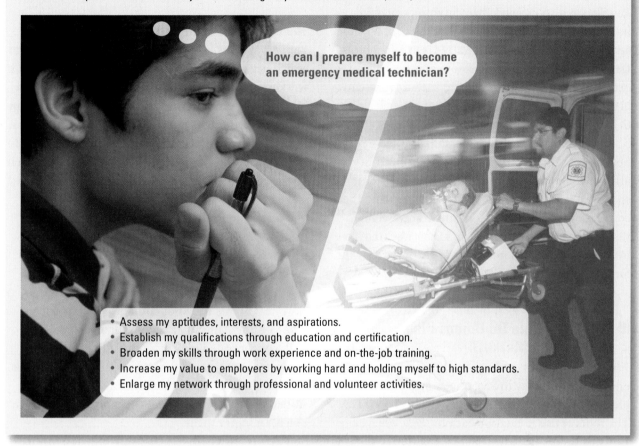

How can I prepare myself to become an emergency medical technician?

- Assess my aptitudes, interests, and aspirations.
- Establish my qualifications through education and certification.
- Broaden my skills through work experience and on-the-job training.
- Increase my value to employers by working hard and holding myself to high standards.
- Enlarge my network through professional and volunteer activities.

who have significant experience and have developed useful job skills. The importance of work experience explains why wages tend to rise the longer a person has been in the labor force.

Of course, getting a job can be difficult when you lack work experience in the first place. But it is not impossible. Some employers prefer to hire people they can train on the job. A restaurant, for example, might hire a cook trainee who would start out doing low-level kitchen tasks. Over time, a cook trainee would learn how the kitchen works and how to prepare items on the menu. For a trainee who is dependable and willing to work hard, on-the-job training can be the first step on a career path.

Another way to get a job when you have no experience is to seek out an entry-level position in a field that interests you. Typically, entry-level jobs—such as office assistant and sales assistant—do not pay much.

But they can provide valuable experience and allow you to start building a work history. By starting at the bottom, you show your willingness to work and to gain the experience and skills you need to move up the job ladder.

Increasing Personal Productivity: Effort and High Standards

The level of energy and enthusiasm that workers bring to a job also increases their value to employers. The workers who stand out are often those who make the greatest effort and hold themselves to the highest standards.

In some jobs, workers are rewarded based on how much they produce. This is true in many sales jobs, for example, where people work on commission and earn a percentage of everything they sell. Other jobs may pay year-end bonuses or offer salary increases based on worker productivity. In either case, workers enhance their job opportunities by making the effort to work hard and excel at what they do.

Building a Personal-Professional Network

People can also develop their human capital by building a personal-professional network of friends and colleagues. One way to do this is to join a professional association, labor union, or other type of occupational group. Belonging to such a group can help people develop work contacts and create a sense of community in their chosen field.

Other ways of building a personal-professional network include getting involved in community affairs, volunteering, or participating in a local sports team. Such activities help people expand their connections within the community. These connections can have positive effects on their working lives by creating new job contacts and new opportunities for professional growth.

◼ 10.5 What Role Do Unions Play in the Labor Market?

On the first Monday in September, many of us attend picnics and other events associated with Labor Day. The roots of this holiday go back to 1882, when labor organizers in New York City held a parade to celebrate the role of workers in American life. The celebration became an annual event and soon spread to other cities. In 1894, Congress passed a law making Labor Day an official national holiday.

The Origins of the Union Movement

Labor Day owes its existence to the union movement, which began in the late 1800s. At the time, many U.S. workers suffered from harsh working conditions in factories and mines. They worked long hours for low pay, often in unhealthy or dangerous circumstances. If workers complained, they were likely to be fired. In response, workers formed unions to help protect their interests. These early unions were relatively small and lacked the power to negotiate with factory owners.

In the late 1800s, however, small unions began to join together to form larger labor federations. The first such federation was the Knights of Labor. Founded in 1869, it brought together both skilled and unskilled workers.

The Knights of Labor soon faced competitors. One was the American Federation of Labor. The AFL concentrated mainly on organizing skilled workers. Another was the Industrial Workers of the World. The IWW sought to unite all workers, both skilled and unskilled, under the motto "an injury to one is an injury to all."

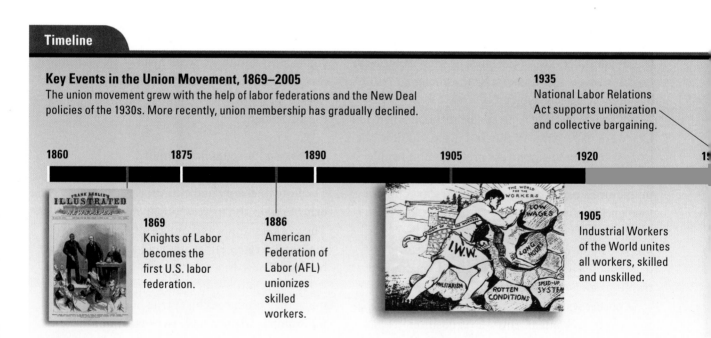

Timeline

Key Events in the Union Movement, 1869–2005
The union movement grew with the help of labor federations and the New Deal policies of the 1930s. More recently, union membership has gradually declined.

1935
National Labor Relations Act supports unionization and collective bargaining.

1860   1875   1890   1905   1920   19

1869
Knights of Labor becomes the first U.S. labor federation.

1886
American Federation of Labor (AFL) unionizes skilled workers.

1905
Industrial Workers of the World unites all workers, skilled and unskilled.

Speaking for their members with one voice, union leaders bargained with employers for better pay and working conditions. If negotiations failed, unions called on workers to strike. During a strike, workers refused to work until their demands were met.

Employers fiercely resisted the union movement. Some used their influence with government officials to block union organizing. Others required employees to sign **yellow-dog contracts,** which prohibited workers from joining unions. Employers responded to strikes by hiring strikebreakers to force the strikers back to work.

The Golden Age of Labor Unions

Despite setbacks, the union movement continued to grow. During the Great Depression of the 1930s, unions enjoyed their greatest success under the New Deal policies of President Franklin D. Roosevelt.

At the president's urging, Congress passed the National Labor Relations Act in 1935. Also known as the Wagner Act, this law guaranteed workers "the right to self-organization, to form, join, or assist labor organizations, [and] to bargain collectively through representatives of their own choosing." The law also permitted closed shops. A **closed shop** is a business that will only hire workers who are union members.

Gaining the right to "bargain collectively" was a breakthrough for unions. **Collective bargaining** is a process in which workers, represented by their union, negotiate with employers for better wages and working conditions. The Wagner Act required employers to bargain in "good faith."

The Wagner Act ushered in a "golden age" of labor unionism. During this period, union membership increased and workers enjoyed rising pay and benefits. Encouraged by such success, several large unions came together in 1938 to form a new labor federation, the Congress of Industrial Organizations. The CIO would later merge with the AFL to create the AFL-CIO.

By the late 1940s, however, many in business and government felt that the Wagner Act had gone too far in empowering labor unions. In 1947, Congress passed the Taft-Hartley Act to rein in the unions. This law outlawed the closed shop and placed limits on the power of unions to organize and strike. It did, however, allow union shops. In a **union shop,** workers are required to join the union after being hired.

The Taft-Hartley Act also permitted states to pass **right-to-work laws**. These laws make it illegal to require workers to join a union as a condition of their employment. In effect, right-to-work laws ban the union shop. Currently there are some 20 **right-to-work states**. Most are located in the South and West.

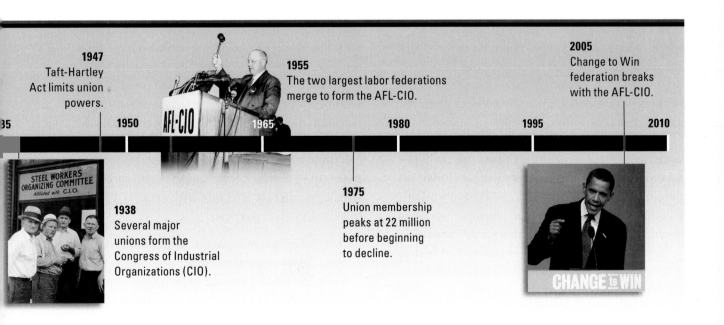

1947
Taft-Hartley Act limits union powers.

1955
The two largest labor federations merge to form the AFL-CIO.

2005
Change to Win federation breaks with the AFL-CIO.

35   1950   AFL-CIO   1965   1980   1995   2010

1938
Several major unions form the Congress of Industrial Organizations (CIO).

1975
Union membership peaks at 22 million before beginning to decline.

CHANGE TO WIN

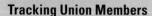

Figure 10.5

Tracking Union Members

As the line graph shows, the percentage of American workers who belong to unions rose and then fell over the past century. The circle graph shows the percentage of union members employed in various parts of the economy in 2006.

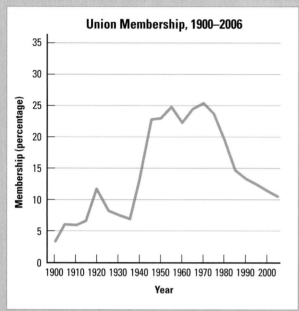

Source: Harold W. Stanley and Richard G. Niemi, *Vital Statistics on American Politics 2007–2008,* Washington, D.C.: CQ Press, 2008.

Sources: AFL/CIO. Bureau of Labor Statistics.

The Modern Union Movement

Despite the restrictions of the Taft-Hartley Act, the number of union members continued to increase into the 1970s. Union membership peaked at more than 22 million in 1975. But by then, as the line graph in Figure 10.5 shows, union membership as a percentage of the total labor force had begun to decline. In 1970, one out of every four American workers belonged to a union. By 2006, that number was closer to one in ten.

The profile of union members has also changed since the 1970s. A generation or two ago, the typical union member was a factory worker. Today, as the circle graph in Figure 10.5 shows, that worker is more likely to be a government employee, such as a teacher or a police officer, than a factory worker.

Economists cite a number of reasons for the drop in union membership. One is the loss of manufacturing jobs and the rise of service industries. Historically, service workers have been difficult to organize. Women, who make up an increasing share of the

labor force, have been less inclined to join unions. In addition, the government now guarantees many of the rights unions once had to fight for, such as workplace safety and an eight-hour workday. Also, polls show that less than 10 percent of workers are dissatisfied with their jobs. The great majority also have a strong sense of loyalty to the companies they work for.

In a bid to reverse the downward trend in union membership, seven major unions representing 6 million members broke away from the AFL-CIO in 2005. They then joined forces to create the Change to Win federation. This new labor federation is largely made up of service-sector unions that represent female, immigrant, and minority workers. Change to Win says of its purpose,

Our mission is to unite the 50 million workers in . . . industries whose jobs cannot be out-sourced and who are vital to the global economy. We seek to secure the American Dream for them, and for all *working people.*

Bread-and-Butter Unionism Today: Wages, Benefits, and Job Security

To reach its goal of expanding union membership, Change to Win is concentrating on **bread-and-butter unionism**. This means focusing on the economic issues that affect workers' daily lives. Change to Win summarizes these issues as "a paycheck that can support a family, affordable health care, a secure retirement and dignity on the job."

By focusing on these bread-and-butter issues, unions perform a vital function for many American workers. They work to secure better pay and improved benefits for their members. They try to save workers' jobs when companies engage in outsourcing and offshoring. They provide information to workers about their rights as employees. Some unions provide training to help workers improve their job skills. By helping to build human capital in this way, unions not only provide benefits to their members, but also to the organizations that employ them.

This brings us back to the question we began with: *Why is it important to develop your human capital?* The answer is both simple and complex. Human capital is one of the most important factors that determine a worker's value in the labor market. But human capital is not a simple set of skills. It also encompasses aptitudes, knowledge, experience, motivation, energy, and attitude. As you prepare to enter the labor market, remember that your human capital is your most valuable resource. The more you develop it now, the more success you will enjoy in the world of work.

Summary

Changes in the labor market are having an effect on the jobs and wages available to American workers. As the labor market evolves, it becomes more important than ever for workers to develop their human capital.

What trends are shaping today's labor market? An influx of women and minorities has changed the labor force in recent decades. In addition, job growth has shifted from manufacturing to the service sector, and knowledge workers have become increasingly important. Globalization is also having an impact as foreign trade and competition have increased both the offshoring and inshoring of jobs.

What determines how much workers earn? Wage rates reflect various factors in the labor market. Wages primarily depend on the skill level of workers and the value of what they produce. Like the price of goods and services, wages are set by supply and demand. Wage rates move toward equilibrium as the demand for workers with the skills needed for a given job and the supply of such workers come into balance.

What can you do to increase your human capital? The first step to increasing your human capital is to identify your abilities, interests, and goals. After that, get the education you will need to meet any licensing or certification requirements. Other key steps include gaining work experience, holding yourself to high performance standards, and building a network of friends and colleagues.

What role do unions play in the labor market? Historically, unions have helped workers defend their rights and improve their pay and working conditions. Although union membership has declined in recent decades, unions today are still helping many workers achieve concrete gains in the workplace.

*Who decides
how much money
superstar athletes
should make?*

Every year, superstar athletes earn millions of dollars playing professional sports. They also rake in big money from commercial endorsements, appearing in ads for everything from luxury cars to snack foods. Where does all this money come from? The ultimate answer is from the fans who buy tickets to sporting events, watch sports on television, and buy the products superstar athletes endorse.

This article analyzes the economics of superstar salaries. As you read, ask yourself, Who decides how much an athlete gets paid? Team owners? Advertisers? Or ordinary fans like you?

The Pro Sports Labor Market

By the Federal Reserve Bank of Boston

Top sports stars are earning more money than top surgeons, and *average* ballplayers are signing multi-million dollar contracts. Has the world gone mad?

Well, believe it or not, the sports labor market is not as crazy as it seems. Team owners who shell out big bucks for superstars are acting rationally. (Whether or not they always spend their money wisely is another question.)

And superstars, who make more in one month than many fans earn in a lifetime, are sometimes underpaid.

Is Anyone Worth *That* Much Money? . . .

Why do pro athletes make so much money?

The answer, once again, is related to supply and demand. Only this time, it's supply and demand in the labor market. Players are selling their skills and talents; team owners are the prospective buyers.

The players' skills and talents—their labor inputs—are in great demand. Why? Because fans are willing to pay top dollar for a chance to see the world's best players at work, and that produces tremendous revenue for team owners.

Rule Number One in the Sports Labor Market: When it comes to salaries, no profit-oriented owner will knowingly pay more than a player is expected to generate in revenue . . .

Yes, owners and general managers sometimes misjudge a player's talent or throw away big money on a player who isn't right for the team. But here's the bottom line: An owner will pay a player millions of dollars only if he or she thinks the player will bring the team even more than that in revenues . . .

Five Things that Affect Salaries

The basics of the sports labor market are pretty straightforward: Owners (buyers) make salary offers based on how much revenue they think a player will add to the team. And players (sellers) make salary decisions based on what they think their talents are worth on the labor market.

But there are a few other points to keep in mind:

1. Demand for pro athletes—especially superstars—has been fairly inelastic. That's

In 2007, home-run hitter **Alex Rodriguez** signed a contract with the New York Yankees worth $275 million over 10 years. He was promised $30 million more if he breaks the all-time home run record of 762.

While still a teenager in 2007, **Michelle Wie** made $23,000 as a professional golfer. But she earned $19.5 million in endorsements.

Star quarterback **Carson Palmer** signed a nine-year contract with the Cincinnati Bengals in 2005 worth nearly $119 million.

LeBron James earned $13 million playing basketball during the 2007–2008 season. He took in another $25 million in endorsements.

By early 2008, **Dale Earnhardt Jr.** had earned more than $42 million as a professional race car driver. He took in another $25 million in 2007 in endorsements.

Sisters **Venus** and **Serena Williams** joined the professional tennis circuit in the mid-1990s. By 2008, each had earned more than $18 million.

partly because there are no readily acceptable substitutes for pro athletes. In most businesses, owners can automate certain jobs. Team owners don't have that option. Maybe a computer can defeat a chess master, but how many computers or robots can hit a big league curveball? (And even if they could, would you really buy a season ticket to watch them do it?)

Human substitutes don't fill the need either. Major League Baseball and the National Football League tried to end labor disputes by hiring replacement players, but the replacement product did not meet the standard of quality that fans expected from a professional team. Hardly anyone showed up for the replacement games—even after owners slashed ticket prices.

2. The decisions that buyers and sellers make will help to determine the level of market prices (or salaries). When a team owner decides to pay a small fortune to a star shortstop, you can bet that other shortstops with similar statistics will be looking for more money when contract time rolls around. Every new blockbuster contract changes the labor market.

3. The supply of players isn't as big as it seems. There are thousands, maybe even millions, of people willing to supply their talents and skills in the sports labor market. But the number of people who even come close to possessing the required level of skill is much smaller—and they are the people that teams are actually competing for.

4. The number of buyers and sellers influences the level of competition in any market. When sports leagues expand, they also increase competition in the sports labor market. The number of teams (buyers) increases, but the number of top players (sellers) remains the same. It's a simple equation: League expansion = Greater demand for players = Stiffer competition for top talent = Higher salaries for superstars.

5. Market size has an impact on how much a player earns. All other things being equal, players who spend their most productive years in "big markets" like New York or Los Angeles will almost always earn more than players who spend their careers in "small markets" like San Diego or Cincinnati.

Underpaid Superstars?
Every big money entertainment business runs on star power. Sports is no exception.

Superstars earn high salaries because they generate lots of revenue for their teams. They are the players fans pay to see —marquee players who draw spectators to games through a combination of exceptional talent and a certain "star quality" that is hard to define but easy to spot. Without them, pro sports would be less exciting and less lucrative.

Nevertheless, lots of people shake their heads over the super size of superstar salaries. And if you are one of those people, this next part will really have you talking to yourself:

If the market for professional athletes were perfectly competitive, superstars could probably earn more than they already do.

Two things prevent superstar salaries from being even higher than they are:

1. The Amateur Draft— Every year, pro teams "draft" (choose) the best college and high school athletes. The draft gives a team "exclusive rights" to a player for a certain number of years, and teams with the worst records get to choose first.

The system is intended to prevent rich teams from signing all the best young prospects. But it also prevents players from shopping around for a higher salary until after they've spent the required number of years with the team that drafted them.

2. The Limited Number of Buyers for a Player's Services—The professional sports labor market has a relatively small number of buyers. In fact, it comes very close to being a monopsony market—a market with only one buyer. Players in each professional sports league have only three choices:

- Sell their services to one of the teams in the league;
- Play for a team in an overseas league; or
- Look for some other type of work.

Owners may fret over the high cost of attracting and keeping top talent, but the fact is that they are parting with their money willingly—if not always cheerfully or wisely—and they never pay more than they expect a superstar to generate in revenue.

In a sense, high salaries are a measure of how prosperous sports have become. If teams didn't have the money, they couldn't afford to pay as much as they do.

Economics of the Public Sector

Chapter 11

How should the U.S. government carry out its economic roles?

Government and the Economy

11.1 Introduction

When you woke up this morning, did you think to yourself, "What is the government going to do for me today?" Probably not. If you are like most high school students, you probably did not think about the government at all this morning. But the government was there. The time log that follows will give you an idea of just how involved the government is in our everyday lives.

6:30 A.M. The clock radio comes on—too early, as always. As you slowly wake up, a song ends and you hear the news begin. "The government has just announced new regulations," the reporter says, "to protect investors against phishing, a form of e-mail fraud."

6:45 A.M. By the time you are up and dressed, the news is over and the radio is back to music. The music comes through loud and clear, thanks largely to a government agency that assigns a separate frequency to each radio station. Otherwise a competing broadcaster using the exact same spot on the radio dial might drown out your station.

6:50 A.M. Still bleary eyed, you stumble into the kitchen to fix breakfast. You put water on to boil while you scramble a couple of eggs. The government is right beside you as you cook. The water that flows from the tap has been analyzed by your local water department to be sure it is safe to drink. Government inspectors made sure the eggs were produced and

Government is involved in many aspects of our everyday lives.

regulation
The establishment, by the government, of rules aimed at influencing the behavior of firms and individuals. Regulation can involve setting prices, establishing product and workplace standards, and limiting entry into an industry.

eminent domain
The power of a government to take an individual's property for public use if the owner is fairly compensated.

regulatory agency
A unit of government created to set and enforce standards for a particular industry or area of economic activity.

merger
The combining of two or more separately owned firms into a single firm.

deregulation
The process of removing government restrictions on firms in order to promote competition or encourage economic activity.

common resource
A resource that everyone has access to and that can easily be overused or destroyed. Examples include the atmosphere and the oceans.

government failure
Inefficient allocation of resources caused by government intervention in the economy.

poverty rate
The percentage of the population that has a family income below a government-defined threshold, or poverty line.

packaged in a way designed to minimize the presence of harmful bacteria.

7:00 A.M. Your grandmother joins you at the kitchen table with the morning paper. She shows you an article announcing an increase in Social Security benefits due to rising living costs. Her pension from the federal government will go up starting next month.

7:06 A.M. As you wait for the school bus, you notice that some potholes in the road have been filled. A paving company hired by the state government has been busy making street repairs.

7:10 A.M. Your bus finally arrives. It is very quiet, and it does not smell of diesel fumes. Your local school district has invested in several battery-powered school buses, and you are lucky enough to ride in one.

7:30 A.M. You reach your destination, a public high school funded by your national, state, and local governments. Governments support public education in part because an educated workforce is key to a productive economy.

Your morning has barely begun, and yet government at every level has already provided you with a multitude of services. In this chapter, you will learn more about the widely accepted roles that the government plays in our market-based economy. You will also explore how the government's intervention affects your life and the lives of all Americans.

■ 11.2 How Does the Government Protect Property Rights?

Government clearly plays a big role in our economic lives. Is this role too big? Many Americans would say it is. But Charles Wheelan disagrees.

> *Good government makes a market economy possible. Period. And bad government, or no government, dashes capitalism against the rocks, which is one reason that billions of people live in dire poverty around the globe.*
> —Charles Wheelan, *Naked Economics: Undressing the Dismal Science,* 2002

Without a doubt, capitalism is alive and well in the United States. But is that because of government involvement or in spite of it?

The Constitutional Basis for Government Involvement in the Economy

The power of the federal government to intervene in the economy comes straight out of Article I of the U.S. Constitution. Among the economic powers that this article grants to Congress are

- to lay and collect taxes.
- to provide for the general welfare.
- to borrow money.
- to regulate interstate and foreign commerce.
- to establish uniform bankruptcy laws.
- to coin money and regulate its value.
- to fix the standard of weights and measures.
- to protect the writings and discoveries of authors and inventors.

Exercising its constitutional powers, the federal government establishes laws and rules designed to influence economic behavior in desirable ways. This process is called **regulation**. All modern government regulation is ultimately based on the powers granted in the Constitution.

Government's Role in Protecting Property Rights

The Constitution lays the foundation for a legal system that protects property rights. We often think of property as land, personal possessions, and other physical assets. But property can also refer to inventions and various forms of expression, also known as intellectual property. No matter what form property takes, property rights entitle the owner to determine how it is used.

Economists argue that protecting property rights is essential for our free enterprise system to flourish. Why? Because incentives matter. Ownership of property creates a number of incentives that promote economic progress, including the three listed here.

Private ownership encourages people to take care of their property. If private owners fail to maintain their property, they are the people who suffer. For example, if you own a house, you have a strong incentive to fix the roof if it leaks. Otherwise the value of your house will decrease.

Private ownership encourages people to make the most productive use of their property. It is in the best interest of owners to use their property in the most productive ways possible. The owner of a farm,

As the incentives-matter principle reminds us, people are motivated to act in ways that promote their well-being. This homeowner has a strong incentive to keep her house in good repair. The value of her home, which may be her most valuable asset, depends in part on how well it has been maintained.

for example, has every incentive to plant crops that make the best use of local soil and climate conditions.

Private ownership encourages people to develop their property in ways that benefit others. Under the law, owners can do whatever they want with their property. But they have the potential to gain by making what they own useful to others. Consider the owners of a health club. Personally, they may have no interest in anything but weight training. Nonetheless, they might decide to offer childcare, nutrition counseling, and spa services to attract more members. By enhancing their health club in ways that benefit others, the owners stand to benefit by increasing the property's value.

Property rights are so basic to our free enterprise system that the government is empowered by the Constitution to protect them. One institution that protects property rights is the court system, sometimes assisted by police forces. Another is the U.S. Patent and Trademark Office (USPTO). This federal government agency protects intellectual property, or property in the form of ideas that have commercial value. It does so by issuing patents, copyrights, and trademarks.

Key Concept

Property Rights

Owners of private property enjoy a number of rights. The three most important are (1) the right to exclusive use of their property, (2) the right to legal protection against trespassers or abusers of their property, and (3) the right to sell or trade their property. These rights give property owners a wide range of options regarding the care and use of their property.

Lend Trade Neglect Own Insure Destroy Enjoy Consume Protect Sell Use Occupy

Eminent domain is the government's right to take private property for public use. In 2005, the Supreme Court ruled that private developers could obtain land through eminent domain as long as their redevelopment pitted projects had public benefits. But do such projects qualify as a public use? Not according to this cartoonist.

An Exception to Property Rights: Eminent Domain

Our nation's founders took property rights seriously. During the Constitutional Convention in 1787, Gouverneur Morris of New York echoed the sentiments of most delegates when he described property as "the main object of Society." Still, the delegates recognized that at times, the government must take private property for a public use, such as the building of a road or courthouse. The government does this through the power of eminent domain.

Eminent domain is the power to force the transfer of property from a private owner to the government for a public purpose. This power existed long before the United States was founded. But the Fifth Amendment to the Constitution added a new element—paying the private owner for property taken under eminent domain. The **Takings Clause** of the Fifth Amendment states,

> No person shall be . . . deprived of life, liberty, or property, without due process of law; nor shall private property be taken for public use, without just compensation.

In 2005, the meaning of *public use* was called into question by a controversial Supreme Court decision. The case before the Court was *Kelo v. City of New London,* which pitted residents of a run-down section of New London, Connecticut, against the city government. The city wanted to use its power of eminent domain to take the residents' property, including land, homes, and businesses, for economic redevelopment.

New London's taking of private property for redevelopment was not unprecedented. In earlier decisions, the Supreme Court had decided that the redevelopment of depressed areas had public benefits that justified a government's use of eminent domain. However, New London did not plan to use the land it had acquired for public projects, such as schools or a civic center. Instead, it intended to turn the land over to private developers who planned to build a hotel, offices, and condominiums on the site for profit.

The city argued that the economic growth that this private development would bring to New London was a public benefit. Some residents who faced the loss of their property disagreed. They argued that the government's taking of their homes and businesses for the benefit of a private developer was not a public use.

In its decision on *Kelo,* the Supreme Court sided with the city. A 5-to-4 majority held that the benefits of economic redevelopment do qualify as public use within the meaning of the Fifth Amendment. Justice Sandra Day O'Connor was one of the four justices who did not agree with the majority. In her dissenting opinion, she wrote that the effect of this decision was "to wash out any distinction between private and public use of property—and thereby effectively to delete the words 'for public use' from the Takings Clause of the Fifth Amendment."

The Supreme Court's decision in *Kelo* provoked a nationwide storm of protest. In response, many states passed laws designed to protect property rights by limiting the use of eminent domain for economic development.

■ 11.3 What Regulatory Roles Does Government Play in Our Economy?

Securing property rights is an important role for government in our economy, but it is not the only role. The federal government is involved in many aspects of the economy by setting and enforcing standards for dozens of industries. Through this regulation, the government seeks to protect the interests of all participants in the economy. One way government does this is by ensuring that markets are competitive.

Government's Role in Maintaining Competition

Like property rights, competition is essential if markets are going to work the way they are supposed to work. The pressures of competition force producers to use resources efficiently, to develop new or better products, and to keep products and services affordable. Because competition is vital to the economy, the government acts to maintain competition when markets fail to do so.

The government's main guardian of competition is the Justice Department. This cabinet-level department, through its Antitrust Division, enforces the antitrust laws that Congress has enacted over the years. It often works closely with the Federal Trade Commission. The FTC is a **regulatory agency**—a unit of government that makes and enforces standards for an industry or area of economic activity.

As modern-day trustbusters, the Justice Department and the FTC prohibit practices that restrict competition. When they uncover such practices, they take the offending companies to court. Successful prosecution can lead to fines and jail sentences for the guilty parties. These illegal practices include the following:

Price fixing. The illegal practice of **price fixing** occurs when competitors agree on a price for a good or service. Price fixing can take many forms, from adopting a formula for computing prices to setting a minimum fee for services.

Bid rigging. Purchasers—including federal, state, and local governments—often acquire goods and services by seeking bids from competing firms. **Bid rigging** occurs when competitors agree in advance who will submit the winning bid. That bid, which is the lowest bid, will still be higher than it would have been in a competitive market. Firms that engage in bid rigging may take turns being the low bidder on a series of contracts.

Market division. The tactic known as **market division** occurs when competitors agree to divide a market among themselves. In one type of scheme, each competitor sells to only certain customers. In another, each competitor sells in only certain geographic areas.

The Justice Department and the FTC also monitor **mergers,** in which two separately owned firms combine into one firm. A merger is illegal if it will substantially lessen competition or tend to create a monopoly.

The government does allow some natural monopolies to exist. A natural monopoly arises when a single firm can supply a product more efficiently than multiple competing firms can. The American

After much study, the Justice Department approved the merger of the XM and Sirius satellite radio networks in 2008. The merger was criticized by many who argued that it gave the new company, Sirius XM Radio, Inc., a monopoly over satellite radio programming. "There are other alternatives out there," answered a Justice Department spokesperson. "We just simply found that the evidence didn't indicate that it would harm consumers."

Telephone and Telegraph Company, better known as AT&T, was once a natural monopoly. In the mid-1900s, it controlled the vast majority of the nation's telephone services.

In the 1970s, however, the Justice Department took action to break up AT&T's monopoly. After a lengthy lawsuit, the company agreed to spin off seven separate regional phone companies, which became known as Baby Bells. AT&T continued to provide long-distance telephone services. Figure 11.3A shows how the Baby Bells later merged into three much larger telecommunication companies.

Government's Role in Protecting Consumers, Savers, and Investors

Caveat emptor. This long-standing rule of the marketplace is Latin for "Let the buyer beware." It serves as a warning to buyers that they purchase goods and services at their own risk. But in today's complex market, buyers may not have all the information they need to make sound judgments about products. Instead, they have come to rely on regulatory agencies to provide such information. Consumers, savers, and investors also look to such agencies to ensure that products are safe and dependable.

Figure 11.3A

Analyzing the Breakup of AT&T

AT&T held a natural monopoly on telephone service until it was broken up into AT&T and seven regional "Baby Bells" in 1984. Over time, the remnants of that breakup pieced themselves back together. By 2006, two companies—Verizon and the "new AT&T"—dominated the telecommunications industry.

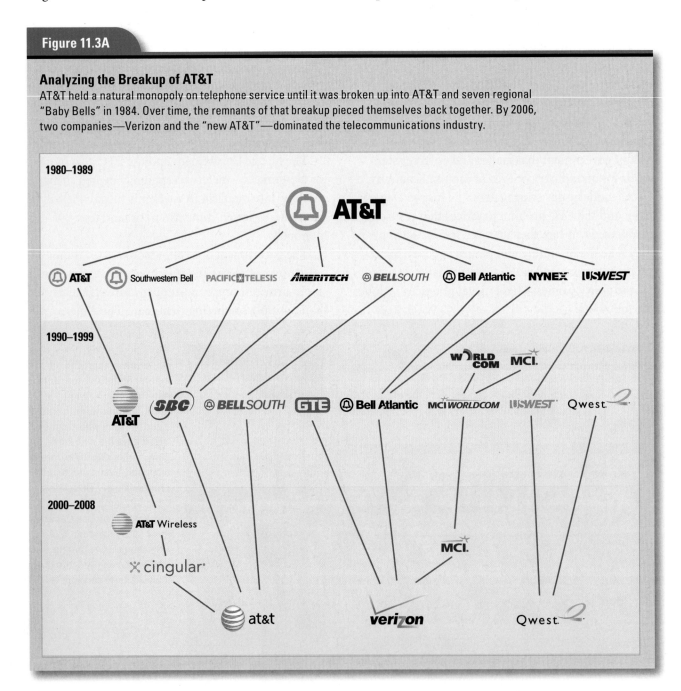

Protecting consumers. Regulation to protect consumers began in the early 1900s. One of the first targets of government regulators was the meatpacking industry. Upton Sinclair, in his novel *The Jungle,* described what went on in meatpacking plants.

> *There was never the least attention paid to what was cut up for sausage . . . There would be meat that had tumbled out on the floor, in the dirt and sawdust, where the workers had tramped and spit . . . meat stored in great piles in rooms; and the water from leaky roofs would drip over it, and thousands of rats would race about on it . . . These rats were nuisances, and the packers would put poisoned bread out for them; they would die, and then rats, bread, and meat would go into the hoppers together.*
> —Upton Sinclair, *The Jungle,* 1906

Thanks in part to Sinclair's stomach-turning prose, Congress passed both the Meat Inspection Act and the Pure Food and Drug Act in 1906. This legislation paved the way for a new regulatory agency, now known as the Food and Drug Administration. The FDA oversees the testing and approval of drugs before they go on the market.

Another wave of consumer regulation began in 1965, triggered by Ralph Nader's book *Unsafe at Any Speed.* Nader claimed that automobiles were unsafe and that the auto industry resisted making cars safer because of the added cost. The next year, Congress passed legislation requiring automakers to install seat belts in all cars. This law led to the creation of an agency to set safety standards for automobiles, the National Highway Traffic Safety Administration.

In 1972, Congress created the Consumer Product Safety Commission to protect Americans against undue risks associated with consumer products. This agency now sets standards for more than 15,000 products, from toys to lawn mowers.

Protecting savers and investors. Of the many banking-related agencies, the Federal Deposit Insurance Corporation may have the most direct role in protecting savers. The FDIC insures nearly all bank deposits for up to $100,000 per depositor.

The Securities and Exchange Commission protects investors by making sure they have the information they need to judge whether to buy, sell, or hold a

In 1965, Ralph Nader's book *Unsafe at Any Speed* spurred Congress to enact safety standards for cars and other vehicles and to establish the National Highway Traffic Safety Administration. Air bags later became a safety feature in cars and even on some motorcycles.

particular security. The SEC establishes and enforces rules to ensure that companies provide that information in a timely and accurate manner.

Such regulatory agencies allow Americans to feel confident when transacting business with total strangers. As the president of a Federal Reserve Bank once observed,

> *It seems remarkable, when you think about it, that we often take substantial amounts of money to our bank and hand it over to people we have never met before. Or, that securities traders can send millions of dollars to people they don't know in countries they have never been in. Yet this occurs all the time. We trust that . . . the person at the bank who takes our money doesn't just pocket it. Or that when we use our credit cards to buy a new CD or tennis racquet over the Internet, from a business that is located in some other state or country, we are confident we will get our merchandise, and they are confident they will get paid.*
> —Jerry Jordan, 2000

The Occupational Safety and Heath Administration monitors workplaces to protect workers from accidents and injuries. According to OSHA, since its founding in 1971, the administration has helped to cut fatal accidents in the workplace by more than 60 percent. OSHA has also been instrumental in reducing workplace illnesses and accidents by 40 percent.

Government's Role in Protecting Workers

The federal government safeguards the interests of workers through the Department of Labor. One of DOL's primary aims is to protect workers' economic rights. It does this by making sure workers get the wages due to them, fostering workplaces that are free of discrimination, and providing unemployment insurance.

Another goal of DOL is protecting workers' physical well-being. To ensure safe and secure workplaces, DOL relies mainly on the Occupational Safety and Health Administration. OSHA sets safety and health standards for industries. When you see construction workers wearing hard hats or highway workers wearing reflective vests, you can be sure OSHA standards are involved. Since OSHA was established in 1971, workplace fatalities have decreased by more than 60 percent and injury rates by 40 percent.

The Perils of Government Regulation

Regulatory agencies are a little like referees. Their role is to make sure that firms play by the rules and that individuals are protected. But referees sometimes make mistakes, and so do government regulators. Economists cite several problems associated with government regulation, including the three described here.

Overregulation. Regulation can be very expensive, both for the regulatory agencies and for the businesses that must comply with the rulings of those agencies. Sometimes regulations are so detailed and complex that they actually discourage economic activity. For example, consider this requirement from an early OSHA standard on ladder safety:

> *The general slope of grain in flat steps of minimum dimension shall not be steeper than 1 in 12, except that for ladders under 10 feet in length the slope shall not be steeper than 1 in 10 . . . Local deviations of grain associated with otherwise permissible irregularities are permitted.*

A building contractor faced with page after page of such regulations might well decide to simply abandon jobs that require ladders.

Balancing costs and benefits. Most people would agree that regulation has benefited society. Everyone wants clean water, for example, and standards enforced by the Environmental Protection Agency (EPA) have done a great deal to address water pollution. But how clean does water have to be? And at what cost?

Consider a lake that was once so polluted that fish could not survive in it. Through regulation, water quality improves and the fish come back. After more regulation and expense, the water becomes swimmable. The water is eventually deemed to be nearly drinkable. But some impurities remain. To remove them would cost as much as has already gone into removing all the other pollutants. Is drinkable lake water a reasonable goal for regulators? Or are the costs of such a level of purity too great to justify?

Regulatory capture. Employees of a regulatory agency need to be familiar with the industry they are regulating. Where better to find qualified employees for an agency than in the industry itself? And when those agency employees leave government service, who will hire them? The same industry that they formerly regulated, of course.

This "revolving door" between government and industry can lead to what economists call **regulatory capture**. This occurs when regulatory agencies are dominated, or captured, by the industries they regulate. Captured agencies act in the best interests of the industry, rather than in the public interest.

One way to address the problems created by regulation is through deregulation. **Deregulation** is the process of removing government restrictions on firms' economic activity. Since the 1970s, Congress has deregulated the banking, airline, cable television, electric power, and interstate trucking industries, among others.

The effects of deregulation have been mixed. In the airline industry, for example, the Civil Aeronautics Board controlled both airline routes and ticket prices until deregulation began in 1978. The result of deregulation, as Figure 11.3B shows, was a dramatic rise in the number of Americans flying as airfares dropped and new routes opened up. At the same time, however, deregulation led to greater crowding at some airports. And as air travel became more competitive, weaker airlines had to shut down or merge with stronger airlines to survive.

■ 11.4 How Should Government Address Externalities and Public Goods?

Government's involvement in the economy takes many forms, from filling potholes to regulating alcohol to enforcing business contracts to inspecting oceangoing vessels. But most of what government does, it does for two basic reasons. The first is to protect individuals in the economy. The second is to make markets—and thus the economy—work better. This second reason is why government intervenes to correct two forms of market failure: externalities and public goods.

The Government's Role in Dealing with Externalities

Externalities are spillover effects resulting from production or consumption. They are costs or benefits that affect someone other than the producer or consumer of a good or service.

Externalities can be negative or positive. Air pollution and secondhand smoke, for example, are negative externalities associated with driving and smoking. Without government intervention, such negative externalities can cause great, if unintended, harm.

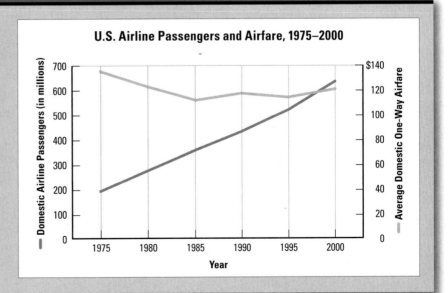

Figure 11.3B

Graphing Gains from Airline Deregulation
Before 1978, the Civil Aeronautics Board controlled both domestic airline routes and fares. After the deregulation that year, any domestic airline judged "fit, willing, and able," was allowed to fly any U.S. route at any price.

- Note the drop in average fares, as calculated in 2000 dollars.
- With lower fares, the number of Americans flying increased between 1975 and 2000.

Source: U.S. Department of Transportation.

The litter you see lining many highways is a negative externality. The companies that produce the plastic bags, soda cans, and other items that litter roads do not bear the cost of cleaning them up. Nor do the consumers who buy and use these items before throwing them away. In many places, cleanup is done by volunteers who adopt a section of highway and work to keep it litter free.

Governments can be equally helpful in promoting activities that have positive externalities. Immunizations, for example, prevent individuals from getting harmful diseases. They also prevent individuals from spreading those diseases to others—a positive externality. To encourage immunization, state governments require children to receive vaccinations against common diseases before enrolling in public school.

Supporting Positive Externalities: Subsidies and Public Provision

Goods and services that generate positive externalities tend to be underproduced relative to their benefits. Higher education is a prime example. People who graduate from college gain the benefit of greater earnings. But education also benefits society by creating a more productive workforce. To support this positive externality, federal and state governments allocate resources to education. They do this through subsidies and **public provision,** which means providing the education itself.

Subsidies. The government subsidizes both the consumers and the producers of education. It gives subsidies to college students in the form of grants, which do not have to be repaid, and low-interest loans. It also gives grants to schools, colleges, and universities.

Vouchers are another form of subsidy. A **voucher** is a coupon to be used to purchase a specific good or service. Some state and local governments provide school vouchers to low-income families to help them send their children to private schools. As Figure 11.4A shows, American are divided in their opinion of school vouchers.

Public provision. If a positive externality is large enough, the government may choose to finance the production of a good or service itself. In the field of higher education, federal and state governments provide most of the revenue needed to support public colleges and universities. Other examples of public provision are the U.S. Postal Service and federal air-traffic control systems.

Limiting Negative Externalities: Command-and-Control versus Market-Based Policies

One of the most widespread and troubling side effects of both production and consumption is environmental pollution. Governments can seek to limit this externality in two ways—through command-and-control policies and through market-based policies.

Command-and-control policies. The term *command and control* comes from the military and refers to the use of authority by a commanding officer to accomplish a mission. The commander exercises authority by issuing orders that others are expected to obey. As one writer puts it, "the idea is that people do what you tell them to do, and if they don't, you yell at them until they do, and if they still don't, you throw them in the brig for a while." Regulatory agencies that adopt

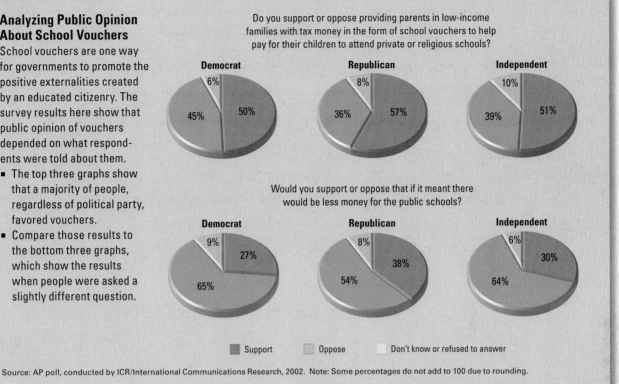

Figure 11.4A

Analyzing Public Opinion About School Vouchers

School vouchers are one way for governments to promote the positive externalities created by an educated citizenry. The survey results here show that public opinion of vouchers depended on what respondents were told about them.

- The top three graphs show that a majority of people, regardless of political party, favored vouchers.
- Compare those results to the bottom three graphs, which show the results when people were asked a slightly different question.

Do you support or oppose providing parents in low-income families with tax money in the form of school vouchers to help pay for their children to attend private or religious schools?

Democrat 6% 50% 45%
Republican 8% 57% 36%
Independent 10% 51% 39%

Would you support or oppose that if it meant there would be less money for the public schools?

Democrat 9% 27% 65%
Republican 8% 38% 54%
Independent 6% 30% 64%

■ Support ☐ Oppose ☐ Don't know or refused to answer

Source: AP poll, conducted by ICR/International Communications Research, 2002. Note: Some percentages do not add to 100 due to rounding.

command-and-control policies follow a similar approach, issuing rules that others are expected to follow.

The Environmental Protection Agency has used command-and-control policies to reduce air pollution. The EPA sets standards for air quality and requires states and cities to meet them. There are problems with this approach, however. As economist Robert W. Crandall observed,

> *The Congress or the EPA may decide to control the wrong substances or to control some discharges too strictly. Congress's own Office of Technology Assessment concluded, for example, that attempting to reach the EPA's goal for urban smog reduction could cost more than $13 billion per year, but result in less than $3.5 billion in improved health, agricultural, and amenity benefits.*
> —Robert W. Crandall, "Pollution Controls," *The Concise Encyclopedia of Economics*, 2008

Market-based policies. Economists generally prefer the use of **market-based policies** to deal with negative externalities. Such policies use incentives, rather than rules and enforcement, to change producers' behaviors.

One market-based policy is a **corrective tax,** which the government levies on producers of pollution. Corrective taxes give producers an incentive to reduce their harmful waste products. These taxes also have the benefit of raising revenue.

Corrective taxes have been used by local governments to reduce the amount of trash that households produce. Under these "pay as you throw" tax schemes, households are charged for each bag of garbage they put out for collection. In response to the trash tax, most households find ways to reduce their output of garbage. The effect has been to reduce the amount of waste that ends up in local landfills.

Another market-based policy is known as **cap and trade**. When using this approach, the government sets a limit, or cap, on the total amount of a pollutant that businesses can emit each year. The government then issues a limited number of **pollution permits** to every firm that emits that type of pollution. The permit gives the holder the right to pollute a certain amount.

As illustrated in Figure 11.4B, this scheme allows firms to sell their pollution permits to one another. Firms that can easily cut their emissions below their caps have an incentive to do so because they can sell their leftover permits. Firms that are unable to cut emissions enough to reach their caps may buy those extra permits to avoid pollution penalties. At the same time, the added cost of buying permits gives heavy polluters an incentive to decrease their emissions as much as possible.

The EPA used a cap-and-trade policy in the 1990s to reduce the output of sulfur dioxide—a major cause of acid rain—emitted from coal-burning power plants. Coal-fired power plants throughout the United States were directed to reduce their sulfur emissions by 50 percent over a fixed period. They were allowed to meet this target in any way they chose, including by buying permits from plants that came in under target early. The approach resulted in sulfur dioxide emissions being reduced more rapidly than anticipated.

Figure 11.4B

Comparing Command-and-Control Regulation with the Cap-and-Trade Approach

This diagram illustrates the cost of reducing emissions from an older and a newer factory, using two regulatory approaches.

- Using a command-and-control policy, each factory is required to make the same reductions, no matter what the cost might be.
- Using a cap-and-trade approach, the two factories are issued pollution permits. The factories have the flexibility to buy and sell permits, thus achieving the same total reduction at a lower cost.

Goal: To reduce total pollution emissions by 200 tons per year

 Plant A emits 1,000 tons per year. Cost to reduce emissions: $100 per ton.

 Plant B emits 1,000 tons per year. Cost to reduce emissions: $50 per ton.

Command-and-Control Regulation

Regulation requires each plant to reduce emissions by 100 tons per year.

Plant A: Cost to cut emissions by 100 tons per year:

$100
× 100
_____
$10,000

Plant B: Cost to cut emissions by 100 tons per year:

$50
× 100
_____
$5,000

Total emissions reduction: 200 tons per year
Total cost: $15,000

Cap-and-Trade Approach

Pollution permits allow each plant to emit up to 900 tons per year.

 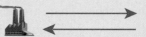

Plant A: Cost to cut emissions by 50 tons per year:

$100
× 50
_____
$5,000

Plant B: Cost to cut emissions by 150 tons per year:

$50
× 150
_____
$7,500

Cost to buy pollution permit for 50 tons per year:

$3,500

Revenue from selling pollution permit for 50 tons per year:

$3,500

Net cost:

$5,000
+ 3,500
_____
$8,500

Net cost:

$7,500
− 3,500
_____
$4,000

Total emissions reduction: 200 tons per year
Total cost: $12,500

The Tragedy of the Commons

These cartoons illustrate the tragedy of the commons, which occurs when a common resource is destroyed through overuse.

- The first cartoon shows a private field, which the owner preserves by limiting the number of cattle that graze there.
- The second cartoon shows a common field, where various farmers take advantage of the free grass to graze as many cattle as possible. Overgrazing turns the once-healthy field into a wasteland.

Negative Externalities and the Tragedy of the Commons

Negative externalities often arise when property rights are not well defined. The air, for example, is what economists call a **common resource**. Everyone has access to a common resource. For this reason, it can easily be overused and even destroyed. Economists call this problem the **tragedy of the commons**. Ecologist Garrett Hardin coined this term.

> *The tragedy of the commons develops in this way. Picture a pasture open to all. It is to be expected that each herdsman will try to keep as many cattle as possible on the commons . . . [One herdsman] asks, "What is the utility to me of adding one more animal to my herd?" . . . The rational herdsman concludes that the only sensible course for him to pursue is to add another animal to his herd. And another . . . But this is the conclusion reached by each and every rational herdsman sharing a commons. Therein is the tragedy. Each man is locked into a system that compels him to increase his herd without limit—in a world that is limited. Ruin is the destination toward which all men rush, each pursuing his own best interest.*
>
> —Garrett Hardin, "The Tragedy of the Commons," *Science*, 1968

Economists apply the tragedy of the commons to a variety of common resources, including Earth's atmosphere and oceans. Pollution and other negative externalities, they argue, result from poorly defined property rights. Without such rights, people lack the incentive to care for common resources and to ensure that those resources are preserved for future use.

Preserving Common Resources: Tolls, Quotas, and Privatization

A number of government policies are aimed at preserving common resources. One policy is to require everyone who uses a common resource to pay a **toll,** or fee. Highway tolls, for example, provide revenue that can be used to maintain roads. They also function as a corrective tax. To avoid paying tolls, some drivers will seek other routes, join carpools, or take public transportation. By providing an incentive to limit use of certain roads, tolls help reduce congestion.

A second way to preserve a common resource is to establish a **quota,** or maximum amount of a resource that a person can use or consume in a given period of time. The ocean, for example, is a common resource, as are the fish that live in it. Like the herders in Hardin's example, people who fish for a living have little incentive to limit their catch. If they do, someone else will come along and take the fish they left behind.

Turning common property into private property is one way to deal with a tragedy of the commons. This cartoonist takes privatization to a new level, suggesting how units of government might be converted into private enterprises.

The predictable result has been overfishing, which threatens to destroy several fisheries in U.S. coastal waters. By setting and enforcing fish-catch quotas, however, the government can control the percentage of the fish stock harvested each year. These quotas will help preserve this common resource.

A third way to deal with a tragedy of the commons is to turn the common resource into a private resource —that is, to **privatize** it. Private ownership restores the incentive to preserve the resource. Consider the problem of overfishing. The government might assign a group of fisheries the property rights to one stock of fish in a particular area. Their "ownership" of these fish gives them an incentive to preserve the resource by limiting the amount they catch each year.

Government's Role in Providing Public Goods

The government plays another widely accepted role in the economy as a provider of public goods. Abraham Lincoln encouraged this form of government engagement when he wrote,

> *The legitimate object of government, is to do for a community of people, whatever they need to have done, but can not do, at all, or can not, so well do, for themselves—in their separate, and individual capacities.*
> —Abraham Lincoln, 1854

Consider a good that could be produced by a private firm, such as a dam to control the flooding of a river. Some people in the river's floodplain might be willing to pay for the protection the dam provides. But the firm would not be able to provide that protection only to those people and withhold it from others. Anyone living in the floodplain would be able to enjoy that protection free of charge.

No profit-seeking firm can be expected to provide a good that consumers do not have to pay for. A government, by contrast, does not seek to make a profit. Rather, it can pay for public goods with tax dollars, thus ensuring that all taxpayers contribute to the cost.

Analyzing the Costs and Benefits of Providing Public Goods

Most people want government to provide public goods, such as national defense and streetlights. But as the scarcity-forces-tradeoffs principle reminds us, no government has the resources to provide everything that people might want. It has to make choices, but how? One way is to analyze the costs and benefits of producing that good.

Consider a proposal before a city council to widen a road in order to relieve congestion. City planners provide the council with detailed estimates of the costs of buying the needed land and hiring a construction company. Estimating the benefits is more challenging. If the road is widened, commuters are likely to spend less time and use less gas stalled in heavy traffic. How much less is uncertain. Nonetheless, estimates of these benefits are made and assigned a dollar value.

At this point, political considerations may also play a part in the council's decisions. If enough voters want a wider road, the council members might decide to approve the project even if the costs seem likely to out-weigh the benefits. The result would be an inefficient use of the city's scarce resources. The funds used to widen the road might well have provided more benefits to more people had they been used differently.

Economists describe situations in which government intervention leads to an inefficient use of resources as **government failures**. Such failures arise for several reasons. Politicians who want to stay in office may support legislation that pleases voters but

is not cost effective. Or they may engage in **logrolling** —agreeing to vote for another lawmaker's legislation if that lawmaker agrees to vote for their own legislation. Such compromises often lead to wasteful spending and economic inefficiency.

Politicians may also be influenced by interest groups when making decisions. Interest groups are organizations dedicated to getting certain policies enacted into law. Although such policies have high utility for a specific group, they may not benefit the economy as a whole.

People who work for regulatory agencies may also contribute to government failure. Staying employed is an incentive for them to find new problems

Figure 11.4C

Analyzing Costs and Benefits of a Public Provision
This graph summarizes the cost-benefit analysis of a proposal to expand preschool education in Ohio. The main cost was that of staffing new preschool classes in public school buildings. The main benefits were estimated to come in four areas.

- *Savings to school systems:* Children who attend preschool come to elementary school better prepared to learn.
- *Increased income tax revenues:* Parents with children in preschool are freed up to work.
- *Justice system savings:* Children who attend preschool are less likely to commit crimes.
- *Savings in health and welfare programs:* Preschools improve child nutrition and reduce child neglect.

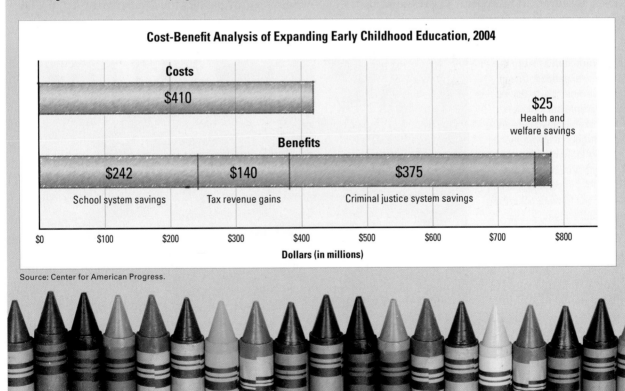

Cost-Benefit Analysis of Expanding Early Childhood Education, 2004

Source: Center for American Progress.

to solve. Government employees may press for more regulation even if it is not the most efficient solution to a problem.

■ 11.5 What Does Government Do to Promote Economic Well-Being?

Before the onset of the Great Depression in the 1930s, the federal government generally followed a hands-off policy toward the economy. Except for times of national emergency, such as the Civil War and World War I, the role of the government in the lives of ordinary people remained small. Then came the stock market crash of 1929, which plunged the nation into the worst economic crisis in its history.

How the Great Depression and World War II Changed U.S. Economic Policy

The 1929 stock market crash triggered a financial crisis that forced thousands of banks to go out of business. Millions of depositors lost their savings. Consumers slowed their spending, and firms cut back production or shut down altogether. The economy took a nosedive, and the Great Depression began.

At first the government did little, assuming that the economy would stabilize on its own. But as the economy worsened, many people looked to the government for help. In 1932, Franklin D. Roosevelt won the presidency by promising a different approach—a New Deal for the American people.

The New Deal greatly expanded the federal government's role in the economy. It created dozens of new programs and agencies aimed at reforming the banking system, helping businesses, and providing jobs. Most New Deal agencies did not outlast the Great Depression. However, the huge federal bureaucracy spawned by the New Deal lived on.

The Depression ended when World War II began. But the federal government did not return to its traditional hands-off role. Instead, it took charge of the wartime economy, overseeing industries as they converted from consumer to military production. To pay for the war effort, the government also sharply increased individual and corporate income taxes.

When the war ended, the federal government ended its supervision of industrial production. But many Americans feared a return to hard times and widespread unemployment. Congress responded to those fears by passing the Employment Act of 1946.

During the Great Depression, the government's role in the economy expanded. One of the government's goals was to put people back to work. The workers shown here were hired through a government program known as the Works Progress Administration. The WPA put some 8.5 million Americans to work constructing roads, bridges, public buildings, parks, and airports.

This act clearly stated an important role for government in stabilizing the economy:

> *The Congress hereby declares that it is the continuing policy and responsibility of the Federal Government to . . . promote maximum employment, production, and purchasing power.*
> —Employment Act of 1946

This act gave the federal government an active role in managing the nation's economy. To carry out that role, the act established the Council of Economic Advisers. This council helps the president formulate sound economic policies. The act also established a Joint Economic Committee that includes members from both houses of Congress. The committee's job is to review the state of the economy and advise Congress on economic policies.

Government's Role in Promoting Economic Stability

Americans clearly benefit from economic stability. In a stable economy, jobs are secure, goods and services are readily available, and prices are predictable. Producers, consumers, and investors can plan for the future without having to worry about sudden upheavals in the nation's economy.

The government promotes economic stability in part by creating a widely accepted currency—the dollar—that maintains its value. The government also promotes stability by stimulating business activity during economic slowdowns. It does this through tax incentives, which encourage businesses to invest in new capital equipment, and through tax rebates, which encourage consumers to spend more money.

In 2008, for example, difficulties in the housing market sent the economy into a tailspin. Reacting to the uncertainty, consumers cut back on spending. To generate more spending, Congress enacted an **economic stimulus** package—legislation specifically designed to stimulate business activity. The package called on the Internal Revenue Service to mail checks of $600 or more, depending on family size, to 130 million households. The nation's leaders encouraged Americans to spend their stimulus checks on consumer goods and services.

Income Distribution and Poverty in the United States

Markets allocate resources efficiently, as Adam Smith noted when he described the invisible hand of the

"I need some short-term economic stimulus."

The government promotes economic stability, in part, by trying to moderate booms and busts. In 2008, with the economy sagging, the government sought to spark business activity with a stimulus package. It sent taxpayers stimulus checks, with the hope that people would spend the money on consumer goods and services.

marketplace. But Smith did not conclude that markets allocate resources fairly. Some people, for example, end up with vastly higher incomes than others.

Every year, the U.S. Census Bureau charts the distribution of income in the United States. It starts by ranking households on the basis of their incomes. Then it divides the entire list of households into five equal parts, called **quintiles**. The bottom quintile contains the lowest incomes, and the top quintile contains the highest incomes.

The Census Bureau also calculates the percent of total income each quintile received. In 2007, for example, the bottom fifth received 3.4 percent of all income, while the top fifth received 50.5 percent. Clearly, income is not distributed equally in the United States.

Another tool for measuring the distribution of income is the **poverty rate**. This rate is the percentage of households whose incomes fall below a certain

Income Distribution

The U.S. Census Bureau measures income distribution by dividing the total number of households into five equal parts, or quintiles. The table shows the range of incomes for each quintile in 2007.
- Note that the circle graph shows the share of the nation's total income received by each quintile in 2007.
- Compare the percentage earned by the top fifth to that earned by the bottom fifth.

Annual Household Income, 2007

Quintile	Income
Top fifth	$100,001 and above
Fourth fifth	$62,001 to $100,000
Middle fifth	$39,101 to $62,000
Second fifth	$20,292 to $39,100
Bottom fifth	$20,291 and below

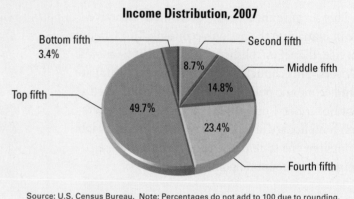

Income Distribution, 2007

Bottom fifth 3.4% · Second fifth 8.7% · Middle fifth 14.8% · Top fifth 49.7% · Fourth fifth 23.4%

Source: U.S. Census Bureau. Note: Percentages do not add to 100 due to rounding.

dollar amount determined by the Census Bureau. That dollar amount, called the **poverty threshold,** is the estimated minimum income needed to support a family.

The poverty threshold varies depending on family size and composition. For example, a family with two adults and one child is expected to live on less income than a family with one adult and four children.

The government considers families to be poor if their incomes fall below their poverty threshold. In 2006, by this measure, about one family in ten lived in poverty. Altogether, the members of those families represented 12.3 percent of the U.S. population. The poverty rate, then, was 12.3 percent in 2006.

Poverty rates vary depending on such factors as age, race, ethnicity, and family composition. It is also worth noting that the Census Bureau's rankings vary from year to year. Just because a family is in the bottom fifth this year does not mean it will stay there. A hallmark of American society is **economic mobility**. People who work hard are usually able to move up the economic ladder. As a result, relatively few families remain in poverty for the long term.

Government's Role in Redistributing Income

For much of our nation's history, the poor relied mainly on friends, family, and private charities to provide for their basic needs. Local communities sometimes established poor houses and poor farms to house the very poor. Otherwise, the poor were left to fend for themselves as best they could.

Then came the Great Depression. With it came an expanded role for government in the economy. New Deal programs aided millions of Americans. The Social Security Act, for example, did much to reduce poverty among disabled and older Americans. However, these programs did not lift every family out of poverty.

During the 1960s, the federal government launched a War on Poverty to help the nation's neediest families. Congress devised dozens of antipoverty programs that together created an economic safety net. Those programs had some success. The poverty rate for families dropped from 18.1 percent in 1960 to 10.1 percent in 1970.

Since the 1960s, most antipoverty programs have involved some form of **income redistribution,** a policy designed to reduce the gap between the rich and the poor. This policy works by taxing wealthier members of a society and then distributing that money to the poor to achieve greater income equality. Redistribution takes a number of forms, including those described here.

Welfare. When most people talk about welfare,

One way the government redistributes income is by issuing food stamps to people with low incomes. Food stamps are vouchers, accessed through an electronic debit card, that can be used to buy food. In addition to promoting well-being, subsidizing food for poor people benefits society as a whole by creating a healthier population. This is a positive externality.

they are referring to Temporary Assistance for Needy Families. The TANF program, funded largely by the federal government but run by the states, provides benefits, services, and work opportunities to needy families. In some states, TANF benefits come in the form of **cash transfers,** or direct payments of cash from the government to individuals.

Other TANF benefits are distributed in the form of goods or vouchers, rather than cash. These **in-kind transfers** include food stamps, public housing, school lunches, and Medicaid. For example, when a person receives health services through the

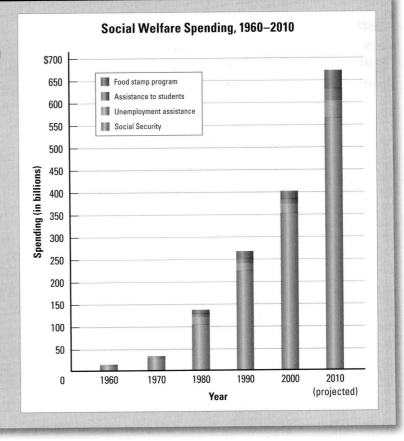

Figure 11.5

Analyzing the Growth of Income-Redistribution Programs
The federal government's role in redistributing income has grown dramatically over the past 70 years. This graph shows changes in spending on four programs since 1960.
- *Social Security:* Supports people with disabilities and retirees
- *Unemployment assistance:* Assists people who are unemployed through no fault of their own
- *Assistance to students:* Provides grants to schools and scholarships and loans to students who continue their education past high school
- *Food stamp program:* Helps low-income families buy food

Social Welfare Spending, 1960–2010

Legend:
- Food stamp program
- Assistance to students
- Unemployment assistance
- Social Security

Spending (in billions) — Year

Source: Budget of the U.S. Government.

This welfare recipient is learning job skills by participating in a welfare-to-work program offered by Goodwill Industries International in Pittsburgh, Pennsylvania. Goodwill has been providing vocational training to the poor since it was founded in Boston in 1902. The goal of this training is to give people the skills they need to move out of welfare and into the workforce.

Medicaid program, the government pays the health care provider. No cash goes to the Medicaid recipient.

Earned income tax credit. The government also helps the working poor through the **Earned Income Tax Credit**. Low-wage workers can claim this credit when they file their federal income tax forms. The credit is applied against whatever taxes are due. Depending on a worker's family size and income, the credit can exceed those taxes. If it does, the worker receives a tax refund.

Unemployment insurance. Employers, through federal and state taxes, contribute to a fund that provides **unemployment insurance** for workers. If workers are laid off from their jobs, the state sends them payments —unemployment compensation—for a certain period of time or until they find another job. Each state administers its own unemployment insurance program, based on federal standards.

The Unintended Consequences of Antipoverty Policies

Through its antipoverty policies, the government redistributes income in a way that is intended to help the poor. Yet critics charge that these policies have had unintended negative consequences for the very people they are meant to help.

These critics worry that antipoverty programs promote dependence on the government and reduce people's incentive to become self-sufficient. TANF, food stamps, Medicaid, and the Earned Income Tax Credit are what economists call **means-tested programs**—that is, they are tied to family income. The more a family earns, the fewer benefits that family can claim. For this reason, recipients of government assistance may have little incentive to get a job and earn money. If their incomes exceed the poverty threshold, they will lose their government benefits.

For welfare recipients with minimal skills and education, getting a job may indeed make them worse off. This is because the kinds of jobs available to low-skill workers usually pay minimum wage and have no benefits. Consider a single mother with less than a high school education. She leaves welfare and takes a low-paying job with no health insurance benefits. She still must struggle to support her children on her low wages. But now, because she is working, she and her children are ineligible for government-provided health services.

Policymakers have developed a variety of proposals to address such problems. One is to provide job training and education for welfare recipients to increase their human capital and help them become self-sufficient. Another is to raise the cap on certain means-tested programs, so that benefits are gradually reduced as income rises. Both of these proposals would lead to higher costs and, most likely, higher taxes to pay for those costs.

A third possible solution is public service employment. As it did during the Great Depression, the government could pay the unemployed to perform useful work. But this might cause a flood of workers to shift from private jobs to more secure government jobs—at great expense to taxpayers.

As always, when resources are limited, whatever choices a government makes will result in tradeoffs. You may not be aware of these tradeoffs now, but at some point you will be. Why? Because government programs are funded by tax dollars, and once you enter the world of work, you will become a taxpayer. In the next chapter, you will learn more about taxes and how they are used to support the many roles government plays in our lives.

Unemployed workers who find a job get the benefits and satisfaction of earning a paycheck. But going back to work may also involve financial tradeoffs. Some workers find they have new costs that erode the value of their earnings.

Summary

The government plays a limited but important role in the economy. It protects property rights, regulates the marketplace, corrects market failures, and promotes the economic well-being of the American people.

How does the government protect property rights? The government is empowered by the Constitution to protect private property rights. It does this through the court system, police forces, and the Patent and Trademark Office. The government may limit property rights through its power of eminent domain.

What regulatory roles does government play in our economy? The government uses its regulatory power to maintain competition; safeguard consumers, savers, and investors; and protect workers. It carries out these tasks through regulatory agencies, which create and enforce standards and regulations for industries.

How should government address externalities and public goods? The federal and state governments implement a variety of policies to limit negative externalities and support positive externalities. They also provide public goods that are deemed necessary or desirable.

What does government do to promote economic well-being? During the Great Depression, the role of the government in the economy greatly expanded. Since then the government has taken on even more responsibility for the economic well-being of its citizens. When necessary to preserve economic stability, the government stimulates the economy by spending more money. The government also redistributes income to combat poverty.

What value would you put on a human life?

What is a human life worth? Can you put a price on it? Can anyone? These seem like impossible questions to answer. Yet this is exactly what government officials are called upon to do when making economic policy decisions.

The case study described on these pages puts you in the shoes of a town council member who must make such a decision. In the process, it explains why and how economists have tried to come up with the value of a human life. When you finish reading the case study, make your own judgment. What is a human life worth?

Case Study: How Much Is a Life Worth?

By N. Gregory Mankiw

Imagine that you have been elected to serve as a member of your local town council. The town engineer comes to you with a proposal: The town can spend $10,000 to build and operate a traffic light at a town intersection that now has only a stop sign. The benefit of the traffic light is increased safety. The engineer estimates, based on data from similar intersections, that the traffic light would reduce the risk of a fatal traffic accident over the lifetime of the traffic light from 1.6 to 1.1 percent. Should you spend the money for the new light?

To answer this question, you turn to cost-benefit analysis. But you quickly run into an obstacle: The costs and benefits must be measured in the same units if you are to compare them meaningfully. The cost is measured in dollars, but the benefit—the possibility of saving a person's life—is not directly monetary. To make your decision, you have to put a dollar value on a human life.

At first, you may be tempted to conclude that a human life is priceless. After all, there is probably no amount of money that you could be paid to volun-tarily give up your life or that of a loved one. This suggests that a human life has an infinite dollar value.

For the purposes of cost-benefit analysis, however, this answer leads to nonsensical results. If we truly placed an infinite value on human life, we should place traffic lights on every street corner, and we should all drive large cars

To determine whether the benefit of a traffic light exceeds its cost, planners must decide how much a human life is worth.

Economists have used a variety of methods to try to determine the monetary value of a human life. This table calculates the benefit of installing a new traffic light based on four different methods.

Expected Benefit from Installing a $10,000 Traffic Light

Source	Basis for the Estimate	Value Placed on a Human Life	Expected Benefit
Economists Orley Ashenfelter and Michael Greenstone	Time saved when speed limits and penalties for speeding change, putting people more at risk of a fatal highway accident	$1.54 million	$7,700
Environmental Protection Agency	Surveys asking people what they think a life is worth	$3.7 million	$18,500
Department of Transportation	Studies of people's willingness to pay to reduce health and injury risks	$5.5 million	$27,500
Economist N. Gregory Mankiw	Studies that compare pay for high-risk and low-risk occupations	$10 million	$50,000

loaded with all the latest safety features. Yet traffic lights are not at every corner, and people sometimes choose to pay less for smaller cars without safety options such as side-impact air bags or antilock brakes. In both our public and private decisions, we are at times willing to risk our lives to save some money.

Once we have accepted the idea that a person's life has an implicit dollar value, how can we determine what that value is? One approach, sometimes used by courts to award damages in wrongful-death suits, is to look at the total amount of money a person would have earned if he or she had lived. Economists are often critical of this approach. It has the bizarre implication that the life of a retired or disabled person has no value.

A better way to value human life is to look at the risks that people are voluntarily willing to take and how much they must be paid for taking them. Mortality risk varies across jobs, for example. Construction workers in high-rise buildings face greater risk of death on the job than office workers do. By comparing wages in risky and less risky occupations, controlling for education, experience, and other determinants of wages, economists can get some sense about what value people put on their own lives. Studies using this approach conclude that the value of a human life is about $10 million.

We can now return to our original example and respond to the town engineer. The traffic light reduces the risk of fatality by 0.5 percentage points. Thus, the expected benefit from having the traffic light is 0.005 × $10 million, or $50,000. This estimate of the benefit well exceeds the cost of $10,000, so you should approve the project.

N. Gregory Mankiw is an economics professor at Harvard University and the author of Principles of Economics.

Chapter 12

Who and what should be taxed?

Taxes and Taxation

■ 12.1 Introduction

On February 14, 1929, in a garage on Chicago's north side, a crime was committed that would shock the nation. Seven men—all but one of whom were members of an organized crime gang—were brutally gunned down by members of a rival gang dressed as police officers. The killings, which made headlines all over the country, were dubbed the Saint Valentine's Day Massacre.

The man believed to have been behind the massacre was Al Capone, one of the most notorious gangsters in American history. Capone, who went by the sinister nickname "Scarface," was a Chicago mob boss during the Prohibition era of the 1920s. At the time, the sale of alcohol was banned by the Eighteenth Amendment. Capone made a fortune from the illegal liquor trade, gambling, and other criminal activities.

By ruthlessly eliminating his rivals, Capone rose to the top of Chicago's criminal world. Federal law enforcement agents, led by Eliot Ness, tried for years to arrest him on murder and racketeering charges. But Capone was slippery—he always had an alibi. In addition, no one was willing to testify against him.

Then, in 1930, a key piece of evidence was found during a routine warehouse raid. Finally, federal prosecutors were able to bring their man to justice. Al Capone—the man branded "Public Enemy Number One"—was charged with the crime of . . . tax evasion.

For several years in the late 1920s, Capone had failed to pay income tax. Yet he lived like a king, spending extravagantly on cars, clothes, and other

Even the notorious gangster
Al Capone had to pay his taxes.

luxuries. The Justice Department knew that such lavish spending was a sign of substantial income, but they could not prove it until they found a coded set of accounts that belonged to Capone. When they filed charges, Capone is said to have responded, "The income tax law is a lot of bunk. The government can't collect legal taxes from illegal money."

But Capone was wrong. In 1931, he was convicted of tax evasion and sentenced to 11 years in prison. He was also forced to pay $80,000 in fines and court costs. His career as a mobster was over.

Capone learned the hard way the truth of Benjamin Franklin's famous saying, "In this world nothing is certain but death and taxes." By comparing taxes to the one truly inevitable event in life—death—Franklin was saying that taxes are an unavoidable consequence of living in society.

Chapter 11 described some of the services and programs provided by government. In this chapter, you will learn about taxes and how they are used to finance government operations. You will read about the various types of taxes and how they are collected and spent by governments at the local, state, and national levels.

12.2 What Are Taxes and How Should They Be Levied?

Most people know what a tax is—a mandatory payment to the government. But ask them if they *like* taxes, and you are sure to get no for an answer. No one enjoys giving up hard-earned income to the government. For many people, the experience is downright painful. The physicist Albert Einstein is reported to have said, "The hardest thing in the world to understand is the income tax."

Taxes: The Price of Civilization

Many people share Einstein's opinion. However, although taxes may be burdensome, they also make government possible. Without taxes, there could be no public institutions—no legislature, courts, or system of law enforcement. Therefore there would be no ordered society. "Taxation," said Supreme Court justice Oliver Wendell Holmes Jr., "is the price we pay for civilization."

Taxes have existed for as long as societies have been organized under common rule. In early civilizations, such as those of Egypt, Mesopotamia, and China, taxation took many forms. Farmers and craft workers had to give up a share of the goods they produced to the government, and traders were taxed on their commerce. In addition, people had to provide labor for building temples, city walls, and other public works. Taxes were paid in the form of goods and labor for centuries, but eventually these were replaced by taxes in the form of money.

Today taxes are collected and used for various purposes. They supply revenues to support the functions of government, such as national defense and criminal justice. They are used to pay for **infrastructure,** such as roads and bridges, and to fund welfare and public services, such as education and health care.

Taxes are also used to promote social and economic goals. For example, a tax may be placed on certain goods and services to limit their use. A tax on cigarettes or alcohol, for instance, can discourage their consumption. Taxes can also be used to redistribute income. For instance, higher taxes might be placed on one group, such as the wealthy, to provide benefits or services to another group, such as the poor.

This stone tablet from ancient Mesopotamia records the payment of a labor tax around 2500 B.C.E. Citizens of Sumer, a local city-state, owed many months of labor tax, or "burden" as they called it. This was only one of many taxes imposed on the people of Sumer.

Despite their many useful functions, taxes have never been popular with the citizens who pay them. Thomas Paine referred to taxes collected by Europe's monarchs as "plunder," or stolen goods. Throughout history, resentment over taxes has given rise to tax protests, riots, and rebellions, including the rebellion that launched our country's fight for independence.

How Our Nation's Founders Viewed Taxation

Taxation was the main issue that sparked the American Revolution. At the time, Britain taxed the American colonies but gave them no representation in Parliament. The colonists believed they should have a say in how they were taxed. The popular slogan "No taxation without representation" became a rallying cry for colonial discontent. As protests mounted, some members of Parliament called on the British government to change its tax policy. "Your scheme yields no revenue," declared the statesman Edmund Burke. "It yields nothing but discontent, disorder, disobedience."

After independence, the American people retained a cautious attitude toward taxation. Although they accepted the need for taxes, they also wanted to limit the government's tax powers.

Some of these limits are written into the U.S. Constitution. Article I, Section 8, Clause 1, which provides the basis for federal tax law, says that Congress shall have the power "to lay and collect Taxes, Duties, Imposts and Excises." But the clause goes on to limit this power in two key ways.

- Taxes can be levied, or collected, only for the country's "common Defence and general Welfare," not for the benefit of individual citizens.
- Federal taxes must be the same in every state.

The framers of the Constitution also inserted a clause that limited the power of Congress to tax individual income. This clause was overridden in 1913, however, by passage of the Sixteenth Amendment, which allowed for the establishment of the federal income tax.

Adam Smith's Four Tax Maxims

Shortly before Americans declared independence in 1776, Adam Smith published *The Wealth of Nations*, his famous book on economics. In it, Smith laid down four maxims, or guiding principles, of taxation that

"You know, the idea of taxation WITH representation doesn't appeal to me very much, either."

Because American colonists had no vote in the British Parliament, they complained about "taxation without representation." As this cartoon implies, however, people need no excuse to complain about taxes.

have influenced thinking about taxes ever since.

Equity. The first of Smith's maxims is equity, or fairness. In his view, wealthy citizens benefit most from government and can most afford to pay its costs. He wrote, "It is not very unreasonable that the rich should contribute to the public expense, not only in proportion to their revenue, but something more than in that proportion." In other words, Smith believed that the rich should pay a higher percentage of their income in taxes than do the poor.

Certainty. Smith's second maxim is that the taxes a citizen owes should be "certain, and not arbitrary." He wrote, "The time of payment, the manner of payment, the quantity to be paid, ought all to be clear and plain to the contributor." Otherwise, government officials may be tempted to abuse the tax system for their own benefit.

Convenience. The third maxim is convenience. Smith wrote, "Every tax ought to be levied at the time, or in the manner, in which it is most likely to be convenient for the contributor to pay it." In other words, the tax system should not be overly complicated. Taxpayers should find the process of paying their taxes simple, straightforward, and predictable.

Efficiency. Smith's fourth maxim—efficiency—is designed to keep the economic costs of the tax system to a minimum. Smith believed that taxes should produce maximum gain for the government, while causing minimum loss for taxpayers. "Every tax," he wrote, "ought to . . . take out and to keep out of the pockets of the people as little as possible over and above what it brings into the public treasury of the state."

The Tax Equity Debate: Who Should Pay and Why?

Most economists would agree in theory with Smith's four maxims. Nevertheless, they often disagree about how to put those maxims into practice. One of the most hotly debated issues is the principle of **tax equity,** the idea that the tax system should be fair. Although economists support the principle of equity, they differ over how best to achieve it.

The crucial issue in the tax equity debate is who should pay. Economists offer two basic approaches to this problem: the ability-to-pay principle and the benefits-received principle.

The **ability-to-pay principle** mirrors Smith's first maxim. It says that citizens should be taxed according to their income or wealth. People with higher incomes should pay more tax. People with lower incomes should pay less tax. Federal and state income taxes are based on this principle. For example, a lawyer who earns $200,000 a year pays a higher percentage of income in taxes than does a teacher who earns $50,000 a year.

The **benefits-received principle** says that those who benefit from a particular government program should pay for it. For example, people who drive should pay for the upkeep of the highway system. Gasoline taxes that fund road repairs are based on this principle, as are highway and bridge tolls.

Who Ends Up Paying Taxes and Why?

One of the difficulties with devising a fair tax system is figuring out who bears the burden of a tax. To many people, the answer seems obvious. The producer or consumer who is legally required to pay the tax bears the burden, right? Not necessarily. The economic burden of a tax—what economists call **tax incidence**—may not fall on the person who pays the tax bill.

To see why, consider the tax on hotel rooms. Many state and local governments levy "occupancy" taxes on the use of hotel and motel rooms. Hotel and motel owners are required to pay this tax revenue

---

Key Concept

Tax Equity

Tax equity begins with the belief that taxation should be fair to all who are taxed. Economists often cite two principles in debates over tax equity: the ability-to-pay principle and the benefits-received principle.

Ability-to-Pay Principle

A tax on luxury items, such as diamond necklaces, is based on the ability-to-pay principle. The idea is that buyers of luxury goods have high incomes and can thus afford to pay more in taxes.

Benefits-Received Principle

Bridge and highway tolls are taxes based on the benefits-received principle. The idea is that drivers—the people who benefit from the road system—should pay the cost of road improvements.

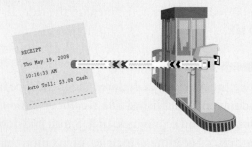

Many states and cities levy occupancy taxes on the use of hotel and motel rooms. Such taxes are typically charged to the customer. But if a hotel lowers its room rates to keep the cost to customers down, the incidence of the tax falls at least in part on the hotel owner.

to the government. Most hotels simply add the tax, which is a percentage of the room rate, onto a customer's bill. When this happens, the customer bears the burden. But this extra cost might cause some hotels to lose customers. If a hotel owner responds by lowering room rates to reduce the overall cost to the customer, then the hotel owner, not the customer, is bearing some of the burden of the tax.

As this example illustrates, tax incidence is affected by elasticity of supply and demand. Elasticity, you may recall, is a measure of sensitivity to a change in price. In a market with very elastic demand, consumers are highly sensitive to price changes. A tax that raises prices may drive some consumers out of the market. If demand is inelastic, however, adding a tax to the price of a good or service will have much less effect on consumers' willingness to buy.

Similarly, in a market with very elastic supply, producers are highly sensitive to price changes. A tax that raises the cost of doing business may drive some producers out of the market. If supply is inelastic, however, adding taxes to other costs will not have much effect on producers' willingness to sell a good or service.

In general, the burden of a tax will fall on the side of the market that is less elastic. If consumers are more likely to leave the market if prices rise, then producers will bear more of the tax burden. But if producers are more likely to abandon the market, the incidence of taxation will fall more heavily on consumers.

Any government hoping to create an equitable tax system must take tax incidence into account. Yet many people are unaware that tax burdens can, and often do, shift. As economist N. Gregory Mankiw points out,

Many discussions of tax equity ignore the indirect effects of taxes and are based on what economists mockingly call the flypaper theory of tax incidence. According to this theory, the burden of a tax, like a fly on flypaper, sticks wherever it first lands. This assumption, however, is rarely valid.

Taxes and Efficiency: Deadweight Losses and the Costs of Compliance

There is less debate among economists about Smith's fourth maxim—efficiency. There are many ways to raise revenue through taxation. One tax system is considered more efficient than another if it raises the same amount of revenue at less cost to taxpayers. Obviously, a tax is, itself, a cost that taxpayers must bear. But taxes also impose two other kinds of costs: deadweight losses and the cost of tax compliance.

A **deadweight loss** occurs when the cost to consumers and producers from a tax—due to lost productivity or sales—is larger than the size of the tax revenue it generates. As economics writer Charles Wheelan put it, a deadweight loss "makes you worse off without making anyone else better off."

Taxes can create deadweight losses by reducing people's incentives to be as productive as they would otherwise choose to be. For example, consider the effect of state and federal income taxes on a job seeker who is offered a position that involves long hours of overtime. If she could keep every dollar she would earn by working the extra hours, the job might look attractive. But knowing that she will have to pay at least a third of her earnings in taxes, she decides it is not worth working that hard. She turns down the job and continues looking for work. Not only is she still unemployed, but the economy has lost what she might have produced had she taken the job. That lost productivity is a deadweight loss.

Another source of tax inefficiency is the cost of complying with the tax code. Every year, U.S. taxpayers spend many hours, and often hundreds of dollars, preparing their income tax forms. Moreover, as Figure 12.2 shows, the overall cost of compliance has been rising yearly. The time and money spent on tax preparation are resources that, if we had a more efficient tax system, could be used productively in other ways.

12.3 What Kinds of Taxes Will You Pay in Your Lifetime?

Every year on April 15, as midnight approaches, post office parking lots fill up around the country. Harried taxpayers hurry inside to get a place in line. The clock ticks. The race is on to get federal income tax forms postmarked before the April 15 filing deadline.

Taxation Basics: Tax Base and Tax Rates

In 2008, that April 15 deadline almost coincided with another tax-related day, known to some as "tax freedom day." This is the date every year when it is estimated that average Americans will have earned enough to pay all their taxes for that year. In 2008, that date was April 23—113 days into the year. This means that Americans spent nearly one-third of 2008 working to pay their federal, state, and local taxes.

Many kinds of taxes make up the average American's tax burden. All these taxes consist of two basic elements: the tax base and the tax rate.

Figure 12.2

Measuring the Cost of Tax Compliance

According to the Tax Foundation, a nonprofit organization dedicated to educating U.S. taxpayers, the cost of tax compliance is rising year by year.

- The foundation estimates that in 2005, individual taxpayers spent 2.8 billion hours filling out 387 million federal income tax forms.
- That same year, the cost of federal tax compliance by all taxpayers—individuals, firms, and nonprofits—was more than $265 billion.

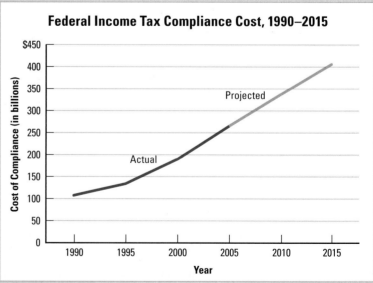

Federal Income Tax Compliance Cost, 1990–2015

Source: The Tax Foundation.

Figure 12.3A

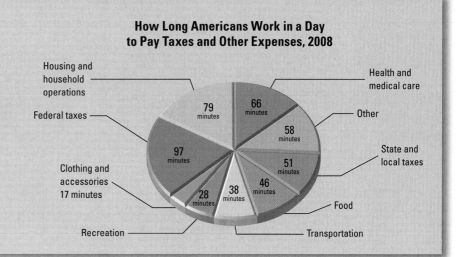

Comparing Taxes with Other Spending Categories
This graph shows how many minutes in an eight-hour day the average American spends working to pay taxes as compared with other major expenses. Note that the number of minutes worked to pay federal and state taxes exceeds any other spending category.

How Long Americans Work in a Day to Pay Taxes and Other Expenses, 2008

Housing and household operations — 79 minutes
Federal taxes — 97 minutes
Clothing and accessories 17 minutes
Recreation — 28 minutes
38 minutes
Transportation — 46 minutes
Food — 51 minutes
State and local taxes — 58 minutes
Other
Health and medical care — 66 minutes

Source: The Tax Foundation.

The **tax base** is the thing that is taxed, such as personal income, a good sold at a store, or a piece of property. Taxes are defined according to their tax base. For example, income tax is based on personal income. A property tax is based on the value of property, such as a home.

The **tax rate** is the percentage of income—or of the value of a good, service, or asset—that is paid in tax. For example, if the income tax rate were set at 20 percent, taxpayers would have to pay an amount equal to 20 percent of their taxable income.

Tax Structures: Proportional, Progressive, and Regressive

Taxes are also defined by their structure, which in turn depends on tax rates. Economists identify three types of tax structures: proportional, progressive, and regressive. Each structure has its advocates and critics.

Proportional taxes. A **proportional tax** is a tax that takes the same share of income at all income levels. For example, a proportional income tax of 10 percent would tax all incomes at that rate.

Critics of proportional taxes argue that such taxes fail the test of fairness, because they tax the rich and the poor at the same rate, even though the poor have less ability to pay than do the rich. A 10 percent income tax levied on a person who makes $25,000 a year, for example, represents a greater sacrifice than the same tax levied on a person who makes $250,000 a year.

Advocates of this tax structure, however, claim that a proportional tax is fair precisely because everyone pays an equal share. They also point out that proportional taxes are efficient because they are simple to calculate and easy to collect.

In recent years, Estonia and several other Eastern European countries have adopted a proportional income tax, or **flat tax**. In Slovakia, for example, rich and poor alike pay a 19 percent tax on income. Since its inception in 2004, the flat tax has helped the Slovakian economy grow by attracting foreign investors. Its simplicity has also led to less tax evasion. Although most Slovakians support the flat tax, a few worry that the low flat tax rate may result in less money for government services.

Progressive taxes. A **progressive tax** is a tax that takes a larger share of income as income increases. A progressive tax is based on the ability-to-pay principle. Most federal taxes, including the federal income tax, are progressive.

The main argument in favor of progressive taxation is the equity argument. A progressive tax gets larger as income increases. Thus it places a greater tax burden on the wealthy—where advocates believe it should be—than on the poor.

Critics of progressive taxation, however, believe that placing an unequal burden on the rich is fundamentally unfair. In effect, they argue, such a tax punishes people for accumulating wealth and may create a disincentive to work, save, and invest. They

Proportional, Progressive, and Regressive Tax Structures

The three basic tax structures differ in how they tax individuals or firms with various levels of income.

Proportional Tax
In a proportional tax structure, tax rates remain fixed as income increases.

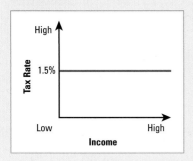

Progressive Tax
In a progressive tax structure, tax rates increase with rising income.

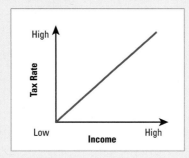

Regressive Tax
In a regressive tax structure, tax rates take a smaller share of income as income increases.

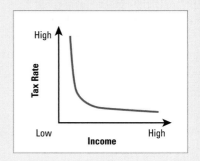

also complain that creating different rates for different income levels leads to a more complex, and therefore less efficient, tax system.

Regressive taxes. The third tax structure, the **regressive tax,** is a tax that takes a smaller share of income as income increases. Governments do not set out to impose higher tax rates as incomes fall. But a tax that is proportional—that applies a single rate to everyone—can effectively function as a regressive tax if it takes a bigger bite out of the incomes of poor people than those of wealthy people.

Sales taxes, for example, are regressive. To understand why, consider a low-income person who earns $20,000 a year and spends $10,000 of it on taxable goods and services. If the sales tax rate is 5 percent, that person pays $500 in sales tax a year. This amount represents 2.5 percent of the low earner's income.

Compare that with the tax burden of a person who earns $100,000 a year and spends $30,000 on taxable goods and services. At the same tax rate, the high earner pays three times as much sales tax, or $1,500. But that figure represents only 1.5 percent of the high earner's income. When the percentage of income claimed by a proportional tax goes down as income goes up, the tax is considered regressive.

Critics of taxes that tend to be regressive argue that they turn the ability-to-pay principle on its head. Instead of taxing most heavily those who are most able to pay, such taxes place the greatest burden on those least able to pay.

Advocates of proportional taxes, however, argue that they need not be regressive. High earners, they point out, may choose to spend the same percentage of their income on taxable goods and services as people with lower incomes. In such cases, the tax is flat, not regressive, with high earners paying more as they consume more.

Individual Income Taxes

The largest share of tax revenue taken in by the federal government comes from individual income taxes. The majority of states also impose an income tax on their residents. The federal income tax and most state income taxes are progressive taxes.

The federal income tax applies to all U.S. citizens and residents with income above a certain minimum level. For example, a single adult who earned less than $8,750 in the year 2007 was not required to file a federal income tax form.

The Internal Revenue Service is responsible for issuing federal income tax forms and processing tax returns. The IRS also works to ensure compliance with the **tax code,** the set of laws that govern federal taxes. Over time, these laws have grown in size and complexity. Between 1954 and 2005, for example, Congress enacted 35 significant changes to the income tax code. These changes have increased the volume of income tax regulations by a whopping 648 percent—to more than 1.2 million words.

The IRS collects taxes from workers using a "pay as you earn" system. Under this system, also known as **withholding,** employers take out a certain amount of tax from each paycheck. At the beginning of each year, most workers receive a **W-2 form,** which lists their wages for the previous year and the amount of tax that was withheld.

Taxpayers submit tax returns between January 1 and April 15. They are required to declare all their income for the previous year, including wages, investment earnings, business profits, and other types of income. If the IRS questions the accuracy of a taxpayer's return, it may order an **audit,** or formal review of the return. Taxpayers who fail to comply with tax laws may face fines or, like Al Capone, imprisonment.

Figure 12.3B shows the federal income tax rates for single adults in various income brackets for 2008. As income rises, the marginal tax rate rises as well. The **marginal tax rate** is the rate at which the last dollar a person earns in a given year is taxed. The table in Figure 12.3B shows six marginal tax rates for single adults in 2008, ranging from 10 to 35 percent. These rising rates make the income tax a progressive tax.

Suppose you earned $15,075 in 2008. The first $8,025 of your income would be taxed at the lowest rate of 10 percent. The remaining $7,050 would be taxed at the next highest rate of 15 percent. This rate—15 percent—would be your marginal tax rate, because it is the rate you would pay on the last dollar earned that year.

Because your income is taxed at two different rates, your average tax rate will be lower than your marginal tax rate. In this case, your average tax rate in 2008 would be just over 12 percent. The graph in Figure 12.3B shows both marginal and average tax rates at different income levels.

Payroll Taxes

The second-largest share of federal tax revenue comes from payroll taxes. A **payroll tax** is a tax on the wages a company pays its employees. Of the several kinds of payroll taxes, the two most important are the Social Security tax and the Medicare tax. Both are used to fund large federal social insurance programs.

The **Social Security tax** is set at a fixed rate, which is paid half by the employer and half by the employee. People who are self-employed pay the entire tax themselves. In 2008, the total Social Security tax rate was 12.4 percent.

Figure 12.3B

Comparing Marginal and Average Federal Income Tax Rates

The federal income tax is a progressive tax. The table shows how marginal tax rates for a single taxpayer rise as income increases. You can see from the graph that the average tax rate for most taxpayers is less than their marginal tax rate. This is true because not all income is taxed at that marginal rate.

2008 Income Tax Rates for Single Adults

Taxable Income	Marginal Tax Rate
$0 to $8,025	10%
$8,026 to $32,550	15%
$32,551 to $78,850	25%
$78,851 to $164,550	28%
$164,551 to $357,700	33%
$357,701 and above	35%

Source: Internal Revenue Service.

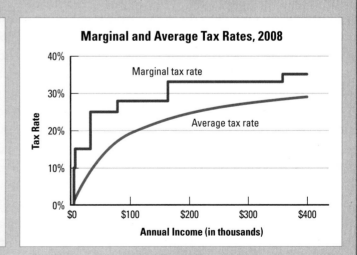

Marginal and Average Tax Rates, 2008

Because its rate is fixed, the Social Security tax appears, at first glance, to be a proportional tax. But it is actually regressive, for two reasons. First, the Social Security tax applies only to wages, salaries, and self-employment income. It does not apply to income from investments. Second, only earnings up to a specified maximum amount, or cap, are taxed. In 2008, that cap was $102,000. Earnings over that amount are not taxed. Thus Social Security claims a smaller share of income as income rises.

The **Medicare tax** is also split evenly between employer and employee. In 2008, the total Medicare tax rate was 2.9 percent, half of which—1.45 percent—was withheld from employees' earnings. The Medicare tax is not capped. It applies the same rate to all taxpayers at all income levels, making it a true proportional tax.

Many states also levy payroll taxes. An **unemployment tax** is a state payroll tax that is used to assist workers who lose their jobs. Some states also levy a **state disability tax,** which funds state programs to help workers who are injured on the job.

Property Taxes

Taxes on property are a major source of revenue for many state and local governments. **Property taxes** are commonly levied on real property, which consists of land and buildings. Some governments also tax personal property, such as cars and boats.

Property taxes are proportional taxes that charge a fixed percentage of the value of a property. That value is calculated by an assessor, a public official who determines the value of a property for taxation purposes. If the **assessed value** of a property changes —a common occurrence in the real estate market— property taxes change, too.

In many communities, property taxes are a major source of revenue for public schools. However, the practice of funding public schools with property taxes has many critics. Some charge that it is unfair to require all property owners to pay such taxes when not all of them use the public schools. Others question the equity of basing school funding on property taxes. These critics point to the fact that lower-income school districts with low property values cannot raise as much revenue as higher-income school districts can. Funding schools in this way puts lower-income students at an educational disadvantage.

Sales Taxes

Another important source of state and local revenue is the **sales tax**. Such a tax levies a percent charge on the purchase of a wide variety of goods and services, from manufactured items to meals served in restaurants.

Sales taxes are relatively easy to collect and provide critical funding for state and local governments. But as you read earlier, sales taxes tend to be regressive, because people with high incomes typically spend less on goods and services as a share of their income than do lower-income individuals. To limit the regressive effects of a sales tax, many cities and states do not tax necessities, such as food and medicine.

Corporate Income Taxes

Governments at all levels levy various types of business taxes. The largest business tax is the federal **corporate income tax,** which is applied to the profits of corporations. Like individual income taxes, corporate taxes are progressive, applying a higher tax rate to higher levels of corporate income.

It might seem that placing high taxes on corporations and other businesses would help relieve the tax burden on ordinary citizens. In reality, the cost of corporate taxes is passed along to individuals—to customers in the form of higher prices, to employees in the form of lower wages, and to shareholders in the form of smaller dividend checks. As one economist put it, "Purely and simply, business taxes, like all other taxes, . . . are paid for by people."

Excise and Luxury Taxes

Federal, state, and local governments also earn revenue from excise and luxury taxes, both of which tax consumption of certain goods and services.

Excise taxes are typically levied on goods and services a government wants to regulate. For example, alcohol and cigarettes are taxed to discourage their use. Because of their association with alcohol and cigarettes, excise taxes are sometimes called **sin taxes**. Like other sales taxes, excise taxes are generally regressive.

Luxury taxes, as the name implies, are levied on the sale of luxury goods, such as fur coats and private jets. Luxury taxes are progressive, because the consumption of luxury goods increases as income increases. The theory behind such taxes is that a person who can afford to buy a fur coat or a private jet can easily afford to pay an extra tax on it.

In practice, however, luxury taxes have not always worked the way lawmakers intended. In 1990, for example, Congress passed a luxury tax on expensive furs, jewelry, cars, private airplanes, and yachts. Because of the tax, wealthy people who might have purchased such products decided not to.

As demand for the luxury goods dropped, the firms that supplied them laid off workers. Within a year, according to a government study, the tax had destroyed 330 jewelry industry jobs, 1,470 aircraft industry jobs, and 7,600 jobs in the boat-building industry. In 1991, these job losses cost the federal

government more than $24 million in lost income tax revenue and unemployment benefits paid to laid-off workers. This amount was more than all of the revenue generated by the luxury tax that same year.

The 1990 luxury tax illustrates the unintended consequences of poorly thought-out tax legislation. In this case, lawmakers failed to realize that the demand for luxury goods is actually quite elastic. In 1993, Congress repealed the luxury tax on everything except cars costing more than $30,000. The luxury car tax expired in 2003.

User Fees and Tolls

Have you ever paid an entrance fee to a national park or a toll on a bridge? Like charges to park in public lots, swim in public pools, or use public highways, these are examples of user fees and tolls. **User fees** and tolls are fixed charges levied on the use of a public service or facility. Fees and tolls are based on the benefits-received principle, because those who use a facility pay the tax.

User fees and tolls are proportional taxes in that everyone pays the same rate, regardless of income. They become regressive or progressive only when a given fee tends to fall more heavily on low-income or high-income taxpayers.

Estate and Inheritance Taxes

The federal government imposes an **estate tax** on assets left to heirs by someone who dies. The heirs, or inheritors of such assets, pay the tax. Many states also levy an estate tax, sometimes called an **inheritance tax,** on top of the federal tax.

Estate taxes are progressive, because larger estates are taxed at a higher rate. Some critics argue, however, that estate taxes are unfair because they impose an additional tax on property and wealth that may already have been taxed during a person's lifetime. Estate taxes may also discourage saving. Critics who oppose the estate tax sometimes call it a "death tax." "Death and taxes may be inevitable," one critic has said, "but they shouldn't be related."

■ 12.4 How Do U.S. Governments Spend the Revenue They Raise?

In 2007, the federal government collected more than $2.5 trillion—that is, $2,500,000,000,000—in tax revenue from its citizens. Such an enormous sum raises an obvious question: what does the federal government do with it all?

Federal Revenue Sources

Most of the federal government's tax revenue comes from four sources. Individual income tax is the largest source, followed by payroll taxes and the corporate income tax. The fourth main source is excise taxes. Figure 12.4A shows these sources, along with the share of total revenue provided by each type.

Figure 12.4A

Analyzing Sources of Federal Revenue

Individual income taxes provide the largest share of federal revenue. Payroll taxes, which fund Social Security and Medicare benefits, are a close second. Because tax revenues did not cover spending in 2007, the government also borrowed money to cover the deficit.

Sources of Federal Revenue, Fiscal Year 2007

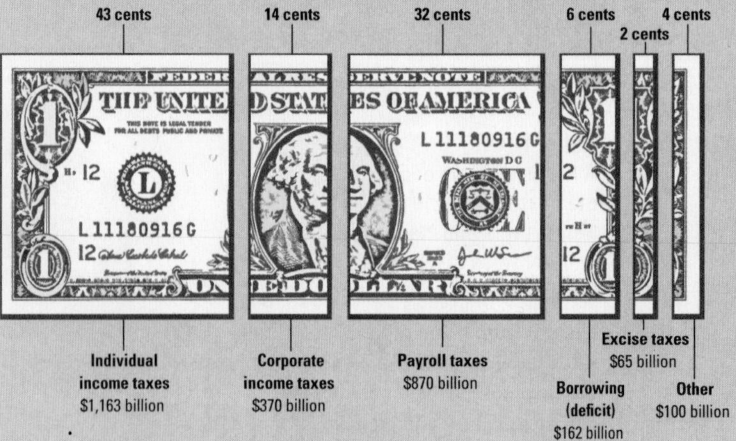

43 cents — Individual income taxes $1,163 billion
14 cents — Corporate income taxes $370 billion
32 cents — Payroll taxes $870 billion
6 cents — Borrowing (deficit) $162 billion
4 cents — Other $100 billion
2 cents — Excise taxes $65 billion

Source: Budget of the U.S. Government.
Note: Amounts do not add to 100 cents due to rounding.

Figure 12.4B

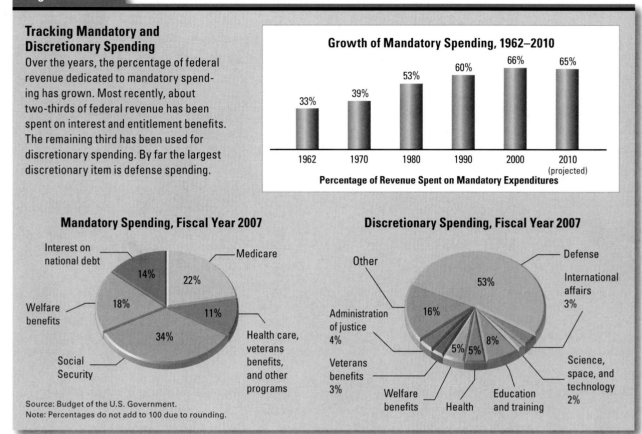

Tracking Mandatory and Discretionary Spending
Over the years, the percentage of federal revenue dedicated to mandatory spending has grown. Most recently, about two-thirds of federal revenue has been spent on interest and entitlement benefits. The remaining third has been used for discretionary spending. By far the largest discretionary item is defense spending.

Growth of Mandatory Spending, 1962–2010

1962: 33%
1970: 39%
1980: 53%
1990: 60%
2000: 66%
2010 (projected): 65%

Percentage of Revenue Spent on Mandatory Expenditures

Mandatory Spending, Fiscal Year 2007

Interest on national debt — 14%
Medicare — 22%
Health care, veterans benefits, and other programs — 11%
Social Security — 34%
Welfare benefits — 18%

Discretionary Spending, Fiscal Year 2007

Defense — 53%
International affairs — 3%
Science, space, and technology — 2%
Education and training — 8%
Health — 5%
Welfare benefits — 5%
Veterans benefits — 3%
Administration of justice — 4%
Other — 16%

Source: Budget of the U.S. Government.
Note: Percentages do not add to 100 due to rounding.

Even with these four major taxes, the government typically does not take in enough revenue to cover all its expenditures. This gives rise to the **federal deficit,** the shortfall between tax revenues and government expenditures in any given year.

To make up this difference, the government borrows money. Federal borrowing takes place through the sale of government bonds, which include Treasury bills, savings bonds, and other government-issued certificates of debt. When the government sells a bond to an investor, it is taking on a debt that it promises to repay with interest in the future.

Selling government bonds to make up for a federal deficit adds to the national debt, however. The **national debt** is the total amount owed by a nation's government as a result of borrowing.

Federal Spending: Mandatory and Discretionary

Every year, the federal government draws up a budget to determine how it will spend its revenues. Like all government budgets, it is based on a fiscal year, rather than a calendar year. A **fiscal year** is a

12-month accounting period. The federal fiscal year begins on October 1 and is identified by the year in which it ends. Fiscal year 2008, for example, ended on September 30, 2008.

In the federal budget, spending is divided into two broad categories: mandatory and discretionary. These broad categories and their subdivisions are represented in the circle graphs in Figure 12.4B.

Mandatory spending is spending that is fixed by law. The only way for Congress to change the amount of money allocated to mandatory spending is to enact new legislation.

The two main categories of mandatory spending are interest on the national debt and entitlements. **Entitlements** are programs through which individuals receive benefits based on their age, income, or some other criteria. Entitlement programs include Social Security, Medicare, and welfare. The amount of money spent on such programs depends on the number of people who sign up for them. As the bar graph in Figure 12.4B indicates, the percentage of federal revenue dedicated to mandatory spending has

Figure 12.4C

Analyzing State and Local Spending and Revenue

State and local governments rely on revenue from various sources and spend their money in different ways. As these graphs show, revenues in 2005 came mainly from taxes and federal funding, while around half of all expenditures went to education and health and social services.

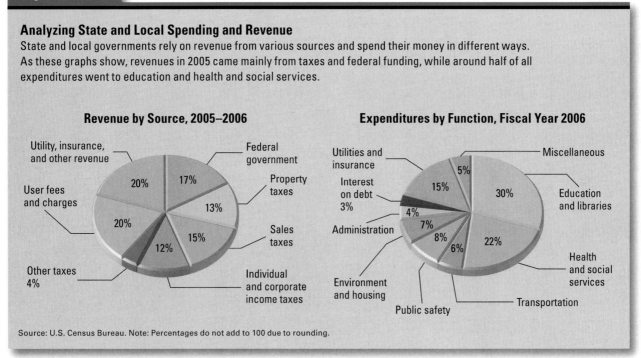

Revenue by Source, 2005–2006

Utility, insurance, and other revenue — 20%
Federal government — 17%
Property taxes — 13%
User fees and charges — 20%
Sales taxes — 15%
Other taxes 4% — 12%
Individual and corporate income taxes

Expenditures by Function, Fiscal Year 2006

Utilities and insurance
Miscellaneous — 5%
Interest on debt 3% — 15%
Education and libraries — 30%
Administration — 4%
7%
8%
6%
22%
Environment and housing
Health and social services
Public safety
Transportation

Source: U.S. Census Bureau. Note: Percentages do not add to 100 due to rounding.

grown significantly over the past several decades.

The other main category of spending, **discretionary spending,** is made up of expenditures that may be raised or lowered as Congress sees fit. As mandatory spending has grown in recent years, the share of revenue available for discretionary spending has shrunk. By far the biggest chunk is spent on national defense. The rest supports government funding for education, scientific research, health care, and foreign aid, among other activities. A portion also funds federal grants to state and local governments.

State and Local Government Revenue Sources

Like the federal government, state and local governments get most of their money from taxes. However, state and local officials face certain problems in raising revenue that the federal government does not face.

Some state constitutions, for example, prohibit state lawmakers from enacting certain types of taxes. Seven states, for instance, ban individual income taxes. Other states limit how much certain taxes can increase from year to year. In Massachusetts, for example, property taxes cannot increase by more than 2.5 percent a year. Such restrictions can be changed only if voters approve amending the state constitution.

In addition, citizens play a much larger role in tax policy at the local and state levels than at the federal level. Many states and localities require voters to approve tax hikes through **tax referendums**— direct popular votes on an issue. Some states, such as California, require a two-thirds majority of voters to approve increases in many types of taxes.

In part because of these limitations, state and local governments rely on certain revenue sources that are not used at the federal level, such as property taxes and sales taxes. Many states also run state **lotteries,** large-scale legal gambling games organized to raise money for a public cause. As of 2008, 41 states, along with the District of Columbia and Puerto Rico, held lotteries. The first graph in Figure 12.4C shows the percentages of state and local revenue that come from various sources.

Spending by State and Local Governments

The second graph in Figure 12.4C shows categories of spending by state and local governments. Unlike the federal government, which spends the bulk of its revenue on entitlements and defense, state and local governments devote large shares of their revenue to services that directly affect young people and their families.

The most important of those services is education. As of 2006, more than 48 million children were enrolled in public elementary and secondary schools throughout the United States. The average amount spent on each of these students was $9,138 per year. More than 90 percent of that money came from state and local governments.

Law enforcement and fire protection are two other responsibilities relegated mainly to local governments. In many communities, police protection is the second-largest public expense after education.

State and local governments also fund a variety of health and social services, often with assistance from the federal government. Typical examples include public health clinics for low-income families, health care centers for the mentally ill, and childcare for low-income working families.

Many other services are funded at the state and local levels. For example, state and local governments spend money to build and maintain roads and bridges. They create and maintain parks and playgrounds for the public to enjoy. They also fund public libraries, civic auditoriums, and museums.

All these services have been developed in response to public demand. The ever-present challenge is finding the money to pay for what the public wants. Because many state constitutions require balanced budgets, states that run short of funds must either raise taxes or cut programs. Either way, people are likely to object.

The fact is that although most people want the services that government provides, few people are happy to pay the taxes needed to fund those services. Former U.S. senator Russell Long once poked fun at this contradiction by reciting this jingle:

> *Don't tax you.*
> *Don't tax me.*
> *Tax that fella behind the tree.*

Taxes may not be a big issue in your life yet. But once you begin earning a regular income, they will be. You may be shocked when you get your first paycheck to see how much is deducted in income and payroll taxes. At that point, the question we started with—*Who and what should be taxed?*—may seem more important. And it should. No matter what form they take, in the end, all taxes are paid by individuals just like you.

Summary

Taxes are necessary to fund government operations and services. The three levels of U.S. government—federal, state, and local—levy various types of taxes to supply the revenues they need.

What are taxes and how should they be levied? Taxes are mandatory payments to some form of government. Ideally taxes should be designed with equity and efficiency in mind, though economists differ on how to achieve these goals. The burden, or incidence, of a tax does not always fall on the person taxed. Instead, it may be divided between consumers and producers, based on the forces of supply and demand.

What kinds of taxes will you pay in your lifetime? Taxes are structured in three basic ways—proportional, progressive, or regressive—depending on their tax rates and effects. Among the main types of taxes are income taxes, payroll taxes, property taxes, sales taxes, and excise taxes.

How do U.S. governments spend the revenue they raise? The federal government spends most of its money on entitlements, interest payments, and national defense. State and local governments spend their revenues on a variety of services, mainly in the areas of education, public safety, and social welfare.

A kinder-gentler or get-tough IRS: Which would you prefer?

The Internal Revenue Service is not the most popular institution in the U.S. government. As the federal agency in charge of enforcing tax laws, it may in fact be the most hated. Although the IRS helps many Americans with their tax returns, it is often seen as hard-hearted and bureaucratic. The prospect of being called in for an audit by the IRS strikes fear in the hearts of most taxpayers.

Yet, as the authors of this article contend, the IRS may actually be too lenient. As you read, consider whether the IRS is being too tough or too easy on American taxpayers.

Filling in the Tax Gap

by Stephen J. Dubner and Steven D. Levitt, *New York Times,* April 2, 2006

This is the time of year when American citizens inevitably think about the Internal Revenue Service and, also inevitably, about how deeply they hate it. But most people who hate the IRS probably do so for the wrong reasons. They think it is a tough and cruel agency, but in fact it is not nearly as tough and cruel as it should be.

The Role of the IRS

The first thing to remember is that the IRS doesn't write the tax code. The agency is quick to point its finger at the true villain: "In the United States, the Congress passes tax laws and requires taxpayers to comply," its mission statement says. "The IRS role is to help the large majority of compliant taxpayers with the tax law, while ensuring that the minority who are unwilling to comply pay their fair share."

So the IRS is like a street cop or, more precisely, the biggest fleet of street cops in the world, who are asked to enforce laws written by a few hundred people on behalf of a few hundred million people, a great many of whom find these laws too complex, too expensive and unfair.

And yet most Americans say they are proud to pay their taxes. In an independent poll conducted last year for the IRS Oversight Board, 96 percent of the respondents agreed with the statement "It is every American's civic duty to pay their fair share of taxes," while 93 percent agreed that everyone "who cheats on their taxes should be held accountable."

On the other hand, when asked what influences their decision to report and pay taxes honestly, 62 percent answered "fear of an audit," while 68 percent said it was the fact that their income was already being reported to the IRS by third parties. For all the civic duty floating around, it would seem that most compliance is determined by good old-fashioned incentives.

The Tax Gap

So which of these incentives work and which do not? To find out, the IRS conducted the National Research Program, a three-year study during which 46,000 randomly selected 2001 tax returns were intensively reviewed. (The IRS doesn't specify what these 46,000 people were subjected to, but it may well have been the kind of inquisition that has earned the agency its horrid reputation.)

Using this sample, the study found a tax gap—the difference between taxes owed and taxes actually paid—of $345 billion, or nearly one-fifth of all taxes collected by the IRS. This sum happens to be just a few billion dollars less than the projected federal budget deficit for 2007; it also amounts to more than $1,000 worth of cheating by every man, woman and child in the U.S.

But most people aren't cheating. And when you take a look at who does cheat and who doesn't, it becomes pretty clear just why people pay their taxes at all. The key statistic in the IRS's study is called the Net Misreporting Percentage. It measures the amount that was misreported on every major line item on those 46,000 returns. In the "wages, salaries, tips" category, for instance, Americans are underreporting only 1 percent of their actual income. Meanwhile, in the "non-farm proprietor income" category—think of self-employed workers like a restaurateur or the boss of a small construction crew—57 percent of the income goes unreported. That's $68 billion in unpaid taxes right there.

Why such a huge difference between the wage earner and a restaurateur? Simple: The only person reporting the restaurateur's income to the IRS is the restaurateur himself; for the wage earner, his employer is generating a W2 to let the IRS know exactly how much he has been paid. And the wage earner's taxes are automatically withheld from his every check, while the restaurateur has all year to decide if, and how much, he will pay.

Incentives Matter

Does this mean that the average self-employed worker is less honest than the average wage earner? Not necessarily. It's just that he has much more incentive to cheat. He knows that the only chance the IRS has of learning his true income and expenditures is to audit him. And all he has to do is look at the IRS's infinitesimal audit rate—last year, the agency conducted face-to-face audits on just 0.19 percent of all individual taxpayers—to feel pretty confident to go ahead and cheat.

As this cartoon suggests, many Americans believe that the IRS audits tax returns to punish taxpayers. Without audits, however, more Americans might cheat on their taxes, leaving honest taxpayers to pay the bill.

So why do people really pay their taxes: because it is the right thing to do, or because they fear getting caught if they don't? It sure seems to be the latter. A combination of good technology (employer reporting and withholding) and poor logic (most people who don't cheat radically overestimate their chances of being audited) makes the system work.

And while it sounds bad to hear that Americans underpay their taxes by nearly one-fifth, the tax economist Joel Slemrod estimates that the U.S. is easily within the upper tier of worldwide compliance rates.

Still, unless you are personally cheating by one-fifth or more, you should be mad at the IRS—not because it's too vigilant, but because it's not nearly vigilant enough. Why should you pay your fair share when the agency lets a few hundred billion dollars of other people's money go uncollected every year?

Stephen J. Dubner and Steven D. Levitt are the authors of Freakonomics: A Rogue Economist Explores the Hidden Side of Everything.

Public Opinion on Tax Compliance and the IRS

Are most people paying their fair share of taxes? According to the public opinion poll below, more than a third of Americans suspect that cheating is widespread. Even more believe that the IRS could do a better job enforcing tax laws.

Do you think most people cheat on their taxes, many people cheat on their taxes, only a few people cheat on their taxes, or do you think almost no one cheats on their taxes?

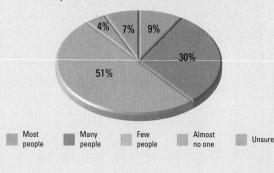

4% 7% 9% 30% 51%

- Most people
- Many people
- Few people
- Almost no one
- Unsure

How good a job do you think the IRS does in enforcing the tax laws so that everyone pays what they should pay? Would you say it does an excellent job, a good job, or a poor job of enforcing the tax laws so that everyone pays what they should pay?

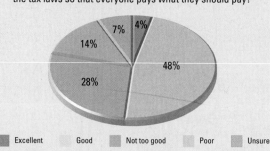

7% 4% 14% 48% 28%

- Excellent
- Good
- Not too good
- Poor
- Unsure

Source: NBC News Poll, Blum and Weprin Associates, April 2005.
Note: Percentages do not add to 100 due to rounding.

Measuring and Managing the Economy

Chapter 13

How do economists measure a nation's economic health?

Measuring the Economy

■ 13.1 Introduction

What does it mean to say that an economy is healthy? Can an economy be sick? Though an economist might not use that exact term, the answer is yes. Consider what happened to Germany's economy after that country's defeat in World War I.

By the time that war ended in 1918, the German economy was in poor shape. To make matters worse, Germany was forced to sign a treaty agreeing to pay for the war damage done to the victors, especially Britain, France, and Belgium. When the bill for war reparations arrived in 1921, it was staggering: 132 billion German marks.

To pay its debts, the German government began printing more money. As the number of marks in circulation soared, their value plummeted. A loaf of bread, for example, that had cost less than 1 mark at the end of the war cost 10 marks in 1921. This same loaf of bread rose to 250 marks in January 1923. Six months later, its price was 3,465 marks.

By November 1923, **inflation** in Germany had spiraled out of control. A simple loaf of bread now cost 200 *billion* marks. A wheelbarrow full of money could not buy a newspaper. Restaurants stopped printing menus because prices were rising too quickly to keep up. A student ordering a second cup of coffee in a cafe found that the price—already inflated at 5,000 marks—had gone up since he ordered the first cup.

Such an extreme and rapid rise in prices is known as **hyperinflation**. At the peak of Germany's hyperinflation, cash was plentiful but so worthless that people burned money in their woodstoves instead of wood. The German economy was indeed very sick.

Economists use various kinds of data to assess the health of an economy.

In the early 1920s, hyperinflation robbed German currency of its value. Germans needed more and more money to purchase the same quantity of goods and services. This woman is stuffing German banknotes into her wood stove. It was more cost effective for her to burn money than to try to buy fuel with it.

The United States has never gone through a period of hyperinflation, but economists are well aware of its devastating effects. They know that even ordinary inflation can be a sign of economic ill health. That is why economists monitor inflation, as well as other aspects of the economy. In this chapter, you will learn how economists gather data about an economy. You will see how they use the resulting statistics, called **economic indicators,** to assess a nation's overall economic health.

■ 13.2 How Do Economists Measure the Size of an Economy?

When economists study a country's economy, they can look at it from two different perspectives. They can study the economic decision making of individuals, households, and firms—the field known as microeconomics. Or, as you will do in this chapter, they can study the workings of the economy as a whole, the focus of macroeconomics. One of the first questions that scholars in the field of macroeconomics ask is, "How big is the economy?"

Gross Domestic Product: What an Economy Produces

The main measure of the size of a nation's economy is its gross domestic product. GDP is an economic indicator that measures a country's total economic output. In formal terms, **gross domestic product** is the market value of all final goods and services produced within a country during a given period of time. A steadily growing GDP is generally considered a sign of economic health.

The job of measuring U.S. GDP belongs to the Department of Commerce's Bureau of Economic Analysis. We can learn a lot about what is involved in this measurement by looking at the formal definition of gross domestic product phrase by phrase.

The market value . . . Our economy produces a vast variety of goods and services, everything from guitar lessons to computers. How can anyone add them all together to come up with a single measure of an economy's output? The Bureau of Economic Analysis does so by attaching a market value to each product. **Market value** is the price buyers are willing to pay for a good or service in a competitive marketplace.

Of all final goods and services . . . GDP is based on the market price of every "final" good or service that can be legally sold in a country. A **final good** is any new good that is ready for use by a consumer. A box of cereal is a final good, as is a new car. Goods that are used in the production of final goods, such as the grains used to produce cereal or the steel and rubber used to manufacture cars, are known as **intermediate goods**. Their market value is not counted in GDP because it is already included in the market value of the final good.

Produced within a country . . . To be included in GDP, goods and services must be produced within the country's borders. The firms that produce the goods and services do not necessarily have to be American owned. Cars manufactured in the United States by the Japanese automaker Toyota, for example, are included in this country's GDP.

During a given period of time. The Bureau of Economic Analysis calculates GDP every quarter, or three-month period. Economists use the calendar year GDP to compare production from year to year or from country to country. This annual GDP includes all final goods and services produced between January 1 and December 31. Goods do not have to have been sold during that period to be included in GDP. For example, a kayak manufactured in 2009 but sold in 2010 would be included in the 2009 GDP.

How Economists Calculate GDP

Economists typically calculate GDP by measuring expenditures on goods and services produced in a country. They divide the economy into four sectors: households, businesses, government, and foreign trade. Each sector's spending makes up one of the four components of GDP: household consumption (C), business investment (I), government purchases (G), and the net of exports minus imports (NX). Economists calculate GDP using this formula:

$$C + I + G + NX = GDP$$

Figure 13.2A shows how this formula was used to calculate this country's GDP for the year 2007.

Household consumption, C. This component of GDP consists of goods and services bought by people in households for personal use. Household consumption ranges from food and fuel to movie tickets and medical care.

Business investment, I. This component consists largely of business investment in capital goods, such as buildings and machinery. It also includes goods produced but not yet sold.

Government purchases, G. Federal, state, and local government purchases of goods and services are also included in GDP. Economists do not count government transfer payments, such as welfare or Social Security benefits, as part of GDP. These payments do not create new production, nor do they involve the purchase of goods or services by the government.

Net exports, NX. In calculating the impact of trade on GDP, economists focus on **net exports**—the value of all exports minus all imports. This makes sense because when a country exports goods and services, those exports bring money back home. The sale of these goods increases the exporting country's GDP. Just the opposite happens, however, when a country imports goods and services. The money used to pay for these imports leaves the economy, thus decreasing the importing country's GDP.

Net exports can be either positive or negative. When exports exceed imports, net exports are positive and increase GDP. When imports exceed exports, net exports are negative and decrease GDP.

Figure 13.2A

Calculating Gross Domestic Product

Gross domestic product is a measure of the total output of an economy. The diagram shows U.S. spending in 2007 on the four components used to calculate GDP. The figures are in billions of dollars. Note that household consumption is by far the largest component. Note also that net exports—exports minus imports—is a negative number. This indicates that Americans spent more on imports than they received for exports that year.

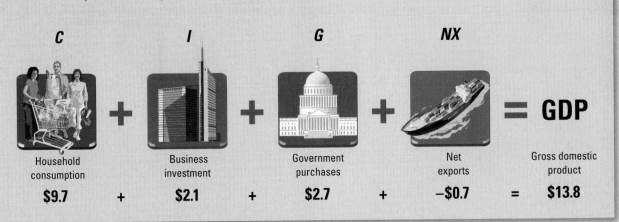

C	I	G	NX	
Household consumption	Business investment	Government purchases	Net exports	Gross domestic product
$9.7 +	$2.1 +	$2.7 +	−$0.7 =	$13.8

Adjusting for Inflation: Nominal vs. Real GDP

Economists use GDP figures to determine not only how big an economy is, but whether it is growing or shrinking and at what rate. For example, the GDP of the United States in 2006 was $13.2 trillion. The GDP in 2007 was $13.8 trillion. The difference between these two figures suggests that the economy grew by some $0.6 trillion, or 4.5 percent, from 2006 to 2007.

But is determining changes in economic output as simple as subtracting an earlier year's GDP from a later year's GDP? The answer is no, and the reason is inflation, which drives up the prices of goods and services over time.

Simply calculating GDP by adding the spending on its four components yields what economists call nominal GDP. **Nominal GDP** measures the output of an economy valued at today's prices, or in current dollars. **Current dollars** reflects the purchasing power of the dollars in the year they are spent. Using current dollars does not take the effect of inflation into account. Inflation can cause prices in current dollars to rise from year to year. And if prices go up, nominal GDP will increase over time, even if the actual output of the economy does not.

To compensate for the effects of inflation, the Commerce Department calculates what is called real GDP. **Real GDP** measures the output of an economy not in current dollars, but in constant dollars. The value of **constant dollars** is fixed at a rate that was current in a specified base year. Because the purchasing power of constant dollars is fixed, real GDP allows us to compare the total output of an economy from year to year as if prices had never changed.

In the example above, real GDP figures show that U.S. economic output grew by only 2.0 percent during 2007, not 4.5 percent as indicated by nominal GDP figures. Figure 13.2B compares nominal and real U.S. GDP over several years.

Adjusting for Population: Per Capita GDP

Economists also use GDP to compare the economies of individual countries. To make accurate comparisons, economists must adjust GDP yet again. This time they do so to take population size into account.

Adjusting for population is accomplished by calculating per capita GDP. *Per capita* means "per person." **Per capita GDP** is a nation's real gross domestic product divided by its population. It is an accepted measure of a society's standard of living.

Consider the United States and Norway, for example. In 2007, the GDP of the United States was about $13.8 trillion. This was more than 55 times the size of Norway's GDP of $0.25 trillion. The difference is not surprising, considering that the U.S. population was more than 300 million and that of Norway just under 5 million. A country with more people generally produces more goods and services, resulting in a higher GDP.

Figure 13.2B

Comparing Nominal and Real GDP

This graph compares nominal and real GDP over time. Nominal GDP measures output for the current year in current dollars. Real GDP measures this same output in constant dollars, the value of which is fixed at a base year, in this case 2000. Constant dollars are adjusted for inflation, so figures for real GDP are less than those for nominal GDP.

- Note that nominal GDP rose from $9.8 trillion to $13.8 trillion over seven years, a 41 percent increase.
- Real GDP, in contrast, rose from $9.8 to $11.6 trillion, an increase of just 18 percent.

U.S. Nominal and Real GDP, 2000–2007

Source: Bureau of Economic Analysis.

When the trees that were taken from this hillside are sold as lumber, their value will be included in GDP. However, GDP will not reflect the negative spillover effects often associated with logging. Such effects include the loss of a valuable resource, the loss of habitat for animals, and soil erosion.

As this example shows, size alone does not provide a complete picture of a country's economy. This is why economists use per capita GDP to compare one nation to another. In 2007, the per capita GDP of the United States was $45,800. The per capita GDP of Norway was $53,000. Despite having a much smaller economy, Norwegians had a higher standard of living than Americans did.

Limitations of GDP as an Indicator of Economic Health

Gross domestic product is a useful tool for measuring economic growth. But as a measure of the overall health of an economy, GDP has several limitations.

GDP leaves out unpaid household and volunteer work. Unpaid activities can have value. A volunteer firefighter, for example, and a parent who stays home to raise children are both doing important work. But because no money is exchanged, such work does not show up in a country's GDP.

GDP ignores informal and illegal exchanges. GDP statistics do not count informal or illegal economic activity as part of a nation's output. An **informal economy** is one that operates without government regulation. Occasional babysitters, for example, are paid for their work. But such transactions are not counted as part of a country's GDP. Barter is another type of informal exchange that is not reflected in GDP.

GDP counts some negatives as positives. A rise in GDP is not always a good sign. For example, after a hurricane, rebuilding can generate economic activity, which in turn can boost GDP. But people are still far worse off than they would have been if disaster had not struck. Over-exploitation of natural resources can also boost GDP. Cutting down a rainforest, for example, will raise GDP in the year of the harvest, but this temporary rise is no guarantee that people will be better off in the future without that resource.

GDP ignores negative externalities. GDP does not reflect the impact of negative externalities such as pollution. A rapidly industrializing country like China, for example, can have a rising GDP even as water and air quality decline. Moreover, GDP turns a negative into a positive when money is spent in response to environmental damage. For example, if a chemical spill from a factory contaminates a drinking well, people's purchases of bottled water are added to GDP.

GDP places no value on leisure time. Citizens of industrialized nations today enjoy more free time than ever before. This leisure time is a major benefit of living in a modern economy. Yet because time is not sold in markets, it is not reflected in GDP.

GDP says nothing about income distribution. A high per capita GDP may suggest that everyone in a society receives a fair share of goods and services.

Studies show a strong link between GDP and literacy rates. High-GDP countries have high levels of education and literacy. This makes sense, since people who have more education, like the students shown here, generally get better jobs and make more money than people with less education.

But per capita GDP is an average. It tells us nothing about how income is distributed in a society. Saudi Arabia, for example, has a high per capita GDP but huge income gaps between its richest and poorest citizens.

As this list of limitations suggests, there is much that GDP does not tell us about a society's economic welfare. As Robert Kennedy once observed,

> [GDP] is indifferent to the decency of our factories and the safety of our streets alike. It does not include the beauty of our poetry or the strength of our marriages, or the intelligence of our public debate or the integrity of our public officials . . . It measures everything, in short, except that which makes life worthwhile.
> —Senator Robert Kennedy, 1968

How GDP Growth Makes People Better Off

For all its limitations, GDP still matters. As a country's per capita GDP increases, so too do other indicators of well-being, such as those listed below.

Literacy and education. Studies show that countries with a high per capita GDP have high levels of education. The **literacy rate**—the percentage of people in these countries who can read and write—is at or near 100 percent. Literacy rates are much lower in countries with low per capita GDP. People with more education generally have better jobs and higher incomes than people with less education.

Health and life expectancy. GDP is related to the health of a population. One measure of health is **life expectancy**—the number of years, on average, that a person is expected to live. People live longer in countries with high per capita GDP than in countries with low per capita GDP. Another measure of health is **infant mortality**—the rate at which babies die during their first year of life. Because people in wealthier countries have better medical care and nutrition, infant mortality rates are lower in countries with high per capita GDPs.

Standard of living. Not surprisingly, people in countries with high per capita GDP tend to be more prosperous than people in low-GDP countries. Their houses are bigger and more comfortable. They have more food and clothing and better access to services. While such material prosperity is surely no guarantee of individual happiness, overall, people are better off living in a society with a high standard of living.

■ 13.3 What Does the Unemployment Rate Tell Us About an Economy's Health?

At any one time, millions of Americans may be out of work. For many of them, the experience is devastating. They struggle to pay bills and to put food on the table. In hard economic times, the number of people who are unemployed rises. When business is booming, the number falls.

The job of tracking unemployment belongs to the Bureau of Labor Statistics. The BLS is a government agency that collects and analyzes economic data. This agency determines the **unemployment rate**—the percentage of the labor force that is seeking work. Like the GDP, the unemployment rate is a useful indicator of the health of an economy. In general, a high unemployment rate means the overall health of the economy is poor.

How the Government Measures Unemployment

Every month, the BLS reports the total number of people who were unemployed for the previous month. To arrive at this figure, the BLS does not attempt to count every job seeker in the country. Instead, it conducts a sample survey each month. By examining a small but representative sample of the population, the BLS can gauge how many people in the entire population are unemployed.

The BLS surveys about 60,000 households each month. Household members who are eligible to be in the labor force are interviewed about their activities during a specific one-week period. The survey excludes those who are under 16 years of age, on active duty in the military, or in an institution such as a prison or nursing home. Based on the interview data, the BLS classifies those who are eligible as employed, unemployed, or not in the labor force.

Employed. Members of the labor force who have jobs are classified as employed. This category includes people who worked for at least one hour for pay or profit during the survey week. It also includes those who worked 15 hours or more without pay in a family-operated business. And it includes workers who were sick, on vacation, or otherwise excused from their jobs during the survey week.

Unemployed. Members of the labor force who are jobless, but are looking for work, are classified as unemployed. To be counted as unemployed, individuals must have actively looked for work in the four weeks preceding the survey week. They had to have inquired about jobs, sent out resumes, filled out job applications, or otherwise sought work. There is an exception: people who have been laid off and are waiting to be called back to their jobs need not actively seek work to be counted as unemployed.

Not in the labor force. Everyone who is eligible to be in the labor force but is neither working nor looking for work is classified as not in the labor force. This category includes full-time students as well as people who are retired, disabled, or prevented by family responsibilities from taking a paying job.

The BLS adds together the number of employed and unemployed people to determine the size of the labor force. To calculate the unemployment rate, it then divides the number of unemployed people by the number in the labor force. The result is multiplied by 100 to express this ratio as a percent, as shown in the formula below.

$$\text{unemployment rate} = \frac{\text{number unemployed}}{\text{number in labor force}} \times 100$$

Figure 13.3A shows how this formula applies to a specific example, drawn from the results of one BLS survey conducted in 2008.

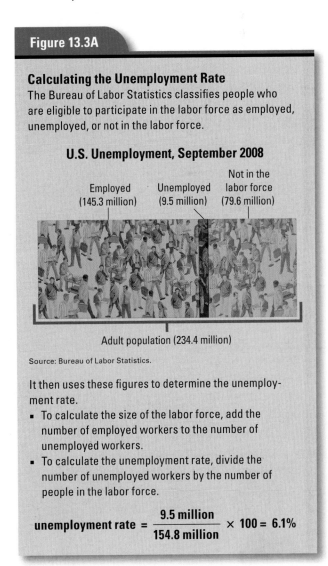

Figure 13.3A

Calculating the Unemployment Rate
The Bureau of Labor Statistics classifies people who are eligible to participate in the labor force as employed, unemployed, or not in the labor force.

U.S. Unemployment, September 2008

Employed (145.3 million) Unemployed (9.5 million) Not in the labor force (79.6 million)

Adult population (234.4 million)

Source: Bureau of Labor Statistics.

It then uses these figures to determine the unemployment rate.
- To calculate the size of the labor force, add the number of employed workers to the number of unemployed workers.
- To calculate the unemployment rate, divide the number of unemployed workers by the number of people in the labor force.

$$\text{unemployment rate} = \frac{9.5 \text{ million}}{154.8 \text{ million}} \times 100 = 6.1\%$$

Unemployment

Unemployment means having no paying job. Economists identify four types of unemployment. The first three—frictional, structural, and seasonal unemployment—can exist even in a growing economy. The fourth, cyclical unemployment, emerges during an economic downturn.

Frictional unemployment happens when a person seeks to enter the workforce or quits one job to seek another.

Structural unemployment happens when advances in technology eliminate jobs.

Seasonal unemployment happens when businesses shut down or slow down for part of the year.

Cyclical unemployment happens when there is a decline in business activity during an economic downturn.

Four Types of Unemployment

In its interviews, the BLS gathers detailed information about people who are unemployed. Based on those data and further research, economists identify four types of unemployment: frictional, structural, seasonal, and cyclical.

Frictional unemployment. Have you ever heard someone talk about being "between jobs"? This situation, which exists when a person has left one job and is looking for another, is what economists call **frictional unemployment**. It applies to people who change jobs as well as to people seeking their first jobs. Frictional unemployment is usually short term, lasting only as long as is needed to find the right job.

Consider Devin, who worked for a year in the electronics department of a retail store at the mall. Though he excelled at his job, he was unable to get a promotion. So he quit, confident he would be able to find a better position at a big electronics store.

Frictional unemployment like Devin's can create temporary hardship for the jobless person. It also represents lost production for an employer trying to fill a position. However, a certain amount of frictional unemployment is unavoidable when people are free to change jobs at will. Changing jobs, as Devin did, is usually good for the economy because it can reallocate labor resources to their best use.

Structural unemployment. People who choose to change jobs are in transition. Their skills are still in demand and the time they spend without a job is usually short. The same cannot be said of those who experience structural unemployment. **Structural unemployment** comes about mainly when advances in technology reduce the demand for certain skills.

Megan, for example, worked as a travel agent for 20 years. People told her where they wanted to go, and she made all the arrangements. She loved her job—until the Internet came along. Online travel services made it easy for people to plan their trips themselves. The demand for Megan's skills dried up. Her job was eliminated, and she became unemployed.

What can people like Megan do to become employable again? They might consider returning to school to develop new skills that employers want. Or they might be able to adapt existing skills to qualify for new job opportunities. Even though structural unemployment is hard on those who experience it, the economy as a whole clearly benefits from the technological progress that creates it.

Seasonal unemployment. In some markets, demand for labor depends on the season. For example, Taylor works for a small construction company in Montana. Winters in Montana are so cold that her company almost always closes during January and February.

For two months, Taylor experiences seasonal unemployment. **Seasonal unemployment** occurs when businesses shut down or slow down for part of the year, often because of weather. Tourism, construction, and agriculture are among the industries that typically lay people off for part of the year.

Cyclical unemployment. Every economy goes through prosperous times and hard times. Such cycles of growth and decline are the cause of **cyclical unemployment**. This type of unemployment occurs during periods of decline. At such times, economic activity slows, GDP drops, and people lose their jobs.

Consider Kai, who in the late 1990s worked as a Web designer for a start-up company that sold pet supplies over the Internet. Like many other Internet-based start-ups—or dot-coms—the company had no trouble attracting investors who were convinced that doing business over the Internet was the wave of the future. The company's stock soared in value, even though the business itself wasn't making a profit. During this period, the price of dot-com stocks rose to dizzying heights.

Then, in 2000, the dot-com bubble burst. Investors rushed to sell off their dot-com shares, and the value of those stocks dropped dramatically. The company that employed Kai went out of business, leaving him and his co-workers unemployed.

People like Kai who experience cyclical unemployment often have trouble finding new jobs that use their skills. Few businesses hire new workers during an economic decline. Moreover, the labor market may be glutted with equally qualified workers who are in the same situation. Many people are forced to take jobs outside their chosen fields or live on unemployment benefits while they wait for the economy to improve.

Full Employment and the Natural Rate of Unemployment

When an economy is healthy and growing, it experiences little cyclical unemployment. But there will always be some frictional, seasonal, and structural unemployment. Some people will always be out of work, even in an economy with full employment. At that point, all of the economy's available labor resources are being used efficiently.

When an economy reaches full employment, jobs exist for everyone who wants to work, even though a certain percentage of those jobs and workers will not yet have been matched together. Economists call this percentage the **natural rate of unemployment**. This rate has varied historically, but has generally ranged between 4 and 6 percent. Figure 13.3B shows unemployment rates over time.

Figure 13.3B

Tracking Unemployment over Time
This graph shows the ups and downs in the unemployment rate over several decades. The horizontal band shows the natural rate of unemployment during the same time period.

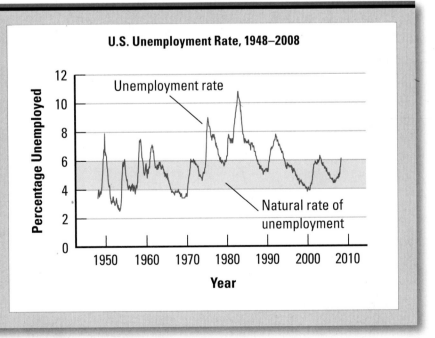

Source: Bureau of Labor Statistics.

Problems with the Unemployment Rate as an Indicator of Economic Health

In determining how many of the country's more than 300 million people are unemployed, the BLS makes every effort to be accurate. Still, critics point to several problems that may make the results less than exact.

The first problem is that at any one time, a number of unemployed people have given up looking for work. Though willing and able to work, they no longer expect to find jobs. These **discouraged workers** do not fit the BLS's definition of unemployed, which counts only those people who are making an effort to find work. Because discouraged workers are left out of BLS calculations, the official unemployment rate, some critics argue, is too low.

The second problem is that the official unemployment rate does not recognize **involuntary part-time workers**. These are people who, unable to find full-time jobs, settle for part-time employment. They work less than 35 hours per week. Others who once worked full time may have had their hours cut back. The BLS counts such part-time workers as employed. However, some economists think these workers should be counted as partially unemployed. For example, someone who works 20 hours a week but wants full-time work might be counted as "half unemployed."

A third problem with the unemployment rate involves people working in informal or underground economies. The **underground economy** is made up of people who earn income from gambling, drug dealing, and other illegal activities. When surveyed by the BLS, they would be unlikely to admit to anything illegal. Instead, their answers would suggest they are unemployed. The same might be true for people in the informal economy who pay no taxes on their earnings. As a result, the actual rate of unemployment might be lower than the official rate indicates.

The Economic Costs of High Unemployment

Despite its flaws, the official unemployment rate serves as a fairly good indicator of conditions in the labor market. And in general, when the rate is high, the overall health of the economy is poor.

The main economic cost of high unemployment is lost potential output. The smaller the number of people who are working, the fewer goods and services the economy can generate. Potential output is lost because labor resources are not being fully utilized. An increasing unemployment rate, then, means a decreasing real GDP.

Unemployed workers also pay a serious economic cost. They and their families lose income and the goods and services that income would have purchased. They may become unable to pay their monthly mortgage, leading to the loss of a home. Unemployment can also mean the loss of medical benefits, which then become an added expense.

High unemployment is also costly for society at

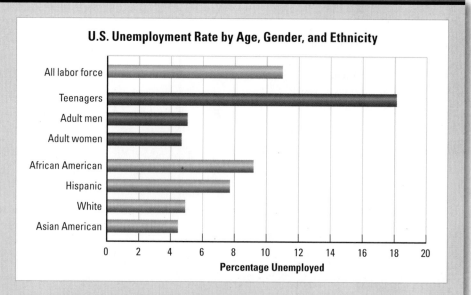

Figure 13.3C

Analyzing the Unemployment Rate
Some groups of Americans have higher unemployment rates than others. Workers who are less skilled or less educated are more vulnerable to job loss than those with more skills and experience. Teenagers have the highest unemployment rate, in part because they have fewer skills and less experience than adults. This graph shows a teenage unemployment rate of 18.1 percent in June 2008.

Source: Bureau of Labor Statistics.

U.S. Unemployment Rate by Age, Gender, and Ethnicity

large. Unemployed workers no longer contribute income taxes to the government. In fact, many begin taking money from the government in the form of unemployment insurance and other benefits. This may call for shifting money from other programs to pay the additional benefits, or it may mean raising taxes on those workers who remain employed.

■ 13.4 What Does the Inflation Rate Reveal About an Economy's Health?

A second cup of coffee that costs more than the first. A pile of money that is more valuable as fuel than as currency. These were some of the bizarre realities of hyperinflation in post–World War I Germany.

The German experience was proof, if any was needed, that runaway inflation can send an economy into a tailspin. That is why economists keep a close eye on a third economic indicator: the inflation rate. The **inflation rate** is the percentage increase in the average price level of goods and services from one month or year to the next. It is tracked by the same government agency that tracks the unemployment rate, the Bureau of Labor Statistics.

Tracking Inflation with the Consumer Price Index

The BLS tracks inflation by gathering information on Americans' cost of living. That is, it studies the cost of buying the goods and services that households like yours purchase every day. As you would expect, the cost of living changes all the time because prices do not stay the same.

Economists at the BLS track changes in the cost of living using what is known as the consumer price index. A **price index** measures the average change in price of a type of good over time. The **consumer price index (CPI)** is a price index for a "market basket" of consumer goods and services. Changes in the average prices of these items approximate the change in the overall cost of living. For that reason, the CPI is sometimes called the **cost-of-living index**. As such, it serves as the primary measure of inflation in the United States.

The CPI market basket is based on surveys of thousands of households about their spending habits. This information is used to develop a detailed list of items to track. Each month, BLS data collectors visit some 25,000 retail stores and record the prices of these items.

The BLS determines the CPI by comparing each month's price information to the prices paid for the same goods and services during a base period. As of 2008, the base period was 1982–1984. The BLS set the cost of goods and services in its market basket during that period at 100.

Using its monthly price data, the BLS can track the change in the CPI between any two periods. For example, the CPI for March 2007 was 205.352. By March 2008, the CPI had increased to 213.528. Based on those numbers, the BLS calculates that the CPI rose 4.0 percent during that 12-month period. In other words, the inflation rate for that one-year period was 4 percent.

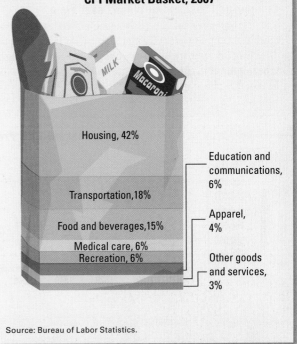

Key Concept

The Consumer Price Index

The consumer price index is an indicator used to track changes in the prices of basic household goods and services. Each group of items in the CPI's market basket is given a "weight," or percentage, that reflects how much consumers spend on it. Average consumers spend the largest part of their income on housing, which includes rent or mortgage payments, property taxes, heat, electricity, and furniture.

CPI Market Basket, 2007

Housing, 42%

Transportation, 18%

Food and beverages, 15%

Medical care, 6%
Recreation, 6%

Education and communications, 6%

Apparel, 4%

Other goods and services, 3%

Source: Bureau of Labor Statistics.

Adjusting for Inflation:
Nominal vs. Real Cost of Living

You have surely heard older people complaining about how much prices have gone up since they were your age. A pair of shoes that once cost $4, for example, cannot be had for less than $40 today. But do higher prices really mean that things cost more than they used to?

The price a person pays for a pair of shoes or any other product is its nominal cost, or its cost in current dollars. The cost in current dollars of all the basic goods and services that people need is the **nominal cost of living**. Like the nominal GDP, the nominal cost of living is based on current prices.

The **real cost of living** is the nominal cost of basic goods and services, adjusted for inflation. Knowing the rate of inflation—established by the consumer price index—allows economists to calculate the real cost of goods and services in constant dollars. The real cost of living can then be used to compare prices over time.

People who complain about how much prices have risen over the years are probably not thinking about the other side of the coin—wages. Consumers pay nominal costs with **nominal wages,** or wages based on current prices. As prices go up, wages generally go up

as well. By using the CPI to adjust for inflation, economists can calculate **real wages** and compare them over time. Figure 13.4A, which tracks presidential salaries since 1789, illustrates the difference between nominal wages and real wages adjusted for inflation.

If wages keep pace with the cost of living, perhaps things do not really cost more than they used to. Thanks to this upward trend, the shoes once purchased for $4 were affordable then and may be just as affordable today at $40. Looking at the cost of living in terms of time, not money, supports this conclusion. As noted in a 1997 Federal Reserve report,

> *The cost of living is indeed going up—in money terms. What really matters, though, isn't what something costs in money; it's what it costs in time. Making money takes time, so when we shop, we're really spending time. The real cost of living isn't measured in dollars and cents but in the hours and minutes we must work to live.*

So how does the cost of a $4 pair of shoes in 1958 compare to the cost of a $40 pair of shoes 50 years later? In 1958, the average wage was around $2 per hour. In 2008, wages averaged around $20 per hour. Which pair cost more in hours worked? The two pairs cost about the same—two hours of time worked.

Figure 13.4A

Comparing Presidential Wages over Time

The first Congress set George Washington's salary as president at $25,000 a year. Two centuries and many pay hikes later, President George W. Bush received $400,000 a year. The difference seems enormous until the effects of inflation are taken into account. When real wages are compared—based on constant 2007 dollars—Washington comes out as the better-paid leader. As a fairly wealthy man, however, Washington declined to accept any salary as president.

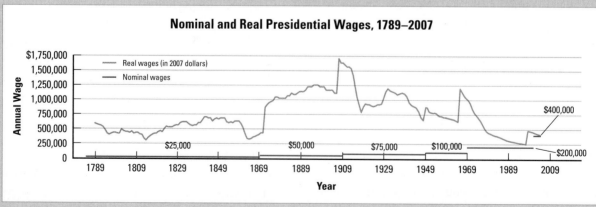

Source: Congressional Quarterly and Robert Sahr, Oregon State University.

Hyperinflation pushed the economy of Zimbabwe to the point of collapse. In this supermarket in the city of Bulawayo in 2008, shelves stand empty. Fuel prices are so high that goods cannot make it to market.

Creeping Inflation, Hyperinflation, and Deflation

In an ideal world, prices would be stable, neither rising nor falling over time. In our real world, prices are always changing. The result can be creeping inflation, hyperinflation, or deflation.

Creeping inflation. In the United States we have come to expect a certain amount of gradual inflation, or **creeping inflation,** every year. Since 1914, the average annual rate of inflation has been about 3.4 percent. For much of that period, the rate has varied widely. But during your lifetime it has stayed fairly close to that average. For Americans, this is normal inflation —the level we are used to.

Hyperinflation. Occasionally inflation goes into overdrive. The result is hyperinflation. Runaway inflation creates extreme uncertainty in an economy. Nobody can predict how high prices will go, and people lose confidence in their currency as a store of value.

A number of countries have experienced hyperinflation since Germany in the 1920s. The African country of Zimbabwe is one example. Zimbabwe began its plunge into crisis in 2000, when the government seized thousands of white-owned farms. Foreign investors fled. Unemployment shot up. Food shortages became severe. The government responded to the crisis by printing money, adding trillions of Zimbabwean dollars to the money supply each year.

As the Zimbabwean dollar lost value, inflation skyrocketed. Vending machines that took coins quickly became unusable. One soda would have required the deposit of billions of coins. By early 2008, the official annual inflation rate had topped 100,000 percent. With the price of goods doubling every few days, farms and factories shut down and standards of living collapsed.

Deflation. The inflation rate is usually a positive number, meaning that the overall price level is rising. But the inflation rate can be negative, a condition that economists call **deflation**. Deflation occurs when prices go down over time.

Deflation is good news for consumers and savers. The value of every dollar they set aside now to spend later will increase over time as prices fall. Deflation is also good for lenders. The dollars they receive from borrowers tomorrow will be worth more than the dollars they lent them yesterday. This increase in the value of dollars can be painful for borrowers, however.

Deflation may also be bad news for businesses. When prices are dropping, people tend to put off spending, hoping for still lower prices later on. As consumer spending slows, businesses cut wages, lay off workers, and may even go bankrupt. The result can be a deflationary spiral, such as occurred in the early days of the Great Depression. In a **deflationary spiral,** falling prices lead to business slowdowns, which lead to lower wages, which lead to still lower prices, and so on.

Demand-Pull vs. Cost-Push Inflation

You are already familiar with one cause of inflation: an increase in the money supply. A dramatic increase in the amount of money in circulation can cause hyperinflation. But even a more modest increase

Figure 13.4B

Analyzing the Wage-Price Spiral

A wage-price spiral is a vicious cycle in which rising prices drive up wages and then rising wages drive up prices. The result is an inflationary spiral that can be hard to break.

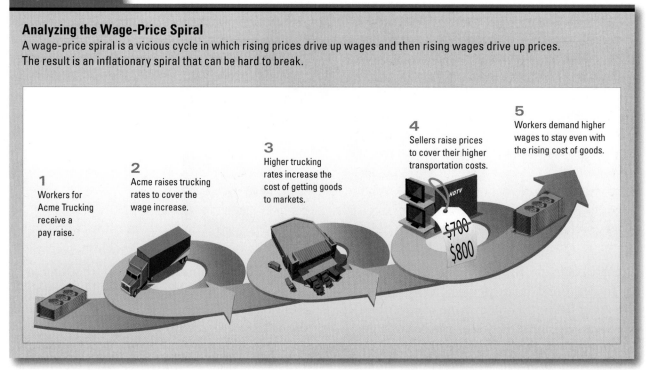

1 Workers for Acme Trucking receive a pay raise.

2 Acme raises trucking rates to cover the wage increase.

3 Higher trucking rates increase the cost of getting goods to markets.

4 Sellers raise prices to cover their higher transportation costs.

5 Workers demand higher wages to stay even with the rising cost of goods.

may trigger inflation if the result is too many dollars chasing too few goods.

A second cause of inflation is an increase in overall demand. The spending that makes up GDP comes from households, businesses, government, and foreign buyers. Sometimes these four sectors together try to purchase more goods and services than the economy can produce. This increase in overall demand results in **demand-pull inflation**. The extra demand by buyers exerts a "pull" on prices, forcing them up.

Inflation can also be caused by increases in the cost of the factors of production. Higher production costs reduce the economy's ability to supply the same output at the same price level. The result is **cost-push inflation**. The rising cost of land, labor, or capital "pushes" the overall price level higher.

Cost-push inflation is often triggered by increases in energy prices. Rising fuel costs affect every link in the supply chain, from farms and factories to the delivery of goods to retail stores. The higher costs of making and moving goods are then passed on to consumers in the form of higher prices.

Whether caused by increased demand or rising costs, inflation can set off a kind of "feedback loop" known as a **wage-price spiral**. This spiral starts when workers demand higher wages in order to keep up

with inflation. Employers pay the higher wages but then raise prices still higher to cover their increased production costs. Higher prices for goods and services once again decrease the real income of the workers, prompting them to call for still higher wages. As their demands are met, wages and prices keep climbing in an inflationary spiral.

Limitations of the CPI as a Measure of Inflation

The BLS relies on the consumer price index to estimate the level of inflation in the United States each month. However, critics point to several biases that may distort the CPI, making the reported inflation rate less than accurate.

Substitution bias. Because the CPI measures the price changes of a fixed list of goods, it does not take into account consumers' ability to substitute goods in response to price changes. For example, when the price of beef rises, many people buy chicken instead to save money. Such savings are not reflected in the CPI.

Outlet substitution bias. The CPI is slow to reflect changing trends in shopping patterns. For example, a growing number of households shop at discount stores, buying clubs, and superstores. The money saved by consumers who shop at these low-cost outlets may not be reflected in the CPI.

New product bias. In a market economy, new products are introduced all the time. Because the BLS cannot predict which new products will succeed, the new products are not incorporated into the market basket until they have become commonplace. For example, the mobile phone was introduced in 1983. However, it was not included in the CPI until 1998. By that time, the price of mobile phones had dropped from $3995 to under $200. None of these pre-1998 price drops were reflected in the CPI.

Quality change bias. Over time, technological advances may improve the quality or add to the lifetime of a product. An example is the automobile tire. Tires today generally last longer than they did in the past. As a result, the cost of tires on a per-mile basis has dropped. Because drivers buy tires less often, longer-wearing tires save money. But these savings are not reflected in the CPI.

The BLS has taken steps to reduce such biases through increasingly sophisticated methods of gathering data. Even so, some economists have estimated that, taken together, these biases in the CPI cause the Bureau of Labor Statistics to overstate the annual inflation rate by as much as 1 percent. Thus the economy may actually be healthier—and Americans better off—than the CPI suggests.

The Economic Costs of Inflation

Between 2000 and 2008, the annual rate of inflation in the United States ranged from a low of 1.6 percent to a high of 3.4 percent. Whether inflation at these relatively low levels is "healthy" for the economy is open to debate. However, we do know that inflation of any amount exacts economic costs.

Loss of purchasing power. Inflation erodes purchasing power—the amount of goods and services that can be bought with a given amount of money. As a result, it undermines one of the basic functions of money: its use as a store of value.

For example, suppose you have your eye on an electric guitar that costs $200. You don't have the money to buy it now, so you save up. When you go back to the store, you discover that the guitar now costs $220. It is the same guitar, but inflation has pushed the price up by 10 percent. The purchasing power of your $200 has eroded by 10 percent.

Multiply this single example across an entire economy and you can see how inflation could affect people's standard of living. Retired people living on fixed incomes are the hardest hit by a continual increase in the overall price level. Working people have less to worry about. As long as wages keep pace with inflation, workers will not lose purchasing power.

Higher interest rates. The expectation that inflation will erode future purchasing power drives up interest rates. In inflationary times, lenders pay close attention to the real interest rate on the money they loan. The real interest rate is the nominal interest rate minus the inflation rate. If the nominal interest rate is 10 percent and the inflation rate is 4 percent, then the real interest rate is 6 percent.

Higher real interest rates on bank deposits

Figure 13.4C

Calculating the Effect of Inflation on Purchasing Power
Because of inflation, the dollar you hold today may not have as much purchasing power tomorrow. This "backpack index" shows the effect of 3 percent inflation on the prices of some everyday items over time.

The Backpack Index

Items in Backpack	Today	In 5 Years	In 10 Years
Pens (12 pack)	$1.49	$1.73	$2.00
Highlighters (6 pack)	$2.99	$3.47	$4.02
Notebook	$5.49	$6.36	$7.38
Calculator	$18.96	$21.98	$25.48
Cell phone	$49.99	$57.95	$67.18
Total	**$78.94**	**$91.49**	**$106.06**

provide an incentive for people to save more. But higher real rates also slow economic growth by making loans too costly. Lower real interest rates discourage saving. At the same time, they encourage borrowing by allowing borrowers to repay most of their loans in dollars that will be worth less tomorrow than they were today.

Loss of economic efficiency. Many economists consider uncertainty about prices to be a bigger problem than loss of purchasing power or higher interest rates. When prices fluctuate due to inflation, buyers and sellers cannot rely on an increase or decrease in prices to give them clear information about market conditions. By making price signals harder to interpret, inflation reduces market efficiency.

■ 13.5 How Does the Business Cycle Relate to Economic Health?

Economies are always changing. Or, as economics writer Charles Wheelan puts it, they "proceed in fits and starts." Wheelan is referring to the recurring periods of growth and decline in economic activity that all economies experience. Economists call this recurring pattern the **business cycle**.

The Four Phases of the Business Cycle

The business cycle consists of four phases. These phases include a period of growth and a period of decline, as well as the turning points that mark the shift from one period to the next.

A period of economic growth is known as an **expansion**. During this phase of the business cycle, economic activity generally increases from month to month. The longest expansion of the U.S. economy lasted a decade, but expansions typically run out of steam in three to five years.

The point at which an expansion ends marks the **peak** of the business cycle. At that peak, economic activity has reached its highest level. The peak also marks the start of a decline in economic activity. Economists do not know when a peak is occurring until they look back at the economic data. At that time they designate one month as the peak phase.

Following the peak comes the contraction phase of the business cycle. A **contraction** is a period of general economic decline marked by a falling GDP and rising unemployment. One of the longest contractions on record—43 months—occurred at the start of the Great Depression. Since 1945, however, contractions have averaged about 10 months.

The lowest point of a contraction is called the **trough**. Like the peak, the trough marks a turning point. Once the economy hits bottom, a new expansion begins.

Economic Indicators and the Business Cycle

The term *business cycle* implies that expansions and contractions occur at regular, predictable intervals. But in fact, the opposite is true. Business cycles are irregular in both length and severity. This makes peaks and troughs difficult to predict. Nonetheless, economists attempt to do just that, using a variety of economic indicators. The illustration on the opposite page shows how three of these indicators—GDP, inflation rate, and unemployment rate—relate to each phase of the business cycle.

Economists categorize the indicators they use to track the business cycle based on whether they signal a future change, an ongoing change, or a change that has already begun.

Leading indicators. Measures that consistently rise or fall several months before an expansion or a contraction begins are called **leading economic indicators**. They are used to forecast the peak and trough of a business cycle, although not very precisely.

The Census Bureau's monthly estimate of housing starts is one such leading indicator. It shows the number of new home-construction projects started in the previous month. A rise in housing starts signals that there is enough money and confidence in the economy to begin preparing for the next expansion. As the economy improves, there will be plenty of people eager to buy new homes. A decline in housing starts indicates trouble ahead as consumers grow more cautious about buying new homes.

Coincident indicators. Coincident economic indicators are measures that consistently rise or fall along with expansions or contractions. They coincide with the phases of the business cycle. Coincident indicators are most helpful in tracking expansions and contractions as they happen.

One of the most reliable coincident indicators is real GDP. As a rule, if total output is increasing in real terms month after month, an economy is expanding. If total output begins to shrink, the economy is contracting. Because inflation also tends to rise and fall with economic activity, economists use the inflation rate as an important coincident indicator as well.

Lagging indicators. Measures that consistently rise or fall several months after an expansion or a contraction are known as **lagging economic indicators**. Economists use lagging indicators to confirm that one phase of the business cycle has ended and another has begun.

One of the most important lagging indicators is the unemployment rate. The reason is that firms are often reluctant to make decisions to lay off or hire workers until they are sure about the direction of the economy. For example, when an expansion begins, firms may delay hiring new workers until they know that the economy is really growing. As a result, unemployment rates do not drop until weeks or months after an economy hits its low point and begins to recover.

Key Concept

The Business Cycle
The business cycle is a recurring pattern of change as an economy expands and contracts. During an expansion, economic activity increases until it peaks and can grow no more. During the contraction that follows, economic activity slows until it sinks into a trough and begins to turn around.

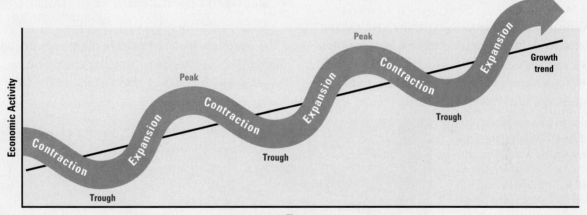

Relating Key Economic Indicators to the Business Cycle

Phase of the Business Cycle	Real GDP	Unemployment Rate	Inflation Rate
Expansion: Period of economic growth	increasing	generally decreasing	generally increasing
Peak: Highest level of economic activity	stops increasing	stops decreasing	stops increasing and may start decreasing
Contraction: Period of economic decline	decreasing	generally increasing	generally decreasing
Trough: Lowest level of economic activity	stops decreasing	stops increasing	stops decreasing and may start increasing

From Boom to Bust to Boom Again

Business cycles are popularly known as periods of boom and bust. A boom is the expansion phase of the cycle. It may also be known as a recovery, upturn, upswing, or period of prosperity. All these terms mean the same thing—the economy is healthy and growing.

One of the key characteristics of a growing economy is an increase in business investment. When firms invest in capital goods, such as factories, machinery, and equipment, their productivity increases. This increased productivity contributes to a rise in real GDP. At the same time, firms hire more people to work in their stores, offices, and factories, thus increasing employment throughout the economy.

Other factors can also contribute to growth. The discovery of new resources, such as by drilling or mining, can boost the quantity of raw materials available for production. Innovations in science or technology can improve efficiency and increase productivity. Such positive "shocks" to the economy can stimulate an expansion.

Consumer confidence is typically high during an expansion. Jobs are plentiful, and both business profits and wages are rising. The future looks bright, leading consumers to borrow and spend money, especially on "big ticket" items such as cars, appliances, and furniture.

An economic expansion can go on for years, leading people to think that it might go on forever. But inevitably, boom turns to bust. The bust, or contraction phase of the business cycle, is also called a downturn, a downswing, or a recession. Most economists define a **recession** as a decline in economic activity lasting at least six months. During a recession, real GDP falls, as do real wages, employment, profits, and production.

Why does an expanding economy stop growing and start shrinking? There is no single answer to that question. A number of different obstacles to growth can push an economy into recession. They include

- a negative shock to the economy, such as rapidly rising oil prices, a terrorist attack, or a stock market crash.
- a rise in interest rates, which makes it harder for consumers and firms to borrow money.
- shortages of raw materials, which can cause price increases.

Consumers typically react to higher prices and higher interest rates by cutting back on spending. As sales slow, businesses begin to see profits fall

America's entry into World War II pulled the nation out of the Great Depression, the worst economic downturn in U.S. history. The war caused an immediate upsurge in demand for fighter planes, ships, arms, and supplies for the troops. This demand spurred an increase in production. Factories started hiring, unemployment fell, and an economic recovery began.

and inventories rise. **Inventory** is merchandise that companies or stores have on hand. Faced with rising inventory, firms cut back production and lay off workers. If profits continue to fall despite these adjustments, firms must cut back further. In this way, an economy enters a contraction phase.

Some recessions are short and relatively mild in their effects. Others are severe. On rare occasions, a recession will last a long time and cause serious damage to the economy. Economists refer to this kind of severe contraction as a depression. A **depression** is a prolonged economic downturn characterized by a plunging real GDP and extremely high unemployment. Americans have suffered through several depressions, with the Great Depression of the 1930s being the worst.

For many people, a recession is a time of anxiety about the economy and their own financial futures. How do consumers regain confidence? What brings bust back to boom? The answer may depend on the severity of the contraction. It took a war to end the Great Depression. The demand for armaments and other goods to fight World War II spurred production and finally turned the slumping economy around.

Recoveries are usually triggered by a combination of events. As business inventories shrink over time, firms begin to increase production. Hiring begins to pick up. Optimism returns and consumers start spending again. A new expansion begins.

The ups and downs of the business cycle may hold little interest for you at this point in your life. This is likely to change once you enter the job market. Should you start looking for work during an expansion, you may find many employers eager to hire you. But should you start your job search during a recession, good jobs may be hard to find. The next chapter explores what the government can—and cannot— do to smooth out the bumps in the business cycle.

Summary

Economists use various indicators to measure the health of an economy. Three key economic indicators are a country's gross domestic product, unemployment rate, and inflation rate. These and other indicators help economists figure out the economy's position in the business cycle.

How do economists measure the size of an economy? Gross domestic product is the main measure of an economy's overall size. Nominal GDP is the measure of the current year's total output. Real GDP measures total output adjusted for inflation. Per capita GDP measures a country's average output per person, allowing for country-to-country comparisons.

What does the unemployment rate tell us about an economy's health? People who do not have jobs but who are looking for work are officially unemployed. A rising unemployment rate is usually associated with an unhealthy economy.

What does the inflation rate reveal about an economy's health? Inflation is a rise in the overall price level. Economists use the Consumer Price Index (CPI) to determine changes in the price level from one period to another. A strong economy is likely to have a low level of inflation. A high inflation rate indicates an unhealthy economy.

How does the business cycle relate to economic health? The business cycle consists of four phases: expansion, peak, contraction (or recession), and trough. As measured by real GDP, the economy grows during an expansion and shrinks during a contraction. The peak marks the end of an expansion and the start of a contraction. The trough marks the end of a contraction and the start of a new expansion.

Which economic indicator would you use to assess the health of our economy?

Gross domestic product is an important and widely used indicator of the health of an economy. But as critics have pointed out, GDP is far from perfect. For this reason, economists have suggested a variety of other indicators that might do a better job of measuring economic well-being. Some of them are presented here. As you read about them, consider the criteria used to devise them. Which one would you choose to measure the health of the U.S. economy?

Five Measures of Economic Well-Being

What says more about the overall economic well-being of a nation: the average amount of money each person in the country spends each year? The amount of pollution the country emits? Or the average height of the adult population?

Nominal GDP

Nominal gross domestic product is the value of all final goods and services produced during a given year, expressed in current prices. This table shows the four largest economies in the world, based on estimated 2007 GDP, followed by a sampling of countries with lower GDPs. Note that the dollar figures are given in billions. For example, $13,811 means $13,811,000,000,000, or $13.8 trillion.

Nominal GDP for Ten Countries, 2007

Rank	Country	GDP in billions of U.S. $
1	United States	$13,811
2	Japan	4,377
3	Germany	3,297
4	China	3,280
11	Russia	1,291
12	India	1,171
14	Mexico	893
15	Australia	822
28	South Africa	278
98	Ghana	15

Source: The World Bank.

Per Capita GDP

Per capita GDP is calculated by dividing a country's GDP by its population. The result —a country's average economic output per person—is a better measure than nominal GDP for comparing the living standards of two or more countries. The number one country in this ranking (though not one of the countries in the table) is tiny Luxembourg. Its estimated 2007 GDP was only $48 billion but its per capita GDP was $99,879.

Per Capita GDP for Ten Countries, 2007

Rank	Country	Per Capita GDP in U.S. $
10	United States	$45,790
16	Germany	40,079
17	Australia	39,098
20	Japan	34,254
44	Russia	9,115
47	Mexico	8,486
61	South Africa	5,883
99	China	2,485
122	India	1,042
143	Ghana	650

Source: The World Bank.

The five economic indicators shown here use these and other criteria to assess the well-being of 10 countries. Four of the indicators are indexes, which use a formula to measure well-being. One—human height—provides comparative data. As you can see, the United States ranks high by some measures and low by others. Which indicator do you think is the most valid?

Human Development Index (HDI)

The Human Development Index is an economic indicator favored by the United Nations. It looks beyond a country's GDP to gain a broader perspective on well-being. The HDI combines per capita GDP with life expectancy, the adult literacy rate, and school enrollment. Based on this measure of well-being, the UN ranks countries according to how well they are doing at promoting human development.

HDI for Ten Countries, 2005

Rank	Country	HDI Value
3	Australia	0.962
8	Japan	0.953
12	United States	0.951
22	Germany	0.935
52	Mexico	0.829
67	Russia	0.802
81	China	0.777
121	South Africa	0.674
128	India	0.619
135	Ghana	0.553

Source: United Nations Development Programme.

Happy Planet Index (HPI)

The Happy Planet Index does not include any measure of GDP. Instead it measures the degree to which a country provides well-being to its people and the planet. The HPI is based on a combination of life expectancy, life satisfaction, and "ecological footprint"—the fairness and responsibility with which a country consumes its resources. The tiny island nation of Vanuatu came in first in this ranking, with a value of 68.2. Zimbabwe came in last.

HPI for Ten Countries, 2006

Rank	Country	HPI Value
31	China	56.0
38	Mexico	54.4
62	India	48.7
68	Ghana	47.0
81	Germany	43.8
95	Japan	41.7
139	Australia	34.1
150	United States	28.8
156	South Africa	27.8
172	Russia	22.8

Source: New Economics Foundation.

Human Height

Scientists who study human growth argue that a population's average height is a better indicator of well-being than GDP or per capita GDP. People grow taller, they say, when they have more healthful diets, greater wealth, better housing, lower levels of pollution, and less disease and stress. Height is largely a function of genes—tall parents tend to have tall children. But nutrition and other environmental factors, these scientists insist, can explain differences in genetically similar populations. In their view, human height and well-being rise together.

Human Height for Ten Countries

Country	Average Male Height	Average Female Height
Germany	5 ft. 10 in.	5 ft. 5 in.
Australia	5 ft. 10 in.	5 ft. 5 in.
United States	5 ft. 9 in.	5 ft. 4 in.
Russia	5 ft. 9 in.	5 ft. 4 in.
Japan	5 ft. 8 in.	5 ft. 3 in.
South Africa	5 ft. 7 in.	5 ft. 3 in.
Ghana	5 ft. 7 in.	5 ft. 2 in.
Mexico	5 ft. 6 in.	5 ft. 1 in.
China	5 ft. 5 in.	5 ft. 1 in.
India	5 ft. 5 in.	5 ft. 0 in.

Note: Data are from various sources and for varying years.

Fiscal and Monetary Policy

■ 14.1 Introduction

For anyone who follows economic news, 2008 was filled with gloom and doom. The year began with uncertainty caused by a meltdown in the housing market. After rising for years, home prices were dropping. Just how far they would plummet, no one knew. In most parts of the country, homes were worth less than they had been just months earlier—sometimes even less than their owners owed on their mortgages. And the bad news was only beginning.

Over the next few months, a breathtaking rise in oil prices caused the price of gasoline to increase from approximately $3.00 to more than $4.00 a gallon. Drivers of large cars and trucks watched in horror as the cost of filling their gas-guzzlers crept to more than $100. The cost of food also rose at an alarming pace. Workers who used to go out to lunch began packing sack lunches at home to avoid soaring restaurant prices. Visits to food banks and soup kitchens increased as more people sought help in the face of rising living costs. Students returning to school in the fall saw the price of a cafeteria lunch go up by an average of 32 cents.

Job losses and falling stock prices added to the country's economic woes. Jobless workers, as well as those who feared for their jobs, cut back on spending. The resulting store closures and business bankruptcies created still more pain and uncertainty. By June 2008, the consumer confidence index, a measure of how people feel about their jobs and the economy,

The federal government and Federal Reserve both work to keep the economy growing smoothly.

fiscal policy
Government policy regarding taxing and spending. *Fiscal* here means "relating to public revenues."

monetary policy
Central bank policy aimed at regulating the amount of money in circulation. *Monetary* means "relating to money."

deficit spending
Government spending in excess of what is collected in revenues.

stagflation
A combination of economic stagnation —or slowdown—and high inflation. During a period of stagflation, gross domestic product growth is slow or zero, unemployment is high, and prices are rising.

multiplier effect
A ripple effect in which a change in spending by one person or business leads to additional changes in spending by another person or business.

easy-money policy
A monetary policy designed to accelerate the rate of growth of the money supply in order to stimulate economic growth.

tight-money policy
A monetary policy designed to slow the rate of growth of the money supply in order to reduce inflation.

crowding-out effect
The possible effect of increased government borrowing on businesses and consumers. By driving interest rates up, high levels of government borrowing may crowd private borrowers out of the lending market.

had sunk to a 16-year low. "If consumers are not spending, then the economy is in serious trouble," said one economist when interviewed about the mood of the country. "I think we're in a recession right now."

"Recessions," points out economics writer Charles Wheelan, "are like wars: If we could prevent them, we would. Each one is just different enough from the last," he adds, "to make it hard to ward off." Moreover, once recessions begin, they tend to spread across borders. If jobless Americans, for example, stop buying German cars, Chinese toys, or Mexican oil, then the economies of those countries will also suffer.

So, who is responsible for monitoring the U.S. economy to prevent recessions, or, at the very least, to minimize the pain they cause? The answer today is the federal government and the Federal Reserve System (the Fed). The federal government uses **fiscal policy,** the government's power to tax and spend, to get a stagnant economy moving again or to address inflation. The Fed uses **monetary policy,** a central bank's control over the money supply and interest rates, to dampen inflation or to stimulate growth. This chapter explores how both approaches are used to stabilize the economy.

■ 14.2 What Are the Origins of Modern Fiscal and Monetary Policy?

Before the 1930s, the federal government rarely intervened in the economy, during good times or bad. The Great Depression, however, caused such widespread misery that when running for president in 1932, Franklin Delano Roosevelt promised he would no longer be bound by this hands-off approach. "I pledge you, I pledge myself," FDR said, "to a new deal for the American people." But just what this "new deal" should be and how it would end the Depression was not clear.

Classical Economics and the Role of Government

When the Depression began, most U.S. economists belonged to a school of thought known as **classical economics**. Begun by Adam Smith, classical economics focused on the decisions of producers and consumers in a free market. Recessions were thought to be caused by events outside the market, such as wars and crop failures. Given time, the market would adjust and return to equilibrium.

Classical economists believed that the government's role in the economy should be minimal. Fiscal policy should focus on keeping taxes and spending low and balancing the federal budget. In their view, every tax dollar spent by the government was one less dollar spent by producers or consumers to stimulate business activity. The government's borrowing to fund a budget deficit only made matters worse by sucking still more money out of the private sector.

Roosevelt, like most politicians, accepted these views when the Depression began. During the 1932 presidential campaign, he blasted his opponent, President Herbert Hoover, for running a budget deficit. If elected, FDR promised to balance the federal budget. After taking office, he launched a flurry of new programs to get the economy moving again.

Like a broken-down car in need of a mechanic, the U.S. economy sometimes needs help from the Federal Reserve to get it going again. During times of economic slowdown, the Fed can use monetary policy—its control over the money supply and interest rates—to help stimulate the economy.

© TCI/Scott Willis

But he never gave up trying to balance the budget—at least not until he encountered the ideas of a British economist named John Maynard Keynes.

The Revolutionary Ideas of John Maynard Keynes

Keynes looked at economics in a different way. Instead of focusing on the role of individuals in the marketplace, he studied the economy as a whole. In his landmark work, *The General Theory of Employment, Interest, and Money,* Keynes sought to explain why economies experience crises like a depression. He also discussed how political leaders could end the Great Depression and avoid similar crises in the future.

Keynes's basic idea was simple. During a recession, overall demand for goods and services decreases because people who are out of work stop spending. In response, businesses cut expenses and lay off workers. Some businesses even close their doors. When that happens, more people lose their jobs, depressing demand still further. The result is a downward economic spiral.

The fastest way to break that downward spiral, Keynes argued, is for political leaders to use fiscal policy to increase overall demand. This increase could be achieved by cutting taxes, which would leave people with more money to spend. Or it could be done by boosting government spending. To be effective, however, increased government spending should be financed by borrowing money rather than by raising taxes. Higher taxes would only take more money out of consumers' pockets.

Taken together, these ideas form the basis of **Keynesian economics**. This school of thought holds that government intervention in the economy is the best way to ensure economic stability. If total spending by individuals and businesses is not enough to stimulate economic growth, then the government should step in to increase demand. Rising demand stimulates production. More production puts people back to work. And the economy begins growing again.

Although widely accepted today, Keynes's ideas were revolutionary in the 1930s. He rejected the view of classical economists, who believed that in the long run, the Depression would run its course and the economy would grow on its own. "This *long run* is a misleading guide to current affairs," Keynes observed. "*In the long run* we are all dead."

The British economist John Maynard Keynes was so influential that an entire school of economic theory bears his name. He argued that during economic downturns, governments should increase spending to shore up overall demand. Once revolutionary, the idea of fiscal stimulus is now widely accepted.

Using Fiscal Policy to End the Depression

In the early years of the Depression, Keynes had a hard time convincing political leaders to try out his ideas. He even paid a personal visit to Roosevelt in 1934, urging him to do more deficit spending to increase overall demand in the economy. **Deficit spending** occurs when a government spends more money than it collects in revenue. To finance such spending, governments often borrow money by selling bonds.

When Roosevelt came out of his meeting with Keynes, he was more confused than convinced. "He left a whole rigmarole of figures," the president complained to his secretary of labor. "He must be a mathematician rather than a political economist."

By 1938, however, Roosevelt was desperate. Despite his efforts to spark a recovery with government spending on public works and job-creation programs, the Depression was deepening again. Reluctantly, FDR gave up trying to balance the budget and decided to give Keynes's ideas a try. "We suffer primarily from a failure of consumer demand because of lack of buying power," FDR

Between 1933 and 1944, President Franklin Roosevelt delivered a series of 30 radio broadcasts. He often used these "fireside chats" to explain and urge support for his New Deal economic programs. Letters poured into Washington after each broadcast, putting pressure on lawmakers to enact the president's proposals.

said in a radio broadcast to the nation. "It is up to us [the government] to create an economic upturn."

Roosevelt went on to propose a multibillion-dollar spending program, much of it to be funded by borrowed money. Even then, the economy was slow to respond. Only with the onset of World War II did the federal government pump enough money into the economy to end the Depression. Between 1939 and 1945, the federal budget deficit soared from under $3 billion to more than $47 billion. At the same time, the unemployment rate dropped from 17 to 2 percent, while the nation's gross domestic product (GDP) almost doubled.

Postwar Economic Policy: "All Keynesians Now"

Keynes died a year after World War II ended. But his ideas lived on in the Employment Act of 1946, which called on the federal government to keep the economy from sliding back into recession. The act did not specify how that was to be accomplished. But by then, most economists agreed with Keynes that the government could and should use its power to stabilize the economy.

Keynesian economics was put to the test in the early 1960s, when growth slowed and unemployment began to rise. To halt the downward slide, President John F. Kennedy called on Congress to stimulate demand by cutting taxes. In an address laying out his plan, the president declared,

> The . . . best means of strengthening demand among consumers and business is to reduce the burden on private income . . . imposed by our present tax system . . . Too large a tax cut, of course, could result in inflation and insufficient future revenues—but the greater danger is a tax cut too little, or too late, to be effective.
> —John F. Kennedy, Address to the Economic Club of New York, Dec. 14, 1962

"I gave them straight Keynes," Kennedy later said of this speech, "and they loved it."

Kennedy was assassinated before Congress took action on his tax proposal. But when finally enacted in 1964, the Kennedy tax cuts sparked a long period of economic expansion. Unemployment declined, just as Kennedy had hoped. At the same time, however, inflation began to rise.

By the end of the 1960s, the idea that the government could use fiscal policy to fine-tune the economy to keep it balanced between inflationary booms and high unemployment busts was widely accepted. Even Richard Nixon, who had campaigned against "runaway government" in 1968, would proclaim after being elected president, "We are all Keynesians now."

Milton Friedman and the Rise of Monetarism

Within a few years, however, cracks began to appear in the Keynesian consensus. One of the most influential critics of Keynes was an American economist named Milton Friedman. Like Keynes, Friedman lived through the Great Depression. But he had a very different explanation for its causes and cure. Along with his coauthor Anna Schwartz, he laid out this explanation in *A Monetary History of the United States, 1867–1960*, published in 1963.

Friedman and Schwartz argued that the Depression was caused less by a lack of demand than by a drop in the money supply. As Figure 14.2A shows, between 1929 and 1933, the amount of money in the economy dropped sharply as banks failed and wiped out the accounts of depositors. As the money supply shrank, people hoarded what dollars they had. Friedman and Schwartz called the result the "great contraction," a period of falling prices, rising unemployment, and declining incomes.

The cure, in their view, lay not in fiscal but in monetary policy. The Federal Reserve should have reacted to the crisis, the economists argued, by expanding the money supply. Later in this chapter, you will read how this expansion is done. With more money in circulation, spending would have picked up and the economy would have started to grow again. As Friedman would later write,

> *The Fed was largely responsible for converting what might have been a garden-variety recession, though perhaps a fairly severe one, into a major catastrophe. Instead of using its powers to offset the depression, it presided over a decline in the quantity of money by one-third from 1929 to 1933 . . . Far from the depression being a failure of the free-enterprise system, it was a tragic failure of government.*
>
> —Milton and Rose Friedman,
> *Two Lucky People*, 1998

Friedman's ideas about the importance of the money supply and monetary policy became the basis for the school of economic thought known as monetarism. According to **monetarism,** changes in the money supply play a primary role in the ups and

Milton Friedman was one of the early recipients of the Nobel Prize for Economics, a recognition of his many contributions to the field. He is best known for his work on monetarism. With his wife Rose, Friedman created a television series on economics called *Free to Choose.*

downs of the economy. If the money supply grows too rapidly, inflation results. With more money in their pockets, consumers demand more goods and services than firms can supply, driving prices up.

Figure 14.2A

Analyzing the Relationship Between the Money Supply and Economic Growth

Milton Friedman argued that the Federal Reserve turned a recession into a depression by allowing the money supply to contract sharply between 1929 and 1932. The line graph shows changes in the money supply during Depression years. The bars show the rate of change in real gross domestic product (GDP). What relationship do you see between the two measures?

Source: U.S. Census Bureau.

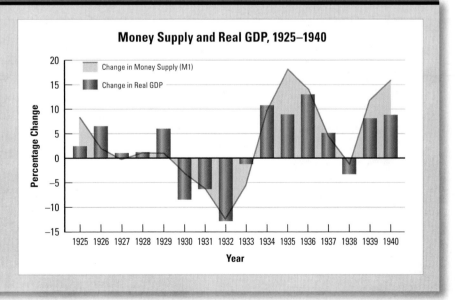

If the money supply grows too slowly, deflation results, and spending and investment slow. Therefore, the goal of monetary policy should be to increase the money supply just fast enough to keep up with economic growth—but no faster.

Friedman died in 2006, but as with Keynes, his ideas have influenced a generation of economists. In a 2002 speech honoring the economist on his 90th birthday, Ben Bernanke, then a member of the Board of Governors of the Federal Reserve System, recognized Friedman's many contributions to economics. Bernanke concluded with this pledge:

Let me end my talk by abusing slightly my status as an official representative of the Federal Reserve. I would like to say to Milton and Anna: Regarding the Great Depression. You're right, we did it. We're very sorry. But thanks to you, we won't do it again.

—Ben Bernanke, Nov. 8, 2002

Using Monetary Policy to Fight Stagflation

The use of monetary policy to stabilize the economy was put to the test in the late 1970s. Early in that decade, the economy received a shock when the Organization of the Petroleum Exporting Countries (OPEC) imposed an oil embargo on the United States and other oil-importing countries. Supplies of oil dwindled, driving up the price of gas. The inflation rate, which had already reached worrying levels, soared into double digits. As the economy struggled with rising prices, business activity slowed, and the unemployment rate climbed. The result was an unhappy economic situation known as **stagflation**.

President Nixon tried to curb inflation by imposing temporary controls on wages and prices. As soon as the controls were lifted, however, prices shot up again. In 1974, President Gerald Ford launched an anti-inflation crusade called Whip Inflation Now, or WIN, but inflation remained a problem. While running for president in 1976, Jimmy Carter scolded Ford for letting the "misery index" rise to more than 13 percent. The **misery index** is the sum of the inflation and unemployment rates. But after taking office, Carter watched helplessly as the index climbed to more than 20 percent.

In 1979, President Carter appointed Paul Volcker as chair of the Federal Reserve Board to bring inflation under control. Influenced by Friedman's writings on monetary policy, Volcker set out to slow the growth of the money supply. The result of his slow-growth policy was a far faster reduction in the inflation rate than most economists thought possible. Inflation dropped from 13.6 percent in 1980 to 3.2 percent in 1983.

This achievement was not without costs, however. During this same period, interest rates soared to historic highs. With the cost of borrowing so high,

Figure 14.2B

Analyzing the Misery Index

The misery index is the unemployment rate added to the inflation rate. Economists studying this index have observed that crime rates tend to rise and fall along with the combined inflation and unemployment rates. As you can see, the index rose throughout the 1970s and peaked in 1980.

U.S. Misery Index, 1960–1985

Legend: Unemployment rate, Inflation rate

Year	Misery Index
1960	7.00
1961	7.76
1962	6.77
1963	6.88
1964	6.44 — Kennedy tax cuts are enacted.
1965	6.10
1966	6.80
1967	6.62
1968	7.83
1969	8.95
1970	10.82
1971	10.25 — OPEC imposes an oil embargo.
1972	8.87
1973	11.02
1974	16.67
1975	17.68
1976	13.45 — Fed implements tight-money policy.
1977	13.55
1978	13.69
1979	17.07
1980	20.76
1981	17.97
1982	15.87
1983	12.82
1984	11.81
1985	10.74

Source: www.miseryindex.us.

business activity plummeted and unemployment reached almost 11 percent—its highest rate since the Great Depression.

The Focus of Fiscal and Monetary Policy Today

Over the past half-century, mainstream economists have come to view both fiscal and monetary policy as useful in managing the economy. Since the end of World War II, both have been used with some success to, as economists put it, "tame the business cycle."

In an ideal world, policymakers using fiscal and monetary policy would keep the economy growing steadily, while keeping inflation and unemployment low. In the real world, the economy still follows the ups and downs of the business cycle. But there is much that can be done to alleviate the worst effects.

■ 14.3 What Tools Does Fiscal Policy Use to Stabilize the Economy?

Fiscal policy consists of decisions made by the government regarding how much money to spend and how much to collect in taxes. At the national level, Congress makes these decisions based on recommendations from the president. Fiscal policy is used to pursue a number of economic goals. These goals include low unemployment, stable prices, and economic growth. The tools that fiscal policymakers use to achieve those goals are aimed at expanding or contracting economic activity.

How Taxes and Spending Expand or Contract the Economy

Early in 2008, Congress enacted an economic stimulus bill in response to worries that the economy was sliding into a recession. More than 130 million households received stimulus checks that year. Payments in the form of a tax rebate—a return of tax money to taxpayers—began at $300 for a single person and rose from there, depending on the size of each family. President George W. Bush described the stimulus as "a booster shot for our economy."

Stimulus checks are just one tool the government can use as part of an **expansionary fiscal policy**. The goal of this policy is to promote economic activity by increasing government spending, cutting taxes, or both. These tools can be used to help businesses grow—for example, by increasing government spending on goods and services. Or they can be aimed at boosting consumer spending, which was the purpose of sending Americans stimulus checks.

Key Concept

Fiscal Policy Tools
When the federal government follows an expansionary fiscal policy, it increases spending or cuts taxes. Both actions put money into the economy, increasing overall demand. When the government follows a contractionary policy, it cuts spending or raises taxes. Both actions pull money out of the economy, decreasing overall demand.

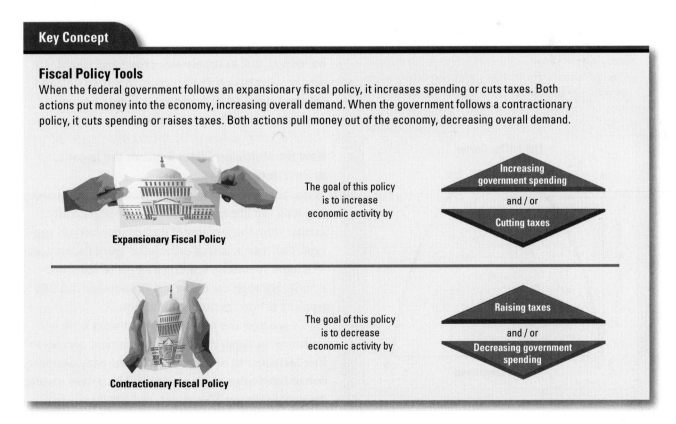

Expansionary Fiscal Policy

The goal of this policy is to increase economic activity by

Increasing government spending

and / or

Cutting taxes

Contractionary Fiscal Policy

The goal of this policy is to decrease economic activity by

Raising taxes

and / or

Decreasing government spending

In contrast, the goal of a **contractionary fiscal policy** is to cool an overheated economy. When buyers demand more goods and services than the economy can produce, overall prices tend to rise. When this happens, Congress can use the same tools to dampen excessive demand. That is, Congress can cut government spending, increase taxes, or both. As demand drops, prices tend to stabilize.

Using Tax Cuts to Stimulate Growth

In the early 1980s, a debate arose over how tax cuts might best be used to encourage economic growth. On one side of the debate were supporters of Keynesian economics. This school of thought is also known as **demand-side economics**. Demand-siders believe that the best way to deal with a sluggish economy is to stimulate overall demand by cutting individual income taxes. As consumers spend their tax savings on goods and services, business will pick up and the economy will begin to grow.

On the other side of the debate were advocates of a theory called **supply-side economics**. Supply-siders

hold that the best way to deal with an economic slow-down is to stimulate overall supply. This can be done by cutting taxes on businesses and high-income tax-payers. As businesses and investors use their tax savings to expand production, the supply of goods and services will increase, spurring economic growth.

Inspired by supply-side theories, President Ronald Reagan pushed for major tax cuts in 1981. In response, Congress lowered the corporate income tax rate at the highest bracket from 48 to 34 percent. It also slashed the top marginal income tax rate from 70 to 28 percent over the next seven years.

Critics of the Reagan tax cuts argued that the cuts would starve the government of needed revenue. In response, supply-siders claimed that the tax cuts would actually increase, not reduce, tax revenues. They supported their claim with a U-shaped graph, known as the **Laffer curve**. Popularized by economist Arthur Laffer, the graph shows a theoretical relationship between tax rates and tax revenues. As shown in Figure 14.3A, the Laffer curve suggests that increasing taxes beyond a certain point may lower revenue. Likewise, cutting taxes at that point may increase revenues.

The results of the Reagan tax cuts were mixed. Over the next few years, the economy grew, just as supply-siders had predicted. Tax revenues also increased, though less rapidly than had been hoped. As a result, budget deficits grew and the federal debt ballooned, just as supply-side critics had feared. To-day, economists generally accept that both demand-side and supply-side approaches should be considered when developing fiscal policy.

How the Multiplier Effect Expands the Impact of Government Spending

When the government spends money on goods and services, the impact on the economy is generally greater than the amount of money spent would suggest. The reason is that each dollar spent encourages still more spending, sending a ripple of economic activity through the economy. Economists call this rippling action the **multiplier effect**.

To see how the multiplier effect works, we will look at what happens when a government decides to hire teenagers to build trails in a local park. Suppose one of those teenagers is paid $1,000 for a week's work. He decides to put 30 percent, or $300, in the bank.

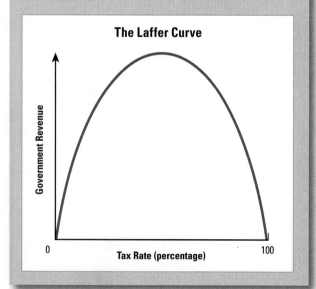

Figure 14.3A

Analyzing the Laffer Curve
The Laffer curve illustrates a theoretical relationship between marginal income tax rates and tax revenues collected by the government. As tax rates rise from a low of 0 percent, government revenues rise as well. But at some point, revenues start to fall as tax rates discourage people from working harder to earn more income. The curve does not tell us, however, just where that turning point is.

The Laffer Curve

Government Revenue (y-axis)

Tax Rate (percentage) (x-axis), 0 to 100

The Multiplier Effect

The multiplier effect explains how money spent by an individual or a government generates additional economic activity as it moves through the economy. As the money passes from one person to another, each dollar of original spending encourages still more spending, benefiting a wider circle of people and creating more overall demand.

Federal government spends $1,000 to pay a week's wages to a teenager for building trails.

The teenager saves $300 and spends $700 on a bicycle.

The bicycle shop owner saves $200 and spends $500 on car repairs.

The auto mechanic saves $100 and spends $400 to hire a painter to paint his fence.

| $1,000 | $1,000 + $700 = $1,700 | $1700 + $500 = $2,200 | $2200 + $400 = $2,600 |

Economic Activity Generated by $1,000 Expenditure

He spends the remaining $700 on a bicycle. That $700 now becomes the bike shop owner's income.

Now suppose the bike shop owner spends $500 of that income on car repairs. That $500 becomes income to the auto mechanic. The mechanic saves $100 and uses the other $400 to hire someone to paint his fence. And so it goes, with the original $1,000 spent by the government rippling through the economy from one person to the next. Each time the money changes hands, some of it is spent again, creating more overall demand.

The multiplier effect works two ways. It can help the economy grow when the government increases spending. Or it can slow economic growth when the government cuts spending. Consider, for example, the impact of a cut in government spending on highways. Construction firms that depended on highway projects would lay off workers. The laid-off workers would cut back on spending. Local businesses would see their sales drop. In this way, a reduction in government spending sends ripples through the economy, reducing demand by some amount along the way.

How Automatic Stabilizers Smooth Out the Business Cycle

Congress increases or cuts highway spending as part of its discretionary spending budget. But discretionary spending accounts for only about one-third of the federal budget. The other two-thirds is devoted to mandatory spending. Mandatory spending includes transfer payments, such as Social Security benefits. These transfer payments, along with taxes, can act as automatic stabilizers. An **automatic stabilizer** helps counter the ups and downs of the business cycle without requiring policymakers to take any action.

Automatic stabilizers work by increasing or decreasing overall demand. Suppose, for example, the economy enters a slowdown. As people spend less, demand for goods and services drops. Businesses respond by laying off workers or reducing their wages. As workers' earnings decline, many of them slip into lower federal income tax brackets. In the lower brackets, their tax bills go down at a faster rate than their incomes. This "tax cut" softens the impact of their reduced wages. Workers spend the money they save in taxes on goods and services, keeping the slumping economy from getting even worse.

Transfer payments also help boost demand during a downturn. As workers are laid off, many become eligible for unemployment benefits. Applications for food stamps and welfare payments also increase. By putting money in people's pockets, these payments encourage spending and keep demand from dropping as rapidly as it otherwise would.

Figure 14.3B

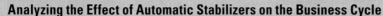

Analyzing the Effect of Automatic Stabilizers on the Business Cycle

Taxes and government transfer payments rise and fall with the business cycle. Since the end of World War II, these automatic stabilizers, combined with discretionary fiscal actions, have worked to limit the ups and downs of the economy. You can see their effect in this graph, which shows the growth of the gross domestic product since 1900.

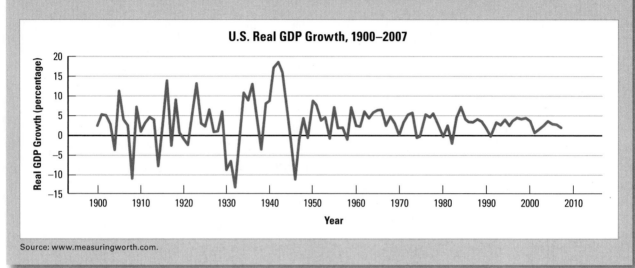

Source: www.measuringworth.com.

Just the opposite happens during upswings in the economy. As earnings rise, wage earners move into higher tax brackets. With more of each additional dollar earned going to taxes, spending cannot rise as fast as wages. This slowing of consumer spending helps stabilize demand. In addition, as employment picks up, the number of people needing transfer payments drops. Government spending declines, just as it would have had Congress deliberately adopted a contractionary fiscal policy.

By themselves, these automatic stabilizers do not have the power to end economic expansions and contractions. But as Figure 14.3B suggests, they may help smooth out the highs and lows of the business cycle.

■ 14.4 What Tools Does Monetary Policy Use to Stabilize the Economy?

Monetary policy consists of decisions made by a central bank about the amount of money in circulation and interest rates. In the United States, the Federal Reserve makes such decisions. Earlier you read about the Federal Reserve's role in overseeing the nation's banking system. The Fed also uses its control of monetary policy to help the economy grow steadily with full employment and stable prices. However, unlike Congress, which controls fiscal policy, the Fed is not an elected body. It has the power to make decisions on its own without the approval of either Congress or the president.

The Structure of the Federal Reserve System

In creating a central bank, Congress gave the Federal Reserve enough power to act independently in monetary policy. At the same time, the Fed's structure ensures that its decisions take into account the needs and interests of all parts of the country.

A seven-member Board of Governors based in Washington, D.C., heads the Federal Reserve System. The rest of the country is divided into 12 Federal Reserve districts. One Federal Reserve Bank operates in each district. These regional Federal Reserve Banks oversee the activities of national and state-chartered banks in their districts. Figure 14.4A shows the 12 districts and their Federal Reserve Banks.

Members of the Board of Governors are appointed by the president and confirmed by the Senate to 14-year terms of office. Once confirmed, a member is limited to one term. In making appointments, the president is directed by law to select a "fair representation of the financial, agricultural, industrial, and commercial interests . . . of the country." To ensure geographic representation, only one member may come from any one of the 12 Federal Reserve districts.

The president also selects one board member to chair the board for a four-year term. Ben Bernanke, who joined the Board of Governors in 2002, became its chairperson in 2006. The chairperson serves as the primary spokesperson for the Fed, both with Congress and with the public.

The Board of Governors is responsible for the overall direction of monetary policy and for supervising the banking system. The board also publishes a wealth of statistics about the U.S. economy.

In addition, all board members serve on the powerful Federal Open Market Committee. The FOMC includes 5 of the 12 Federal Reserve Bank presidents as well. The president of the New York Federal Reserve Bank is always on the FOMC, in recognition of New York City's status as the country's financial center. The other Federal Reserve Bank presidents rotate to fill the four remaining slots.

The FOMC holds eight regularly scheduled meetings each year to assess the state of the economy. At these meetings, the committee examines a wide range of economic indicators. From this information, it determines what changes, if any, the Fed should make in its monetary policy. As with fiscal policy, the decisions of the Fed may be expansionary or contractionary in their effects.

Fighting Recession and Inflation with Monetary Policy

The Fed adopts an expansionary monetary policy when it believes the economy is in danger of sliding into a recession. Also known as an **easy-money policy,** an expansionary monetary policy is intended to speed the growth of the money supply. As the amount of money flowing into the economy increases, interest

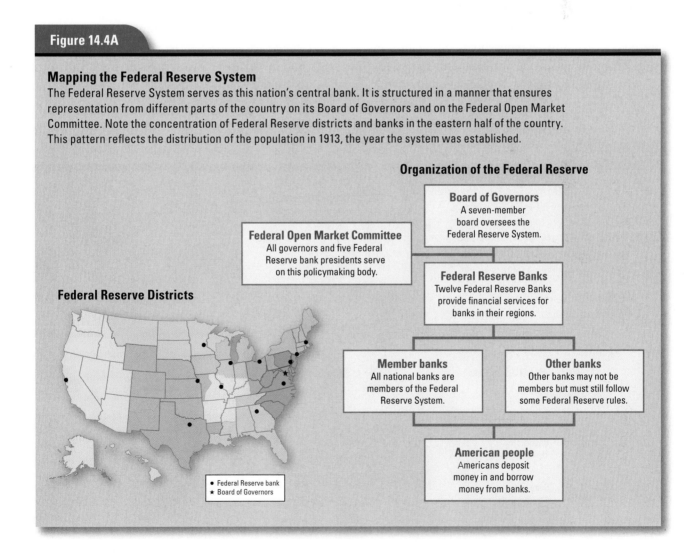

Figure 14.4A

Mapping the Federal Reserve System
The Federal Reserve System serves as this nation's central bank. It is structured in a manner that ensures representation from different parts of the country on its Board of Governors and on the Federal Open Market Committee. Note the concentration of Federal Reserve districts and banks in the eastern half of the country. This pattern reflects the distribution of the population in 1913, the year the system was established.

Organization of the Federal Reserve

Board of Governors
A seven-member board oversees the Federal Reserve System.

Federal Open Market Committee
All governors and five Federal Reserve bank presidents serve on this policymaking body.

Federal Reserve Banks
Twelve Federal Reserve Banks provide financial services for banks in their regions.

Federal Reserve Districts

Member banks
All national banks are members of the Federal Reserve System.

Other banks
Other banks may not be members but must still follow some Federal Reserve rules.

American people
Americans deposit money in and borrow money from banks.

- Federal Reserve bank
★ Board of Governors

Easy-Money vs. Tight-Money Policies

The Federal Reserve follows an easy-money policy to encourage economic growth and thus lower the unemployment rate. The Fed adopts a tight-money policy in an effort to slow economic growth and thus decrease the inflation rate.

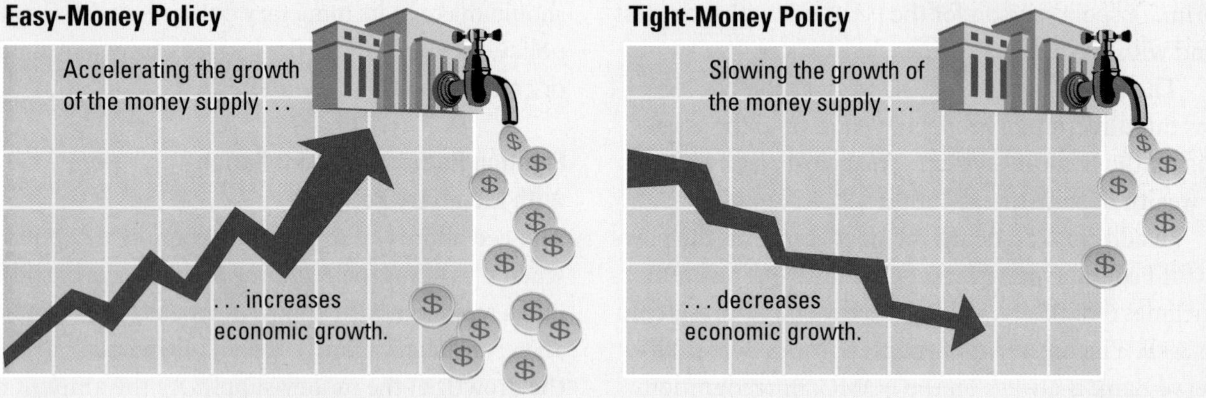

Easy-Money Policy

Accelerating the growth of the money supply . . .

. . . increases economic growth.

Tight-Money Policy

Slowing the growth of the money supply . . .

. . . decreases economic growth.

rates drop and borrowing becomes cheaper and easier. With loans easier to get, households and firms spend more on goods and services. Demand increases, leading to more production, stronger economic growth, and a drop in the jobless rate.

On the other hand, the Fed pursues a contractionary monetary policy when rising prices threaten to trigger an inflationary wage-price spiral. Also known as a **tight-money policy,** a contractionary policy is intended to slow the growth of the money supply.

Figure 14.4B

Analyzing How Banks Create Money

Banks create money by using the deposits in checking accounts to make loans. This illustration shows how the money-creation process works, starting with a gift of $1,000.

- Notice that each time a bank receives a deposit, it keeps 10 percent in reserve and loans out the rest.
- Remember that the money supply includes both currency in circulation and deposits in checking accounts.

$1,000	Currency in circulation
$1,000	Deposits in checking accounts
$1,000	Cumulative money supply

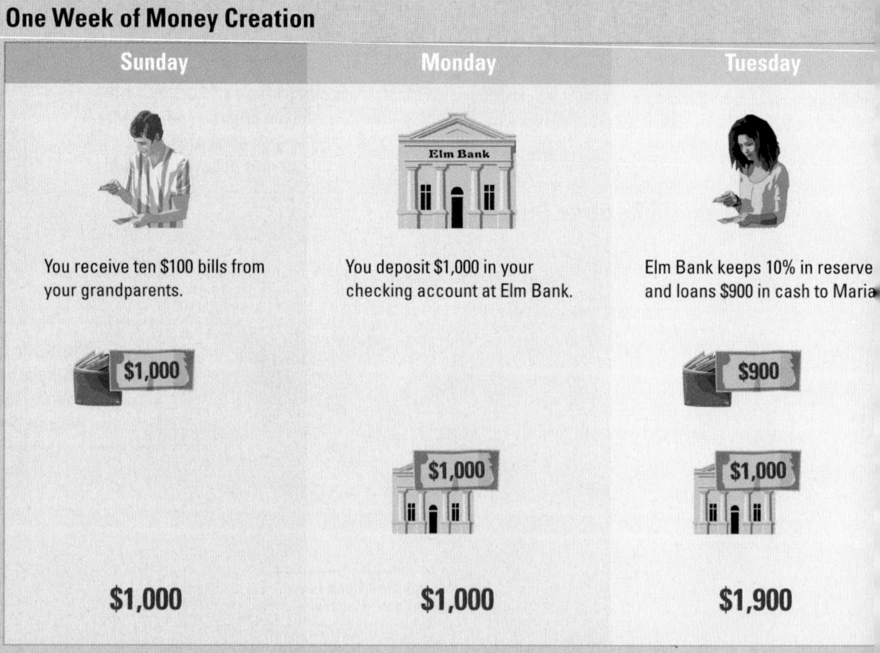

One Week of Money Creation

Sunday	Monday	Tuesday
You receive ten $100 bills from your grandparents.	You deposit $1,000 in your checking account at Elm Bank.	Elm Bank keeps 10% in reserve and loans $900 in cash to Maria.
$1,000		$900
	$1,000	$1,000
$1,000	**$1,000**	**$1,900**

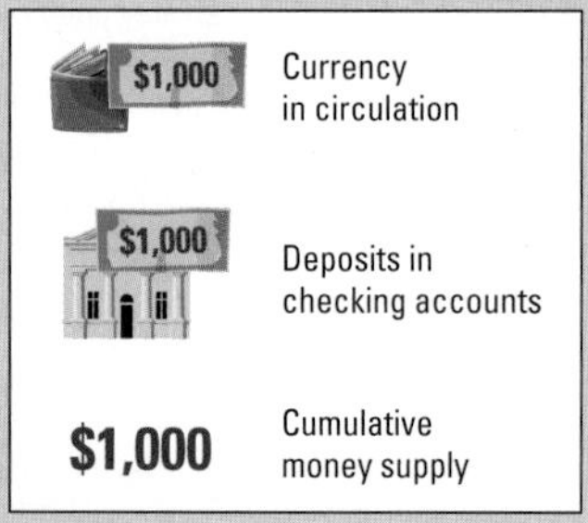

With less money flowing into the economy, interest rates rise and loans become costlier and harder to get. Households and firms cut back on borrowing as well as spending. Demand shrinks, leading to less production, weaker economic growth, and a drop in the inflation rate.

How Banks Create and Destroy Money

To understand how the Fed regulates the money supply, we need to look at how banks create or destroy money. Banks are in the business of taking in money from depositors and using it to make loans. They make their profit from the interest they charge on those loans. However, because of the **reserve requirement**—the regulation that banks must keep a certain percentage of deposits on hand to repay depositors—banks cannot loan out all the money they take in. They must hold some cash in their vaults or on deposit in a Federal Reserve Bank as a reserve fund.

Because it is not readily available for use, money held in reserve by banks is not considered part of the M1 money supply. M1 is the most common measure of the amount of money circulating in an economy. It includes all bills and coins in use, as well as traveler's checks and money in bank checking accounts.

When you deposit money in a bank account, it goes into the bank's reserves along with everyone else's deposits. Your account is credited with the amount of your deposit, which becomes part of the money supply. The bank can then loan the portion of your deposit that is not required to remain in reserve to someone else. The money loaned may be used to buy goods or services. Or it may end up in the borrower's checking account. Either way, that money is now also part of the M1 money supply. In this sense, the bank has "created" money by making a loan.

The reverse happens when a borrower repays a bank loan. The money used to pay off the loan leaves the borrower's checking account and goes back into the bank's reserves. As the borrower's checking account shrinks, the money supply also shrinks. In this sense, paying off a bank loan "destroys" money—at least until the bank loans that money out again.

The Federal Reserve can speed or slow money creation by making it easier or harder for banks to make loans. Whether its goal is to increase or decrease the money supply, the Fed uses the same three tools: open-market operations, the reserve requirement, and the discount rate. Of these, open-market operations are the most important.

Wednesday	Thursday	Friday	Saturday
Maria deposits $900 in her checking account at Oak Bank.	Oak Bank loans $810 to Cody, who spends it on a new computer.	The computer store deposits $810 in its checking account at Ash Bank.	Ash Bank makes a loan of $729 to Rasheed.
	$810		$729
$1,900	$1,900	$2,710	$2,710
$1,900	$2,710	$2,710	$3,439

The Fed's Most-Used Tool: Open-Market Operations

The Federal Reserve can inject money into the economy or pull it out using open-market operations. An open market is a market that is open to all buyers and sellers. The Fed's **open-market operations** involve the buying and selling of government securities in the bond market. The securities can be Treasury bonds, notes, bills, or other government bonds.

The decision to expand or contract the money supply in this way is made by the FOMC. When the FOMC adopts an easy-money policy, it instructs the Fed's bond traders to buy government securities. Every dollar the Fed pays for bonds increases the money supply.

When the FOMC adopts a tight-money policy, its bond traders sell securities in the bond market. The public pays for these bonds with cash or money taken out of banks. As this money goes out of circulation, the money supply shrinks. Moreover, because banks end up with smaller deposits, they have less money to lend, which also slows the growth of the money supply.

Open-market operations are relatively easy to carry out. They allow the Fed to make small adjustments in the money supply without new laws or banking regulations. For these reasons, the sale and purchase of securities is the monetary tool the Fed uses most to stabilize the economy.

The Fed's Least-Used Tool: The Reserve Requirement

The Fed's least-used monetary tool is its power to set the reserve requirement for banks. The Fed's Board of Governors could expand or contract the money supply by adjusting the **required reserve ratio**. This ratio is the minimum percentage of deposits that banks must keep in reserves at all times. Lowering the ratio would allow banks to make more loans and create more money. Raising the reserve ratio would force banks to keep more cash in reserve and out of the money supply. This, in turn, would leave banks with less money to lend, slowing money creation.

In practice, changes in the required reserve ratio are infrequent—and for good reason. Think about what a change in the requirement might mean for

---

Key Concept

Open-Market Operations
The Federal Reserve buys and sells government securities in the bond market to expand or contract the money supply. This diagram shows how these open-market operations ripple through the economy in an effort either to encourage economic growth or to fight inflation.

| What the Fed Does to Encourage Economic Growth | The Fed buys government securities in the bond market from banks. | Banks have more money to loan. Interest rates drop. | Borrowing, spending, and demand increase. | GDP increases, unemployment rate decreases, and inflation rate increases. |

| What the Fed Does to Fight Inflation | The Fed sells government securities in the bond market to banks. | Banks have less money to loan. Interest rates rise. | Borrowing, spending, and demand decrease. | GDP decreases, unemployment rate increases, and inflation rate decreases. |

banks. A lower percentage might not be a problem. Banks would be happy to have more money to lend. To meet a higher ratio, however, a bank would have to scramble for extra cash. It could borrow the needed money, but it would have to pay interest on the loans. Or the bank could refuse to renew loans as they come due. To avoid these negative impacts, the Fed seldom uses reserve requirements as a tool of monetary policy. For many years, the reserve requirement ratio has been 3 or 10 percent, depending on the amount of a bank's deposits.

The Fed's Third Tool: The Discount Rate

Even when the reserve requirement remains stable, banks sometimes need to borrow money to keep their reserves at the proper level. This might happen because a bank has made too many loans. Or it could be a result of unexpectedly large withdrawals. Whatever the reason, banks can borrow money from a Federal Reserve Bank to shore up their reserves. The interest rate on such loans, known as the **discount rate,** is the last tool in the Fed's toolbox.

The Federal Reserve Board of Governors controls the discount rate. A low rate makes it less costly for banks to borrow from the Fed. Banks can then use that money to make loans to customers, thereby expanding the money supply. Raising the discount rate has the opposite effect by discouraging banks from borrowing from the Fed. With money tight, banks make fewer loans, keeping the money supply in check.

Unlike the reserve requirement, the discount rate changes frequently over time. Between 1990 and mid-2008, it ranged from a high of 7.0 percent to a low of 0.75 percent. Whatever the rate, banks usually view the Federal Reserve as a lender of last resort. Borrowing from the Fed, they worry, may send a signal that the bank is in trouble.

Instead, banks generally borrow the funds they need from other banks. Knowing this, the Fed does not use the discount rate as its principal tool for managing interest rates. Instead, it targets the rate that banks charge one another for loans.

Targeting the Federal Funds Rate

When the Fed makes news, the story is almost never about changes in the money supply or the discount rate. Instead, the report is usually about a change in the **federal funds rate**. This is the rate that banks

"I told you the Fed should have tightened."

The speaker in this cartoon believes that the Federal Reserve should have used its monetary policy tools to keep inflation in check by implementing a tight-money policy. The fact that the hot dog vendor is charging $25 for a hot dog is a clear sign that inflation is out of control.

charge one another for very short—as short as overnight—loans. Such lending is common between banks with excess reserves and banks that need a quick loan to maintain their required reserves.

Unlike the discount rate, the federal funds rate is not a monetary policy tool. Banks, not the Fed, decide what they charge one another for loans. Still, the Fed has an interest in making sure that the rate banks are charging one another is in line with its general monetary policy. Therefore, the FOMC sets a target for the federal funds rate based on its view of the economy. It then uses open-market operations to nudge the federal funds rate toward that target.

The FOMC focuses on the federal funds rate for two main reasons. First, it is the easiest bank rate for the Fed to change using open-market operations. Second, interest rates on everything from saving accounts and bonds to mortgages and credit cards are affected by the federal funds rate. Thus, a small change in the federal funds rate can have a powerful effect across the entire economy.

As with all of its activities, the Fed has two goals in mind when targeting the federal funds rate. One is

Figure 14.4C

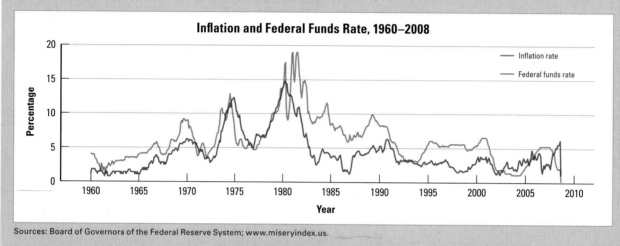

Analyzing the Impact of Interest Rates on Inflation

The Federal Reserve targets the federal funds rate—the rate banks charge to loan each other money—to control inflation. In the early 1980s, Federal Reserve chairman Paul Volcker fought inflation by pushing the federal funds rate up to record highs. You can see the effects of his tight-money policy on this graph.

Inflation and Federal Funds Rate, 1960–2008

Sources: Board of Governors of the Federal Reserve System; www.miseryindex.us.

to control inflation, as you can see in Figure 14.4C. The other is to maintain healthy economic growth. Getting the rate right to do both is a challenging task, especially because it can take months for a change to work its way through the economy.

14.5 What Factors Limit the Effectiveness of Fiscal and Monetary Policy?

Despite the best efforts of policymakers, booms and busts still happen. One reason may be that the business cycle is simply a fact of life in a market-based economy. But other factors may also keep fiscal and monetary policy from being as effective as economists would like.

Time Lags Can Complicate Policymaking

At least two types of time lags plague economic policymaking. One lag comes from the time it takes to compile accurate economic data. Early estimates of GDP growth, for example, are often too high or too low. As a result, economists may miss the start of a recession. Only when the indicator is corrected months later does the actual state of the economy become clear. By then, corrective action may be too late to do much good.

Another time lag comes from the time it takes for actions begun today to work their way through the economy. The multiplier effect of federal spending can take months to stimulate or dampen overall demand. After studying efforts to use fiscal policy to combat recessions since World War II, historian Bruce Bartlett concluded,

> The history of anti-recession efforts is that they are almost always initiated too late to do any good . . . The enactment of stimulus plans is a fairly accurate indicator that we have hit the bottom of the business cycle, meaning the economy will improve even if the government does nothing.
>
> —Bruce Bartlett, "Maybe Too Little, Always Too Late," *New York Times,* Jan. 2008

In general, monetary policy can be enacted more quickly than fiscal policy. Even so, a change in interest rates may take six months or more to have an effect on economic output or the inflation rate.

Economic Forecasts Can Mislead Policymakers

To implement economic policy successfully, policymakers must be able to forecast how the economy will behave months or even years into the future. To make such forecasts, economists monitor several economic indicators. They also use economic models and computer programs to make sense of these data. Based on their models, they make educated guesses about the future. Policymakers use these forecasts to decide what actions to take to head off recessions or fight inflation.

Predicting the future is never easy, and sometimes forecasters guess wrong. An example of a prediction that did not come true occurred in 2001. As the first graph in Figure 14.5A shows, the federal government began that year with a budget surplus. The Congressional Budget Office responded with a report forecasting continued surpluses through 2011. The CBO also predicted that by 2009, the accumulated surplus would be large enough to pay off the national debt. The second graph in Figure 14.5A shows just how wrong these forecasts turned out to be.

Concerns About the National Debt May Limit Government Spending

Worries about the size of the national debt may also complicate policymaking. When Keynes urged President Roosevelt to increase deficit spending, he did not mean that the federal government should run deficits forever. The result, Keynes realized, would be an ever-increasing national debt. Such a debt would not be in the long-term interests of the economy.

Figure 14.5A

Tracking Federal Budgets and the National Debt

The federal budget is in deficit when spending exceeds tax revenue. It is in surplus when revenue exceeds spending. Every budget deficit adds to the national debt, just as every surplus subtracts from the debt. Since 1975, budget deficits have been the rule, not the exception. As a result, the national debt topped $10 trillion by late 2008.

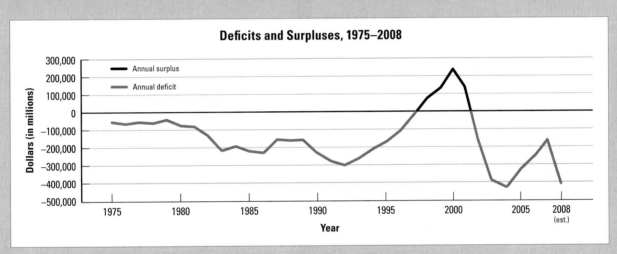

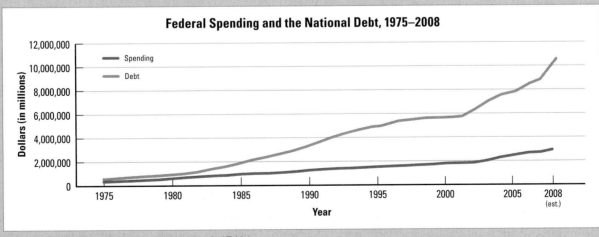

Source: Budget of the U.S. Government FY2009, Historical Tables.

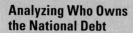
Figure 14.5B

Analyzing Who Owns the National Debt

Economists often describe a portion of the national debt as money we owe ourselves. As this graph shows, however, about one-quarter of the debt is foreign owned. Some Americans view foreign ownership of U.S. government securities as a sign of confidence in the strength of the U.S. economy. Others worry that the federal government has become too dependent on foreign lenders.

Source: U.S. Treasury.

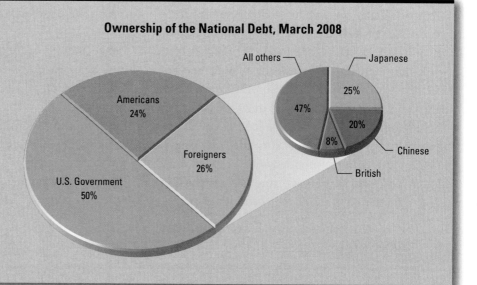

Ownership of the National Debt, March 2008

Americans 24%

U.S. Government 50%

Foreigners 26%

All others 47%

Japanese 25%

Chinese 20%

British 8%

Instead, most economists advise that deficit spending be limited to times of national emergencies. Such emergencies include wars, natural disasters, and recessions. During good economic times, they say, Congress could run surpluses. These surpluses could then be used to pay down the national debt, balancing the federal budget over time.

That is the theory. Since the 1970s, however, the federal government has generally spent more than it receives in revenue in both good times and bad. The inability of Congress to keep spending under control has led some politicians to call for a constitutional amendment requiring a balanced budget. The Senate approved an early version of such an amendment in 1982. The House approved a later version in 1997.

Meanwhile, deficit spending continues. By December 2008, the national debt had climbed to about $10.6 trillion. Each individual's share of that debt amounted to around $35,000. The size of the national debt has many Americans deeply worried. Listed below are some of their concerns.

Fear of government bankruptcy. Some people worry the national debt will eventually bankrupt the federal government. Most economists, however, doubt that will happen. As long as the government can increase taxes or refinance the debt, it will not go into bankruptcy. To refinance the debt, the government sells new bonds and then uses that money to repay bondholders whose bonds have matured.

Concern about the burden on future generations. Many people are concerned about the burden that a large nation debt will place on the next generation—namely, you and your friends. Once again, however, many economists believe this worry is overblown. As shown in Figure 14.5B, about three-quarters of the national debt is owned by American individuals or institutions. Economists look at this portion of the debt as money we owe ourselves.

Taxpayers do bear the burden of paying interest on that debt. But much of that money goes right back to Americans who own government securities. Many retired people, for example, depend on the interest from government bonds to support themselves. They have no wish to ask any generation, including yours, to "pay off" the national debt.

Unease about foreign-owned debt. Citizens, government agencies, and financial institutions in foreign countries own about one-quarter of the national debt. This is not debt that we owe to ourselves. Foreign ownership of so much of the national debt concerns Americans for two reasons. First, they do not like seeing all of the interest owed to foreign bondholders flowing out of the U.S. economy. Second, they worry that Congress is becoming too dependent on foreign lenders to support its deficit-spending habits. What will happen, they ask, if foreigners suddenly decide they no longer want to buy U.S. government securities?

Many economists share these concerns to some degree. However, they point out that payments to foreign bondholders enable those bondholders to buy U.S. goods and services. Economists also note that many Americans invest in bonds issued by foreign governments. The interest these bondholders receive helps offset U.S. payments to foreigners. Finally, as long as our economy is strong, foreigners are unlikely to stop buying U.S. government securities.

Worries about the crowding-out effect. A widespread concern about the growth of the national debt is that federal government is crowding private borrowers out of the lending market. This **crowding-out effect** is said to happen when government borrowing drives interest rates up so high that people are no longer willing to borrow money to invest in businesses. This could trigger an economic downturn.

Economists agree that crowding out is a potential problem. However, they note that the negative effect of the government's borrowing on long-term growth depends on how the money is spent. Government spending on highways and airports benefits private enterprise. So does spending on education and research, which improves this country's human capital.

Do all of these limitations and concerns mean the economy would be better off if policymakers did nothing to stabilize it? Some critics of fiscal and monetary policy would answer yes. But mainstream economists see an important role for both fiscal and monetary policy in keeping the economy healthy.

In your lifetime, you are likely to live through both recessions and periods of high inflation. Either situation can create hardships that you would rather not face. Still, knowing that the government has tools to help the economy recover from such ills may help you face them with confidence. For having learned how these tools work, you now know that the bad times will not last forever.

Summary

Governments and central banks use two broad policies to keep their economies running smoothly. Fiscal policy is based on the government's power to tax and spend. Monetary policy is based on the power of the Federal Reserve over the money supply and interest rates.

What are the origins of modern fiscal and monetary policy? British economist John Maynard Keynes championed the use of fiscal policy to fight recessions. Keynesian economics holds that government spending should be used to stimulate demand during recessions. American economist Milton Friedman promoted the use of monetary policy to control inflation. Monetarism holds that the control of the money supply is key to keeping inflation in check.

What tools does fiscal policy use to stabilize the economy? Expansionary fiscal policy tools include increased government spending and tax cuts. Contractionary fiscal policy tools include decreased government spending and tax increases. Automatic stabilizers can also serve to expand or contract the economy.

What tools does monetary policy use to stabilize the economy? The Federal Reserve works to stabilize the economy by managing the growth of the money supply and interest rates. Its tools include the power to establish bank reserve requirements and the discount rate. Through its open-market operations, it also regulates the federal funds rate.

What factors limit the effectiveness of fiscal and monetary policy? A number of factors keep fiscal and monetary policy from maintaining a stable course for the economy. These factors include lack of timely information, inaccurate forecasts, and time lags between actions and their effects.

What would you do with a stimulus check?

In 2008, Congress implemented an expansionary fiscal policy to stimulate the economy. The stimulus package took the form of a tax rebate, or a return of tax money to taxpayers. As soon as the president announced the plan, articles began appearing in the news media offering advice about what to do with a stimulus check. The article you see here is one of them.

Suppose you have just received a stimulus check for $600. Read the article. Then ask yourself, "What would I choose to do with my stimulus check?"

Rebates: Spend, Invest, or Pay Off Bills?

by Barbara Mlotek Whelehan

Over the next several weeks, 130 million Americans will get some easy money, compliments of Uncle Sam. Well, it's actually courtesy of ourselves, the taxpayers.

But Congress and the president decided that giving Americans rebate checks is a great way to boost the economy.

The idea: Put some money back in the hands of Americans, who can be counted on to squander it. It's almost our patriotic duty to do so.

But we don't have to go along with this idea. We live in a free country, after all. So we can take advantage of this opportunity to bolster our personal finances.

This economic stimulus check serves as a reminder that every day we make financial choices that have a trickle-down effect on our lives.

Decisions Involve Trade-Offs

For example, if you spend money you have today on a flat-screen TV, that money isn't available for future needs or desires. If you instead invest that money for tomorrow, it's not available for your present desire to watch "American Idol" on that beautiful plasma screen.

Lastly, if you spend money you don't have today by financing a TV purchase, you commit future earnings to this expenditure. Since interest is normally levied in this scenario, your purchase could end up costing a heck of a lot more than the original price of the TV, making this the least attractive of all options.

Yet we routinely choose that option. According to a recent article in *The Wall Street Journal*, Americans are heaping on more debt, with average credit card balances up 9.5 percent in the first quarter of 2008 over the year before . . .

So, are you planning to buy a big-screen TV in time for the HDTV conversion? Or have you traced the route to the Grand Canyon on a road map in anticipation of a cross-country trip? Or are you going to cave to that pretty gold bracelet?

Hey—here's a chance to stash away some money. These rebate checks will range in value from $300 to $1,200, and couples with young children will get up to $1,800.

Practical Uses for the Extra Cash

During a recent visit to my home, the pest control guy started griping about the dire state of the economy. I asked him what he planned to do with his rebate check, and he said he's going to use it to pay bills. "I know that's not what I'm supposed to do with it," he added quickly.

Actually, he's in good company. A recent survey by H&R Block found that nearly half of Americans—45 percent—will pay bills with their rebate checks and their tax refunds from the 2007 tax year. Two out of 10 (21 percent) will buy necessary goods or services (food, car repairs, etc.) with their rebate checks, while just 18 percent will invest it. Only about 16 per-cent of Americans will splurge on such things as electronics, jewelry or a vacation.

That's great news—Americans are taking the opportunity to pay down their bills. The so-called bad news is that this might not help our economy all that much, 70 percent of which depends on consumer spending . . .

In that H&R Block survey, by the way, more than 40 percent of the respondents said they wished the government would use the $168 billion economic stimulus package for a higher purpose, such as to reduce the national debt (37 percent), im-prove health care (32 percent), shore up Social Security (17 per-cent) or to improve education (15 percent).

I have to agree that I'd like lawmakers to address these problems, too. But I don't object to getting this check.

Sage Advice from the Experts

What does the smart money say you should do with this influx of cash? . . .

Bud Hebeler, author of "Get-ting Started in a Financially Secure Retirement," says that people should be encouraged to put the forthcoming govern-ment check into 1) paying off some credit card debt; 2) their

The government issues stimulus checks to boost the economy. But what is the best way for taxpayers to use that money?

WHEN SOMETHING GOOD COMES YOUR WAY...

TAKE IT...

ADMIRE IT...

FEEL IT...

SMELL IT...

"...PAY IT FORWARD"

CREDIT CARDS

GAS

FOOD

BAGLEY THE SALT LAKE TRIBUNE '08

© 2008 Pat Bagley, The Salt Lake City Tribune and PoliticalCartoons.com

Enjoy It While You Can

It's nice to get a stimulus check. Even though it's really a tax rebate—a portion of what you've already paid the government—it feels like a gift. As this cartoon points out, however, most of the money quickly disappears into the hands of others.

mortgage; or 3) into retirement savings—perhaps in that order. "I know this isn't what is wanted by the feds, brokers, retailers, etc., but it would be the best thing for the vast majority of baby boomers," he adds.

The National Association of Personal Financial Advisors suggests readers should strengthen their financial security several ways.

Best way to use your rebate money:

1. Contributing to an IRA.
2. Paying off high-interest credit card debt.
3. Saving for college.
4. Building a rainy-day fund.
5. Paying off long-term debt such as a student loan or mortgage.

Any one of these actions will contribute to your financial health and by extension, that of the overall economy, because you'll be less dependent on social support systems to get through a crisis.

A Look at Your Options

So let's take a look at what you can do with a hypothetical payout of $1,200, assuming you're married and your spouse goes along with your decisions.

You can invest it in an IRA. And if you get a return of 8.5 percent on average, in 25 years it'll be worth $9,244. OK, that's not enough to retire on, but if you use it as seed money and continue to invest $1,200 a year for 25 years earning that return, it'll be worth $94,401. You have to admit, that's not chump change.

Or you can use it as a down payment for a big-screen Sony LCD HDTV selling at $3,000 and finance the $1,800 balance. If your credit card interest rate is 13 percent and you make only minimum payments each month, it will take you 13 years and three months to pay it off, and you will have paid $1,198 in interest. That's a total of about $4,200 for that $3,000 TV.

So if you're already saving money for retirement and your other goals, plus you have a healthy rainy day fund stashed away as well as no debt, then go ahead and splurge! You deserve it, and so does the economy.

But if you need the money for something, go ahead and use it wisely. You deserve it, and the economy will understand.

Barbara Mlotek Whelehan is a financial journalist who specializes in personal financial planning.

Unit 6

Globalization and the Global Economy

How do countries conduct trade in the global economy?

The United States and the Global Economy

■ 15.1 Introduction

In 1971, Marc McCreary and his family opened a T-shirt factory in Florence, Alabama. Within a few years, his business was booming, with over 1,000 employees and millions of dollars in sales. Other T-shirt factories also opened in Florence, as people hoped to cash in on the growing market. Florence began calling itself the "T-Shirt Capital of the United States."

But then the boom went bust. In the early 2000s, imported T-shirts from China and other low-wage countries began flooding the U.S. market. These shirts were comparable in quality to American shirts, but much cheaper. Florence's factory owners tried to boost productivity and lower costs, but in the end they could not compete. "You can't fix this by working harder," McCreary later told a reporter for National Public Radio. "This is a global situation. None of us could figure this out."

In 2003, McCreary had to close his factory and lay off his workers. The other T-shirt firms in Florence also shut down. Thousands of people lost their jobs, and the economy of Florence suffered a major blow.

For a few years the city struggled with the effects of the plant closings. Then it began to recover. Some laid-off workers enrolled in retraining programs to learn new skills. Others opened their own small businesses. Outside firms, including some foreign

Trade among countries plays an important role in shaping the U.S. economy.

China has become a major exporter of T-shirts and other clothing to the United States. Low wages and efficient production methods make Chinese goods highly competitive in American markets.

companies, relocated to Florence to take advantage of the area's skilled workforce. Although some laid-off workers had trouble getting back on their feet, most moved on to new and even better jobs.

The story of Florence and the T-shirt industry reflects changes in the American economy as it becomes increasingly tied to the global economy. The **global economy** is the system of markets and trade that links the countries of the world. Economists generally agree that, despite the challenges of foreign competition, the benefits of participating in the global economy far outweigh the costs. This chapter focuses on one of the most important aspects of the global economy—global trade—and its role in shaping the U.S. economy. It also looks at the financial system that makes trade across borders possible.

■ 15.2 Why Is Global Trade Growing in Importance?

Take a look at the label on your shirt. Does it say "Made in U.S.A."? Chances are good it does not. Although Americans can still buy clothing made in U.S. factories, most of the apparel sold in this country is produced in other countries. The same is true for electronic goods and many other products. The abundance of foreign-made goods in American markets underscores the increasing importance of global trade.

The Growth of Global Trade

As Figure 15.2 shows, international trade has grown dramatically since the end of World War II. Over the past half-century, the worldwide trade in merchandise, which includes all types of goods, has expanded more than 120 times, or by 12,000 percent. A number of developments have combined to make this increase in global trade possible.

First, advances in transportation have had a major impact on cross-border trade. It is easier to move goods around the world than ever before. Ships are far larger today than they were 50 years ago, enabling them to carry more goods at a lower cost per unit. Container ports have facilitated shipping by allowing the loading and unloading of whole containers of goods. The development of wide-body, long-distance jet planes has made air transport cheaper and faster. As a result, perishable goods such as fresh fruits and vegetables can be shipped thousands of miles without spoiling.

Improved communications have also fueled the growth of global trade. Satellite systems now link computers and telephones around the world, making it possible to communicate almost instantly across great distances. A company in one country can serve its customers in another almost as easily as if they were in the same city. Global business can be transacted, and money can be exchanged, with just a few keystrokes.

Figure 15.2

Graphing the Growth of International Trade

Global trade has increased sharply since the 1950s.

- The first graph shows the rising value of merchandise exports—the overseas trade in goods—around the world between 1948 and 2005.
- The second graph shows that over that same time span, the share of total global trade generated by the United States has decreased.

World Merchandise Exports, 1948–2005

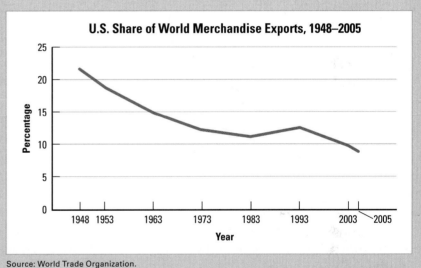

U.S. Share of World Merchandise Exports, 1948–2005

Source: World Trade Organization.

A shift in the types of goods being produced and traded has further promoted global commerce. At one time, much of the trade between countries was in bulk commodities, such as grains, coal, and steel. These items were heavy and relatively hard to ship. Today a large share of global trade is in lighter manufactured goods, such as computers and other electronic devices, which are easier to transport and which sell for much higher prices.

Why Countries Trade:
Absolute and Comparative Advantage

Countries trade with each other for the same reason individuals do: to get the goods and services they value at the lowest cost. Most countries lack either sufficient resources or large enough markets to produce everything their people would like to consume for themselves. A country like the United States, however, is rich enough and big enough to produce virtually everything it needs.

Nonetheless, the United States and other large, wealthy countries still engage in trade with other countries. Why? Because even rich countries benefit when they specialize in the production of some goods and services and trade those products for other goods and services. Decisions about what to specialize in reflect a country's absolute and comparative advantages.

As you read earlier, a country has an absolute advantage in trade if it can produce something more efficiently than other countries can. Such an advantage might come from a country having access to a scarce resource or having the ability to produce something more cheaply than other countries can. For example, South Africa's rich diamond deposits give it an absolute advantage in diamond production.

A country has a comparative advantage in trade when it can produce a good or service at a lower opportunity cost than its competitors can. For example, the United States and Canada are both capable of producing jet airplanes and wood products. But the opportunity cost of producing timber is lower for Canada than it is for the United States. And the opportunity cost of producing jet airplanes is lower for the United States than it is for Canada. So it makes sense for the United States to trade its relatively cheaper airplanes for Canada's relatively cheaper timber. By specializing, both countries get the goods they want at a lower cost than if they tried to produce both goods for themselves.

One country's comparative advantage over another might stem from any of several differences between them. Three of the most important are differences in climate, factors of production, and technology.

Differences in climate. Many countries have a comparative advantage in the production of certain crops based on climate. Tropical countries export warm-weather crops like mangos, bananas, and coffee. Countries with temperate climates trade grains like wheat and corn. Seasonal variations between the

Northern and Southern hemispheres can also play a part. For example, during the winter months the United States and Europe buy fruits and vegetables from southern countries such as New Zealand and Chile, which are then in their summer growing season.

Differences in factors of production. Countries with an abundance of a particular factor of production—land, labor, or capital—may have a comparative advantage in the production of goods derived from that resource. Canada, for example, with its extensive forestland, has a comparative advantage in timber products. China, with its huge population, has an advantage in the production of goods like clothing that require large amounts of low-cost labor. Japan, with its high national savings rate, is able to specialize in industries that require a lot of investment capital, like automobile manufacturing.

Differences in technology. Countries that have developed high levels of technology also enjoy a comparative advantage in producing high-value goods. Japan's advantage in auto production is in large part a result of advances in engineering and production methods. Similar advances in the software and pharmaceutical industries have given the United States and Europe a comparative advantage in those fields.

Differentiated Products Promote Global Trade

Global trade is not solely a matter of absolute or comparative advantage. After all, many countries are

South Africa, with its abundant diamond deposits, has long enjoyed an absolute advantage in diamond production. In recent years, however, scientists have managed to grow gem-quality synthetic diamonds using machines like the one shown to the right. Experts say these lab-grown diamonds are comparable to natural stones and could impact the diamond market.

Differentiated Products

The three animated movies shown here are examples of differentiated products. Produced in the United States, Japan, and Great Britain, all three have entertained worldwide audiences. But they differ in style and in their approach to storytelling. Consumer demand for such varied products promotes global trade.

Howl's Moving Castle
This Japanese anime film tells a fairy-tale story of a young woman coming of age in a fantasy world of the late 1800s.

Yu-Gi-Oh!
This U.S.-Japanese production, done in a manga, or comic-book, style, follows a young hero's struggle against an ancient Egyptian god.

**Wallace and Gromit:
The Curse of the Were-Rabbit**
This British comedy, filmed in stop-motion animation, tells the story of a village plagued by a mutant rabbit.

equally efficient at producing all kinds of goods—cars, foods, movies, clothing. They don't have a particular advantage in the production of such goods, and yet they trade them nonetheless.

The reason is simple. Consumers enjoy the variety created by differentiated products. **Differentiated products** are products that are essentially the same, but are distinguished from each other by variations in style, materials, or taste.

Consider a commonplace food like cheese. All cheese is basically the same—a product made of cultured milk. Looked at that way, one type of cheese is pretty much the same as another. But consumers who buy cheese don't look at it that way. Cheese is a differentiated product. The unique tastes and textures of the many varieties are strong selling points for consumers. Shoppers tend to seek out specific cheeses—French brie, Greek feta, Italian parmesan —to suit their particular tastes and menus. This demand drives the international trade in cheeses.

The same principle applies to other products and countries. Consumers may seek out leather shoes and handbags from Italy, popular music from Great Britain, or animated movies from Japan. Economists note that differentiated products like these are an increasingly important factor in global trade.

■ 15.3 What Goods and Services Do Countries Trade?

In 2005, Sara Bongiorni and her family carried out an unusual experiment. They tried to live the entire year without buying any products made in China. Bongiorni chronicled the experience in her book, *A Year Without "Made in China": One Family's True Life Adventure in the Global Economy*. The author discovered that Chinese goods are everywhere in the American marketplace. Even American flags are made in China. She came away from that year with a deeper understanding of U.S. ties to the global economy.

The United States not only imports products from abroad. It also exports goods and services to other countries. **Imports** are products made in another country and sold domestically. **Exports** are products made domestically and sold in another country. In the global trading system, one country's exports become another country's imports, and vice versa.

Figure 15.3A

Analyzing U.S. Imports and Exports

The United States imports and exports a wide variety of goods and services. The first graph shows U.S. imports by category in 2007. The second graph shows U.S. exports in the same categories. Products within each category may vary greatly. For example, footwear and furniture are both included in the consumer goods category. Capital goods include machinery and equipment used in production.

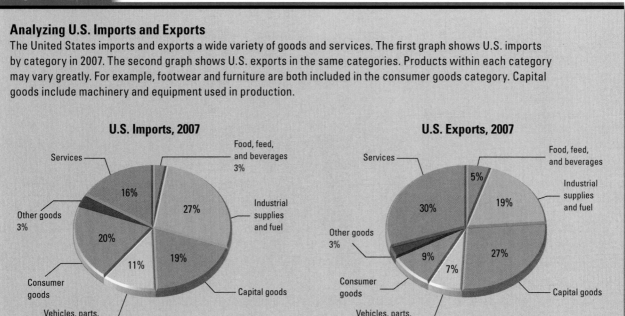

Source: U.S. Census Bureau. Note: Due to rounding, percentages do not add to 100.

The United States as a Major Importer

As Sara Bongiorni found out in her year without China, the United States is the world's leading importer of goods and services. In 2007, its share of world imports was almost equal to that of the next two largest importers, Germany and China, combined.

The first graph in Figure 15.3A shows the kinds of goods and services the United States imported in 2007 by category. The largest category that year was industrial supplies and fuels. This category includes chemicals, minerals, wood products, cotton, petroleum products, and other fuels. Within this category, far more money was spent on imported crude oil than on any other good.

Consumer goods other than automobiles ranked second. This category includes all types of products for personal and home use, ranging from household appliances, televisions, and furniture to clothing, jewelry, and cosmetics.

The third largest category of imports in 2007 was capital goods. Included in this group are goods that are used in the production of other goods and services. Examples include machines, computers, measuring instruments, and telecommunications equipment.

The United States as a Major Exporter

The United States is also one of the world's top three exporting countries, along with Germany and China. Its exports range from farm products, minerals, and manufactured goods to financial and transportation services. The second graph in Figure 15.3A shows the kinds of products U.S. producers export by category.

Capital goods make up the bulk of U.S. exports. Among the most valuable exports in this category are semiconductors, civilian aircraft, industrial machinery, and telecommunications equipment. The United States has a comparative advantage in such high-tech goods because of its high levels of human capital.

At first glance, it might seem odd that the United States both imports and exports the same types of goods, such as automobiles and telecommunications equipment. The explanation for this paradox lies in product differentiation. German cars and American cars, though similar, are not the same. There is a market for German cars in the United States and a market for American cars in other countries.

In the case of telecommunications equipment, the products differ more substantially. The United States imports cell phones and exports satellite communications equipment. The United States does not have a comparative advantage in cell phone production, but it does have an advantage in satellite technology. Therefore, it makes sense for the United States to export satellite devices and import cell phones.

The Growth of Service Exports

Services also make up a significant share of U.S. exports. In 2007, services accounted for almost one-third of all exports. The illustration below shows the kinds of services the United States exports by category. As with manufactured goods, service exports reflect the country's comparative advantage in fields requiring a highly trained workforce. Such fields include engineering, education, and information services.

You might be wondering how a service, which is not a physical object, can be exported. Every time an American company sells a service to a foreign customer, whether in the United States or abroad, it is exporting that service. For example, when a foreign student pays to attend college in the United States, that education is considered a service export. Likewise, when a foreign traveler pays for a hotel stay in a U.S. city, that payment is classified as a service export. American banks, airlines, insurance companies, and shipping agencies all add to U.S. export totals when they do business with foreign clients. So, too, do entertainment companies when they sell American movies or musical recordings to customers overseas.

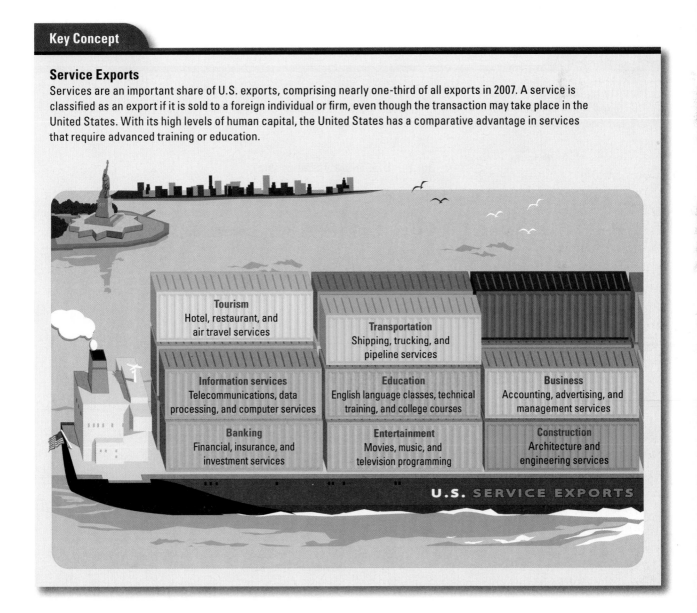

Key Concept

Service Exports
Services are an important share of U.S. exports, comprising nearly one-third of all exports in 2007. A service is classified as an export if it is sold to a foreign individual or firm, even though the transaction may take place in the United States. With its high levels of human capital, the United States has a comparative advantage in services that require advanced training or education.

Tourism
Hotel, restaurant, and air travel services

Transportation
Shipping, trucking, and pipeline services

Information services
Telecommunications, data processing, and computer services

Education
English language classes, technical training, and college courses

Business
Accounting, advertising, and management services

Banking
Financial, insurance, and investment services

Entertainment
Movies, music, and television programming

Construction
Architecture and engineering services

U.S. SERVICE EXPORTS

America's Trading Partners

The United States trades with most countries in the world. However, it conducts more than half of its foreign trade with just ten countries. Figure 15.3B shows America's top ten trading partners in 2007.

Canada has long been America's chief trading partner. The long border between the United States and Canada and the traditionally good relations between the two countries have contributed to the growth of U.S.-Canadian trade. In 2007, Canada accounted for 18 percent of all U.S. foreign trade.

After the signing of the North American Free Trade Agreement (NAFTA) in 1994, Mexico became this country's second most important partner in trade. From time to time, however, growing trade with China has pushed Mexico into third place.

Around half of U.S. trade is with wealthy, industrialized countries such as Germany and Japan. The other half is with newly industrialized countries such as China and oil-exporting countries like Venezuela and Saudi Arabia.

The Benefits of Global Trade for U.S. Consumers

Trade with other countries has many benefits for U.S. consumers. Global trade gives us access to an enormous variety of goods and services. We also enjoy low prices for many goods because we import these goods from low-cost producers. This makes us better off. As economics writer Charles Wheelan points out, "Cheaper goods have the same impact on our lives as higher incomes. We can afford to buy more." As a result, our standard of living improves.

Figure 15.3B

Identifying U.S. Trade Partners
The United States conducts most of its foreign trade with just ten countries. This graph shows the percentage of total U.S. foreign trade carried out with each of those key trade partners.

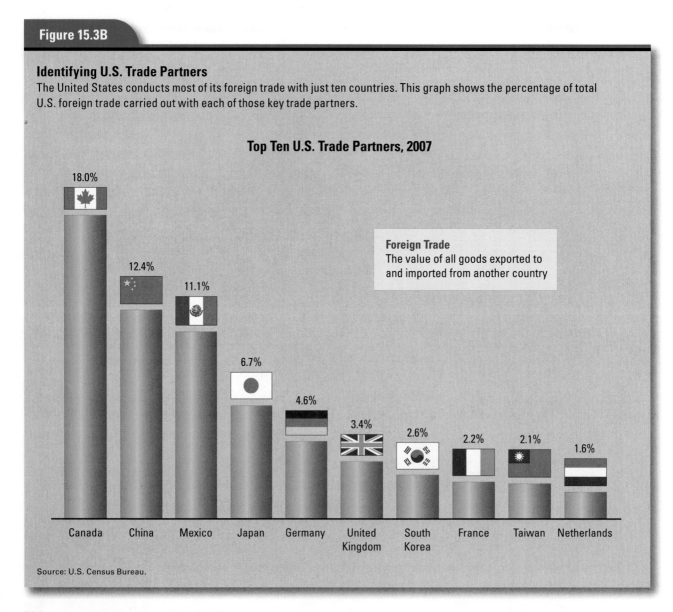

Top Ten U.S. Trade Partners, 2007

Foreign Trade
The value of all goods exported to and imported from another country

- Canada 18.0%
- China 12.4%
- Mexico 11.1%
- Japan 6.7%
- Germany 4.6%
- United Kingdom 3.4%
- South Korea 2.6%
- France 2.2%
- Taiwan 2.1%
- Netherlands 1.6%

Source: U.S. Census Bureau.

In 2000, Alabama native Natalie Chanin, a fashion designer who had worked abroad for many years, returned to her home state to set up a new business. Her company, based in Florence, employs local artisans and suppliers to create clothing, fabrics, and other fashion goods that reflect local traditions.

Global trade also increases competition among producers. This may cause some producers to go out of business, as it did the T-shirt makers of Florence, Alabama. At the same time, it creates new opportunities for innovative or low-cost producers to enter the marketplace. Moreover, the producers that survive become more efficient and productive, thus contributing to a healthier economy. For example, competition from Japanese and European automakers gives U.S. carmakers a strong incentive to make better vehicles at a lower cost. The resulting improvements benefit anyone who buys an American car, whether in this country or abroad.

Finally, global trade enhances the flow of ideas around the world. The movement of products and services among countries opens societies to new ways of doing things. This exchange of new ideas and technologies promotes further innovation.

The Impact of Global Trade on U.S. Workers

As the story of the Florence, Alabama, T-shirt boom and bust makes clear, global trade can also have negative effects on American workers, at least in the short term. Workers who are employed in industries that fail in the face of foreign competition may lose their livelihoods as a result of global trade. In most cases, laid-off workers find new jobs. But some never manage to recover their former standard of living. This results in real hardship for people and communities.

While some workers may have suffered as a result of global competition, the labor force as a whole has not. In 1971, when Mark McCreary opened his Florence T-shirt factory, the U.S. labor force participation rate was 60 percent. By 2003, the year his factory closed because of cheap imports, the percentage of adults in the labor force had risen to 66 percent.

In the long run, global trade increases economic activity. This, in turn, promotes economic growth. Workers who lose their jobs but retrain themselves for new careers generally improve their circumstances. As in any market, competition among buyers and sellers produces winners and losers. But for countries that use their resources wisely and exploit their comparative advantages, the gains created by global trade outweigh the losses.

■ 15.4 How and Why Do Countries Regulate Trade?

Have you ever tried to mail a package to another country at the post office? If so, you probably had to fill out a customs declaration. It asked you to list the items you were sending and to indicate whether they were gifts or goods to be sold. This information is required by **customs**—the government department responsible for examining goods entering a country and enforcing any trade restrictions on them.

Economists have long argued against trade restrictions. Nonetheless, few countries have ever fully embraced **free trade**—the unrestricted movement of goods and services across borders. Over the years, countries have found many reasons to regulate foreign trade.

Trade Barriers

The main reason countries erect barriers to trade is to protect their domestic industries from foreign competition. This cartoon illustrates the four main types of trade barriers.

© TCI/Scott Willis

Types of Trade Barriers: Tariffs, Quotas, Embargoes, and Voluntary Restraints

Many countries restrict imports in order to shield domestic markets from foreign competition. Such behavior is known as **protectionism**. Countries do this mainly to satisfy political demands at home. There are many types of trade barriers. The four main types are protective tariffs, import quotas, trade embargoes, and voluntary export restraints.

Protective tariffs. The most common type of trade barrier is the **protective tariff**—a tax on imported goods. Countries use tariffs to raise revenue and to protect domestic industries from competition from cheaper foreign goods. Tariffs are among the easiest taxes to impose, since they arouse little domestic protest and can be easily applied to goods before they enter the country.

While protective tariffs may help specific domestic producers, they do not benefit consumers. Tariffs push up the prices of imported goods. So instead of having to lower prices to compete with cheap imports, domestic producers can raise prices to the inflated price level of the imports. Thus, tariffs make all goods more expensive for consumers.

If they are set high enough, protective tariffs can also have negative effects on the entire economy. The Hawley-Smoot Tariff Act, passed by Congress in 1930, raised the average tariff rate on imported goods to more than 40 percent. Although 1,028 economists petitioned President Herbert Hoover to veto the bill, he signed it into law. In response, other countries raised their tariff rates. Foreign trade came to a halt, helping to turn a recession into a worldwide depression.

Despite these drawbacks, most governments are still persuaded that tariffs are needed to protect their country's workers and industries. In 2008, for example, the United States imposed a 4.7 percent tariff on imported pianos, a 6.8 percent tariff on cut roses, and a 4 percent tariff on felt-tip pens.

Import quotas. While tariffs make foreign goods more expensive, they do not limit the quantity of goods that can be imported. An **import quota,** on the other hand, places a limit on the quantity of a good that can be imported during a specified period of time. For example, an import quota on textiles might limit textile imports from a given country to 10 million garments per year. Once that limit is reached, textile imports from that country must stop for that year.

Beginning in the 1960s, textile quotas were used by the United States and other countries to shield their domestic clothing industries from competition from low-wage countries. The phasing out of these quotas in the 1990s caused an upsurge in inexpensive clothing imports. Many U.S. apparel companies went out of business as a result, including the T-shirt makers of Florence, Alabama.

Like tariffs, quotas are designed to protect domestic industries. But they do not raise revenue for the government. They may also lead to corruption and smuggling as producers look for ways to exceed quota limits. Like tariffs, import quotas raise prices for consumers as costlier domestic items replace cheaper imports once the quota limit is reached.

Trade embargoes. A **trade embargo** imposes a ban on trade with a country or group of countries, usually for political reasons. For example, in 1960 the United States imposed a trade embargo on Cuba to protest its revolutionary government's seizure of American-owned property. In 1986 the U.S. Congress imposed an embargo on South Africa to oppose its apartheid policy of racial segregation.

Trade embargoes have a mixed record. When successful, they pressure countries to change their policies. South Africa, for example, abandoned its racial segregation policies when faced with trade embargoes from many countries. In contrast, as of 2008, the decades-long U.S. trade embargo against Cuba had failed to bring about a change in the country's government or policies.

Voluntary export restraints. The fourth type of trade barrier is known as a **voluntary export restraint,** or VER. This type of barrier limits the quantity of a good that can be exported from a country during a specific time period. In effect, it is an export quota, self-imposed by the exporting country.

In most cases, however, a VER is not truly voluntary. It is usually established at the insistence of an importing country. It is designed to avoid harsher restrictions, such as tariffs or import quotas. For example, Japan imposed a VER on its automobile shipments to the United States in the 1980s when faced with U.S. threats to restrict Japanese auto imports.

The Debate over Trade Restrictions

People have long debated the merits of free trade versus protectionism. Economists generally agree that free trade promotes economic growth and is good for consumers. Still, domestic producers, labor unions, and political leaders continue to make the case for trade restrictions. They base this position on a number of key arguments.

The jobs argument. This argument assumes that allowing cheap imports into a country destroys jobs by forcing domestic companies to cut costs, lay off workers, or even go out of business. Protectionists might point to the collapse of the Florence, Alabama, T-shirt industry to support this case.

According to the jobs argument, highly paid workers in a wealthy country like the United States simply cannot compete with low-wage workers in poorer countries. The only way to protect American jobs is to

Import quotas caused this shipment of cotton pants from China to be held up at the port of Antwerp, Belgium. An import quota limits the amount of a good that can be brought into a country in a given period of time. If the quota is exceeded, the good can be refused entry and blocked by customs officials.

Figure 15.4A

Analyzing the Costs and Benefits of Trade Restrictions

Trade restrictions do not just affect the industries they are meant to protect. They also have an impact on consumers and on producers in other industries. This table summarizes the costs and benefits of the four trade barriers. Overall, most economists say, the economic costs of trade restrictions outweigh the benefits.

Trade Barrier Pros and Cons

Trade Barrier	Benefits	Costs
Protective tariff	Saves jobs in protected industries Reduces competition in protected industries Raises revenue for government	Raises prices for domestic consumers Raises costs of production in related industries May cause job losses in related industries
Import quota	Saves jobs in protected industries Reduces competition in protected industries	Limits product choices for consumers Raises prices for domestic consumers May lead to corruption and smuggling
Trade embargo	May bring about policy changes in the targeted country	May lead to economic hardship for people in the targeted country Encourages smuggling
Voluntary export restraint (VER)	Reduces risk of trade restrictions being imposed by another country	Hurts domestic producers by limiting their foreign sales

make cheap imports more expensive by imposing tariffs or to limit their availability by imposing quotas.

Economists reply that tariffs and quotas cost more jobs than they save. For example, in the 1980s the United States imposed tariffs on imported steel to protect the domestic steel industry. The tariffs led to higher steel prices. Higher steel prices raised the cost of producing goods made with steel, from pots and pans to automobiles. This hurt domestic producers of such goods, who had to compete with foreign producers using cheaper steel.

By one estimate, the steel tariffs earned roughly $240 million in profits for U.S. steel companies and saved 5,000 jobs. But they cost domestic industries that use steel $600 million in profits and 26,000 jobs.

Most economists also dismiss the idea that American workers cannot compete with foreign labor. Low wages in poor countries, they say, reflect low productivity. The cost to an employer of a high-wage worker who is very productive may be less than that of a low-wage worker who is less productive. Free trade encourages firms to specialize in those activities in which their workers are relatively more productive.

Finally, economists note that while free trade destroys some jobs, it also creates jobs. It does so by expanding the industries in which the United States has a comparative advantage. It helps U.S. export industries, since buying imports from foreign countries gives those countries the purchasing power to buy American goods. It also creates jobs for retailers and businesses that sell and service imported goods.

The national-security argument. This argument states that industries that are vital to national security must be protected. Included in this category are defense industries and producers of critical resources like oil and steel. Some would even extend this argument to include the production of basic foods, such as wheat and corn. Those who make this argument say trade restrictions are needed to avoid dependence on foreign suppliers during times of conflict.

Most economists would agree that when the country's security is at stake, trade barriers may be justified to protect key industries. But they are skeptical when calls for such protection come from industry representatives rather than military or intelligence agencies. Industries that are facing stiff foreign competition have an interest in proclaiming their own importance to the country's security.

The infant-industry argument. Sometimes a newly formed industry needs time to become competitive. According to this argument, such "infant industries" will eventually become strong enough to stand on their own. In the meantime, protectionists say, tariffs may be necessary to protect them from cheaper imports.

Economists typically respond that even if one accepts this argument, it is difficult to put into practice. It requires that the government identify which infant industries will eventually make a profit and are therefore worth protecting. In reality, making this selection is notoriously difficult, and the process is all too easily influenced by politics.

Economists also object to the infant-industry argument on principle. New firms, they argue, must be willing to accept losses when starting up if they believe they can become profitable in the long run. Moreover, many new firms have grown into industry giants.

The unfair-competition argument. This argument asserts that trade is fair only if all countries play by the same rules. For example, protectionists argue that some countries "cheat" by providing subsidies to their industries to help them compete with foreign firms. They say that trade barriers are justified to protect domestic industries from subsidized foreign imports.

Protectionists also contend that some countries "dump" their products in foreign markets to force competitors out of business. Dumping means selling a product for less than it cost to produce it. Dumping is considered an unfair trade practice by most trade organizations, and most countries disavow it.

Economists typically reject both parts of the unfair-competition argument. First, they assert that the benefits to consumers of cheap imports outweigh the costs to domestic producers, regardless of whether the imported products are subsidized or not. Second, they say it is nearly impossible to detect dumping because it is difficult to determine a foreign firm's costs. "Often," write economists Campbell McConnell and Stanley Brue, "what appears to be dumping is simply comparative advantage at work."

The protection-as-bargaining-chip argument. This argument states that trade restrictions can be a useful bargaining tool in trade negotiations with other countries. Its advocates claim that the threat of a tariff or import quota can be used to persuade another country to remove or reduce its barriers to trade.

Economists point out that this strategy can easily backfire. When that happens—when the threat of a new trade restriction does not produce the desired result—the country faces a dilemma. It either has to make good on its threat and impose the restriction (which might harm its economic welfare) or back down (which can harm its reputation). Either of these results leaves the country worse off than before.

The environmental-and-labor-standards argument. Some people contend that countries with lax environmental or labor laws have an economic advantage over countries that must comply with stricter laws. To make trade fair, they say, countries with stricter laws should impose tariffs against countries that do not uphold similar standards.

The problem with this argument, say most economists, is that lax standards are most common in the world's poorer countries. These countries have few resources to devote to worker and environmental protection. As they develop their economies, in part through global trade, they will be able to pay more attention to labor and environmental standards. Restricting trade with such countries only slows the pace at which such improvements can be made.

Why Trade Restrictions Are Still Widespread

If the view of most economists is correct and trade restrictions do more harm than good, then why do political leaders and the general public still support them? The answer lies in the political process. Producers and workers who are threatened by foreign competition typically organize to seek trade protection. They lobby members of Congress and educate the public on the subject.

On the other hand, those who benefit from free trade—the great majority of consumers—may not even realize that their interests are at stake. And so, as the following analysis points out, they do little to oppose trade restrictions.

The overall cost of tariffs and quotas typically greatly exceeds the benefits. It is not uncommon to find that it costs the public $200,000 or more a year to protect a domestic job that pays less than one-fourth that amount. Moreover, because these costs are buried in the price of goods and spread out over millions of citizens, the cost born by each individual citizen is quite small. In the political arena, the voice of the relatively few producers demanding protectionism is loud and constant, whereas the voice of those footing the bill is soft or nonexistent.

—Campbell R. McConnell and
Stanley L. Brue, *Economics: Principles,
Problems, and Policies*, 2008

Reducing Trade Barriers Through International Agreements

Countries do have incentives to promote free trade, however. The chief incentive is to be able to sell their products abroad and earn export revenues. For that reason, countries have negotiated international trade agreements to reduce trade barriers. Figure 15.4B shows U.S. free-trade agreements around the world.

Some trade agreements involve just two or three countries or a particular region. For example, the North American Free Trade Agreement includes just Canada, Mexico, and the United States. The European Union, established in 1993, included 27 member countries by 2009. Both these regional agreements reduce tariffs and promote trade among their members.

The first trade agreement to involve a large number of countries was the General Agreement on Tariffs and Trade. When adopted by 23 countries in 1948, GATT lowered tariffs on tens of thousands of goods.

In 1995, the members of GATT formed the World Trade Organization. Since its formation, the WTO has overseen various international negotiations aimed at reducing trade barriers. It has also worked to resolve trade disputes among its members. By 2009, the WTO consisted of 153 member countries, all of which agree to abide by WTO rules.

Figure 15.4B

Mapping U.S. Free-Trade Agreements

The United States has numerous trade agreements with other countries. The Office of the U.S. Trade Representative is the government agency responsible for negotiating such agreements. This map highlights the countries with which the United States has or is negotiating a trade agreement, the status of the agreement as of 2008, and the year the agreement was made effective.

U.S. Free-Trade Agreements, 2008

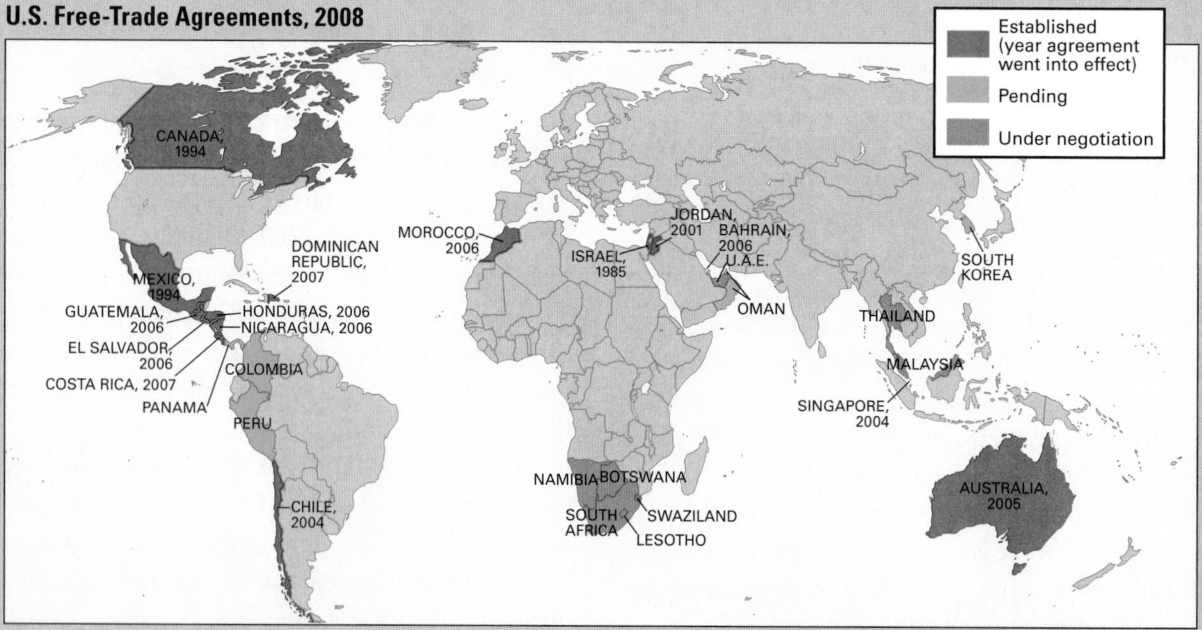

Legend:
- Established (year agreement went into effect)
- Pending
- Under negotiation

CANADA, 1994
MEXICO, 1994
DOMINICAN REPUBLIC, 2007
GUATEMALA, 2006
HONDURAS, 2006
NICARAGUA, 2006
EL SALVADOR, 2006
COSTA RICA, 2007
COLOMBIA
PANAMA
PERU
CHILE, 2004
MOROCCO, 2006
ISRAEL, 1985
JORDAN, 2001
BAHRAIN, 2006
U.A.E.
OMAN
SOUTH KOREA
THAILAND
MALAYSIA
SINGAPORE, 2004
AUSTRALIA, 2005
NAMIBIA BOTSWANA
SOUTH AFRICA
SWAZILAND
LESOTHO

Strong Dollar, Weak Dollar

The value of the dollar rises or falls depending on the demand for dollars relative to other currencies.

- When the dollar is strong relative to another country's currency, U.S. importers benefit because goods from that country cost less in dollars.
- When the dollar is weak relative to another country's currency, U.S. exporters benefit because their goods cost less in that country's currency.

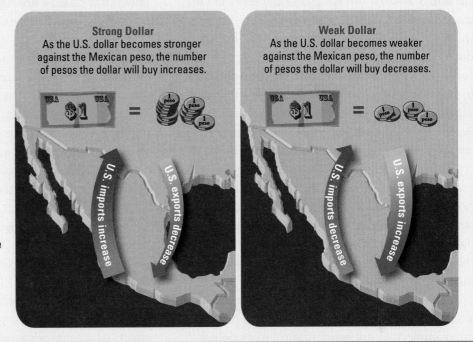

Strong Dollar
As the U.S. dollar becomes stronger against the Mexican peso, the number of pesos the dollar will buy increases.

Weak Dollar
As the U.S. dollar becomes weaker against the Mexican peso, the number of pesos the dollar will buy decreases.

■ 15.5 How Is Global Trade Financed?

For countries to trade goods and services, they must also trade their currencies. If you have ever visited a foreign country, such as Mexico, you know that you must exchange your dollars for Mexican pesos in order to shop while you are there. The same is true for U.S. businesses that want to buy goods or services in Mexico. Likewise, a Mexican firm that wants to buy American goods must trade its pesos for dollars. The process of converting one currency to another is known as **foreign exchange**. Without the exchange of currencies, little or no global trade would take place.

Foreign Exchange and Exchange Rates

Foreign exchange takes place on the **foreign exchange market**. This market is made up of major banks and financial institutions around the world that buy and sell currencies.

Each currency traded in the foreign exchange market has an **exchange rate**. This rate indicates the value of one currency in terms of another. For example, if you can exchange one U.S. dollar for 10 Mexican pesos, the dollar exchange rate is US$1 = 10 pesos. The Mexican peso exchange rate would be 1 peso = US$0.10.

Exchange rates typically fluctuate based on supply and demand. If Americans are buying lots of goods and services from Mexico, they will need lots of pesos. Because the price of something generally rises with demand, a strong demand for pesos tends to raise the price of pesos in terms of dollars. That is, it will take more dollars to buy the same number of pesos. The exchange rate might fall from US$1 = 10 pesos to US$1 = 9 pesos. The dollar would then be worth less in pesos. When one currency loses value relative to another currency, we say **depreciation** has occurred.

Conversely, if Mexicans are buying lots of U.S. goods and services, the demand for dollars in Mexico will increase. That, in turn, will cause the price of the dollar to rise relative to the peso. So, for example, instead of getting 10 pesos for one dollar, you might get 11 pesos. When one currency gains value relative to another currency, we say **appreciation** has occurred. Note that when comparing two currencies, the appreciation of one means the depreciation of the other.

When a currency appreciates in value, it is said to get stronger. When it depreciates, it is said to get weaker. Thus, a **strong dollar** has a higher exchange rate and trades for more foreign currency than a **weak dollar**.

Whether a country's currency is strong or weak has important effects on its cross-border trade. When the dollar is weak, foreign goods and services cost more in dollars. This tends to discourage imports into the United States. At the same time, a weak dollar makes U.S. exports relatively cheap for other countries, since their currencies are strong relative to the dollar. Thus, a weak dollar is likely to boost U.S. exports. When the dollar is strong, the reverse occurs. Imports from other countries become cheaper, while exports become more expensive.

Although many people regard a strong dollar as good and a weak dollar as bad, it is really a matter of perspective. A weak dollar can be hard on consumers, who pay more for imports, but good for those producers who primarily export their products. When the dollar is strong, on the other hand, consumers may benefit and producers may suffer.

There are exceptions to this general rule. Producers who depend on imported parts for their products, for example, may not benefit from a weak dollar. And consumers whose jobs depend on exports may not benefit from a strong dollar. Generally, countries try to strike a balance between high and low exchange rates while achieving some stability relative to other currencies.

Foreign exchange occurs wherever people change money around the world. Currency exchange offices, such as this one at London's Gatwick Airport, are common in many large cities.

Exchange Rate Systems: Fixed and Floating

An exchange rate that fluctuates based on supply and demand is called a **floating exchange rate** because rates "float" up and down based on the market. This is the dominant system in the world today.

Some countries take a different approach, however. They establish a **fixed exchange rate** to keep their currency stable. Under a fixed system, the government typically fixes, or "pegs," its currency to another major currency, such as the dollar. For example, Mexico might establish a fixed exchange rate of 10 pesos to the dollar and seek to maintain that rate rather than let the peso's value float up and down on the open market.

Both types of exchange rates have their advantages and disadvantages. The main advantage of floating rates is that they reflect supply and demand in the financial markets. The main disadvantage is that they are unpredictable. An unexpected rise or fall in a currency's exchange rate can have negative effects on a country's economy by disrupting trade.

Fixed rates, on the other hand, are predictable. They allow businesses and the government to make economic plans based on a constant value for the currency. Nevertheless, a fixed rate system runs into trouble when a currency's exchange rate no longer reflects what the market says it is worth. When this happens, a government may have to intervene in financial markets to preserve the value of its currency. It does so using reserves of currency, which it holds for this purpose.

For example, if the value of the peso compared to the dollar were to fall too low, the Mexican government could buy pesos on the open market. It would pay for them with dollars from its currency reserves. This would increase the demand for pesos while reducing their supply, thus increasing their value. At the same time, it would increase the supply of dollars on the market, decreasing their value. The result would be to push up the value of the peso.

Were the value of pesos to climb too high, the government could step in to devalue its currency. It would do so by selling pesos from its reserves for dollars. This action would increase demand for dollars while reducing their supply. And it would decrease demand for pesos while increasing their supply. The result would be a **devaluation** of the peso relative to the dollar.

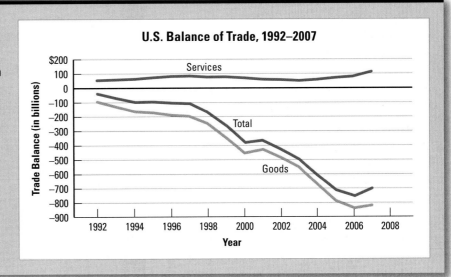

Figure 15.5A

Graphing the Trade Balance
This graph shows the U.S. balance of trade in goods and services from 1992 to 2007. Note the area in which the United States has a positive balance of trade. What does that say about this country's comparative advantage in the global market?

U.S. Balance of Trade, 1992–2007

Source: Bureau of Economic Analysis.

Since the 1970s, most industrialized countries, such as the United States and Japan, have allowed their currencies to float in a managed way. Other countries with less stable currencies have pegged them to a major currency, such as the dollar or the euro, the common currency of the European Union.

Imports, Exports, and the Balance of Trade

Another way countries try to manage the value of their currency is by regulating their balance of trade. **Balance of trade** is the difference between the value of a country's exports and the value of its imports. Also known as net exports, it is calculated by subtracting imports from exports.

A country's balance of trade can be positive or negative. If a country exports more than it imports, it has a positive balance of trade, or a **trade surplus**. If it imports more than it exports, it has a negative trade balance, or a **trade deficit**. Figure 15.5A shows the U.S. balance of trade in goods and services over time.

A trade surplus helps to strengthen a country's currency. Think about what would happen if the United States had a trade surplus. The number of dollars coming into the United States from the sale of exports would exceed the number of dollars we send to other countries to pay for imports. As the supply of dollars held by people in other countries dropped, the value of the dollar would likely rise.

In the same way, a trade deficit tends to weaken a country's currency. Again consider the situation of the United States, which has run a trade deficit for years. To pay for all of its imports, the United States has to send more and more dollars to its trading partners. As the supply of dollars held by people in other countries rises, the value of the dollar is likely to drop. Thus, by exporting more or importing less, a country can have some effect on the strength of its currency.

Just as a weak currency is not necessarily bad, a trade deficit does not necessarily signal a struggling economy. In 2007, the U.S. trade deficit amounted to more than $700 billion. Yet the United States also had the world's largest economy that year.

Financing the U.S. Trade Deficit

When the United States runs a trade deficit, it means that the country is buying more than it is selling in world markets. How does the country manage to do this year after year?

The United States finances its trade deficit by borrowing dollars from foreign lenders and by selling U.S. assets to foreign investors. In other words, foreigners enable the United States to run deficits. They are willing and able to do this because they have so many surplus dollars from selling us their goods.

Foreigners holding dollars can lend their dollars to the United States by buying Treasury securities or other types of bonds. In 2007 foreigners held more than $2.5 trillion in U.S. Treasury securities alone.

Chapter 15 The United States and the Global Economy **313**

Figure 15.5B

Graphing Foreign Direct Investment

Foreign direct investment is capital invested by foreign interests in another country's businesses. FDI promotes economic growth and helps balance the U.S. trade deficit.

- The bar graph shows the dollar value of FDI flowing into the United States from 1990 to 2006.
- The line graph shows the dollar value of American FDI flowing into other countries.

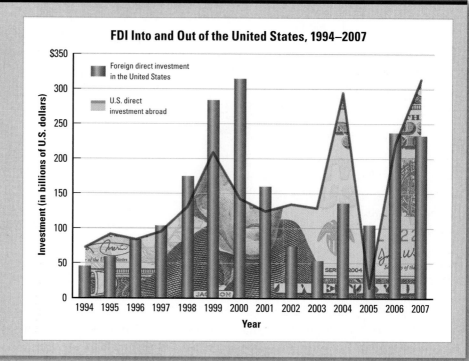

FDI Into and Out of the United States, 1994–2007

Legend:
- Foreign direct investment in the United States
- U.S. direct investment abroad

Y-axis: Investment (in billions of U.S. dollars)
X-axis: Year (1994–2007)

Source: Bureau of Economic Analysis.

This amounted to about 40 percent of all publicly held U.S. government bonds.

Foreign investors can also purchase stock in American companies or buy U.S. assets, such as farmland and office buildings. Some foreign companies use their dollars to buy American companies or to establish new businesses in the United States.

Investment by a firm in a business enterprise in a foreign country is known as **foreign direct investment** (FDI). A German or Japanese auto company creating an assembly plant in the United States is an example of foreign direct investment. In 2007, FDI in the United States was around $230 billion.

Growing Concern About the U.S. Trade Deficit

How concerned should Americans be about the steady rise in trade deficits since the 1980s? The answer depends on whom you ask. A 2005 *Wall Street Journal* editorial found little cause for concern: "On the list of economic matters to worry about, 'the trade deficit' is about 75th—unless politicians react to it by imposing new trade barriers or devaluing the currency." The *New York Times,* on the other hand, in reporting on the 2006 trade deficit, wrote, "A growing trade deficit acts as a drag on overall economic growth."

Many Americans are understandably concerned about trade deficits. Such concern is rooted in personal experience and common sense. After all, if you spend more than you earn, you go into debt. If you borrow to finance your debts, you go deeper into debt. This endless borrowing can get a person into serious financial trouble.

Many people view the U.S. trade deficit in much the same way. The United States, they argue, cannot continue to run large deficits and finance them with foreign borrowing forever. At some point, we may have to pay off all that debt, which could prove painful. Moreover, many Americans do not like the idea of foreign firms owning and controlling U.S. land and businesses.

Economists differ on the significance of the trade deficit and the resulting U.S. debt owned by foreigners. Thomas Sowell notes that the United States has been a debtor country for much of its history. In the 1800s, foreign loans and investment helped finance the country's economic development. "There is nothing wrong with this," he writes, and continues,

By creating more wealth in the United States, such investments created more jobs for American workers and created more goods for American

consumers, as well as providing income to foreign investors . . . Neither the domestic economy nor the international economy is a zero-sum process, where some must lose what others win. Everyone can win when investments create a growing economy. There is a bigger pie, from which everyone can get bigger slices.
—Thomas Sowell, *Basic Economics,* 2007

Sowell and other economists point out that the trade deficit is not a problem as long as our economy grows. When times are good, foreigners view the United States as a safe place to invest their dollars. But the deficit and debt could become an issue if the economy falters. Foreigners may then become less eager to make new loans to the U.S. government. And old loans will have to be repaid—by taxpayers like you. As economists Robert Frank and Ben Bernanke note,

Foreign loans must ultimately be repaid with interest. If the foreign savings are well invested and the U.S. economy grows, repayment will not pose a problem. However, if economic growth . . . slackens, repaying the foreign lenders will impose an economic burden in the future.
—Robert H. Frank and Ben S. Bernanke, *Principles of Economics,* 2007

The trade deficit may not be high on your personal worry list. But the global economy is bound to play a large role in your life. You are already a participant in that economy every time you buy goods made in other countries. And whatever career you choose, it is likely to involve the global marketplace in some way. Understanding how global trade works will help you make better choices, whether you are hunting for the best deal or the ideal job.

Summary

The United States plays an active part in the global economy. U.S. trade with other countries has expanded in recent decades and has contributed to economic growth both at home and abroad.

Why is global trade growing in importance? Various factors have contributed to the growth of global trade. Chief among these are advances in transportation and communications, which have made it easier for countries to do business and move goods around the world. New and differentiated products have also stimulated global trade.

What goods and services do countries trade? Manufactured products are the main category of exports among nations. Agricultural and mineral commodities—notably oil—are also important. Services in such areas as finance, transportation, education, and information also make up a key component of overseas trade.

How and why do countries regulate trade? Although free trade makes economic sense, most countries find reasons to restrict trade. Usually they do so for political reasons, erecting trade barriers—such as tariffs and quotas—to limit imports in order to protect domestic industries. Such restrictions benefit specific industries at the expense of consumers and producers in other industries.

How is global trade financed? Importers and exporters finance global trade by trading currencies on the foreign exchange market. Exchange rates fluctuate based on supply and demand. Governments may try to influence rates through trade policies and other means. When countries have a negative balance of trade, or a trade deficit, they generally finance their deficit by getting loans or investment capital from abroad.

Could you, or should you, live without imports?

Opinion polls show that many Americans favor buying products made in the United States over imported goods. They believe that by "buying American" they can help protect U.S. industries and save American jobs.

What do you think? Would you be willing to check product labels every time you shop to avoid buying imported goods? Before you answer that question, you may want to read about one family's experience of living for a year without buying goods made in China.

A Year Without "Made in China"

by Sara Bongiorni, *The Christian Science Monitor,* **Dec. 21, 2005**

BATON ROUGE, LA—Last year, two days after Christmas, we kicked China out of the house. Not the country obviously, but bits of plastic, metal, and wood stamped with the words "Made in China." We kept what we already had, but stopped bringing any more in.

The banishment was no fault of China's. It had coated our lives with a cheerful veneer of toys, gadgets, and $10 children's shoes. Sometimes I worried about jobs sent overseas or nasty reports about human rights abuses, but price trumped virtue at our house. We couldn't resist what China was selling.

But on that dark Monday last year, a creeping unease washed over me as I sat on the sofa and surveyed the gloomy wreckage of the holiday. It wasn't until then that I noticed an irrefutable fact: China was taking over the place.

It stared back at me from the empty screen of the television. I spied it in the pile of tennis shoes by the door. It glowed in the lights on the Christmas tree and watched me in the eyes of a doll splayed on the floor. I slipped off the couch and did a quick inventory, sorting gifts into two stacks: China and non-China. The count came to China, 25, the world, 14. Christmas, I realized, had become a holiday made by the Chinese. Suddenly I'd had enough. I wanted China out . . .

On Jan. 1 we launched a yearlong household embargo on Chinese imports. The idea wasn't to punish China, which would never feel the pinprick of our protest. And we didn't fool ourselves into thinking we'd bring back a single job to unplugged company towns in Ohio and Georgia. We pushed China out of our lives because we wanted to measure how far it had pushed in. We wanted to know what it would take in time, money, and aggravation to kick our China habit.

We hit the first rut in the road when I discovered our son's toes pressing against the ends of his tennis shoes. I wore myself out hunting for new ones. After two weeks I broke down and spent $60 on sneakers from Italy. I felt sick over the money; it seemed decadent for a pair of children's shoes. I got used to the feeling. Weeks later I shelled out $60 for Texas-made shoes for our toddler daughter.

We got hung up on lots of little things. I drove to half a

dozen grocery stores in search of candles for my husband's birthday cake, eventually settling on a box of dusty leftovers I found in the kitchen. The junk drawer has been stuck shut since January. My husband found the part to fix it at Home Depot but left it on the shelf when he spotted the telltale "Made in China."

Mini crises erupted when our blender and television broke down . . . We killed four mice with old-fashioned snapping traps because the catch-and-release ones we prefer are made in China. Last summer at the beach my husband wore a pair of mismatched flip-flops my mother found in her garage. He'd run out of options at the drug store.

Navigating the toy aisle has been a wilting affair. In the spring, our 4-year-old son launched a counter-campaign in support of "China things." He's been a good sport, but he's weary of Danish-made Legos, the only sure bet for birthday gifts for his friends. One morning in October he fell apart during a trip to Target when he developed a sudden lust for an electric purple pumpkin.

"It's too long without China," he wailed. He kept at me all day.

The next morning I drove him back so he could use his birthday money to buy the pumpkin for himself . . .

My husband bemoans the Christmas gifts he can't buy because they were made in China. He plans to sew sleeping bags for the children himself . . . but I fear he will meet his match with thread and needle.

"How hard can it be?" he scoffed.

The funny thing about China's ascent is that we, as a nation, could shut the whole thing down in a week. Jump-start a "Just Say No to Chinese Products Week," and the empire will collapse amid the chaos of overloaded cargo ships in Long Beach harbor. I doubt we could pull it off. Americans may be famously patriotic, but look closely, and you'll see who makes the flag magnets on their car bumpers. These days China delivers every major holiday, Fourth of July included.

I don't know what we will do after Dec. 31 when our family's embargo comes to its official end. China-free living has been a hassle. I have discovered for myself that China doesn't control every aspect of our daily lives, but if you take a close look at the underside of boxes in the toy department, I promise it will give you pause.

Our son knows where he stands on the matter. In the bathtub one evening he told me how happy he was that "the China season" was coming soon.

"When we can buy China things again, let's never stop," he said.

After a year without China, I can tell you this: You can still live without it, but it's getting trickier and costlier by the day. And a decade from now I may not be brave enough to try it again.

Sara Bongiorni is the author of A Year Without "Made in China": One Family's True Life Adventure in the Global Economy.

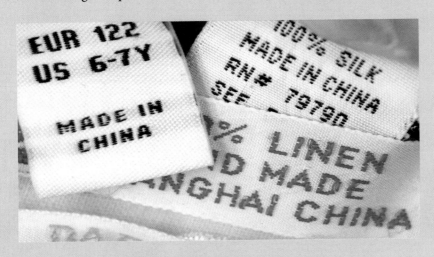

Pintu Gates A1-A11, B1-B11

Imigresen Immigration
入国管理

Tuntutan Bagasi Baggage Reclaim
手荷物受取所

Summit ends in failure

DEFEND OUR FOREST CLEARCUT THE WTO

The Costs and Benefits of Globalization

16.1 Introduction

Globalization is a complex process. At its heart, it represents the growing integration of economies and societies around the world. For some of us, the most visible sign of globalization may be the availability of products from many different nations in food stores and shopping malls. For others, it may be shuttered factories, as work once done in the United States moves to other countries. As economist David Hummels observes, our views of globalization are mixed.

> The word globalization *has been used to mean many different things. It may conjure up visions of fleets of container ships moving goods worth trillions of dollars across all the world's oceans, giant multinational firms with operations in every time zone, brand names and advertisements known by consumers on six continents, and telephone call centers in India providing customer service to American consumers . . . To some, globalization also conveys broader concerns and even fears, such as the erosion of labor and environmental standards or the loss of national sovereignty to international institutions that are not accountable to citizens of any nation.*
> —David Hummels, *Focus: Globalization*, 2006

Globalization is also controversial. To its supporters, the benefits of globalization far outweigh any

Globalization is a hotly debated political and economic issue.

costs it might bring with it. They argue that the easy movement of people, goods, ideas, and technology around the world promotes economic growth and reduces poverty. They also believe that globalization encourages global cooperation in efforts to solve broad social and environmental problems.

Critics of globalization, in contrast, charge that its costs exceed its benefits. As evidence they point to a deteriorating global environment and the persistence of poverty in much of the world. Not only has globalization failed to solve these problems, they argue, but may well be making them worse.

The debate over globalization made headlines in November 1999 when protesters gathered in Seattle, Washington, to disrupt a meeting of the World Trade Organization. The antiglobalization demonstrators blamed the WTO for contributing to a host of economic, social, and environmental problems, from job losses in the United States to global warming. As they marched through the streets, they chanted, "Hey hey, ho ho, the WTO has got to go."

The United Nations plays an important role in the globalization debate. The UN examines key economic and political issues and seeks solutions to global problems. Here, UN delegates meet to discuss human rights.

To clear the streets, Seattle police used tear gas and rubber bullets in what newspapers called the "Battle of Seattle."

This chapter examines the debate between supporters and critics of globalization. It also considers some of the costs and benefits of the globalization process for both people and the environment.

■ 16.2 Who Are the Main Players in the Globalization Debate?

At the Seattle protests, concerns about globalization focused on the World Trade Organization. However, the WTO is just one of many players in the globalization debate. These players can be divided into four main groups: international organizations, nongovernmental organizations, multinational corporations, and sovereign nation-states.

International Organizations
Some of the main targets of globalization critics are international organizations like the WTO. Other key players in this group are the United Nations, the World Bank, and the International Monetary Fund.

World Trade Organization. As the body mainly responsible for drawing up and enforcing international trade agreements, the WTO stands at the center of the globalization debate. Its critics argue that the WTO works to protect the interests of wealthy countries and corporations at the expense of poor countries. They also charge that WTO policies endanger the environment and the rights of workers.

WTO officials see these charges as misguided. "Trade is the ally of working people, not their enemy," declared WTO director-general Mike Moore at the Seattle gathering in 1999. "As living standards improve, so too does education, health, the environment and labor standards."

United Nations. Founded at the end of World War II as a peacekeeping organization, the United Nations has become a key player in the globalization process. As part of its mission, the UN analyzes economic issues and provides aid to poor countries. It also brokers international agreements designed to protect the environment, defend human rights, and preserve cultural

Despite global efforts to relieve poverty in Africa, Africa remains the world's poorest continent. A large foreign debt is part of the problem. Yet, as this cartoon implies, even if Africa were to break free of its debt, it would still be shackled with severe problems.

traditions. These activities put the United Nations squarely in the middle of the globalization debate.

World Bank. Also founded as World War II drew to a close, the World Bank has seen its mission change over time. Its initial goal was to help Europe recover from the war. Later, its focus shifted to helping poor countries develop their economies.

As part of this second effort, the World Bank has funded large projects aimed at improving the economic infrastructure of poor countries. Examples include hydroelectric dams and highways. Critics charge that many of these projects have benefited wealthy business interests and corrupt governments far more than the poor.

Critics also point out that some projects, such as a program to help settlers move into the Amazon rainforest, have led to widespread environmental destruction. Others, such as dam projects in Asia, have hurt poor people by forcing them to relocate out of areas to be flooded. In response to such criticism, the World Bank has shifted its focus to projects more directly aimed at eliminating poverty.

International Monetary Fund. Founded at the same time as the World Bank, the International Monetary Fund has seen its mission evolve as well. Its first task was to reconstruct the world's battered international banking system after World War II. Today the IMF offers economic advice and assistance to countries with financial problems.

The IMF is often called on to help countries experiencing a financial crisis. Such a crisis typically arises when a government accumulates too much **foreign debt**. A country's foreign debt is the amount of money it owes to lenders in other countries.

When debt levels rise too high, a poor country may have trouble servicing its debt. **Debt service** is the series of payments of interest and principal a borrower agrees to pay a lender over the life of the loan. To make payments on time, a government may need to borrow still more money. But as soon as signs of trouble appear, lenders may demand higher interest on new loans. Or they may stop loaning money to the government altogether. The result is a debt crisis.

The IMF uses a two-pronged approach to end such a crisis. First, it acts as a kind of lender of last resort. The IMF agrees to loan money to the troubled government at a lower interest rate than other lenders are demanding. This enables the government to continue servicing its debt.

Second, as a condition for such loans, the IMF requires the government to adopt austerity measures. Usually this means reducing the government's budget deficit by cutting spending. Once this is done, the government has less need to keep borrowing more and more money.

Critics charge that such measures harm poor countries. When forced to cut spending, governments often eliminate programs that help the poor, such as food subsidies. As a result, critics say, the costs of IMF policies fall most heavily on those least able to bear them. The benefits, in contrast, flow to banks and other lenders in wealthy countries whose loans are protected.

Critics also charge that IMF policies trap poor countries in a cycle of debt they can never repay. A better approach, they say, would be **debt forgiveness,** or the cancellation of debts owed to foreign lenders. Eliminating foreign debts, they argue, would help poor countries escape the debt cycle.

Defenders of the IMF reply that no country is forced to accept an IMF loan with its austerity measures. Moreover, canceling debts would only reward countries that have failed to control their budgets. It would also eliminate any incentive for poorly managed governments to make needed fiscal policy reforms.

Nongovernmental Organizations

Another set of players in the globalization debate consists of **nongovernmental organizations**. NGOs are nonprofit organizations that operate outside of governments. The term NGO often refers to organizations that focus on helping lift people out of poverty around the world. Funding for NGOs typically comes from member contributions and grants from private foundations.

Many of the NGOs in the globalization debate are concerned about the effects of global trade on the environment. Among these are such groups as the Sierra Club, Greenpeace, and the World Wildlife Fund. Other NGOs speak out on social issues associated with globalization. Examples include Oxfam International, CARE, the Global Fund for Women, and Save the Children.

The Seattle protests brought together representatives from hundreds of NGOs supported by students, farmers, and church groups. Members of labor unions were also there to voice their concerns about losing jobs to global trade. "I never got on with environmentalists," commented a laid-off steelworker from Michigan, "until I realised we were all fighting for the same thing."

Multinational Corporations

Multinational corporations are both central players in the globalization process and prime targets of globalization critics. Multinationals are companies that have a home base in one country and operations in other countries. These large companies promote globalization by moving goods, capital, information, and people across borders to do business.

Some multinationals have economic assets that dwarf those of many nations. In 2002, the United Nations Conference on Trade and Development (UNCTAD) reported that 29 of the 100 largest economic entities in the world were companies, not countries. The economic output of Exxon/Mobil, for example, was about the same as that of Pakistan. General Electric ranked just above Kuwait, Romania, and Morocco. Toyota's output of goods and services was twice that of Guatemala.

The economic power of these giant corporations concerns critics of globalization. Critics fear that multinationals might become a law unto themselves, wielding power with little restraint from national governments. Critics also worry that in their search for profits, multinationals will move their operations to countries that are unable to protect their workers or the environment from abuse. The result, critics fear, will be a "race to the bottom" in terms of wages, working conditions, or pollution.

Supporters of globalization counter that multinational corporations generate trade, investments, jobs, and other economic benefits in countries where those corporations do business. The multinationals also train workers in new technologies and business methods, increasing the host country's human capital.

In the 1970s, for example, Daewoo, a South Korean multinational, decided to expand its garment-making business to Bangladesh. The company invited 130 Bangladeshi workers to Korea to learn how to make shirts. Over time, 115 of those workers left Daewoo and used what they had learned to set up their own garment companies. Clothing soon became Bangladesh's leading export. By 2006, its garment industry employed 3 million workers who produced $5 billion worth of clothing for export each year.

Sovereign Nation-States

The last major players in the globalization debate are the world's sovereign nation-states. A **nation-state** is an independent political body with full authority over its territory and inhabitants. The members of the United Nations are all nation-states.

A nation-state, in theory, has the sovereign power to regulate trade and capital flows across its borders. **Capital flows** are movements of money and investments from one country to another. To secure the benefits of global trade, however, many nation-states have agreed to limit their use of trade barriers by signing free-trade agreements and joining the WTO.

A frequent complaint about the WTO is that its rulings on trade barriers restrict national sovereignty. As one protester in Seattle put it, "The WTO can rule that a country's laws and regulations are barriers to free trade, regardless of the fact that those laws were passed by the people or in the public interest."

This protester might have been referring to a decision made by the WTO a year earlier in a dispute over the use of synthetic hormones to stimulate the growth of cattle. The European Union (EU) had banned imports of meat from hormone-treated cattle as a health risk. The United States appealed the ban to the WTO, saying that it was an unfair restraint on trade. The WTO found no health risk and ruled that the ban was an illegal trade barrier.

Regardless of how you feel about hormone-treated cattle, what is important to note here is that the WTO's ruling could not and did not force the European Union to change its policy. Members of the WTO retain their full sovereign powers. However, the ruling did give the United States the right to raise tariffs on European imports to make up for the cost of the EU ban to U.S. beef exporters.

The Globalization Index

As you would expect, some nation-states are more open to globalization than others. To see how nations rank in this area, *Foreign Policy* magazine has created the Globalization Index. This index measures a country's global outlook in four broad areas: trade and investment, personal contacts, technological connectivity, and political links. The 72 countries that were ranked in 2007 accounted for 97 percent of the world's gross domestic product (GDP) and 88 percent of the world's population.

A country's ranking in the Globalization Index indicates how much or how little it has opened itself up to trade and contact with other countries. Perhaps not surprisingly, the highest-ranked countries, such as the United States, Australia, and the nations of Europe, are among the world's wealthiest. Lower-ranked countries, such as India, Nigeria, and Peru, are marked by widespread poverty.

This contrast raises the question of cause and effect. Are the top-rated countries wealthy because they have embraced globalization? Or have they embraced globalization as a means to grow wealthier?

Figure 16.2

Graphing Globalization

According to the Globalization Index, some countries are more global than others. The index ranks countries in terms of their interactions with the rest of the world in the four categories listed on the graph.

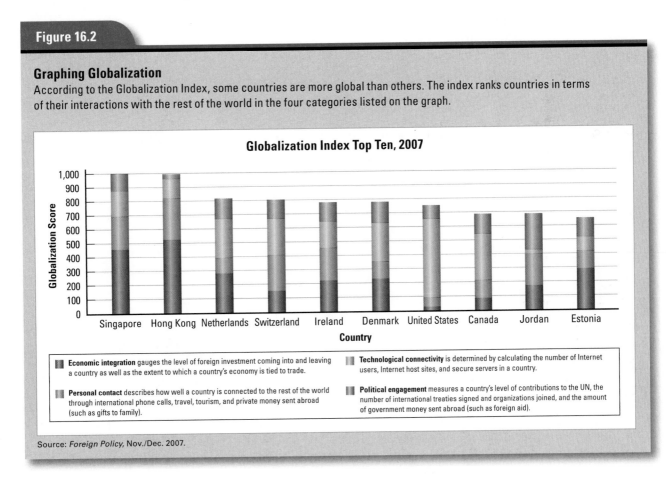

Globalization Index Top Ten, 2007

Economic integration gauges the level of foreign investment coming into and leaving a country as well as the extent to which a country's economy is tied to trade.

Personal contact describes how well a country is connected to the rest of the world through international phone calls, travel, tourism, and private money sent abroad (such as gifts to family).

Technological connectivity is determined by calculating the number of Internet users, Internet host sites, and secure servers in a country.

Political engagement measures a country's level of contributions to the UN, the number of international treaties signed and organizations joined, and the amount of government money sent abroad (such as foreign aid).

Source: *Foreign Policy*, Nov./Dec. 2007.

■ 16.3 Has Globalization Helped or Hindered Economic Development?

Most economists believe that globalization contributes to economic development by increasing trade and investment across borders. **Economic development** is the process by which countries increase their economic output and improve the lives of their people. Economic development brings with it improvements in social welfare, including better nutrition, health care, and education. However, these benefits have not been spread uniformly among the world's more than 6 billion people.

Measuring Economic Development

The World Bank and the IMF have a number of ways to measure economic development. Most of those methods focus on such economic indicators as per capita GDP. Using these indicators, these organizations are able to classify countries by level of development. The three general classifications most commonly used are developed, developing, and least developed countries.

Developed countries. The world's wealthiest nations are considered developed countries. A **developed country** has an advanced, industrial economy and a relatively high annual per capita GDP.

Developed countries typically have stable political and legal institutions. Their courts can enforce property laws and contracts. They also have public services that are essential for economic growth. These include power and water services, transportation systems, telecommunication networks, and schools. Although poverty exists in these countries, the gap between rich and poor is not as great as it is in poorer nations.

The United States, Canada, Japan, Australia, New Zealand, Israel, and most of the countries in Western Europe are considered developed countries. Singapore, South Korea, Taiwan, and South Africa are included in this group as well.

Developing countries. The majority of nations in the world are developing countries. A **developing country** is in the process of modernizing its economy. Most people have enough income to meet their basic needs. However, they have less access to goods and services than the average person in a developed country.

Levels of development and wealth differ widely among developing nations. A few, sometimes called **newly industrialized countries,** are making a rapid transition from agricultural to industrial economies. China and Brazil are two examples. Others, such as Saudi Arabia and Kuwait, have high per capita GDPs because of their oil wealth, but they lag behind developed countries in other ways.

Key Concept

Developed, Developing, and Least Developed Countries
As these photographs illustrate, countries differ in terms of their levels of economic development.

Developed countries are highly industrialized and have an annual per capita GDP of more than $10,000 (as of 2008).

Developing countries are in the process of industrialization and have an annual per capita GDP of $1,000 to $10,000 (as of 2008).

Least developed countries are not yet industrialized and have an annual per capita GDP of less than $1,000 (as of 2008).

Figure 16.3A

Mapping Human Development

The Human Development Index is based on the idea that a country's true wealth is its people. The index rates countries on three dimensions: life expectancy, education, and living standards. This map shows the HDI rankings in 2008.

Human Development Index Rankings, 2008

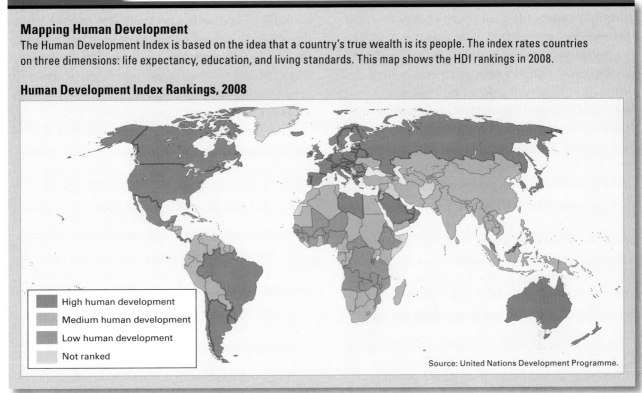

High human development
Medium human development
Low human development
Not ranked

Source: United Nations Development Programme.

A common characteristic of developing countries is a wide income gap between rich and poor. In Brazil, for example, a small percentage of wealthy families enjoy a high standard of living. Meanwhile, the majority of Brazilians live in poverty.

Many developing countries are still struggling to develop governments that can ensure the rule of law. Examples include Kenya, Lebanon, and Peru. In addition, their public services may not be well developed. As a result, many of their people may lack access to electricity and clean water.

Least developed countries. A smaller group of the world's poorest nations are classified as least developed countries. A **least developed country,** or LDC, has barely begun to modernize its economy. Poverty is widespread and often severe.

Most of the people in LDCs earn a meager living from **subsistence agriculture**. They raise crops or livestock mainly for personal consumption rather than for sale. The great majority of these countries are in Africa. Liberia, Ethiopia, and Mali are a few of Africa's very poor countries. Most of the remaining LDCs are located in Asia, including Afghanistan, Cambodia, and Nepal.

The Human Development Index

The United Nations has adopted a broader approach to classifying nations. This approach, the Human Development Index, is based on the belief that people are the real wealth of nations. The United Nations sees economic development as a means to help people develop their full potential and lead productive lives —but not as an end in itself.

The HDI measures a country's level of human development along three dimensions. The first is life expectancy, an indicator that reflects the general health of a population. The second dimension is education. The level of education is measured by combining the adult literacy rate and the **enrollment ratio**—the percentage of school-age children attending school.

The third dimension is standard of living. This dimension is measured by looking at a country's per capita GDP. The more money people have to spend, the better off they are in terms of material goods. These three measures are combined to arrive at a country's overall HDI ranking.

The map in Figure 16.3A shows how 177 countries scored on the Human Development Index in 2008. The top-ranked country in the "high human development" category was Iceland. The United States ranked twelfth. The "medium human development" category included China and India. These two countries are home to more than one-third of the world's people. The countries in the "low human development" category were all located in Africa.

The Costs of Globalization for Poor Countries

However one measures development, it is clear that globalization has not ended global poverty. Between 1990 and 2005, a period of rapid globalization, many developing countries experienced healthy GDP growth. But not all of them did.

During this same period, per capita income in some LDCs remained stagnant or fell. In Haiti, for example, per capita GDP declined by 2 percent. In Guinea-Bissau, it fell by nearly 3 percent. In a report released not long after the Seattle protests, Oxfam International, an NGO working to help the world's poorest countries, observed,

> *Over the past twenty years the income gap between people living in the LDCs and in the industrialised world has widened. Twenty years ago, the ratio of average income in the LDCs to average income in the industrialised world was 1:87. Today it is 1:98, and the gap is widening at an accelerating rate.*
> —Oxfam International, "Rigged Trade and Not Much Aid: How Rich Countries Help to Keep the Least Developed Countries Poor," 2001

To critics of globalization, such statistics are evidence that free trade is hurting, not helping, poor countries. These critics point out that nearly a billion people—around one-sixth of the world's population—live in extreme poverty. In 2008, the World Bank defined **extreme poverty** as a state of severe economic hardship in which people live on less than $1.25 per day.

Globalization hurts poor countries, critics say, because most trade agreements have been written to serve the interests of wealthy countries, not LDCs. As Oxfam pointed out in its 2001 report,

> *Average tariffs in the EU, the United States, Canada, and Japan . . . are relatively low, at approximately five per cent. However, the average obscures very high tariffs in sectors of most relevance to poor countries. Tariffs on some agricultural commodities are more than 300 per cent in the EU and, as in the case of groundnuts [peanuts], over 100 per cent in the USA.*

The products that LDCs are best able to export tend to be farm products and goods that are easy to manufacture, such as clothing. As long as wealthy countries block imports of these products with high tariffs and import quotas, globalization will remain, as its critics maintain, a game with "rigged rules."

The Benefits of Globalization for Poor Countries

Supporters believe that globalization holds out the best hope for relieving poverty around the world.

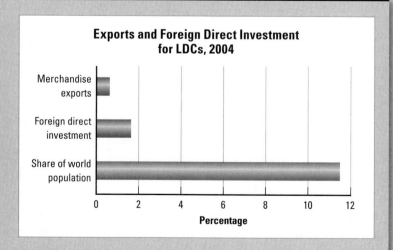

Figure 16.3B

Analyzing the Participation of Least Developed Countries in Globalization
As this graph shows, the world's least developed countries are not getting their "fair share" of export trade or foreign direct investment in terms of their populations. One reason may be trade barriers and agricultural policies in developed countries that discourage merchandise exports from LDCs. Low levels of human development may also discourage outside investors from starting new businesses in LDCs.

Source: UN Office of the High Representative for the Least Developed Countries, Landlocked Developing Countries, and Small Island Developing States.

Exports and Foreign Direct Investment for LDCs, 2004

Merchandise exports

Foreign direct investment

Share of world population

0   2   4   6   8   10   12
Percentage

Economics writer Charles Wheelan summed up the benefits of trade for poor countries as follows:

Trade paves the way for poor countries to get richer. Export industries often pay higher wages than jobs elsewhere in the economy. But that is only the beginning. New export jobs create more competition for workers, which raises wages everywhere else. Even rural incomes can go up; as workers leave rural areas for better opportunities, there are fewer mouths to be fed from what can be grown on the land they leave behind. Other important things are going on, too. Foreign companies introduce capital, technology, and new skills. Not only does that make export workers more productive; it spills over into other areas of the economy. Workers "learn by doing" and then take their knowledge with them.

—Charles Wheelan, *Naked Economics*, 2002

As the pace of globalization has picked up, GDP growth in poor countries has often exceeded that of wealthy countries. In 2006, for example, the World Bank reported that the growth rate for the developing world as a whole since 2000 was more than double that of developed countries. Growth in many LDCs was even higher. However, some poor countries saw their per capita GDP drop because their populations grew faster than their economic output.

The benefits of globalization are also reflected in the Human Development Index. A number of countries with low HDI scores in 1985 have improved significantly since then. Examples include China, India, and Indonesia. Many economists attribute this improvement to the fact that these countries opened themselves up to global trade.

Globalization has also helped lift millions of people out of poverty. The number of people living in extreme poverty has declined since 1981. This is true despite the addition of more than a billion people to the world's population in the same time period.

Supporters of globalization recognize that the benefits of opening up poor countries to trade come with costs. Small businesses may fail when faced with competition from giant multinationals. Poor farmers may not be able to compete with factory farms in rich countries. People who move from farms to cities in search of work may find life there harsher than

it was in their rural villages.

"It is necessary to acknowledge that globalization benefits people unevenly," wrote IMF official Flemming Larsen, "and that it *can and does* produce losers as well as gainers." On the whole, however, supporters argue that globalization has produced—and will continue to produce—far more gainers than losers.

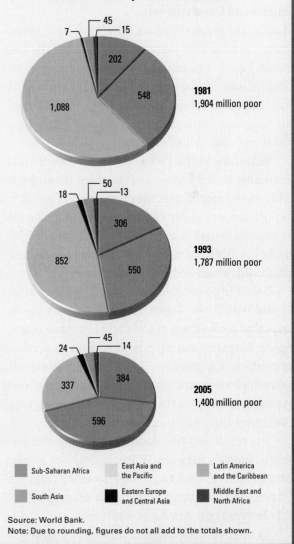

Key Concept

Extreme Poverty

In 2008, the World Bank defined extreme poverty as living on less than $1.25 a day. Since the 1980s, the number of people living in extreme poverty has declined, despite global population growth. By 2008, the world's poorest people were concentrated in South and Central Asia, sub-Saharan Africa, and the mountains of Central and South America.

Extreme Poverty Around the World

1981
1,904 million poor

1993
1,787 million poor

2005
1,400 million poor

Sub-Saharan Africa
East Asia and the Pacific
Latin America and the Caribbean
South Asia
Eastern Europe and Central Asia
Middle East and North Africa

Source: World Bank.
Note: Due to rounding, figures do not all add to the totals shown.

Singapore is one of the Four Asian Tigers—along with South Korea, Taiwan, and Hong Kong—that benefited from export-led development. As Singapore's economy grew, gleaming skyscrapers replaced older slums. In 2007, Singapore was the world's fifth wealthiest country, as measured by per capita GDP.

The Four Asian Tigers: A Case Study of Export-Led Development

Among the greatest gainers benefiting from globalization are the four economies nicknamed the Four Asian Tigers. The name refers to the countries of South Korea, Singapore, and Taiwan, along with the former British colony of Hong Kong. In the 1960s, all four were relatively poor. Today they rank among the world's developed economies.

Beginning in the 1970s, the Tigers adopted an economic model known as **export-led development**. This model emphasizes the production of goods for export as a way of expanding an economy. The sale of exports brings in money to buy machinery for factories. With the new machines, more goods are produced, which adds to economic growth.

Following a pattern established by Japan after World War II, the Tigers developed export industries that took advantage of their low labor costs. South Korea, for example, became a major producer of clothing and sneakers. Taiwan built factories that assembled electronic goods. At the same time, their governments kept tariffs high to protect their new industries from foreign competition.

The result was two decades of spectacular economic growth. Between 1970 and 1989, the average annual GDP growth in the Tigers ranged from 7 to 10 percent. In contrast, the world average growth rate hovered between 3 and 4 percent.

As their economies grew, the Tigers invested heavily in education and other services to improve the lives of their citizens. As a result, their levels of human development rose rapidly. Today all four rank in the "high human development" category.

The success of the Four Asian Tigers was so impressive that the IMF and World Bank began recommending the export-led development model to their clients. From China to Chile, developing countries embraced the new model. By the 1990s, the Tigers faced fierce competition from countries like Vietnam and Bangladesh, which had even lower wage rates. As a result, the Tigers' GDP growth began to slow.

Critics of export-led development point to a number of problems with this model. The most obvious is that it depends on a high level of demand for exports in wealthy countries, especially the United States. If that demand drops because of an economic downturn, countries that rely on U.S. consumers to buy their exports will also suffer. As has often been observed, "When America sneezes, the world catches a cold."

■ 16.4 Has Globalization Helped or Hurt the Environment?

Many of the protesters at the 1999 WTO meeting in Seattle were concerned about globalization's effects on the environment. To show their concern, some came dressed as sea turtles, a reference to a WTO decision made the previous year.

The WTO ruling involved a U.S. law designed to protect sea turtles. The law banned imports of shrimp caught in nets that also trap and kill sea turtles. Asian countries that depend on shrimp fishing charged that the U.S. law violated WTO trade agreements. The WTO ruled that the shrimp ban, like the EU's ban on hormone-raised beef, was an illegal trade barrier.

Unlike the European Union, however, Congress chose to revise U.S. law to comply with the WTO ruling. Its decision to do so upset environmentalists seeking to protect an endangered species. It also underscored what critics saw as the WTO's indifference to environmental issues.

Economic Development Creates Environmental Problems

The plight of sea turtles caught in shrimp nets is a reminder that economic development is hard on the environment. Countries exploit natural resources and develop industries to promote economic growth. But such development may also cause pollution, destroy landscapes, and endanger wild species.

Almost all human activity has some impact on the environment. When farmers clear forests and grasslands to plant crops, they are also destroying the habitats of plants and animals. As developing countries shift from agriculture to industry, their environmental problems multiply. If left unregulated, factories spew smoke into the air and pour toxic waste into waterways.

The latest environmental challenge confronting the world is climate change. This term refers to variations in Earth's overall climate over time, ranging from decades to millions of years. Historically, climate change was caused by natural processes. Such processes include volcanic eruptions and variations in the intensity of sunlight reaching the planet's surface.

Many scientists now believe that human activity is causing the global climate to become warmer. The main culprit is the burning of fossil fuels in power plants, factories, and vehicles. When coal, oil, and natural gas are burned, they release carbon dioxide

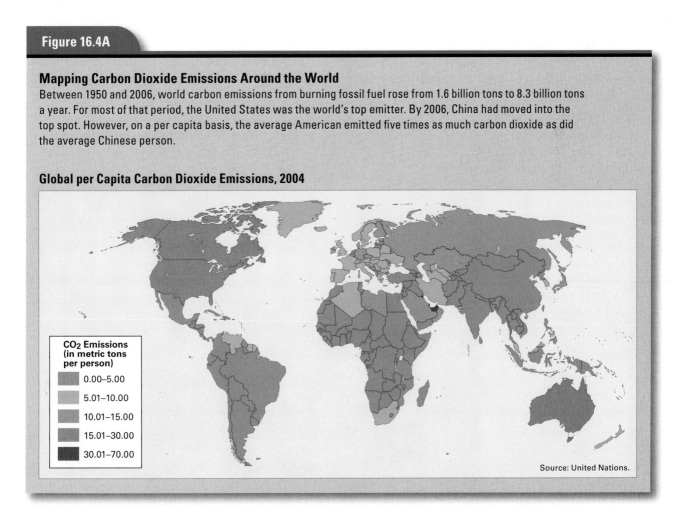

Figure 16.4A

Mapping Carbon Dioxide Emissions Around the World
Between 1950 and 2006, world carbon emissions from burning fossil fuel rose from 1.6 billion tons to 8.3 billion tons a year. For most of that period, the United States was the world's top emitter. By 2006, China had moved into the top spot. However, on a per capita basis, the average American emitted five times as much carbon dioxide as did the average Chinese person.

Global per Capita Carbon Dioxide Emissions, 2004

CO_2 Emissions (in metric tons per person)

- 0.00–5.00
- 5.01–10.00
- 10.01–15.00
- 15.01–30.00
- 30.01–70.00

Source: United Nations.

and other gases. These gases act like a greenhouse in the atmosphere, trapping energy from the sun near Earth's surface.

A 2007 UN report on climate change warned that average global temperatures are likely to rise between 3.5 and 8 degrees Fahrenheit by the end of this century. Environmental writer Fred Pearce detailed the effects of this global warming:

> *Melting glaciers and precipitation are causing some rivers to overflow, while evaporation is emptying others. Diseases are spreading. Some crops grow faster while others see yields slashed by disease and drought. Strong hurricanes are becoming more frequent and destructive . . . Clashes over dwindling water resources may cause conflicts in many regions.*
>
> *As natural ecosystems—such as coral reefs— are disrupted, biodiversity is reduced. Most species cannot migrate fast enough to keep up, though others are already evolving in response to warming.*
>
> —Fred Pearce, "Instant Expert: Climate Change," NewScientist.com, 2006

The Costs of Globalization for the Environment

Environmentalists do not blame all of these problems on global trade. But they worry about the impact that rapid economic growth has on the environment. Markets may do well at coordinating trade, environmentalists concede. But by putting profits first, markets often overlook the environmental costs of economic activity. As one environmental economist wrote,

> *Though the market is a powerful tool for economic progress, where its edges meet the planet it is mainly [used] as a saw, shovel, or smokestack—as an instrument of destruction rather than protection.*
>
> —David Malin Roodman, *The Natural Wealth of Nations: Harnessing the Market for the Environment*, 1998

Environmentalists are not opposed to economic development. But they believe development should be sustainable over time. **Sustainable development** is designed to meet people's present needs without having a negative impact on future generations' ability to meet their needs. For example, a lumber company that plants as many trees as it cuts down each year is practicing sustainable development.

Unfortunately, say environmentalists, most current development is not sustainable. Globalization is making millions of people in the developing world rich enough to live like Americans. As a result, global demand for luxury goods, such as computers and cars, is rising. The same is true for the fossil fuels

Before China globalized its economy in the 1990s, few of its citizens could afford their own cars. But by 2008, the number of privately owned cars in China topped 15 million. One result has been a rapid rise in pollution. According to the World Bank, China had 16 of the 20 most air-polluted cities on Earth in 2006.

Figure 16.4B

Analyzing the Relationship Between Income and Environmental Quality

The environmental Kuznets curve illustrates a theoretical relationship between per capita income and the quality of a country's environment.

- As incomes begin to rise, environmental quality declines. This may be due to industrialization or lifestyle changes as people begin to consume more.
- At some income level, people begin to demand a cleaner environment. From that point on, increased per capita income leads to improved environmental quality.

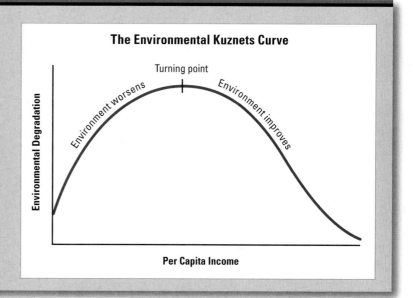

The Environmental Kuznets Curve

needed to power them. "Trying to meet that kind of demand," cautioned environmentalist Bill McKibben, "would stress the earth past its breaking point."

Environmentalists also worry that globalization may encourage multinational corporations to move their operations to "pollution havens." A **pollution haven** is a country that attracts polluting industries because of its weak or poorly enforced environmental laws. "'Pollution havens' . . . have failed to materialize," reported the World Bank in 2000. "Instead, poorer nations and communities are acting to reduce pollution because they have decided that the benefits . . . outweigh the costs." But the possibility that such havens might emerge remains a concern.

More worrisome yet is the link between globalization and climate change. Moving people and goods around the globe by air and sea produces more than 6 percent of the world's carbon emissions. And as the economies of developing countries grow, their consumption of fossil fuels increases as well. This adds still more greenhouse gases to the atmosphere.

If nothing is done to reduce these emissions, environmentalists warn, the effect on the environment could be devastating. "In this century, human activity could trigger an irreversible melting of the Greenland ice sheet and Antarctic glaciers," wrote Fred Pearce. "This would condemn the world to a rise in sea level of six metres—enough to flood land occupied by billions of people."

The Benefits of Globalization for the Environment

Supporters of globalization recognize that development has environmental costs. They argue, however, that the best way to address those costs is not by slowing economic growth. The answer, they say, is to speed it up.

To explain why, economists point to the **environmental Kuznets curve**. This theoretical curve shows pollution increasing as a country begins to industrialize. When incomes start to increase, people are more interested in raising their living standards than in controlling pollution. As they grow wealthier, however, this attitude begins to change. People become concerned about dirty air and waterways and demand that their governments do something about it. The wealthier that people become, the more resources they seem willing to devote to improving the environment.

There is historical evidence suggesting that people will do more to protect their environment as they grow richer. The city of London, for example, had far worse air pollution a century ago than it does today. Lake Erie was pronounced "dead" in the 1960s. Today, the lake has one of the world's largest freshwater fisheries. And as recently as 2008, China's government announced that it was shifting from growth at the expense of the environment to "putting equal emphasis on both."

Given this history, some economists describe a clean environment as a luxury good. However, they also note that the relationship between income and environmental protection is strongest for visible pollution. Examples include smoggy skies and sewage-choked rivers. It is weaker for problems that people do not see every day, such as carbon emissions and loss of forests. "The quick and dirty rule seems to be that if you can't see it or smell it in your local urban neighborhood," noted economics writer Andrew Leonard, "then, no matter how rich you are, you aren't going to do much about it."

Globalization may also benefit the environment by fostering international cooperation to solve problems. For example, in 1985, British scientists discovered that synthetic chemicals were thinning the ozone layer in Earth's atmosphere. The ozone layer protects the planet from harmful ultraviolet rays given off by the sun. Overexposure to these rays can cause skin cancer and damage eyes.

Recognizing the danger, world leaders met in 1987 to sign the Montreal Protocol on Substances that Deplete the Ozone Layer. Hailed by the U.S. Environmental Protection Agency as "the world's most successful international environmental treaty," the protocol ended production of the most harmful chemicals. Since the treaty went into effect, the thinning of the ozone layer has stopped. Full recovery, however, may take many lifetimes.

Whaling: A Case Study of Global Environmental Cooperation

Another example of global cooperation to protect the environment is the Save the Whales campaign.

Begun in the 1970s, this campaign brought together the International Whaling Commission, sovereign nation-states, and NGOs in an effort to protect endangered whale species.

For centuries, whales had been hunted for their meat and oil. By the 1950s, however, modern whaling methods had brought many whale species to the brink of extinction. The number of blue whales, for example, had dropped from between 30,000 and 40,000 in the 1930s to 2,000 or fewer in the 1960s.

The International Whaling Commission was established in 1946 to manage whale harvests. In 1982, under immense pressure from NGOs, the commission imposed a moratorium, or ban, on whaling. The moratorium applies only to commercial whaling. Whales may still be caught for scientific purposes or by native peoples who depend on whales for food.

The Save the Whales campaign was evidence of the growing power of NGOs. Working together, antiwhaling groups persuaded people around the world that protecting whales was important. As a result of the hunting ban, the stocks of many whale species are no longer in decline. Some are even on the rebound.

The world has done less well in protecting other forms of marine life. Because of overfishing by commercial fishing fleets, around 75 percent of fish stocks are being harvested at unsustainable levels. As a result, many fish species are in danger of extinction. Making matters worse, the oceans are being polluted at an alarming rate. Whether the world can come together to save the oceans and marine life, as it did whales, remains an open question.

As part of its effort to protect whales, the International Whaling Commission promotes whale watching as "a sustainable use of cetacean [sea mammal] resources." Whale-watching tours earn welcome tourist dollars for former whaling communities. At the same time, these tours allow the public to see whales in their natural environment.

■ 16.5 Does Globalization Enrich or Threaten Local Cultures?

On August 12, 1999, a group of farmers and anti-globalization activists drove their tractors into a town in southwestern France. There they destroyed a McDonald's restaurant that was under construction, dumping the rubble on the outskirts of town. "I believe that the French people," declared José Bové, the group's leader, "are with us in this fight against junk food and against globalisation."

For Bové and his supporters, globalization—as symbolized by McDonald's—was a threat to French culture. In their eyes, it undermined local traditions of fresh food and small-scale agriculture. For many other people, however, globalization is a positive force that enriches local cultures.

The Global Reach of American Culture

Bové's attack was not only directed at globalization. It was also an assault on Americanization—the spread of American customs and culture to other countries. For many of its critics, globalization and Americanization are one and the same.

Over the past several decades, American fads, foods, and fashions have spread rapidly around the world. Much of this Americanization has been carried out by multinational corporations. American-based companies can be found in almost every corner of the globe. On a visit to Beijing, China, anthropologist James L. Watson noted,

> *Looming over Beijing's choking, bumper-to-bumper traffic, every tenth building seems to sport a giant neon sign advertising American wares: Xerox, Mobil, Kinko's, Northwest Airlines, IBM, Jeep, Gerber, even the Jolly Green Giant. American food chains and beverages are everywhere in central Beijing: Coca-Cola, Starbucks, . . . Baskin-Robbins, Pepsi, TCBY, Pizza Hut, and of course McDonald's.*
> —James L. Watson, "China's Big Mac Attack,"
> *Foreign Affairs,* 2000

Americanization is also evident in popular culture. American music, movies, and television shows are popular throughout the world. Some of these cultural products have been created with the global market in mind. Such globalized films may deal with inter-

American business interests, including the entertainment industry, have carried U.S. culture to the far reaches of the globe. Disneyland is one example. The first overseas Disneyland opened in Tokyo, Japan, in 1983. Two more parks followed: Disneyland Paris, in France, and Disneyland Hong Kong.

national issues or feature non-American actors in starring roles.

Commercial interests are not the only force driving the spread of American culture. Language also plays a part. English is one of the most widely spoken languages in the world, used by as much as one-fifth of the world's population. Many people around the world also respect the American traditions of freedom and democracy. They admire the spirit of openness and innovation in American life.

Nevertheless, the spread of American culture concerns many critics of globalization. Some see it as **cultural imperialism,** the imposing of one country's culture or language on another country. Usually, the charge of cultural imperialism is made by people in a small or weak country who fear domination by a larger, more powerful country.

The Costs of Globalization for Local Cultures

The main criticism of globalization from a cultural perspective is that it weakens local traditions. Like José Bové, many people worry that their own way of

Language Extinction

More than half the world's 7,000 languages are expected to go extinct by 2100. Languages die when their community of speakers chooses to speak the tongue of the dominant culture for economic or social reasons. This map shows several key areas of language extinction. Some of these areas include many small language communities, each with its own native tongue.

Language Extinction Around the World, 2007

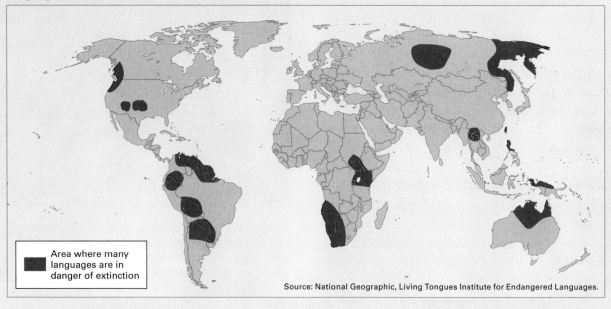

Area where many languages are in danger of extinction

Source: National Geographic, Living Tongues Institute for Endangered Languages.

life will be lost amid a flood of imported culture.

Critics point to the rapid extinction of languages as one cost of globalization. As the English language and Western cultural influences spread across the world, many smaller, local languages are dying out. Language experts predict that more than half of the world's 7,000 languages will disappear by the end of the century. The map above shows areas of language extinction around the world.

Language is an important vehicle for the preservation of culture. This is especially true for native peoples in the developing world, who may not have a written language. When a language dies, it takes with it a wealth of human knowledge, especially about the natural world. "Most of what we know about species and ecosystems is not written down anywhere," observed linguistics professor David Harrison. "It's only in people's heads. We are seeing in front of our eyes the erosion of the human knowledge base."

Along with the loss of language, many peoples are seeing their own traditions crowded out by cul-

tural imports. In many villages, for example, people have swapped their traditional clothing for jeans and T-shirts. Teenagers are more interested in television shows and popular music from abroad than traditional folklore and music. They choose hamburgers and pizza over traditional foods.

This problem is not limited to developing nations. In the 1960s, U.S. movies earned only about 35 percent of European box office revenues. Today that figure ranges between 80 and 90 percent. In response, some countries have enacted laws to preserve local cultural products. France and Canada, for example, have imposed limits on cultural imports, such as American magazines, movies, and television programs.

Cultural evolution is nothing new, of course. It is a natural process that has been taking place for thousands of years. But critics warn that globalization is speeding up the process of cultural change, often with commercial interests in mind. They fear that the rich, vibrant mosaic of world culture will be replaced by a bland "McWorld," where all cultures resemble that of the United States. As Julia Galeota, who at the age of 17 wrote a prize-winning essay on cultural imperialism, observed,

> Throughout the course of human existence, millions have died to preserve their indigenous culture. It is a fundamental right of humanity to be allowed to preserve the mental, physical, intellectual, and creative aspects of one's society. A single "global culture" would be nothing more than a shallow, artificial "culture" of materialism.
>
> —Julia Galeota, "Cultural Imperialism: An American Tradition," 2004

The Benefits of Globalization for Local Cultures

Supporters of globalization see a different result from the interaction of world cultures. They contend that globalization enriches local cultures by exposing people to new ways of doing things. Rather than a bland "McWorld," they say, the result is a "global village," where cultures share ideas and customs but retain their distinct identities.

"Critics of cultural imperialism charge that rich cultures dominate poor ones," wrote economist Tyler Cowen. What they fail to see is the degree to which "local culture commands loyalty." In India, for example, domestic recordings dominate 96 percent of the music market. "Western culture often creates its own rivals," Cowen observed, "by bringing creative technologies like the recording studio or the printing press to foreign lands."

Although globalization is often seen as a one-way flow—from rich to poor nations—it goes the other way, too. Customs and traditions from developing nations also influence the developed world. The fact that restaurants in the United States serve food from Thailand or Ethiopia is a sign of globalization. So is the fact that Americans watch Bollywood movies from India, listen to Afro-pop music from Nigeria, and furnish their homes with crafts from Indonesia.

Artists and artisans in developing countries benefit from the chance to sell their products in the developed world. By gaining a larger market for their work, many are able to preserve their art, music, and traditional crafts.

The idea that cultures should be protected from change is wrongheaded, say supporters of globalization. No one is forced to speak English or eat at McDonald's. People make such choices voluntarily. "China has become more open partly because of the demands of ordinary people," observed Watson. "They want to become part of the world."

In Nepal, the people who live near Mount Everest have adopted new customs through contact with foreign tourists. Mountain climber Jon Krakauer sees some of these changes as negative. But he also says

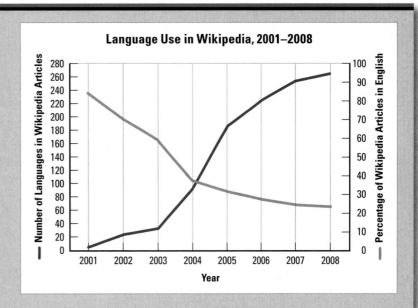

Figure 16.5

Tracking Online Language Use
When first developed, the Internet was dominated by English-language speakers and articles. In recent years, however, it has become a vehicle for language preservation by linking speakers of endangered tongues. This graph shows a rapid increase in the number of languages used in articles written for Wikipedia, the online encyclopedia, between 2001 and 2008. As a result, the percentage of articles written in English has decreased sharply.

Language Use in Wikipedia, 2001–2008

Source: Wikipedia.

This McDonald's restaurant in New Delhi, India, is much like a McDonald's in the United States. But the menu reflects the fast food chain's adaptation to local culture. The Maharaja Mac—made from mutton—and the vegetable burger are both designed to appeal to Indian tastes.

that local people have benefited from global contact. Money from tourism and grants from international organizations have funded new schools, medical clinics, and many other improvements. Krakauer wrote,

> Most of the people who live in this rugged country seem to have no desire to be severed from the modern world or the untidy flow of human progress. The last thing [they] want is to be preserved as specimens in an anthropological museum.
> —Jon Krakauer, *Into Thin Air,* 1997

Cultural diffusion—the process of sharing ideas and knowledge across cultures—is often disruptive. But it is also productive and leads to new ways of life. It can even help spread universal ideals, such as respect for human rights and freedoms. As Cowen observed,

> Culture is not a zero-sum game, so the greater reach of one culture does not necessarily mean diminished stature for others. In the broad sweep of history, many different traditions have grown together and flourished. American popular culture will continue to make money, but the 21st century will bring a broad mélange of influences, with no clear world cultural leader.
> —Tyler Cowen, "Some Countries Remain Resistant to American Cultural Exports," *New York Times,* Feb. 22, 2007

McDonald's: A Case Study of Cultural Adaptation

McDonald's is a powerful symbol of globalization for supporters and critics alike. The American fast food chain has more than 30,000 outlets in more than 119 countries around the world. Many critics claim that McDonald's imposes American cultural values wherever it goes. But the reality is more complex. Although McDonald's has brought changes to other countries, it has also adapted to local cultures.

Everywhere McDonald's sets up a branch, it follows certain standard practices. The menu is the same —burgers, fries, and shakes—and the restaurant is clean and modern. Over time, however, many branches have changed their menus to suit local tastes. In Norway, you can get a salmon sandwich. In India, where many people do not eat beef or pork, you can order a mutton burger, called a Maharaja Mac. Or, if you do not eat meat, you can get a spicy vegetarian patty made of peas and potatoes. French diners can order espresso coffee and brioche along with their burgers and fries.

The style of the restaurants can vary, too. In France, for example, many branches have been remodeled to reflect local architecture. "Far from being cookie-cutter copies," Shirley Leung reported in *The Wall Street Journal,* "each of the remodeled restaurants features one of at least eight different themes—such as 'Mountain,' complete with a wood-beam ceiling reminiscent of a ski chalet. The company has even begun to replace its traditional red-and-yellow signs with signs in muted tones of maroon and mustard."

At the same time, McDonald's has had an impact on local cultures. In China, for example, people do not traditionally celebrate children's birthdays. After McDonald's introduced American-style birthday parties, however, many Chinese families adopted the custom. McDonald's also introduced a higher standard of cleanliness—including clean public bathrooms—than was typical of Chinese restaurants. As a result, many Chinese customers began demanding similar standards of hygiene elsewhere.

One custom the Chinese have not adopted is the "eat and run" style of dining typical of a McDonald's in the United States. At Chinese branches, customers may linger for hours, socializing, reading the newspaper, or doing their homework. Such behavior would be unusual, and probably discouraged, at an American fast food restaurant.

All of this suggests that globalization is neither simple nor predictable. It is a complicated process, with many costs and benefits, that is changing the world in unforeseen ways. What does seem clear is that as long as countries continue to trade and interact, globalization in some form will continue. As economist Lester Thurow wrote,

Fifty years from now few of us will be apt to say we work in the U.S. economy or the Japanese economy. We live in the United States or Japan, but we work in the global economy.
—Lester Thurow, *Fortune Favors the Bold: What We Must Do to Build a New and Lasting Global Prosperity*, 2003

Summary

Globalization means many things to many people. In essence, it is the integration of economies and societies around the world. Critics emphasize its costs, however, while supporters point to its benefits.

Who are the main players in the globalization debate? Four main groups play key roles in globalization: (1) international organizations, such as the World Trade Organization; (2) nongovernmental organizations, such as the World Wildlife Fund; (3) multinational corporations, such as McDonald's; and (4) sovereign nation-states.

Has globalization helped or hindered economic development? For many developing countries, globalization has been the key to growing their economies and raising living standards. However, some of the world's less-developed countries have failed to experience such economic gains.

Has globalization helped or hurt the environment? Although globalization is not the root cause of most environmental problems, it may contribute to them by encouraging industrialization. However, as countries develop, they also begin to do more to protect the environment. Globalization may help solve problems like climate change by promoting international cooperation.

Does globalization enrich or threaten local cultures? Globalization brings cultures together in ways never experienced before. In some cases, the flood of Western products and ideas may crowd out local traditions and customs. At the same time, globalization enriches cultures by introducing new ideas, technologies, foods, and arts that can be adapted for local use and enjoyment.

What can you do to fight global warming?

As an individual, there is little you can do to shape the course of globalization. But there are things you can do to limit some of its negative effects. You can buy Fair Trade products, for example, thus helping producers in developing countries raise their standard of living. You can become a member of an NGO or other group that works on globalization issues. Or you can take steps to curb the carbon emissions that you contribute to global warming.

The following article examines ways that people can reduce their carbon footprints. As you read the article, think about the changes you and your family might make to help slow global climate change.

Reducing Your Carbon Footprint

**by Clayton Sandell,
ABC News, June 7, 2006**

Erik Daehler loves to travel. But every time he gets on an airplane, he knows his carbon footprint gets bigger . . . What, might you ask, is a carbon footprint?

A carbon footprint is the measure of the amount of carbon dioxide—the major man-made global warming greenhouse gas—that goes into the atmosphere as you go about your daily life. Almost everything you do affects it: turning on a coffee maker, driving a car, buying food—and in Daehler's case—taking a ride on a passenger jet.

Air travel accounts for about 3.5 percent of the human contribution to global warming, according to the Intergovernmental Panel on Climate Change. The good news is you can offset—if not eliminate—your carbon footprint by making choices that can even save you money . . .

Making these kinds of choices has become a growing trend among people who want to reduce the size of their carbon footprints. At the same time, they must grapple with the question of whether their actions really make any difference.

Many people have employed a number of low-tech ideas that all play a small part in reducing their footprints: reusing canvas shopping bags, taking shorter showers, and walking or riding a bicycle for short trips around town.

Increasingly, many have turned to Web sites that offer carbon calculators, which add up how much carbon dioxide gas their lifestyle puts into the atmosphere. You increase your carbon footprint by driving a sport utility vehicle, for example, or reduce it by driving a hybrid.

Energy Efficiency

Experts say one of the first things you can do to reduce your carbon footprint is to get smart about energy efficiency . . . "Efficiency is the least expensive way to cut down on your carbon footprint," said John Steelman, director of the climate program at the Natural Resources Defense Council [NRDC].

On average, every American is responsible for about 22 tons of carbon dioxide emissions every year, according to statistics compiled by the United Nations. That is far above the world average of 6 tons per capita. Thus, experts say there are lots of ways to reduce your carbon footprint inexpensively by taking some simple steps at home.

How? Web sites like stopglobalwarming.org have carbon calculators that offer dozens of suggestions for cutting emissions around your house. For example, the site says that moving a thermostat down two degrees in winter and up two degrees in summer will save 2,000 pounds of carbon dioxide and $98 a year.

If every household in America replaced just three bulbs with energy-efficient fluorescent bulbs, we would all save $60 a year and collectively keep a trillion pounds of CO_2 out of the atmosphere, according to the site.

Daehler has replaced all his light bulbs with energy-efficient bulbs and has watched his electricity bill drop 12 percent. He said many people often don't realize that electronic devices like VCRs and stereos that stay plugged in all day are also drawing power, even if they are turned off.

These items, which include cell phone and iPod chargers, draw what is known as a phantom load. "They call them vampires," said Daehler, who makes sure to unplug his chargers when he's not using them. "They constantly draw about a watt of energy," he said. "And if you have 10 of those

in your house, always plugged in, that's 240 watt hours a day" . . .

Tony Napolillo, a marketing manager with a green energy company in Texas, makes reducing his carbon footprint a part of everyday life. He credits the city of Austin with providing incentives and rebates on, for example, air conditioners and landscaping—things that helped him transform his home into a model of energy efficiency.

"The programmable thermostat and the compact fluorescent light bulbs were all provided by the city," he said. "It's made a huge difference on what my house uses and loses."

Kym Trippsmith, a writer for a financial Web site, would like to go a step further and install a solar panel system for her California home. "But it's $40,000," she said, too expensive an upfront cost to install all at

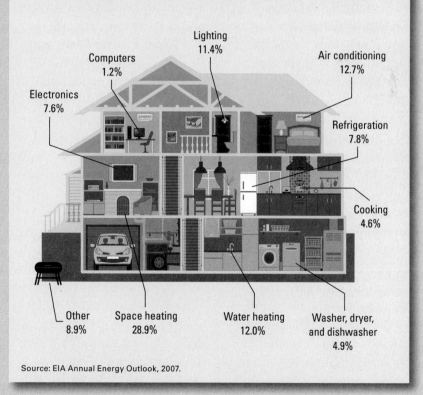

Sources of Household Carbon Emissions
The electricity, natural gas, and fuel oil used by households account for about 18 percent of all U.S. carbon emissions. Motor vehicles produce even more. The average car emits twice its weight in carbon dioxide each year.

Computers 1.2%
Lighting 11.4%
Air conditioning 12.7%
Electronics 7.6%
Refrigeration 7.8%
Cooking 4.6%
Other 8.9%
Space heating 28.9%
Water heating 12.0%
Washer, dryer, and dishwasher 4.9%

Source: EIA Annual Energy Outlook, 2007.

once. But if she could make it happen, she said her footprint would shrink and her wallet would grow. "I hope to save $6,000 a year," she said. "Within eight years, that system would completely pay for itself."

Buy Local

Practically everything we buy has a carbon cost associated with it that consists of things like transportation costs and the amount of electricity that goes into manufacturing a product or packaging.

Even natural foods often have a carbon impact. For example, fruits and vegetables are transported on trucks that drive an average of 1,500 miles from field to supermarket, according to a 2001 U.S. Department of Agriculture study. So Daehler buys fruits and vegetables only from local farmers' markets . . .

Transportation

Personal transportation choices can also shrink a carbon footprint. Many people choose to walk, ride a bicycle or a scooter on short trips around town. Some cut their emissions by shopping at stores—or even by taking jobs—that are closer to home.

Another choice requires giving up the gas-guzzling car you have now for something more efficient . . . If you can afford a hybrid, stopglobalwarming.org says you can save 16,000 pounds of CO_2 and $3,750 a year . . .

"Green Tags"

Many people are now asking their utility companies for "green power" options in which they pay a little extra for power that is generated by cleaner wind or solar technology. If your utility doesn't offer a green option, a growing number of private companies offer "green tags" that help you offset your carbon emissions from electricity.

"The average residential utility usage in the United States is about 1,000 kilowatt hours, or one megawatt hour a month," said Tom Starrs at Bonneville Environmental Foundation in Portland, Ore.

Bonneville offers green tags that cost $20 to $24 a month, depending on what combination of clean power you choose . . .

"When you offset your usage through a green tag purchase, you're preventing about 1,400 pounds of CO_2 and other greenhouse gas emissions a month, or about 16,800 pounds a year," said Starrs . . .

Impact?

The real question, of course, is whether individual efforts to reduce carbon footprints will have a positive effect on cutting greenhouse gases, or be worth the sacrifice. Some are not optimistic.

"I drive a Prius. I have a garden," said Trippsmith. "We have a smaller footprint than most. But it's a drop in the bucket . . ."

Daehler said that his indi-vidual contribution to reducing greenhouse gas pollution is small, but has begun to see anecdotal evidence that people are changing their ways . . .

"It seems insignificant," he said. "But what you find is, the more people you touch, and give the word to and talk to, the more it moves.

"When I first bought my first hybrid three years ago," Daehler adds, "no one I knew had one . . . Now I can name a dozen friends who have hybrids. So you start to see a cumulative effect."

But even reducing your footprint to zero and living a so-called carbon neutral life may not be enough, said the NRDC's Steelman.

"You can take yourself out of the equation," he said. "But that doesn't change that coal plant into a clean power generation plant. So, in addition to making changes in your own life, it's holding politicians accountable and raising your political voice to solve the problem."

But Tony Napolillo said he won't wait for politicians to act.

"Everybody has to realize they have personal responsibility," he said. "They can't just wait for the government or the corporate world to do something about it. If everybody could strive to be carbon neutral, this would be a greater world."

Clayton Sandell is a reporter for ABC News.

Resources

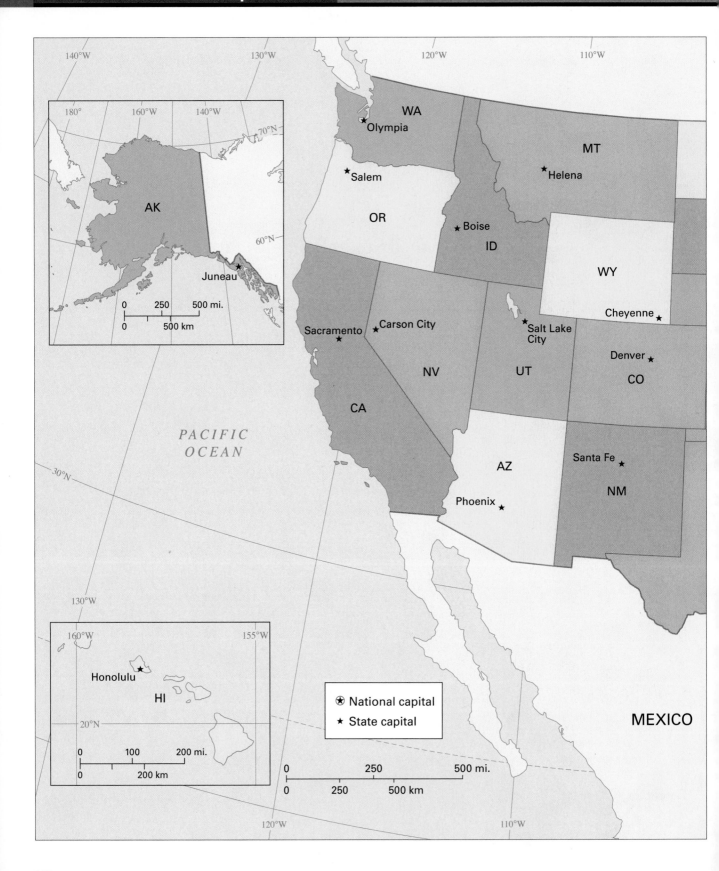

WA
★ Olympia

★ Salem

OR

MT
★ Helena

★ Boise
ID

WY
Cheyenne ★

Sacramento ★ ★ Carson City

NV

Salt Lake ★
City

UT

Denver ★
CO

CA

AZ

Santa Fe ★

NM

★ Phoenix

140°W 130°W 120°W 110°W

180° 160°W 140°W
70°N

AK

60°N

Juneau ★

0   250   500 mi.
0   500 km

30°N

PACIFIC
OCEAN

130°W

160°W 155°W

Honolulu ★

HI

20°N

0   100   200 mi.
0   200 km

⊛ National capital
★ State capital

0   250   500 mi.
0   250   500 km

MEXICO

120°W 110°W

CANADA

ND
★ Bismarck

MN
St. Paul ★

WI
Madison ★

MI
Lansing

ME

Montpelier ★
VT   NH
Concord ★
Albany ★   MA
NY   ★ Boston
Hartford ★   ★ Providence
CT   RI

Pierre ★
SD

IA
Des
Moines ★

PA
Harrisburg ★
Trenton
NJ
★ Dover
MD   DE
★ Annapolis
Washington, D.C.

NE
Lincoln ★

IL
Springfield ★

IN
Indianapolis ★

OH
Columbus ★

WV
Charleston ★

Richmond ★
VA

KS
Topeka ★

MO
Jefferson
City ★

Frankfort ★
KY

NC
Raleigh ★

OK
Oklahoma
City ★

AR
Little
Rock ★

Nashville ★
TN

Columbia ★
SC

ATLANTIC
OCEAN

AL
Montgomery ★

Atlanta ★
GA

N
W   E
S

TX
Austin ★

MS
Jackson ★

LA
Baton
Rouge ★

Tallahassee ★
FL

Gulf of Mexico

Tropic of Cancer

40°N

30°N

20°N

100°W   90°W   80°W   70°W

90°W   100°W

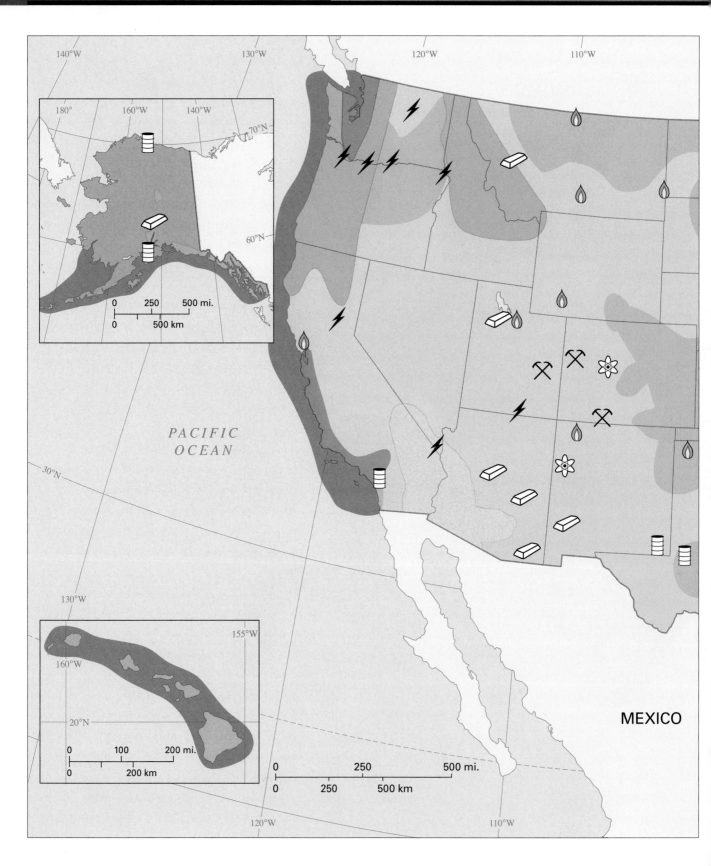

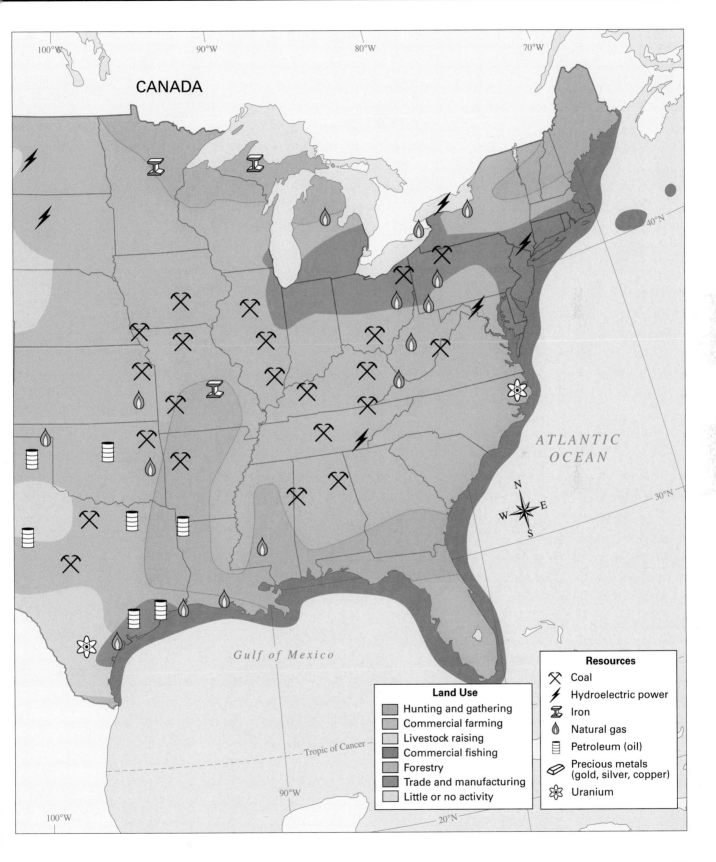

CANADA

ATLANTIC
OCEAN

Gulf of Mexico

Tropic of Cancer

Land Use
- Hunting and gathering
- Commercial farming
- Livestock raising
- Commercial fishing
- Forestry
- Trade and manufacturing
- Little or no activity

Resources
- ⚒ Coal
- ⚡ Hydroelectric power
- ⚙ Iron
- 🜕 Natural gas
- ▯ Petroleum (oil)
- ◊ Precious metals (gold, silver, copper)
- ⚛ Uranium

100°W · 90°W · 80°W · 70°W

40°N

30°N

20°N

90°W

100°W

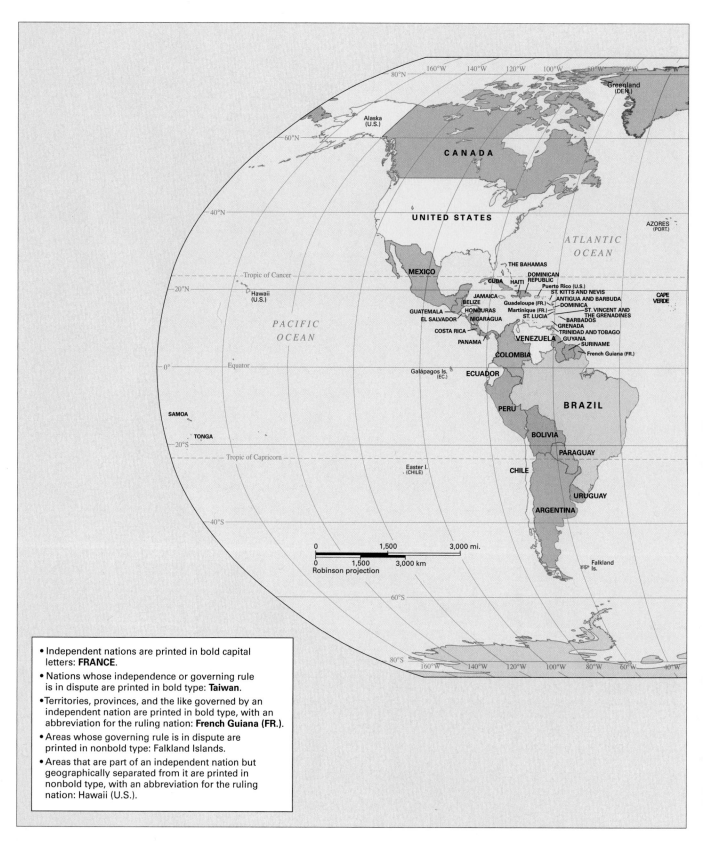

80°N
160°W 140°W 120°W 100°W 80°W 60°W 40°W

Greenland (DEN.)

Alaska (U.S.)

60°N

CANADA

40°N

UNITED STATES

ATLANTIC OCEAN

AZORES (PORT.)

Tropic of Cancer

MEXICO

THE BAHAMAS

DOMINICAN REPUBLIC

20°N

Hawaii (U.S.)

CUBA HAITI

Puerto Rico (U.S.)
ST. KITTS AND NEVIS
ANTIGUA AND BARBUDA
DOMINICA
ST. VINCENT AND
THE GRENADINES
BARBADOS

CAPE VERDE

JAMAICA

GUATEMALA
BELIZE
HONDURAS
EL SALVADOR NICARAGUA
COSTA RICA

Guadeloupe (FR.)
Martinique (FR.)
ST. LUCIA

GRENADA
TRINIDAD AND TOBAGO
GUYANA
SURINAME

PACIFIC OCEAN

PANAMA

VENEZUELA

French Guiana (FR.)

COLOMBIA

0°
Equator

Galápagos Is. (EC.)

ECUADOR

PERU

BRAZIL

SAMOA

BOLIVIA

TONGA

20°S

PARAGUAY

Tropic of Capricorn

Easter I. (CHILE)

CHILE

URUGUAY

ARGENTINA

0   1,500   3,000 mi.

0   1,500   3,000 km
Robinson projection

40°S

Falkland Is.

60°S

80°S
160°W 140°W 120°W 100°W 80°W 60°W 40°W

- Independent nations are printed in bold capital letters: **FRANCE**.
- Nations whose independence or governing rule is in dispute are printed in bold type: **Taiwan**.
- Territories, provinces, and the like governed by an independent nation are printed in bold type, with an abbreviation for the ruling nation: **French Guiana (FR.)**.
- Areas whose governing rule is in dispute are printed in nonbold type: Falkland Islands.
- Areas that are part of an independent nation but geographically separated from it are printed in nonbold type, with an abbreviation for the ruling nation: Hawaii (U.S.).

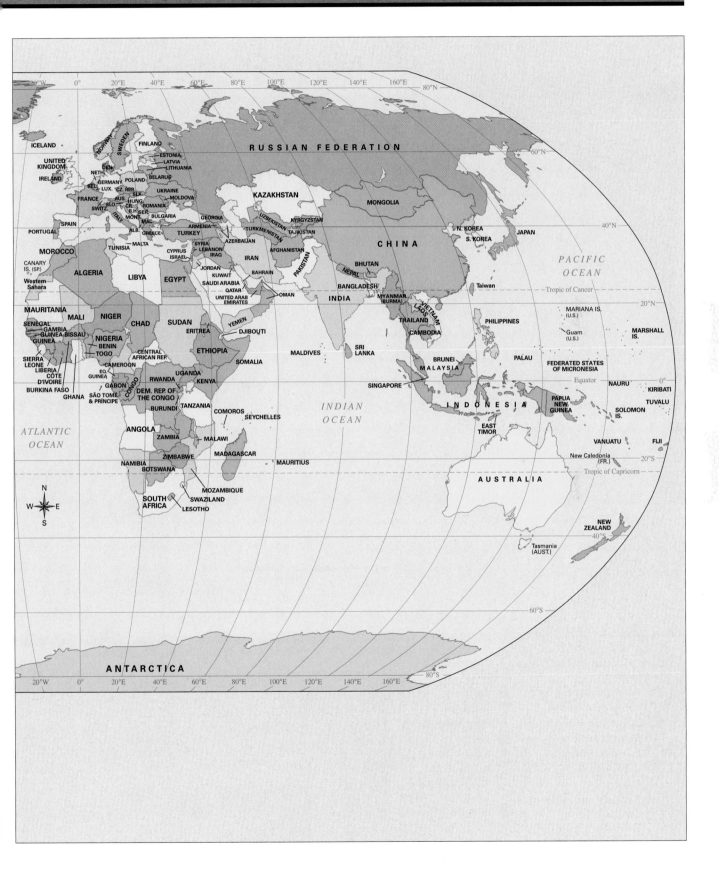

ICELAND

UNITED
KINGDOM

IRELAND

NORWAY

SWEDEN

FINLAND

RUSSIAN FEDERATION

ESTONIA
LATVIA
LITHUANIA

DEN.
NETH.
BEL. GERMANY POLAND BELARUS
LUX. CZ. REP.
SLK. UKRAINE
FRANCE AUS. HUNG. MOLDOVA
SWITZ. SLO. CR. ROMANIA
ITALY B.H. SER.
MONT. BULGARIA
MAC.
ALB. GREECE

KAZAKHSTAN

MONGOLIA

PORTUGAL SPAIN

GEORGIA

ARMENIA
AZERBAIJAN

TURKEY

UZBEKISTAN KYRGYZSTAN

TURKMENISTAN TAJIKISTAN

N. KOREA
S. KOREA

JAPAN

40°N

MOROCCO

TUNISIA

MALTA

CYPRUS
ISRAEL

SYRIA
LEBANON
IRAQ

AFGHANISTAN

CHINA

PACIFIC
OCEAN

CANARY
IS. (SP.)

ALGERIA LIBYA EGYPT

IRAN

BHUTAN

Western
Sahara

JORDAN
KUWAIT
SAUDI ARABIA
QATAR
UNITED ARAB
EMIRATES

BAHRAIN

PAKISTAN

NEPAL

BANGLADESH

Taiwan

Tropic of Cancer

MAURITANIA

MALI NIGER

CHAD SUDAN

OMAN

INDIA

MYANMAR
(BURMA)

VIETNAM
LAOS

MARIANA IS.
(U.S.)

20°N

SENEGAL
GAMBIA
GUINEA-BISSAU
GUINEA

NIGERIA
BENIN
TOGO

ERITREA

YEMEN

DJIBOUTI

THAILAND

CAMBODIA

PHILIPPINES

Guam
(U.S.)

MARSHALL
IS.

SIERRA
LEONE
LIBERIA
CÔTE
D'IVOIRE
BURKINA FASO
GHANA

CENTRAL
AFRICAN REP.

CAMEROON

EQ.
GUINEA

GABON

SÃO TOMÉ
& PRÍNCIPE

ETHIOPIA

SOMALIA

UGANDA

RWANDA

DEM. REP. OF
THE CONGO

CONGO

KENYA

MALDIVES

SRI
LANKA

SINGAPORE

BRUNEI

MALAYSIA

PALAU

FEDERATED STATES
OF MICRONESIA

Equator

NAURU

KIRIBATI

0°

BURUNDI

TANZANIA

COMOROS

SEYCHELLES

INDIAN
OCEAN

INDONESIA

PAPUA
NEW
GUINEA

TUVALU

SOLOMON
IS.

ATLANTIC
OCEAN

ANGOLA

ZAMBIA

MALAWI

MADAGASCAR

EAST
TIMOR

VANUATU

FIJI

ZIMBABWE

New Caledonia
(FR.)

20°S

NAMIBIA

BOTSWANA

MAURITIUS

Tropic of Capricorn

AUSTRALIA

N
W E
S

MOZAMBIQUE

SOUTH
AFRICA

SWAZILAND

LESOTHO

NEW
ZEALAND

40°S

Tasmania
(AUST.)

60°S

ANTARCTICA

80°S

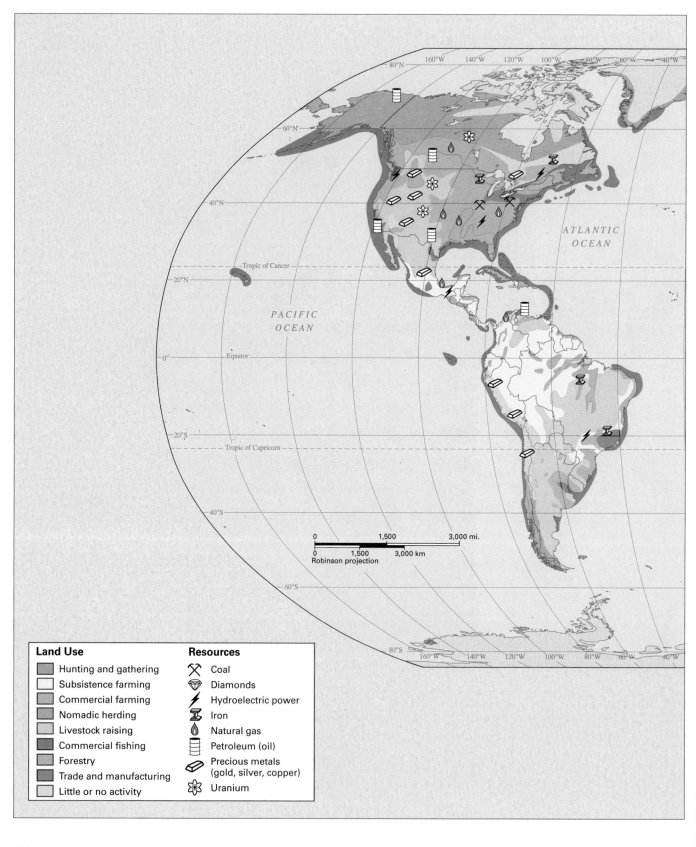

160°W 140°W 120°W 100°W 80°W 60°W 40°W

80°N

60°N

PACIFIC
OCEAN

40°N

Tropic of Cancer

20°N

ATLANTIC
OCEAN

PACIFIC
OCEAN

0° Equator

20°S

Tropic of Capricorn

40°S

| 0 | 1,500 | 3,000 mi. |
| 0 | 1,500 | 3,000 km |

Robinson projection

60°S

80°S

160°W 140°W 120°W 100°W 80°W 60°W 40°W

Land Use

- ▨ Hunting and gathering
- ☐ Subsistence farming
- ▨ Commercial farming
- ▨ Nomadic herding
- ☐ Livestock raising
- ▨ Commercial fishing
- ▨ Forestry
- ▨ Trade and manufacturing
- ☐ Little or no activity

Resources

- ⚒ Coal
- ♦ Diamonds
- ⚡ Hydroelectric power
- ⚖ Iron
- ◊ Natural gas
- ▤ Petroleum (oil)
- ▭ Precious metals (gold, silver, copper)
- ✳ Uranium

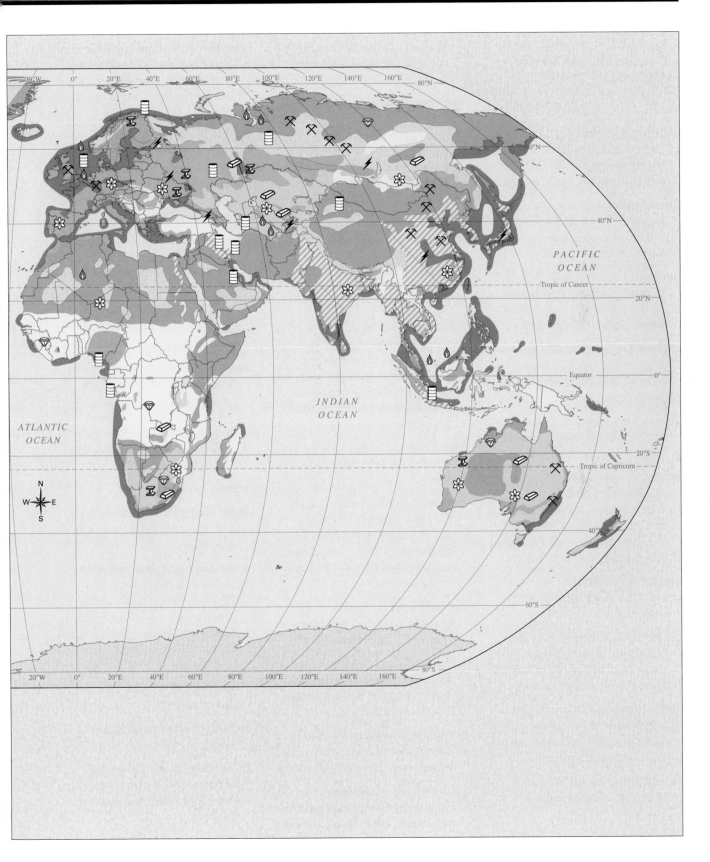

Glossary

*Speaking of Economics terms appear in **blue** type. Other key terms are in **black** type.*

A

ability-to-pay principle the idea that citizens should be taxed according to their income or wealth; one of two basic approaches to tax equity

absolute advantage the condition that exists when someone can produce a good or service using fewer resources than someone else

affirmative action policies designed to promote the hiring of individuals from groups that have historically faced job discrimination

antitrust law legislation designed to limit the formation of monopolies or combinations of firms that act to restrict competition

appreciation a rise in the value of one currency relative to another, based on supply and demand

articles of incorporation a legal document required for the establishment of a corporation that details the firm's objectives, structure, and planned operations; also called a corporate charter

articles of partnership a legal agreement that states the terms of a partnership

assessed value the value of a piece of property for tax purposes, as determined by a public official known as an assessor

asset allocation a method of dividing investment assets among different types of investments, such as stocks, bonds, and cash

asset anything owned to which a market value can be assigned

audit an official review of an income tax return to assess the return's accuracy

automatic stabilizer a fiscal tool that helps counter swings in the business cycle without direct action by the government; examples include transfer payments and taxes, which help stimulate or limit overall demand and stabilize the economy

axis one of two perpendicular lines in a coordinate system, used to locate a point in space

B

balance of trade the difference between the value of a country's exports and the value of its imports; this figure can represent a surplus (more exports than imports) or a deficit (more imports than exports)

bank a business whose main purpose is to receive deposits and make loans

banknotes an early form of paper currency, issued by banks to clients who made deposits of gold or silver; these notes could be exchanged for gold or silver "upon demand"

barrier to entry an obstacle that can restrict a producer's access to a market and limit competition

barter the direct exchange of goods or services without the use of money; a typical feature of traditional economies

bear market a prolonged period of falling stock prices, accompanied by widespread investor pessimism

benefit what is gained from something in terms of money, time, experience, or other improvements

benefits-received principle the idea that citizens who benefit from a particular government program should pay for it; one of two basic approaches to tax equity

bid rigging an illegal, anticompetitive practice in which two or more firms agree in advance which one will submit the lowest bid for a contract offered through a competitive bidding process

black market an illegal market in which goods are traded at prices or in quantities higher than those allowed by law

board of directors a governing body of a corporation elected by the shareholders

bond an investment that represents a loan to a government or corporation and guarantees the lender a fixed rate of interest over the term of the loan, with repayment of the principal at the end of the term

brand a trade name

brand loyalty the tendency to favor one company over all others in a market

bread-and-butter unionism efforts by labor unions to improve the basic economic conditions that affect workers' daily lives; wages and health care benefits are typical bread-and-butter issues

brokerage a company that buys and sells stocks and bonds for investors

budget a plan for spending and saving

bull market a prolonged period of rising stock prices, accompanied by widespread investor confidence

business association an organization that represents the interests of businesspeople in a geographical area

business cycle a recurring pattern of growth and decline in economic activity over time

business ethics principles of right and wrong that guide the actions of a company and its employees

business franchise an arrangement in which a parent company, or franchiser, distributes its products or services through independently owned outlets

business license a legal document that allows a business to operate in a state, city, or town; also called a business permit

business name the legal name under which a business operates

business permit a legal document that allows a business to operate in a state, city, or town; also called a business license

C

cap and trade a policy that limits the amount of pollution a firm may legally emit each year but allows firms to trade with each other to obtain additional pollution permits

capital the tools, machines, and buildings used to produce goods and services; one of the factors of production

capital flow the movement of money into and out of a country through foreign investment and other financial activities

capital goods the manmade objects —tools, machinery, buildings, or other fabricated goods—used in production; also called physical capital

capitalism the free market economic system

capitalist an individual investor who accumulates capital, such as machinery, factories, and railroads

cartel an organization of producers established to set production levels and prices for a product; cartels are illegal in the United States but do operate in global markets

cash transfer a direct payment of cash by the government to an individual

certification official recognition that a person is qualified in his or her field

ceteris paribus the assumption, used in economic models, that all factors other than those being considered remain the same; from a Latin expression meaning "other things being equal"

change in demand an increase or decrease in demand (the quantity of a good or service that consumers are willing and able to buy) as a result of a change in factors other than price; a shift of the demand curve to the left or right

change in quantity demanded an increase or decrease in quantity demanded (the amount of a good or service that consumers are willing and able to buy at a specific price) as a result of a change in price

change in quantity supplied an increase or decrease in quantity supplied (the amount of a good or service that producers are willing and able to offer for sale at a specific price) as a result of a change in price

change in supply an increase or decrease in supply (the quantity of a good or service that producers are willing and able to offer for sale) as a result of a change in factors other than price; a shift of the supply curve to the left or right

check a signed form instructing a bank to pay a specified amount to the person or business named on it

checkable deposits money in bank checking accounts

check clearing the transfer of funds from one bank or account to another as a result of cashing a check

chief executive officer the highest-ranking person in charge of managing a corporation

circular flow model a diagram that shows the circular movement of money, resources, and goods and services among households and producers in an economy

classical economics an economic philosophy, originating with Adam Smith, that focused on how free markets and market economies work; this philosophy, which dominated economic thinking until the Great Depression of the 1930s, held that capitalism was self-regulating and required few government controls

closed shop a business that only hires workers who are union members

closely held corporation a corporation owned by an individual or a small group of individuals that allows only a select group of people to buy stock; also known as a privately held corporation

coincidence of wants a situation in which each of two individuals has something the other wants; the basis for barter

collective bargaining negotiations between an employer and a group of employees, usually represented by a labor union, to determine the conditions of employment

collusion an arrangement in which producers cooperate on production levels and pricing; collusion is illegal in the United States

command and control policy a policy approach—often applied to environmental policy—that relies on rules and enforcement, rather than market incentives, to influence behavior

command economy an economic system in which decisions about production and consumption are made by a powerful ruler or government

Commerce Clause Article I, Section 8 of the U.S. Constitution, which gives Congress the power to regulate interstate trade

commercial loan money borrowed by a business to pay expenses

commodity a product that is exactly the same no matter who produces it

commodity-backed money currency that can be exchanged for a specific commodity, such as gold or silver; bank notes are an example

commodity money any good used as a medium of exchange; examples include gold, silver, and salt

common resource a resource that everyone has access to and that can be easily overused or destroyed; examples include the atmosphere and the oceans

communism a political and economic system in which all property and wealth is collectively owned by all members of society; the final stage of socialism in Marxist theory

comparative advantage the condition that exists when someone can produce a good or service at a lower opportunity cost than someone else

complementary good a product that is used or consumed jointly with another product; tennis rackets and tennis balls are one example

compounding the ability of an investment to generate earnings that can be reinvested to produce still more earnings

compound interest interest paid not only on the original amount deposited in an account but also on all interest earned by those savings

concentration ratio the proportion of a market controlled by a fixed number of companies; for example, a four-firm concentration ratio shows how much of a market is controlled by the four largest firms in that market

constant dollars the value of the dollar fixed at a specified base year; a measure of the dollar's value adjusted for inflation to reflect purchasing power over time

consumer loan money borrowed by an individual to make major purchases

consumer price index (CPI) a measure of price changes in consumer goods and services over time; the CPI shows changes in the cost of living from year to year

contract an agreement between a buyer and a seller

contraction a period of general economic decline marked by falling GDP and rising unemployment

contractionary fiscal policy a policy designed to lower inflation and cool an overheated economy by cutting government spending, increasing taxes, or both

cooperative a business organization that is jointly owned and operated by a group of individuals for their mutual benefit

copyright a legal protection that gives creators and publishers of books, music, software, and artistic works the sole right to distribute, perform, or display that work

corporate bond a bond issued by a corporation to raise money for its operations

corporate bylaws rules that govern the management of a corporation

corporate charter a legal document required for the establishment of a corporation that details the firm's objectives, structure, and planned operations; also called articles of incorporation

corporate income tax a tax applied to the profits of a corporation

corporate officer a senior executive who oversees specific areas of a corporation's business

corporate responsibility the idea that businesses should take responsibility for the impact of their actions on society

corporation a business owned by shareholders who have limited liability for the firm's debts

corrective tax a tax on producers that is designed to reduce negative externalities, such as pollution

correlation a relationship between two factors, pieces of data, or other variables

cost what is spent in money, effort, or other sacrifices to get something

cost-benefit analysis a way to compare the costs of an action with the benefits of that action; if the benefits exceed the costs, the action is worth taking

cost-of-living index a measure of change in the overall cost of goods and services; another term for the consumer price index

cost-push inflation a rise in the price of goods and services caused by increases in the cost of the factors of production

costs-versus-benefits principle the idea that people choose something when the benefits of doing so outweigh the costs

credit an arrangement that allows a person to buy something with borrowed money and pay for it later or over time

credit card a card authorizing the user to buy goods and services with funds borrowed from the bank, store, or other business that issued the card

credit history the record of a person's borrowing and repayment of loans

creeping inflation a gradual, steady rise in the price of goods and services over time

crowding-out effect the possible effect of increased government borrowing on businesses and consumers; by driving interest rates up, high levels of government borrowing may crowd private borrowers out of the lending market

cultural diffusion the process of sharing ideas and knowledge across cultures

cultural imperialism a process by which one country imposes its culture or language on another country, often through the influence of economic forces

currency bills and coins circulating in the economy

current dollars the value of a dollar in the year it is spent; a measure of the dollar's value that reflects current purchasing power, without taking inflation into account

curve a line representing data points on a graph

customs the government agency that examines goods entering a country and enforces trade restrictions

cyclical unemployment a type of unemployment that results from a period of decline in the business cycle; unemployment caused by a contraction

D

data factual information, often in numerical form

deadweight loss a loss of productivity or economic well-being for which there is no corresponding gain

debit card a card authorizing the user to access his or her own funds on deposit in a bank account; a debit card can be used to buy goods or services or to withdraw money directly from an account

debt forgiveness the cancellation of all or part of a debt

debt service the series of payments of interest and principal a borrower agrees to pay a lender over the life of a loan

deficit spending government spending in excess of what is collected in revenues

deflation a fall in the price of goods and services; the opposite of inflation

deflationary spiral a downward trend in prices, wages, and business activity; a deflationary pattern in which falling prices cause a business slowdown, which in turn leads to lower wages, a further fall in prices, and even less business activity

demand the quantity of a good or service that consumers are willing and able to buy at various prices

demand curve a graph of the relationship between the price of a good or service and the quantity buyers are willing and able to buy

demand schedule a list of the quantities of a good that one person will buy at various prices

demand-pull inflation a rise in the price of goods and services caused by an increase in overall demand

demand shifter a factor other than price that can cause a change in demand for a good or service; examples include changes in consumer incomes or tastes

demand-side economics the theory that the best way to ensure economic growth is to stimulate demand by putting more money in the hands of consumers, either by increasing government spending or cutting taxes on lower-income earners, or both; this theory, which is associated with Keynesian economics, assumes that consumers will spend this additional money on goods and services, thus stimulating the economy

depreciation a fall in the value of one currency relative to another, based on supply and demand

depression a prolonged economic downturn characterized by plunging real GDP and extremely high unemployment

deregulation the process of removing government restrictions on firms in order to promote competition or encourage economic activity

devaluation a lowering of a currency's exchange rate in a fixed-rate system; this reduces the currency's value relative to other currencies

developed country a wealthy, industrialized country in which the majority of people have more than enough income to meet their basic needs and maintain a high standard of living

developing country a low- to medium-income country in which most people have less access to goods and services than the average person in a developed country

differentiated products goods that are essentially the same, but are distinguished from each other by variations in style, materials, or other characteristics

discount rate the interest rate the Federal Reserve charges on loans to private banks

discouraged workers unemployed workers who have ceased to look for work; discouraged workers are not considered part of the labor force and are not factored into the unemployment rate

discretionary spending expenditures that can be raised or lowered as a legislature sees fit; spending that is not mandatory

disequilibrium a situation that exists when the quantity of a product demanded by consumers does not equal the quantity supplied, resulting in a shortage or a surplus

diversification a method of lowering risk by investing in a wide variety of financial assets

dividend a portion of a firm's profits paid to owners of the firm's stock

division of labor the allocation of separate tasks to different people, based on the principle of specialization

double taxation taxation of a corporation at both the corporate level and the shareholder level

E

Earned Income Tax Credit a tax reduction given to low-wage workers when they file their federal income tax forms; its goal is to raise the incomes of poor people without discouraging them from working

easy-money policy a monetary policy designed to accelerate the rate of growth of the money supply to stimulate economic growth

economic development the process by which a country makes economic progress and raises its standard of living; development includes improvements in agriculture and industry, the building of roads and other economic infrastructure, and investments in human capital

economic efficiency the result of using resources in a way that produces the maximum amount of goods and services

economic enigma a puzzle or riddle that may be explained through economic analysis

economic equity the fairness with which an economy distributes its resources and wealth

economic freedom the ability of people to make their own economic decisions without interference from the government

economic growth a condition in which an economy is expanding and producing more and better goods and services

economic indicators statistics that help economists judge the health of an economy

economic interdependence the characteristic of a society in which people rely on others for most of the goods and services they want

economic mobility the ability of people to raise their standard of living and improve their economic status

economic model a simplified representation of reality that allows economists to focus on the effects of one change at a time

economic planning the process by which economic decisions are made or influenced by central governments rather than by private individuals

economic security the idea that the less fortunate members of society should get the economic support they need to live a decent life

economic stability a condition in which the goods and services people count on are available when they want them

economic stimulus a policy or action designed to promote business activity and stimulate economic growth

economic system a society's way of coordinating the production and consumption of goods and services

economics the study of how people choose to use their limited resources to satisfy their unlimited wants

economies of scale the greater efficiency and cost savings that result from large-scale or mass production

economy a system used to manage limited resources for the production, distribution, and consumption of goods and services

elastic responsive to a change in price, applied to either supply or demand; the supply or demand of a good or service is said to be elastic when the quantity supplied or demanded changes significantly with a change in price

elasticity a measure of the degree to which the quantity demanded or supplied of a good or service changes in response to a change in price

elasticity of demand a measure of the sensitivity of consumers to a change in price

elasticity of supply a measure of the sensitivity of producers to a change in price

eminent domain the power of a government to take an individual's property for public use if the owner is fairly compensated

enrollment ratio the percentage of school-age children attending school

entitlement a government program that provides benefits to individuals based on their age, income, or some other criteria

entrepreneur a person who assembles and organizes the resources necessary to produce goods and services

entrepreneurship the willingness and ability to take the risks involved in starting and managing a business

environmental Kuznets curve a graph showing a theoretical correlation between higher per capita income and reduced environmental pollution; according to the theory, pollution first increases with a rise in income but then declines as living standards continue to improve

equilibrium price the price at which the quantity of a product demanded by consumers in a market equals the quantity supplied by producers

equilibrium quantity the quantity of a good or service demanded by consumers and supplied by producers when the market is in equilibrium

equilibrium wage the rate of pay that results in neither a surplus nor a shortage of labor; a wage rate that is too high will attract too many workers, whereas a rate that is too low will attract too few

estate tax a federal tax on the assets left to heirs by someone who dies

excess demand a situation that exists when the quantity demanded of a product exceeds the quantity supplied, thus producing a shortage

excess supply a situation that exists when the quantity supplied of a product exceeds the quantity demanded, thus producing a surplus

exchange rate the value of one currency in terms of another

excise tax a tax on the consumption of certain goods and services; sometimes used to discourage consumption, as on cigarettes

excise tax a tax on the manufacture or sale of a good

excludable a characteristic of a good or service whose use can be denied to those who do not pay for it; a feature of private goods

expansion a period of economic growth

expansionary fiscal policy a policy designed to promote economic activity by increasing government spending, cutting taxes, or both

export-led development an economic model that emphasizes the production of goods for export as a means of economic growth

exports goods and services produced domestically and sold in other countries

externality a cost or benefit arising from the production or consumption of a good or service that falls on someone other than the producer or consumer; a spillover or side effect of production or consumption

extreme poverty a condition in which people are too poor to meet their basic survival needs, including food, shelter, and clothing

F

factor market a market in which households sell land, labor, and capital to firms

factor payment income earned when an individual sells or rents a factor of production that he or she owns; for example, wages are a factor payment made to workers in exchange for their labor

factors of production the resources used to produce goods and services; defined as land, labor, and capital

federal deficit a shortfall between government revenues and expenditures in any given year

federal funds rate the interest rate banks charge each other for loans from their excess reserves; the Federal Reserve helps determine this rate—also known as the overnight rate—by regulating the money supply through open market operations

fiat money currency not backed by gold or silver; all paper money today is fiat money

final good any new good that is ready for consumer use; final goods are included in the calculation of GDP

financial capital money used for investment or production

financial institution a firm that deals mainly with money, as opposed to goods and services; examples include banks and stock brokerages

financial intermediary a business, such as a bank, that brings together savers (sellers) and borrowers (buyers) in financial markets

firm an organization that uses resources to produce and sell goods or services; a business

fiscal policy government policy regarding taxing and spending

fiscal year a 12-month accounting period

fixed exchange rate an exchange rate set by a government at a fixed value relative to another currency

flat tax a proportional income tax that applies the same tax rate to all taxpayers, regardless of income

floating exchange rate an exchange rate that fluctuates based on supply and demand

foreign debt the part of a country's total debt that is owed to foreign creditors

foreign direct investment (FDI) capital invested by foreign interests in a business enterprise in another country; FDI may be used to buy an existing company or to set up a new operation

foreign exchange the trading of one national currency for another

foreign exchange market the market for buying and selling currencies around the world, carried out through banks and other financial institutions

foundation an organization created and supported by donated funds or property

fractional reserve banking a system in which banks keep a portion of deposits in reserve and make loans with the rest

franchisee a business owner who buys the license and distributes the products of a franchiser

franchiser the parent company in a business franchise

free enterprise system an economic system in which the means of production are mostly privately owned and operated for a profit

free market economy an economic system in which the workings of the market are not planned or directed

free trade the policy of eliminating barriers to international trade; free trade allows goods and services to move more freely across borders

free-rider problem a free rider is someone who enjoys the benefit of a good or service, such as roads or public schools, without paying for it; free riding becomes a problem when it leads to underproduction of that good or service

frictional unemployment a type of unemployment that results when workers are seeking their first job or have left one job and are seeking another

fringe benefits nonwage compensation offered to workers in addition to pay; examples include health care and vacation benefits

full employment a condition in which everyone who wants to work can find a job

future-consequences-count principle the idea that decisions made today have effects in the future

G

general partner an owner in a general partnership

general partnership a form of business in which all co-owners have unlimited liability, or full responsibility, for any business debts

global economy the system of economic interaction among the world's countries, including international trade and transfers of money, resources, and technology

globalization the process by which people and economies around the world are becoming increasingly interconnected; the term is often used to refer to economic globalization, the integration of national economies into the global economy

good a physical article that has been produced for sale or use

government failure an inefficient allocation of resources caused by government intervention in the economy

graph a visual representation of the relationship between two sets of data

gross domestic product (GDP) the market value of all final goods and services produced within a country during a given period of time

H

household a person or a group of people living together

human capital the knowledge and skills people gain from education, on-the-job training, and other experiences

hyperinflation an extreme and rapid rise in the price of goods and services

I

imperfect competition any market structure in which producers have some control over the price of their products; in such a market, prices are no longer set by supply and demand

import quota a limit on the quantity of a good that can be imported during a specified period of time; a type of trade barrier

imports goods and services produced in other countries and sold domestically

incentive something that motivates a person to take a particular course of action

incentives-matter principle the idea that people respond to incentives in generally predictable ways

income redistribution a policy designed to reduce income inequality by taking money from the rich and distributing it to the poor

Industrial Revolution a period of rapid industrial growth and development during the 1700s and 1800s

inelastic not responsive, or only slightly responsive, to a change in price, applied to either supply or demand; the supply or demand of a good or service is said to be inelastic when the quantity supplied or demanded does not change significantly with a change in price

infant mortality the rate at which babies die during their first year of life; a key indicator of a nation's health and well-being

inflation an increase in the overall price level of goods and services produced in an economy

inflation rate the percentage increase in the average price level of goods and services from one month or year to the next

informal economy a sector of the economy that operates without government regulation or monitoring and is not officially recorded or taxed; the informal economy is not included in the calculation of GDP

infrastructure the basic public facilities and installations that help an economy function, including roads, bridges, airports, power and water systems, and other utilities

inheritance tax a state tax on the assets left to heirs by someone who dies; similar to the federal estate tax

initial public offering (IPO) the first sale of a new corporation's stock

in-kind transfer a government benefit in the form of goods or vouchers, such as food stamps and public housing

input a resource used in the production process; also known as a factor of production

inshoring the process of bringing work and jobs into a country; the opposite of offshoring

inside director a member of a firm's board of directors who comes from within the firm

installment loan borrowed money that is typically paid back in equal monthly payments

intellectual property creations of the mind that have commercial value, such as inventions and works of art

interest a periodic payment for the use of borrowed funds; interest is paid on a loan

intermediate good a good used in the production of a final good; intermediate goods are not included in the calculation of GDP

inventory merchandise that companies or stores have on hand

investing using money with the intention of making a financial gain

invisible hand Adam Smith's metaphor to explain how an individual's pursuit of economic self-interest can promote the well-being of society as a whole

involuntary part-time workers people who settle for part-time employment because they are unable to find full-time work

J

junk bond a low-quality corporate bond that earns a relatively high rate of interest based on its higher risk

K

Keynesian economics a school of thought, pioneered by John Maynard Keynes, holding that government intervention in the economy is necessary to ensure economic stability; Keynesians support demand-side policies to revive economic growth

knowledge worker a person who works with information or who develops or applies information in the workplace

L

labor the time and effort people devote to producing goods and services in exchange for wages; one of the factors of production

labor force the portion of the population that has paid work or is seeking work; the labor force does not include active members of the military

labor union an organization of workers in a specific industry that seeks to improve working conditions, wages, and benefits for its members

Laffer curve a U-shaped graph associated with supply-side economics that shows a theoretical correlation between tax rates and tax revenues; according to the graph, raising marginal tax rates beyond a certain point reduces tax revenues

lagging economic indicators measures that consistently rise or fall several months after an expansion or contraction begins

laissez-faire the principle that government should not interfere with the workings of the economy; a French term meaning "let them do"

land all the natural resources, including energy, that are used to produce goods and services; one of the factors of production

law of demand an economic law stating that as the price of a good or service increases, the quantity demanded decreases, and vice versa

law of diminishing marginal utility the general observation that as the quantity of a good or service consumed increases, the benefits for the consumer of each additional unit decrease

law of supply an economic law stating that as the price of a good or service increases, the quantity supplied increases, and vice versa

law of unintended consequences the general observation that the actions of people and governments always have effects that are not expected or intended

leading economic indicators measures that consistently rise or fall several months before an expansion or a contraction begins

least developed country a country that suffers from severe poverty and low standards of living

legal tender currency that must be accepted as money for purchases and as payment for debts

liability the legal responsibility to repay debts and to pay for damages resulting from a lawsuit

license a legal permit to operate a business or enter a market

life expectancy the number of years, on average, that a person is expected to live; a key indicator of a nation's health and well-being

limited liability less than full responsibility for repaying business debts; liability in this case does not extend to the owner's personal property

limited liability company a business in which the proprietor's liability extends only to whatever he or she has invested in the business

limited liability partnership a partner-ship that allows co-owners to operate like general partners while enjoying the protection of limited liability

limited partner a partner in a business who contributes financial capital but plays no role in day-to-day operations; also known as a silent partner

limited partnership a form of business consisting of at least one general partner and one or more limited partners

liquid assets items of value that can be used as cash or easily converted into cash; examples include traveler's checks and money deposited in bank checking accounts

liquidity the ease with which assets can be converted into cash

literacy rate the percentage of people in a country who can read and write

loan a transaction in which a lender gives money to a borrower, who agrees to repay the money at some point in the future

logrolling a practice in which lawmakers agree to vote for each other's legislation

lottery a large-scale gambling game organized to raise money for a public cause

luxury tax a tax levied on the sale of high-priced luxury goods, such as diamond jewelry and private jets

M

M1 money circulating in the economy that includes cash and assets that can be easily converted into cash

M2 money circulating in the economy that includes M1 plus less liquid deposits in various kinds of accounts or funds

macroeconomics the study of the workings of the economy as a whole

mandatory spending government expenditures that are fixed by law and can only be changed by new legislation; spending that is not discretionary

margin the border or outer edge of something

marginal benefit what is gained by adding one more unit to an activity

marginal cost what is given up by adding one more unit to an activity

marginal tax rate the rate at which the last dollar a person earns in a given year is taxed

marginal utility the extra satisfaction or pleasure achieved from an increase of one additional unit of a good or service

market an arrangement that brings buyers and sellers together to do business with each other

market-based policy a policy approach—often applied to environmental policy—that relies on market incentives, rather than regulation, to influence behavior

market-clearing price the price at which the quantity demanded of a product equals the quantity supplied; another term for equilibrium price

market demand the sum of all the individual quantities demanded in a market

market division an illegal, anticompetitive practice in which two or more firms agree to divide a market among themselves, selling only to certain customers or in certain geographic areas

market economy an economic system in which economic decisions are left up to individual producers and consumers

market equilibrium the point at which the quantity of a product demanded by consumers in a market equals the quantity supplied by producers

market failure a situation in which the market fails to allocate resources efficiently

market index a way of measuring changes in the value of a group of stocks, bonds, or other investments

market power the ability of producers to influence prices

market price the price a willing consumer pays to a willing producer for a good or service

market share a firm's proportion of total sales in a market

market structure the organization of a market, based mainly on the degree of competition; there are four basic market structures: perfect competition, monopolistic competition, oligopoly, and monopoly

market supply the sum of all the individual quantities supplied in a market

market value the price buyers are willing to pay for a good or service in a competitive market

markets-coordinate-trade principle the idea that markets are usually the best way to coordinate exchanges between buyers and sellers

mass production large-scale manufacturing

means-tested program a government benefit that is tied to family income so that benefits are reduced as income rises; examples include food stamps and welfare payments

Medicare tax a federal payroll tax designed to fund Medicare, the national health insurance program for the elderly and disabled

merger the combining of two or more separately owned firms into a single firm

microeconomics the study of the economy at the level of individuals, households, and businesses

middle management a group of mid-level corporate managers who report to the senior officers and supervise the firm's workers

minimum wage the lowest hourly rate, or wage, that employers can legally pay their employees; a price floor on wages

misery index the sum of the inflation rate and the unemployment rate

mixed economy an economic system in which both the government and individuals play important roles in production and consumption; most modern economies are mixed economies

monetarism a school of thought, based on the ideas of Milton Friedman, holding that changes in the money supply are the main cause of inflation and of economic expansions or contractions

monetary policy central bank policy aimed at regulating the amount of money in circulation

money a generally accepted medium of exchange that can be traded for goods and services or used to pay debts

money supply the total amount of money in the economy

monopolistic competition a market structure in which many producers supply similar but varied products

monopoly a market structure in which a single producer supplies a unique product that has no close substitutes

mortgage money borrowed to buy a house, an office building, land, or other real estate

multinational corporation a corporation that does business in more than one country

multiplier effect a ripple effect in which a change in spending by one person or business leads to additional changes in spending by another person or business

municipal bond a bond issued by a state or local government to raise funds for public projects

mutual fund a collection of securities chosen and managed by a group of professional fund managers

N

national debt the total amount owed by a nation's government as a result of borrowing

nation-state an independent political body with full authority over its territory and inhabitants

natural monopoly a market controlled by a single firm for reasons of efficiency; in a natural monopoly, one firm can provide a good or service at a lower cost than two or more competing firms

natural rate of unemployment the percentage of the labor force without work when the economy is at full employment; a condition in which the economy is strong and there is no cyclical unemployment

near-money an asset similar to money, such as a savings account, that serves as a store of value but cannot be used to buy things directly

negative externality a cost of production or consumption that falls on someone other than the producer or consumer; a negative side effect

negative utility a lack of pleasure or satisfaction from consuming a product or service or taking an action; the opposite of utility

net exports the value of all exports minus all imports

newly industrialized country a developing country that is making a rapid transition from an agricultural to an industrial economy

no-free-lunch principle the idea that every choice involves tradeoffs; a restatement of the scarcity-forces-tradeoffs principle

nominal cost of living the cost in current dollars of all the basic goods and services needed by the average consumer

nominal GDP a measure of a country's economic output (GDP) valued in current dollars; nominal GDP does not reflect the effects of inflation

nominal wages wage levels based on current dollars

nonexcludable a characteristic of a good or service whose use cannot be denied to anyone; a feature of public goods

nongovernmental organization (NGO) nonprofit organizations that operate outside of governments, often with a focus on humanitarian or environmental concerns

nonprice competition the use of product differentiation and advertising to attract customers

nonprofit organization an organization that functions much like a business but does not operate to make a profit; nonprofit organizations focus on public or private goals, such as the promotion of human rights, environmental preservation, or medical research

nonrenewable resource a natural resource that cannot be replaced once it is used; examples include oil and coal

nonrival in consumption a characteristic of a good or service that can be used or consumed by more than one person at the same time; a feature of public goods

normative economics the branch of economics that makes value judgments about the economy; its focus is on which economic policies should be implemented

O

offshoring relocating work and jobs to another country; the opposite of inshoring

oligopoly a market structure in which a few firms dominate the market and produce similar or identical goods

open-market operations the purchase and sale of government bonds by the Federal Reserve for the purpose of regulating the money supply and controlling interest rates

opportunity cost the value of the next best alternative that is given up when making a choice; a measure of what you must give up to get what you want

output the goods or services generated by the production process

outside director a member of a firm's board of directors who comes from outside the firm

outsourcing a business practice in which work that was once done within a company is sent to outside contractors

P

partnership a business owned by two or more co-owners who share profits from the business and are legally responsible for the business's debts

patent a legal protection that gives inventors the sole right to make, use, or sell their inventions for a fixed number of years

payroll tax a tax on the wages a company pays its employees; examples include the Social Security tax and the Medicare tax

peak the highest point of an expansion, or period of economic growth; a peak is followed by economic decline

per capita GDP a nation's real GDP divided by its population; a measure of average economic output per person

perfect competition a market structure in which many producers supply an identical product and no single producer can influence its price; in such a market, prices are set by supply and demand

perpetual resource a natural resource that is widely available and in no danger of being used up; examples include sunlight and wind

personal saving rate the proportion of a household's income that its members save each year

physical capital the manmade objects—tools, machinery, buildings, and other goods—used in production; also called capital goods

pollution haven a country that attracts polluting industries because of its weak or poorly enforced environmental laws

pollution permit a government license, issued under a cap-and-trade system, that allows a producer to emit a certain amount of pollution

positive economics the branch of economics that uses objective analysis to find out how the economy actually works

positive externality a benefit of production or consumption that falls on someone other than the producer or consumer; a positive side effect

poverty rate the percentage of the population that has a family income below a government-defined threshold, or poverty line

poverty threshold the estimated minimum income needed to support a family

price ceiling a maximum price set by the government to prevent prices from going too high

price controls government-imposed limits on the prices that producers may charge in the market

price fixing an illegal, anticompetitive practice in which two or more firms agree to set a common price for a good or service

price floor a minimum price set by the government to prevent prices from going too low

price index a measure of the average change in price of a type of good over time

price leadership the ability of the dominant firm in an oligopoly to set price levels that other firms then follow

price setter a producer that can set a price for a product, rather than accepting the market price

price taker a producer that has no influence over the price of a product; price takers must accept the market price

price war an intense competition among rival firms in an oligopoly in which they successively lower prices to increase sales and win a larger share of the market

principal the amount of money borrowed, or the amount of money still owed on a loan, apart from the interest

private goods goods and services that are sold in markets; distinct from public goods

privately held corporation a corporation owned by an individual or a small group of individuals that allows only a select group of people to buy stock; also known as a closely held corporation

privatize to convert a publicly owned resource or institution to private ownership

product differentiation the attempt by firms to distinguish their goods and services from those of other firms

production equation a formula used to represent the production process: land + labor + capital = goods and services

production possibilities curve a graph showing the combinations of two goods that can be produced with a given set of resources

production possibilities frontier a simple model of an economy that shows all the combinations of two goods that can be produced with the resources and technology currently available

productivity a measure of the efficiency with which goods and services are produced, stated as a ratio of output per unit of input

product market a market in which firms sell goods and services to households

professional organization an organization that represents the interests of people who work in a particular profession

profit the money earned by a business after subtracting its operation costs

profit motive the desire to make a profit

progressive tax a tax that takes a larger share of income as income increases; the federal income tax is progressive

property rights the rights of those who own land, buildings, or other goods to use or dispose of their property as they choose

property tax a tax levied on real property—land and buildings—and sometimes on personal property, such as cars and boats

proportional tax a tax that takes the same share of income at all income levels; a flat tax is proportional

prospectus a legal document that provides information about a security offered to investors

protectionism the policy of erecting trade barriers to shield domestic markets from foreign competition

protective tariff a tax on imported goods designed to protect domestic producers from foreign competition; a type of trade barrier

public franchise a contract issued by a government entity that gives a firm the sole right to provide a good or service in a certain area, such as a national park

public goods goods and services that are used collectively and that no one can be excluded from using; public goods are not provided by markets

publicly held corporation a corporation that offers stock for sale to the general public and has many shareholders

public provision the supplying of a good or service by the government; examples include the services provided by publicly supported schools and universities

public works government-financed projects such as dams, highways, and bridges

purchasing power the value of a unit of money in terms of what it can buy

Q

quantity demanded the amount of a good or service that consumers are willing and able to buy at a specific price

quantity supplied the amount of a good or service that producers are willing and able to offer for sale at a specific price

quintile any one of the five groups of a population that has been divided into fifths for the purpose of data analysis; for example, the top quintile of a country's population in terms of income represents the top fifth of all earners

quota the maximum amount of a resource that a person is allowed to use or consume in a given period of time

R

rate of return the ratio of the money gained or lost by an investment relative to the amount invested; often expressed as the percentage gained or lost in a year

rational-behavior model the idea that people behave in ways that are based on reason and self-interest

rationing the controlled distribution of a limited supply of a good or service

real cost of living the cost in constant dollars of all the basic goods and services needed by the average consumer; the nominal cost of living adjusted for inflation

real GDP a measure of a country's economic output (GDP) valued in constant dollars; real GDP reflects the effects of inflation

real rate of return the ratio of the money gained or lost by an investment relative to the amount invested, adjusted for the effects of inflation

real wages wage levels based on constant dollars; nominal wages adjusted for inflation

recession a period of declining national economic activity, usually measured as a decrease in GDP for at least two consecutive quarters (six months)

regressive tax a tax that takes a smaller share of a family's income as that income increases; a sales tax is generally regressive

regulation the establishment, by the government, of rules aimed at influencing the behavior of firms and individuals; regulation can involve setting prices, establishing product and workplace standards, and limiting entry into an industry

regulatory agency a unit of government created to set and enforce standards for a particular industry or area of economic activity

regulatory capture a situation in which a regulatory agency is dominated, or captured, by the industry it regulates; a captured agency tends to favor the industry it is meant to regulate more than the public interest

renewable resource a natural resource that, with careful planning, can be replaced as it is used; examples include forests and fresh water

rent control a legal limit on the amount a landlord can charge a tenant; a price ceiling on rents

required reserve ratio the minimum percentage of deposits that banks must keep in reserves at all times

reserve requirement the regulation that requires banks to keep a certain percentage of deposits on hand at all times to repay their depositors

resource anything used to produce an economic good or service

revenue the amount of money a firm receives in the course of doing business

revenue table a table that lists the various prices for a given product along with the quantity expected to sell and the revenue that would be earned by the producer at each price

right-to-work law a law that prohibits employers from making union membership a requirement for getting or keeping a job

right-to-work state a state with right-to-work laws, which forbid mandatory union membership

risk the chance of losing money or of failing in some way

rival in consumption a characteristic of a good or service that cannot be used or consumed by more than one person at the same time; a feature of private goods

royalty a share of earnings paid to a franchiser or to an inventor, writer, or artist for the sale or use of that person's work

rule of 72 a method of calculating how long it will take to double the value of an investment; the number 72 is divided by the investment's annual rate of return to determine its doubling time

S

sales tax a tax on the purchase of goods and services

saving setting aside a portion of income for use in the future

scarcity the condition that results because people have limited resources but unlimited wants

scarcity-forces-tradeoffs principle the idea that limited resources force people to make choices and face tradeoffs when they choose

scientific method a method of rational inquiry with five steps: (1) posing a question, (2) researching the question, (3) developing a hypothesis, (4) conducting studies and collecting data, (5) analyzing the data, and (6) evaluating the hypothesis

seasonal unemployment a type of unemployment that results when businesses shut down or slow down for part of the year, often because of weather

securities investments, such as stocks, bonds, and mutual funds, that give their holders the right to receive some sort of return, or profit

service work done by someone else for which a consumer, business, or government is willing to pay

shareholder an investor who buys shares of a company's stock

shortage a lack of something that is desired

silent partner a partner in a business who contributes financial capital but plays no role in day-to-day operations; also known as a limited partner

sin tax an excise tax placed on certain goods or services to discourage their consumption; examples include excise taxes on alcohol, cigarettes, and gambling

Social Security tax a federal payroll tax designed to fund Social Security benefits, including old-age pensions and income for people with disabilities

socialism a political and economic philosophy based on collective or government ownership of a society's resources and means of production, with the goal of achieving social and economic equality

sole proprietorship a business owned and managed by one person

specialization the development of skills or knowledge in one aspect of a job or field of interest

stagflation a combination of economic stagnation—or slowdown—and high inflation; features of stagflation include slow or zero economic growth, high unemployment, and rising prices

stakeholder someone who has an interest in, or is affected by, a company's actions

start-up costs the initial expense of launching a business

state disability tax a state payroll tax that funds programs to help workers who are injured on the job

stock an investment that represents ownership in a business

stockbroker a person who buys and sells stocks and bonds for investors

stock certificate a legal document that certifies ownership of a specific number of shares in a corporation

stock market the market in which stocks and bonds are bought and sold

strong dollar a dollar with a high exchange rate; a dollar that has risen in value, or appreciated, relative to other currencies

structural unemployment a type of unemployment that results when the demand for certain skills declines, often because of changes in technology or increased foreign competition; under such conditions, workers may need retraining to find new jobs

subsidy a government payment to a supplier of goods or services, designed to help that supplier continue to operate

subsistence agriculture the raising of crops or livestock mainly for personal consumption rather than for sale

substitute good a product that satisfies the same basic want as another product

supply the quantity of a good or service that producers are willing and able to offer for sale at various prices

supply chain the network of people, organizations, and activities involved in supplying goods and services to consumers

supply curve a graph that shows the relationship between price and the quantity that producers are willing and able to supply

supply schedule a table that shows the quantities supplied at different prices in a market

supply shifter a factor other than price that can cause a change in the supply of a good or service; examples include changes in technology and government policy

supply-side economics the theory that the best way to ensure economic growth is to stimulate overall supply by cutting taxes on businesses and high-income taxpayers; this theory assumes that producers and investors will use their tax savings to expand production, thereby stimulating the economy

sustainable development a pattern of resource use and economic growth designed to meet current needs while preserving the environment and ensuring that future generations will also be able to meet their needs

T

Takings Clause a clause of the Fifth Amendment to the Constitution stating that the government must pay private owners when their property is taken for public use under the power of eminent domain

tax base something that is taxed, such as personal income or a piece of property

tax code the set of laws that govern federal, state, or local taxes

tax equity the idea that a tax system should be fair

tax incidence the allocation of the burden of a tax between consumers and producers; tax incidence is said to fall on the group that actually bears the burden of the tax, no matter from whom the tax is collected

tax rate the percentage that is levied on the value of whatever is being taxed, such as income or property

tax referendum a direct popular vote on a proposal to raise taxes

technology spillover a benefit that results when technical knowledge spreads from one company or individual to another, thereby promoting new innovations

telecommuting the practice of working at home or at another location outside the workplace and using phones, computers, or other means to stay connected with the workplace

temporary worker a person who is employed for a limited period of time, often on a project basis or to fill a short-term need

thinking-at-the-margin principle the idea that many decisions involve choices about using or doing a little more or a little less of something rather than making a wholesale change

tight-money policy a monetary policy designed to slow the rate of growth of the money supply in order to reduce inflation

toll a fee for the use of a common facility, such as a bridge or highway

total revenue the total amount received by a business for selling a good or service; it is calculated by multiplying the quantity of a good or service sold by its price

total revenue test a tool used by producers to gauge the impact of a change in price on revenues earned; it is also used by economists to determine the elasticity of demand for a good or service

trade association an organization that represents the interests of people and businesses working in a particular industry

trade barrier a government measure that limits international trade, such as a protective tariff or an import quota

trade deficit a negative balance of trade, in which imports exceed exports

trade embargo a ban on trade with a country or group of countries, usually for political reasons; a type of trade barrier

trade-makes-people-better-off principle the idea that people benefit by focusing on what they do well and then trading with others, rather than trying to do everything for themselves

trademark a distinctive name or symbol that identifies a firm and its products or services and that has been legally registered as the property of that firm

tradeoff the exchange of one benefit or advantage for another that is thought to be better

trade surplus a positive balance of trade, in which exports exceed imports

traditional economy an economic system in which decisions about production and consumption are based on custom and tradition

tragedy of the commons a circumstance in which a shared resource is overused or destroyed because users take no responsibility for its preservation

transaction costs the time and money consumers spend shopping for the best product at the best price

transfer payment a government payment to a household or firm for which the payer receives no good or service in return; examples include Social Security checks and unemployment benefits

traveler's checks checks that can be used like cash by travelers to pay for goods and services

trough the lowest point of a contraction, or period of economic decline; a trough is followed by economic growth

trust a combination of firms; in the late 1800s, trusts worked to eliminate competition and control prices, but were later banned under antitrust laws

U

underground economy a sector of the economy based on illegal activities, such as drug dealing and unlawful gambling

unemployment insurance a government program providing limited cash payments to workers who lose their jobs

unemployment rate the percentage of the labor force that is not employed but is actively seeking work

unemployment tax a state payroll tax used to assist workers who lose their jobs

union shop a business in which workers are required to join a union after being hired

unitary elastic demand a condition that exists when the percentage change in the quantity demanded of a good or service equals the percentage change in price; a demand elasticity equal to exactly 1

unitary elastic supply a condition that exists when the percentage change in the quantity supplied of a good or service equals the percentage change in price; a supply elasticity equal to exactly 1

unlimited liability full responsibility for repaying business debts; liability in this case extends to the owner's personal property

user fee a fixed charge on the use of a public service or facility; examples include bridge tolls and park entrance fees

utility the pleasure, satisfaction, or benefit a person receives from consuming a product or service or from taking an action

V

variable a quantity that can vary, or change

venture capital money from an individual investor or organization that invests in a new business in exchange for a share of ownership

voluntary exchange the act of willingly trading one item or service for another

voluntary export restraint (VER) a limit on the quantity of a good that can be exported from a country during a specified time period; a type of trade barrier

voucher a coupon used to purchase a specific good or service

W

W-2 form an official document that lists a worker's wages for the previous year and the amount of tax that was withheld; W-2 forms are filed with federal income tax returns

wage discrimination the practice of paying some workers less than other workers in the same job because of their race, ethnicity, gender, or other personal characteristics

wage gap a difference in the wages earned by various groups in society, such as between men and women or between white Americans and black Americans

wage-price spiral an upward trend in wages and prices; an inflationary pattern in which rising prices lead to demands for higher wages, causing producers to raise prices further and workers to demand additional wage hikes

weak dollar a dollar with a low exchange rate; a dollar that has fallen in value, or depreciated, relative to other currencies

wealth the total value of all the things a person or a group of people owns

withholding a system in which employers deduct a certain amount of tax from workers' paychecks

Y

yellow-dog contract a work agreement prohibiting workers from joining a union

yield the income return on an investment, such as interest paid on a bond or dividends paid on a stock

Z

zoning permit a legal document certifying that a business meets certain criteria to operate in a particular section, or zone, of a town or city

physical characteristics, and
    nonprice competition, 131
Pixar Animation Studios, 165
"Pollution Controls" (Crandall), 217
pollution haven, **331**
pollution permits, **217**
poor countries, and economic
    development, 326–327
Popov, Vladmir, 46
portability of money, 143
positive economics, **3**, 5–**6**
positive externalities, 132, **133**, 216
poverty
    antipoverty policies, unintended
        consequences of, 226–227
    extreme, **319, 326,** 327
    income distribution and, 223–224
poverty rate, **207, 223**–224
poverty threshold, **224**
"The Power to Choose"
    attending college, 16–17
    carbon footprint, reducing,
        338–340
    comparative advantage, 70–71
    credit scores, 160–161
    economic indicators, 270–271
    ethical consumers, 96–97
    global warming as negative
        externality, 136–138
    human life, determining value of,
        228–229
    Internal Revenue Service, role of,
        246–248
    living without imported goods,
        316–317
    maximizing utility of free time,
        34–35
    minimum wages, 116–117
    moving from unfree to free
        market, 54–55
    social responsibilities of business
        organizations, 182–183
    stimulus checks, 292–294
    superstar athletes, salaries for,
        202–204
price ceilings, **99, 112**–113
price controls, **99, 112,** 114–115

price fixing, **211**
price floors, **99, 112**
price index, **261**
price leadership, **129**
price setters, **124**
price takers, **121**
price war, **129**
prices
    allocation of resources and, 111
    equilibrium price, **99, 101,**
        105–108
    incentives to work and produce
        and, 109–110, 111
    information to consumers and
        producers and, 109, 111
    interaction with supply, 82–85
    market balance and, 102–103
    market structure and, 121
    markets and, 99–100
    monopolistic competition, 131
    monopoly, 124
    oligopoly, 129
    perfect competition, 121–122
    response of markets to changing
        conditions, 110–111
    role in modern mixed economy,
        108–111
    shortages, 103–104
    surpluses, 104–105
    time needed to reach equilibrium,
        105
principal, **141, 149**
principles of economic thinking, 11
Principles of Economics (Frank &
    Bernanke), 315
private goods, **134**–135
private ownership, incentives for,
    208–209
privately held corporations, 172
privatization, **220**
pro sports labor market, 202–204
producer expectations, 87
producers
    how to produce, 38–39
    market structure and, 120
    monopolistic competition, 130
    monopoly, 123

    number of, 86
    oligopoly, 128
    perfect competition, 121
    what to produce, 38
    for whom to produce, 39
product differentiation, **130–131**
product market, **44**
product safety, 180
production equation, **22**
production incentives, 109–110, 111
production information, and prices,
    109, 111
production possibilities, 63
production possibilities curve, 30
production possibilities frontier
    (PPF), **19, 30**–33
productivity, **19, 26,** 32, 62
products
    market structure and, 120
    monopolistic competition,
        130–131
    monopoly, 123
    oligopoly, 128
    perfect competition, 121
professional jobs, 191
professional organizations, **178**
profit, **52**
profit motive, 51, **52**
profitability, of sole proprietorships,
    168
progressive taxes, **231, 237**–238
property rights
    eminent domain and, 210
    private ownership, incentives for,
        208–209
    U.S. economic system and, 51, 52,
        208–210
property taxes, **240,** 241
proportional taxes, **231, 237,** 238
prospectus, **158**
protection as bargaining chip, 309
protectionism, **297, 306**
protective tariffs, **297, 306,** 308
public franchises, **125**
public goods, **119, 134**–135, 220–222
public libraries, 47
public provision, **216**

public works, **47**

publicly held corporations, **172**

purchasing power, **143**, 265

Pure Food and Drug Act, 213

Q

quality change bias, 265

quantity demanded, **76**–77

quantity supplied, 82–**83**

quintiles, **223**

quotas, **219**–220

R

rainy-day funds, 152

*A Ranking of the Most Influential
     Persons in History* (Hart), 4

rate of return, **154**

rational-behavior model, **14**–15

rationing, **99, 114**

Reagan, Ronald, 280

real cost of living, **262**

real GDP, **254**

real rate of return, **157**

real wages, **262**

rebate checks, 292–294

recessions, **268**–269
     2008 recession, 273–274

recyclable products, 97

recycled content, 97

Red Cross, 178

Redel, Timothy, 168

redistribution of income, 224–
     226

registered trademark symbol,
     179

regressive taxes, **231, 238**

regulation. *See* government
     regulation

regulatory agency, **207, 211**

regulatory capture, **215**

renewable resources, **23**

rent control, **113**

required reserve ratio, **286**–287

reserve requirement, **285**, 286–287

resource monopolies, 124–125

resources, **5**, 20–21

restrictions on business
     partnerships, 170–171
     sole proprietorships, 168

retirement funding and savings,
     152–153

revenue, **75, 84**

Revitalizing the Soviet Economy
     (Shmelev & Popov), 46

rewards of investments, 154, 157

Ricardo, David, 62–63

Richards, Keith, 19–20

right-to-work laws, **185, 199**

right-to-work states, **199**

risk, **148**

risk takers, 25

risks of investments, 154, 157

rival in consumption, **135**

Robinson Crusoe (Defoe), 29

Rockefeller, John D., 124, 166

Rodriguez, Alex, 203

Rolling Stones, 19, 20

Romania, 322

Roodman, David Malin, 330

Roosevelt, Franklin D., 199, 222,
     274–276

royalties, **176**

rule of 72, 154, 155

Russia, 45

S

Saint Valentine's Day Massacre, 231

sales taxes, 238, **240**, 241

Sandell, Clayton, 338–340

satellite radio network merger, 211

satisfaction of economic wants,
     22–26

Saudi Arabia, 324

Save the Whales campaign, 331

saving(s), **141, 147**
     about, 150–151
     achievement of goals and, 151
     budgeting and, 153
     economic growth and, 151
     economic hardship and, 151–152
     government's role in protecting,
          212–213
     retirement funding and, 152–153

savings deposits, **147**–148

scarcity, **3, 6**
     of money, 143
     reasons for, 20–22
     resources and, 21
     shortages and, 21–22

scarcity-forces-tradeoffs principle,
     6–7

Schwartz, Anna, 276–277

scientific method, **12**

sea turtles, protecting, 328–329

seasonal unemployment, 258–**259**

Seattle, WA, 320

Second Life, 185–186

securities, **154**

Securities and Exchange
     Commission (SEC), 158, 213

self-sufficiency, 61–62

Selkirk, Alexander, 29, 30
     castaways' dilemma, 61–65

semiskilled jobs, 191

service exports, 303

service mark symbol, 179

services, **19, 21**, 131

shareholders, **157**

Sherry, Paul H., 116–117

Shmelev, Nikolai, 46

shopping with a conscience, 96–97

shortages, 21–22, 103–104

silent partners, **170**

sin taxes, **240**

Sinclair, Upton, 213

Singapore, 50, 324, 328

Sirius satellite radio network, 211

Sixteenth Amendment, 233

size of labor force, 186

skilled jobs, 191

skills inventory, 72

Sklar, Holly, 116–117

Smith, Adam, 3–4, 9, 10, 14, 43, 58,
     59, 223, 233–234, 274

social responsibilities of business
     organizations, 182–183

Social Security, 152

Social Security taxes, **239**–240

socialism, **45**

sole proprietorships, **163, 167**–169

Chapter 1

4: Adam Smith, *An Inquiry into the Nature and Causes of the Wealth of Nations,* ed. Edwin Cannan (London: Methuen, 1904/1776), at www.econlib.org. Steven D. Levitt and Stephen J. Dubner, *Freakonomics: A Rogue Economist Explores the Hidden Side of Everything* (New York: HarperCollins, 2005). Steven E. Landsburg, *The Armchair Economist: Economics and Everyday Life* (New York: Free Press, 1993). Levitt and Dubner, *Freakonomics.* **5:** Alfred Marshall, *Principles of Economics* (London: Macmillan, 1920/1890), at www.econlib.org. **8:** Landsburg, *Armchair Economist.* Levitt and Dubner, *Freakonomics.* **9:** Smith, *Wealth of Nations.* **10:** Smith, *Wealth of Nations.* Henry Hazlitt, *Economics in One Lesson: The Shortest and Surest Way to Understand Basic Economics* (New York: Three Rivers Press, 1979 [originally published in 1946]). **12:** Levitt and Dubner, *Freakonomics.* **14:** Smith, *Wealth of Nations.* **16–17:** Ryan Allis, "Should I Go to College?" at www.zeromillion.com.

Chapter 2

19: "YOU CAN'T ALWAYS GET WHAT YOU WANT" Written by Mick Jagger & Keith Richards. © 1969 Renewed ABKCO Music, Inc. www.abkco.com. Used with permission. All rights reserved. **19–20:** Keith Richards, in Robert Greenfield, *The Rolling Stone Interviews: Keith Richards* (New York: St. Martin's Press/Rolling Stone Press, 1981). **20:** Sean Egan, ed., *The Rough Guide to the Rolling Stones* (London: Rough Guides, 2006). Mick Jagger in Jann Wenner, "Jagger Remembers: The Rolling Stone Interview," *Rolling Stone,* Dec. 14, 1995, at www.rollingstone.com. **24:** Charles J. Wheelan, *Naked Economics: Undressing the Dismal Science* (New York: Norton, 2002). Gary Becker, in Wheelan, *Naked Economics.* **25:** Nolan Bushnell, in Steve L. Kent, *The Ultimate History of Video Games: From Pong to Pokemon and Beyond . . . The Story Behind the Craze That Touched Our Lives and Changed Our World* (Roseville, CA: Prima, 2001). **26:** Jagger, in Wenner, "Jagger Remembers." **34–35:** Barbara Hagenbaugh, "Full Activity, Study Schedules Have Many Teens Just Saying No to Jobs," USA TODAY. April 7, 2005. Reprinted with Permission.

Chapter 3

38: Boris Yeltsin, *Against the Grain: An Autobiography* (New York: Summit Books, 1990). **43:** Smith, *Wealth of Nations.* **44:** Ibid. **45:** Karl Marx, *Critique of the Gotha Programme,* 1875, at www.bartleby.com. **46:** Nikolai Shmelev and Vladmir Popov, in Thomas Sowell, *Basic Economics: A Common Sense Guide to the Economy,* 3rd ed. (New York: Basic Books, 2007). **47:** Smith, *Wealth of Nations.* **54–55:** Mart Laar, "How Estonia Did It," in The Heritage Foundation, *2003 Index of Economic Freedom* (Washington, DC: 2002).

Chapter 4

58: Robert H. Frank and Ben Bernanke, *Principles of Economics,* 3rd ed. (New Delhi: Tata McGraw-Hill India, 2005). Smith, *Wealth of Nations.* **59:** Smith, *Wealth of Nations.* **60:** Wheelan, *Naked Economics.* James D. Gwartney, Richard L. Stroup, and Dwight Lee, *Common Sense Economics: What Everyone Should Know About Wealth and Prosperity* (New York: St. Martin's Press, 2005). **67:** Paul Heyne, Peter J. Boettke, and David L. Prychitko, *The Economic Way of Thinking* (Upper Saddle River, NJ: Pearson Prentice Hall, 2006). **68–69:** Gwartney, Stroup, and Lee, *Common Sense Economics.* **69:** Tim Harford, *The Undercover Economist: Why the Rich Are Rich, the Poor Are Poor—and Why You Can Never Buy a Decent Used Car* (New York: Oxford University Press, 2006). **70–71:** From COMMON SENSE ECONOMICS by James D. Gwartney, Richard L. Stroup, and Dwight R. Lee. Copyright © 2005 by the author and reprinted by permission of St. Martin's Press, LLC. **72:** NCEE Skills Inventory, used with permission and adapted from Focus Globalization, page 93. Copyright © 2006 National Council on Economic Education, New York, NY. All rights reserved. Adapted from the University of Technology, Sydney's "Job Skills" Inventory at www.careerdevelopment.uts.edu.au/whatican/skills. For more information visit www.ncee.net or call 1-800-338-1192.

Chapter 5

79: David Henderson, ed., *The Fortune Encyclopedia of Economics* (New York: Warner Books, 1993). **96:** Ellis Jones, *The Better World*

Shopping Guide: Every Dollar Makes a Difference (Gabriola Island, BC: New Society Publishers, 2007).

Chapter 6
99: Brad Beckwith, in Julie Jargon, "Heartland Sees Boom with Grains in Demand," *Wall Street Journal,* Feb. 15, 2008. 100: Beckwith, in Jargon, "Heartland." **107:** Sowell, *Basic Economics.* **110:** Michael Burdette, in James R. Healey, "Storm Worsens Oil, Gas Problems," *USA Today,* Aug. 29, 2005. **111:** Sara Kehaulani Goo and Justin Blum, "Gas Supplies Tight; Bush Asks Drivers to Conserve," *Washington Post,* Sep. 2, 2005. Sowell, *Basic Economics.* **112:** Henry Hazlitt, in Hans Sennholz, ed., *The Wisdom of Henry Hazlitt: A Collection of Essays by Henry Hazlitt* (Irvington-on-Hudson, NY: Foundation for Economic Education, 1993). **116–117:** Holly Sklar and Paul H. Sherry, *A Just Minimum Wage: Good for Workers, Business, and Our Future,* produced by the American Friends Service Committee and the National Council of Churches USA in support of the Let Justice Roll Living Wage Campaign, at www.letjusticeroll.org. Thomas Sowell, "A Glimmer of Hope," www.realclearpolitics, by permission of Thomas Sowell and Creators Syndicate, Inc.

Chapter 7
119: Bob Sullivan, *Gotcha Capitalism: How Hidden Fees Rip You Off Every Day and What You Can Do About It* (New York: Ballantine Books, 2007). **123:** Robert Heilbroner and Lester Thurow, *Economics Explained: Everything You Need to Know About How the Economy Works and Where It's Going* (New York: Touchstone, 1998). **136–138:** Robert F. Kennedy

Jr., "Global Warming: A Real Solution," *Rolling Stone,* June 18, 2007.

Chapter 8
141: Kyle MacDonald, June 12, 2005, oneredpaperclip.blogspot.com. **142:** MacDonald, July 8, 2006, oneredpaperclip.blogspot.com. **152:** David Bach, *The Automatic Millionaire: A Powerful One-Step Plan to Live and Finish Rich* (New York: Broadway Books, 2003).

Chapter 9
163: Oprah Winfrey, in Sara McIntosh Wooten, *Oprah Winfrey: Talk Show Legend* (Berkeley Heights, NJ: Enslow Publishers, 1999). **164:** Oprah Winfrey, in Janet Lowe, *Oprah Winfrey Speaks: Insight from the World's Most Influential Voice* (New York: Wiley, 1998). Linda Alvarado, in Hector V. Barreto, *The Engine of America: The Secrets to Small Business Success from Entrepreneurs Who Have Made It!* (Hoboken, NJ: John Wiley and Sons, 2007). Mary Kay Ash, at www.secretsofsuccess.com. **165:** Andrew Carnegie, in Dan Fitzpatrick, "Only Known Recording of Andrew Carnegie Gives Voice to History," *Pittsburgh Post-Gazette,* Oct. 30, 2007, at www.post-gazette. com. Madam C. J. Walker, at "Two American Entrepreneurs: Madam C. J. Walker and J. C. Penney," www.nps.gov. Vera Wang, in Gloria Nicola, "Conversation With: Vera Wang Reflects on Weddings, Modernity, and the Most Incredible Accessory—Eyewear," *2020mag,* Feb. 2002, www.2020mag.com. Steve Jobs, commencement address at Stanford University, June 12, 2005, at news-service.standford.edu. **166:** Debbi Fields, at www.mrsfields.com. Thomas Edison, at www.thomas edison.com. Mary Kay Ash, at

entrepreneurs.about.com. Alvarado, in Barreto, *Engine of America.* John D. Rockefeller, in Connie Robertson, ed., *The Wordsworth Dictionary of Quotations* (Hertfordshire, UK: Wordsworth Editions, 1998). Bill Gates, at www.brainyquote.com. David Birch, in Frances McGuckin, *Business for Beginners: From Research and Business Plans to Money, Marketing, and the Law* (Naperville, IL: Sourcebooks, 2005). **167:** Walker, in Larry Chang and Roderick Terry, eds., *Wisdom from the Soul of Black Folk* (Washington, DC: Gnosophia Publishers, 2007). Winfrey, in Lowe, *Oprah Winfrey Speaks.* Stephen Fairchild, in Jack Canfield, Mark Victor Hansen, Dahlynn McKowen, Tom Hill, John Gardner, Elizabeth Gardner, and Kyle Wilson, eds., *Chicken Soup for the Entrepreneur's Soul* (Deerfield Beach, FL: Health Communications, 2006). Jerry Greenfield, at "Ben Cohen and Jerry Greenfield," www.businesswings.co. uk. **178:** www.gatesfoundation.org. **180:** Visualscope Studios, "Code of Ethics," www.visualscope.com. **182–183:** Milton Friedman, "The Social Responsibility of Business Is to Increase Its Profits," *The New York Times Magazine,* Sep. 13, 1970. Reprinted by permission. John Mackey, "Rethinking the Social Responsibility of Business: Putting Customers Ahead of Investors," *Reason,* Oct. 2005, from *Reason* magazine and Reason.com.

Chapter 10
185: Catherine Winters, in Wagner James Au, *The Making of Second Life* (New York: Harper Collins, 2008). **186:** Winters, in Au, *Making of Second Life.* **190:** Wheelan, *Naked Economics.* **191:** Robert H. Frank,

The Economic Naturalist: In Search of Explanations for Everyday Enigmas (New York: Basic Books, 2007). **198:** Industrial Workers of the World, www.iww.org. **200:** Change to Win, www.changetowin.org. **201:** Ibid. **202–204:** "Inning 6: The Pro Sports Labor Market," www.bos.frb.org, Public & Community Affairs Department, Federal Reserve Bank of Boston.

Chapter 11

208: Wheelan, *Naked Economics*. **210:** Gouverneur Morris, in James Madison, *The Debates in the Federal Convention of 1787*, July 5, 1787, at www.constitution.org. *Kelo et al. v. City of New London et al.,* 545 U.S. 469 (2005), at caselaw.lp.findlaw.com. **211:** Thomas O. Barnett, in Peter Whoriskey and Kim Hart, "Justice Dept. Approves XM-Sirius Radio Merger," *Washington Post,* Mar. 25, 2008, at www.washingtonpost.com. **213:** Upton Sinclair, *The Jungle,* 1906, at www.online-literature.com. Jerry L. Jordan, "How to Keep Growing 'New Economics,'" *Economic Commentary,* Aug. 15, 2000, www.clevelandfed.org. **214:** Robert S. Smith, "Compensating Wage Differentials and Public Policy: A Review," *Industrial and Labor Relations Review* 32 (1977): 339–352, in Frank and Bernanke, *Principles of Economics.* **216:** Joel Spolsky, "The Command and Control Management Method," Aug. 8, 2006, www.joelonsoftware.com. **217:** Robert W. Crandall, "Pollution Controls," *The Concise Encyclopedia of Economics,* at www.econlib.org. **219:** Garrett Hardin, "The Tragedy of the Commons," *Science* 162 (1968): 1243–1248, at dieoff.org. **220:** Abraham Lincoln, July 1854, in Paul M. Angle and Earl Schenck Miers, eds., *The Living Lincoln* (New York: Barnes and Noble, 1955), at books.google.com. **228–229:** From MANKIW, *Principles of Economics,* 4E. © 2007 South-Western, a part of Cengage Learning, Inc. Reproduced by permission. www.cengage.com/permissions.

Chapter 12

232: Al Capone, at "Exhibit: Al Capone Verdict," www.archives.gov. Benjamin Franklin, in Mankiw, *Principles of Economics.* Albert Einstein, at www.quotationspage.com. Oliver Wendell Holmes Jr., in Peter L. Bernstein, "Don't Like Taxes? Consider the Alternative," *New York Times,* Feb. 10, 2008, at www.nytimes.com. **233:** Edmund Burke, in Sowell, *Basic Economics.* Smith, *Wealth of Nations.* **234:** Smith, *Wealth of Nations.* **235:** Mankiw, *Principles of Economics.* Wheelan, *Naked Economics.* **240:** Gwartney, Stroup, and Lee, *Common Sense Economics.* **242:** J. C. Watts Jr., at www.quotegarden.com. **245:** Russell Long, in Mankiw, *Principles of Economics.* **246–248:** Stephen J. Dubner and Steven D. Levitt, "Filling in the Tax Gap," *New York Times,* Apr. 2, 2006, at www.nytimes.com.

Chapter 13

256: Robert Kennedy, speech at the University of Kansas, Mar. 18, 1968, at www.jfklibrary.org. **262:** "Time Well Spent: The Declining *Real* Cost of Living in America," Federal Reserve Bank of Dallas, Annual Report, 1997, www.dallasfed.org. **266:** Wheelan, *Naked Economics.*

Chapter 14

274: Bernard Baumohl, in Lara Moscrip, "Consumer Confidence Tumbles to 16-Year Low," June 24, 2008, CNNMoney.com. Wheelan, *Naked Economics.* Franklin Delano Roosevelt, address accepting the presidential nomination at the Democratic National Convention in Chicago, July 2, 1932, at www.presidency.ucsb.edu. **275:** John Maynard Keynes, *A Tract on Monetary Reform,* 1923, at www.quotationspage.com. Franklin Delano Roosevelt, in Robert Reich, "John Maynard Keynes," *Time,* Mar. 1999. **275–276:** Franklin Delano Roosevelt, Apr. 14, 1938, at www.mhric.org. **276:** John F. Kennedy, address to the Economic Club of New York, Dec. 14, 1962, at www.americanrhetoric.com. John F. Kennedy, in David Shreve, "President John F. Kennedy and the 1964 Tax Cut," *Presidential Recordings Project,* 2001, at tapes.millercenter.virginia.edu. Richard Nixon, in Reich, "John Maynard Keynes." **277:** Milton Friedman and Rose D. Friedman, *Two Lucky People: Memoirs* (Chicago: University of Chicago Press, 1998). **278:** Ben S. Bernanke, address to the Conference to Honor Milton Friedman, Nov. 8, 2002, at www.federalreserve.gov. **279:** Paul Krugman, Robin Wells, and Martha Olney, *Essentials of Economics* (New York: Worth, 2007). George W. Bush, in "Bush Signs Stimulus Package into Law," Feb. 13, 2008, www.msnbc.com. **288:** Bruce Bartlett, "Maybe Too Little, Always Too Late," *New York Times,* Jan. 23 2008, at www.nytimes.com. **292–294:** Bankrate.com. N. Palm Beach, FL, 2008. © 2008 Bankrate.com. All rights reserved, used by permission.

Chapter 15

297: Marc McCreary, in Adam Davidson, "U.S. Town's Economy

Shifts Away from T-Shirt Business," *All Things Considered*, Apr. 28, 2005, www.npr.org. **304:** Wheelan, *Naked Economics*. **309:** Campbell R. McConnell and Stanley L. Brue, *Economics: Principles, Problems, and Policies* (Boston: McGraw-Hill/Irwin, 2008). **310:** Ibid. **314:** "Animal Spirits and the Fed," *Wall Street Journal*, Feb. 1, 2005, at www.atlanticpacificalliance. com. Jeremy W. Peters, "U.S. Trade Deficit Grew to Another Record in '06," *New York Times*, Feb. 14, 2007. **314–315:** Sowell, Basic Economics. **315:** Frank and Bernanke, *Principles of Economics*. **316–317:** Sara Bongiorni, "A Year Without 'Made in China,'" *The Christian Science Monitor*, Dec. 21, 2005. By Sara Bongiorni. Reused with permission from the December 20, 2005 issue of The Christian Science Monitor (http://www.csmonitor.com). © 2005 The Christian Science Monitor. All rights reserved. For permissions, contact copyright@csmonitor.com.

Chapter 16
319–320: David Hummels, "The Debate over Globalization," in *Focus: Globalization* (New York: National Council on Economic Education, 2006). **320:** Mike Moore, in Don Knapp, "Activists to WTO: Put People over Profits," Nov. 29, 1999, www.cnn.com. **322:** Dan Petrowski, in John Vidal, "Real Battle for Seattle," Dec. 5, 1999, *The Guardian*, www.guardian.co.uk. **323:** Jane Cover, Dec. 3, 1999, at "The WTO History Project," depts.washington. edu. **326:** Oxfam International, "Rigged Trade and Not Much Aid: How Rich Countries Help to Keep the Least Developed Countries Poor," May 2001, www.oxfam.org. uk. **327:** Wheelan, *Naked Economics*.

Flemming Larsen, "Globalization, the NGOs, and the IMG: A New Dialogue," *Le Monde*, Sep. 19, 2000, at www.imf.org. **330:** Fred Pearce, "Instant Expert: Climate Change," *New Scientist*, Sep. 1, 2006, www.NewScientist.com. David Malin Roodman, *The Natural Wealth of Nations: Harnessing the Market for the Environment* (New York: W. W. Norton/Worldwatch, 1998), in John Micklethwait and Adrian Wooldridge, *A Future Perfect* (New York: Random House, 2000). **331:** Bill McKibben, *Deep Economy: The Wealth of Communities and the Durable Future* (New York: Times Books/Henry Holt, 2007). The World Bank, *Greening Industry: New Roles for Communities, Markets, and Governments*, Vol. 1 (New York: Oxford University Press, 2000). Pearce, "Instant Expert." "White Paper: China's Policies and Actions on Climate Change," china.org.cn. **332:** Andrew Leonard, "How the World Works: Outsourcing Pollution," Aug. 22, 2006, www.salon.com. Environmental Protection Agency, "Backgrounder: The 20th Anniversary of the Montreal Protocol: A Landmark Environmental Treaty," www.epa.gov. International Whaling Commission, "Whalewatching: Recognition and Development of Whalewatching Issues Within the IWC," www.iwcoffice.org. **333:** José Bové, in "Bové Appeals over McDonalds Rampage," Feb. 15, 2001, news.bbc.co.uk. James L. Watson, "China's Big Mac Attack," *Foreign Affairs*, May/June 2000, in Katrin Sjursen, ed., *Globalization* (New York: H. W. Wilson, 2000). **334:** David Harrison, in Stefan Lovgren, "Language Racing to Extinction in Five Global 'Hotspots,'" Sep. 18, 2007,

news.nationalgeographic.com. **335:** Julia Galeota, "Cultural Imperialism: An American Tradition," *The Humanist*, May/June 2004, www.thehumanist.org. Tyler Cowen, "Some Countries Remain Resistant to American Cultural Exports," *New York Times*, Feb. 22, 2007, www.nytimes.com. Watson, "China's Big Mac Attack." **336:** Jon Krakauer, *Into Thin Air: A Personal Account of the Mount Everest Disaster* (London: Macmillan, 1997). Cowen, "Some Countries." **336–337:** Shirley Leung, "McHaute Cuisine: Armchairs, TVs, and Espresso—Is It McDonald's?" *Wall Street Journal*, Aug. 30, 2002. **337:** Lester Thurow, *Fortune Favors the Bold: What We Must Do to Build a New and Lasting Global Prosperity* (New York: HarperCollins, 2003). **338–340:** Clayton Sandell, "Reducing Your Carbon Footprint: How You Can Lower Your CO2 Contributions to the Environment," ABC News, June 7, 2006, abcnews.go.com.

Photographs

Front Cover
Sigfried Layda/Getty Images

Front Matter
i: Sigfried Layda/Getty Images **v:** RF/Corbis **v:** Emil Muench/Photo Researchers Inc. **v:** James Green/ Robert Harding **v:** AP Photo **v:** RF/ Corbis **v:** RF/Corbis **v:** Michael Ochs Archives/Corbis **vi:** RF/Corbis **vi:** RF/Corbis **vi:** AP/Photo **vi:** RF/ SuperStock **vi:** RF/Getty Images **vi:** Inga Spence/Photo Researchers Inc. **vi:** RF/Corbis **vii:** Denis Farrell/AP Photo **vii:** AP Photo **vii:** V1/Alamy **vii:** age fotostock/SuperStock **vii:** Kevin Foy/Alamy **viii:** John G. Mabanglo-AFP/Getty Images **viii:** Travel Excellence/Alamy **viii:** Matin Mejia/ AP Photo **viii:** RF/Corbis **viii:** RF/ Alamy **viii:** Bill Bachmann/Alamy

Unit 1 Opener
1 A: Pete Oxford/Robert Harding **1 B:** Mark Peterson/Corbis **1C:** RF/Corbis **1 D:** Emil Muench/Photo Researchers, Inc. **1 E:** Michael Ochs Archives/Corbis **1 F:** Atlantide Phototravel/Corbis **1 G:** AP Photo **1 H:** RF/Corbis **1 I:** Alison Wright/Photo Researchers Inc. **1 J:** RF/Corbis

Chapter 1
2 A: RF/Corbis **2 B:** RF/Corbis **2 C:** RF/Corbis **2 D:** RF/Corbis **2 E:** RF/ Corbis **2 F:** RF/Corbis **2 G:** Michael Reynolds/Corbis **2 H:** RF/Corbis **4:** The Granger Collection, New York **5 R:** RF/Getty **5 L:** RF/Getty **7:** Guy Crittenden/Images.com/Corbis **8 R:** Reed Saxon/AP Photo **8 L:**

Cate Gillon/Getty Images **9 R:** age fotostock/SuperStock **9 L:** RF/Super-Stock **10:** Tim Boyle/Getty Images **11 BR:** (inset) Cate Gillon/Getty Images **11 T:** Getty Images **11 CR:** Romilly Lockyer/Getty Images **11 TC:** (inset) Peter M. Fisher/Corbis **11 BL:** (inset) RF/Masterfile **11 BR:** RF/Getty Images **11 BCL:** Foodfolio-photocuisine/ Corbis **11 BCR:** RF/Corbis **11 BL:** Joson-zefa/Corbis **11 CR:** (inset) Torleif Svensson/Corbis **11 TR:** (inset) RF/Corbis **11 TR:** RF/Corbis **11 TC:** Phil Schermeister/Corbis **11 TL:** (inset) Playboy Archive/Corbis **11 TL:** Owaki-Kulla/Corbis **13:** RF/Super-Stock **14:** William Colgin-Mississippi Press/AP Photo

Chapter 2
18 A: Michael Ochs Archives/Corbis **18 B:** AP Photo **18 C:** Bettmann/Corbis **18 D:** AP Photo **18 E:** GAB Archives/Redferns/Retna Ltd. **18 F:** Courtesy of the Sanchez Collection **20:** Yves Herman/Reuters **21:** Amit Dave/Reuters Pictures Archive **23 BCR:** Kaj R. Svensson/Photo Researchers Inc. **23 C:** Getty Images **23 BL:** Andrew McClenaghan/Photo Researchers Inc. **23 BCL:** RF/Index Stock **23 BR:** RF/Alamy **23 T:** Charlie Riedel/ AP Photo **25:** © Martin Klimek **29:** Images.com/Corbis **31:** Dennis Galante/Getty Images **32:** Dennis D. Potokar/Photo Researchers Inc.

Chapter 3
36 A: Mark Peterson/Corbis **36 B:** Chuck Savage/Photolibrary **36 C:** FoodPix/Jupiter Images **36 D:** Food-Pix/Jupiter Images **36 E:** Mike Randolph/Masterfile **36 F:** RF/Corbis

36 G: SuperStock **36 H:** RF/Corbis **38:** Bettmann/Corbis **40:** Andy Reynolds/Getty Images **42:** David Keith Jones/Alamy **43:** RF/Corbis **45:** The Granger Collection, New York **47:** Bo Zaunders/Corbis **51 BL:** age fotostock/ SuperStock **51 TR:** RF/Alamy **51 BC:** RF/Getty **51:** RF/SuperStock **51 BR:** RF/SuperStock **51 TL:** Occupational Safety and Health Administration **52:** © The New Yorker Collection 1993 Mort Gerberg from cartoonbank.com. All Rights Reserved. **55:** Panoramic Images/Getty Images

Chapter 4
56 A: Emil Muench/Photo Researchers Inc. **56 B:** Alison Wright/Photo Researchers Inc. **56 C:** Leonard Lee Rue III/Photo Researchers Inc. **56 D:** Alison Wright/Photo Researchers Inc. **56 F:** Marco Simoni/Robert Harding **56 G:** Gavin Hellier/Robert Harding **56 H:** Pete Oxford/Robert Harding **56 I:** James Green/Robert Harding **56 J:** Marco Bianchi/Robert Harding **58:** Richard List/Corbis **59:** Swerve/Alamy **60:** © Andrew Toos/ CartoonStock.com **62 TL:** RF/Corbis **62 TR:** Marielle-photocuisine/Corbis **66:** George Contorakes/Masterfile **68 L:** Apple/epa/Corbis **68 R:** Motorola **71:** Matt York/AP Photo

Unit 2 Opener
73 A: RF/Corbis **73 B:** Michael A. Keller/zefa/Corbis **73 C:** F. Micelotta-American Idol 2008/Getty Images for Fox **73 D:** Reggie Casagrande/Getty Images **73 E:** RF/Corbis **73 F:** Jon Riley/Getty Images **73 G:** age fotostock/ SuperStock **73 H:** Inga Spence/Photo Researchers Inc. **73 I:** AP/Photo

© The New Yorker Collection 1993 Bernard Schoenbaum from cartoonbank.com. All Rights Reserved. **225:** Tim Boyle/Getty Images **226:** Joe Appel/AP Photo **228:** RF/SuperStock

Chapter 12
230 A: AP Photo **230 B:** RF **230 C:** AP Photo **230 D:** Popperfoto/Getty Images **230 E:** AP Photo **230 F:** Wright's Reprints **230 G:** Bettmann/Corbis **231 H:** Bettmann/Corbis **230 I:** Susan Ragan/AP Photo **232:** Penn Museum object 33-59-19 image #175612 **233:** © The New Yorker Collection 1970 J. B. Handelsman from cartoonbank.com. All Rights Reserved. **235:** RF/Alamy **236:** RF/Corbis **247:** www.CartoonStock.com

Unit Opener 5
249 A: Raif-Finn Hestoft/Corbis **249 B:** Frank Vetere/Alamy **249 C:** V1/Alamy **249 D:** RF/SuperStock **249 E:** Marcio Jose Sanchez **249 F:** Kevin Foy/Alamy **249 G:** Brendan Smialowski/Getty Images **249 H:** Joel Stettenheim/Corbis

Chapter 13
250 B: John Gillmoure/Corbis **250 D:** Walter Weissman/Corbis **250 E:** Kevin Foy/Alamy **250 F:** Wright's Reprints **250 G:** Joel Stettenheim/Corbis **250 H:** Marcio Jose Sanchez **250 J:** Gabe Palmer/Alamy **250 K:** RF/SuperStock **250 L:** Raif-Finn Hestoft/Corbis **252:** The Granger Collection, New York **255:** Calvin Larsen/Photo Researchers Inc. **256:** Jeff Greenberg/Alamy **263:** John Moore/Getty Images **265:** RF/SuperStock **268:** Bettmann/Corbis

Chapter 14
272 A: V1/Alamy **272 B:** Brendan Smialowski/Getty Images **272 C:** Frank Vetere/Alamy **272 D:** Wright's Reprints **272 E:** AP Photo **272 G:** Chris Hondros/Getty Images **272 H:** Doug Mills/AP Photo **272 I:** Charles O'Rear/Corbis **272 J:** V1/Alamy **275:** Tim Gidal-Picture Post/Getty Images **276:** Laurie Platt Winfrey/The Art Archive **277:** Roger Ressmeyer/Corbis **287:** © The New Yorker Collection 1997 Robert Mankoff from cartoonbank.com. All Rights Reserved. **293 L:** Don Ryan/AP Photo **293 R:** Michael Maloney-San Francisco Chronicle/Corbis **294:** © 2008 Pat Bagley The Salt Lake City Tribune and PoliticalCartoons.com

Unit Opener 6
295 A: Caro/Alamy **295 B:** Matin Mejia/AP Photo **295 C:** Travel Excellence/Alamy **295 D:** David Butow/Corbis **295 E:** RF/Corbis **295 F:** RF/Alamy **295 G:** RF/Alamy **295 H:** GIPhotoStock Z/Alamy **295 I:** Fabrice Coffrini-AFP/Getty Images **295 K:** Bill Bachmann/Alamy **295 L:** John G. Mabanglo-AFP/Getty Images

Chapter 15
296 A: Greg Probst/Corbis **296 B:** RF/Corbis **296 C:** David Butow/Corbis **296 D:** Martial Trezzini/AP Photo **296 E:** Fabrice Coffrini-AFP/Getty Images **296 F:** Caro/Alamy **296 G:** RF/Alamy **296 H:** RF/Alamy **296 I:** GIPhotoStock Z/Alamy **296 J:** GIPhotoStock Z/Alamy **298:** SCPhotos/Alamy **299:** RF/Corbis **300 L:** E. R. Degginger/Photo Researchers Inc. **300 R:** Max Aguilera-Hellweg **301 L:** Walt Disney Pictures-Zuma/Corbis **301 C:** Courtesy of Warner Bros.-Bureau L. A. Collection/Corbis **301 R:** DreamWorks Distribution LLC/Special Anti-Pesto Still (Aardma-Bureau L. A. Collection/Corbis **305:** NY Times/Redux **307:** Virginia Mayo/AP Photo **312:** Ace Stock Limited/Alamy **317:** Jens Buttner-epa/Corbis

Chapter 16
318 A: John G. Mabanglo-AFP/Getty Images **318 B:** Bill Bachmann/Alamy **318 C:** Travel Excellence/Alamy **318 D:** Yang Liu/Corbis **318 E:** John G. Mabanglo-AFP/Getty Images **318 F:** Matin Mejia/AP Photo **320:** AFP/Getty Images **321:** © 2005 Christo Komarnitski and PoliticalCartoons.com **324 L:** Uriel Sinai/Getty Images **324 C:** Lakruwan Wanniarachichi-AFP/Getty Images **324 R:** Atlantide Phototravel/Corbis **328:** R. Ian Lloyd/Masterfile **330:** Iain Masterton/Alamy **332:** Tom Brakefield/Corbis **333:** Issei Kato/Reuters **336:** Dourglas E. Curran-AFP/Getty Images **341 A:** Viviane Moos/Corbis **341 B:** Ariel Skelley/Corbis **341 C:** RF/Corbis **341 D:** RF/Corbis **341 E:** RF/Corbis **341 F:** Chuck Savage/Corbis

Art

Chapter 1
6: QYA Design Studio **8:** QYA Design Studio **11:** Don Taka **12:** QYA Design Studio **13:** QYA Design Studio

Chapter 2
22: QYA Design Studio **24:** QYA Design Studio **26:** QYA Design Studio **28:** QYA Design Studio **29:** Scott Willis **30:** QYA Design Studio **31:** QYA Design Studio **32:** QYA Design Studio **35:** QYA Design Studio

Chapter 3
39: QYA Design Studio **41:** QYA Design Studio **44:** QYA Design Studio **46:** QYA Design Studio **48:** QYA Design Studio **49:** QYA Design Studio **51:** QYA Design Studio

Chapter 4

61: QYA Design Studio 62: QYA Design Studio 63: QYA Design Studio 64: QYA Design Studio 65: QYA Design Studio 67: QYA Design Studio 68: QYA Design Studio

Chapter 5

77: QYA Design Studio 78: QYA Design Studio 80: QYA Design Studio 81: QYA Design Studio 82: QYA Design Studio 84: QYA Design Studio 85: QYA Design Studio 86: QYA Design Studio 89: QYA Design Studio 93: QYA Design Studio 94: QYA Design Studio 97: QYA Design Studio

Chapter 6

100: QYA Design Studio 101: QYA Design Studio 104: QYA Design Studio 106: QYA Design Studio 107: QYA Design Studio 108: QYA Design Studio 110: QYA Design Studio 111: QYA Design Studio 113: QYA Design Studio 115: Scott Willis

Chapter 7

121: QYA Design Studio 123: QYA Design Studio 124: QYA Design Studio 127: QYA Design Studio 130: QYA Design Studio 134: QYA Design Studio

Chapter 8

143: QYA Design Studio 145: QYA Design Studio 147: QYA Design Studio 148: QYA Design Studio 150: QYA Design Studio 152: Scott Willis 153: QYA Design Studio 155: QYA Design Studio 157: QYA Design Studio 158: QYA Design Studio 161: QYA Design Studio

Chapter 9

166: QYA Design Studio 168: QYA Design Studio 169: QYA Design Studio 171: QYA Design Studio 173: QYA Design Studio 174: QYA Design Studio 176: QYA Design Studio 177: QYA Design Studio

Chapter 10

187: QYA Design Studio 189: QYA Design Studio 191: Scott Willis 192: QYA Design Studio 195: QYA Design Studio 197: QYA Design Studio 200: QYA Design Studio

Chapter 11

209: QYA Design Studio 212: QYA Design Studio 215: QYA Design Studio 217: QYA Design Studio 218: QYA Design Studio 219: Scott Willis 221: QYA Design Studio 224: QYA Design Studio 225: QYA Design Studio 227: Scott Willis

Chapter 12

234: QYA Design Studio 235: QYA Design Studio 236: QYA Design Studio 237: QYA Design Studio 238: QYA Design Studio 241: QYA Design Studio 242: QYA Design Studio 243: QYA Design Studio 244: QYA Design Studio 248: QYA Design Studio

Chapter 13

253: QYA Design Studio 254: QYA Design Studio 257: QYA Design Studio 258: QYA Design Studio 259: QYA Design Studio 260: QYA Design Studio 261: QYA Design Studio 262: QYA Design Studio 264: QYA Design Studio 267: QYA Design Studio

Chapter 14

274: Scott Willis 277: QYA Design Studio 278: QYA Design Studio 279: QYA Design Studio 280: QYA Design Studio 281: QYA Design Studio 282: QYA Design Studio 284 T: QYA Design Studio 284–285: QYA Design Studio 286: QYA Design Studio 288: QYA Design Studio 289: QYA Design Studio 290: QYA Design Studio

Chapter 15

299: QYA Design Studio 302: QYA Design Studio 303: QYA Design Studio 304: QYA Design Studio 306: Scott Willis 311: QYA Design Studio 313: QYA Design Studio 314: QYA Design Studio

Chapter 16

323: QYA Design Studio 326: QYA Design Studio 327: QYA Design Studio 331: QYA Design Studio 335: QYA Design Studio 339: QYA Design Studio